RED HERRINGS
AND
WHITE ELEPHANTS

RED HERRINGS
AND
WHITE ELEPHANTS

ALBERT JACK
WITH ILLUSTRATIONS
BY AMA PAGE

metro

Published by Metro Publishing Ltd,
3, Bramber Court, 2 Bramber Road,
London W14 9PB, England

www.blake.co.uk

First published in hardback in 2004

ISBN 1 84358 129 9

British Library Cataloguing-in-Publication Data:

A catalogue record for this book is available from the British Library.

Design by www.envydesign.co.uk

Printed in Great Britain by Creative Print and Design (Wales)

9 10 8

Papers used by Metro Publishing are natural, recyclable products made
from wood grown in sustainable forests. The manufacturing processes
conform to the environmental regulations of the country of origin.

This book is dedicated to the memory of
Albert Victor Childs (1916–1998)

CONTENTS

ACKNOWLEDGEMENTS

Thanks in the first place go to Martyn Long, whose trivial conversation at the inns around Guildford sparked the idea in the first place. That master of triviality then provided enough inspiration for me to crawl through dirty libraries with dusty librarians (although in some cases that was the other way round) and research the origins of some of our favourite phrases.

Special thanks also go to Ama Page, all the way out there in Botswana, for the wonderful illustrations, and to Tony Banks MP for offering to host the book launch in the House (and I don't mean his house). Thanks also go to the following for contributing ideas, answers, leads and suggestions. In no particular order, then: Andy McDaniel, Bruce Foxton and Steve Grantley of the Stiff Little Fingers fame (make of that what you will) who are responsible for a couple of the little gems you will later read. Then thanks to Claire Miller for the illustration of me. The Teswaine trio of Peter Patsalides for the Greek translation, Paul Ryan for his spiritual guidance and fatherly advice and Tony Henderson for his support. Nigel Harland for lunch at the Lords, followed by the Commons and then followed by a visit to their respective libraries (no dusty librarians in there). It should also be recorded that David Dickie's suggestions (set enough traps in the woods and you are going to catch a badger) weren't quite what I had in mind but made us all laugh just the same. Peter Gordon should get a mention in here somewhere and so must my sister Julie Willmott and cousin John Harris. Thanks to Martin Foale for his suggestion, Lucian Randall and all at Blake Publishing.

If this book is a roaring success then all of them should share the credit in some small way. If, however, it turns out to be an unmitigated disaster, then they can have all the credit themselves and leave me out of it.

Albert Jack – Guildford, October 2004

ACKNOWLEDGEMENTS

Albert Jack supports the MacKinnon Trust, a registered charity working to raise awareness in mental-health issues such as schizophrenia and the care needed by those who suffer and their families. Their website can be found at www.mackinnontrust.org

INTRODUCTION

In the course of a day, we all use many examples of what is known as an idiom. Idioms are words and phrases which those of us with a native English tongue take for granted, as we have grown up to recognise their meaning. That is despite the words being used having absolutely nothing to do with the context of a conversation we are having.

For example, if I explained I am writing this preface 'off the cuff', you would immediately recognise it as an unprepared piece being written in one take (which, by the way, it is). But why do I call that 'off the cuff' when it has nothing to do with my cuffs, much less being either on or off them?

If I suggest everything in this book is absolutely true, I can emphasis that statement by insisting every word in here is 'straight from the horse's mouth'. Again, we all know that means it has come directly from the source of information and is therefore reliable. But I haven't got a horse. I have never spoken to one and unless I can find one that wins more often, even when I hedge my bets, then I might have nothing to do with any of the beasts again.

These phrases appear in conversation all over the English-speaking world every minute of the day and we take them for granted. Have you ever heard someone say they had a bone to pick with you or they could smell a rat? Have you wondered what on earth they were talking about? No, probably not, because we all grow up knowing what these phrases refer to, but, if you were overheard by anyone learning our beautiful language, they'd think we were all mad.

However, have you ever wondered where those phrases come from in the first place and why we use them? I did, when I was sitting in a pub with a friend, who was feeling a little groggy and under the weather, as he had been out painting the town red the previous night. I suggested a hair of the dog was in order and the bar-person, who was an English student from

Colombia, and a very good one at that, thought we were crazy. She told us dogs weren't allowed in the pub. How we all laughed.

It was wintertime, and cold enough to freeze the balls off a brass monkey, so cold, in fact, I believe it was snowing in the ladies. So we sat by the fire, hair of the dog in hand, and started wondering where those sayings originated and why they are so natural to use. The pub's guv'nor eventually fetched us up a square meal, but we'd been there a while and before we all reached the end of our tethers I decided to leave for home. It was raining cats and dogs outside, so I bit the bullet and made my way through the cold and started researching these little phrases. Within minutes I had discovered that many of them do have traceable origins and some even emerge from a particular event in history. Some are unbelievable but, by and large, many make immediate sense. Some have more than one suggested origin, in which case, I have chosen the source that had the best supporting evidence. Therefore, I can assure the reader, there is only one cock and bull story among them.

It took months of painstaking research, working mainly between the hours of closing time and opening time, before I finally had it in the bag and the fruit of that labour is now in your hand. I know there are many missing idioms (thousands of the rascals, in fact), but we deliberately selected only the best-known sayings with interesting origins. The idea was not to create a definitive dictionary of well-known phrases, but to choose the ones we could have some fun with and those that you, the reader who sent a shilling in my direction, would enjoy.

Thanks to my brilliant illustrator, Ama Page, there are also some top-notch cartoons to help you along the way. If this volume proves to be popular, there will be a second edition to which you are invited to contribute by sending suggestions to info@albertjack.com.

But there is another benefit to reading this book. Everybody loves trivia, but nobody likes a smart Alec. So, the next time you are caught in a corner with somebody talking a load of old codswallop, tell them where that phrase comes from and then start reciting a few of the other shaggy dog tales from this collection. That should get rid of them for you.

1: NAUTICAL

To be **Taken Aback** suggests someone has been taken truly by surprise and stopped in their tracks. 'Aback' is the nautical term for sudden wind change, in which the sails flatten against the mast. In some cases, out on the high seas, tall square-rigged ships may not only be slowed down by a sudden wind change, but also driven backwards by strong gusts. The phrase used in such circumstances is 'taken aback'.

To **Have Someone Over A Barrel** means that somebody is totally at the mercy of third parties and unable to have any influence over the circumstances surrounding them. In medieval Britain it was standard practice to drape a drowning, or drowned, person face down over a large barrel to try and clear their lungs. As the victim was usually unconscious it was obvious they were totally reliant upon third parties and whatever action they took would determine their fate. Not really an ideal situation to be in for many reasons – especially in the Navy.

The **Bitter End** is the absolute end. This phrase has its origins at sea and is nothing to do with taste. On the sailing ships of past centuries, the anchor was fixed to the deck by solid bollards made of iron and wood known as 'bitts'. Coloured rags were tied to the rope near the deck end and once they were revealed crewmates knew the anchor could not be let out much further. The rope between the anchor and rag was known as the bitt end or the bitter end. To be at the 'bitter end' meant there was no rope left and the water was too deep to set the anchor.

If something **Goes By The Board** it means it is cast aside, lost in the events. On the old wooden tall ships the 'board' was the side of the boat. Anything falling off a ship and lost forever was regarded as gone past the board, or 'by the board'.

By And Large is a phrase we use as a substitute for 'broadly speaking' or dealing with a subject in general terms rather than in a detailed way. The phrase is a nautical one and dates back to day when ships relied on the wind in their sails. Sailing 'by' means to steer a ship very close to the line of the wind, and sailing 'large' means the wind is on the quarter. This technique made it easier for helmsmen to keep a ship on course during changing winds and in difficult conditions but not in a particularly accurate way, just generally in the right direction. Large ships were assessed on their ability to sail 'by and large'. The phrase was a standard part of the nautical language by 1669 and in wider use by the turn of the following century.

When you have **Had Your Chips** your luck has run out and you are close to failing altogether. Often this is thought to relate to gambling casinos and the gaming chips they use as stake money. This certainly does ring true and can illustrate a situation where a desperate gambler, trying to win back his losses, could be told, 'You have had all your chips now.' But there is an earlier suggestion. An old naval story indicates workers in a dockyard were allowed to take home off-cuts of timber, known as chips, as a perk of the job. It was not uncommon for some men to fall out of favour with the foreman, perhaps for trying to take too many, and to have this privilege removed. In which cases they were told they had 'had all their chips'.

To **Cut And Run** describes pulling rapidly out of a difficult situation and escaping without disadvantage. The phrase was first recorded in 1704 and has a nautical meaning. Hauling a heavy anchor was a difficult task and took many men a considerable time to both free it and raise it back into the sling. Ships coming under attack from the shoreline could suffer considerable damage before the anchor could be dislodged and raised, so it became standard practice to chop the hemp anchor line with an axe and to allow the ship to 'run on the wind'. By 1861 the phrase to 'cut and run' was a standard naval expression.

Dead In The Water means an idea or scheme has no momentum and no chance of success. This is a nautical expression, dating back to the days of the sailing ships. On a windless day, with nothing to propel the vessel, a boat sitting motionless in the sea was known as 'dead in the water', going nowhere.

To be **At A Loose End** describes a time when we would normally be sitting around with nothing to do. We go back to the old tall ships to define this phrase. Any ship using sails would have thousands of ropes making up the rigging. Each of these lengths would need to be bound tight at both ends to prevent them from unravelling, which would be disastrous during a storm. When the ship's captain found seamen sitting around with nothing to do, he would usually assign them mundane labour such as checking the rigging for loose ends, and re-binding them. Therefore, idle men would find usually themselves 'at a loose end'.

On The Fiddle has nothing at all to do with the previous saying. Instead it implies someone is involved in something not entirely within the rules, and perhaps gaining more than they should be. This is a nautical saying and associated directly with the square ship plate (see **Square Meal**). Those square plates had a raised rim (as did the tables), which prevented food falling off in high seas and these rims were called 'fiddles'.

Crew would become suspicious of a fellow sailor with so much food it piled against the rims and they became known as 'on the fiddle' (taking or being given more than they should).

First Rate means something is the best available, near perfect or as good as you can get. From the time Henry VIII began organising the English Navy in the 16th century, war ships were rated on a scale of one to six (a grading that lasted more than 300 years). Then, as now, size mattered and the smallest ships were given a sixth rating, while the largest and best armed were regarded as first rate. Therefore, the best ships to command or crew were known as the 'first rate' vessels, a term that became synonymous with the best of anything.

To **Flog A Dead Horse** is to waste time and energy on a situation that will clearly have a negative outcome. Far out to sea, the Horse Latitudes can be found 30 degrees either side of the Equator, where the subsiding dry air and high pressure results in weak winds. According to naval legend, the area was so called because the tall sail ships, relying on strong winds, always slowed considerably or even stalled altogether. Often it took months to pass through the Horse Latitudes, by which time sailors had worked off what was known as the 'Dead Horse' – the advance wages they had received when signing on. As seamen were paid by the day, the slow passage was to their benefit and there was no incentive to expend much effort in the Horse Latitudes as they worked off their advance wages. Therefore this period of months in the painfully slow mid-ocean became known as 'flogging the dead horse'.

When somebody **Passes With Flying Colours** they have achieved something with distinction, or been successful in a difficult task. The earliest known reference dates back to 1706 and the English Navy, whose term for flag was 'colours'. Victorious and sailing back into London, fleets would demonstrate their success at battle by keeping the battle flags high on the mast and word would soon spread that the Navy had passed by 'with its colours flying', a sure sign of victory.

To feel **Groggy** means to feel generally run down and unwell, often as the result of drinking too much. In 1740 Admiral Vernon, the commander in chief of the West Indies, replaced the neat rum which was then issued to all sailors twice daily, with a watered-down version. The Admiral was a well-known figure and had the nickname 'Old Grog' because of his trademark Grogam coat (a rough mixture of mohair and silk). Thomas Trotter, a sailor on board the *Berwick*, wrote the following passage in 1781:

A mighty bowl on deck he drew
And filled it to the brink
Such drank the *Burford*'s gallant crew
And such the gods shall drink
The sacred robe which Vernon wore
Was drenched within the same
And hence his virtues guard our shore
And Grog drives its name

According to The *Guardian*'s *Notes & Queries, Series I,* the unhappy sailors of the fleet soon began calling the new watered-down ration 'Grog' and as a natural progression drunk sailors were considered 'groggy'.

Making money **Hand Over Fist** alludes to the practice of making steady financial gain, and usually pretty quickly. Back in the 18th century the term was originally 'hand over hand' and was a nautical term meaning 'to make fast and steady progress up a rope'. Later modified to 'hand over fist', alluding to a flat hand passing over the fist gripping the rope, the phrase widened to describe any steady progress in the forward direction, never backwards, such as a boat race. By the late 19th century the financial markets, where often the largest sums could be made out of industrial shipping, had adopted the expression.

The expression to be **Left High And Dry** describes being stranded in a situation without support or resource. It's quite simply a nautical phrase, in use from the early 1800s (around the time of the Battle of Trafalgar in 1805), and used to describe a ship left grounded and vulnerable as the tides goes out. A ship's captain who had been left 'high and dry' could do nothing to resolve his situation until the tide returned and refloated his boat. In the meantime the ship was exposed and vulnerable.

To be **Put Through The Hoop** means to be punished or chastised for a wrongdoing. This is a nautical phrase related to the ancient marine custom of 'running the hoop'. The punishment comprised four or more convicted sailors being stripped to the waist, and having their left hands tied to an iron hoop. In the other hand each would hold a length of rope known as a nettle. The bosun would then hit one sailor with a cat o' nine tales and he in turn would have to hit the man in front of him. Being put 'through the ordeal of the hoop' later became shortened to the phrase we know today. Originally, it was a form of horseplay when the ship was in calm waters, but as each blow landed the angry recipient would land a harder blow on the man in turn. As it went on the blows became harder, leading to its effectiveness more as a punishment rather than a game.

Telling a person to **Shake A Leg** means encouraging them to get on with a task. In recent centuries the phrase was well used in public school dormitories, prisons and other institutions where people sleeping in communal rooms would be ordered out of bed at dawn every day. The origin of the saying dates back to the time when civilian women were first allowed on board a ship. At that time the bosun's mate would traditionally rouse the sailors with the cry 'Shake a leg or a purser's stocking.' When a stocking-clad female leg appeared the lady was allowed to stay in her bunk until the men were all up and departed. This was an obvious attempt to preserve her modesty while dressing, but it would seem fair to suggest that a lady on board a ship full of 18th-century sailors may not have had much modesty left worth preserving.

When a person **Splices The Mainbrace**, they are celebrating the successful outcome of an event. The phrase is another dating back to the days of the tall ships that relied upon the wind in their sails. During heavy seas the bosun granted extra rum rations to the sailors who undertook the dangerous duty of climbing the highest rigging, known as the mainbrace. Such sailors were able to celebrate a little more than the others who were given more menial tasks to perform.

Money For Old Rope is simple to explain. In days long gone, when the tall ships returned to their ports, some sailors were allowed to claim old rigging damaged during the voyage. Although of no use to the ships needing long undamaged lines for their sails, parts would still be in good condition and sought after by local traders. Sailors profited by selling it on and, as no effort was required on their part (it was regarded as a perk amongst senior shipmen), some jealousy occurred. The chosen few were criticised for making 'money out of old rope'. These days estate agents have replaced favoured crewmen.

When it is cold enough to **Freeze The Balls Off A Brass Monkey**, we really had better wrap up warm. But who ever heard of such a thing? Old nautical records provide the answer. The guns on 18th-century men-of-war ships needed gun-powder to fire them, and this was stored in a different part of the ship for safety reasons. Young boys, usually orphans, who were small enough to slip through tight spaces, carried this powder along tiny passages and galleys. Because of their agility the lads became known as 'powder monkeys' and by association the brass trays used to hold the cannonballs became known as the brass monkeys. These trays had 16 cannonball-sized indentations that would form the base of a cannonball pyramid. Brass was used because the balls would not stick to or rust on brass as they did with iron, but the drawback was that brass contracts much faster in cold weather than iron. This meant that on severely cold days the indentations holding the lower level of cannonballs would contract, spilling the pyramid over the deck, hence 'cold enough to freeze the balls off a brass monkey'.

When something is **In The Offing** it is considered to be likely to happen, possibly imminently. The origin of this saying can be found on the high seas in the 17th century. 'Offing' was nautical slang for 'offshore' and a ship approaching a port or coastline, close enough to be seen from land, was considered to be 'in the offing'.

To **Push The Boat Out** is used to describe a large celebration or expense. This is obviously a nautical expression and relates to the large parties and celebrations sailors would have before setting out on long voyages. A 'pushing the boat out' celebration was always a popular one to attend.

When we look out of the window and it is **Raining Cats And Dogs**, it is too wet to go out. There are several suggestions for the origin of this phrase, one alluding to a famous occasion when it actually rained frogs. Apparently many were lifted into the air during a howling gale and then dropped to the ground around startled pedestrians. Cockney rhyming slang then substituted 'cats and dogs' for 'frogs'.

But I prefer the ancient nautical myth, which led sailors to believe that cats had some sort of influence over storms. According to the Vikings dogs were also a symbol of storms and they always appear in illustrations and descriptions of their own Norse god of storms. (Odin, father of Thor, was the god of thunder and is described as an old bearded man with one eye who wore a cloak and wide-brimmed hat. Many claim he was the inspiration for JRR Tolkien's character Gandalf in *The Lord Of The Rings*.) Because of this connection, ancient mariners believed that when it rained it was the cats who caused it, and when the gales appeared they were brought by the dogs, leading to the phrase 'raining cats and dogs'.

The phrase first appeared in literature in 1738 when Jonathan Swift wrote in his book *A Complete Collection Of Polite And Ingenious Conversation*, 'I know Sir John will go, though he was sure it would rain cats and dogs.' In 1653 Richard Broome wrote in his play *City Wit*, 'It shall rain dogs and polecats,' suggesting he too alluded to the old nautical tales.

You Scratch My Back And I'll Scratch Yours is a saying with its origins in the English Navy. These days we use it to suggest two people will do each other a favour, or look out for each other so that both parties benefit from one another's actions. During the 17th and 18th centuries the English Navy was traditionally brutal and punishments for disobedience or absenteeism were unimaginably harsh. It was common for a crewmember to be tied to a mast after being sentenced to a dozen lashes, with a 'cat o' nine tails', for minor offences such as being drunk. A 'cat' was nine lengths of thin knotted ship rope bound at one end into a handle. These punishments were usually carried out in full view of the crew, by one of the victim's crewmates. But it was also likely that the crewmate would himself be a victim of the cat o' nine tails at some stage on a voyage, so would be lenient with his victim by applying only light stokes and merely 'scratching' his back. He himself would then receive equally lenient treatment by another shipmate if and when he was on the receiving end.

When you find a person **Three Sheets To The Wind** they are roaring drunk and capable of very little. There are two suggested origins for this phrase. The first is that a windmill with only three sails (sheets) would rotate badly and wobble like a drunk. But the second is far more likely, especially as, like so many phrases, it has a nautical origin. The sails of a tall ship were controlled by rope (the rigging) and these ropes were – and still are – called 'sheets'. Two sheets controlled each sail and the story is that if one of the sheets wasn't properly handled, then the other three (of the two sails) would be 'to the wind'. The boat would then be blown about from side to side and not under full control, much like a drunk trying to navigate his way home.

Shipshape And Bristol Fashion is used to say that everything is neat, tidy and in good order. In the days before Liverpool became a major English port, Bristol was the premier western port from which most ships would embark on transatlantic voyages. It was also a naval port and prided itself on its reputation for efficiency and neatly packed cargoes. The traditional high standards of ships leaving Bristol lead to the phrase passing into the English language.

To **Sling Your Hook** is often used as a 'polite' instruction for somebody to go away. There are several possibilities for this, some referring to the hooks miners or dockers hung their day clothes on during a shift. But the earliest reference is again a nautical one with the hook being a ship's anchor and the sling being the cradle it rests in while at sea. To 'sling the hook' meant to be upping anchor and leaving harbour.

Son Of A Gun began as a dismissive, contemptuous remark, although now it has developed into a more friendly expression, often implying shock and disbelief. Back on the high seas, in the days when women were allowed to live on board the ships, unexpected pregnancy was a regular occurrence. The area behind the mid-ship gun, and behind a canvas screen, was usually where the infant was born. If paternity was uncertain, and it isn't hard to imagine this happened more often than not, the child would be entered into the log as the 'son of a gun'.

Another nautical phrase widely used is **Spick And Span**. These days it indicates something that is new, clean and tidy. Back in the ancient shipyards a 'spick' was a nail or tack (a spike) and a 'span' was a wooden chip or shaving. Newly launched ships, with wooden shavings still present and shiny nails, would be regarded as 'all spick and span' – brand new.

A **Square Meal** is used to describe a good, solid dinner. It is a nautical phrase dating back centuries. Old battleships had notoriously poor living conditions and the sailors' diet was equally bad. Breakfast and lunch would rarely be better than bread and water but the last meal of each day would at least include meat and have some substance. Any significant meal eaten on board a ship would be served on large square wooden trays which sailors carried back to their posts. The trays were square in design to enable them to be stored away both easily and securely, hence the phrase 'a square meal'.

These days **Swing The Lead** is a metaphor used to describe somebody who is avoiding work by giving the appearance of toiling, but not actually doing anything. It is a phrase with its origins in naval history. Aboard ship it was the job of a leadsman to calculate the depth of water around a coastline by dropping a lead weight attached to a measuring line at the bow end. As the easiest job on board it was usually given to a sick or injured seaman and many feigned illness in an attempt to secure such light work. The phrase came ashore and is now used to describe anybody making excuses or simply going through the motions.

A **Washout** is a general failure where no trace of any effort has been made. This expression has its origin in the way the old tall ships passed messages to each other. Naval signals would be read and then chalked on to a slate before being passed to the correct authorities. Once the message had been received, the slate would be washed clean so that no traces of the message would be left other than in the correct hands. This was known as a 'washout' and it is easy to see how the phrase spread into wider use on land.

To be **Under The Weather** means to feel unwell and unable to function properly, and is yet another phrase with its origin out at sea. In days gone by when a sailor was ill he would be sent below decks where he could recover. Under the decks and 'under the weather' his condition could begin to improve.

If we are told to **Whistle For It** the inference is that we are highly unlikely to get the result we want. This is another expression dating back to the early sailing ships circumnavigating the world. The belief among some sailors was that when the day was still, and the sails empty, they could summon the wind by whistling for it. Other sailors disagreed and felt whistling was the Devil's music and instead of a gentle wind arriving a fierce storm would appear. This also explains the origin of the phrase '**whistling in the wind**'. Often, whistling would bring no change in the weather at all (no surprises there) but it did lead to yet another saying, '**neither a fair wind nor a storm**', meaning the action altered nothing at all.

2: MILITARY

Once **The Balloon Has Gone Up** you know there is trouble ahead. During the First World War, observation balloons would be sent into the sky at the first suspicion of an enemy attack, in order to monitor distant enemy troop movements. To most this was a sign of impending action. During the Second World War, strong barrage balloons connected to the ground with thick steel cable were raised around English cities. The idea of these was to impede enemy aircraft, which might crash into them in the darkness or clip their wings on the steel cable. Often they also protected cities from enemy missiles, which would hit a balloon and explode before reaching its target. Their success was immeasurable but to city folk the sign of 'the balloon going up' meant an impending air raid. Trouble was indeed ahead.

To **Beat A Hasty Retreat** means to abandon something, to leave quickly and avoid the consequences of remaining in the same position. This term dates back to the time when a marching army would take its orders from the drummer. Positioned next to the commanding officer, the drummer boy would beat the orders to an army on a battlefield. At night time, or during a battle when things were not going well, the drummer would be ordered to beat a 'retreat' and on hearing the signal a fighting army would immediately cease battle and return to company lines as quickly as they could.

To **Bite The Bullet** is to carry out a task against the doer's wishes. It means getting on with something that just 'has to be done'. This phrase has its origins in the British Empire as the Victorians made friends around the world at the point of a gun. At the time of the Indian Mutiny, gun cartridges came in two parts with the missile part being inserted into the base and held in place by grease made of either cow or pork fat. To charge the bullets the two parts had to be bitten apart and the base filled with gunpowder before they could be fired. This task was usually left to low-ranking Hindu soldiers to whom pigs are holy animals, sacred and not to be desecrated. However they were forced, against their wishes, to 'bite the bullet' in times of battle.

To **Chance Your Arm** is to take an uncalculated risk, where the outcome is completely unknown: a blind bet, if you like. There are several suggestions for the origin of this saying, one being that military men, whose rank was displayed in the way of stripes on their sleeves, would take battlefield risks, which could equally lead to promotion or demotion, depending on the outcome.

A better explanation (at least one that is more fun) dates back to Ireland as long ago as 1492. During a feud between two distinguished families, the Kildares and the Ormonds, during which Sir James Butler, the Earl of Ormond, and his family took sanctuary inside St Patrick's Cathedral in Dublin. The Kildares laid siege outside until Gerald Fitzpatrick, the Earl of Kildare, decided the feud had gone too far and attempted a reconciliation. But the Ormonds were suspicious of his offer of peaceful settlement and refused to leave the cathedral. As a desperate measure to prove his good intentions Fitzgerald ordered a hole to be cut into the cathedral door and then thrust his outstretched hand through, putting his arm at the mercy of those inside as it could easily have been cut off. Instead, Butler took his hand and peace was restored. It is not known if that is actually the origin of the phrase, but it should be.

To be **Sent To Coventry** is to become a social outcast and be ignored by everybody. But why Coventry? During the English Civil War in the mid-1600s Coventry was a strong Parliamentarian town, and Royalist soldiers, captured during the early battles in the Midlands, would be sent to nearby Coventry where they could be certain of a frosty reception. Long before the days of prison camps soldiers loyal to the King could only wander around town looking for food or work but locals would refuse to speak with them, and would even turn their backs and ignore their presence completely. Back then the only entertainment to be found was in local inns but Royalists were barred. Coventry was clearly no place for them but, short of walking back to London, and starving on the way, there was little option but to stay and scavenge. In some cases Royalist soldiers who were deemed useless or not quite committed to the cause would also be garrisoned near Coventry, assuring them of a miserable posting by way of punishment. The idea was that, as no loyalist wanted to be sent to Coventry, they might show more commitment to the King in battle and avoid the posting.

A **Feather In Your Cap** means you have done something well and it has been duly noted, although not rewarded by any tangible means other than by having a 'feather placed in your cap'. Its origin seems easy to explain. Any Indian brave fighting for his tribe in America, who killed an enemy, was rewarded by having a feather placed in his head-dress. The most prolific braves would have a headband full of feathers. However, four hundred years prior to this, in medieval England, battlefield bravery was rewarded in a similar way. Knights who had shown great courage were also afforded plumes to wear in their helmets. The Black Prince, 16-year-old Prince Edward, the Prince of Wales of his day, showed such courage at the Battle of Crecy in 1346 (the first great battle of the Hundred Years War) he was awarded the crest of one of his defeated enemies, John of Bohemia. That crest, of three ostrich feathers, remains the crest of the Prince of Wales to this day.

The phrase **Pull Your Finger Out** is associated these days with encouraging someone to get a move on, or hurry up and complete a task more quickly. Like so many English phrases it has a military or naval origin. Loaded cannons would have gunpowder poured into a small ignition hole and held in place with a wooden plug. But in times of battle, when speed was of the essence, the powder would be pushed in and then held in place by a gun crewmember using his finger. Impatient artillerymen, anxious to fire their cannons at the enemy, would shout at the crewmember to 'pull his finger out' so that the gun could be fired. It has not been recorded how many digits were lost on the battlefields.

Flash In The Pan is used to describe something or somebody making a great impression at the outset but ultimately failing to deliver any real result. Of military origin the phrase emerged during the use of early flintlock muskets. Sometimes gunpowder would ignite with a flash in the lock-pan but the main charge failed to light, meaning the shot in the barrel did not discharge, so no harm could come to man nor beast that time round. It was a 'flash in the pan' and the expression was in regular use by 1741.

To **Throw Down The Gauntlet** is to lay a challenge, originally of combat but latterly to any form of contest. A gauntlet is a medieval armoured glove, forming part of a knight's suit of armour. Traditionally a knight would challenge another to a duel by throwing down his gauntlet. If his opponent picked it up it meant he was accepting the challenge and battle would begin. **Taking Up The Gauntlet** has since been a phrase used for accepting a challenge. The Swedish word 'gantlope' (see **Run The Gauntlet**) was anglicised to 'gauntlet' as a result of this tradition, but 'running the gauntlet' and 'throwing down the gauntlet' are not otherwise connected.

Hanging Fire is often used to describe a pause before beginning a task. Sixteenth-century muskets were always slow to fire their charge due to the delay between lighting the gunpowder in the touch-hole and detonation. This was known at the time as 'hang-fire' and the expression was soon used to describe any person delaying or slow to take action.

To Be Hoisted By One's Own Petard means to become a victim of your own deceit, or caught in your own trap. In medieval times a petard was a thick iron container which was filled with gunpowder and set against medieval gates, barricades and bridges. The wicks, however, were unreliable and often detonated the gunpowder immediately, blowing up the engineer in the process. In which case he was 'hoisted (blown up) by his own petard (container of gunpowder)'.

To take someone **Down A Peg Or Two** means to reduce their status among their peers. It is possible the origin of this phrase is found at sea, and the peg used to fly a ship's colours. The lower the peg, the less impressive the achievement. But there is also a reference dating as far back as the 10th century and King Edred's anger at the amount that his army was drinking. Aware that he needed his soldiers sober for the great battles against the Vikings, Edred ordered pegs to be put into the side of ale barrels and no man was allowed to drink below the level of the peg in a single sitting. But as soon as this rule was applied soldiers would drink from other people's kegs and take them down a 'peg or two'.

3: LITERATURE

Dickens was certainly good at inventing phrases. One of them was **Artful Dodger**, which is used to describe somebody involved in crafty or criminal practice. One of Dickens's characters in *Oliver Twist* (1837) was Jack Dawkins, a wily pickpocket and expert member of Fagin's gang of thieves. During the story the author gave Dawkins the nickname 'The Artful Dodger'. Almost immediately the Victorian public adopted the phrase and it was used to describe any crafty rogue.

To have **Cold Feet** indicates a loss of nerve or to have doubts about a particular situation. This phrase has its origins in the gaming world, albeit a fictional one. In 1862 Fritz Reuter, a German author, described a scene in one of his novels during which a poker player fears losing his fortune but does not want to lose face by conceding defeat. Instead he explains to his fellow poker players his feet are too cold and he cannot concentrate. This gives him a chance to leave the table and then slip away from the game. It is not known whether Reuter was drawing on a real life experience (as many novelists do) but his scene certainly appears to be the origin of the phrase.

To **Curry Favour** is a phrase used to describe keeping on the good side of somebody, carrying out acts to keep in favour. The origin of this phrase does not lie in Indian culture, but in the 'Roman de Fauvel', a French satirical poem written in 1310 and popular for centuries. Fauvel was the name of the centaur (half-man, half-horse) who was a beast of great cunning and danger, and to keep on the right side of him sycophants would spend time grooming Fauvel to keep him in a good mood. The art of grooming or dressing a horse is known as 'currying' the animal and therefore those seeking to keep in the centaur's good books could be found 'currying Fauvel'. Over the centuries, and through translation, 'Fauvel' became 'favour'.

A **Dark Horse** is something of an unknown quantity, perhaps somebody whose abilities are not yet fully known but soon will be. In the 16th century the phrase 'to keep something dark' meant keeping something quiet but Benjamin Disraeli created our phrase in his debut novel *The Young Duke*, published in 1831. (At that time Disraeli was only 27 years old and another 37 years away from being Prime Minister.) In his story he describes a horse race in which the two favourites are beaten to the finishing line by an unfancied third. Disraeli wrote, 'a dark horse which never had been thought of rushed past the grandstand in sweeping triumph.' It was common for owners to conceal the potential of their best new horses until the actual day of

the race, and almost immediately, throughout
the racing world, such animals became known as
'dark horses' regardless of their colour.

Dickens To Pay is used as a threat: 'If you do
that again there will be Dickens to pay.'
Charles Dickens wasn't a frightening character
so as a threat it seems mild to say the least. But
the 19th-century novelist has nothing to do

with it. As long ago as the 16th century the word 'Devil' was, in fact, 'Devilkin' and having 'the devilkin to pay' meant a passage straight to Hell for one's misdemeanour. Devilkin was usually pronounced 'Dickens', or at least it was in 1601 when William Shakespeare included the line 'I cannot tell what the Dickens his name was' in his play *The Merry Wives Of Windsor* – more than 200 years before Charles Dickens was born.

To describe somebody as a **Good** or **Bad Egg** would suggest they were either decent, dependable and reliable or not. The expression 'bad egg' was first used in 1855 in Samuel A Hammett's novel *Captain Priest* which included the phrase, 'In the language of his class the Perfect Bird generally turns out to be a bad egg.' The analogy he draws is with an egg that on the outside may appear fresh, but when the shell is broken it may be rotten inside. At the beginning of the 20th century students began reversing the phrase and describing decent people as a 'good egg'.

The phrase **As Sure As Eggs Is Eggs** is used to describe absolute certainty about something. In fact, it is a simple misquote which has passed into common usage. In formal logic and mathematics the formula 'x is x' is used to describe complete certainty. It is unclear how or when 'x is x' became 'eggs is eggs' but it is known Charles Dickens used the phrase 'eggs is eggs' in *The Pickwick Papers*, published in 1837. Maybe Dickens was joking, or playing on words, or possibly it was a simple mistake that proved amusing enough to be left unchanged.

At One Fell Swoop is used to indicate 'in a single movement' or all at the same time, and conjures up an image of a bird of prey swooping down on its target. It is one of Shakespeare's creations. In the Bard's 1606 play *Macbeth*, the character Macduff, on learning his wife and children have all been killed, cries out, 'What, all my pretty chickens, and their dam, at one fell swoop?' The word 'fell' has been used since then to mean 'evil' or 'deadly'.

Sending someone off with a **Flea In Their Ear** implies they have been told off, and in no uncertain terms. The analogy is that of a dog with a flea in its ear, running around in distress shaking its head. The phrase has been used since 1579 when the popular Elizabethan author John Lyly (Lillie or Lylie) published *Euphues, Or The Anatomy Of Wit*. In it he included the line – 'Ferardo... whispering Philautus in his eare (who stoode as though he had a flea in his eare), desired him to kepe silence', as he described a scene where the lord of the manor rebuked a servant.

The phrase **Going For A Song** is used to indicate that something is cheap and priced well below its true value. The actual song, which describes the origin, is in fact a long poem called 'The Faerie Queene', presented to Queen Elizabeth I by Edmund Spenser. At the time it was regarded as Spenser's most popular work but Lord Burleigh, the Lord High Treasurer, was unimpressed. When he heard the Queen intended to pay Spenser £100 for the work, he famously exclaimed, 'What! All this for a song?' The Queen, much to Burleigh's dismay, insisted the money was handed over. The incident was widely reported and the phrase became English slang, although meaning of low value instead of high. The reason for this was the pennies and small change people would toss to buskers and singers entertaining in the hostelries around old London town.

To **Kill The Goose That Lays The Golden Egg** is to destroy a source of income, or other benefit, through sheer greed. The origin of this saying can be found in one of Aesop's fables, which was translated into English by William Caxton in 1484. In the story Aesop tells the tale of a peasant who discovered a goose that laid golden eggs. In his excitement, and desire to become instantly wealthy, the hapless peasant immediately cut the goose open in order to retrieve the rest of the hidden fortune, killing it in the process and consequently losing his chance of great wealth. The moral of the fable is to be content and have patience, and to caution against greed.

To **Go The Whole Hog** means to do something thoroughly and completely without reservation. Although this is unlikely to be the origin of the phrase, the first reference to it can be found in William Cowper's 1779 poem 'The Love Of The World; or Hypocrisy Detected'. As Cowper describes Muslim leaders trying to work out which part of the hog was edible, he says, 'But for one piece they thought it hard, from the whole hog to be debarred.'

The passing of the phrase into wider use came

from the sales tactics of American meat men. Starting in Virginia, enterprising butchers offered joints of meat for sale by the pound, but anybody buying the whole animal would be charged a much cheaper rate, pound for pound. Buying the whole hog and then sharing it around friends and neighbours soon became standard practice for those looking for good discounts on their meat prices. In 1828 Andrew Jackson often used the phrase 'going the whole hog' in his presidential campaign. The election was notable as being the first involving ordinary Americans and campaign leaders organised rallies, parades, dinners and barbecues in order to win votes. Slogans were also used for the first time and Jackson's 'going the whole hog' (going all the way) became known all over America. Jackson won the election, considered at the time as the dirtiest campaign ever witnessed.

How The Other Half Lives is a friendly phrase alluding to the life styles of the rich. The expression can be traced as far back as 1532 and the French book *Pantagruel* by Rabelais and was in use in England by 1607. Jacob Riis used the phrase as the title of a book in 1890 but somewhere along the line the saying has completely changed its meaning. Originally it was a condescending expression used by the rich to describe the poor, but these days it is a light-hearted expression used by the less fortunate to describe the rich.

Ignorance Is Bliss is used to suggest that lack of knowledge equals lack of concern. Originally the phrase alluded to the innocence of youth described in 1747 by Thomas Gray in his poem 'Ode On A Distant Prospect Of Eton College' in the lines 'Thought would destroy their paradise / No more where ignorance is bliss / Tis folly to be wise'. The context Gray uses for the word ignorance is one of limited knowledge rather than the impoliteness or arrogance the word can also be associated with.

Living in an **Ivory Tower** is a mildly pejorative expression used to describe those who live sheltered lives, away from the harsh realities and problems faced by others. It is of French origin and can be traced back as far as the early 1800s, to a poet named Alfred de Vigny. Alfred led a life of disappointment and in his later years withdrew almost completely from society, while continuing to write. In 1837, in a poem called 'Pensees d'Aout' ('Thoughts of August') written by a critic called Sainte-Beuve, de Vigny's lifestyle was described as isolated, and it was suggested he lived in a secluded 'tour d'ivoire' (an 'ivory tower'). The phrase was then widely used to describe other academics who had the reputation of living in a world away from harsh realities, suggesting they knew little about real life.

A **Jekyll And Hyde** character is a person who has two very different sides to his personality. One side is sweet and loving and the other dark and menacing. *The Strange Case Of Dr Jekyll And Mr Hyde* is a story by Robert Louis Stevenson first published in 1886 to instant acclaim. In the story Stevenson describes a doctor (Jekyll) who discovers a drug enabling him to create a separate personality to express his own evil instincts. He calls his new personality 'Mr Hyde'. As the story unfolds Hyde becomes more and more wicked and eventually Dr Jekyll finds the drug too powerful to overcome and he is unable to return to his natural state of calm and reason, leading to his eventual suicide.

A **Leap Of Faith** or a **Leap In The Dark** is a step into the unknown where an outcome cannot be reliably predicted. It is famously suggested the final words of English philosopher Thomas Hobbes (1588–1679) were, 'Now I am about to take my last voyage, a great leap in the dark.' Almost immediately others picked up his words. In 1697 Sir John Vanbrugh wrote in his play *The Provoked Wife*, 'Now I am for Hobbes' voyage, a great leap in the dark.' Other celebrated writers, such as Disraeli, Defoe and Byron, later quoted Hobbes, although over the years the phrase has developed to mean any general uncertainty, rather than the leap into eternity.

To be in possession of **The Lion's Share** is to have the larger part of something, more than anyone else involved. This phrase is another originating from Aesop's fables. One story tells of a lion and three other animals, all hunting together, who catch and kill a stag for their supper. The meal was divided into four equal parts but, just as the animals are about to tuck in, the lion stops them. He insists the first portion is for him as he is king of the jungle and therefore their ruler. He then claims a second portion for himself on the basis he is the strongest of them all and finally a third because of his infinite courage. The lion then allows the other three animals to share the last portion between them but warns them only to touch it if they dare.

Namby Pamby is a phrase used to emphasise weakness and childish manner in an adult. The original Namby Pamby was the poet Ambrose Philips (1674–1749), a fellow of St John's College, Cambridge. Philips had achieved success with both *The Distrest Mother* (1712) and his later adaptation of Racine's *Andromaque*, but his infantile language was ridiculed by the great poets of his day. It was Henry Carey who bestowed on Philips the nickname 'Namby Pamby' because his verses were addressed mainly to babies, and it was quickly adopted as part of the English language.

If something is **Piping Hot** it is extremely hot. The pipes that amplified the sound of the old pipe organs found in cathedrals and large churches would hiss in the same way as water does when it steams. When something was 'pipe hot' it was known to be boiling or steaming. The phrase was first recorded during the 1300s and can be found first in Chaucer's *Canterbury Tales* when he wrote, 'Wafers piping hot out of the gleed'. A wafer is a kind of thin cake, baked between wafer-irons, and 'gleed' is the hot coals of a fire.

Our **Salad Days** are the carefree periods of youth when mortgages, insurance and the taxman have yet to enter our minds. The weekend is for living, our partners still look forward to seeing us and the divorce court is a place for old people. The phrase is a simple one with a simple origin provided, once again, by Shakespeare. In 1606 the Bard wrote the play *Antony And Cleopatra*, which includes the line: 'They were my salad days, when I was green in judgement.'

To be **As Happy As A Sandboy** means you are in a state of joyous contentment. This phrase passed into regular usage courtesy of Charles Dickens. In 1840 Dickens published *The Old Curiosity Shop* which includes an inn called The Jolly Sandboys that displayed a sign outside depicting three drunken sandboys. But what was a sandboy? Dickens is known to have spent time in Bristol, which is referred to throughout *The Pickwick Papers*, published in 1836. Around that time it is recorded that the town's landlords would spread sand on the floor of their establishments which would soak up any spillage, much in the same way as sawdust would be used in other places. In Bristol the Redcliffe Caves are full of sand and innkeepers would send boys off into the caves to provide them with a regular supply. These youngsters were paid partly in ale and consequently they were usually half-cut (merry or jolly), hence Dickens's inn sign and the origin of our phrase.

To have a **Skeleton In The Cupboard** is to have a shameful secret hidden away. I remember as a small boy asking my mother, after watching a programme about missing siblings, if I had any brothers or sisters I didn't know about. She told me we didn't have any 'skeletons like that in our cupboards', which scared the life out of me as I wondered how many children had been locked up forever in cupboards for being naughty. Until 1832 it was illegal to dissect a human body for the benefit of medical research, but of course many a physician still did, and the skeletons had to be hidden somewhere. It is also true that, after dissections became legal, grave robbers would dig up newly buried corpses and sell them to unscrupulous doctors in an underhand way. This practice was so frowned upon that medical men would try to keep their secrets hidden away in locked cupboards. The phrase was first used in print during an article in *Punch* magazine, written in 1845 by William Thackeray, and has been in common usage ever since. My parents probably still wonder where the keys to all the wardrobes in our house went. I imagine they are still over the fence behind next door's shed.

Sour Grapes is a phrase used to describe someone who is sulking or jealous of not having something that others do have. It stems from a simple and popular fable of Aesop called 'The Fox And The Grapes', in which the fox spends a long time trying to reach a bunch of grapes high on the vine, but eventually fails. The fox then comforts himself by explaining he didn't really want them after all, as they looked sour.

An **Ugly Duckling** is a gaunt and awkward child who grows up to be beautiful. This phrase comes from a fairy tale written by children's author Hans Christian Andersen. It tells the story of a duck that mistakenly nests a swan's egg. When the egg is hatched the startled mother duck cannot understand how she has produced such an awkward, ungainly child, which is notably different from the rest of her brood. The cygnet is ridiculed for its dull appearance and hides away in the tall reeds in shame. However, come the spring, the clumsy cygnet emerges from her hideaway having been transformed into a beautiful swan. Danny Kaye's song 'The Ugly Duckling', which was released in the 1950s, popularised the story all over the world.

4: LANGUAGES

To call someone a **Berk** is generally regarded as a mildly humorous put-down without malice, but the origin of the phrase suggests it was very different to begin with. Berk derives from a simple piece of cockney rhyming slang where anybody referred to as a 'Berkshire Hunt' was on the receiving end of one of the most offensive uses of rhyming slang. 'Berkshire Hunt' was shortened to 'Berk' as a replacement for the original meaning, but these days, berk is not at all linked to its original meaning by those using it.

To go **Berserk** means to be in an uncontrollable state, wild and violent. Norse mythology tells the tale of a warrior who would work himself into a frenzy before going into battle and would cast his weapons aside to fight barehanded. Dressed only in a bearskin coat the warrior was universally feared, as were his 12 sons who each had a fearsome reputation. Their battle dress earned them a nickname. Bear is a 'bern' in old Norse and coat is translated as 'serkr' and from this combination they revelled in their reputation of 'berserkers'. Many Viking warriors emulated their example and the word crossed the North Sea to England during the Viking invasion in 865.

To **Blackmail** somebody is to demand money by threats, usually to expose secrets. This word, or phrase, originated in the Highlands of Scotland in the 1600s. The 'mail' in blackmail is the old Scottish word for rent, usually spelled either 'maill' or 'male', which in turn evolved from the Old Norse word 'mal' meaning agreement or contract. In those days tenants paid their rent in silver coins which used to be known as 'white money' but in the 1600s the Highland clan chiefs began a protection racket, threatening farmers and traders with violence if they didn't pay to be protected from other clans. This informal tax, or additional rent, soon became known as 'black money' or 'black rent', being the opposite of white, and so 'blackmaill' became part of the language as a word used to describe the practice of obtaining money by threat of violence. During the 1900s the art of demanding money not to divulge somebody's secrets was established and the use of the word 'blackmail' extended to describe this.

Blighty is an affectionate old-fashioned term for Britain. This developed during the British Empire campaign in India and is taken from the Hindi word 'Bilayti', meaning foreigner. Empire soldiers used the term to refer to their homeland and the expression was in regular use by the time of the First World War by soldiers who talked of Britain.

Getting down to **Brass Tacks** means that early discussions are complete and we now need to get to the heart of the matter, the details. Some suggestions point to the origin of this phrase being the American drapery stores, where brass-headed tacks were nailed into the counter and used for measuring out fabric. The idea being that, once the customer had taken time to choose their material, putting it to the 'brass tacks' meant actually getting down to the sale. Another explanation is that the phrase stems from the brass tacks found in furniture, which can only be seen when the item is taken apart for restoration. For the real origin we need to look no further than our good old cockney rhyming slang, in which 'facts' are dubbed 'brass tacks'.

Cockney rhyming slang is responsible for many phrases, and **A Load Of Cobblers** is another of them. These days 'cobblers' means something said is unbelievable or evident nonsense. It is an extension of 'a load of balls', a phrase widely used for centuries in England. A cobbler's awl is a tool used for making lace holes in shoes or boots. In cockney rhyming slang 'balls' became 'cobblers awls', or cobblers. In the Queen's English it means you are talking **codswallop**.

To be **Cut To The Quick** implies deep and emotional hurt. This is a simple phrase to explain as the Old English word for 'living' is *cwicu*. Back in ancient England to be 'cut to the *cwicu*' meant receiving a deep flesh wound.

Having A Dekko is a common phrase for having a look at something. It is often mistaken for cockney rhyming slang but the phrase for that is 'butcher's hook' ('hook' rhymes with 'look'). In fact, having a 'dekko' was introduced to the English language by troops returning from India in the 1800s, during the Empire-building campaigns. 'Dekko' is the Hindustani word for 'look' (or to see).

To describe a person as having **Gone Doolally** is to suggest they have gone mad. In the late 19th century, as the British Empire dominated the world, the British Army established a military base at Deolali, 100 miles north of Bombay in India. The base had an asylum, into which unstable battle-weary troops would be sent, but it also doubled as a transit camp where soldiers, at the end of their duty tour, would be stationed to await the boat home. But ships only left for Blighty between November and March so some soldiers had months to wait for their transportation. The ensuing drawn-out weeks of heat, exhaustion and boredom often resulted in strange and eccentric behaviour. This behaviour would be explained, on their return to Britain, as the man having 'gone through Deolali'. Doolally was recorded as military slang in 1925. (See also **Basket Case**.)

A **Doss House** is used to describe living accommodation that is basic in the extreme and a **Dosser** is an unkind word used to describe somebody living there or in any other cheap, temporary place. The phrase is traced back to Elizabethan England during the late 16th century when a basic straw bed was known as a 'doss', taken from the French word 'dossel' meaning bundle of hay. Farmers and other landowners would rent out straw beds in barns, or other basic shelters, to the homeless and these places, lined with 'dossels' were known as doss houses.

To **Egg On** is a term used to urge or encourage somebody, usually into doing something foolish or risky. The phrase is almost as old as eggs themselves and its origin can be found in the old Anglo-Saxon language where the word 'eggian' means to spur on, or from the Old Norse word 'eggja', meaning to incite. To 'eggian' a person was to encourage or incite them.

To **Run The Gauntlet** means to place one's self at risk of attack from all sides, either physically or verbally. It is of Scandinavian origin. In the 1600s the Swedish military would punish soldiers or sailors by forming two lines of men, each armed with a short length of rope or a baton. The offender was then forced to run down between the lines, while his comrades beat him as hard as they could. The Swedish word for passageway is 'gantlope' and this was later anglicised to 'gauntlet' by the English military, who discovered this form of punishment during the Thirty Year War (1618–48). The practice was abolished in 1813 but remained a method of public school bullying well into the 1900s.

To **Wreak Havoc** means to cause major confusion and destruction. The expression began life as 'Cry Havot' which is the old French expression for 'plunder'. In widespread use by the 13th century, the phrase evolved into Anglo-French as 'Cry Havoc'. During a military campaign the cry of 'havoc', by the generals, was the signal that the battle was won and the pillaging and looting could begin. In 1386 Richard II banned the use of the phrase on pain of death but Shakespeare used the term in several of his plays, which is how it passed over into wider use.

Hob Nobbing with somebody implies keeping their company or associating with them. This expression is the perfect example of how, as the English language progresses, word corruption often occurs. Originally the phrase used was 'hab nab' which was shortened from the Old English word 'habban', meaning 'to have', and 'nabban', meaning 'not to have'. This expression then took on the meaning of 'to give and take' in the context of drinks. But in 1811 the *Oxford English Dictionary* tells us that in the corner of an open fireplace there was usually a small ledge called a hob, which was used to warm cold wine or beer. The table this was then served upon was called a 'nob', suggesting that 'hob and nobbing' was a term for sharing drinks. By 1861 Charles Dickens had used the phrase in his novel *Great Expectations* and it passed over into wider use as a term for associating with someone.

If we are **In Cahoots** we are planning an event in secrecy. An American term, it has developed from the French word 'cahute', meaning 'small hut'. The phrase was used by native Americans to describe the French settlers during the 17th century and has come to mean groups of people colluding with each other unseen in confined spaces.

To put the **Kibosh** on something usually means it is stopped in its tracks, effectively ended. This sounds like a Jewish word and sure enough its origin can be found in Hebrew, where 'kabash' means to subdue or to bring into subjection.

If you **Lambast** someone, they are on the receiving end of a very severe rebuke or reprimand. Emanating from the Old Norse word 'lamia' meaning 'to make lame', the phrase entered the English language as 'Lam' meaning 'to beat soundly'. 'Baste' is the Old Norse word for 'thrash', or 'flog', and over time the two words have connected to provide the phrase in use today.

To **Be At Large** is usually applied to a prisoner who has escaped and is free from custody. It is one of those strange phrases that appear to have no basis in the English language, and indeed it doesn't. The French have the phrase 'prendre la large' which means 'to stand out and be free to move', from which our expression has developed.

When somebody is **Larking About** they are playing around in a silly manner. There is a suggestion that the phrase is linked to skylarks, who frolic around in the sky on summer evenings, but the expression derives from the Middle English word 'Laik' which means to play and the Old English work 'Lac' meaning a contest. By the 18th century the word 'lark' was established as part of the English language meaning 'amusing adventure or escapade'.

To **Use Your Loaf** means to show some common sense and intelligence. The origin for this is simple – 'use your loaf of bread', which is 'head' in cockney rhyming slang.

To be **Left In The Lurch** means you have been left at a disadvantage, usually by someone close to you. There is an old French game of dice called 'lourche', the object of which is to leave your opponent way behind you on the score card. When this happens, the trailing opponent incurs a lourche (a disadvantage). The phrase became anglicised via the card game of cribbage. During the scoring process if a player reaches 51 holes on the cribbage board, before another reaches 31, the trailing player is deemed to have been left in the lurch. It can also be noted that, once a winner has placed his peg in the final hole of the score board, causing the game to be over, he is considered to be **Pegged Out**, a phrase used to described being exhausted, or finished for the time being.

When somebody makes a **Moot Point** they are suggesting something so vague and ambiguous that it is open to debate. 'Moot' derives from a wonderful old Anglo-Saxon word 'gemot' which means 'meeting'. Saxon society was made up of many different assemblies where public issues could be debated. A 'wardmote' was a ward meeting, a 'burgmote' was a town meeting and the grand 'witenagemote' was a meeting of prominent wise men. During the 16th century the moot courts, or the mootings, were established at the Inns of Court in London. This was the place where young law students were able to practise their powers of argument and debate by taking part in hypothetical trials. It is a practice that continues to this day and forms the origin of this phrase.

Mufti Day is a day many school children look forward to as it means they can spend the day in their own choice of clothes, rather than in school uniform. In the work place many companies now also have a 'mufti day' and employees can dress casually for a small donation to charity. The phrase is a military one and originates in the Middle East where British officers and their troops would relax in dressing gowns, smoking caps and slippers. This appearance was similar to that of a costume worn by experts in Muslim law, who are called 'muftis'. The expression returned to Britain with the military and passed into wider use during the 19th century.

A **Phoney** is regarded as fake, not the genuine article. 'Fainne' (pronounced 'fawnya') is a Gaelic word meaning circle or ring. In the 18th century some Irish gold was not regarded as genuine and by 1811 gold rings from that country were known as 'fawney', which became an English slang word meaning fake. During the 1920s imitation gold rings passed on by American confidence tricksters were also regarded as 'fawney', although their accent led to a corruption and the word became 'phoney'.

A **Plum Job** or a **Plum Role** is considered to be one of the best and most important a person can have. During the 1600s the slang term in England for £1,000 was 'plum', in the same way as a 'monkey' is now £500 and a 'score' is £20. Back then £1,000 was a seriously large amount of money but it was the fixed amount some politicians received for certain government roles. This was considered by the average layman to be a vast sum of money for doing very little and these posts became known as 'plum jobs'. It is easy to see how this phrase caught on and is applied to this day to easy or privileged positions, although it is often used in admiration rather than the contempt the expression started with.

Point Blank range means very close to and is usually used in relation to gunfire, as in 'shot at point blank range'. The origin is a military one and stems from the French word 'point blanc' which means centre, or bullseye. It was used to describe the flight of an arrow that flies directly at its target. In other words, you are close enough to the target for no arcing to take place. To tell someone point blank, as in 'I told him point blank the answer was no' also suggests the conversation was held at very close range, face to face.

Not A Sausage is a way of describing either something as free of charge or one's own self as being penniless. It is derived from another example of the colourful cockney rhyming slang of London, where sausage and mash was a staple diet between the 17th and 18th centuries. To be without 'sausage and mash' is to be without cash.

To suggest a person is **No Great Shakes** is to imply they are not particularly effective, and not up to a given standard. The word 'shakes' in this context comes from the Old English word 'schakere', which means to boast or brag. This was a phrase used frequently in the 13th century and the phrase 'of no great schakere' meant a person had nothing to boast about. A second widely held belief is that the phrase comes from the game of dice, suggesting a poor player wasn't any good because his 'shakes' were not effective enough.

To be **In A Shambles** is to be in a state of complete disarray. This phrase is usually used as a criticism of a person, group of people or a situation. The word 'shambles' derives from the Old English word 'sceamul' (pronounced 'shamell') which means 'stool' or 'table' as in a butcher's workbench. During the medieval period most towns had certain streets exclusively occupied by a single trade. There would be whole rows of fishmongers, greengrocers and butchers, which were known as 'shambles'. Some old towns such as York still have streets called The Shambles. Street butchers were supplied by the slaughterhouses and such was the mess of blood and animal parts by the butchers' workbenches they too became referred to as 'shambles'. This then became a metaphor for general mess and chaos.

Thick As Thieves is a term used to imply two or more people are on very close, friendly terms with each other, often with a common purpose. It stems from a French phrase 'like thieves at a fair', which describes groups of villains working in close collusion, which then hopped the Channel during the Norman Conquest in 1066. In England the saying was first used by author

Thomas Hook in his novel *The Parson's Daughter*, which was published in 1833. Contrary to popular belief, the phrase 'thick as thieves' is not a reference to the intellect of those residing at Her Majesty's Pleasure.

To **Take Umbrage** means to take offence at somebody's remarks or behaviour. The word 'umbrage' has its roots in the Latin word 'umbra' meaning shade (which is also where the word 'umbrella' comes from). In England, 'umbra' was used to describe the shade or shadow cast by a line of trees and came to mean the shadow or shade a person is put under by suspicion or doubt. To be put in such a shadow will give rise to resentment and ill feeling, hence 'taking umbrage'.

Without Batting An Eyelid is a common phrase used to describe a person taking a situation in their stride, without even blinking in surprise. 'Bate' is a long obsolete English word meaning 'to flutter' or 'to beat the wings' as a butterfly might. When a person reacted, to something without showing any signs of surprise (blinking) they were regarded as 'not even bateing an eyelid', which later mutated into the phrase we use today.

To get off **Scot Free** means to have escaped punishment and avoided the consequence of a bad deed. The origin of the phrase is traced to Scandinavia (not Scotland as it would appear) and the word 'scot' meaning 'payment'. Around the 13th century a great municipal tax called 'scot' was imposed on the Scandinavian people. All households were required to pay according to their means but the peasants were exempt. They were known as 'scot-free'. In England the scot tax lasted in some places for hundreds of years, finally petering out during the Westminster electoral reforms in 1836.

It is also known that during the Middle Ages innkeepers would hold a record of a person's drinking on a slate called a scot and to leave an establishment without paying was known as 'going scot free'.

5: THE ANCIENTS: GREEKS AND ROMANS

An **Achilles' Heel** is a perceived weakness in someone or something otherwise considered solid and perhaps infallible. As the ancient Greek legend goes, Thetis dipped her son Achilles into the river Styx with the intention of making his skin armour like and impenetrable. But she held him by his heel, which remained out of the water and as a result his only vulnerable spot. Achilles grew up to be an invincible soldier but his deadly enemy, Paris, learned of his weakness and killed him during the Trojan War with an arrow shot straight at his heel. Homer told the full story in his *Iliad*.

To **Add Insult To Injury** suggests a second remark or action makes an already bad situation worse by adding another problem. It is suggested the origin of the saying dates back to 25 BC and a book of fables by the Roman writer Phaedrus. In his story 'The Bald Man And The Fly', Phaedrus describes a fly stinging a bald man on the top of his head. Angry at being bitten the man attempts to kill the fly with a hard slap, but the insect sees this coming and jumps off, leaving the man to slap only his head. The fly then insults the man for trying to kill it over a simple insect bite. The bald man had not only received an injury, in the shape of a bite on the top of his head, but also suffered the indignity of making it worse and being insulted by the fly.

To keep something **At Bay**, such as danger or illness, means to fend it off and not be affected by it. In ancient history the bay tree was thought to possess great protective powers, as they never seemed to be struck by lightning. Romans and Greeks would seek shelter under a bay tree during storms and warriors took to wearing bay leaves as a means of protection against both the enemy and thunderstorms in an attempt to keep them 'at bay'.

During the Great Plague of London in 1665 city folk did the same in the hope they would avoid the disease and keep the plague 'at bay'.

To have the **Bit Between Your Teeth** means to go about a task with such enthusiasm and determination that nobody can stop you. This term relates to the metal bar in a horse's mouth attached to the reigns enabling a rider to steer and control the animal. This bar is known as the 'bit' and needs to be positioned at the softer back of the mouth where the horse can feel it. If the bit gets caught further forward, between the teeth, the horse becomes insensitive to a rider's instructions and therefore uncontrollable. The expression dates back to the year 470 BC and Greek culture when Aeschylus remarked, 'You take the bit in your teeth like a new-harnessed colt.'

When somebody is described as a **Real Brick** they are complimented on their reliability and their solid and dependable nature, somebody beyond the call of duty. The ancient Greek legend of the city of Sparta tells a story of its king, Lycurgus, who had failed to build defensive walls around his kingdom, as was the custom of the day. When questioned about this King Lycurgus is said to have pointed to his soldiers and replied, 'But I have a wall, and every man is a brick.'

If we **Burn Our Bridges**, we are putting ourselves in a position from which there is no return, often to our great cost. This phrase can be traced back to the Roman Army, whose generals adopted the practice of burning the bridges their soldiers crossed on their way into battle, removing any thought of retreat from their minds. They also used to **Burn Their Boats** after sea invasions, once again eliminating any idea of withdrawal.

'My **Ears Are Burning**' is a remark made by a person to suggest they are being talked about by others at that moment. Quite often we experience a tingling or slight burning sensation in either ear and the superstitious Romans believed all such things were signals. 'It is acknowledged that the absent feel a presentiment of remarks about themselves by the ringing of their ears' (*Naturalis Historia*, AD 77). As the Romans also firmly believed everything on the left signified evil and on the right implied good, the theory was that the left ear burning suggested evil intent and the right ear praise. Sir Thomas Brown (1605–82) in his book *Extracts From Christian Morals* suggested guardian angels were responsible and they touched the right ear if the talk was favourable and the left if unfavourable.

Eat Your Heart Out is a phrase we use in good humour to taunt another person. The suggestion is that they should be envious of and worried about another's achievement. The saying was a favourite Jewish expression in showbusiness circles during the 20th century but was certainly in use much earlier. Diogenes Laertius credited Pythagoras with saying 'Do not eat your heart' meaning 'Don't waste your life worrying about something.' And that was 2,500 years ago.

To **Fiddle While Rome Burns** is a phrase often used to describe somebody being occupied by small details while a greater disaster is taking place unnoticed. Roman legend has it that in AD 64 Emperor Nero wanted to see what Troy had looked like as it burned to the ground, so he set light to Rome. It was said that he watched the blaze for six days and seven nights while he played his fiddle and enjoyed himself. Nero strongly denied the claims and blamed the disaster on the Christians, who were then ruthlessly persecuted. Historians have confirmed Nero was nowhere near Rome when the fire started, supporting his defence. Instead he was probably out enjoying himself at the School of Charm run by Caligula.

To **Go With The Flow** means not to have a strong opinion and thus follow the majority. Often thought to be of American origin, the phrase in fact predates the Yanks by about 1,600 years. Marcus Aurelius was crowned Emperor of Rome on 7 March 161. His turbulent reign was characterised by war and disaster but also, above all, intellectual thought. Marcus dealt with his turmoil through stoic philosophy and much of this is expressed in his writings *The Meditations*, in which he displays the tension he felt between his position as emperor and his prevailing feeling of overall inadequacy. Much of Marcus's philosophy is based around the flow of thought and the flow of happiness and he concluded that 'all things flow naturally'. Marcus also expressed the opinion it was better to 'go with the flow' rather than try to change the natural course of events.

The phrase **Beware Of Greeks Bearing Gifts** is a friendly warning against trickery and deception. This phrase refers to the most famous Greek gift of all, the Trojan Horse. During the Trojan Wars the Greeks had besieged the city of Troy for over ten years. Finally, as they made plans to leave, they built a huge wooden horse as an offering to the gods and a sign of peace. The horse was left at the gates of Troy and, once the Greeks had withdrawn, the people of Troy opened their gates, for the first time in a decade, to receive the apparently harmless gift. However, as soon as the horse was inside, Greek soldiers poured out of the wooden structure and destroyed the city. Virgil, in the *Aeneid* (II.49) has Laocoon warn the Trojans about accepting the horse, saying, 'I still fear the Greeks, even when they offer us gifts.'

When something **Hangs By A Thread** it means a situation could change in an instant. The phrase alludes to the sword of Damocles that was hung from a ceiling by a single hair. The Roman philosopher Cicero tells the story that in 400 BC Dionysius the Elder, ruler of Syracuse, became tired of one of his courtiers, Damocles, for his slimy bootlicking. To remind the young servile how fortunate his position was, and how tenuous it might be, Dionysius sat Damocles beneath the sword during a banquet. Not only did the sword 'hang by a thread' but so did Damocles's life. Cicero used the incident to illustrate that he understood how tenuous his own privileged position was.

When somebody claims they **Don't Give A Jot** they are implying they care nothing at all about a circumstance. The phrase is thousands of years old and is exactly the same as the expression **I Don't Give One Iota**. The origins for both can be found in the early Greek language. A jot is the letter 'iota' which is the smallest in the Greek alphabet. It was used at the time to imply 'the least of anything'.

A situation that is in the **Lap Of The Gods** is one where the outcome is unclear and cannot be influenced in any meaningful way. Early suggestions for the origin of this saying predictably pointed to the practice in many cultures of leaving gifts with statues of gods in the hope of answered prayers. But Homer's *Iliad* probably holds the answer. In the story

Patrocolos, a friend of Achilles, is killed by the Trojans who then intended to parade his severed head to demoralise their opponents. With the battle in the balance, and the outcome uncertain, Automedon declared, 'These things lie on the knees of the gods.' On hearing this Achilles returned and led an unexpected rout of the Trojans, confirming to all that the gods were well and truly on the side of the famous warrior.

To **Lick Something Into Shape** means to mould something (or someone) to suit a particular task or situation. Bizarrely, some races used to believe that some animals, particularly bears, gave birth to formless offspring and then licked them into the shape of their breed. This is possibly because many animal offspring are born covered in a thick afterbirth, sometimes making them almost unrecognisable until a mother has cleaned it off. Around AD 150 Aulus Gellius wrote, 'For he said that as the bear brought forth her young formless and misshapen, by licking gave it form and shape.' And we thought the Romans were knowledgeable.

Lily Livered is a term used for cowards, or cowardly behaviour. The ancient Greeks had the custom of sacrificing an animal on the eve of each battle and the animal's liver was considered a major omen. If it was red and full of blood all the signs were positive but, if the liver was pale and lily-coloured, it was thought to signify bad tidings. The Greeks also believed the liver of a cowardly person was pale and lily-coloured.

When a person is described as **Mealy Mouthed** the implication is they are unwilling to speak plainly or openly about something, in case what they have to say offends. It is often used as a derogatory term for somebody who is trying to please others. Its origin can be found as a phonetic adaptation from the ancient Greek 'melimuthos' which means, literally, 'honey speak'.

To make a **Mountain Out Of A Molehill** means to exaggerate something out of all proportion. The original phrase was 'to make an elephant out of a fly' and dates back to the ancient Greek satirist Lucian, who lived in AD 2. But in 1548 Nicholas Udall wrote *Paraphrase Of Erasmus* which includes the line: 'Sophists of Greece could, through their copiousness, make an elephant of a fly and a mountain of a molehill.' The original expression has long been forgotten but Udall's replacement remains a commonly used phrase.

The **Rule Of Thumb** is a rough estimate based on experience rather than formal calculation. The expression has been in wide use since the late 1600s and there are several suggestions for its origin. One of them emanates from the ale-makers where, in the days before accurate thermometers were available, the brewer would test the temperature of fermenting beers by dipping his thumb in. If this was the phrase's origin one would expect to find pubs called The Brewer's Thumb, but I can find none.

Another suggestion dates back to the Middle Ages when it was legal for a man to beat his wife with a cane no thicker than his thumb. Evidence of this comes to light in the *Biographical Dictionary Of The Judges Of England* written by Edward Foss in 1864. In the text Foss suggests that a 'husband may beat his wife, so that the stick with which he administers the castigation is not thicker than his thumb'. It should also have been possible for a wife to beat the man who put that law on the statute book with a stick no thicker than he was. Instead we go back to the Romans who used the tip of the thumb (from the knuckle upward) as a unit of measurement, as any thumb would fit roughly 12 times into the next unit of measurement, a foot. There is definitely a connection here, as the French word for inches is 'pouces' which translates as 'thumb' and that remained a standard unit of measurement until metrification. The Roman bricklayers used their thumbs to estimate measurements and the phrase has been in standard use ever since.

If a person is **Not Worth His Salt** they are regarded as not very good at their job and not worth the wages. During the days of the Roman Empire salt was an expensive commodity and soldiers were actually paid partly in salt, which they carried in leather pouches. This payment was known as 'salarium', from the Latin word 'sal', meaning salt. The modern word for wages, 'salary', also originates from this source.

The origin of the phrase **Taken With A Pinch Of Salt** goes as far back as AD 77 and the Latin *Addito Salis Grano* written by Pliny the Elder. The elderly Pliny had discovered the story of King Mithridates VI, who once ruled Pontus and built up his immunity to poisoning by fasting and then taking regular doses of poison with a single grain of salt in an effort to make it more palatable.

Scallywag is a word used particularly around the Liverpool area, to describe a boisterous, energetic and disruptive young male who has little regard for authority. The word started life as 'scurryvag', which comes from the Latin phrase 'scurra vagus' meaning 'wandering fool'. In London the word 'scurryvag' was used to describe a scurrilous vagrant (a merging of the two words) which later became scallywag thanks to the Liverpool accent.

To **Spill The Beans** is a widely used term for giving away a secret. A tradition that began in ancient Greece for electing a new member to a private club was to give each existing member a white and brown bean with which to cast their votes. The white bean was a yes vote and the brown meant an objection. The beans were then secretly placed in a jar and the prospective member would never know how many people voted either for or against him. Unless, that is, the jar was knocked over and the beans spilled. Then the club members' secret would be out.

Spondulics is a slang word for money. According to the *Oxford English Dictionary* it is a word of 'fanciful origin' but my Greek friends have managed to trace it back to their ancient language and the word 'spondulikos', which derives from 'spondulos', a type of seashell. Apparently this shell was once used as a currency and is very likely to have been the origin of our slang phrase. In addition, the Greek word for spine, or vertebrae, is 'spondylo' and a stack of coins could resemble a spine. This suggestion is supported by John Mitchell in his book *A Manual Of The Art Of Prose Composition*, first published in 1867, in which he lists 'spondulics' as a 'coin pile, ready for counting'.

Leaving **No Stone Unturned** is a phrase we use to describe having made all possible efforts to complete a task. After the Greeks defeated the Persians at the battle of Plataea in 477 BC, Polycrates set about finding the treasure he thought had been left in the tent of the Persian general Mardonius. After searching everywhere he turned to the oracle at Delphi who advised him to 'move every stone' in his search. Polycrates took that advice and subsequently found the treasure. The phrase soon became popular and only a few years later, in 410 BC, Aristophanes called it 'that old proverb'. At nearly 2,500 years old, 'no stone unturned' may even be our oldest idiom.

To **Swear On Your Testicles** (stop laughing at the back) is an old phrase dating back to the Romans and their apparent courtroom practice of swearing the truth of a statement on their testicles. In fact, there is some truth in this, as the Latin word for a witness is *testis*, which is taken from the old Indo-European word for the number three. The Romans regarded an impartial witness, who could look at events in an objective way, as a third party, which is how testis developed as the word for witness. But they did also use the word 'testis' as a witness to a man's virility, which is how the word testicle also evolved and how the two are connected. But, when a Roman was swearing on his testicles, he was actually swearing on his witness. No doubt this has had Latin students sniggering for generations.

To **Thread Your Way** through a crowd is an old English phrase dating back to the mid-1500s. Back then the good and the great would entertain themselves for hours in a new modern puzzle called mazes. However, many people soon realised it was just as hard to find their way out of a maze as it was to reach the centre. Some adopted the practice of taking a clew (a cheap yarn or thread) and fixing one end at the beginning, enabling them to find their way back out again and that lead to the term 'threading your way through'. But this wasn't a new trick, even in the 1500s. It was borrowed from the ancient Greek myth in which Theseus finds his way back out of the Minotaur's labyrinth after slaying the beast, by using a 'clew' of thread. A slight variation of the word 'clew' led to 'clue' becoming used in modern English language as the term for anything helping to unravel puzzles or mysteries. The word 'maze' itself stems from the word 'amazing', which was used to describe the popular new game.

When somebody is described as **Two Faced** it is suggested they are hypocritical, prepared to share one opinion with a person and then a conflicting viewpoint with another. The inference is they have a separate face for each contrary opinion. Janus was a Roman god with responsibility for the gates of heaven. Legend tells us he had two faces, one in the usual position and one on the back of his head, enabling him to see in both directions at once. From that Roman legend grew the idea that anybody able to see two sides to an argument, and agree with both, must have two faces just like Janus. This extends itself to meaning any person who is able to say one thing to one person and a conflicting thing to another must also need two faces, like Janus.

To **Set Off On The Wrong Foot** means to start something badly. This phrase finds us back with the Romans and their superstitions about left-sided things being evil and guided by evil spirits (the Latin word for left is 'sinister'). Gaius Petronius (AD 27–66), author of *Satyricon* and Emperor Nero's adviser in matters of luxury and extravagance, insisted his fellow Romans only ever entered or left a building by the right foot. Such was his obsession that guards were placed at the entrance to every public building to ensure his rule was obeyed. Most Romans shared Petronius's belief that to start a day by leaving the house by the left foot meant an unlucky day during which disaster might strike. (See also **Get Out Of Bed On The Wrong Side** and **Ears Are Burning**.)

Get Out Of Bed On The Wrong Side is a phrase we use when someone is being grumpy or bad tempered during the day. An ancient superstition suggests that evil spirits lay during the night on a particular side of the bed. It was unlucky to emerge in the morning on that side as it would mean those evil spirits and their influence would possess the body during its waking hours and this would only be put right the following dawn by not repeating the mistake. The wrong side, incidentally, is the left-hand side. (See also **Set Off On The Wrong Foot**.)

6: SPORT

Across The Board means all encompassing, wide-ranging and including everyone or everything. At 19th-century race meetings large boards would be used to display the odds on a horse to come first, second or third in a given race. A popular bet was to place an even amount of money on one horse to finish first, second or third. This was known as an 'across the board bet'. Obviously the bookmakers' odds would be calculated and only when a horse finished in the position a bookmaker least expected it to would a punter win more than the sum of his three stakes.

All Over Bar The Shouting is used when any controversial event is said to be technically settled, but arguments about the outcome continue, albeit with little effect on the result. In use since 1842, the phrase is from the world of sport, in particular boxing. Once a referee's decision was made, the crowds would either cheer or argue the judgement and shout appeals. But usually the referee's verdict stood and the contest would be over, apart from the subsequent cheering and shouting.

When suggestions are **Bandied About** it means they are either put up for discussion or repeated by one party to many. For example, 'They bandied about the suggestion all afternoon before deciding not to proceed any further with it' or 'The lies she bandied about all over town did his reputation no good at all'. For the origin of the use of this word we travel to France and the game of Bander, which was an early form of tennis and involved hitting a ball to and fro. Later, in the 1600s, the Irish invented a team game that formed the origins of hockey, which required a group of people 'bandying' a ball between them. They called the sport 'Bander' after the French game because of the similarities between the two ideas. The crooked (or bowed) stick they used led to the term 'bandy-legged' being applied to those with bow legs.

When someone has **Lost Their Bottle** they have lost their nerve and their bravery. This phrase originates from the world of bare-knuckle prize-fighting during the late 19th and early 20th centuries. In a fighter's corner one of his seconds was known as 'the bottle man' and his job was to supply water to a fighter between rounds. Without water a fighter was unable to continue and sometimes it was known for a bottleman to be asked to walk away and leave when a fighter was taking a beating, to provide an excuse for him not continuing. The phrase 'lost his bottleman' was later shortened and widely used to describe cowardly behaviour.

Not enough room to **Swing A Cat** is a reference to small tight spaces. It is often thought the phrase originates from 17th-century sailors needing space in which they could swing the cat o' nine tails but there is other evidence from two centuries earlier. Cat lovers read no further. In the 15th century, there was a 'sport' involving the swinging of cats (by the tail) into the air where they would become moving targets for archers at fetes, fairs and country festivals. Crowded festivals would be described as having no room to 'swing the cat'.

To knock the **Daylights** out of somebody would be to put them on the receiving end of a pretty impressive beating. In days gone by 'daylights' was slang for a person's eyes. In early bare-knuckle boxing parlance, to darken a fighter's daylights would mean to give him a black eye, and to beat the daylights out of him meant both eyes were so badly swollen he could no longer see.

Down To The Wire is used to describe a contest, sporting or otherwise, where the outcome will not be determined until the very last. Before the days of televised horse racing, American and British racetracks would string a wire across the finishing line above the riders' heads. A steward would then be placed at a vantage point, looking down the line so that a winner could be more easily established during neck-and-neck finishes. In 1889 the following appeared in *Scribers Magazine*: 'As the end of the stand was reached, Timarch worked up to Petrel, and the two raced down to the wire, cheered on by the applause of the spectators. They ended the first half mile of the race head and head, passing lapped together under the wire, and beginning in earnest the mile which was yet to be traversed.' The race had gone 'down to the wire' and the expression has been widely used since then.

At The Drop Of A Hat is used to imply something would be carried out immediately. The phrase is easily traced to the 19th century when sporting referees, who usually wore hats, would raise one into the air, alerting competitors to be ready, and then drop it to signal the start of an event. The method was commonly used in boxing or horseracing and such events were considered started 'at the drop of a hat'. It is sometimes thought to be of American origin but the practice has long been used on both sides of the Atlantic.

A **Hat Trick** is the common phrase used to illustrate three of anything, but is most often associated with goals scored by footballers. But the origin of the phrase is found in a different sport, cricket. Traditionally any bowler dismissing three batsmen with three consecutive deliveries would be awarded a new cricket cap by his team in honour of the achievement, which became known as a 'hat trick'. Supporters at cricket matches seldom witness a hat trick as it only happens on rare occasions. In football it is far easier to achieve and thus much more common.

To **Keep It Up** means to persevere at a task and a person should carry on in the same manner. But what is 'it' – and why should it be 'up'? The origin for this can be found in the Victorian penchant for playing badminton in the gardens of country houses during summer months. Quite simply the shuttlecock needed to be kept up and the phrase 'keep it up' was frequently shouted during rallies.

To **Knuckle Down** means to concentrate and apply more effort to a task. Surprisingly this term emanates from the world of marbles where an important rule of the game is that the knuckle must be placed in the exact spot a player's previous marble had come to rest. Those not concentrating and playing carelessly with their knuckle off the ground would quite simply be told to put their 'knuckle down'.

To **Knuckle Under** means to submit and admit defeat. In the late 17th century when arguments raged in the drinking taverns of London, there was a custom that when a person admitted defeat he would knock the underside of a table with his knuckle. There is also a suggestion dating from around the same time that bare-knuckle prize-boxers would keep their fists down, with their knuckles under their hands, when they no longer wanted to fight, and to have them up facing an opponent when they did. Over the years this phrase has also corrupted to '**buckle under**'.

When something gets done in the **Nick Of Time** it has been done at the very last possible minute, before it was too late. During the Middle Ages a tally man would keep the scores for team games. This chap would do so by carving a nick in a piece of wood each time a team scored and if the winning nick was added during the last minute it was known as the 'nick in time'.

To **Play Fast And Loose** is used to describe a person who cannot be trusted, usually with another's affections. Fast and loose was, for centuries, a popular gambling game played at race meetings, fairgrounds and market places all over Europe. Originally known as 'pin and girdle' it was played with loops made of leather straps being tossed over peg. The 'fast' in the phrase is used in the sense of an immovable object (the peg) and the 'loose' began as 'loops' before developing in the 15th century to become the idiom we have today. The game was apparently played with 'carefree abandon' which is how it became applied to the carefree and shallow attitude some of us adopt at times.

The phrase **To Come Up To Scratch** is closely linked. In early bare-knuckle boxing or prize-fighting bouts, long before the Marquis of Queensberry produced any rules, a line would be scratched in the ground midway between each fighter's corner at the start of the bout. Any boxer who was knocked down would be given 30 seconds to gather his senses and return to the scratch and show he was fit (or willing) enough to continue fighting. Any boxer 'coming up to the scratch' would be allowed to continue, but a boxer not coming up to the scratch was deemed the loser.

To **Start From Scratch** is a saying we use to illustrate starting again from the beginning, regardless of how much we have already achieved of a task. This is easily explained as during medieval horse races competitors would start at a line 'scratched' into the ground by either a sword or a javelin. If competitors cut corners, or strayed from the set course of the race, they would have to start again from the scratch.

To **Throw Your Hat Into The Ring** means you are signalling an intention to join an event or enterprise, or by taking up a challenge. The phrase can be traced back to the days of prize-fighters who would tour the country with travelling fairs giving local people the chance to win money by trying to beat them in the ring. The way any local would enter the competition was to throw his hat into the ring, which would then be placed in a pile with the others and later shown to the crowd as an invitation for the owner to step forward.

A **Turn Up For The Book** is a pleasant surprise, although not necessarily for everybody. This is a horse-racing phrase dating back to the time the sport was even shadier than it is now. A 'book' is traditionally a record of bets laid on a race kept by the bookmaker. There were occasions, when the favourites were backed heavily and expected to win, that a bookmaker could lose his livelihood on the outcome of a single race meeting. At these times it would be in his interest for an unfancied horse, with very few bets on it, to romp home in one of the last races and save the bookmaker's hide as he then got to keep all the money staked on more popular horses. The sport of kings had a relatively small community and it wasn't uncommon for favours to be called in at times. It was known that some owners would allow their champion horse to turn up and run under the name of an inferior nag, beat the field and thereby save a friendly bookmaker's business. As a result otherwise slow horses racing well and surprising 'everyone' by winning was known as a 'turn up for the book'. The horse had turned up especially to assist the bookmaker's book.

To have the **Upper Hand** implies a person will win a contest or social situation. This phrase dates back to the 15th century and a pastime involving two or more contestants. The first player grips a staff at the bottom end while the next places their hand just above it. This goes on, hand over hand, until the upper end of the shaft is reached: the last person to be able to take a grip has the 'upper hand'. This method of finding a random winner was often used in baseball and cricket in the 1900s when hands would be placed on a bat and the last to take a grip got to play the game first.

To be **Batting On A Sticky Wicket** is to be faced with a difficult problem that requires great care to resolve successfully. It is a cricketing term alluding to the difficulty a batsman has playing on a wet and tricky wicket. These days a wicket is protected from the rain by covers quickly pulled over if the clouds burst overhead. But earlier cricketers often played on a wet surface and great care was needed. The West Indian team fell foul of a 'sticky wicket' at the Kensington Oval in 1935 and it was later reported that the 'West Indians have a remarkable record here having only lost once in 1935 on a sticky pitch.'

A **Wild Goose Chase** is a fruitless pursuit with no hope of successful outcome. Its origin comes from the earliest form of horse racing during the 1500s in England. First the lead horse would be sent off in no particular direction with the rider able to choose his own route. After a delay a second rider would be sent off in pursuit, followed by all other competitors at regular intervals. As none of the pursuing riders knew which route the lead horse had taken they all set off in different directions akin to wild geese scurrying after their leader. The term was regularly applied to the sport but it appears to have been Shakespeare who altered the meaning to one of hopeless pursuit.

To **Win Hands Down** suggests a very comfortable victory. This is a widely used expression in the world of sport and its root can be found in the sport of kings, horse racing. Even today, when a jockey is winning comfortably he can gallop down the finishing straight without using his whip to encourage the nag along. Instead he can place both hands back on the reins, canter to the line and 'win with his hands down'.

7: WORK AND TRADE

To go **Against The Grain** suggests something moving against the natural flow of events or feelings. For example, a wife, who hates football but will attend a Cup Final with her husband who loves the sport, might say, 'Well, even though it goes against the grain, I will go along.' It is a woodcutter's saying, in use since the 1600s. To work by cutting or carving along the grain of wood is notably easier than cutting across (or against) the grain. Working with the grain is considered smooth and easy; against it is hard and unnatural.

At Full Blast is associated with something going at full speed or operating at the maximum limit.

Back during the Industrial Revolution foundries would use a huge blast furnace for the smelting of iron. When the foundry was at the limit of its production it would be regarded as 'operating at full blast'.

If we are not fit to **Hold A Candle** to somebody it means we are not in their league and should not be working in the same place. This phrase is traceable to the day when craftsmen would employ unskilled labour (usually children) to hold candles illuminating their work. Being told one wasn't fit to 'hold the candle' was an insult indeed and usually used as a derogatory term to an inferior craftsman or street entertainer.

To **Carry The Can** means to take reluctant responsibility for something, usually that has gone wrong. Originally a military term, the saying stems from the duty of one man to carry a large can (bucket) of beer between the mess and a group of men. The one carrying the can was responsible for both the beer and for returning the empty bucket. The phrase was in regular use by 1936 but a second theory dates further back. During the 19th century, explosive was regularly used in both coal and tin mines. One person would be given the unenviable task of carrying a can of explosives to the mine face each day, hence a reluctance to 'carry the can'.

When the **Cat Is Let Out Of The Bag** it means some sort of secret has been revealed. In the days of the medieval market deceptions were often played on unsuspecting buyers, and one of those involved piglets and cats. Having been shown a suckling piglet a purchaser would then start haggling with the vendor over price. While this was going on the piglet would be bagged up ready to be taken home but a cat was often substituted while the buyer's attention was diverted. The deception would only be revealed when the buyer reached home and let a 'cat out of the bag'.

If we are told we have **Our Work Cut Out For Us** we know there is a lot to be done and a difficult task lies ahead. The phrase stems from the craft of tailoring but at first glance it would seem the work is being made easier (by having someone cut out patterns before the stitching begins). But, in fact, such a practice makes life more difficult for the tailor, as cutting the work out in advance is much quicker than actually tailoring a suit and therefore piles of material would mount up making it hard for the tailor to keep up. Therefore it is quite easy to imagine a tailor explaining he is busy as he has his 'work cut out for him' and would be hard at it for the foreseeable future. The first recorded appearance of the phrase meaning 'more than one can handle' turned up in *A Christmas Carol*, a Charles Dickens novel first published in 1843.

The expression **Dyed In The Wool** is used to describe somebody who is fixed in their opinions and inflexible. The phrase came into use in English wool mills and is first recorded in 1579. Quite simply wool that had been dyed before it was treated would retain its colour much better than if it were dyed after weaving (known as 'dyed in the piece'). Therefore 'dyed in the wool' became a phrase applied to anything that wasn't easily altered by other processes, such as persuasion.

Fired – Prior to the invention of toolboxes all English craftsmen and tradesmen carried their tools around in a sack. To be given their sack meant being discharged from employment and the worker would carry his tools either home or on to his next job (see **The Sack**). However, miners who were caught stealing coal or other materials, such as copper or tin, would have their tools confiscated and burned at the pit head in front of the other shift workers, a punishment that became known as 'firing the tools' or 'being fired'. This meant the offender would be unable to find other work and repeat his crime elsewhere. Other trades adopted the practice and the phrase quickly established itself.

Mad As A Hatter is a term used to describe unpredictable behaviour. In the Middle Ages making felt hats involved the use of a highly toxic substance called mercurous nitrate. This acid was known to cause trembling in some people, a little like the symptoms of Parkinson's Disease, and those who suffered the effects in this way were assumed to be mad or crazy. During the 17th century tales were told of a man called Robert Crab, an eccentric who lived in Chesham, who was easily identified because of his distinctive hat and was known to locals as 'the mad hatter'. He apparently gave away all his wealth to the poor and lived his life eating anything he could find in the countryside, such as grass, berries and dock leaves. The phrase passed over into the English language in the 19th century, thanks to Lewis Carroll and his novel *Alice In Wonderland*. In the story Carroll invented a mad hatter but he may have been inspired by a real-life figure.

To **Strike While The Iron Is Hot** means to take action early enough, ensuring a favourable result. The phrase is a medieval blacksmith's term, alluding to shaping an iron horseshoe at exactly the time the metal was at the correct temperature and not giving it time to cool, when it would become harder to work with.

Having **Too Many Irons In The Fire** is an extension of the expression, originating at around the same time. It means that a person has too many activities taking place at one time, preventing them from giving enough time to any one of them. It must be tempting for a blacksmith to try and speed up his work by having more irons in his fire than he is capable of working with. The result would be that all of them either became too hot and soft, or cooled down again before he has had time to shape some of them properly.

If somebody is described as **On The Level** it means they are trustworthy and reliable. In the 14th century the freemasons' membership was exclusively made up of skilled stone workers. A level base or platform for a building or other structure was the most important part of a whole building project. Because of that the 'level' used to ensure a flat foundation was the most important tool a freemason had in his case, leading to a common phrase at the time describing anything, including a person, as 'level' (true, honest and dependable).

Something going at **Nineteen To The Dozen** is operating very quickly indeed. Back in the 18th century coal-fired, steam-driven pumps were used to clear water out of Cornish tin and copper mines. Hand-powered pumps were slow and ineffective but at full power the steam version could clear 19,000 gallons of water for every dozen bushels of coal burned, which is how the expression became used.

To **Pay On The Nail** means to make a prompt cash payment for good or services. Back in the bustling medieval market place, dealers were known by their round, pillar-like counters, called nails. It is thought the phrase referred to the practice of a buyer placing his cash openly and in full public view on the nail. This routine is recognised to this day by the four bronze nails that still stand outside the Exchanges in Bristol and Limerick. The expression is not unique to Britain, however: Holland and Germany have a similar saying.

To make a **Pig's Ear** out of something is to attempt a task and get it so badly wrong the effort is useless. The phrase dates back to the Middle Ages when it is said that the only part of a pig that could not be eaten or used in any way was the ear. Therefore, any craftsman or (usually) apprentice making something ineffective or unusable was considered to have produced a 'pig's ear'.

To **Stretch A Point** is to exceed or to suggest something beyond what is usually acceptable. The phrase alludes to the tagged laces in 18th-century costume which were called 'points'. To 'truss a point' meant to tie the laces together and to 'stretch a point' meant to allow them to adjust and provide room for growth beyond the clothing's original intended size, such as after a feast or during early pregnancy.

To find yourself in **Queer Street** is to be in some sort of financial trouble, possibly even bankrupt. The phrase originates from the word 'query' which tradesmen and merchants would write in their ledgers against the column of customers who were late in paying. The word would be written as a reminder to enquire of the debt the next time that person attended their premises for business. Carey Street, off Chancery Lane in London, housed the bankruptcy courts and through that became affectionately known as 'Queer Street'.

When somebody **Queers Your Pitch** they are deliberately attempting to prevent a successful outcome to your venture. During the 18th and 19th centuries market traders began calling the area set aside for their barrows and stalls a 'pitch', a term still used in Britain's market places. It is not clear why the word 'pitch' was adopted as market slang but it could possibly have links to 'pitching' an idea. For hundreds of years prior to that the word 'queer' had been used as English slang for anything that was wrong or worthless. In the vibrant and competitive market places of centuries gone by it was common practice for rival traders to attempt to spoil each other's trade, sometimes in an underhand way and sometimes legitimately by using better banter or cheaper goods. Rendering a rival stall worthless became known as 'queering a pitch'.

Later in the century stage actors adopted the phrase when other cast members stole the audience's attention during a scene, evidence of which can be found in an 1866 review of Shakespeare's *Macbeth*. 'The smoke and fumes of "blue fire" which had been used to illuminate the fight came up through the chinks of the stage, fit to choke a dozen Macbeths, and – pardon the little bit of professional slang – poor Jamie's "pitch" was "queered" with a vengeance.'

To be **Given The Sack** is to lose your job, or be discharged from duty. This expression dates back to the day when craftsmen, tradesmen and labourers would travel from place to place, sometimes working on a project for only a few days and at other times for many years. Long before toolboxes, these workers would carry the tools of their trade around in a large sack, which would be given to their employer for safe keeping and then returned when their services were no longer needed. To be given the sack was to be given the means to carry their tools to another place of work, unlike being **Fired** when the tradesman had been caught stealing or breaking the rules, and his tools would be burned to ensure he would be unable to work elsewhere.

Being **Tarred With The Same Brush** is to be part of a group regarded as all having the same faults and weaknesses but, by inference, often unfairly. The expression is an old farming term, which derives from the practice of treating the sores of an entire flock of sheep. The sores could be coated by a brush dipped in tar. The same brush would be used on all of the stricken sheep but never on a healthy animal for fear of passing the infection on, in which case all infected sheep were 'tarred with the same brush'.

If a person is **Never Going To Set The Thames Alight** they are unlikely ever to do anything impressive or notable, usually in respect of either their work or studies. Many believe the allusion here is to the river Thames but the root of our expression is actually a 'temse'. During the 1700s farmers used a tool called a temse, which was a sieve given to labourers or farmhands during the harvest months. Hard-grafting farm boys would joke with each other they had worked so fast their temse had caught fire. Equally, lazy scallywags would 'never be able to set their temse alight'.

Being **On Tenterhooks** means being under great stress or tension while waiting for a result or outcome. It has been suggested the phrase stems from tent hooks, which are used to hold a canvas under great tension, keeping it watertight, but its origin is far older. In bygone days newly produced cloth would be attached to hooks and stretched across large frames known as 'tenters', coming from the Latin word 'tendere', meaning 'to stretch out'. Anyone, or anything, stretched to the limit later became known as being 'on tenterhooks'.

8: THE BIBLE

The **Apple Of One's Eye** is somebody (usually a child) who is regarded as precious and irreplaceable. Over a thousand years ago, the pupil of the eye was known as the 'apple'. The modern word, pupil, is Latin and did not form part of the English language until the 1500s. Sight was regarded as the most valued of all the senses and therefore the 'apple' was precious and irreplaceable. King Alfred, in the late ninth century, actually linked the two and applied it to somebody he was affectionate towards, but it is not known who. The first recorded reference is in the Bible: Deuteronomy 32:10 says, 'He kept him as the apple of his eye,' suggesting he watched over him to ensure his safety.

At The Eleventh Hour indicates something has occurred at the very last moment. First used in the Bible (Matthew 20:9), the phrase can be traced to the parable of the labourers and the practice of a 12-hour working day. In the vineyards the very last of the day's labourers would be taken on during the eleventh hour (around 5pm) in an effort to finish the day's scheduled work on time.

To have **Feet Of Clay** suggests a real weakness in something (or someone) otherwise considered strong and infallible. This is a Biblical phrase and comes from a story in the Book of Daniel 2:31–5. Daniel describes a 'great statue' in Nebuchadnezzar's dream, which had a head of gold, breast and arms of silver, stomach and thighs of brass, legs of iron and feet of iron mixed with clay. But iron doesn't mix easily with clay, leaving a great weakness in an otherwise mighty monument that is not obvious to the eye.

Having a **Fly In The Ointment** is an expression used to describe a tiny thing that is hindering the outcome of something altogether much larger and more important. Thousands of years ago, before doctors, apothecaries (an early version of chemists) dealt with all medical treatment, and their sought-after potions and ointments would be dispensed from large vats. These vats could treat a vast number of people but a single fly or other insect found floating in them was thought to spoil the whole amount. The earliest reference to this phrase can be found in the Bible, in Ecclesiastes (10:1), which includes the phrase 'Dead flies cause the ointment of the apothecary to send forth a stinking savour.'

To be made a **Scapegoat** is to take responsibility for, and be blamed for, another's mistakes. This phrase dates back to an ancient Hebrew ritual for the Day Of Atonement set out by Moses himself in his *Laws Of Moses*. He decided that two goats should be taken to the altar of the tabernacle where the high priest would draw lots for the Lord and for Azazel (a desert demon). The goat selected as the Lord's would then be sacrificed and, by confession, the high priest would transfer all of his, and his people's, sins on to the second goat. The lucky mammal would then be sent into the wilderness, taking all the sins with it. If only it were that easy these days.

The **Final Straw** is a small insignificant event producing a situation that is intolerable overall. It has a Biblical origin and an old proverb states, 'It is the last straw that breaks the laden camel's back', which means that one small thing may bring about a catastrophe in the greater scheme of events. In the 17th and 18th centuries the expression in England used to be 'the last feather that breaks the horse's back' but Charles Dickens rescued the old proverb in his novel *Dombey And Son* in 1848. It caught on so successfully that it is 'last straws' and not 'last feathers' we talk about today.

To **Separate The Wheat From The Chaff** means to divide the valuable from the worthless. It is easy to see how, during a harvest, it is important to thresh corn to separate the grain from the husk. But the answer to how it became a popular and widely used expression can be found in the Bible and the suggestion that the 'wheat' are those loyal to Christ, and the 'chaff' are those who have rejected his ideals. Luke 3:17 has a passage including the line 'His winnowing fork is in his hand to clear his threshing floor and to gather the wheat into his barn, but he will burn up the chaff in his fire.'

A **Wolf In Sheep's Clothing** is a person who appears pleasant and friendly but carries a hidden menace. This expression can be found in another of Aesop's fables, dating back 1,400 years. In one of his stories a wolf wraps himself up in a sheep's fleece and sneaks past the shepherd into the paddock. Once inside he immediately eats one of the lambs before his deception can be discovered. But the actual origin can be found in the Bible: Matthew 7:15 says, 'Beware of false prophets, which come to you in sheep's clothing. Inwardly they are ravening wolves.'

9: PEOPLE AND PLACES

The **Blurb** is the curious name given to a short, written promotional sales pitch. Loosely speaking it is a rough but positive general explanation. The American comedy writer Gelet Burgess invented a comic book in 1907, which featured a Miss Belinda Blurb on the cover. The publication was to be given away at a book festival and Belinda was a parody of the type of artwork often found on the jackets of more serious novels at the time. When later asked what the name meant, Burgess described it as 'self praise and making a noise like a publisher'. A simple example of inspired alliteration, the phrase caught on immediately.

As Bold As Brass is applied to anyone with the courage of their conviction and not afraid to be seen either succeeding or failing. It is recorded that the phrase dates back to the late 1770s and refers to a London magistrate called Brass Crosby. At that time it was illegal for the workings of Parliament to be published for public knowledge. However, one London printer produced a pamphlet revealing some of the proceedings and was immediately arrested. He was brought before Brass Crosby's court and the magistrate, in tune with public opinion, let the printer off. Crosby was immediately arrested for treason and himself thrown in jail. But such was the public outcry in support of the magistrate that Brass was released and he became something of a hero. His brave stand against authority was widely reported, leading to the term 'as bold as brass' passing into common parlance.

To **Stage A Boycott** means withdrawing from social or commercial arrangements, either as a protest or punishment. The phrase is one of remarkably few to emanate from southern Ireland. In the 1870s Captain Charles Cunningham Boycott, an Englishman, was working as a land agent for Lord Earne at Loughmask in County Mayo. In September 1880 a campaign, organised by the Irish Land League, was calling for a reform of the system of landholding, and protesting tenants demanded Captain Boycott initiate a substantial reduction in their rents. Boycott refused, even ordering anyone in arrears be evicted, whereupon Charles Parnell, the President of the Land League, made a speech calling for everybody in the local community, not only Boycott's tenants, to refuse to have anything to do with the unpopular agent.

The result was that labourers refused to work for him, shop and innkeepers declined to serve either him or his family and even the postal staff refused to deliver his letters. Boycott had to go to the expense of having his food brought in, under guard, from great distances away, and of employing 50 labourers from as far away as Ulster for the harvest, all protected by 900 guard. This action by the locals was so successful and aroused so much passion (it was even reported in *The Times* during November 1880) that the Land League called upon all Irish men and women to treat similar landlords, or their agents, like 'Boycott'. Within weeks the phrase was adopted by newspapers around Europe and subsequently worldwide. By the time the captain died in 1887, after returning to England, his name had become a standard part of the English language.

A **Cock And Bull** story is likely to be untrue and without any real facts supporting it. Some suggest the phrase originates from old fables in which animals speak to each other, but there is a much more reliable source. Stony Stratford is a Buckinghamshire town located almost directly halfway between London and Birmingham and Oxford and Cambridge respectively. During the great coaching era of the late 18th and early 19th centuries, the town was an important and thriving stop-over point for travellers, tradesmen and mail coaches. The two main coaching inns were called The Cock and The Bull and both became known throughout the country as the centre of all news travelling either on foot or by horse. The competing inns established a rivalry as to which could produce the most exciting and scurrilous travellers' tales to be passed on to the major cities and as a result many unbelievable stories were dismissed as 'Cock and Bull' tales.

Codswallop means that something is worthless, rubbish or nonsense. Wallop is Australian slang for beer or ale. In 1875 Australian inventor Hiram Codd developed the first bottle with a lid which kept sparkling water fizzy until it was opened, but Aussie beer drinkers were unimpressed by the new craze of drinking fizzy water, which they regarded as rubbish, and dismissed it as 'Codd's Wallop'.

If something is **Too Dicey** it is considered to be risky or dubious and should be treated with great caution. The BBC's *Antiques Roadshow* suggested an origin for this phrase in May 1999 when a presenter was given an antique map to value. He explained to the owner that there was once a crooked map-seller who, in the 1800s, used old and worn map plates to print new copies on to old paper and sell them on as original antiques. The map seller was called Mr Dicey and when he was caught and punished the phrase entered the language as a byword for anything that could not be relied upon.

The **Full Monty** means the whole lot – the maximum available. There are several suggestions for its origin but the earliest can be traced back to the turn of the century. In 1904 the tailors Montague Burton (later shortened to Burtons) established their first hire shop in Chesterfield. They made it possible for men not only to hire a suit for special occasions, but also to hire a complete outfit of suit, shirt, tie, shoes and socks and those opting for the full set were known to be wearing the 'Full Monty'. The saying re-emerged in the mid-1980s as part of the *Coronation Street* dictionary *Street Talk*. It has since been used as the title of several books and a film.

To have **Hobson's Choice** is to have no choice at all. In the early 1600s Thomas Hobson owned a well-known livery stable in Cambridge. Hobson insisted on hiring out his horses strictly on a rotation basis to ensure each animal was evenly worked and nobody was allowed to select a favourite, as was common practice in other liveries at the time. The author and poet John Milton seems to be responsible for the phrase passing into wider English use as he mentions Hobson in two of his epitaphs. Milton was at Cambridge University around 1630 so it is quite possible he was one of Hobson's customers.

The Real McCoy is the genuine article, not a fake or a copy. One story goes back to the 1890s. American welterweight boxer Kid McCoy dominated his sport during the late 19th century and was well known throughout his land. McCoy had many imitators who would earn money in boxing booths and fairgrounds all across America, challenging locals to take on the champion. In the end few people believed, and rightly so, the champion was fighting in booths. During the 1920s, long after McCoy had retired, the little boxer was having a quiet drink in a bar when a lumbering drunk picked an argument with him. McCoy's associates warned the giant off by insisting he was provoking a champion boxer but the fat man would have none of it, challenging McCoy to prove who he was. Eventually the ageing boxer reluctantly floored the persistent drinker with a single punch and then went back to his whisky. Apparently when the man regained consciousness his first words were 'Godammit, he *is* the real McCoy.' It's a great story, but it isn't the origin of the expression.

Elijah McCoy was born in Colchester, Ontario, Canada, on 2 May 1844, the son of former slaves who had fled north from Kentucky. McCoy trained as a mechanical engineer in Scotland before travelling to America and settling in Detroit. In 1872 he designed an automatic lubricator for steam engines, his first of 57 patented inventions to revolutionise industry in America. Others included the ironing board and the lawn sprinkler. McCoy became famous and his popular inventions were copied all over the world, although many buyers would insist on buying only 'the real McCoy'.

A **Mickey Finn** is a drink that has been drugged in one way or another, usually to render a person helpless so that a crime can be committed. Mickey Finn was the owner of both the Palm Garden Restaurant and the Lone Star Saloon located on Whiskey Row, Chicago. Neither establishment was quite what it seemed; both were havens for pickpockets and petty thieves, mostly trained by Finn himself. One of Finn's common methods was to lace drinks with chloral hydrate (knock-out drops) and then fleece his victims before dumping them down the road. Unsurprisingly the two bars were closed down in 1903, although Finn escaped jail and found work as a barman where he sold his recipe to other unscrupulous vagabonds.

His Name Is Mud is a derogatory phrase used to describe a person who is unpopular or completely out of favour due to some act. The obvious allusion might seem to be one of someone so low in society's opinion that they are no better than mud, but this is not the origin of the phrase. On 14 April 1865 John Wilkes Booth assassinated President Abraham Lincoln in the Ford Theater, Washington DC. As he made his escape Booth broke his leg, but still managed to reach his horse and ride away. When he reached the countryside he looked for the house of Dr Samuel Mudd who treated his injury. Mudd had no idea of the events of the evening but, when he heard of the assassination the following day, he immediately informed the authorities he had seen Booth. Despite his innocence, the doctor was arrested and later convicted of conspiracy and sentenced to life imprisonment. In 1869 Mudd was pardoned and released from jail, but the American public never forgave him for his implied involvement in the assassination plot. It would be another hundred years before Mudd was finally declared innocent and his name cleared.

Murphy's Law is the theory that if anything can go wrong it probably will. This phrase began to be used in 1949 at the Edwards Air Force Base test centre in California. Captain Edward A Murphy was an engineer working on Project MX981, which was a series of experiments to find out how much deceleration the human body can stand in a plane crash. One morning Murphy found a transducer had been wired up the wrong way and wasn't working. The young engineer fixed the problem and claimed of the technician responsible 'If there is ever a wrong way to do something, he will find it.' During the tests the project manager kept a list of theories, or 'laws' as he called them, and added Murphy's comment under the title 'Murphy's Law'. A little later Dr John Paul Stapp, an Air Force doctor, was involved in similar deceleration experiments and gave a press conference to reveal his team's results. During the press session Dr Stapp recorded that the project's excellent safety record was due to a firm belief in 'Murphy's Law', which was to try and foresee anything that could go wrong and avoid it happening by advanced planning. Over the following years aerospace manufacturers picked upon the phrase and used it widely in their advertising, leading to 'Murphy's Law' becoming used all over the English-speaking world.

When we describe something as **OK**, we regard it as acceptable and good for use. The expression seems to have first appeared in print during 1839 in the *Boston Morning Post* and later popularised during the 1840 election campaign of Martin Van Buren of Kinderhook, New York. He was known as 'Old Kinderhook' – OK for short. Twenty years later, during the American Civil War, soldiers relied on a biscuit called Orrin Kendall for rations, and a port in Haiti called Aux Cayes was famous among American sailors for its rum, known as 'OK Rum'. But before all of this there lived a popular native American chief called Old Keokuk who signed all his treaties by using only his initials.

A **Parting Shot** is a final blow or withering remark that a victim has no chance of responding to. The Parthians were an ancient race living in south-west Asia. They were skilled warriors whose battle tactics included mounted archers riding away from their enemy, giving the impression of a retreat. They would then twist backwards in their saddles and fire with deadly accuracy at the pursuing enemy. The first references were made to the Parthians in English literature during the 17th century and the phrase 'parthian shot' became a well-known phrase for 'parting blow' until the early 20th century when the similarity between 'parthian' and 'parting' led to a corruption of the original phrase.

A **Peeping Tom** is a male person who tries to watch something they shouldn't – usually with sexual connotations – in the hope nobody catches them. The expression has a wonderful origin connected to everybody's favourite naked horsewoman, Lady Godiva. During the 11th century the Earl of Mercia, Leofric, was one of the three great English earls and he ruled a vast area of the country. In 1040, according to legend, he tried to impose heavy taxes on his countrymen and there was uproar in the streets. Leofric's compassionate and charitable wife Godgifu (which has evolved into Godiva) sided with the people and begged her husband to lower the taxes. Leofric told his wife he would lower taxes after she had ridden naked through the streets of Coventry. Now Godiva was a game girl and her hapless husband hadn't reckoned on her spirit, so she agreed to the challenge. Not surprisingly the people of Coventry were delighted but as a show of respect all agreed to stay indoors, close their shutters and face the other way as the lady passed by. All of them kept their word, except Tom the Tailor who couldn't help himself and peeped out through the shutters. According to legend the 'peeping Tom' was then struck blind. Lady Godiva was a real person, but the story is probably only just that.

To **Plug A Song** or **Book** is to promote it and make as many people aware of it as possible. In the early part of the 20th century Radio Normandie was one of the first independent stations and was broadcast from northern France. Radio Normandie was also the first commercial radio station to transmit to England during the 1930s and one of their sources of income was to receive payments to play records and promote them throughout the country. The station's founder and main broadcaster was a Captain Leonard Plugge, which was probably how the phrase originated.

Sweet FA does not stand for Sweet Fuck All, as many people believe. In fact, it stands for Sweet Fanny Adams. Fanny was an eight-year-old girl living in Alton, Hampshire, who was found murdered, her body cut into pieces and thrown into the River Wey. At around the same time the English Navy changed their rations from salted tack to low-grade tins of chopped-up sweet mutton. The new ration was both tasteless and unpopular, and with macabre humour sailors suggested the new meat was the remains of the murdered girl and christened the ration 'Sweet Fanny Adams'. On land the phrase was adopted to describe anything boring, monotonous and not worth describing (as was the ration and not poor Fanny) hence 'Sweet FA'.

10: POLITICS

In The Bag is a phrase used to describe something of an absolute certain outcome. Since the beginning of the English Parliament, tradition has it that all petitions brought before the House of Commons, which had a successful outcome, would be placed by the Speaker in a large velvet bag hung from the back of the Speaker's chair. Therefore politicians, or reporters, describing a petition as 'in the bag' would be confirming its favourable outcome. The bag, although now only symbolic, still hangs behind the Speaker's chair.

To **Jump On The Bandwagon** means to join in, often uninvited, an already successful venture and gain some sort of self-benefit. In the Deep South of America travelling bands would once perform on their wagons in front of political or other rallies. Usually the bands would be a highlight of an event, attracting the largest crowds, so it was common for political or religious leaders to climb up on to the wagon, interrupting the music (sometimes with prior agreement) and gain themselves an immediate captive audience. Crowds would often tolerate this knowing the musicians would be back in due course. The practice had continued for over a hundred years before it was first recorded during William Jennings Bryan's presidential campaign in the early 1900s.

A **Battle Axe** is a comic, if not offensive, term for belligerent and stubborn old woman. Its origins can be found in America and the early years of the women's rights movement. The phrase itself was originally meant as a rallying or war cry but backfired when the movement published a journal called *The Battle Axe* (to signify their resolve). Instead, the phrase was quickly used as a derogatory term for the domineering and hostile nature of the majority involved in that movement and as a reflection of what many, including less aggressive women, thought of its members.

Beyond The Pale is usually applied to someone who has committed an unspeakable act or behaves immorally. A Pale, historically, is an area around a town or a city, which was subject to a particular jurisdiction and was governed by the King or one of his lords. Areas outside the Pale were generally regarded as lawless and uncouth, so unaccountable peasants of medieval England, Ireland and France (the English-held towns of Calais and Dublin established their own Pales) were regarded by relatively civilised town-folk as from 'Beyond the Pale'.

Bob's Your Uncle is often used to describe something that is resolved in your favour without much effort, such as 'Just send the form in and Bob's your uncle'. The phrase was in regular use in Britain from the 1890s and comes from the promotion in 1886 of Arthur Balfour to Secretary of State for Ireland. Balfour was a surprise choice for the position and few regarded him as qualified for the post. But when it became known he was the nephew of Prime Minister Robert Gascoyne-Cecil, Third Marquis of Salisbury, the joke circulated that, if Robert was your uncle, a deed was as good as done.

Hear Hear is often used in political circles to suggest agreement or endorsement of something being said. Originally any disagreement with a speaker, either in the Commons or the House of Lords, would be expressed by loud humming from those with opposing views, in an attempt to drown out the speech being made. But members agreeing and in favour of the speaker would call for those humming to listen by shouting 'hear him, hear him'. This phrase has evolved over the years to the one used today.

When somebody is told to **Toe The Line**, they are expected to follow the rules and submit to authority. Originally this phrase refers to the lines drawn along the two front benches in the House of Commons which still exists. The two lines are strategically placed at a distance far enough apart to prevent opposing members reaching each other with their swords, should the debating become heated enough. Any member becoming animated enough during an argument to step over a line would be called to order and told to 'toe the line'. Tradition still prevents members from 'crossing the line' but these days none of them carries swords or other weapons, although it would be much more fun if they did.

It is no surprise to find the Americans claiming the origin of this historic British tradition. The US Navy website states, 'The space between each pair of deck planks in a wooden ship was filled with a packing material called "oakum" and then sealed with a mixture of pitch and tar. The result, from afar, was a series of parallel lines a half-foot or so apart, running the length of the deck. Once a week, usually on Sunday, a warship's crew was ordered to fall in at quarters with each group of men into which the crew was divided and lined up in formation in a given area of the deck. To ensure the neat alignment of each row the sailors were directed to stand with their toes just touching a particular seam.' Also, a naval punishment for boys too young to be flogged was to stand for hours on end in any weather with their toes touching the line. If they moved their punishment would be extended.

When an idea is **Pie In The Sky** it is thought to be a good idea but unlikely to amount to a successful conclusion, especially for the person suggesting the plan. The original use of the phrase was, in fact, quite cynical. It comes from a trade union parody often used during the years of the Great

Depression early in the 20th century. The hymn, entitled 'The Sweet By And By', goes like this: 'You will eat, bye and bye / In that glorious land above the sky / work and pray, live on hay / You'll get pie in the sky when you die.' And through that popular movement the phrase passed over into wider use.

11: THE LAW

A **Baker's Dozen** is 13, not 12. There are two established theories as to the origin of the phrase. The first is set in medieval England and identifies the sales techniques of tradesmen such as bakers and fishmongers. When selling directly to the public, merchants would have a fixed price for their wares. But when selling to bulk buyers such as town market stall-holders the merchant would gift an extra item for every dozen bought. In such cases the 13th loaf or fish would represent the stall-holder's profit on the items he buys and then sells at market.

The second theory dates back to the 13th century when bakers had the reputation of selling underweight loaves, although sometimes unfairly as the baking process sometimes made the bread 'thin' on the inside. In 1266 regulations were brought in to standardise weights of various loaves and the penalty for being underweight could mean a day in the stocks. To avoid this, bakers began to add an extra loaf, known as a vantage loaf, to every dozen sold, to make sure they stayed within the new laws.

A **Barrack Room Lawyer** is a derogatory term meaning they are unqualified or inexperienced at what they are attempting to achieve (usually in professional circles). Since the 19th century the Queen's (or King's) Regulations have enabled soldiers without any formal legal training to conduct their own defence, make a formal complaint to superiors or promote their own interests. But those who did so were held in contempt by their commanding officers, who bestowed the uncomplimentary tag upon them. The phrase had passed into common usage by the beginning of the 20th century.

If we **Have A Beef** it usually means we have something to moan about or a quarrel to pick. The earliest record of the phrase is found in the

1811 *Dictionary Of The Vulgar Tongue*, which suggests to 'cry beef' meant to give the alarm. Prior to that, in criminal London, it was known that the traditional cry of 'stop thief' was mocked and drowned out by passing fellow criminals who loudly called 'hot beef' instead, in a bid to confuse law-abiding passers-by and allow their colleague to make his getaway.

To suggest somebody has a **Brass Neck** is to imply they have some nerve and will try anything to suit their own purposes, usually with the reluctant admiration of others for their cheek. The origin of this phrase appears to lie with the legend of a highwayman who was sentenced to hang from a tree for his crimes. This method of hanging brought about a slow death by choking so the highwayman came up with a cunning plan. He would swallow a piece of brass tube, with a wire attached to it and held inside his mouth, in the hope this would prevent his throat being crushed and allow him to breathe long enough for the crowd to disperse. All he then needed was an accomplice who could cut him down, remove the tube and save his life. Unfortunately it is not known if this is actually true (I hope it is) but the legend is certainly where the term 'brass neck' came from.

To be thrown in **The Clink** means to be locked away in jail. It is sometimes thought the clink is a reference to the sound of the irons and chains placed on a convict. In fact, The Clink is the name of one of the oldest prisons in England, located in

the London borough of Southwark since the 13th century. The Liberty Of Clink was the name of the district in which the prison was located; it was south of the river and exempt from the jurisdiction of the City of London. In other words, it could make up its own rules. Originally owned by the Bishop of Winchester, The Clink had a fearsome reputation with punishments including boiling in oil, the rack, breaking on the wheel, being forced to stand in cold water until a prisoner's feet rotted, being slowly crushed under weights and starvation. The only way to avoid such treatment was to pay bribes and therefore The Clink provided a vast source of income for the Church from those prisoners on the receiving end of its barbaric practices. Finally destroyed by rioters in 1780, The Clink is now a museum, built on the foundations of the original building and a fitting reminder of London life throughout the Middle Ages.

A **Hijack** is usually associated with the forced or violent theft of a mode of transport, normally aircraft. But it is also often applied to a person taking over any proceedings that have already begun. The earliest reference to its origin can be traced to the old English highwaymen who would steal coaches at musket point and traditionally used the words 'Hold 'em high, Jack', meaning everybody on the coach had to hold their hands in the air while he took control.

By Hook Or By Crook is an expression we use to explain achieving something by any means possible, either honestly or otherwise. For its origin we need to know that a hook is a blunt billhook and a crook is a curved shaft a shepherd uses to gather his flock. In medieval feudal England a law was passed preventing the cutting down of trees or lopping of branches in order to gather firewood. But the law permitted the poor to gather dead wood from forests and deemed anything they could collect with a blunt hook or shepherd's crook was allowable. The Bodmin Register of 1525 states, 'Dynmure Wood is open to the inhabitants of Bodmin… to bear away on their backs a burden of lop, hook, crook and bag wood.'

An **Ignoramus** is somebody of low intelligence and who applies little or no thought to a situation. Much of our legal language derives from Latin and many modern terms of law can be traced to the original use of that language. In Latin 'ignoramus' means 'we don't know [why this case was brought]' and the word would traditionally be stamped on legal documents rejected by the courts as badly thought-out and without basis. The expression has been in general use since George Ruggle wrote a play in 1615 called *Ignoramus* in which the title character, a lawyer, demonstrated the ignorance of the common lawyers of that time.

A **Laughing Stock** is a person exposed to a wide number of other people for their stupidity. In medieval England the stocks were used in many villages to hold a petty criminal or daft soul who had been caught doing something silly, in front of their own community. Their hands and feet would be secured in the wooden frame and the village folk would gather round to laugh at and humiliate the hapless person, often by pelting them with rotten vegetables.

To be pushed from **Pillar To Post** means to be in a constant state of flux and probably harassed at the same time. In the Middle Ages each town and village in England had both a pillory and a whipping post. A pillory (also known as the stocks) was a place where petty criminals or traders who had swindled their customers would be clamped by their head and arms, and local people would gather round to humiliate them. In the case of a more serious crime, offenders would first be put in the pillory and then taken to the whipping post, being jostled along the way, for a public flogging. So the phrase began as 'from the pillory to the post' but evolved into the idiom we use these days.

The phrase **Possession Is Nine Tenths Of The Law** began life as Possession Is Nine Points Of The Law. The phrase was used by anybody claiming an advantage in a legal situation, especially over the ownership of property, whether it belonged to them or not. Prior to the 17th century the expression was 11 out of 12 and it is not known why it was later reduced. However, the nine points are: patience, money, a just cause, a good lawyer, good counsel, witnesses, a true jury, a good judge and good luck.

To **Read The Riot Act** is an expression used when an individual or group of people are given a severe rollicking about their bad behaviour. The original

Riot Act was passed by the British government in 1715 as an attempt to increase the powers of the civil authorities when a town was threatened by riotous behaviour. The Act made it a serious crime for groups of 12 or more people not to disperse within one hour of it being read out to the mob.

The Act read: 'Our Sovereign Lord the King chargeth and commandeth all persons being assembled immediately to disperse themselves, and peaceably to depart to their habitations or to their lawful business, upon the pains contained in the Act made in the first year of King George for preventing tumultuous and riotous assemblies. God save the King.'

Those failing to disperse risked penal servitude for not less than three years or imprisonment with hard labour for up to two years. Actually reading it out took extraordinary courage and often, during serious disturbances, many didn't hear it anyway. After the infamous Peterloo Massacre near Manchester in 1819 many of the convicted demonstrators claimed not to have heard the Act being read and the same defence was put during trials for the 1743 Gin Riots, 1768 St George's Massacre and the 1780 Gordon Riots. The Act remained on the statute book until the 1970s, but little use had been made of it for over a century, apart from when I come home late from the pub, singing loudly.

Rigmarole is an unusual word with an interesting origin. It is used to describe something disconnected, rambling and difficult to see a way through. It is now well over 700 years old and dates back to 1291 when the Scottish noblemen signed a deed of loyalty to King Edward I of England. Each of them fixed their seal to it and when all the attachments were joined together and presented to the King it was 40ft long. The deeds were known as the Ragman Roll and it was a dishevelled mix and match of all the Scottish deeds, both confusing and complicated. Ragman Roll morphed into 'Rigmarole' and became used to describe anything of a troublesome, time-consuming and awkward nature.

If something **Rings True**, or has the **Ring Of Truth** to it, it is generally thought to be the genuine article, despite possible alternatives. Centuries ago, coins of the realm were made of pure metals instead of the hard-wearing alloy that makes up modern currency. But pure metals such as silver have a sonorous ring to them when dropped on a hard counter, so it was quite possible to tell the difference between a genuine coin and a counterfeit by the ringing sound it made when tested.

To Be Screwed is a widely used term for being cheated, or placed at a disadvantage. During the 19th century English prisons were intended to be cruel places of punishment (hard labour) to deter prisoners from returning. One of these forms of punishment was to force a convict to turn a crank handle up to 10,000 times a day. These handles were designed in a way that the hard labour could be made even worse by a warder turning a simple screw, which increased the resistance of the handle. In such barbaric places, bribery and corruption were commonplace and any prisoner who did not agree to a warder's demands could find himself being 'screwed' the next time he was on the handle.

A **Soap Opera** has become the accepted term for a regular radio, and later TV, drama shows usually based around normal life. Each episode ends in suspense to ensure listeners and viewers return to find out what happens next. The origin of the phrase lies in America during the 1920s with a popular weekly radio programme called *Amos And Andy*. As the show was always broadcast during prime time, and for family viewing, the soap manufacturers Proctor and Gamble started to advertise their products during the breaks and later sponsored the programme. Soon afterwards other similar shows (and soap manufacturers) followed suit and a critic, writing in 1938, began referring to them generally as 'soaps'. The word 'opera' was then borrowed from the popular 'horse operas' (a term for cowboy films) of the 1930s.

On The Treadmill is another saying relating to Victorian hard labour, one the great writer Oscar Wilde was subjected to during his prison sentence in the late 1800s. Today it is used to describe exhausting, never-ending work that is usually without even acknowledgement. In Oscar's day a treadmill was a primitive version of modern-day step machines found in every gym or fitness centre. It was a row of evenly spaced wooden planks joined at each end by a large round cog. Poor Oscar and his fellow convicts were forced to walk the treadmill all day long, akin to walking up an endless staircase but without actually leaving the bottom step. As the playwright himself said at the time, 'If this is the way the Queen treats her prisoners, she doesn't deserve to have any.' Needless to say none of his clothes still fitted when he eventually left Reading Gaol. And today, in fitness centres, they all pay to do it.

When something has **Gone West** it is generally lost forever. Usually it is a plan, project or perhaps business deal that 'goes west' when something major goes wrong. There is a suggestion that the sun setting in the west may be the root of the phrase but it is more likely to be the Tyburn gibbet, a place of execution once situated near the site of Marble Arch in central London, where we uncover the secret. London's main prisons at either Newgate or **The Clink** were both located on the east side of the city and a condemned man would be loaded on to a cart and taken west to meet his fate. Nobody ever returned from the journey west.

12: MUSIC, THEATRE AND PERFORMANCE

A **Blonde Bombshell** is a cliché now used to describe any dynamic or attractive blonde lady, usually a singer, actress or film star but often applied to politicians or business figures. The original 'Blonde Bombshell' was Jean Harlow, an American actress, mistress of the one-line witticism and star of the 1933 film *Bombshell*. When the film was later released in the UK producers, worried it might be perceived as a war film, changed its title to *Blonde Bombshell* and the phrase immediately passed into the English language.

To hope somebody **Breaks A Leg** is in fact a message of goodwill and good luck, usually reserved for a stage actor or musician prior to a performance. Some claim the expression originates from the assassination of President Abraham Lincoln who was shot dead in his private box at Ford's Theater in Washington DC, on 14 April 1865. His murderer John Wilkes Booth, a renowned Shakespearean actor, broke his leg jumping down on to the stage to make his escape. The claim is that the saying arose as a form of black humour in relation to that event. But in fact the phrase was known centuries before that when a measure of the success of a stage performance was the number of times an audience called the performers back to the front of the stage for applause. Each time the curtain was reopened the actors bowed or curtsied, and the more often that happened the greater the chance of 'breaking a leg'.

That **Old Chestnut** is a phrase used to describe an old joke or excuse, something that has been heard many times before. The origin of the saying dates back to 1816 when the play *The Broken Sword* by William Diamond was staged in Covent Garden, London. One of the play's characters, Captain

Xavier, often repeats the same joke about a cork tree, with slight variations each time. At one point another character, Pablo, interrupts with the punchline and says, 'It's a chestnut. I have heard you tell the joke 27 times and it's a chestnut.' At some point later American actor William Warren was playing the part of Pablo and while he was being entertained at a society dinner one evening, another guest began to recite an old, well-known joke. Warren interrupted and said with a flourish, 'It's an old chestnut, that's what it is,' much to the amusement of everybody there. That is how the expression passed into the English language.

Putting The Dampers on something means to discourage or to tone down the enthusiasm somebody is showing for an idea. This saying has a musical origin and relates to the piano. A damper is operated by a foot pedal, which presses it against the strings to reduce the instrument's sound. To 'put the dampers' on a concert performance was a phrase used to describe toning the sound of the orchestra down.

To have **Egg On Your Face** implies a decision or choice has been made which later turns out to be a mistake, leaving a person looking foolish. Some suggest this is a relatively recent phrase and originates in America during the election campaigns of the 1960s and 1970s. At the time it was common for opponents of a candidate to throw eggs at them in order to make them look foolish. There is, however, strong evidence to suggest the Victorian theatres hold the real origin. At the time, during the slapstick comedies of the era, the fall guy would usually have eggs broken on his forehead to make him look foolish, not unlike taking a custard pie in the face. Those crazy Victorians!

To **Face The Music** has two possible origins. The first is that nervous (often terrified) actors and actresses, on an opening night, would have to go out on stage at the start of their performance and quite literally 'face the music' (as the orchestra pit sat directly in front of the stage with the musician facing the actors). In this case 'facing the music' meant the actor actually went out and performed, rather than **losing their bottle** (their nerve). The second explanation suggests that a dishonourable military discharge would always result in the disgraced serviceman being marched off barracks to the sound of drummers playing (being 'drummed out'), in which case he too had 'faced the music'.

As Fit As A Fiddle is used to indicate a person or an animal is in good condition, lively and energetic. But since its origin we seem to have lost a letter along the way. Back in the days of medieval court the fittest person was thought to be the fiddler as they danced and scampered about as they played their music throughout the crowds. The phrase widely used at the time was 'as fit as a fiddler', which makes a lot more sense.

To indulge in **Horseplay** is to behave in a boisterous but friendly manner. The origin of this saying lies with the English Morris dancers. At country fairs players riding wooden hobbyhorses usually accompanied Morris dancers. These 'horses' were expected to engage in wild and uncontrollable antics to entertain the crowds, much as a clown does in a circus, and the 'horseplay' became a popular and important part of the Morris dancers' act.

Jumping The Shark is a phrase used to describe good television shows that have run out of steam and become average at best. This has been the case with many classic comedies, which run for one series too many and standards and ratings start to fall. One of the great TV shows of the 1970s was *Happy Days*, featuring The Fonz, the Cunningham family and their friends. All of America and Britain seemed captivated by the show until the writing became tired, and during the last series viewers started to switch off. The final straw seems to have been a scene in which The Fonz (Henry Winkler) was waterskiing in his leather jacket and motorcycle boots and literally jumped over a shark. For many critics enough was enough and that scene marked the end for the show, though not of its well-earned cult status.

When something is **On The Nose** we take it to be right on time, exact and precise. The reason this phrase is used can be found in the studios of the very early live radio broadcasts where a programme producer would signal to the performers in the sound-proofed booths when they went 'on air and live' by touching his nose.

To **Play It By Ear** means to take a situation as we find it and then adapt our actions as we have to.

In other words to wait and see what happens before reacting. This is a musical expression and can be traced back to the time prior to recording equipment. In those days composers and songwriters had to craft out a piece of music on a piano, and write it down as they went along to remember how the melody went. Musicians also had to listen to one or two instruments and then pick out their parts by ear, which was known as 'playing it by ear'. These days musicians who can play their part just by listening to a record are said to be 'playing it by ear', but that is a lot easier now than it used to be.

To **Pull Out All The Stops** implies a big, concerted effort is being made to complete a task in time. This is a simple one and alludes to the grand church organs, which used 'stops' to tone down the volume of the instrument. At vast gatherings, with many people present, an organist would 'pull out the stops' to increase the sound of his organ, enabling everybody at the back to hear it clearly.

Living The Life Of Reilly is one of the strangest sayings of all. It suggests that the person referred to lives a charmed life of ease, and anyone blessed with good fortune is considered to be doing the same. The origin of the phrase is unclear, but it could perhaps lie with the earliest recorded reference, which is found in a song called 'My Name Is Kelly', written by H Pearse in 1919. It was a popular music hall song and included the lines 'Faith and my name is Kelly, Michael Kelly, but I'm living the life of Reilly just the same.' This lyric is a reference to an earlier song performed in the music halls during the 1880s, which described a character called O'Reilly who was a working-class Irish immigrant. He always claimed to be on the verge of hitting the big time, making himself and everyone around him rich in the process.

If you ask somebody to **Put A Sock In It**, you are asking them to quieten down. In the early days of sound recording and radio broadcasting, the ability to control instrument volumes was severely limited, but orchestras and bands, the forerunners of the modern pop band, were in high demand. Usually the horn sections would drown out the wind instruments and strings in the enclosed studios. In an attempt to even the sound out, horn players muffled their instruments by literally stuffing a sock into the mouth of their instruments, bringing them down to the same sound level as the rest of the band.

Back To Square One means back to the beginning. The origin of the phrase is easily traced to the 1930s when commentary on football matches began to be broadcast by the BBC. The BBC's schedule magazine, *The Radio Times*, devised a numbered grid system which they published enabling commentators to indicate to listeners exactly where the ball was on the pitch. Square one was the goalkeeper's area and whenever the ball was passed back to him, signalling the start of the forward movement of the team, play was referred to as being 'back to square one'.

When someone **Steals Your Thunder** they are taking credit for something that you should properly be credited for. The phrase was in regular use by 1900, especially by jealous politicians claiming their brilliant and original ideas had been stolen by another. The expression was coined in the early 1700s by the playwright and critic John Dennis, who discovered the sound of thunder could be reproduced to great effect by pummelling large tin sheets backstage at the Drury Lane Theatre in London. At a time when sound effects were virtually unheard of, his idea considerably added to the drama and drew much attention. His play, on the other hand, did not attract attention and was replaced by *Macbeth* in a matter of weeks. Shortly afterwards the embittered Dennis saw a performance of *Macbeth* and was furious to hear his thunder being reproduced without his permission. Writing a review the following day, he raged, 'See what rascals they are. They will not run my play and yet they steal my thunder.'

13: THE USA

If we are **Barking Up The Wrong Tree** we have misunderstood something and are now pursuing the wrong course of action. This is a phrase of north American origin and comes from the old practice of racoon-hunting dating back to the 1800s. Racoons are nocturnal animals and hunters would roam around the forests in darkness, using dogs to pick up a scent. Frightened racoons would scurry to safety in the branches of trees but hunting dogs would stand with their paws on the base of a trunk barking. A hunter would then climb the tree for the catch, but would sometimes find the racoon nowhere to be seen. When that happened it was said the dog had been 'barking up the wrong tree'.

Bootleggers are well known for selling items, originally alcohol, without proper permission and avoiding tax or other duties, making them cheaper and therefore popular. These days a bootlegger is better known for making copies of music or films

and selling them without the artist's or producer's permission and without paying any royalties due. The expression was first recorded in the mid-1800s and applied to those who sold illegal liquor to Indians in the Far West. Those making the sales would ride out to the reservations with thin bottles of alcohol concealed in their riding boots and quickly became known by the authorities as 'bootleggers'. The phrase travelled across the sea to the UK and was soon applied to anyone involved in counterfeit activity.

If we are **On The Breadline** we are poor and on the verge of destitution, the inference being very close to disaster. This is an American phrase, which travelled across the Atlantic in the 1870s. Around that time a celebrated bakery, run by the Fleischman family in New York, was famous for the quality and freshness of its bread. The reason was that all the bread was baked in the morning and any left over at the end of each day was given to the poor and starving for free, rather than kept for the following day's customers. A queue, in America, is known as a line, so at the end of each day a 'breadline' would form outside the premises, and those on it were close to starvation.

A **Bucket Shop** is a place to buy cheap tickets, usually airline or theatre tickets. But, before that term was coined, such places were usually illegal brokerage houses that cheated their customers. The original 'bucket shops' were seedy American bars where patrons could buy cheap beer by the bucketful and these bars often cheated their customers who had no way of measuring out the amount of beer in the bucket, other than by the glass. But the time they had drunk the bucketful, customers had, more often

than not, lost their senses, their bearings, the use of their legs and, more importantly for the innkeeper, count.

Someone is said to have a **Chip On Their Shoulder** when they are looking for an argument for no apparent reason, at least not one that is obvious to anyone else. Its origin can be found 200 years ago, in a custom used by American schoolboys to challenge each other to a fight. One would place a twig or piece of bark (a chip of wood) on his shoulder and challenge another to knock it off. If he did a fight started. Then, as now, it is a phrase used to describe someone who is spoiling for a row.

Being on **Cloud Nine** describes a feeling of total happiness and content, or euphoria. Between the 1930s and 1950s the American Weather Bureau divided clouds into classes numbered one to nine. The highest, cloud nine, is the cumulonimbus, which reaches 40,000ft and can appear as white mountains, even on a sunny day. During the 1950s a popular US radio show, *Johnny Dollar*, ran an episode during which the hero was often knocked unconscious and then transported to 'cloud nine' where he was revived and lived to be a hero again in other episodes. It was through that association that 'cloud nine' passed into the English language as a popular phrase for the peak of existence.

A **Deadline** is the final date or time by which a task has to be completed. Originally the deadline was a white line painted at Andersonville prisoner of war camp in America during the American Civil War. Without the use of wire and fencing Andersonville simply had marksmen placed around the perimeter and any prisoner crossing the white line was shot dead, no questions asked. Since then the phrase has been applied to newspaper writers who had to have their article submitted by a certain time before a publication went to print. If they missed the deadline their story was considered dead as it would be out of date by the following day's print run.

To say somebody is **Dressed To Kill** is to suggest they are smart, fashionable and set to make a romantic conquest. The origin of this phrase appears to have come from the *Cambridge Tribune*, an American newspaper. On 10 November 1881 an army recruit, resplendent in his new shiny uniform, was asked how he felt about his appearance. Unimpressed by either the splendour or the question, the soldier simply replied to the interviewer 'I am dressed to kill.'

If something is described as **Fair To Middling**, it is generally accepted as being around average, or just above. The phrase was originally used in the American cotton industry in the mid-1800s. Commercial cotton was graded in categories ranging between inferior and fine. Average was known as 'middling' and just above it the grade was called 'fair'. The term was in wide-ranging use across the water by 1837 and in October of that year the *Southern Literary Messenger* of Richmond, Virginia, reported the following: 'A dinner on the Plains, Tuesday September 20th – given at the country seat of JC Jones, Esq for the officers of the Peacock and Enterprise. The viands [items of food] were fair to middling.' In England the phrase was first listed in the *Century Dictionary* of 1889 as meaning 'moderately good'.

When something is **Flavour Of The Month**, it is temporarily in fashion. The phrase is one of the most enduring advertising slogans of the last century and originates in the American ice cream parlours during the 1950s. To encourage customers to try different flavours and increase the sales of less popular types of ice cream, parlours would lower the price of a certain flavour for a month-long promotion. That month's cheap ice cream would be widely promoted as 'the flavour of the month'.

To **Get Someone's Goat** means to really irritate and annoy a person. This is an American phrase from the early part of the 20th century. Goats have long been considered to have a calming influence on horses and for this reason were often the stable mates of highly strung race horses, especially while being stabled at an unfamiliar race track. But sometimes a fancied stallion's chance of success would be torpedoed by shady opponents, who would slip into the stable and take the goat away. The result was an irritated and nervy racehorse who performed badly in the race.

To hear something **On The Grapevine** means to have obtained information through gossip and rumour while remaining unaware of the true source. William Morse invented the telegraph in America and first used it in a demonstration to Congress on 24 May 1844. Such was the enthusiasm for this new system of communication that companies all over America rushed to put up telegraph lines, often cutting many corners. In 1859 a Colonel Bee began work on a line between Virginia City, Nevada and Placerville, California and to save time and money decided to use trees instead of fixed telegraph poles. But the natural movement of trees soon pulled and stretched the line, leaving it coiled and tangled resembling one of the wild grapevines in California. From then on any general source of information was known in that area as 'the grapevine' and the term quickly spread throughout the land.

When something has **Gone Haywire** it is considered to be an uncontrollable rambling mess. The expression originated in the early 20th century in America with the introduction of a strong, thin metal wire, which was used to bind hay bales. Once snipped, the taut haywire would spring dangerously through the air and then be piled up in the corner of a yard in a tangled mass.

Later farmers would use the rusting haywire to make temporary repairs to fences and tools and the overall chaotic mess with everything connected with the haywire resulted in the phrase being used to describe general untidy disorder.

Hobo is an American term for a travelling worker, rather than a 'tramp' (who travels without working) or a 'bum' who does neither. The origin of the phrase is the word 'hoe-boy', a **freelance** farm worker travelling with his tools (hoes) looking for work.

To **Hold The Fort** is to maintain normality and keep things running in the absence of others. During the American Civil War (1861–65), General Sherman immortalised the phrase during the battle of Allatoona in 1864. When gathering his army on top of Mount Kennesaw, near Atlanta, Georgia, Sherman signalled down to General Corse that reinforcements were arriving and he must 'hold the fort' until he had gathered enough men to mount an attack on the siege soldiers. The phrase made its way to Britain via the poet Philip Bliss (1838–76), who wrote about spiritual assistance in times of difficulty: 'Hold the fort for I am coming, Jesus signals still.' Popular

American evangelists Moody and Sankey introduced the poem to the British public during their religious campaign in 1873.

Keeping Up With The Joneses is an expression for attempting to stay the financial and social equals of better-off friends or neighbours. Of American origin, the phrase began in a popular comic strip-cartoon of the same name by Arthur R. Momand. Beginning in 1913 *Keeping Up With The Joneses* ran for 28 years and was syndicated throughout US newspapers. Momand based the comedy around his own family's real-life attempt to maintain a show of material wealth on a limited income. Years later, in 1955, Momand wrote to CE Funk explaining his ideas. 'We had been living way beyond our means in our endeavour to keep up with the well-to-do class which lived around us in Cedarhurst. I also noticed most of our friends were doing the same: the $10,000 chap was trying to keep up with the $20,000-a-year man. I decided it would make good comic-strip material, so sat down and drew up six strips. At first I thought of calling it *Keeping Up With The Smiths*, but in the end decided "Jones" was more euphonious [pleasant sounding].'

A **Kangaroo Court** is an irregular (or illegal) tribunal that is conducted with complete disregard for due legal process. In America during the 19th century it was common for court procedure to miss out legal steps in order to obtain a popular or convenient conviction. This was known as jumping though the procedure of justice. It was first recorded in America in 1853 and has clear links with the Californian gold rush of 1849, which was joined by many Australian prospectors. During this time informal courts were set up to deal with so-called illegal prospectors who were known as claim jumpers. Many of these were Australian and it isn't difficult to see how the phrase passed over into wider use. It became a well-known phrase in Britain when applied to the dubious tribunals used by trade unions to deal with members who were regarded as strike-breakers.

To **Knock The Spots Off** means to beat easily, without too much effort. This phrase is of American origin and can be traced back to the mid-19th century when it was in common use. At carnivals and festivals all over America one of the most popular side shows was the shooting gallery, where cowboys, farmers and children would all pit their skills on the firing range. The most commonly used target, and the one in greatest supply, was a playing card and each sharpshooter would aim to remove as many of the 'spots' on the card as possible. The one who shot them all off would emerge as the winner.

Lock, Stock And Barrel is a phrase used to indicate something in its entirety. This phrase has an American origin and can be traced to a US senator who persuaded the Senate to manufacture muskets in three parts: the lock, the stock and the barrel. This way the weapons could be easily transported in separate parts, preventing theft, and damaged guns could be rebuilt using spare parts from others. The idea was adopted and from that day onwards, soldiers found they needed the 'lock, stock and barrel' (everything) in order to make up a weapon.

A person **Throwing Mud Around** is generally bad mouthing and slandering somebody. The origin of this expression is nothing to do with the hapless Dr Mudd (see **Name Is Mud**), but a section of the American newspaper media in the early 1800s.

Journalists who sullied other people's reputations were regarded as 'mud slingers' and their newspapers 'the mud press'. More recently it has become known as 'the gutter press'.

Your **Neck Of The Woods** is used to imply a person's neighbourhood. Way back in the early history of colonial America, the British began putting names to places in an attempt to give that new country some sense of its own identity. In doing so there was a deliberate attempt to avoid traditionally English-sounding names such as Dell, Fen, Moor, Heath and Ford. Instead words like Hollow, Fork, Stick and Foot were used. The only word that seems to have travelled is 'neck', which had been used in England since the mid-1500s to describe a narrow strip of land surrounded by water. But the settlers across the pond used the word to describe narrow strips of woodland in the new country and native Indian settlements, often located in the forests, were identified by which 'neck of the woods' they could be found in.

To be **Sold Down The River** means to have been misled and that a promise or other assurances have not been met. It is an American phrase by origin and relates to slavery in the 1800s. Wealthy landowners would hand pick the slaves they regarded suitable to live on the estates with their families in relative comfort. Some were even promised such a lifestyle as they left Africa, India and the East Indies in search of a better future. The reality, however, was that those regarded unsuitable to live with the families were put on a boat and sent down the Mississippi river where they were sold to the plantations as slave labour. There the living conditions were appalling and the wretched folk had been well and truly 'sold down the river' by the land of opportunity.

A **Straw Poll** is an expression used to describe a study of general opinion. It is widely used in politics to assess the overall views of the people by taking small random samples of opinion and using that to measure wider feeling. The use of the phrase began in America in 1824 when reporters from the *Harrisburg Pennsylvanian* questioned a sample of voters in Wilmington in an attempt to predict the overall result. Their findings proved accurate and were considered such a success that the idea caught on and has been used in almost every election ever since. The actual wording comes from the practice of throwing a handful of straw into the air to determine the direction of the wind.

Taking A Rain Check is a term used when declining an invitation on one occasion, but keeping it open for another day. The phrase began during the 19th century when American baseball clubs noticed dwindling crowd levels during the winter months. It became obvious that fair-weather fans were not interested in games played on cold or wet days, especially if there was any chance of bad weather stopping play. That was until one bright marketing spark came up with the idea of promising a 'rain check' (or rain ticket) to any fan who wanted to leave, up to a certain point during a match, because of bad weather. The 'rain check' became a safety net for fans as it would entitle them to attend a game on another day if the one they paid for was washed out, ensuring their entry fee had not been wasted. The best part for the club was that they not only kept the money, but also guaranteed the fan would return again another day *and* they retained his goodwill for the future. The practice spread and it later became common for American baseball fans to 'take a rain check' halfway through dull and boring games, whatever the weather.

Talking Turkey means to have frank and direct discussions, which can be blunt in their delivery. Turkeys were first found in America among the native Indians. At first European settlers confused the bird with the guinea fowls (natives of Africa) they had in their home countries. Thinking the bird was from Turkey, they developed a taste for it and soon the gobbler was in high demand at the settlements and reservations. As a result all serious discussions with the native Indians soon became known as 'talking about turkey' and the phrase became part of the English language in America, before crossing the water to Britain. *Brewer's Dictionary* offers a second suggested origin of the practice of turkey hunters attracting their prey by imitating its gobbling noises ('talking turkey'). Apparently the birds would then return the call and reveal their whereabouts for the hunter. Take your pick.

There Is More Than One Way To Skin A Cat is a common saying to indicate there are several ways in achieving a particular goal. Cat lovers will be relieved to know this has nothing to do with their feline friends. Instead it relates to catfish – long a popular source of food and easy to snare, but the skin is difficult to remove. I am reliably informed there are several ways to skin a catfish successfully, the best being to drop the fish into boiling water, which allows the skin to be easily peeled away from the meat.

There Is No Such Thing As A Free Lunch means that nothing actually comes for free and, even when it seems to, there is usually a hidden cost. In the 1840s American bars and restaurants began attracting customers by offering a free lunch to anyone buying a drink. But these lunches were usually only salty snacks that, once eaten, would encourage the customer to drink more and quench his subsequent thirst. It was soon noted these drinkers were spending more than they originally intended and didn't even benefit from a proper lunch. Such tactics still work and are the reason why so many modern pubs and bars can be found offering free bowls of salted crisps and peanuts to drinkers. John Farmer, in his book *Americanisms*, published in 1899, noted: 'The free lunch fiend is one who makes a meal of what is really provided as a snack, but shamefacedly manages to get something more than his money's worth.'

To put in your **Two-Penny's Worth** means to add an opinion, which could be regarded as almost worthless. The origin of this phrase is found in America when the US Treasury issued a two-cent coin in 1864, along with three- and 20-cent coins. They were the first US coins bearing the phrase 'In God We Trust'. The two-cent coin, being the lowest in value, was soon used as a self-deprecating and modest way of offering an opinion and by the late 19th century 'let me have my two cents' worth' was a standard preamble to offering suggestions. This was done because if an opinion was later regarded as worthless a person could claim they had warned in advance it may have had a low value. The phrase crossed the Atlantic in the early 20th century and has been in use in Britain ever since.

To be **On The Wagon** means a person is no longer drinking alcohol. In the US water carts and wagons began carrying drinking water, or water for cleaning the streets, in 1900. At that time, a person who was known to have given up alcohol could often be found waiting for the water wagon to arrive so they could quench their thirst. People would flock around as the wagon arrived and reformed heavy drinkers were said to actually ride on the wagon around town so they could take on as much water as possible and help quash the craving for alcohol. Many Americans, including criminals who had blamed drink for their crimes, were encouraged to sign a pledge that they were 'on the water wagon', which meant they would rather drink water from the wagon than the demon whisky. The expression became widely used in America throughout the 20th century.

14: FOOD AND DRINK

Barmy Army is a phrase used to describe a rowdy group of people, usually sports fans who are excitable, volatile and often drunk. 'Barm' is the froth produced by fermenting alcohol and in English prisons inmates used to feign madness by 'putting on the barmy stick' (frothing at the mouth). In 1912 Fred Murray wrote and published a popular song which includes the lines 'Ginger you're barmy, why don't you join the army.' This formed part of a popular limerick during the First World War when the lines 'you'll get knocked out by a bottle of stout, Ginger you're barmy' were added. In 1994 rowdy English cricket fans, who had followed the national team to Australia for the Ashes tour, were affectionately nicknamed the

'Barmy Army', an obvious equivalent of Scotland's Tartan Army of football fans.

When somebody **Brings Home The Bacon** they have achieved something notable, or won a prize or award. There are two possible explanations for this phrase. The first is an ancient game, popular at country fairs up and down the land. Men would chase a heavily greased pig around a ring and whoever finally caught and held on to the pig was given it as a prize to take home. Such winners were said to have 'taken home the bacon'. The second, and far more likely, explanation originates from a tradition known as the Dunmow Flitch Trials. Established by a noblewoman called Juga in 1104, at Great Dunmow in Essex, the trial was a challenge to all married couples in England to live for a year and a day in complete harmony, without so much as a cross word between them. The prize offered was a flitch of bacon (a whole side) but in over 500 years there were only eight winners. The tradition was re-established in 1855 and these days are held every four years, often with celebrities taking part. Claimants of the flitch are required to stand in front of a jury of 12 (six maidens and six bachelors of Great Dunmow) and prove their worthiness during a day-long family event. The winners 'take home the bacon'. These days, it would seem, the noblewoman's bacon is safe.

As Drunk As A Lord is used to describe anyone in an advanced state of intoxication. During the 18th and 19th centuries heavy drinking was popular among the nobility and men of fashion prided themselves on their talent to consume vast amounts of wine. As lords and noblemen rarely worked, they would indulge themselves throughout the day and by the time a hunting party retired to nearby hostelries in the evening they would often be rolling drunk. Villagers and farm workers could rarely afford such behaviour, but when one of them did they were described as 'drunk as a lord'.

Eating Humble Pie is used to indicate somebody who has to admit to being wrong in public, perhaps in humiliating fashion, and is looked down upon by those once considered equal. This hierarchy was established during the medieval hunts and the subsequent banquets. During the feast the lord of the manor, and his peers, would be served the finest cuts of venison. But the entrails and offal, known at the time as 'umbles', would be baked into a pie and served to those of a lower standing or out of favour. It was common practice for people to be humiliated by finding themselves sat at the wrong end of the table and served 'umble pie'.

In *David Copperfield*, the Charles Dickens novel published in 1850, one of the characters, Uriah Heep, said, 'I got to know what umbleness did and I took to it. I ate umble pie with an appetite.' That's how the phrase was popularised in Britain.

Gone For A Burton is a phrase used to indicate that somebody has had an unfortunate mishap, or that something or someone has been lost altogether. Before the Second World War, Burton's Ales ran an advert depicting a football team with one player missing from the line-up, leaving a gap in the team photograph. The caption explained that the player had 'Gone for a Burton'. This slogan was picked up by the RAF during the war and used as slang for a missing pilot who had crashed in action into the sea (aka the drink) and was affectionately referred to as having 'gone for a Burton'. He would be missing from photographs in future.

Gone To Pot is widely used to describe something that is no longer of any real use, or a person not in the fit condition they used to be in. A reference dating back to the 16th century show that cuts of meat which, in those pre-refrigerated days, were on the verge of hardening and no longer edible, would be chopped into small pieces and cooked up in a stew-pot. Therefore meat beyond its best would be described as having 'gone to the pot'.

The phrase **Hair Of The Dog** is a shortened version of 'the hair of the dog that bit you'. Early English medical theory suggested rubbing the hair of a particular dog into the wound of its bite would cure the ill effects and heal the wound. The phrase was used in many variations until settling down as a hangover remedy. These days a few more drinks the day after a major session is said to cure the effects of a hangover and is known as 'the hair of the dog'.

15: HUNTING

To **Beat Around The Bush** is to approach a subject indirectly without tackling the central point directly. The saying is a 300-year-old hunting phrase relating to beaters, who use sticks against a bush or undergrowth (wherever game has taken refuge) with the intention of scaring it out and into the line of the hunters' guns. That is known as catching a quarry by 'beating around the bush'.

When something or someone is **Clapped Out**, it is worn out, exhausted and unable to continue. For the origin of this phrase we delve into the sport of hare coursing, a centuries-old custom and the forerunner of today's greyhound racing. While greyhound racing is relatively civilised, its predecessor was barbaric and cruel. In the name of fun a pair of greyhounds would be set after a hare in a race to catch it. Often, in the countryside, the chase would take quite some time and the hare, in a bid to catch its breath, would find a chance to stop and sit up on its haunches. Its fear and exhaustion was so great, and its breathing so heavy, that the hare's chest heaved in and out, forcing the front legs to move backwards and forwards in time, giving the appearance of clapping. This is what led to the phrase 'clapped out' entering the English language.

Fair Game is used to describe somebody, or something, that may be legitimately pursued and assaulted. In the 1700s King George III introduced 32 new hunting laws in a bid to reduce poaching and protect landowners, such as himself, from theft of livestock. The idea was to keep hunting the privilege of the aristocracy, but was cloaked in the notion that without controls game stock would be severely depleted. By the beginning of the following century it was illegal for anyone to remove game from any land apart from the squire and his eldest son. Anybody taking even a single pheasant could be transported to Australia for seven years. But some small animals and birds, mainly vermin, were not included in the legislation and these were listed in the regulations as 'fair game'.

The Game Is Up is used to suggest a secret scheme or a plot has been revealed. It is often thought to relate to a sporting event that has come to an end, but in fact its origin lies in hunting. Those hunting game on country estates employ beaters who drive pheasants and other game birds out into the open (see **Beating Around The Bush**). The shout 'the game is up' suggests the bird's hiding place has been found and they have been driven up into the path of the guns. The shoot can begin.

To take something **Hook, Line And Sinker** means to be gullible enough to believe a dubious tale in its entirety. A hungry and gullible fish will not only swallow a baited hook but also the lead weight (a sinker) and some of the line.

Taking **Pot Luck** means to take whatever is randomly given. This expression was widely used in the Middle Ages when a cooking pot containing a range of ingredients, such as a stew, was always on the fire. Any visitor being offered a meal would be ladled out whatever was in the pot and they called that 'pot luck'. This is also the origin of the phrase **Pot Shot**, which meant the hunter would shoot at any animal he saw, rather than track a particular game, to go in the family cooking pot.

Red Herring is used to describe something that provides a false or misleading clue, often in a detective story. In the 18th and 19th centuries herring was one of the most widely caught fish in the seas around Britain. In those pre-refrigerated days it would be preserved by salting and smoking. This smoking process would turn the herring a deep brownish red colour. Heavily smoked herring would also have a particularly strong and pungent smell. For the origins of the phrase we turn to hunting in the early 1800s and hunt saboteurs. It's true: there must have been an early version of the modern fox lover as on hunt days the strong-smelling fish would be dragged along the hunt route and away from the foxes. This confused the hounds, which followed the scent of the 'red herring' rather than that of the fox. So effective was this tactic that the phrase passed into common English usage.

A **Stalking Horse** is a name given to someone who is put forward to mask another's ambitions and mislead an opponent. Stalking horses rarely benefit from their own actions; instead they agree to act in order to gauge support for a challenge to an incumbent leader. The phrase stems from an old English hunting practice, dating back to 1519, whereby a huntsman would walk behind a specially trained horse and reach his target without alarming it, as he would have done if he went towards it unhidden and on foot. Once within range the hunter could bag the unsuspecting game with relative ease.

189

16: SIMPLE PHRASES, SIMPLE ORIGINS

When something is **Above Board** it implies everything has been carried out honestly and in the proper way, and there is no need for suspicion. This is a gaming term and relates to the practice of a player keeping his hands above the gaming board at all times, where the other players could see them. This way nobody could be accused of cheating. Even a player simply scratching his knee could lead to suggestions the game had not been played fully 'above the board'.

Alive And Kicking is used to suggest someone or something is lively and active. In the last century the origin was thought to relate to a market fishmonger who used the phrase to indicate his fish were so fresh they were still 'kicking' in the trays. But there is an earlier theory which will have us believe the phrase was in use during the Middle Ages when, during pregnancy, expectant mothers would describe their unborn as 'alive and kicking' in the womb.

All In The Same Boat is an expression used to illustrate a group of people all facing exactly the same benefit, or adverse affect, of a particular event. The phrase has a nautical origin and alludes to sailors in high seas all facing exactly the same peril should the ship go down, regardless of whether they were the captain or a lowly deck hand. Everybody faced the same risk.

As Bright As A Button is used to describe somebody who is mentally alert and quick-witted. The expression dates back to early military uniforms that had metal buttons, which needed to be kept polished and sparkling.

To **Bank On Someone** means to rely upon or completely trust a person. Prior to the modern bank many people kept whatever wealth they had either about their person or hidden away in as safe a place as possible. In medieval Venice, once the centre of world trade, men set up benches or counters in the main squares and would trade the various world currencies that passed around the city. These men were universally trusted and relied upon and traders could borrow, exchange and even leave money with them while they returned to their native countries. The bench men would then trade that currency with other travellers and traders would often collect even larger sums than they left behind the next time they returned to Venice. The system was an early form of world banking and the Venetians were regarded as people who could be 'banked upon' (or with). The Italian word for bench or counter is 'banco'.

To **Barge In** on something is to intrude or abruptly interrupt a situation. Since the 17th century development of the English waterways, which linked most major towns and cities, the boats used have been flat-bottomed barges. Due to the cumbersome handling of these vessels, collisions were common and by the late 1800s schoolboys used the term for bumping into or 'hustling' somebody. By the turn of the century the phrase had entered the common English language meaning to interrupt without invitation, sometimes with physical force.

If you are dressed in your **Best Bib And Tucker** you are wearing your finest outfit, your Sunday best. In the 17th century it was common for all society men to wear fashionable bibs to protect their morning and dinner suits from spills. The women wore lace or muslin, which was tucked into the top of low cut dresses (to protect their modesty) and known as tuckers. Couples dressed in their finest for special occasions were known to have gone out in their 'best bib and tuckers'. The phrase is now applied to either sex in their best clothes.

A **Bigwig** is a slang term for somebody in authority. In 17th-century England the fashion was for gentlemen to wear wigs, a tradition that lasts to this day in areas such as the law courts and the House of Lords. Back then gentlemen's wigs were not only fashionable but also indicated social status – the aristocracy, bishops and High Court judges were all afforded full-length wigs which represented their position at the top of society. This level or class became known as the 'bigwigs'. The tradition is fading these days as many High Court judges opt not to wear the traditional head-dress, believing it makes the judiciary look remote and out of touch.

To **Bite Off More Than You Can Chew** is an expression we use to indicate someone has taken on more than they can manage, perhaps greedily. This is an American phrase traceable to the 1800s and the popular habit of chewing tobacco. Such tobacco was produced in lengths and it was as common to offer others a 'bite' as it is these days to offer somebody a cigarette from a packet. The greedy would take such a large bite they were unable to chew it properly but tried instead to break it down and save some for later, without their benefactor realising it. Naturally people became wise to this, hence the admonition 'don't bite off more than you can chew'.

To be in the **Black Books** is to be out of favour and disgraced. Originally a black book held the names of those who were to be punished. Henry VIII, during his battle against the Pope in the 16th century, compiled a black book listing monasteries he regarded as promoters of 'manifest sin, vicious, carnal and abominable living'. Using the Black Book as evidence, the King was able to persuade Parliament to dissolve the monasteries and assign their wealth to the Crown. Given that burning at the stake and public disembowelment were among Henry's favourite methods of persuasion, it paid not to be in his Black Book, and it was Henry's purges that give rise to the idiom we use. Later in the century merchants used black books to make lists of people who failed to pay for goods and of those who had been made bankrupt. In 1726, *The Secret History Of The University Of Oxford* records that the Proctor had a 'black book' and that 'no person whose name was listed may proceed to a degree'.

A **Black Leg** is a person who continues to work when his colleagues are out on strike. Originally a northern mining term which evolved from working miners being identifiable by their black boots and coal-covered black trousers. To see a 'black leg' walking past during a strike meant you saw a strike-breaker.

A **Blacklist** is a list naming those who have broken laws or other agreements and codes. This is closely associated to Henry's **Black Book** but as a list, once compiled, names were neither added nor removed as they might be in a running book. The first Blacklist was compiled during the 1660s after Charles II was crowned King. One of the first things the Restoration Parliament did was to have a list of names drawn up of all those held responsible for the trial and execution of his father, Charles I, in 1649. Those on the list were ruthlessly hunted down and publicly executed in an act of revenge. The new King, however, was opposed to the bloodshed and fought, unsuccessfully, for clemency. In the end only nine of the original 60 names on the blacklist, were publicly slaughtered.

To have a **Bone To Pick** with someone suggests some sorting out until all the facts of a particular dispute are apparent to all parties. The phrase stems from the 16th century and relates to a dog biting and chewing on a butcher's bone until it was picked

clean. A **Bone Of Contention** suggests an argument or a fight and also originates in the 16th century relating to two dogs fighting over a bone.

To **Buttonhole** a person is to detain and talk to somebody who may have previously been avoiding the conversation. The phrase is a reference to the practice, dating back to the 18th century, of gentlemen discreetly slipping a finger into the buttonhole of another's morning suit, ensuring they stay and listen to what they have to say. A variation of this was to hold on to the suit's buttons (button-hold). Either way it was a tactful manner of restraining somebody for a quiet word.

When something is or has been **On The Cards** it means it was predictable and very likely to happen. This is a simple phrase with a simple origin. In the late 18th century, fortune-tellers were a very popular part of society and tarot cards were regularly used to predict a person's future. When a predictable event took place it was common to conclude that it had previously been 'on the cards'.

To be **Carpeted** is to be reprimanded in a severe way by a superior. The saying can be traced to the days of the Victorian civil service where status was of utmost importance and to attain a level which afforded a civil servant an office with a carpet was success indeed. To be reprimanded in such a way as a person was moved back to an office with wooden floorboards was considered serious and shameful. Status-conscious Victorians would want to avoid a 'carpeting' at all costs. How did they ever create that Empire?

Off The Cuff means speaking without notes or carrying out a task with no real preparation. In Victorian times men wore shirts with stiff, detachable collars and cuffs, making them easier to keep clean. In order to give the impression they were speaking to an audience from the heart politicians and after-dinner speakers wanted to address gatherings without any visible script or notes. They would, however, write key notes about topics they would like to cover on their cuffs which they could refer to from time to time. They might also make additional notes during the speech of a fellow politician so they would be reminded to counter any points made by their opponents. This all gave the impression the speaker was fully prepared and articulate enough not to need a script but in fact they had notes all the time, written out 'on the cuffs'.

As Dead As A Dodo means long obsolete, finished and no longer available. A dodo was a large flightless bird that can thank the Portuguese for its name. Being flightless, because its wings were too small for its fat body, the dodo would be taken on board a ship at harbour and, unable to escape, kept alive as fresh meat to be eaten by hungry sailors as required. When the Portuguese found them on the island of Mauritius they named them 'doudo', meaning stupid in their language. By the end of the 17th century they had been eaten into extinction (becoming one of the first recorded species to do so) and the expression passed over into the English language.

A **Dead Ringer** is somebody who looks just like another. In medieval Britain the medical profession was not quite as refined as it is now, and often anybody found not to show signs of life was regarded as dead, when they might have been simply unconscious. (This was also before comas were fully understood.) It was not uncommon for bodies to be exhumed later and corpses found with their fingers worn to the bone, an obvious indication somebody had returned to consciousness and tried to claw their way out of a coffin. So horrific was this image that the English gentry began mistrusting medical opinions and buried their loved ones with string attached to their wrists, connected to a bell above the grave. Anybody who returned to consciousness and found themselves prematurely buried could attract attention by ringing the bell and it has been recorded this actually worked. Many 'bodies' were exhumed after bells were rung and some people carried on with their normal lives. But when spotted in the street startled acquaintances would cry to each other, 'That looks just like Jack Jones – I thought he was dead' to which they would receive the reply, 'Yes, he must be a dead ringer.' And that, believe it or not, is true.

Somebody who has **Gone To The Dogs** is thought to be down on his luck and whose appearance and behaviour has deteriorated. At the great medieval dining tables scraps and partially eaten food was usually thrown out for the dogs. Often beggars and the starving could be found rooting around with the dogs trying to find something to eat.

To **Earmark** something is to intend to set something aside as your own. The origin of this saying is found in the ancient art of marking cattle ears with a ring or a tab. Owners, or potential owners at market, would set cattle aside in this way, indicating an intention to buy. Centuries prior to that this practice even included human property: slaves would have 'their ears borne through with an awl' to identify ownership. This practice is also the root of the later fashion of wearing earrings. In relatively recent years the term spread to the wider use it has today.

Eavesdroppers are people who deliberately try to overhear another's conversation without detection. Centuries ago houses in England had no gutters and drain pipes. Instead the roofs extended far past the walls of the house enabling rainwater to drip to the ground away from the building. The area between the dripping rain and the walls was originally known as the 'eavesdrip' and latterly the 'eavesdrop'. The eavesdrop also served as a shelter for passing pedestrians who would stand close to the walls of a building and out of the rain, but they could also overhear conversations going on inside a house, and became known as 'eavesdroppers'.

At The End Of My Tether means I am at the very limit of my patience and self-control. In the Middle Ages a grazing animal would often be tethered to a post, ensuring it didn't stray beyond a certain small area. But, once the animal arrived at the limit of its tether, unable to quite reach pastures new, it would become frustrated, irritable and sometimes traumatised to the point of despair. Sound familiar?

To **Fly In The Face** of something means to do the opposite of what is usually expected, and often at some risk. This phrase has been in use for centuries and relates to hens who, when attacked by foxes, fly around their faces in an attempt to confuse and distract the wily old predator. Risky business indeed.

Freelance workers – often self-employed writers, journalists or musicians – are not continuously employed by a single organisation. In the Middle Ages when knights and lords fought for supremacy (and land), a freelancer was exactly that, a lance soldier for hire. The word used these days is mercenary but once upon a time a 'free lance' was exactly how it sounded. The phrase passed into modern English language as late as 1820 when Sir Walter Scott wrote in his novel *Ivanhoe*: 'Ivanhoe offers Richard the services of my Free Lancers.'

Having a **Frog In The Throat** suggests a person is unable to speak easily and clearly. There was a time, prior to clean drinking water being freely available, that folk would drink water drawn from ponds and streams. Medieval legend will have us believe that people feared swallowing frogspawn lest tadpoles would hatch in the stomach. The idea of a live frog trying to make an escape by way of the throat isn't a pleasant one (although with garlic and a little white wine sauce it doesn't seem too bad to the French).

To **Haul Somebody Over The Coals** means to give them a severe tongue-lashing, and perhaps find out the truth of a matter. In the 15th century, heresy (practising unorthodox religions) was regarded as a crime against the Church and the punishment was death. The problem was that the crime of heresy was almost impossible to prove as few ever confessed to adopting their own religious opinions, so the powers that be came up with an ingenious method of deciding. Anybody accused of heresy would be tied and dragged over a burning bed of charcoal. If they died it was accepted the person was a heretic and deserved such a fate. However, if they lived they were freed, as it was thought God had protected the accused. So, while the supposed heretics died, the innocents were merely roasted. Brilliant!

When we **Break The Ice** we are taking the initiative in breaking down a formality and getting started on a project. This idiom is more than 500 years old and is common in many European languages. Years ago many major European rivers would ice over at the bank sides during the cold and bitter winters. The River Thames used to freeze completely and carnivals and fairs were held on the surface. But those relying on the rivers for their livelihood didn't enjoy those times quite so much and every morning, before they could set about their business, they would have to break the ice around the boats and cut a path out to where the water still flowed. For them 'breaking the ice' meant getting started on their day's work.

Ill-gotten Gains is a term for money, or other reward, obtained by dishonest means. The phrase we use today has been shortened from its original form: 'Ill-gotten gains never prosper.' The phrase first appeared in the early 16th century and was applied to the pirates of the English coastline and their booty. In 1592 William Shakespeare popularised the phrase in his play *Henry VI Part 3* when he included the line 'Didst thou never hear that things ill got had ever bad success?'

When something is **Near The Knuckle** (usually a comment or remark) it is regarded as on the limit, as far as one should go. When carving a joint of meat a butcher will cut the flesh right down to the knuckle bone which would be the limit of the cut, therefore a remark near the knuckle is on the limit. The expression **Close To The Bone** means exactly the same thing.

A person who is **Long In The Tooth** is considered to be old and wise. There is no real proof as to whether the origin of this phrase comes from humans or animals, particularly horses. Our equine friends do not benefit from dental hygiene and therefore as they age their gums recede, leaving the teeth appearing longer in the mouth (see **Don't Look A Gift Horse In The Mouth**). However, our forefathers didn't have the benefits of modern dentistry either, so our elderly ancestors were affectionately regarded as being 'long in the tooth'.

To be described as having **No Flies On You** means you are quick-witted, alert and active. The expression can be traced to the cattle ranches of both America and Australia and is first recorded during the mid-1800s. Quite simply the lively, active cattle and horses attracted few flies that preferred instead to settle on the slow, sluggish animals who would stay still for the longest period of time. The phrase became widely used very quickly and in the early 1900s even the Salvation Army put it to general use by adopting a hymn entitled 'There are no flies on Jesus'. It even included the classic observation 'There may be flies on me and you / but there are no flies on Jesus.'

To **Pigeon Hole** a person is to classify them and give them a specific identity when more than one might be more appropriate. The English used to keep pigeons as domestic birds, although not as pets, but for food. Pigeons generally do not stray too far from a place they are being fed, so folk would set small openings into walls, or build boxes with recesses that pigeons would naturally make their home, without realising they would later be eaten. These were known as pigeonholes. During the 18th century offices would have small compartments built into the furniture to file documents and, owing to the resemblance, these also became known as pigeonholes. These pigeonholes would each have categories and the documents in them would all have a similar theme, decided by the filing clerk. When a document had more than one reference it was up to the clerk to decide where it was to be placed and hence a document was 'pigeonholed'. But not always correctly.

If you are asked to do something **Post Haste** you are being asked to do it quickly, without delay. When, during the 16th century, the English postal system began to develop around the country, it relied on horseback messengers. Because of the nature of the work, horses needed to be rested every 20–30 miles. This led to the emergence of posthouses all over the country which all provided fresh horses for messengers to use on longer journeys. The royal post was regarded as a priority and post-boys would gallop into stable yards shouting 'post haste' in order to attract attention and then swap their horse for a rested one to continue his journey. The same system was also the origin for the expression **By Return Post**, meaning immediate reply. A messenger who was asked to bring a reply to a letter back on his return journey was asked to wait until the recipient provided such a reply.

To **Ride Roughshod** over a person is to treat them harshly and without consideration of their feelings. Horses that are roughshod have nails deliberately left protruding from the shoe to provide extra grip in wet or icy conditions. To be trampled on or kicked by a horse with roughshod shoes would be uncomfortable to say the least. For a short time during the 1700s it became common practice for cavalry soldiers, from many countries, to ensure their horses were roughshod or had other sharp objects attached to their hooves. The idea was that during a charge the war-horses would cut and damage enemy mounts, but they soon found the shoes did as much damage to themselves and each other, so the practice was stopped.

The **Silly Season** is a period of time when most of the stories we hear are unlikely to be true, or something minor or superficial given undue prominence. The real silly season is during August and September when Parliament traditionally rises for its summer recess and MPs return to their constituencies. This deprives the newspapers of a steady stream of news: political rows, bad judgements, poor behaviour and general

Westminster gossip. With big gaps in their publications to fill, journalists would make the most of silly stories, such as tales about the Loch Ness Monster, UFO sightings, giant marrows and student capers. One early story about a giant gooseberry led to the season being called the 'Big Gooseberry Season' but over time this became the 'silly season'.

To **Smell A Rat** is used when someone is suspicious of something, without actually having any demonstrable cause. In English towns and villages rats were a common problem and many people used dogs, whose highly sensitive sense of smell enabled them to sniff out rats and then kill the vermin. A person whose dog suddenly started sniffing around a house or barn would often say 'looks like he has smelled a rat', long before the pest could be seen or detected by humans.

If you find somebody **On The Warpath** it is better to stay well out of their way as it suggests they are in an aggressive mood and preparing for a fight. Before proper roads were mapped out the countryside was criss-crossed by bridle paths and other narrow ways. In North America feuding natives would regularly cross territories to confront their enemy, and the pathways flattened by foot soldiers and horsemen between the two camps quickly became known as 'war paths' as, essentially, the only time they were used was en route to war.

If I **Pull The Wool Over Your Eyes** I have tricked or deceived you. This expression is linked to the term **Bigwigs**. Centuries ago a man's status was confirmed by the size of his wig and such people were considered well worth robbing by the city scallywags and vagabonds. Some rogues developed the trick of approaching a victim from behind and pulling the wig down over a victim's eyes to disorientate him and make it easier to steal his possessions before running away.

17: MISCELLANEOUS

An **Acid Test** is the accepted process of finding out beyond any doubt if something is genuine or not. Gold is one of the few precious metals not affected by the majority of acids but it does react with a mixture of hydrochloric and nitric acids. When first used in the Middle Ages this mixture was given the Latin name 'Aqua Regia', meaning 'royal water', as it dissolved the king of metals. The first recorded use as an idiom was on 8 January 1918, as the First World War drew to a close, when US President Woodrow Wilson said to Congress, 'The treatment accorded Russia by her sister nations in the months to come will be an acid test of their goodwill.' The 'acid test', or 'fizz test' as it has become known, is used these days mainly by geologists to differentiate between limestone and other types of rock.

A **Basket Case** is a light-hearted, although not entirely affectionate, way of describing somebody who cannot communicate properly, is mentally unstable and unable to cope emotionally. At the end of the First World War, the Surgeon General of the US Army was quoted in the *US Official Bulletin* (28 March 1919) that he 'denies there is any foundation for the stories being circulated of the existence of "basket cases" in our hospitals'. It is a clear reference to trench soldiers suffering shell shock and related mental illness. At the time basket weaving was a regular activity in both British and American mental hospitals, such as the one at Deolali (see **Doolally**). The phrase was known to be British Army slang during the First World War.

Saved By The Bell – Although the phrase is associated with boxing for obvious reasons, the origin is supposed to lie at the Horse Guard Parade in London. One night, during the Victorian era, a guard was famously accused of being asleep on duty. He denied the charge and claimed he had heard the main bell of Big Ben chime 13 times at midnight, instead of the usual 12. Such was the seriousness of the charge the clock mechanism was checked and it was discovered a cog was out of line and Big Ben would indeed chime 13 times instead of 12. On that evidence, the guard was freed – well and truly saved by the bell.

To suggest somebody has **Gone Round The Bend** is to unkindly infer they have gone mad. In the 1900s, the Victorians built hospitals in which to confine the mentally unsound. At the time stately homes were built with long, straight driveways in order that the building could be seen from the main road in all its splendour, albeit from a distance. The mental homes were placed at the end of long, curved driveways so that they would remain unseen, and therefore if a person had 'gone round the bend' it meant they had been confined.

To **Give Somebody A Break** means to give somebody an opportunity, usually after they have done something wrong or been perceived to do so. This phrase derives from the early street performers who would be given a break halfway through their act, during which they could pass a hat around and collect money for their performance. During the 19th century the phrase was picked up by the criminal and vagrant community who would pass a hat around each other for a friend on their release from prison so they would not have to return to the world totally penniless. That person was deemed to have been 'given a break'.

A **Busman's Holiday** means a person is spending his time away from work, doing exactly what he would during his working day. This idiom stems from the turn of the 20th century, when buses were horse-drawn. It was tradition that a bus driver would spend his days off travelling in the rear of his bus to make sure the relief driver was looking after his horses properly. As the horse was very much the means of his income, the animal's welfare was essential and drivers took few chances – even on their holidays.

Crocodile Tears are considered to be false tears or showing insincere sorrow. In fact, crocodiles, after eating, shed excess salt from glands located just beneath each eye, giving the impression of tears.

According to ancient Egyptian legend, after the animal had devoured its victim it would immediately appear to be crying with remorse. The Egyptians coined the phrase and applied it to their double-dealing country folk who showed insincerity or false sorrow for their actions.

Digs is a word used to describe temporary accommodation or lodgings, usually for students. During the Californian gold rush, which began in 1849, miners raced to the area and had to live rough in shelters they dug for themselves into the hillsides. These became known as 'diggins'. Some enterprising folk dug out entire rows of them and rented out diggins to other prospectors arriving in the area. The term was shortened to 'digs' by the time it came into use in England a decade later.

In the 17th century **The Dutch** were both military and trading rivals of England. The English attitude towards the Dutch can be found in the diaries of Samuel Pepys, whose work covered this period in English history. Such entries include 'several seamen came this morning and said they would go and do all they could against the Dutch' and 'And so to home where my heart aches as the Dutch have burned our ships.' It was common for the English to refer to the Dutch in derisory fashion and surprisingly many of the phrases continue to be used nearly 400 years later. Here are a few examples:

Ending an assurance with the suffix 'or I am a Dutchman' implies total confidence in a suggestion or the one giving the guarantee will allow the recipient to call them a Dutchman, inviting the lowest form of insult. For example: 'My chickens are the finest in London sir, if I am found to be wrong then I'm a Dutchman.'

Dutch Auction – An auction that goes the wrong way, with the reserve figure being set too high in the first place and the auctioneer having to gradually decrease the price until a bid is finally made.

Dutch Bargain – A one-sided deal, and not a bargain at all.

Dutch Comfort – No real comfort at all.

Dutch Concert – An expression used to

describe a shambles of a performance during which the singers sang different songs and the musicians played the wrong notes.

Dutch Courage – False bravery that has to be summoned up by alcohol.

Dutch Gold – A German alloy of copper and zinc which is gold in colour and often passed off as gold to unsuspecting dealers.

Dutch Party – Where the guests contribute their own food and drink.

Dutch Talent – Ability and results obtained through brawn rather than by intellect.

Dutch Treat – A gift for which the recipients pay themselves.

Dutch Uncle – A person who criticises severely, and often unfairly.

Double Dutch – A person speaking gibberish, which cannot be understood by an Englishman.

Triple Dutch – Like **Double Dutch**, only even more preposterous.

To **Go Dutch** means a gentleman expects his lady guest to pay for herself. Fair enough these days but not the behaviour of an English gentleman 400 years ago, the inference being that it was normal behaviour for a Dutchman.

Forking Out is used to describe handing over money, sometimes reluctantly. Many years ago the word fork was thieves' slang for finger and 'forking over' or 'forking out' became slang for paying or handing out money.

Funnybone – Nobody who takes a blow on the nerve between the elbow bones ever laughs; instead they experience a painful tingling sensation. So why is it called the 'funnybone'? The reason is a medical pun: the long bone in the upper arm connected by this nerve is called the 'humerus'. The joke stuck and had passed over into wider use by 1867.

Why do we say **Good Health** when we are about to drink alcohol, which is far from good for us? The answer lies in 19th-century England and the deadly outbreak of cholera between 1848 and 1849 in particular. In August 1849 cholera reached epidemic proportions in the Broadwick Street area of Soho in London, resulting in 344 deaths in only four days. But there were almost none in any neighbouring areas. Local physician Dr John Snow suggested cholera was linked to drinking polluted water and proved this when he found that 87 victims out of the 89 he examined were known to have drunk from the Broadwick Street well. Snow called for the authorities to take the handle off the pump, and almost immediately the outbreak was halted. For a long while afterwards the locals would avoid water and drink only ales and wines. When drinking they would toast each other with 'to your good health', knowing they were safe from the disease. Appropriately enough there is a pub called the John Snow on Broadwick Street today.

When we **Hedge Our Bets**, we are supporting more than one cause and increasing the possibility of a favourable outcome. The phrase is attributed to old English peasants and vagabonds who plied their trade overtly between or underneath hedges. Hedge was also a widely used expression applied to the lower classes. A 'hedge-priest' was a poor or untrustworthy man of the cloth, a 'hedge-writer' a Grub Street author and a 'hedge-marriage' was a clandestine union performed by a 'hedge-priest', possibly referring to a bigamous marriage. In 1811 the dictionary tells us the use of the word 'hedge' had become used as a term for protecting oneself against losses on a wager, suggesting that a gambler who 'hedges in' their bets is taking precautions against losses.

To find yourself **In A Hole** is to be in difficulty, particularly financially. American writer John P Quinn gave the best suggestion for this phrase in his 1892 book *Fools Of Fortune*. Poker tables in dimly lit gambling dens had a hole in the centre into which gamblers dropped a percentage of their stake money payable to the house. Losses to the dealer were also dropped into the hole, which was collected in locked iron boxes underneath. The owners would then collect their money at the end of each session. The expression is used these days to express any misfortune but back in the 19th century a losing gambler had all his money well and truly 'in the hole'.

In The Limelight implies being the centre of attention or in the public eye. When calcium oxide (lime) is heated, it produces a bright white light. In 1826 a Scottish army engineer called Thomas Drummond used this discovery to aid map-making in poor weather. The intense, highly visible limelight could be seen from a great distance and was used to mark out distances accurately. Shortly afterwards scientists developed his invention to produce other powerful lights, which were then used in lighthouses and later as spotlights in theatres, to focus attention on the main performer. So somebody who was standing 'in the limelight' was at the focus of attention.

Something **In A Nutshell** is explained in as few words as possible. Thousands of years ago important documents were carried around in walnut shells which would then be bound and kept waterproof. The idea of having something 'in a nutshell' means a shortened version that still covers every main point but there are examples of long and celebrated works being written in such small handwriting the document would still fit inside the shell of a walnut.

Something done **In A Jiffy** is done extremely quickly. 'Jiffy' might seem like a slang word but in fact it is a scientific term meaning 'unit of time'. Originally a jiffy was one sixtieth of a second, although it is now more commonly known as one hundredth of a second and occasionally even a millisecond. Some scientists use the word to describe the time light takes to travel one foot in a vacuum (a nanosecond). Whatever the duration, whenever we are told something will be done 'in a jiffy', it never is.

Jumping Over The Broomstick means a wedding that has taken place informally and without any real preparation. It started out as a custom for the medieval underclasses such as gypsies, wandering labourers and other people of no permanent address. All the happy couple had to do in bygone days was to jump together over a broomstick to secure their status as man and wife.

If someone got their **Just Deserts**, it is generally thought that they got what was coming to them, what they deserved. The confusion over the origins of this phrase lies in the spelling: 'deserts' is spelled like the word that means a vast sandy part of Egypt, but sounds like that spotted dick and custard we sometimes have after dinner, which is why the phrase is often explained as 'well, he deserved a pudding like that after what he did'.

When somebody is **Having Their Leg Pulled** they are on the receiving end of a deception, or a joke. An old Scottish rhyme dating from 1867 seems to reveal its origin with the lines 'He preached and at last pulled the auld body's leg, sae the Kirk got the gatherins o' our Aunty Meg.' The suggestion is that old Aunt Meg had been hanged for a crime and the preacher hauled on her legs to ensure she died quickly and without too much pain. Aunt Meg was known to have been the victim of much deception and trickery, which placed her at the gallows for a crime she did not commit, leading to the belief that having her leg pulled was the result of such deception.

To **Read Between The Lines** is to find the real message hidden away in a situation which is not at first obvious. The origin of this expression is found in cryptography and early attempts at passing coded messages. One method of secret writing was to place the real message on alternate lines and weave an unrelated story on to the other lines. On first reading a simple story or letter could be read, but only on reading the alternate lines could the hidden message be decoded.

People at **Loggerheads** are considered to be confronting each other. In the 15th and 16th centuries a 'logger' was the name given to a heavy wooden block fastened to the legs of grazing horses, enabling them to move slowly around a field but not to jump fences or stray too far. Frequently the loggers tangled with each other, leaving horses connected at close quarters and becoming agitated and hostile to each other. The phrase passed over into wider uses via Shakespeare's play *The Taming Of The Shrew*, during which two of the main characters are seen to be at 'loggerheads' with each other.

There is a second possible origin for the phrase dating to ancient nautical warfare. Sailors used a weapon called a loggerhead, which was a long pole with a cup fixed to the end. These were used to project flaming tar at enemy ships in close quarters to create injury and fire on board. Naturally both sides used similar weapons and such battles were known as 'being at loggerheads'.

Not to **Mince Your Words** is to speak plainly, frankly and with brutal honesty. The phrase is always used in the negative sense, as in 'not to' – we never hear complaints of somebody mincing their words. The first recorded use of the expression can be traced to 1649 and Joseph Hall's *Cases Of Conscience*. Some things we are told are unpleasant to swallow and difficult to digest, and the allusion is drawn from butchers who mince cheaper cuts of meat to make them easier to digest. A person 'not mincing his words' is not making any effort to soften their message.

Minding Your Ps And Qs is a gentle warning to behave in a correct and polite manner. There are two suggestions for the origin of this phrase and both have a reasonable claim. First up is the civilised surroundings of the French court during the 17th century. The aristocracy were expected to dance delicately when they took to the floor and dance instructors were in high demand. During their lessons pupils were encouraged to mind their 'pieds' (feet) and 'queues' (the tails of their wigs).

But my favourite can be found in the old London taverns, where the bartender would keep an account of how much beer their customers had been drinking by marking their pints under the letter P and their quarts (two pints) under the letter Q. Customers were well advised to watch their Ps and Qs to make sure they were not overcharged at the end of a session.

Mum's The Word means to convey no secrets and remain silent. This has nothing to do with mothers and more to do with the 'mmmm' we use with tightly closed lips indicating we have nothing to say on a subject. The phrase was first recorded in 1540 but is thought to be at least 200 years older still.

Mumbo Jumbo is the expression we use for language that seems nonsense and to have no discernible meaning. For the origin of this saying we travel to Africa with the explorers and missionaries of the 18th century. One of these travellers, Francis Moore, wrote a book of his adventures called *Inland Parts Of Africa*, published in 1738. In one part Moore includes the passage 'A dreadful bugbear to the women is called Mumbo Jumbo, which keeps the women in awe.' Mumbo Jumbo was a legendary spirit in villages across Africa who was used by male tribal leaders in order to keep the women of their tribes in line. One of the major tribal customs was for a man to have several wives and bitching between them was a frequent occurrence. When an outbreak of backbiting became intolerable, the husband would dress up as Mumbo Jumbo and visit the main culprit in the dead of night and scare her rigid by shrieking and hollering. The trouble-making missus was then tied to a tree and given an old-fashioned thrashing by Mumbo Jumbo. Clearly he was not to be messed with. The phrase travelled back to England and became associated with the meaningless rantings of 'Mumbo Jumbo'.

A **Nest Egg** is a person's savings, which they will try to keep adding to. In the English countryside, prior to factory farming, chickens used to live naturally and lay their eggs in nests. To encourage hens to be more productive it was common practice for farmers to place a porcelain egg, known as a 'nest egg', into the breeding ground. Apparently it worked. Likewise, a small sum of money given to a person as a 'nest egg' was thought to encourage them to add to it.

To **Grasp The Nettle** is an expression used to describe facing an unpleasant task or problem with determination. Stinging nettles cause pain and discomfort when lightly touched or brushed against, but have been used over the centuries for their medicinal and nutritious content. The best way to collect nettles is to grab the leaf firmly; trying to do it softly or hesitantly will lead to a brush and an itchy rash or two.

To find somebody **As Drunk As A Newt** is never a pleasant experience, but at least they will be all right in the morning. But no one has ever found an intoxicated newt ricocheting up the high street on a Saturday night, so why the reference? It seems that during the 17th and 18th centuries 'newts' was the nickname gentlemen gave boys who looked after their horses while out on the town for the night. As they spent their evenings in gaming houses, bars and opium dens our forefathers were good enough to send out 'warm-up' drinks to the newts who would then usually be found rolling drunk by the time the horses were collected, hence the saying.

When somebody feels **As Right As Ninepence**, they are in tip-top condition and ready for anything. Silver ninepenny pieces were in common use in England until 1696, and were one of the highest-value coins in circulation. Also, the popular silver coin was often given as a token of love or affection and for those two reasons people were always pleased to have them. But some people believe the phrase is a simple corruption of the saying 'right as ninepins', which is a reference to the English pub game of skittles. Once the ninepins were all upright the game could begin.

To **Pay Through The Nose** is an odd expression. It is taken to mean we have paid a price far too high for goods or services. The origin of this lies in the Viking invasion of the British Isles during the ninth century. The Danes had particularly strict tax laws, which were applied with relish every time they invaded a foreign land. In Ireland the Vikings levied an especially high tax which they called the 'Nose Tax'. The reason for that was any citizen failing to pay had their nose either slit open or cut off altogether. This charming behaviour continued until the genial Viking leader, Eric Bloodaxe, was killed by the English warrior King Edred at the Battle of Stainmore in 954.

When something has gone **Pear Shaped** it has gone wrong, or at least not quite according to plan. The 1940 film *My Little Chickadee*, starring WC Fields and Mae West, contains the line 'I have some very definite pear-shaped ideas' and the phrase certainly originates around that time. However, it is widely thought that early RAF pilots are responsible for popularising it. While practising loops a trainee pilot would often fail to make a perfect circle and would flatten the plane's flight during the bottom section. These mistakes were referred to as 'going pear shaped'.

When the **Penny Finally Drops** it means somebody has finally understood something. This saying dates back to the Victorian era and the popular penny slot arcades. Often, in the old wooden slot machines, the penny would stick halfway down and users would have to either wait or give the machine a thump before the 'penny finally dropped' and they could start the game.

Pin Money is now used as a term for small amounts of money, but the sum was not always small. In the 14th and 15th centuries pins were very expensive and only allowed to be sold on the first two days of January. Husbands gave their wives money saved for the purchase. As time went by pins became ever cheaper and the money could be spent on other things. However, the expression remained.

To **Rob Peter To Pay Paul** is to take or borrow from one source to contribute to another, thereby solving one problem but creating another. Use of this expression is traceable back to 17 December 1540 when the church of St Peter in Westminster, London, became a cathedral. But its elevated status lasted only 10 years when the diocese of Westminster was placed back under the authority of St Paul's Cathedral and St Peter's became merely a church again. To **add insult to injury**, much of the land and property of St Peter's was then sold off to fund repairs to St Paul's. There was public outcry at the robbing of St Peter's to prop up St Paul's, and the expression became popularised.

There is, however, evidence that the phrase dates back centuries earlier. This is provided by the Oxford priest and theologian John Wyclif, who wrote in 1380, 'How should God approve that you rob Peter and give this robbery to Paul in the name of Christ?' (*Select Works III*). While it is possible that 16th-century Londoners applied this phrase to the events surrounding their cathedrals, it is clear that the phrase had been coined in the mid- to late-1400s.

Ruling The Roost is a phrase used to suggest a person is in charge and demonstrating their authority. The obvious allusion is to a chicken run, where the cockerel rules over all the hens. But not so fast. The phrase has been in use since the 16th century and was popularised by Shakespeare when he wrote in *Henry VI Part II* (1590): 'Suffolk, that new made man that rules the roast.' Indeed, tradition has it that the master of the house carves and serves the roast meat and in 1637 Thomas Nabbes wrote in *Microcosmus*, 'I am my lady's cook, and king of the kitchen where I rule the roast.'

This origin is further supported by the fact that in Anglo-Saxon English the word roast was pronounced with a long 'o', so it sounded like roost. So it seems that in days gone by, ruling the roast was indeed a demonstration of authority.

The phrase **Above** or **Below The Salt** describes a person's status. This phrase comes straight from the great banqueting rooms where the silver salt cellars would be placed in the centre of the table. Those sitting on the same side of the salt as the host (above it) were considered the most important guests and those further away (below) were less valued guests.

To be **In Seventh Heaven** is to be truly delighted, over the moon and on cloud nine. According to Muslim beliefs there are seven heavens, each of them relating to one of the seven planets ruling the universe. The suggestion is that every level of heaven consists of a precious stone or metal and a servant of the Most High inhabits each one. The seventh heaven is considered the most glorious and is occupied by Abraham who presides over everything and who is the most loyal to God. During the Middle Ages the Cabbalists, who were

Jewish mystics steeped in the occult, reinforced this belief by interpreting the seventh heaven as the domain of God and his holy angels. Therefore to be 'in seventh heaven' is to be in a place of eternal bliss.

A **Shaggy Dog Story** is a story of unconvincing origin, not necessarily to be believed. The origin of this phrase is, in fact, a real shaggy dog story which, when told on the London social scene during the 1800s, wasn't believed by everybody but is still a good story. Apparently a wealthy gentleman, who owned a grand residence in Park Lane, lost his beloved shaggy dog during a walk across Hyde Park opposite his home. The man was heartbroken and advertised extensively in *The Times* for the return of his companion. An American living in New York heard the news and took pity on the dog's owner. He vowed he would search for a pet matching the description of the lost hound and deliver it to London on his next business visit, which he duly did. But when the New Yorker presented himself at the London mansion he was met by a po-faced butler who looked down at the dog, winced and exclaimed, 'But not as shaggy as that, sir!' The story caused howls of laughter across London's social circuit, but was not entirely believed by everybody. A 'shaggy dog story' indeed.

To **Get Shirty** means to become aggressive and look for an argument or a fight. This phrase has a direct link back to the 18th century when it was customary for a gentleman to remove his shirt before engaging in fisticuffs, ensuring it remained clean, tear-free and could be worn again afterwards.

To give a person **Short Shrift** is to dismiss their opinions or feelings without much consideration. The word 'shrift' means a confession given to a priest, after which absolution is given. It derives from the verb 'shrive' meaning 'to hear a confession', and its past tense is 'shrove' as in Shrove Tuesday, the day prior to Lent when pious folk attend confession. During the 17th century, when criminals were taken out and executed almost immediately after the ultimate sentence was passed, they were given a few moments to save their souls by confessing their sins to a waiting priest. This was usually on the gallows platform and time would have been short, which is how the phrase 'short shrift' passed over into wider use.

To **Sleep Tight** is to sleep well and have a good night's rest. In this context the word 'tight' is generally thought to be about pulling the bedclothes tightly around ourselves. But the first beds to be mass-produced in England were made with straw mattresses held by criss-crossed ropes attached to the bed frames. Sooner or later the ropes would slacken off and the mattress would become uncomfortable. For this reason all beds were sold with an iron tool, similar to a large clothes peg, which was used to wind the ropes tighter whenever they became loose. Therefore to suggest a person 'sleeps tight' was to remind them to tighten their mattress ropes and have a more comfortable bed to sleep in.

To **Get Hold Of The Wrong End Of The Stick** means to misunderstand something entirely and to misinterpret a situation. The phrase can be traced back to the 1400s and began life as 'the worse end of the staff' (or lance), with the wording changing during the 1800s. It is also said to date back to Roman times and their use of communal toilets where people sat side by side. For personal hygiene reasons the Romans used a short staff with a sponge tied to one end and everybody took great care not to get hold of the wrong end when reaching out to use it. Not only did they give us roads, sanitation and great architecture, but also, it appears, an early version of Andrex.

To **Up Sticks** is to leave a place and move on to pastures new. There are several suggestions for the origin of this phrase. One is that in the days of horse travel a mount would be tethered to the ground by a picket (rope) tied to a stick driven into the earth. These sticks would be carried around by horsemen and used whenever they arrived at a place, upping them again on departure. Alternatively, a ship's mast was known as a stick, and when they were raised the vessel was ready to depart. Either way the phrase is relatively recent and first recorded during the 1800s.

Why do we call a level of a building a '**Storey**'? The word 'story' derives from the ancient Greek word 'historia' meaning 'account of events'. Back in the 14th century, the word 'story' was used in architecture in the sense that stained glass windows and stone carvings or sculptures on the outside of a building had real stories as their theme. The more rows of pictures, the more stories they told. The higher the window or the building, the more stories it could have. This developed in time to mean an entire level of a building was known as a storey.

Straight From The Horse's Mouth is a term used to describe accurate, first-hand information. In bygone days a horse was a valuable commodity and there were few ways of reliably assessing a horse's age before buying one. Everybody was afraid of spending good money on an old horse with very little work left in it. One of the better ways of reassurance was to look at the teeth of the animal and find out how far they had worn, or how far its gums had receded, to determine the age of a nag. First-hand inspection would reveal the truth. **Don't Look A Gift Horse In The Mouth** is directly related to the same practice. It was regarded as extremely rude to check the teeth of a horse (to see if it was worth anything) if it had been given as a gift.

There But For The Grace Of God Go I is used by people noting another's misfortune and suggesting it could easily have befallen themselves. The popular Protestant preacher John Bradford first used this phrase while being held in the Tower of London on the trumped-up charges of 'trying to stir up a mob'. In fact, all he had done was to save a Catholic preacher named Bourne from a baying Protestant mob. But this happened during the reign of Mary I, whose restoration of the Catholic Church saw the persecution of many Protestants. While in the Tower, Bradford witnessed many being taken away for execution and each time would remark, 'There but for the grace of God goes John Bradford.' But Bradford was soon charged with heresy and later burned at the stake in Smithfield market on 1 July 1555.

To **Tie The Knot** is commonly understood to mean marriage. The phrase means very little to any western wedding ceremony, but we can find it in many other cultures around the world. In Sikh weddings both the bride and groom wear silk scarves and the bride's father knots them together as the happy couple honour the Sikh scriptures. Chinese Buddhists honour the deity Yue Laou by uniting couples with a silken cord after which nothing can break their unity, and during Hindu ceremonies several garments of the committed are tied together as they walk around a holy fire. In western ceremonies the knot has a much lower-key role as it is only the ribbons of a bridal bouquet that are tied together. In all cases the knot is there to symbolise love, unity and a bond that cannot ever be broken in any circumstances. (The divorce lawyers can stop laughing right now.)

Once a thing is **Up The Spout** it is gone and lost forever. A spout was a tube found in pawnbroker shops or bookmaker's. Articles to be pawned, or wagers placed, would be put into the spout and whisked off to the office above where it was safely stored away. It was commonly known for a man's weekly wages to have gone 'up the spout' before the weekend was over, or for an object of value to go the same way during troubled times.

Upper Crust is an expression used to describe England's upper or ruling classes. The origin of this phrase dates back as far as the mid-14th century when the upper, crusty part of a loaf of bread would be reserved for the master of the house and his honoured guests, while the softer underside was given to the minions. It became widely used in America in the early 18th century when it was applied to the 'upper layers' of society.

When something has **Gone To The Wall** it is finished, over and can never be recovered. This phrase apparently has a rather morbid origin and relates to the practice of placing the dead next to the churchyard wall bordering the graveyard, prior to a funeral service. But there are other suggestions for its use in our language. Four hundred years ago the city streets were narrow and unlit, and invited crime. After dark, innocent passers-by were always at risk from thieves or muggers and a person cornered in a dark alley with their back to the wall really was vulnerable.

Another suggested origin comes from medieval chapels, such as the one found in Dover Castle, which provided stone seating around the walls to support the elderly and infirm. The rest of the congregation were required to stand and the expression used at the time was that 'the weak had gone to the wall'. Take your pick from those.

To ask for something **Warts And All** is to require that no attempt be made to cover any defects or hide unsavoury detail. Oliver Cromwell was a radical parliamentarian who overthrew the English monarchy in the mid-17th century. At the time portrait painters would soften the features of their subjects by removing blemishes and facial lines from their work (a sort of early air-brushing) and the end result would always be flattering. But when Cromwell, as Lord Protector, commissioned Sir Peter Levy to paint his portrait, he issued the artist with the following instructions: 'I desire you would use all your skill to paint my picture truly like I am and not flatter me at all. Remark all these roughness, pimples, warts and everything as you see me, otherwise I will never pay you a farthing for it.' The end result does include a large wart, just below Cromwell's lower lip.

A **Wheeler Dealer** is a crafty business person with an eye for a quick profit, possibly dishonest. It is possible the phrase originates in the gambling casinos or saloons where roulette is played on a wheel and dealers handle cards. In this context a 'wheeler dealer' could be a professional gambler, therefore having no established profession or trade.

However, there is a second possibility. Billingsgate Fish Market in London was once one of the busiest markets in England and a place where underhand business often took place. In the days before automated transport, the barrows loaded with fresh fish would be wheeled up from the dockside so that the dealing could take place. It is thought the fishmongers at Billingsgate were known as 'wheeler dealers'.

To have a **Whip Round** is to take an informal collection, usually for money to buy a collective gift or make a donation. This phrase comes from a combination of sources, namely the British Parliament, an army officers' mess and the hunting ground. The phrase 'whipper-in' is still used in fox-hunting circles as the name for a huntsman's assistant who keeps the hounds in their pack by using a whip. In the mid-1800s this phrase was shortened to 'the whip' and later broadened again to 'whip-up' meaning to generate enthusiasm or interest. In Parliament those appointed by a party to keep members in line and ensure they vote for the right motions are still known as 'The Whips'. Army officers, no doubt with a hunting background, extended this phrase even further during their long nights socialising in the officers' mess. At official dinners for large gatherings, officers solved the problem of who would pay for the large rounds of wine by assigning an orderly in the role of a whip. He would go around the table collecting sums from each gentleman in a wine glass and then be sent off to pay for further rounds. This became known as a 'whip round' and that is how it passed over into the English language. It was further established in 1861 when Thomas Hughes wrote in his novel *Tom Brown At Oxford*, 'If they would stand a whip of ten shillings a man then they may have a new boat.'

A **Whipping Boy** is a person who takes the punishment for a misdemeanour committed by somebody else. In the Middle Ages it was quite common for a boy of ordinary, or even peasant, stock to be educated alongside a prince or the sons of the aristocracy. As a result the commoner benefited from great privileges and in some cases the position was sought after. However, there was a down side. It was considered inappropriate for a schoolmaster or tutor to punish a member of the aristocracy and in the case of a prince he simply would not dare. Instead, when the toff misbehaved or failed in his studies, it would be the innocent commoner who received a thrashing in his place. But there are well-recorded exceptions. When George Buchanan, the Latin master to King James I, decided the boy needed punishing, he thrashed the prince himself, despite the presence of a whipping boy. The brave Buchanan threatened to do it again if the misdemeanour was repeated.

The practice wasn't confined to the schoolroom. When the French King Henry IV converted to Catholicism in 1593 he sent two ambassadors to the Pope who were symbolically whipped to atone for the King's previous Protestantism. They were both well rewarded and made cardinals soon afterwards.

As Clean As A Whistle is known to mean bright, shiny and spotless. It could also mean untarnished in the sense of getting away from something 'as clean as a whistle'. There are several suggestions for the root to this phrase. One is the bright shiny locomotive with its polished brass whistle. Others point to a freshly carved wooden whistle or to the sound a shining sword makes as it swishes through the air.

A **White Elephant** is an expression used to describe something useless that has, or will, become a huge burden to those who possess it. For this we travel to Thailand, in the days when it was known as Siam. According to the legend white elephants were so highly prized that whenever one was discovered it automatically belonged to the King. It was considered a serious offence to neglect, put to work or even to ride a white elephant so they were of no use to an owner, yet still highly revered. The King, it appears, was a wily old devil and used them in ruthless fashion. He decided that any subject causing him displeasure would be given a white elephant as a special royal gift. The subject was obviously unable to refuse a royal gift but the beast had to be cared for and could not be made to pay its way. Such gifts could ruin a man financially. The phrase arrived in England in the mid-18th century after the Empire builders brought it home with them, applying it to expensive but otherwise useless public buildings or monuments.

To be awarded the **Wooden Spoon** doesn't say much about your performance as it is given to those who finish last. The custom began in 1811 at Cambridge University where each year there were three classes of honours degrees awarded. The first class winners were called Wranglers, and said to have been born with golden spoons in their mouths. Following them were the Senior Optimes (silver spoons) and the third class went to the Junior Optimes (lead spoons). The last of the Junior Optimes was called the 'wooden spoon' and the University adopted the custom of presenting a wooden spoon to the graduate who had the lowest exam result in the Maths Tripos. But it was still a pass!

INDEX TO PHRASES

Praise for Cathy Kelly's irresistible storytelling:

'Honest, funny, clever, it sparkles with witty, wry observations on modern life. I loved it'
Marian Keyes

'Comforting and feel-good, the perfect treat read'
Good Housekeeping

'This book is full of joy – and I devoured every page of it gladly'
Milly Johnson

'A heartwarming story about family, love and love'
The Lady

'Packed with Cathy's magical warmth'
Sheila O'Flanagan

'Cathy Kelly shines an insightful light on female insecurity and the healing power of self-belief and family support'
Woman & Home

'Filled with nuggets of wisdom, compassion and humour, Cathy Kelly proves, yet again, that she knows everything there is to know about women'
Patricia Scanlan

'Love, laughter, tears and understanding are the perfect ingredients for a fabulous read'
The Sun

'An involving, heartwarming read about family, friends, love and disappointment'
Fanny Blake, *Sunday Express*

other women

Cathy Kelly

ORION

First published in Great Britain in 2021 by Orion Books,
an imprint of The Orion Publishing Group Ltd
Carmelite House, 50 Victoria Embankment,
London EC4Y 0DZ

An Hachette UK company

1 3 5 7 9 10 8 6 4 2

A CIP catalogue record for this book is
available from the British Library.

ISBN (Hardback) 978 1 4091 7926 9
ISBN (Export Trade Paperback) 978 1 4091 7927 6
ISBN (eBook) 978 1 4091 7929 0

Typeset by Input Data Services Ltd, Somerset

Printed and bound in Great Britain by Clays Ltd, Elcograf S.p.A.

MIX
Paper from
responsible sources
FSC® C104740

www.orionbooks.co.uk

To Murray and Dylan, I'm so proud of you both,
all my love, Mum xxC

Prologue

I park the car on a grass verge at the hospital, ignoring all the signs warning me that it will be clamped.

I don't care about clamping. I have to get into the emergency department. What does a car matter?

I half run because the heaviness in my chest since I got the phone call from the hospital won't allow me to run properly. Or breathe. I need deep, calming breaths.

Screw deep calming breaths.

I need to be with him.

Now. Sooner.

I can keep him alive. No doctor can do it: he needs me, holding his hand, willing him back to life.

I don't have time for the information desk – I know this hospital, see the double doors leading into the actual A & E itself, see a man pushing out of them, and I race, grabbing one swing door just before it shuts.

And I'm in.

Scanning. Peering in past half-drawn cubicle curtains. A man throwing up vile black stuff.

Two cops standing outside another cubicle. A woman on a heart monitor.

And then there he is.

I see his hand lying limply. A hand that's caressed me so many times.

I stand at the edge of the already-full cubicle, about to speak when a doctor hangs her stethoscope round her neck and says: 'I'll talk to the wife.'

She's gone instantly and I follow her, see her approach another woman. The doctor puts a comforting hand on the woman's forearm.

'I'm the wife!' I say, my voice frantic.

And then, as the doctor spins round, I see the other woman, recognise her, see the horror on her face.

'I'm his wife,' I say, 'not her.'

PART ONE

Autumn Leaves Falling

I

Sid

Oscar Wilde was right – work is the curse of the drinking classes. Not that there's any drinking done in Nurture itself. I wend my way through the hordes in The Fiddler's Elbow, neatly avoiding a guy who thinks – mistakenly – that small, dark-haired women in their thirties are only in pubs on a Friday to find handsy hunks like himself, and congratulate myself on not sweeping his feet from beneath him. Krav Maga is a great self-defence tool but there's a time and a place for everything.

I'm heading for the snug at the back of the pub where my Nurture colleagues will be settled in.

Nurture is an advocacy group, semi-funded by the state, set up to improve the health of the people of Ireland and to educate anyone who thinks curry chips, a deep-fried burger and a sugar-laden soft drink is a fully balanced meal.

However, education is a tough job and we need a Friday-night decompress as much as any other worker, so on Fridays, even the most goji-berry-loving among us move blindly en masse across the road to The Fiddler's Elbow to reward ourselves for a week of meetings, phone calls, Zoom meetings and enough unanswered emails to bury us with guilt till kingdom come.

Because of how bad the optics would be if the health gurus were spotted regularly having a drink, eating salt-laden pub snacks and enjoying that ritual of workplace comparing whose week was worse, we converge in the pub's small closed-off snug where nobody can see us.

'The figures came in today from the Department of Health.

Diabetes Two is on the rise, despite the campaign. A year-long campaign,' laments Robbie, who's been in Nurture thirteen years, as long as I have, and is also a campaign director. I'm responsible for school health, which is like trying to hold back a flood with a very small bucket.

I pat a disconsolate Robbie on the back, trying not to spill what looks like a big brandy, and find an empty stool beside Chloe, an intern on a gap year who seems so young, she makes me feel seventy instead of just thirty-four.

Right now, Chloe looks miserable.

'Sid!' she says, eager and anxious in equal measure, and I can sense more misery coming on.

'Adrienne shouted at me today, *shouted*,' she tells me. 'Just because we were out of the coffee pods she likes. It's not my job to replace them, is it? Do you think she has a psychiatric illness?'

Chloe, a wet week out of school and not yet toughened up enough to cope with actual shouting in an office, stares at me over the top of her drink and waits for me to answer. She can't be twelve or else she couldn't be interning, but she looks it, despite the carefully applied modern eyeliner, very grown-up suit and the I-am-clever big-framed glasses.

I think of all the things I could say: 'Adrienne's good at her job but, sometimes, it gets the better of her and she goes into the kitchen for a little meltdown and a caffeine hit.'

Chloe only knows teachers, who are not supposed to shout.

Therefore a workplace meltdown has to be incorrectly categorised into a mental-health box and can't be normal people at the end of their tether. Apart from babysitting, I'd say we are her only work experience.

'This job is not what I thought it would be,' Chloe goes on. 'How do you handle it, Sid?'

Chloe has seen me with my kid sister, Vilma, who is nineteen, and I'm getting the vibe that she thinks I am Vilma's mother, therefore a nurturing sort.

I am not a nurturing sort. Not by a long shot.

Plus, she can't really think I'm Vilma's mother? I'm thirty-four, not forty-four, although my skincare regime is a little lax, if I'm honest.

The barman finally hands me my large glass of wine and I'm about to test how acidic it is before replying when I think, who am I kidding? I'd drink battery acid at five-thirty on a Friday. Still, the battery acid works and I sigh deeply after my first deep drink.

'Chloe, without meaning to sound unhinged, sometimes I go into the office kitchen and have a little rant at the microwave. It lets off steam.'

I had a mini-canteen breakdown yesterday when a frantic phone call came in about a pancake-and-cream franchise setting up shop right beside a school which famously has no sports area whatsoever. I tell Chloe this.

'But you didn't shout at anyone, did you?' says Chloe, sounding younger every moment.

Patience has never been one of my finer qualities, but I try my best.

'Work can push people, Chloe. Adrienne's brilliant at her job; passionate. It was nothing personal, I'm sure, but I'll talk to her if you like. Did she say sorry?'

Chloe blushes. 'Yes, several times, but that's not the point, is it?'

'The workplace can be a tense environment,' I say, thinking that the pub is doing its job and I am relaxed enough to stop myself throwing the contents of my glass over Chloe to show her how people can really react when they're irritated.

'Want a nacho?' I hand Chloe the packet to change the subject.

'I don't eat processed foods,' she says piously.

'Suit yourself.' I snap my packet back.

Chloe hasn't a clue as to what work is really like as opposed to what young people think it is going to be. The microwave getting shouted at and that accountant who'd faked his CV and nearly lost us our government funding because of the subsequent funds-going-missing fall-out are about the worst things that have ever happened there. The money's not great and I'd be better off if I'd moved jobs years ago, but Nurture is a nice, steady place to work, despite the setbacks like cream-and-pancake franchises. Nurture is truly my second family.

If Chloe knew what horrors some offices held in store for newcomers, she'd take being screamed at in the kitchen any day.

When I finish my wine, I use an app to call a taxi from the only taxi company I ever use. Everyone else has different systems and can't understand why I prefer to wait twenty minutes for someone I know to turn up and bring me home, but I don't care. When the text comes that my driver's here, I say goodbye to everyone and try not to get sucked into any more open-ended discussions about terrible work traumas. Everyone is relaxed by now and it's a good time to go. My own couch, possibly a hot bath and a box set await me. I never drive into the office on Fridays and walk in because my bijou apartment – very bijou – is only two miles away from our city-centre offices. But I never do the walk home.

Tonight, my driver is a lovely man called Gareth, who looks like a bouncer and has a husband and two apricot-coloured chugs (pugs crossed with chihuahuas: 'Their breathing's much better, Sid, love, when they're mixed breed') at home. As he's finishing his shift, he's perfectly happy to sit without much conversation – the chugs are losing weight as per the vet's instructions, thankfully – and listen to Lyric FM playing quietly over the radio.

I phone Vilma from the car: 'Hi, Vilma, tell me – do I look old enough to be your mother?' I ask.

My little sister snorts down the phone, then hits protective mode: 'No! Who said that?'

8

I sink into the back seat. 'A girl in my office, about eighteen, an intern. She's probably seen you come to get me for lunch because I had the distinct feeling she thought I was your mother.'

'Don't be an idiot.'

'Really.'

'What did she say?'

'It's not what she said – it's that she thinks I'm the motherly type,' I mutter, sorry I started this.

'You're the "take down the patriarchy" and the true sisterhood type,' says Vilma. 'You look out for the women you work with. You dumbass.' She uses the term with affection. 'You like them to be prepared, same way you prepared me for life after school, and *in* school for that matter. That's why my friends love you. You tell us to take no shit and we don't. You're our special ops trainer, Sid: leave no woman behind. Sort of like the Army Rangers – be ready for anything.'

I say nothing for a moment: I always wanted Vilma and her friends to be prepared for life because women are notorious for playing by the rules when the other half of the human race long since ripped up the rule book. I adore Vilma – nobody is going to hurt her on my watch.

'That's probably it,' I say, aiming for cheerful.

'Besides, you've got Mum's skin: olive and anti-ageing, horrible sister. I've got Dad's: pale and liable to burn after five minutes in the sun. You look way too young to be my mum . . . You'd have to have had me when you were fifteen, and in all the pictures I've seen of you at fifteen you look like you're considering entering a convent.'

'I was a nerd,' I protest. 'Nerds wore undistressed jeans and fluffy sweaters with cats on them.'

Vilma laughs.

She and I are technically half-sisters and she takes after my beloved stepfather, Stefan, who required no make-up when he'd adoringly dress up as a vampire to accompany her and other small children on the endless Hallowe'en rounds. He is actually Lithuanian but has the bone structure and height of someone who just drove down from the Carpathians in a black coach. Vilma, whose name means 'truth' in Lithuanian, is the same as Stefan – pale skin, pale eyes, hair like the woods at midnight. I'm like my mother: my hair's chocolate with what Vilma fancifully likes to call bronze highlights, and my eyes are like Mum's, hazel. But Mum's a perfect hippie with her hair long and trailing, which goes with her Stevie Nicks' vibe, while mine's short. And if anyone ever catches me in a hippie outfit, kill me immediately.

'What're you up to tonight?' I ask Vilma, imagining her in the bedroom she shares in a college house, deciding whether it's a jeans night or time to break out the big guns and wear one of the floaty skirts she borrowed from Mum – to be worn ironically, of course.

'Going to Jojo's for a Netflix binge. Drag Race old seasons.'

I can hear the rattle of clothes hangers as she speaks.

'What—'

I know what's coming next.

What are you up to tonight?

'Just here,' I say, as if here is somewhere exciting instead of outside my building. I can't face Vilma's sadness at the fact that my life revolves around almost nothing social. 'Talk tomorrow and be—'

'—safe, yes,' she replies. 'Love you.'

'Love you more.'

It takes another few minutes to get me home.

'Thanks, Gareth,' I say, climbing out right in front of the steps to my apartment-block door. That's the great thing about my taxi guys. There's none of that, 'We'll just drop you on the corner here and sure, you can walk the rest of the way' with them. I tip well and I always ask to be brought as close to the door as possible.

I'm on the tenth floor, which is utterly wonderful from the point of view of getting burgled, because there's a great shortage of ten-storey ladders. Any would-be intruders would have to come from inside the building and, given the concierge system and security cameras all over the place, which I do not regret paying for in my management fees, it's very unlikely that anyone in our apartments would ever get burgled. Plus, I have three locks on the door. And a baseball bat inside it.

Marc, who'd been my significant other for twelve years, hadn't said a word when I insisted on getting three locks. It was one of the many things I loved about him.

Loved: is there a sadder word?

I open my three locks, step inside, relock them quickly and walk through the hall, which, finally, is no longer bare-looking, because Vilma had persuaded me to give her money for frames for some art prints, which we then hung with sticky wall hangers because we are both lethal with hammers.

Marc had taken all his pictures when he'd left.

'Sid, you really don't care about interiors, do you? It looks like you just rent the place and expect to be evicted at any moment,' said Vilma one day when she was visiting. 'Give me a few quid and I'll find pictures to give some vague sense that you're staying longer than a week.'

And she had.

Vilma is a wonderful sister, a conduit to another world. I'm not sure how I would have got by this past year without her because Marc and I were like an old married couple with our own happy routines. Without him, I was rudderless.

There was no one to make me morning coffee, no one to cook up scrambled eggs when we'd run out of groceries, no one to sit with in companionable peace while we surfed the TV stations and our various cable subscriptions.

Sometimes, when I get home, it feels as if somebody has died and left me alone in my little universe.

I conquer this by watching more and more TV and making cocktails – only at weekends – from *The Butler's Friend*, a vintage book from the 1920s which has taught me to make the perfect Boulevardier, where the secret is not just rye whiskey, sweet vermouth and Campari, but to stir and never shake.

Apart from trips home to see Mum and Stefan, my stepfather, and when Vilma comes to see me, I exist in a world of work, home and online supermarket deliveries.

If making the perfect Boulevardier, staying in all weekend and having a loving relationship with my couch cushions were what it took to keep me sane, then that's what I'd do. Marc's leaving had shocked me and made me feel stupid all at the same time. Because, under the circumstances, our relationship was hardly built to last. It was a miracle it had lasted as long as it did, but still, I missed him. We'd grown into adulthood together but that childhood-sweethearts-lasting-forever thing is a hard trick to pull off.

Still, what we'd had was special and I knew I'd never have it again. Besides, I needed another man in my life like I needed a hole in the head. I had everything I wanted. Except for those new biker boots I was longing for.

Who needs men when you've got fabulous boots, right?

2

Marin

I have my hand on the handle of conference room four and I'm steeling myself to open it.

I take a deep breath, hold it for a count of five, and let it out again slowly – a concept brought to me by my daughter, Rachel, who says nobody breathes properly.

'We'd all be dead, then,' pointed out Joey, my other child, nine and three quarters and hilariously determined to annoy his elder sister.

'*Properly*, dopey head,' said Rachel. 'We tense up and don't use the correct muscles.'

She might have a point. To open the door to conference room four, I think I need a brown paper bag to breathe into because I know exactly what I'll find in there and, some days, I just can't cope with the toxicity.

Eighteen years of working as an estate agent has taught me that the early gut impression of a disintegrating marriage can be as good as being their divorce mediator.

In other words: you'd be surprised how much you can tell about people when you are selling their home.

The Ryans, inside the room, are enriched uranium toxic.

Like when I do Pilates and think my stomach might explode with the pain of unused muscles being worked out, I force myself past the feelings and enter the room.

The Ryans are each glaring at the window behind the desk.

They both accompanied me on the initial valuation of their three-bed, semi-detached house in the lovely suburb of Glenageary. Every opened door was a failure of their life together.

For example, the two unused children's bedrooms, one of which was where Charlotte Ryan now stored her clothes.

Leo opened one closet door aggressively: 'See? Half of this stuff still has tags on it. Unworn.'

I like to think I'm always professional but I nearly needed the brown paper bag then, too. Unworn clothes. *Expensive* unworn clothes. I yearned to sort through the piles with Charlotte and offer her anything to try them on. She's probably my height, five six, about the same size – twelve – and is clearly a shopaholic, with money.

There the similarity ends because her hair is expensively highlighted while mine is at the growing-out-the-mistake-fringe stage, and is my natural chestnut colour, constantly tied up at the back of my head and nourished with dry shampoo.

Still, the thought of her wardrobe haul is affecting my brain like the thought of a line of cocaine must affect a coke addict. I stifled the urge but the clothes haunted me all the way around the house.

If only I had the perfect clothes, then everything in my life would be wonderful. I'd feel complete, not less-than.

Random female clients wouldn't look at me as if I was the downtrodden hired help in my black trousers – where are the fashion people hiding the perfect ones? – worn to hide my big hips. My mother wouldn't remark every time she saw me in work clothes that it was a pity my firm didn't have a uniform. My mother has a normal nose but she can look down it as if it was a ski jump in Val d'Isère.

If I had the right jeans, trousers and crisp white shirt, I'd like me more and Nate, my husband, would fancy me the way he used to fancy me back in the days when dinosaurs roamed the earth. But then, maybe marriages are like that, right? Wild lust in the beginning settles down to 'Did you put out the bins?'.

Now that they've accepted my valuation and have chosen Hilliers and McKenzie to sell their property, the Ryans are here in person to discuss the reams of paperwork required to sell a house and sign the company contract. Today.

Charlotte's wearing Isabel Marant. Hideously expensive and, like most high-end clothes, utterly impossible to sell on after being worn. I know because occasionally I shop for expensive clothes, then find out they don't suit me, and try to sell them on.

I know I have a problem, OK? For some people, it's chocolate. For others, wine o'clock.

Anything to fill the gaping hole of emptiness.

For me, it's frantic, addict-level shopping until I'm sitting breathlessly in the car with my haul and I realise, again, that this has all been a mistake. Like all addictive things, my chronic compulsive shopping hits my pocket ruthlessly.

I cannot ask a client about her clothes.

Get a grip, Marin Stanley, I tell myself firmly. You are a professional.

I therefore adopt my professional smile, which is clearly set to 'far too friendly' as its appearance elicits a diatribe from Charlotte about how Leo is keeping the house like a pit and they'll never sell unless he opens some windows and swears off the beer.

'The place smells like a brewery!'

In turn, this makes Leo kick off about how Charlotte had better not start on him now because he can't take any more of her bitching.

I am suddenly annoyed with these people. I steel myself to sound brisk and do what a mentor had told me years ago: carry on as if the argument simply is not happening.

'Your contract with Hilliers and McKenzie,' I say, rapping said document onto the desk. 'I'll go through the details again.'

They shut up.

After an hour of hostility so intense it could run the national grid, I escape the small office to lean against the wall near the giant ficus which brings the dual benefits of oxygen and a discreet hiding space into the office.

From her desk, which is, as ever, perfectly tidy, our office administrator, Bernie, sees me. For once, she appears not to be on the phone, although her ever-present headset is still plugged into her ear. She leaves her chair and is at my side in a moment.

'Do we need someone to go in and clean up the bodies?' she asks.

'No, but I was tempted,' I tell her.

'Ha!'

'I need caffeine,' I mutter, 'then I'll go back in.'

Bernie pats my arm. 'Leave it to me,' she says.

She swoops into the office and closes the door. I imagine her telling Leo and Charlotte that once we get all the paperwork signed and have their booking deposit, we can move on to the other important issues like solicitors, contracts, PSRA forms, money-laundering legislation forms – all the important details of estate agents in a modern age.

I have briefly discussed all of this with them and I should be in there now but, luckily, Bernie can tell when anyone in the office is suffering from Separating Couple Anxiety. Empathy is both very useful and a hindrance in an estate agent.

Five minutes pass and I check the emails on my phone.

She glides gracefully out of the office.

'I have given them all the papers,' she says. 'I considered asking if they wanted more tea or coffee, but thought they might throw hot liquids and we'd get sued.'

We grin at each other.

'Quick, I gave them only one pen. So there is something physical to argue over. Coffee,' she says.

We hurry into the little office kitchen where Bernie, after one crisp conversation with one of the senior partners, had a coffee-shop-standard machine installed. It would be the envy of every other estate agent in the country, I imagine, if they knew about it. But then we are a high-value agency and I doubt if anyone has an office administrator like Bernie. Deftly, she makes us two strong shots of espresso and we drink them, hers straight, mine with a little hint of sugar.

In the interests of full disclosure, I also like sugar, biscuits and chocolates.

'It's sad,' Bernie says thoughtfully, 'how sometimes the separating ones are so full of rage against each other. It's not good for the soul.'

'I don't know how you subdue them,' I say ruefully. 'It felt as if they were about to kill each other and every word was a knife thrown.'

'They are angry with the world and it spills over. We'll let them sit in there on their own for a while and then I will go in and charm them. Don't take on their rage.'

Finally, the Ryans leave the building and I find that Rachel is right. I am breathing better.

I take up my phone to message her something funny about this and find that because my phone was on silent for the meeting, I've missed a call, a text from my mother and that Nate has messaged me.

My mother texts like people once sent telegrams, as if words cost money. Particularly ones like 'please', 'thank you', and 'love': I MUST talk to you about your brother! Phone soonest.

I add so many kisses and hearts to Rachel's messages that they're often a sea of pink and red. I know that when Joey gets a phone, in the very distant future, I shall have to call a halt to this outpouring of love. Boys go off to school holding their mothers' hands, but by the time Joey is twelve and gets a phone, he'll be teased mercilessly at any sign of a heart emoji.

Nate's message is better than my mother's but not much:

Talked to Steve earlier. I asked him and Angie to dinner tomorrow. Know it's a bit last minute but you're fabulous at pulling rabbits out of hats. Asked Finn too. He's coming alone. What about Bea and Luke? Nate

Nate is not a man given to kisses at the end of messages. He finds my outpourings of adoring emojis ludicrous and he teases me mercilessly about them.

In person, however, he's very affectionate, so I can live without smiley faces and hearts. He's also the sort of man who'd have been called a bon viveur in another era. He's tall, strong and muscular from lots of exercise, has a fine singing voice and is always delighted to get his old electric guitar out at parties, so he and his two best friends, Finn and Steve, can sing the folky rock they used to perform when they busked during their college years.

My Nate loves parties, always has, always will. He's never happier than when the house is full of our friends, but these days, I feel too tired to entertain so much. The endless cycle of work, housework, grocery shopping and making dinner is getting to me.

Sometimes, I simply need time to relax with just us. But I can't break his heart like that.

I fire off a couple of messages, telling Nate it's fine – although it's not, really – and texting my mother that I will phone her on the way home.

At my desk, instead of working, I scribble a few frantic menu ideas. I love dinners with my family. Weekend cooking is the best: when there's no rush, I can mess around with recipes and we all have a lazy dinner where there's no studying, homework or anything to hurry us. I don't even mind lazy last-minute dinners where I throw the takeaway menus on the table and we come to a consensus, but there's no hope of that with Steve and Angie.

I like Steve. He and Finn are Nate's oldest friends: they met at college through the running club and now, two and a half decades later, they're still friends. The fourth part of the gang was Jean-Luc, Bea's husband, who died in a car accident nearly ten years ago.

We've kept our friendship going through those awful years

after Jean-Luc was killed, when Bea couldn't cope with get-togethers because it was too painful to remember how it used to be. Somehow, we got her back into the fold because, as Nate insisted, she was part of us. We'd be letting both her and Jean-Luc down if we didn't try.

Bea is amazing: she's raised their son, Luke, on her own, works part-time as a secretary in a dental and medical clinic, so she is always there to collect Luke from school, and she's a lioness protecting him, trying to give him everything his dad isn't there to give. Her coming back to our group is partly because of Luke – he and Joey are the same age and, I like to think, because the three men provide role models for a fatherless son.

I like Steve but I admit to loving Finn like a brother. He's kind, warm, clever and, since he broke up with his long-term girlfriend, Mags, has demonstrated unerringly bad taste in girlfriends. I wish I could find someone fabulous for him; I had hopes for him and Bea, to be honest, but they are just friends.

Plus, I don't think you can make other people fall in love with each other – it happens organically or not at all.

Steve used to fly through women as if he thought the world was ending and spreading his seed was paramount. Then he met Angie.

I can't honestly say how I feel about Angie because she makes me feel inadequate on so many levels that I've never managed to reach the bedrock of knowing whether I like her or not. There: I've said it. I feel guilty saying it because she's so nice but I can't help it. Some people push us into being our worse selves.

First time I met her, I saw this vision of sexy, beautifully dressed blondeness getting out of a taxi at the restaurant and my insecurities covered me like a warm, sticky blanket. I felt like I used to when I was a child and my mother was listing my imperfections.

That night, Angie was perfectly pleasant to everyone, talked warmly to me and Mags and discussed work – it would have been easier if she'd been beautiful and brainless but no, she's an award-winning architect in a practice with another woman. She enthralled every guy at and near our table. Her existence pushed every button in me, the ones that said my hair is wrong (goes frizzy so easily), my clothes are wrong and I could lose six pounds without it putting a dent in my overall body mass.

Eleven years later, nothing has changed.

Duh.

A dinner with Angie will mean me pulling out all the stops on my precious Saturday morning off.

Maybe not all the stops, I remind myself, because the grocery bank account is not looking particularly healthy right now. The mortgage is still not paid off and even though people assume that any financial job like Nate's is the equivalent of having a money-printing press in the basement, we are not rich.

I tell myself to go through the bank direct debits and payments this weekend. A financial audit. Although that scares me, because an audit will make me face up to why I bought Lululemon – *Lululemon!* – track pants for running when I never run. But the leggings were so soft and lovely, I just thought, maybe with the right leggings I *would* run? Hopefully?

I work my way through a pile of paperwork, make some phone calls, write some emails and finally finish for the day.

In our business, the working day is anything but a nine-to-five one. Evening and Saturday showings are part of the business and if you're a mother, you need a brilliant child minder.

But I have been in Hilliers and McKenzie for a long time and have moved up the ladder enough to ease that pressure. Happily for me, gone are the days of standing for several two-hour bursts in a series of show houses where you cannot use the facilities, make tea or barely sit on one of the mini-sized couches brought in to make the rooms look bigger, all the while fingering speed dial on your phone in case a weird viewer comes in and you are alone. Now, I am a senior negotiator and handle bigger-value properties and the one-offs, which means I have more power over my own diary. I still have to spend plenty of Saturdays and late nights showing houses but I can arrange it all myself, rather than the more junior staff members who have their showings assigned.

As I head out into the winter rain, I phone my mother and prepare myself for the onslaught.

'Your father's still in the allotment. He should have married that allotment,' my mother shrieks, full volume, down the line.

Dominic, my younger brother who is currently living back home, is in his room 'all hours, never cracks open the window and he doesn't know how to put on a wash!'.

I could mention that if my mother had taught my ditzy thirty-nine-year-old brother how to wash his own clothes when he was a teenager, he might still be married and not be back in the family home clogging the place up like a free-loading guest without the skills to cook, buy groceries, wash towels, clean the bathroom after he's used it, or offer to pitch in with rent money.

But I never point out what my mother *should* have done. My mission, should I choose to accept it, is to listen, agree with her and then nod silently at *how could his wife throw him out of the house?* The irony of this never escapes me.

There are three kids in my family and Dominic, the youngest, could do no wrong in my mother's eyes until recently during the year-long-catastrophe that is Dom's marriage break-up. His wife got tired of being married to a child-man who thinks there's a laundry/cooking/cleaning fairy.

Dominic is not my problem. April, my sister, a woman who believes in romantic fairy tales, is not my problem either. April's the oldest of us three but I definitely parent her. How did this happen? I can't afford the therapy to find out.

As the family fixer, I'm the one who gets the annoyed phone calls from my mother and the begging ones from my father. Last week's instalment in this long-running saga: 'Marin, can you say you need a babysitter next Wednesday? Pretty please? Your mother's got the book-club women in.'

The 'book-club women' are Ma's friends who prefer bitching about their other halves to reading. When they're there, she loudly discusses how bad her life is with my poor father able to hear every word from the tiny den next door, even when he has the sound turned up on the telly.

Being the family fixer also means getting exhausted calls from Dom's wife, Sue-Who-Deserves-Sainthood, who needs Dom to appoint a lawyer so they can get on with the legalities; and then calls from my mother again, who must have got some of the lawyer-type calls from Sue too, because she's got bursitis in one of her knees owing to back-to-back novenas, praying for Dom's marriage. My mother doesn't believe in divorce.

If Ma knew about April's life choices, all of which involve married men, I'd have to call an ambulance.

I know my duty: calm my mother down or she'll have bursitis in the other knee too.

'I'll talk to Dominic, Ma,' I say. 'I think Dad's been planting some Christmas bulbs he wants to force for you. He knows how you love hyacinths,' I add, which is a white lie, because I told him to plant something to keep her happy. 'There's something about the scent of them in the house for the holidays, isn't there?'

Ma is thrilled with this vision of her taste and is mollified. Mollifying my mother is tricky but I am good at it: I've had enough practice, after all. Somehow, after her extracting a promise from me to phone Dom's wife, Sue, I hang up.

Sue's a decent woman who deserves better than Dominic, much and all as I love him. Until he grows up, there is no hope for him having a sensible relationship.

Ideally, he needs to get out of my parents' house, live on his own and reflect that the real world is hard.

Saying you're in love with someone in front of a church full of your friends and relatives is not what marriage is about. It's about respect, compromise, caring, affection, kindness and, sometimes, making dinner for glamorous people who intimidate you because it will make your spouse happy.

It's Saturday evening, I've been out all afternoon showing a lovely late Edwardian house to scores of people who are all interested, but none interested enough to put in an offer. This means that as I stand in the kitchen sweating over a hot stove, I'm feeling irritated and somewhat put upon because of having to cook instead of ordering take out and collapsing in front of the telly. Bea and Luke are late, which is a pity, as Bea is a marvellous cook and always helps, and Luke could play Xbox with poor Joey who is currently sitting silently with Alexandra, Angie and Steve's ten-year-old daughter, while she plays with her mother's phone.

It's my fault: 'Be polite to her,' I always say and he does his best. They're in the same class at school and don't really get on, so I know he feels aggrieved to be stuck with her at the weekend as well as during the week.

Rachel is out at her friend Megan's house, where they're doing something that involves watching TV simultaneously with their friend in college in Galway. It's at moments like this that I question Rachel's – and Megan's – decision to have a gap year before starting college late next September. In March, they'll have earned enough from their various jobs to start a six-month travel fest around the world. The problem is that they're enjoying themselves so much, I don't know if they'll ever go to college.

Her evening out means I'm in the kitchen alone. I have pulled out as many stops as I can and spent far too much buying expensive beef with which to make a teriyaki beef stir fry. No matter how much prep you do beforehand, stir-frying for nine means you end up with two woks and sweat breaking out on your forehead.

'Can I help?'

It's Angie, who always offers to help and I always say no.

Tonight, as ever, she looks immaculate. To a clothes-obsessed woman like myself, I can see that she has the right sneakers (expensive), worn with ankle skimming jeans (also expensive) and a cream silk and cashmere zipped hoodie that clings. You can tell it's got silk in there: the fineness of the cashmere is the key. There's a translucency there to the expert/obsessive eye.

I almost moan. I've seen most of the outfit on Net à Porter: not in the sale part of the site, although that's where I spend hours scrolling. Not buying. Just scrolling.

Angie is perfect.

In her presence, I feel diminished and then ashamed at feeling so. How can I be a fit mother to a nearly grown daughter when I let such stupid things as clothes and body image affect me so badly?

'No, really, Marin. Let me do something. The men are talking work and I am fed up of work.'

She does try but I can't let her.

'You'll ruin your clothes if you fry,' I say. 'How about moving the drinks into the dining area and warming the plates,' I improvise.

'Sure.'

By the time dinner is served, with Angie having carried the plates to the table and having called everyone, I feel like the scullery maid in a period film with Angie as the elegant lady hostess.

'It looks gorgeous,' says Nate, his hand resting on Angie's shoulder as he walks round her to his seat at the table.

He smiles adoringly at Angie – adoringly! There's no other word for it and at that moment, I hate her. She's one of *those* women, I decide furiously, the ones who think nothing of flirting with other women's husbands. Does she want Nate?

Bitch.

'Really, this looks wonderful,' Nate says again and I feel my blood boil.

I cooked it, I want to say. She warmed the plates, nothing more. But then Nate gives me a one-armed hug and says: 'Fabulous little chef, our Marin,' and before I know it, they're all holding glasses up, even the kids with their orange-juice ones, and I'm supposed to smile, even though I'm sweaty, still wearing my apron and reeking of kitchen.

Nate hands me wine and I take a gulp before whisking off the apron.

I fix a smile to my face. *Fabulous little chef?* I'm over-reacting, that's all.

'Enjoy,' I say, and take two more gulps of the wine. Feeling bitchy brings out my inner alcoholic tendencies.

Nate and Steve had argued over which was better: the wine Nate had chosen or the bottles Steve had brought. I hate the stupid male competitiveness between them. But right now, I don't care which wine it is, I finish my glass far too quickly and fill it up again.

It will serve a purpose. And stop me hoping the competitiveness doesn't extend to wives.

When the doorbell rings, I leap to my feet.

'Bea and Luke,' I guess, delighted that a female ally has arrived.

Bea looks so cold, she's actually shivering. Her dark hair is plastered to her face, any mascara she'd applied earlier has slid down her cheeks and I swear there's a blue tinge to her.

'The tyre went flat and we had to fix it!' says Luke, erupting happily into the house and charging off to see Joey.

Bea holds out her hands, which I now see are filthy. 'It's so long since I changed a tyre, I'd almost forgotten. We were stuck because I couldn't get one of the nuts off the tyre and then this man stopped –'

'You let a stranger help?' says Finn, coming into the hall. 'You should have phoned – I'd have come out.'

'I can take care of myself,' says Bea, waggling a penknife she's produced from her coat pocket.

'Hold on, Mr Attacker: just let me get the knife part out – oops, that's the bottle opener, now wait: which end is up?' says Finn.

'Thanks, smartarse,' says Bea, grinning. 'I'm sorry I'm so late, Marin. Go ahead and eat but I'm filthy and wet. Can I borrow something?'

'You'll have to borrow something of Rachel's,' I say, feeling a wobble in my self-esteem. Am I menopausal? That could explain it. 'My stuff will swim on you.'

Bea's tall and naturally slender with legs that genuinely go on forever and, despite all this slenderness, has actual boobs. When I first met her, she was going out with Jean-Luc, I was newly dating Nate, and Bea had been his previous girlfriend. We were early twenty-somethings. Stuff like that happened then. Everyone had said that Bea was so beautiful, I was more nervous of meeting her than of gaining the approval of Nate's pals. But she was so likeable, an intense student studying French and history, which was how she and Jean-Luc had hooked up; he was making a mint giving French tutorials given his Auvergne heritage.

The thing is, Bea is nothing like Angie – she never makes me feel less-than. She never notices her beauty now just as she never noticed it when we were in college and I felt both gauche and encased in puppy fat alongside her slender, fey cleverness.

If Steve had died, would I still be inviting Angie into our lives? Sexy Angie? No.

But Bea's different. Bea has been in my life for twenty years, she's my friend.

I grab her hand. 'Come on upstairs. We can rifle through Rachel's things and find you something dry.'

Upstairs, Bea refuses a shower but towels off and I find her something of Rachel's to wear. Rachel's twenty-seven-inch-waist jeans are perfect, as is a silky black blouse.

'I couldn't get a leg in those jeans,' I say mournfully.

'Nonsense.'

Bea is there, hugging me. She is so very affectionate and I feel for her with only Luke to be affectionate with now and no husband to hug.

'You're gorgeous. You're the sexy, curvy one. I'm the one with bony knees who spent college elbowing people because my limbs had suddenly grown too large.'

We laugh at the memory.

I'd expected to dislike this tall, slim girl with the cloudy auburn hair because Nate had gone out with her before me. But two minutes in Bea's presence had sorted that out. She'd been sitting with them all, chatting mainly to Finn, when Nate introduced me.

'Nate Stanley, in the name of the sisterhood, I am ordering you to be nice to lovely Marin and don't leave her waiting for you in random pubs,' she'd said.

'Yes, or we'll make you suffer,' said Finn lazily. 'He has no manners. Too macho,' he confided to me.

'I am not,' said Nate, stung.

'He's a sweetie,' Bea had whispered to me, 'but don't tell him I said that. He's like the big brother I never had. If he steps out of line, tell me or Finn.'

I wish I could tell her that something feels out-of-line right now but there's nothing I can put my finger on. Besides, Bea has enough to cope with. Life as a widow with an almost ten-year-old boy is not easy. She's been alone since a car crash took her beloved Jean-Luc ten years ago. She doesn't need me moaning on with my wild imaginings about Angie wanting to get her hands on Nate. Because that's all they are.

Bea lost the man she loved in one fatal moment when she was eight and a half months pregnant with their child.

If anyone gets to moan, it's Bea.

3

Bea

'Kite-surfing or hang-gliding?' asks Shazz.

'I'm so much more a kite-surfing sort of gal,' I say sarcastically, hauling the newly changed duvet onto the bed and making everything neat. I love having fresh bedclothes at the weekend. Ironed and everything. The first time Shazz realised I iron my sheets, she said, 'You're fucking kidding me, right?'

'No,' I said. 'I like ironed sheets and a pretty bed, so shoot me. And watch the language – the kids will hear.'

The kids are my Luke and her Raffie, born around the same time, introduced at the health clinic when they were a month old and both of us were single mothers with newborns, reeling with exhaustion. I was thirty-three, Shazz was twenty-three. We had nothing in common except our babies, but we clicked.

Raffie's over here for a play date and there's much giggling from downstairs as they create baby chickens on Minecraft, the current craze. Shazz has stayed to chat and Christie and the girls are coming later.

'They hear bad language everywhere,' says Shazz now, and she's right. Fighting the onslaught of bad language and the fear of social media awaiting them mean mothering is tricky, to say the least.

I neatly arrange the fake mohair blanket in a seafoam colour at the end of the bed, fix my cushions on the pillows and admire my hard work.

Shazz, one of my best friends since that day in the health clinic and a woman whose ultra-pink hair is almost definitely visible from space, is sitting on the floor against the radiator not helping in the slightest.

But then Shazz has seen me at my worst in this bed, like that time when the kids were tiny when Luke and I both had a vomiting bug and she came over to take care of us, which is not something everyone would do. Anyone who's stripped the bed and remade it, while I retched loudly in the bathroom, and then tucked me back into bed with rehydration salts and said; 'Sleep, babes, I'll take care of everything,' never has to bother helping again. They have earned the right to sit on the floor and drink coffee.

'Is kite-surfing that one where they look as if they're being dragged out to sea?' I ask, starting dusting.

'Yeah, I think,' she says, which is her version of ignoring me. She's busy on her tablet writing me up a dating profile despite my protests that hell will freeze over before I go on another date. In the past eight years – since Shazz and our other friend, Christie, started pushing me to try again – I've been on a few dates. Disaster does not come near describing any of them.

At the top of my list of shame stars Ed. He was a set-up by an old school friend and in her fantasy world, her cousin Ed and I – two lonely people – were going to fall madly in love with each other.

This type of behaviour makes a woman wonder exactly what her old friends think of her when they stick cousin Ed on a platter and say, 'Now, there you are! A man! He's just your sort.'

Ed was *nobody's* sort. He had limited small talk unless it was about the rise of right-wing European politics (he was all for it) or model trains. Ed had been searching for love for years. Years. Women were picky, he said with narrowed eyes. Women expect men to buy them dinner into the bargain. Did they think he was made of money?

It was a summer party, so I excused myself to the bathroom, had no coat to find, and headed for home. I'd had the most amazing, wonderful husband and he'd been snatched from me, leaving me a widow at thirty-three. And people were trying to set me up with losers like Ed?

'You're thinking about Ed,' says Shazz, long neon and diamante purple-gel nails working the keypad, looking for hunks who'd fancy single mothers. 'You have an Ed look on your face.'

'Delayed shock,' I say.

'You do French, right?' she asks.

Jean-Luc was French and we met when I was brushing up my French at an evening course he was teaching.

'Yeeees,' I say, dragging the word out. I can see sheer filth coming out of this online profile. Shazz could have so much fun with my ability to do things French-style.

'I *speak* French, Shazz. Mentioning anything else French is asking for trouble.'

'Oh, don't be so picky,' she say blithely, tap tapping away.

I left the dating scene because it was so horrendous and because I'd largely relied on the comfortable route of meeting men via friends. Internet dating scares me. I don't want to swipe my way to love on my phone – Shazz has swiped left many times since she's been a single mum and frankly, I don't know why there aren't more crime shows on how much guys lie about themselves on their profiles, not to mention using other people's photos so that they are entirely unrecognisable.

Shazz found the love of her life, Zephaniah, online, which is why she's keen to get me set up again. She's a born-again romantic. But I'm stalling. I have post-traumatic dating syndrome.

The nail in the coffin, so to speak, was at a party held by Moira, a woman I once worked with. She met me at the front door, utterly excited: 'Bea, I have just the guy for you. Trust me.'

Trust me is what people say when they're about to lie to you.

Startlingly, the guy in question wasn't a weirdo. He was nice, just not my type in the slightest because when it came down to it, I thought ruefully, my type was lying in the cold ground.

The problem turned out to be a guy called Joe who was there with his wife, about whom Joe conveniently forgot as soon as he set eyes on me.

After many glasses of wine, *I* was Joe's type. He happily decided that I was there for him. The nice guy and I agreed that we weren't each other's dream date, so he went off in search of craft beer and a long conversation with some other people about the Champions League. I decided to find my coat with Joe following me around like a dog snuffling for biscuits.

I wanted to escape quietly and I didn't know where the coats were being kept, and Joe followed me into one of the bedrooms on my search. Worse, his wife thought I was encouraging it.

'Leave him alone,' she said, finally pinning me in a corner.

'I do not want Joe,' I said angrily. 'In fact, I have no interest in Joe. I came here for a few drinks with my friend, and it turns out she has a man lined up for me.' I pointed towards the dining-room table area where the food was laid out. 'There he is over there, talking about football and beer. While your husband,' Joe was slinking further and further away all the time, 'has decided he is for me. I have no interest in him. So why don't you bring him home, sober him up and tell him not to run after strange women at parties.'

'It's your fault,' she screeched. 'You skinny bitches with your long hair and no baby fat! You dangle yourselves and your breasts in front of him!'

Clearly this was an ongoing problem and one of the reasons it had not been nipped in the bud was because Mrs Joe always blamed whatever woman Joe had got in his sights, instead of getting Joe and nailing his knee caps to the floor. Also, I am on the bosomy side and Mrs Joe was not. Having big boobs is not all it's cracked up to be but clearly mine had sent Mrs Joe over the edge.

I pushed away from her and said: 'Next time, blame your husband, don't blame the poor woman he is pursuing.'

Still shaking, I found my coat in a chaotic pile in a spare bedroom, walked up to Moira and said hotly, 'I am never coming to your house again. You left me to that mad woman.'

'She gets a bit like that when she's had drink . . .'

'What's Joe's excuse?'

'Over-excitable, loves women.' She looked guilty.

'Why didn't you rescue me?' I demanded. 'In future, we meet for coffee and only coffee. You're buying!'

In the taxi on the way home, I pondered that hitting men like Joe over the head was the only answer. Then, I came to the conclusion that really, the only answer was not going out to parties until people decided that I had actively chosen the celibate life.

But Shazz was convinced in her lovestruck state that I needed pairing up too. Christie – lesbian mother of two exquisite twin girls born via IVF and now living with a female police inspector, Gloria – was on Shazz's side.

The get-Bea-dating-again adventure has been going on for weeks now and I have already seen more dating profiles than I ever cared to. From my glimpse into this world, every man is a hiking, scuba-diving dude who has an Idris Elba/Lionel Messi thing going and plays guitar, or else, they're sex-starved maniacs who imply that what's in their trousers can also be seen from space.

'Can you play a musical instrument?' asks Shazz.

'Does the ukulele count?' I enquire.

'No, smartarse,' she replies. 'Playing the spoons is out too.'

We both laugh.

'I'm going to put saxophone,' she says, concentrating.

'So it's a complete tissue of lies?' I say, the laughing actually beginning to hurt my sides now.

'Absolutely. My cousin Tonya said she kept fit by pole dancing and she went on loads of dates.'

'What are you waiting for, then? Go on! Stick in pole

dancing: I'll practise at bus stops. Far be it from me to get in the way of horny men looking for one-night stands.'

'You're not taking this seriously,' Shazz mutters. 'I'll put in the saxophone. It's very sexy.'

'But I don't play it –' I begin to protest, then try another tack. 'I only said I'd try the Internet once and I want it to be an honest profile.'

'*Nobody* does an honest profile! Relax. This is like leaving bird seed out. You scatter seeds to see what comes along.'

'I know exactly what'll come along if you imply I'm a French-speaking sex kitten who plays the saxophone: sex-starved men. I'm too old, too worn out, Shazz. I want normal. I want romance,' I add wistfully. My bedroom was romantic. From my sea-foam throw to my ruched, frilled cushions, it was a haven for romance. It just never saw any.

'You're never too old for love,' Shazz says, while I hope that there must be one decent, kind, affectionate man out there who will hold me in his arms and make me feel better.

Falling in love with him would be different – in my experience, love hurts too much. Also, people like to believe in an endless supply of true loves. If one dies, you search till you find another one, yes?

No.

But since Shazz fell in love, she wants everyone to be in love. I wish it was that easy.

Late at night, I wonder how being raised without a strong male influence in his life will affect Luke. He has Finn, Nate and Steve, but they have their own lives. We are on the outside, no matter what they think.

I console myself with the psychological tenet that one good parent is all a child needs: I was told that once and I still cling to the idea like a drowning person clinging to a rock in the sea.

When Luke was younger, I used to talk to him about Jean-Luc, show him pictures of his dad, but I do it less now.

We've almost lost contact with Jean-Luc's family in France. His older brother is a lot older, has grown up kids, and has always been too busy to stay in touch, while Jean-Luc's mother, Celine, could barely cope for a long time with seeing the growing little boy who looked so like her own little boy, so our Skype calls have dwindled to almost nothing in the past few years. Honestly, it suits me because I'm terrified Celine would want Luke to come to her for holidays and I can't bear the thought of letting him go.

He's not alone, either: another consolation point. Two kids in his class in school have never set eyes on their fathers, either, although they're still alive. Just vamoosed.

In the case of Shazz, whose boyfriend walked out on her and Raffie when he was a newborn, said boyfriend is looking at certain and very painful death should he ever walk back in.

'That Bastard,' she calls him.

Obviously, That Bastard vanished so comprehensively that he doesn't pay child support. So Shazz does gel nails and beauty treatments from her front room and manages brilliantly.

Since Zephaniah, who is as kind as he is handsome, arrived on the scene, Shazz never talks about That Bastard. She talks about how she never believed in love before but does now.

'Jeez, Bea: you'll be a born-again virgin if you don't get some action soon.'

'Who says I don't get action?' I demand. 'If you could see the way the electricity meter reader and I are together . . .'

'Sparks fly?'

'Exactly.'

Her phone rings and gives me a chance to go downstairs to make coffee for us both. The boys are building a Lego fort with great intent. They play very limited computer games in my house because I won't let them. Since they're both nearly ten later this month, this is still possible but who knows how long my power will last.

Now that she has Zep in her life, Shazz says it's lovely to

have a father figure around for Raffie. She doesn't say it to upset me but to spur me to 'get on with my life'.

'What happens when Luke's grown up? What then?'

'I'll get cats. Or play tennis.'

'Or get the cats to play tennis,' she replies sarcastically. 'He's dead ten years, Babes: nobody said you had to throw yourself on the funeral pyre. Poor Lukey will never be able to leave home: he'll think you've dedicated your life to him and he can't go. I'm joking,' she adds. 'Well, sorta.'

'I don't want to guilt him into never leaving,' I say heatedly, 'but what are the odds of a forty-three-year-old widow with a son falling in love with someone new?'

'You could do with someone to hug who isn't nine and three quarters,' continues Shazz. 'Besides, the dreaded family-tree school project is coming up soon and, apparently, even a hint of "My mum has a boyfriend" makes it easier.'

We've been warned about the Family-Tree project by a friend of Shazz's. In theory: it's a lovely idea. A big chart with as many of the pupil's family members pictured or drawn on it as possible. Lovely if you come from a traditional family but tricky if you're one of the three kids in Luke's and Raffie's class without an actual father.

'Don't remind me,' I groan.

We always talk gently about Jean-Luc the night before Luke's birthday which is coming up. Hearing about the fatal car crash sent me into instantaneous labour. My son was born hours after his father died. I can't see that fitting well onto the Family-Tree project.

As time progresses, I find it harder and harder to remember a time when it was myself and Jean-Luc, when we were a blissfully married couple with a baby on the way. I must have been another person then.

Now, I'm Bea, single parent, widow, adoring mother of Luke, with a tough shell on the outside that I let very few people penetrate.

I was thirty-eight weeks pregnant when my husband died, which means that Jean-Luc never saw his son and Luke, my baby boy who has recently turned gangly and long limbed, never saw his dad.

This is not a sob story – I don't believe in that. I don't want pity. If people dole it out, I smile and mentally give them the bitter version of Taoism: shit happens.

It's true. Appalling things happen amidst the most wonderful of love stories, destroying them.

Love does not stop drunk drivers ploughing into cars.

Love does not mean that your beloved husband will be miraculously revived at the scene of the accident.

Love does mean that when your waters break when you hear the news your husband has died, you fight to bring your son into the world and vow that nothing will ever hurt him.

Actually, that's mother love. The tough kind, the anyone-who-hurts-my-son-will-regret-it love.

Being solely responsible for a child toughens you up. We mothers will do anything for our kids. But for ourselves? Who has the time to do anything for themselves?

Mothers never stop looking after their children. When Jean-Luc's anniversary and Luke's birthday arrives, my mother will bring me flowers and hug me extra hard.

'Love you, darling girl,' she'll say. 'Wherever he is, Jean-Luc is looking down on you and he's so proud of how you're raising Luke.'

My dear mum: I couldn't have got through any of it without her. But I'm not sure Jean-Luc is gazing down at me from anywhere. I truly believed in heaven until he was killed and then – then, I didn't believe in any heaven or deity because no decent God would rip my unborn baby's father away so cruelly.

I've never felt Jean-Luc's presence, although I've dreamed of his arms around me. Once, when that happened, I woke up and cried.

Now, the truth has seeped into my dreams too. I dream of him gone and I'm searching for him, aware that time is ticking and that if I don't find him, it will be too late.

It's hard to know which is worse.

I decided that when Luke was very small and I was weeping – yes, such a biblical word, but it's how it felt – weeping over the only man I think I could ever love, that I would go on because of Luke. I have my friends, mainly women, but I try to hide my vulnerability by holding that rod of steel in my back because it's better that people don't see how broken hearted I am. Fake it till you make it, right?

I feel that dear Finn, one of the people left over from that other life when Jean-Luc and I were together, somehow knows how wounded I still am. Finn will phone and invite me out to dinner for Jean-Luc's anniversary. Loyal, lovely natured and clever, Finn cannot cook, so we have to go out and we have fun choosing restaurants. But I hold my pain close to my heart.

And Marin and Nate, whom I dated years ago when I was a twenty-year-old idiot, will call and say they're having a few people over for supper and would I come?

'Just bring yourself and Luke, no cooking dessert or anything. It's going to be jeans and sweatshirts at the kitchen table, promise.' That's what she always says.

Even though Luke and Joey get on like a house on fire, and I know everyone well, those dinner parties sometimes make me consumed with sadness.

They're a memory of a life I no longer lead.

The doorbell rings snapping me back to the here and now and the two boys yell that it's Christie with the girls.

She's the third part of our triumvirate of square pegs in the round holes of school mums. The girls, Daisy and Lily, who are the girliest girls you will ever see, erupt into the house. Shazz and I go down to meet them. They're non-indentical twins. Daisy is blonde and favours Heidi-style pigtails at the moment with sparkles on everything. Lily is dark and looks like she was ordered from a Parisian catalogue. On her, the cheapest garment looks chic, even at age eight.

'How's the online profile going?' says Christie, herself a stunning blonde with a blunt haircut and a razor-sharp mind.

'I am a French sex kitten with hidden talents,' I murmur, as the four kids get together.

'Shazz!' says Christie.

I cheer up. Lesbian dating websites must be more honest. Or are women inherently more honest? I ponder.

'The picture's the vital ingredient,' Christie goes on. 'Just slap a photo up. That one from summer on the beach where she's in the bikini. No man can resist tits.'

'Tits? Really? Where has the romance gone?' I demand, going into the kitchen and putting the kettle on to boil.

'You got to find the guy first,' says Shazz, 'then work on the romance.'

I give in.

I let them scroll through my phone for photos, saying a clear no to said bikini shots.

One of Shazz's boyfriends once said I had 'a nice rack' and I was mortally embarrassed about this, and have been heading for the minimiser section of the bra department ever since.

We finally settle on a picture of me – fully clothed – on the beach that same evening, a blanket wrapped around me, smiling because the children were all happily tired out and we were heading back to the house we'd rented in Wexford, hungry but full of cheer.

I look just like my mum: hair the colour of the russet apples that used to fall from the tree in our old garden, eyes that are amber in some lights, a honeyed pale gold in others. I know I can look cautious now, as if ready for the next blow.

Tragedy might teach you resilience but it also teaches you to be over-alert about the next pain coming down the tracks.

It's a good photo of me because I'm smiling.

I might be the one faking it on this profile, I think: implying a happy inner world when, in reality, I often feel so lonely and worried about everything.

But still, Shazz and Christie are madly set on this. And I can't let them down.

4
Sid

Vilma's got tickets with all her friends to see some band I've never heard of who are doing a one-off gig in a small venue at the weekend.

'You've got to come!' she says and I can almost see her eyes sparkling with happiness telling me this.

I'm sitting at my desk staring at my inbox, which is full. Again. I've only been out of the office for two hours for a working lunch and despite the new directive from Adrienne that we are too busy to engage in the corporate world's ass-covering cc emails, everyone's still at it.

I start deleting with a vengeance.

'I got a pint of beer spilled on me at the last gig you dragged me to,' I say mutinously, aware that I am sounding childish. 'Plus, it's freezing. Who wants to leave their fire to go out at night in bloody November?'

I do not have a fire, but still. Vilma, who is in college studying political science and seems to have about three lectures a week, laughs.

'You are coming if we have to drag you out of the apartment,' she announces. 'You've had a year of barely ever going out at night, no matter what the weather. It's either one gig every few months or myself and the girls kidnap you and drag you to our flat.'

As their flat is a hotbed of both men and women arriving and departing like a train station, I could not cope with it. I like my peace and not sharing the couch with various happy student types.

'You've got to get over him,' Vilma said as a parting word.

'Fine,' I said in resignation, before hanging up and crossly deleting a few more emails. She didn't understand about Marc and I, but then, I'd never explained it to her. Marc and I were each other's safe harbours in every sense, but I'd messed it up.

Still, his leaving had shocked me because I pride myself on being watchful – hell, I can read a room in seconds – and I hadn't seen the signs.

People always thought we were perfect for each other and in our slender, fine-bonedness, we could almost be brother and sister, although he's taller and his hair is darker than mine.

I'd once had long hair but I kept it in a short cut now: not a pixie but something with a hint of avant-garde to it, half like I went at it with the kitchen scissors, half like some tricky hairdressing genius did it over three hours of aloof thoughtfulness. Nobody ever believes I get it cut in a tiny salon close to the office where most of the customers are lovely elderly ladies having their hair set. I love old ladies – there's not a shred of romantic notions left in them. They've seen Life and know exactly what it brings.

Not that surprising, really, that my world is all safely contained within a couple of miles' radius. Home, the office, the pub. 'You could work anywhere,' Marc would say to me in those early days.

'I like what I do and it's important work,' I said.

And it was. Plus, Adrienne, boss of the organisation, ran the place so wonderfully that it felt like the safest place on earth. Nurture by name and nurture by nature.

During my second year there, when I decided it was the right place for me, Marc and I moved in together. Buying a two-bedroom apartment meant we could afford almost no furniture but as time went on, things improved. We splashed out on a grey velvet couch we could both almost sleep on and a rug in a modern print. And cushions. I adore cushions, the squashier and more velvety the better.

Apart from the cushion fetish, I'm a minimalist. Marc's wallet is testament to his messiness. Receipts hang out of it and if he didn't have me to accompany him around shops, he'd be dressed like a tramp.

Oh but I'm doing it again. Saying 'if he didn't have me'.

It's all past tense now. So past tense that the tumble weeds are rolling through the remains of our relationship.

Nearly a year ago, Marc left me the couch and the rug and I began to think about getting a cat.

'He's gone? Just like that? How dare he dump you. You should have dumped him first,' Vilma said as I told her the news that night on the phone. Vilma, eighteen at the time, was heavily into female empowerment and the belief that girls rule the world. I did not tell her that, in my experience, this was unfortunately not the case.

'I did not know it was over, so he got to do the dumping, which is fine,' I assured her, sounding calm because I was self-medicating with vodka tonics and Haribos instead of dinner. At least nobody could see me, Nurture Department Head, public purveyor of the Sugar is Evil message, doing this.

While Vilma gave out stink about men and how, if she had a staple gun, she'd sort bloody Marc out, with a few well-judged staples and when was I going to tell our mother, Giselle, because she'd be devastated, I ruminated on pets. Cats don't need to be walked. If I had a dog, it would have to come into the office with me and no dog would survive the noisy chatter of our office. A cat wouldn't mind vodka tonic nights. Cats can look after themselves. I didn't want to be alone. Alone scared me.

'Why did you say that about cats?' Vilma asked, confused.

The vodka:tonic ratio was 50:50 at this stage, I should point out. Desperate times and all that.

'I'm just upset,' I improvised. 'He said it was time to end it.'

Vilma hissed, which is what all younger sisters do when their big sister's boyfriends leave. It's a comfortingly feral noise. I adore my sister.

It was just as much my fault as Marc's, but to tell Vilma would be to ultimately hurt her, so I couldn't. But I did miss him, missed having someone to watch telly with or get takeaway with.

Which said it all, really: when TV and takeaway are the things you miss most about your relationship, you know it's over.

Vilma's and her friends' delight is infectious as they queue up to get into Whelan's, the venue where an amazing band called Granny's Fruitcake will be on stage from ten.

They've all decided I am to 'have a fun night out!' and are taking this seriously: before long, they have commandeered a high table near the stage, are treating me like bodyguards taking care of a celebrity, and have put a mini bottle of wine, an actual glass and a packet of crisps in front of me. All young men who attempt to infiltrate the group are warned off by them, like lionesses warding off attack.

Despite several nights out with the girls, I am not sure exactly what Vilma told them, but am guessing it involves how poor Sid is lonely, needs to get out more and still isn't over being dumped.

There's no point correcting this version of events and I am happily going along with it because I have no choice, it might be fun and I am out of box sets. Even *I* know it's worrying how I put calendar reminders on my phone diary when new ones are due on Netflix. Life lived through Netflix series is the sort of thing you probably regret when you are dying. But, who knows?

There are five young women: Vilma and her best sister-pack – Rilla (trainee police officer), Sinead (beauty therapist), Svetlana (working in a gym and doing fitness coach qualifications) and Karla (training to be a nurse). They've been friends since school apart from Karla, who's an honorary member of the team because she and Rilla are dating.

I love their protectiveness. I am halfway down my packet of crisps before I get a chance to try my wine.

'The wine's crap here,' says Karla, her spiky haircut coloured an unlikely red. 'Are you sure it's OK for you, Sid?' she asks, as if I am a wine connoisseur.

'Watch her glass, Karla,' says Vilma, looking left and right. 'I don't trust glasses: anybody can slip a drug into one. Bottles are better.' She waved her beer bottle at me.

'Put it down and never pick it up again,' recites Rilla, who has rippling blond hair and the look of a fairy-tale princess, but she's a self-defence genius who learned unarmed combat from her army dad from the age of twelve. I love Rilla.

I pull my wine glass into my embrace and think that if it makes me look like a wino, it's better than being dragged off into the night drugged out of my brain on GBH.

'We take care of each other,' Vilma says, reciting the mantra I taught her. 'Nobody goes to the loo on their own. We travel in pairs. Check in.'

I feel a surge of pride at seeing Vilma and her friends taking care of each other.

'I feel like the older Sarah Connor in *Terminator*,' I say, grinning, 'the one with the amazing combats and boots who has her own rocket launcher. '

We all high-five each other as the band starts up. Their delight is infectious.

Granny's Fruitcake will never be on my playlist but they are earnest, sweet, trying so hard. The lead singer is the youngest, possibly only shaves twice a week and has a lovely huskiness to his voice but the music isn't my thing. Still, that wasn't the point.

After the gig, all of us – happily undrugged by strangers – wander off for something sweet in a cake-and-coffee shop Rilla suggests.

The Cake Shop Café is accessed through a second-hand bookshop that I've been in before. With a mezzanine where books cover every square metre, it would take days to examine all the stock with your head sideways to read the spines before serious neck strain set in. At night, when the bookshop is closed, the café with its outside pergola seating area can be reached by a teeny lane. The pergola area with its trailing plants, fairy lights draping the overhang and tea lights in tiny jars on the tables is buzzing. Heaters keep it warm and there are cheap blankets for anyone who wants added cosiness. The girls slither into a small space and I take the tea and cake orders.

The café's a lovely mix of people, from those retreating after nights in music venues to those having a post-prandial coffee and dessert.

I leave my girls chattering and laughing, exchanging photos and uploading social media things, and collide neatly with a tall man holding an empty tray and staring at the cakes and sugar-laden health balls behind the glass counter.

'Sorry.'

'Fine,' I mutter.

'Did I hurt you?' he asks, staring down at me. I hate being stared down at. Being short is a definite disadvantage in life.

I shake my head. 'Fine,' I say again, about to move past. It was past my bedtime and, jacked up on the 'strangers will put date-rape drugs in your drink' message, I wasn't in the mood for random men talking to me.

'Snap. You've been out with a gang of youngsters in Whelan's,' he says and I stare up, eyes narrowed. Stalker? Random nutter? Nice normal man? It's so hard to tell, as anyone who has ever watched the crime channels will tell you.

'I took my nephews and I saw your gang in there,' he explains, pointing to two lanky youths with broad shoulders who are sitting at a table staring at their phones. 'Actually, they took me,' he adds, semi-bemused. 'I felt like an ancient uncle.'

I can't help myself and I laugh.

'You too, huh?'

'My sister and her friends,' I say, making a snap decision that

45

we were in a public place and my girls would attack him if he tried to slip anything dodgy into my tea.

'Girls' night out?'

'Women,' I say, hackles up. 'We're women.'

He holds up his hands. 'Sorry! Women! No offence. I'm old school in some ways. My nephews seem like boys to me and everyone younger does too. So I say girls . . .' He grimaces. 'I'm making this worse. I suppose I'm saying that they're girls and you, on the other hand, are a woman –'

Poor man is digging a hole so deep, he'll only get out with crampons, some rope and a mountaineer shouting instructions.

I take pity on him. 'It's all right. I'm not going to hit you over the head with my copy of *Feminism Rules*,' I say, 'so cut the cheese.'

He smiles. 'Sounds like an old book title. *Who Moved My Cheese?*'

Against my better judgement, I laugh. 'It's a new title: *Women Who Love Pinterest and Rabbits More Than Men, So Cut The Cheese.*'

'Catchy. I should read it. Shamefully, my own rabbit habit is getting out of hand . . .' he deadpans and it's inexplicably not cheesy. 'I should point out that I am not hitting on you. I was making conversation, that's all. If it helps, I don't date. I'm appalling at it. I have decided to retire from the ring.'

My superpower is a hard-won, near-perfect analysis of people. Near-perfect. I am not counting Marc because just before he left, my superpower obviously left me.

But it's back and I decide that the man beside me is not joking. He is over with dating. He's right: why bother? I chance a look at him.

He's handsome with a lean face, kind flinty grey eyes, a Borzoi-long nose, with short sandy hair going grey in narrow streaks. He could be anywhere from thirty to forty in the dim light of the café. His night out gear is the defiantly undressy: hiking jacket, jeans and an Aran sweater, and his long legs have the hint of someone who trains obsessively for marathons.

'Runner?' I ask.

'Used to be.' He sounds miserable.

'Now you cycle because your knees are banjaxed.'

His turn to laugh. 'Correct. I also swim but am not insane or young enough for triathlons. I like my joints and want to hang on to them. Meanwhile, you work in banking and your idea of a night out is entertaining clients in posh restaurants?' he ventured, taking in my trench coat and trousers, which are from my work wardrobe. Sweatpants were too casual for tonight and my last acceptable pair of jeans have an inconvenient hole in the inner thigh. I am not a shopper.

'Excellent guess,' I lie. 'I have an entire team at my disposal and I scream at them if they annoy me or if my coffee's the wrong temperature. I have two assistants, one I throw my coat at and one who buys my lunch.'

'They'd never have you in the intelligence world, what with being able to lie with ease,' he says, grinning.

I think, *Oh yes, they would.*

'I've seen *The Devil Wears Prada,*' he adds.

'Did sisters or girlfriends make you watch it?'

'My niece – my sister's little girl, Danielle.'

He had, I allowed myself to notice, a nice smile.

'I am putty in her hands. So are her brothers. I was babysitting some years ago, it was a toss up between a Transformer movie or *The Devil Wears Prada,* which is her favourite movie, and she won. Some day, she will be running the country.'

'You are a new man. Congratulations.'

'Thank you.' He inclines his head modestly. 'New man, single man, that's me. Can't get a woman to save my life so have just given up.' He stops dead. 'Sorry – don't know where that's come from. Thinking out loud. All those young people in Whelan's gazing into each other's eyes and making plans for later. I felt both a hundred years old and entirely out of the game. I realised a long time ago that it was time to get out of the game, but a band venue with young people really gets the message across.'

He rubs the bridge of his nose thoughtfully and I think he might be as tired as I am.

We're getting closer to the counter and are standing side by side.

'Do you think,' I say, and I wonder if maybe my mini bottle of wine has pushed me over the edge here, 'that people really weren't meant to date? That somewhere in the whole theory of evolution people are supposed to exist in little extended family groups. And sometimes, if they are very lucky, they make it as couples, but otherwise not?'

He gives me a long searching look.

'You might be on to something there,' he says. 'I thought I had it right with my last girlfriend and – and then I didn't.'

I held up a hand. 'I'm not listening to how she was a horrible bitch, you hate her and she ruined your life,' I say, only half kidding.

'No,' he says. 'It was – forgive the cliché – complicated. But I don't diss and tell.'

He actually sounds forlorn and I think I'll send him over to Vilma so she can counsel him on getting over people. In my experience, straight men don't allow male friends enough emotional access to counsel them past relationship pain.

It was his go with the person behind the counter, and he began politely ordering all sorts of carb-related things to fill the two young guys in the corner. I'd typed in everyone's order on my phone, because I knew I'd never remember it – between chai, lattes and matcha teas and buns with no nuts in them, unless they had anything with Nutella involved, and then the nut-free thing didn't count . . .

'How about your dating history?' the man says as we stand beside each other in what feels like a companionable silence. 'What I mean is, why have you come to the conclusion that dating is over?'

'I lived with a guy for nearly thirteen years and broke up a year ago. Nobody since.' It felt important to say this. The new me was laying the facts out there. I live on my own: so what? 'I'm perfectly happy with my box sets.'

'Me too,' he says. 'Box sets are brilliant.'

'Box sets, a takeaway and a single, perfect glass of wine. Hangovers are just horrendous when you get older,' I add, shuddering. When I make my cocktails at the weekend, I only drink one now. The first post-Marc month involved far too much wine. I do not want to be the single woman statistic who drinks her way through her weekends and gets the shakes on Monday mornings without a shot of vodka.

'It must be age – I can't cope with hangovers either,' he says. 'I swim a lot and I can't go for pints with the lads anymore because I'm not prepared to pay the entertainment tax.'

Suddenly I smile up at him, the irony of it all hitting me as it so often does when I think of the way I live my life now.

'These are supposed to be some of the best years of our lives,' I say, half to myself. 'We are youngish, free, and clearly reasonably solvent if you have a racing bike and we spend our lives eating takeaways and watching Netflix.'

The man looks at me. 'I disagree. The rules of life are societal constructs. Who says these are the best years and to enjoy them properly we have to live in pairs and have children?'

'Teacher?' I ventured.

'University lecturer,' he said, then added, 'I'm Finn. Why can't men and women merely be friends? Honestly, genuinely just friends and let someone else fulfil their biological imperative.'

I raise an eyebrow and decide he's broken up recently too. Only the really recently broken-up talk like this. It's as if being uncoupled pulls out a little stopper in your brain and lets all these random truths out.

We shuffle along as our various teas and foodstuffs are put onto trays.

'You and I should be able to see a film or an exhibition and not feel we have to pair up like little robots.'

'Are you asking me out?' I say, grinning, knowing he wasn't.

'I'm sorry,' he says, 'I shouldn't have asked that; you'll think it's a trick. But it's an idea, an experiment. Let's go out – as friends. Then everyone will leave me alone about not having a girlfriend.'

My superpower is still working and he's not tricking me but still . . .

'Tell your friends to leave you alone. I don't do male friends unless I work with them.' He seemed like a decent guy. In another universe, we could have dated – but not in this one. 'Sorry,' I add, 'no dice. Not my thing.' I pick up the tray of coffees and goodies that has handily just materialised in front of me and head back to my crew.

'OK, then. Very nice to meet you.' He smiles at me.

Back at the table, Vilma gives me the laser-eye look. 'So, that dude you were talking to. He was into you, wasn't he?'

'He wasn't,' I say. 'We were discussing how dating is over-rated and humanity should get used to living life alone.'

'Ugh,' says Rilla, without looking up from her phone. 'What about sex?'

I feel Vilma's hand on my thigh and realise she's glaring at me. 'You have no friends, Sid: none, except the people you work with. And us, although I practically had to kidnap you to get you out. You need some life. For fuck's sake, go out with this guy – as a friend. You've got plenty of home-made pepper spray in case he's stalker material, but he looks OK.'

I'm shocked into silence.

Vilma has looked up to me her whole life and now she's staring at me as if I am the weirdest person she's ever met: her crazy sister, the recluse, who never goes out.

I am not going to cry. I never cry. I am going to get angry. Anger works better.

'Fine,' I say furiously, as if I'm raising the stakes on a poker game, 'fine. Let me out, Karla.'

I wriggle out and march up to the table where Finn is now sitting with his two nephews, who are wolfing down cake as if they've been on a keto diet for a month.

They all stare at me.

'Just friends,' I say, ignoring the two younger men. 'No funny business. First sign of it and I'm off.'

'Me too,' he says, looking only a hint startled. 'Film? I have to tell you that I cannot watch – er,' he considers his words, 'sad movies where people cry.'

'Me neither. I like ones where women get to avenge themselves on men. With guns. Flamethrowers, castration, that sort of thing.'

One of the nephews winces.

Finn considers this and nods approval. 'Good plan.'

He extracts himself from the open-mouthed nephews and we move away.

'My name is Sid, short for Sidonie. Never call me Sidonie.' I am aware that I am talking very fast but I think that I may run if I consider how unlike me this is.

'OK, Sid, to keep the ball entirely in your court, I will give you my phone number and if you really want to do this you can ring me, and maybe you should give me your card in case you think I'm being, er, big headed by expecting you to ring me. Because the man rings the woman?'

'That worked in the nineteenth century, but not anymore,' I say gravely. 'Besides, we're in the Friend Zone, which has different rules.'

He grins and it turns out that he really has the most amazing smile. I shuffle around in my purse and take out a card. We manage to swap with only the faintest touch of fingers. But that still feels pleasurable.

'Tomorrow, when we are in our right minds and we have had

some sleep, we will phone each other. And whoever phones first gets to pick the film,' I barter.

'Deal.'

We shake hands and then with one last, bursting grin, he salutes me.

'Comrade friend,' he says.

'Smartass,' I mutter, pretty sure he can hear me.

5

Marin

I can hear my brother and mother arguing before I'm even in the house.

Not all the words are audible but the ones I can hear make me want to run out the door. My mother can start an argument in an empty room. Now she's roped Dom in.

'Lazy . . . taking me for granted . . . disgrace!'

'You said Sue was beneath me!'

My heart actually sinks. Nobody heard me arrive. I could sneak out and –

'Marin!' hisses Dad.

I turn in the hallway and find him peering out from the den where Ma keeps her crafting supplies and where Dad hides himself away during book-club nights and any other night when Ma is in a mood.

'In here.'

I slip in and he shuts the door, delighted to see me.

We hug and I smell that quintessentially Dad smell of Old Spice and fresh ginger. Dad loves ginger and drinks it with lemon, cloves, fresh thyme and hot water every morning. His father gave him the recipe for his arthritis and he's been drinking it for years now, even though Ma rubbishes it as 'an old cure and not worth a patch on modern medicine'.

Ma also has arthritis and now takes a roll call of medicines to cope with the effects of anti-inflammatories on her stomach lining.

'What's the row about this time?' I ask, sitting down on the old worn couch that my father sits on every night to watch his beloved documentaries or gardening shows on TV.

'Divorce,' says Dad. 'Dom told her he was definitely getting divorced and it hasn't gone down well. You'd think he was planning a satanic ritual in the back garden.'

We both giggle. In truth, I think the reason my father has survived so many years with my mother is because he has such a good sense of humour. It's either that or he's growing cannabis in the allotment.

'I've got an old black satin skirt we could repurpose for the altar,' I suggest. 'Doesn't fit me anymore. My hips have spread.'

'I could plant next year's bulbs into a pentagram shape,' Dad says.

We both giggle again.

'I did try to tell her that divorce was a good plan so they could start again with other people but she stormed out,' Dad goes on.

'That was brave of you,' I say, surprised. Dad is very mild mannered and rarely, if ever, goes up against my mother. He gets the full silent treatment for days when he does.

He looks guilty. 'She was going to Mass. Didn't want to be late.'

'Ah.'

My mother goes to daily Mass, is first in line for communion and disapproves of everything the Vatican says she should disapprove of, no matter how cruel.

Her motto in life is 'what will people/Fr Leonard think?'

It's a very hard motto for us flawed human beings to live up to.

'You have to get her to face facts, Marin,' Dad continues. 'With Dom living here, it's like being on the front line. He needs another place to hang around in his old T-shirts and boxers – which he was wearing when he opened the door to Gladys from choir, I might add. I'm too old to be living with this.'

I close my eyes briefly at my father's begging and wonder exactly how I'm going to manage this one.

I'm not sure when I became the family member who was chosen to handle my mother but, somewhere along the way, it happened.

April, despite being the eldest, was always too dizzy and lost in her romantic novels to be of much use. Dominic was a little wild child, everyone's favourite because he's so much fun if utterly unable to do things on his own. Dad is incapable of handling the immoveable force that is my mother. I have wondered many times how they got married in the first place and then remind myself that Ma would have said: 'Denis, church, twelve on Saturday, second one in June, next year. Yes?' And Dad would have nodded.

Which left me, second-born, to keep the peace in our lopsided family. Keeping up appearances has always been the beating heart of our family. We all had to be suitably dressed for morning Mass on Sunday, where my mother would hold her head high and search out those who had not managed this feat of family management.

Dom once naughtily told Ma that sitting in church didn't make her religious any more than sitting in the garage made him a car, but she batted that one right back at him and added a cuff round the ear for good measure. Pure steel, that woman is.

'I'm sleeping badly,' Dad points out, looking mournful.

I give him a stern look: 'That's emotional blackmail.'

'Ah go on, Marin, she listens to you.'

'She listens to you, too.'

'Yes but only for a short while and then she sulks with me. Dom doesn't notice the sulking: he's always been immune. I really can't sleep, you know. I wake up early. That's a sign of stress: I looked it up.'

'Fine. Fill me in, then. Why did Dom tell her he was getting a divorce? He was hell-bent on getting back with Sue last time I talked to him.'

'Sue's moved on. She went out for drinks with an old flame,'

Dad whispers, as if keeping the volume down will make the news easier to impart.

I was getting the picture, finally: my mother has looked down on Sue for years. But now that Sue was moving on, divorce was suddenly in the future and Fr Leonard, very much of the old school of Catholicism, would need CPR if he heard. No wonder there was screaming.

'OK. Let me at them.'

Dad reached under his couch and retrieved an open box of cheap chocolates. 'Have a few. Get your blood sugar up.'

'If she finds these, you're dead,' I say.

Ma prides herself on her figure and does not allow treats in the house.

His mouth full of toffee chocolate, Dad grins. 'I won't tell if you won't.'

The kitchen is uncharacteristically messy when I enter to find Dom, barefoot, wearing ratty sweatpants and a jumper, making coffee in an old Moka machine with the remains of a toasted sandwich on a plate.

The diametric opposite is my mother, who is wearing a neat tweedy-looking skirt to the knee, beige nylons, sedate heels and one of those pale pink twinsets you see in newspaper special offers. Her hair is sprayed into a helmet of frosted curls which dare not move. She is sitting on a kitchen chair, toe tapping, a china cup in front of her and is mid-diatribe.

'. . . You cannot make those vows and then abandon them. New jacket?' she says, catching sight of me and switching her attention from one child to another in a flash.

Ma's intonation is practically weaponised: nobody else can endow two words with such a negative meaning. My mother has been criticising my clothing for so long that this latest statement is like water off a duck's back.

'Work clothes,' I say cheerfully.

'I still think Hilliers should have a uniform,' she says,

reverting to a very old, oft-revisited topic. 'Something classy, a heather tweed, maybe with a plain blazer. Black makes you look old. But a uniform . . .'

She angles her head a little as if to imagine this dream, heather tweed outfit on me. 'Or maybe not. Tweed does add weight around the middle if one isn't careful.'

Fantasy Marin would tell my mother that people in glass houses shouldn't throw stones – my mother is at least two stone overweight – but Real World Marin knows better.

'We can't all have your figure, Ma,' I say, again cheerfully. Because when you deliver a whopper of a lie like this you have to throw in a bit of toadying.

'I know,' says Mum, smoothing down her tweedy skirt.

I often think the problem with my mother is that she has a very limited sense of self awareness. Her focus is always dedicated towards looking at other people's flaws, never her own. I feel sure there is a whole segment of psychoanalysis devoted to this but even when I read *Psychologies* mag, I still can't find the bit to help.

'Hi, Dom,' I say, going over and patting him briefly on the back. 'Is there enough in that Moka for another cup?'

'Yeah, sure,' he says, laid back as ever.

Up close, he has several five o'clock shadows and yet still looks recklessly handsome. All the girls loved Dom at school. But my mother clearly doesn't right now, hence the pained text from Dad begging me to drop in.

Dom has made an almighty mess of the kitchen constructing a toasted cheese sandwich and he stinks. I can see why my mother gets annoyed. But then, she smiled when Dom did this as a young man. Said it was his wife's job to tidy up after him – what does she expect?

Still, I have to make an effort for Dad.

The Moka splutters explosively on the stove top telling us that the coffee is ready. Dom stands watching it, which makes me aware that he's expecting me to take it off the stove and pour the coffees. I am a woman, hence I perform the domestic duties. Poor Dom: he's going to have to cop on.

I have no idea how Sue put up with him for so long. She's a lovely, clever woman – she must have really loved him.

I pour two coffees – I wouldn't dream of asking my mother if she wants one, because she's a tea person through and through – and add sugar into mine.

'Do you want to talk about what's upsetting you, Ma?' I ask gently, hoping to bring the heat in the kitchen down.

'Oh, only that my children have no respect for me or the Church.' She eyes the sugar-laden cup of coffee in my hand like it's an illegal substance. Ma is very anti-sugar. She gave it up one Lent and never went back. Now she views all people who take it in their tea or coffee as people who do not under-stand the value of sacrifice for one's religion. I much prefer to do things for Lent – help the homeless, that type of thing. Not Ma.

'Respect goes two ways, Ma,' says Dom loyally.

'Oh does it?' she snaps back. 'If you respected me, you wouldn't expect to live under my roof while getting a divorce. How will I ever hold my head up at Mass again? Have you any idea what Father Leonard will say? Imagine the way they'll look at me in the choir.'

'Choir? You all sing like ferrets being strangled.'

I have to hide a grin. He's being childish but, sadly, accurate.

'Dominic!' she shrieks in rage.

Ma is building up a head of steam here and I feel myself assuming the role I always used to as a child: fixer-in-chief. Children do when they're trying to cope with rage and anger.

I feel that familiar tension in my chest and my breathing turns shallow. I can remember the endless arguments at home, arguments out of nowhere that my mother started and Dom somehow ignored, that made April run to her bedroom, pick up another romance novel and escape into it. Dad ran to the allotment and I tried to calm it all.

No wonder we are all the way we are, I think. April in fantasy world hoping that her current married boyfriend will leave his wife; Dom with his head in the sand, ignoring the fact that he has screwed up his own marriage.

I go to the biscuit cupboard and find some very plain biscuits, which are what my mother thinks are suitable offerings in the confectionary department. The only time she bakes nice things are when she is baking for church socials or fetes.

'You're getting a divorce then, Dom?' I say quietly.

'Yep,' he says. 'Sue went out with that bastard Liam the other day. D'you remember him from school? He always said she was the hottest thing. Bastard. I can't believe she'd do that to me.'

'Do what to you?' I say.

'You know, go off with someone else.'

'But you moved out. The two of you have been fighting for about three years, so yeah, I guess she wants to move on.'

'Marin, how can you say such a thing,' growls my mother.

I'm reminded slightly of the satanic voice in *The Exorcist*. I finish my coffee and feel the caffeine and the sugar hit my system.

When home feels like a horror movie, it's time to leave. You never see that embroidered on cushions.

'Ma,' I say gently, 'you can't stop Dom and Sue getting divorced.'

'I can,' she says fiercely. 'I can and I will. I just need somebody to talk some sense into him,' she goes on. 'He got married in a church. Your cousin, Father Michael, came over from Canada to perform the ceremony.'

'Michael was here anyway to visit Auntie Silvie; he didn't fly over on purpose,' huffs Dom.

'That's not the point,' shrieks my mother, and the bell rings for round two.

I roll my eyes and leave them at it, go back into the hall and find Dad in his den.

'Sorry, I didn't help much.'

He reaches under the couch for his chocolates.

'It was lovely to see you, all the same,' he says, offering me another one. 'I'm going to pretend to be asleep if she comes in here.'

I'm almost at the front door when Dom appears.

'Sorry,' he mutters. 'You didn't need to get dragged into all of that.'

I hug him and he leans into me.

'I was thinking,' he begins. 'I need to get out of here and, well, the Sue situation . . . we need time to work it out. I've been investigating flats and I can rent from a pal who's going away but I'll need a deposit.' Dom grins. 'It's just I'm a bit strapped, what with paying my half of the mortgage on our house –'

Dom works in software development and while he could probably write code to make a high-tech fridge do the salsa across the kitchen floor, he's hopeless with money.

'Of course,' I say automatically. 'I'll sell my gold ingots . . .'

We both laugh.

'Seriously, let me check. I'm sure I can manage something. Take care, darling.'

'You're the best, Marin,' says Dom, and I feel so sorry for him. He is a lovely man – just caught in a strange man-child cycle.

I hug him again. 'Love you.'

'Love you, big sis,' he says, and I head off.

When finally I get home, having picked up Joey from the childminder's, Nate's already there and Rachel's left a note on the fridge saying she's got an evening shift in the pizza restaurant, which is her new job. I examine whether tonight's dinner has defrosted.

It has, so I high-speed it into the oven, get vegetables ready for the steamer and am ready to race upstairs to change when Nate wanders into the kitchen.

He's changed out of his suit, is now in jeans and a sweater, and is unruffled because he hasn't gone eight rounds with my mother and brother. He's on the phone, chatting happily: something about a football match and I feel a sudden intense blast of irritation.

I am home late, the oven isn't even turned on, and it would have taken nothing, *nothing*, for him to open the fridge and bung tonight's meatballs topped with mozzarella into the oven. But then, I have made myself indispensable to this family the way I did to my family of origin.

Marin will do it.

From purchasing food to cooking dinner, to laying the table and serving up the meal. Fix, fix, fix. There is nothing Nate has to do except arrive home, change and open wine if he feels like it. I'm the one who's always done the school runs in the morning and picked up the children from childminders: this means Nate has always been free to swim first thing with Steve and Finn.

He's fighting fit and I struggle to do an online Pilates class once a month.

He idly picks up an apple and bites into it. 'What's up?' he asks, seeing my face.

'Bad day,' I mutter, not wanting the fight, but then the irritation refuses to lie buried and squelches out of me, the way my belly does when I wear shaping knickers.

'You could have put dinner in the oven,' I say.

'You should have rung. I would have,' he says equably. 'I can lay the table for you,' he adds.

Lay the table *for me*? It's like, 'I can do the shopping *for you* if you're really stuck.'

It's for all of us. Not just me.

Me wants to lie in a bubble bath, read a novel and not have to look after everyone.

'Really bad day?' he asks, cocking his head to the side.

I have a sudden flashback to the household I have just left where anger ripples through the air.

Taking a deep breath, I say: 'Yes, but I'm OK. Please, do lay the table. Open wine, maybe?'

'That I can do,' says my husband with a charming grin. He kisses me on the cheek, goes to the cupboard in the utility room where he keeps his precious bottles.

Wine will help, I decide. I am lucky. I mustn't forget it.

But to really cheer myself up, I log on to my current favourite account: Vestiare, where delicious and designer things are sold second-hand, so I have a hope in hell of buying them. Vintage clothes porn has got to be the purest art form for the shopaholic, I think, as I begin to scroll. Just something small, perhaps.

Nobody has to know . . .

6

Bea

I'm sitting in morning traffic, edging forward as rain lashes the windscreen and thinking that I'll be at my desk at seven-fifty. According to the car radio traffic updates, there's a blockage up the road due to an oil spill and I wish, as I often do, that my job was on a direct public transport route instead of being inconveniently situated.

In summer, getting to the big medical and dental clinic, where I work as secretary to the medics, means a walk and two buses. In winter, it means either three buses or just two and Scott of the Antarctic outer garments.

I hate the cold, which is why I keep holding off on getting a dog, despite Luke's increasing begging for one.

'Muuum,' he begs. 'I'd look after it. He could sleep in my bed and I'd feed him and walk him and everything.'

His idea of the perfect dog is a Husky, which needs lots of walking, apparently.

Parental Skills Update 2.0 means I know that I will be walking, feeding and cleaning up the poop of said Husky, so we will not be getting one, no matter how beautiful they look. I cannot fit in ten kilometres a day in all weathers. I've been researching, though. Sadly, there doesn't appear to be any breed which doesn't require much walking and is happy to sit at home watching the telly while I'm at work.

Still, making sure Luke never loses out is something of a mission of mine. Maybe it is time for a dog.

In place of a father figure, get a fluffy thing to love?

It does take a village to rear a child and, in our case, that village is almost an all-female one. Alongside myself, Shazz and Christie – or the Single Momma's Club, as Shazz calls us – we have a pretty excellent support system going. My mum, Patricia, is one part of the village. Next up is Shazz's mum, Norma, whom Shazz calls Normal.

I should point out that, sometimes, Shazz calls me Bea-ch for a laugh. You've got to love her sense of humour, and we do spend a lot of time laughing in the Single Momma's Club. 'As long as we're not *Real Housewives of Beverly Hills*,' jokes Christie, which always makes us crack up.

As three women supporting our own kids, anything less like the Beverly Hills ladies would be impossible to imagine.

The final part of our support system is Christie's dad, Vincent. He adores the twins, Daisy and Lily. Christie's mother, on the other hand, has never even met her exquisite twin granddaughters.

'Why?' I couldn't help but ask, the second time we met up, Shazz and I pushing Raffie and Luke in their buggies in the park close to both our homes. Christie, small and with short blonde curls, had her two teeny, gorgeous babies sound asleep in a double buggy and we began, as mothers with small children do, to talk.

Feeding, sleeping, nappies, the great breast-feeding versus bottle-feeding debate: we ran through all the big stuff first, and eventually worked our way round to real life.

'She wanted me to have a happily married, two-point-five-children relationship and I haven't. She thinks there's something wrong with me because I don't fit the mould.'

'You not married, is that it?' asked Shazz, who likes to know all the facts straight up.

For Shazz, it's a point of principle not to let us happily marrieds into our gang.

'No,' said Christie.

'Partner or did he do a runner?' Shazz went on.

Shazz, brought up by a single parent herself, believes that all men leave one way or the other.

Christie gave us an assessing look. 'I'm on my own,' she said.

'Us too,' replied Shazz, happy to have found another member of the tribe. 'My bastard legged it, Bea's fella died. What about you?'

There was a beat.

'I'm lesbian,' Christie said finally. 'It was always going to be just me.'

'Their dad's a turkey baster,' said Shazz in delight. 'Least you don't have to worry about getting child support off it.'

She cackled to herself while I waited anxiously to see if Christie would take offence. People quite often did with Shazz and she'd outdone herself this time.

But no.

Christie grinned. 'I can see I'm going to have to educate you cis girls – that's straight to you. And no, I wouldn't have put it that way myself,' she said, 'no turkey baster involved. The girls were born with donor sperm.'

'I might as well be a bloody lesbian,' continued Shazz, ignoring any hint that she might not be the poster child for political correctness. Shazz doesn't care who someone sleeps with or whether they're gender fluid or celibate as long as they're what she calls 'good people' and enjoy a bit of fun. 'I mean, for all the action I've been getting, I could have turned gay and not even noticed. Not that I haven't tried but the men out there – they run at the sight of a new baby. Since Raffie was born, I'm practically a born-again virgin.'

One of Christie's babies, Daisy, yawned a tiny baby yawn and we all sighed.

Sex means different things to different people. Shattering orgasms, babies or simply the comfort of another human being's arms around you. Sex can but doesn't always mean friendship. Once myself, Shazz and Christie joined forces, we had a friendship force field around us that gave the most earth-shattering sex a run for its money.

We're family, an all-woman village raising four children. I'd do anything for Shazz and Christie, because they'd do anything for me.

Finally, there's a break in the traffic and I manage, with a sneaky five-hundred-metre trip down a bus lane, to get to work on time. I work in a suburban dental and medical clinic, where there are three dentists and five doctors and a multitude of patients coming in and out all the time. I work in the medical section and our desks are in a huge glassed-off area in reception. I spend a lot of time either on the phone or typing up doctors' letters, arranging blood tests, keeping all the doctor-patient communication running smoothly. It's a nice place to work, and I get on really well with the other women who work in the reception area. The other benefit is that I can work part time; I do mornings and share my particular load with another staff member called Antoinette. Up to one o'clock everything is mine; after one o'clock, it's hers. It might not be my true calling but it pays the bills. Ask any single mother and they'll tell you job security is worth its weight in gold, and, most brilliantly, it means I can always be there to pick up Luke from school. Plus, working in such a big practice, you don't necessarily get too close to the people who are coming in, in the same way as you would in a smaller surgery, which suits me just fine. Antoinette used to work for just one doctor and she says it was really difficult.

'You get to know people and you see everything and you see their pain, and I just couldn't do that anymore.'

'Sounds terrible,' I say. And I know I couldn't do it.

I know my mother thinks that Jean-Luc's death has made me hard: on the contrary, it's made me soft, I merely manage to hide it because I can't bear to go through anything like that again. So working here is perfect. I make appointments, type

66

up letters, I'm kind to the people who come in and out, smile at their children. But above all, I do not have to get personally involved with their pain.

The morning's busy and by one o'clock, I'm looking forward to belting out of here and racing home via the supermarket where I'll get some stuff for dinner. The last patient is a red-haired woman who beams as she pays and tells me how lovely Dr Lee is, and how he must be so nice to work for.

'He is,' I assure her as I pass over the credit card machine. In my pocket, I feel my mobile phone vibrate with a text message. When my patient is gone, there's nobody left in reception so I quickly check my phone.

And laugh out loud.

Shazz has sent me a WhatsApp with a selection of photos from her current favourite dating website, which is not quite Tinder but has certainly a hint of its cheeky, straight-to-the-point sexiness.

Yes? texts Shazz beside the picture of one man who obviously owns his own gym or else does not have a job, such is the beauty of his muscles, all on view as he is not wearing a shirt. He has definitely oiled himself up for the photo.

I call her. 'Is he interested in kite-surfing and a girlfriend who's easy-going and loves sexy clothes?' I ask.

'What's wrong with that?'

'I'm a medical secretary. I'm wearing sedate navy trousers, ballet pumps, a navy sweater and you think you can pimp me out to Mr Fun Lovin' Leather Trousers . . .?'

We both laugh.

'How do you know he's wearing leather trousers?' she asks.

'Intuition.' Just so I don't sound like Ms Never Having Fun Ever, I add: 'One day, if we can find me a clever, kind, wise man who happens to be handsome, then sure: I could date him but –'

'Idris Elba's taken,' sighs Shazz. 'There's no hope for you now.'

'Pity, that,' I agree.

I finish tidying up, ready to leave, when Laoise, one of my colleagues, sidles over to my desk looking as if she's about to faint. She's pale at the best of times but now looks so blanched, it's scary.

'Laoise? Are you all right?' I ask, leaping up and steering her to my seat.

'No,' she whispers. 'Bea, I went in to drop some letters to Dr Lee, and he was on the phone. I don't think he even noticed me. He can be very obtuse sometimes.'

I wait patiently for her to get to the point.

'But whoever he was talking to, it was about the practice. They're thinking of downsizing when Dr Ryan retires and breaking up the practice. Dr Lottie wants to work with a woman's menopause clinic, so she'd go too. Dr Lee was talking about some premises they need to look at. A smaller one. I stayed for as long as I could – he was facing the window, you know the way he does when he's on a call, so he honestly didn't notice me. They won't need so many staff, Bea – our jobs –'

I feel an instant clenching of my guts as both my frontal cortex and my intestinal brain do inner shrieks of horror. It's not called the gut-brain axis for nothing.

I also do a rapid mental scan of the staff of the clinic and think that if five doctors suddenly become three, then they have far too many medical secretaries to go around. And the ones who work part-time are certain to go first.

'Of course, we don't know for sure –'

Laoise's trying to talk herself out of the catastrophic thinking but I can't.

She's married, so she has the safety net of another person's salary. I don't.

It's utterly terrifying, one of those moments when the pluses of single motherhood get wiped away by the very precariousness of it all.

'We don't know for sure,' I repeat back to her, and I'm not sure which one of us I'm trying to convince.

68

7
Sid

Five days have elapsed since I met Finn in the coffee shop, and I still haven't rung, texted or WhatsApped him. His card isn't exactly burning a hole in my handbag, but it's simmering in there.

Vilma has texted me about it several times: Did you ring that guy yet?

Busy. Haven't got around to it. I text back breezily.

On the fifth day she rings. This time, no punches are pulled. 'Have you been talking to that sexy Finn bloke from the coffee shop yet?'

'No, I've been swamped at work,' I protest. 'You have no idea, Vilma: we're juggling so many projects.'

This sounds fabulous and I immediately wonder why I'm not a professional liar. I'd make a fortune. If only I could play poker, I'm sure I could combine the lying with the gambling and earn a fortune.

'I smell bullshit,' says Vilma. 'Ring him.'

OK, scratch that.

'Vilma, honey, the decision to ring him all happened after some wine, it was late at night,' I begin. 'Your generation can do that sort of thing, but mine? Not so much.'

'Millennials get such a tough time,' she says narkily, 'but your generation are the weird ones. What are you? X? Y? Baby boomer?'

'I'm not a baby boomer,' I say, shocked, 'they're ancient.'

'Oh sorry, I forgot, you're the "Nothing good is ever going to happen, so I'm going to just sit here in the dark" generation.'

I have to laugh. 'OK, sis. No, I haven't rung him because I made a decision not to. It was a crazy impulse in the first place. I don't know what came over me.' I'm on a roll with the lying again. 'Plus, I have friends; I don't need any more.'

'No, you don't,' she says, in the way only a sister can. '*I* have friends, loads of friends, while you could probably count your actual friends on one hand and still have a couple of fingers left over for typing.'

'I have loads of friends I work with,' I say, stung.

'What about friends *outside* work, friends from school, from college?'

'You're different to me, Vilma,' I grumble. 'You're good at holding on to people.'

I didn't hold on to people – I'd jettisoned them all. Being alone was the only way forward for me all those years ago.

'I thought you were brave and were going to have a new male friend to go for coffee or see a film with.'

I hesitate.

'Just coffee, then?' she says. And I can almost hear her smiling down the phone, like she's boxed me into a corner.

'You're very manipulative, Vilma,' I mutter, 'has anyone ever told you that?'

'Yes,' she says, and now I know she's smiling.

'One of us has to be manipulative. You're a bit clueless, to be honest, Sid, I don't know how you've survived this far.'

For a moment I almost can't breathe because sometimes I'm not entirely sure I *have* survived this far, but Vilma doesn't need to know that.

Existed: that's the word. Some days, I just exist. I don't try to have a good day – I just try to have a day full stop, where I get up, take care of my body, sit at my desk, drink my coffee shakily, and get into bed at night with relief, so glad it's all over.

'What do you suggest?' I say, wrenching myself out of this train of thought.

I've always wanted Vilma to be able to look up to me, to show her that you can have a wonderful, marvellous life and be strong. But I've faked it a lot of the time.

I didn't want to be a horrendous role model for the rest of her life, the cautionary tale. I didn't want to be her sad older sister who never did normal things, never fell in love or settled down.

Vilma thought I'd had a lovely, normal relationship with Marc but I could never explain it to her. Now that he's out of my life, she merely wants me to be happy – and apparently lots of friends is the secret to this.

'Just one coffee,' she wheedles.

'OK, one coffee.' I sigh. 'I'll text him now.'

'Good. Now when you meet people you don't really know, you've got to meet them somewhere really public, never night time, and in a busy area, OK?'

'No shit, Sherlock?' I reply laughing, the big sister letting herself be schooled by the baby of the family. If there's one person I can't say no to, it's Vilma.

I spend so long at my desk composing the text, that I probably could have written an entire report on the negative impact of soft-drink machines in schools in the time it takes me. In the end, I look at my masterpiece and sigh.

Hi, Finn, Sid here. No good films on. Will we meet for a coffee and talk about work?

I send it before I can stop myself. And then I think how lame is that: can we meet for coffee and talk about work? I've basically set us an agenda.

I can feel myself blushing. Me? A woman with biker boots blushing.

I turn my phone to silent and stuff it into my pocket. I don't want to see what he sends back; in fact, he probably won't send anything back because, under the circumstances, why would he? I have made him wait five days and nobody waits five days. Plus, he'll think I'm a nutcase because we discussed the concept of being friends and friends don't say, *Let's talk about work*.

Unless they have no life at all, which makes sense. I have no life at all.

'Are you OK, Sid?' I look up; it's Chloe, innocent intern. She's wearing false eyelashes and I have to admit they look amazing. She's no longer wearing her *I'm intelligent* glasses though: the lashes would probably keep banging into the lenses. I read that somewhere; the two don't go together terribly well.

'Just running through some work problems in my head,' I say with false calm.

In case she asks, I make up a work problem on the spot. I am good at lying, definitely.

Is there an Olympics for that? I was never sporty and it seems that all my skills – being quirky as hell, having weird hair, dressing all in black – are not ones with Olympian categories. But Chloe just nods and floats away, leaving me to ponder my non-existent problems.

The rest of the afternoon passes and I refuse to look at my phone. If the apartment is burgled, the alarm company have my work number as well as my home number. If something happens with Mum, Vilma or Stefan, they all have my work number too. So people can get me.

I stay in the office until six and I'm one of the stragglers, the last to leave.

'Night,' says Eddie, going off with his rucksack. Eddie is a cyclist and makes a round trip of twenty miles every day to get into the office. I have no idea how he hasn't been squashed before now, because I certainly wouldn't cycle along Dublin's roads, but the exercise looks good on Eddie. He is certainly a lean, mean fighting machine.

'See you, Eddie,' I say, 'careful of those trucks.'

'Yes, sir,' he says, saluting me.

Finally, I'm at the door of the office. There's nobody else there except me and the cleaners who are beginning to arrive. I greet them, chat to everyone, particularly Imelda, who's one of my favourites. Imelda has a large and noisy family and it only takes the slightest encouragement for her to start discussing them. Three of her nephews are now in a band.

'I told them they might as well stand at traffic lights washing car windscreens for money because they'll make more cash that way,' she cackles.

I'm comfortable with Imelda, because she's a woman. And I'm comfortable with women. Which is probably why it was days before I texted Finn, and yet I was comfortable with him – so maybe I can be comfortable with some men?

Over the years, I've honed my skills at men-reading. I used to be over-cautious, I have to be honest. But now, I get on well with all the men in the office, have nice chats with the barman in The Fiddler's Elbow on Fridays, say hello to motorbike couriers who arrive, sweating in the office. But I still wouldn't get into a lift with a man, any man. Even if I've known him for years. Politeness has cost many women too much. How often do women feel uneasy at getting into a lift alone with a man, yet do so all the same because not to would be rude?

In my world, be rude. Be as rude as you bloody like. I'm taking the stairs, mate.

'See ya, Imelda,' I say, as I head down in the blissfully empty lift. I pull my phone out of my pocket and look at it and there, top of the list, is a text from Finn.

Hey, Sid, would love to have a coffee. When are you thinking? This evening is good for me or tomorrow lunchtime?

Lunch was pushing it: in fact, lunch was outrageous, ripe with the sense of a date. Coffee was different. I stared at myself in the lift mirror. I looked OK. My hair did look messy, but then it often does as I run my fingers through it a lot and it's not had a cut for ages. I haven't seen my lovely old ladies in the salon for yonks. They're pistols, those women. Seen it all, done it all and can still laugh. I hope I'm like that when I'm older.

I start a text to Finn and by the time I'm in the building's reception, before I have a chance to really think about it, I press send.

Just finished work, been busy, yeah coffee, I can do a quick one, half six, seven, just for half an hour?

As soon as it's gone, I cringe. But it seems the cringe factor is one-sided. His reply is instantaneous.

I'd love that, how about that little place on Nassau Street. Vanilla?

I know the one, sure.

See you there in twenty-five minutes?

Great. I stuff my phone back in my pocket and think: *What have I done?*

Everyone outside is windswept. I pull into a shop, find a mirror and decide that at least my eye make-up has stayed on pretty well since half seven this morning. I like a goth eye: habitual ultra-black liner, helped with espresso brown shadow and a hint of silver that brings out the silver in my eyes.

Vilma says she thinks I like this because it makes me look tough, which is actually entirely accurate. I want my eye make-up to say what I could never say: watch out.

Anyone who thinks make-up is all about sexual allure will never understand that for some of us, it's our warpaint. Like tribal markings when the world's first peoples marked their faces for battle. My eye liner is just the same.

Beware: that's what I hope it says.

Vilma thinks I'm just one pair of leather trousers away from going to a heavy metal concert but says I'd look 'cute' in them.

'I am not cute,' I always say in retort. 'It's just I'm short and you're tall, that's all.'

Little is not all it's cracked up to be, I'd like to add. It makes people think you're soft. Hence the all black clothing and the goth eye make-up.

I was soft once, yes. Not anymore.

I scan the rest of me. I'm wearing my normal work uniform of black shirt, black cardigan, of which I have loads in varying shades of greyness, and black jeans. Add to that my equally exciting black runners and black waterproof puffa jacket and I look like I'm hiring for a job as a band roadie.

My hair adds to the look: chaotic and a bit tough, I hope. Rain never bothers it, so I duck back out into the rain and driving wind, nearly at my destination. I have never been in this coffee shop and it's up a laneway off Nassau Street. Presumably the sort of place college lecturers go at lunchtime to mutter about college politics.

When I get there, I see it's a nice mixed crowd of people of all ages and colours. Finn is at the counter having an animated discussion with a tall woman with dreadlocks.

'Sid,' he says, and he smiles, a smile that really lights up his face, and I feel the weirdest quiver inside me, which is scary. I'm not sure where these feelings are coming from or what they are, but they're not bad. There are no internal warning bells over Finn. Instead, I feel . . . warm.

Firmly pushing down any non-friend feelings, I say, 'Hi, Finn,' and give him a manly punch on the arm which comes out stronger than I mean it to.

'Ow, what was that for?'

'Friendly greeting,' I say.

75

He introduces me to the girl behind the counter. We chat for a moment and she tells me the best coffee of the day is a lovely Colombian roast.

'That's what you always say, Asha,' laughs Finn, and I look at him, eyes narrowed. Is he flirting with her? He's older. She's what – twenty-three, twenty-four? I stare at him, waiting to see something that backs up my suspicion, but he seems genuine. The familiar nervous quiver is somewhere inside me but it's not emerging. Something is holding it back. My hands aren't shaking at all.

'Yeah, professor,' says Asha loudly, 'I say that because it sells well and I get more tips, trying to put myself through college here.'

'Fair enough,' he says, grinning back. 'Just checking you weren't being made to push the Colombian or I'll have to have words with Phil. Phil owns this place,' Finn says to me as an aside. 'I have to keep him on his toes about treating my students with respect.'

He and Asha fist bump.

'Are you really a professor?' I say as we take a seat up against a wall, where all the tables are crammed incredibly close together.

'Yes,' he says. 'I am really a professor. I even have the round-rimmed glasses for work. Joke.'

'Wow,' I say.

He hasn't added any sugar to his coffee. No sweet tooth, then. I'd really like one of the pastries they have on the counter, but I feel a bit shy about getting food. Shy but not tensed up. That's something. Maybe I can do this once and never do it again. Block his number, something like that. *Get a grip, Sid. Just think of him as a work colleague.*

'Are you hungry?' he says. 'You have that hungry look about you.'

'I was working through lunch, though I had a bit of a sandwich,' I say.

'What do you want?' He gets up quickly. 'I'll get us something sweet, savoury? I know you have only half an hour, but let me feed you.'

'I'll have one of those Portuguese tarts,' I say.

'Nice choice, I'll have one too.'

He's back in a moment and we start biting into the tarts.

The glory of the creamy lemony filling lets my lungs expand and warm feelings flood me.

'That's lovely,' I say. 'Sometimes sweet things are the answer.'

'I agree,' he says.

'I thought you cyclists were very careful about what you ate?'

'We are, but that doesn't mean we can't have something nice now and then. Go on, tell me about your day; you wanted to talk work.'

'Well, what else are we going to talk about? We don't know each other.'

'We could discuss our childhoods.'

'New friends don't normally get on to their childhoods until at least the third or fourth meeting. So let's go with work OK? Pretend we are colleagues.'

I blink at him, hoping that didn't sound as mad out loud as it does in my head. I'm not normally like this. I'm a professional, can have professional conversations, but, right now, I feel a little unhinged.

'OK. So, tell me about your work, maybe?' Finn leans in, nodding in encouragement.

I sit a bit more comfortably into my chair now we're on solid ground and I start. He does that lovely thing of listening, of not interrupting every five moments, which was what Marc did, but then, that was different.

'And the people?' he prompts, when I've finished telling him about my new project.

'The people are great. Adrienne is our boss and she's fearless.

I really admire that about her.' I pause, tart gone, halfway down my coffee. 'She's genuinely afraid of nobody.'

I realise suddenly that I've let all my protective barriers down and I can feel the stinging in my eyes signalling that without immediate intervention, my eyes are going to fill with tears.

Startlingly, I get the sense that he has picked up on this too.

'That must be cold,' he says in kind tones, looking into my cup. 'I'll get us more.'

He's back in a minute but it's enough time for me to have recovered, to have dabbed at my eyes and bitten the inside of my mouth, which is a painful but effective 'come back to the here and now' technique they don't teach in cognitive behavioural therapy.

He sits down and says lightly: 'Now, my work. Can't have you hogging the limelight. You need to know what you're getting yourself into. My oldest friends don't ask me about work anymore because they say I get carried away . . .'

I am suddenly annoyed on his behalf. 'Talk,' I command. 'I want to know it all.'

We sit there another half an hour, having gone through his work and then moved on to his family – he's the eldest, has two sisters and five nieces and nephews, both parents living. And then he wants to know about mine.

'My little sister is a lot younger,' I say. 'Vilma, you met her. I was fifteen when she was born.'

'Really? It must have been like being an only child. Was that lonely?'

'No,' I add thoughtfully. If this had been a date I would have stopped there, wary of sharing too much, but since we were doing the friend thing there was no need. It's very freeing, this friend-without-benefits thing. There are no expectations.

'My mum's a bit unusual. When I was younger –' I pause.

'Do not laugh or snigger when I say this,' I warn, 'but our house was a sort of commune for a while.'

Finn's mouth forms a lovely O.

'And you a professor of history and everything,' I said. 'I thought you'd know about communes.'

'I do know about communes, I've just never met anyone who was brought up in one.'

'There is always the odd commune around if there are a couple of hippies. "When two hippies are joined together, there will always be some magical place with weed, a smelly blanket and anecdotes about how life was good when you could drive a VW combi van around Morocco and live the free life." I don't know the rest of the saying,' I said. 'But basically, how it works is that you get a few people who are completely broke and one of them has a house but no money, so they live together and cook horrible things with lentils. My entire childhood was spent farting.'

Finn laughs. 'You do paint with words.'

'Thank you,' I say awkwardly, pleased.

'We also made a lot of jam because we had gooseberry and blackberry bushes in the garden. You have no idea how good I am at making jam.'

He laughs again and we are off, joking, chatting. It's funny and easy. In a way it's like talking to Vilma and her friends: light, interesting, with no side. He's not looking for anything from me except someone to have an enjoyable cup of coffee with.

'Why are you finished with dating?' I ask, and add at speed, 'As a friend. And nothing else. This is not me asking for romantic purposes, OK?'

He nods. 'Message received. I was in a long-term relationship for a few years and we – this is going to sound so clichéd – we began to feel like brother and sister eventually.'

My turn to nod. I understand that one far better than he could know.

'We met just a few years after college and we sort of grew up together, you know the way you're still in your twenties and life's still a big adventure with no plans. Then, somewhere along the way, it stopped working.'

He looks down into his coffee cup now and I'm pretty sure he's not lying. But then, how to be sure?

'Did she feel the same way?'

'She ended it.'

'What's her name?'

'Mags.'

'Are you still friends?' I'm interested because I've only seen Marc once since, and even then it was by accident. When he left, he disappeared.

'No.' He shrugs. 'We tried, honestly tried, but we couldn't go back to that way. We'd messed with the dynamic. I don't think you can date for that long and go back to being friends. Well,' he amends, 'you would if you had children, but not us. Hey, the human race is weird, right? What about you?'

'I was with a guy called Marc for a long time. It ended a year ago.'

Suddenly, I feel anxious. I've talked enough about me. I can't talk about Marc. It's too revealing.

I take a glance at my phone and realise that over an hour has gone by.

'I'm going to be late.'

Which is an absolute lie because I'm only going to be late to my own couch, which never complains either way.

He nods and says, 'Sorry, didn't mean to keep you so long.' He stands as I do and even though he's tall, I don't feel any fear. There is nothing, absolutely nothing predatory about Finn.

'Yeah, this was fun, we can do it again.' I'm surprised by the words as they leave me, and that I mean them.

'We can go on a hike,' he says, 'there isn't anything on in the cinema, it's all useless at the moment.'

'A hike?' I say.

'A hike,' he repeats, grinning. 'I hike with a load of people at the weekend; it's fun, you'd like it.'

'How do you know I'd like it? People are always telling me I'm going to like something. Like skateboarding when I was fourteen. Hated it. Fell off and wrecked my elbow. What's that about, insisting that people are going to like the things you like?'

'Don't know, I'll talk to someone in the psychology department tomorrow. Bound to be a syndrome,' he says, straight-faced. 'But I thought you might like being up the mountains, all the space, feeling the wind in your face.'

'I have had the wind in my face all evening,' I say. 'Do you know what it was like getting here? Twenty-five minutes of rain and wind.'

'No, seriously, Sid, it makes you feel free.'

I look at him for a beat and his face is animated.

'I reckon you'll enjoy it, and two hours up the mountains will show you if you do or not. If you don't, you never have to do it again. And I will then do something that you really want to do like –' his eyes glint – 'rollerblading?'

'Why would I want to go rollerblading? Because I'm a girl?' I sniff. 'I was actually very good at rollerblading when I was younger. I could go backwards and everything. Never knew why I wasn't good on the skateboard.'

'I just fell off the blades,' he says, 'I think I was too tall, the centre-of-gravity issue meant it didn't work. My sisters made me go out with them and they loved watching me fall. But seriously, a hike?'

'How do I know you are not going to bring me up the mountains, attack me with an industrial stapler, kill me and bury the body?'

'There is that,' he agrees. 'But I've got away with it so often before . . .'

His wicked grin is actually lovely. He has a dimple in one cheek.

'Of course, you could tell someone where you are going. Give that younger sister of yours access to your phone's location so she knows where you are at all times.'

Sounds fair. 'When will we do this hiking thing?'

'Saturday? It's supposed to be a beautiful day. I was thinking of going up myself, but everyone who hikes with me is busy. The lure of Christmas happening in the distance is hauling people away from the outdoors and into shopping centres. But I just have to get out: it clears my head, has this meditative quality that I love.'

'OK,' I say, 'if you promise not to attack and kill me, then bury me up the mountains – in which case, I will haunt you forever.'

'Understood. First, you have proper boots, right? Bring a rucksack, water, something to eat and warm clothing.'

'I thought we were going up the mountains for a bit, not to the Antarctic for a week.'

'It's pretty cold up there this time of the year; beautiful, but cold, and it will be sunny, so maybe a bit of sun block.'

'Sun block *and* hiking gear.'

'You're going to love it. I'll send you the details. And if you are going to duck out at the last minute or if it's raining or if there's a gale force blowing, tell me, I'll be going up there anyway.'

'OK, thank you.' I reach into my bag for my wallet and he says, 'Oh, I paid.'

'You are not supposed to pay, we are supposed to be going Dutch on all this stuff, friends do the equal-paying thing.'

'Well, after we have hiked, if we have coffee and buns or whatever, then you can pay, right?'

'Deal.'

'Deal.'

I don't punch him on the shoulder when I go. But I grin at him.

'I'd better enjoy this hiking or our friendship is over. I'm going to have to buy hiking boots; this is a big investment.'

He stares at me thoughtfully for a moment and I have absolutely no idea what he is thinking. His face is so still but his eyes are searching mine.

'A totally worthwhile one,' he says.

As I walk off into the wind and the rain, I'm smiling.

8

Marin

It's a glorious Friday night. No one is coming over at the weekend, there's nothing that needs doing, and I'm feeling the joy of knowing I have got my Christmas shopping in the bag nice and early. Or in the basket, as the case may be. Because I never have time to hit the shops (well, sometimes . . .). I have done most of my Christmas shopping online now before all the good stuff gets snapped up. I have long ago given up the idea of trying to get the perfect present for everyone, because there isn't a perfect present for everyone. Darling April is always happy with beautiful romantic perfumes. And body lotions from Victoria's Secret thrill her to bits. Everything from Victoria's Secret thrills her to bits, even though I feel she's probably older than the target market. But she loves it in there. All those floors of frilly things destined to make the man in her life fall in love with her all over again. Mum is impossible to shop for, always has been, always will be. I get Dad sweets and a jigsaw and a wonderful book about wildlife, same thing every year and he's happy. Over the years I have got him all sorts of things for the allotment. But he now has enough trowels and string and gardeners' hand cream to last him several lifetimes. Dom is getting help with his deposit, which I know he'll appreciate more than any present. Nate is super tricky to buy for, because he's so particular about his clothes. However, I refuse to give him gift vouchers. Instead, every year, I buy him one elegant polo shirt from an expensive brand and he seems pleased. Buying for Rachel and Joey is a total joy, because they both do a list for me about two months before Christmas. It's one of our family traditions. Sort of like a treasure hunt of lovely things, lots of little gifts and one bigger present.

Anyway, the shopping is pretty much done, though it's anyone's guess what I'll be given come Christmas Day.

'Mum, I've done all my homework,' says Joey hopefully, peering into the kitchen. 'Can I have a go on the Xbox now?'

'*All* the homework, honey?' I say, because Joey has been known to fib a smidge when it comes to his weekend homework. Our plan is to get it done on Friday evening and then he's free for the weekend.

'Wait till you're going to secondary school,' Rachel likes to tease him sometimes, 'then you'll be doing homework all weekend.'

'I won't, Mum, will I?' says Joey, horrified.

'Oh it's not that bad,' I always say, giving Rachel the side eye. 'And the older you get, the more homework you're capable of doing,' I add, which is also fibbing.

'Will I check your homework journal and tick everything off, sign it?' I say now.

'Yeah, sure.'

Once the homework notebook has been checked – I see there's a note in there that it's a school photograph day on Monday, and that all the uniforms had better be clean, shiny and the correct colour – I sign the notebook. I give Joey a hug and he belts off to his beloved Xbox.

'You do know that the next generation of children are going to have bizarrely enlarged thumbs from playing games,' says Rachel, who has wandered into the kitchen, holding the takeaway menu.

Sometimes we do takeaways on Fridays and I love it, because it means I don't have to cook. Sheer bliss.

'You are pretty good with the old thumbs yourself,' I say, grinning at her. 'What have you decided? I need to phone the order in now. Dad said he wanted Kung-Po chicken.'

'Oh I don't know, I was thinking more Thai.'

'Ah, honey, it's Chinese this week; we agreed.'

'I don't know if I want Chinese,' she says. 'Megan and I have been discussing how we have to try lots of different foods to acclimatise ourselves for when we go around the world. And we're going to spend a lot of time in Thailand. So I just need to be more into the culture and the food.'

'When you're in Thailand, you can eat Thai food, but tonight we are getting Chinese. Dad's picking it up on his way home, he's not going to two places.'

'Don't see why not,' she grumbles.

Eventually she agrees, chooses a dish and wanders off moodily. I wonder when the difficult teenage years end, because she's eighteen now, nearly nineteen, and there's no end in sight.

Louise, Megan's mother, and I have recently discussed exactly how moody and difficult to live with Rachel and Megan are lately, and we – their mothers – worry about letting two such innocents off on a gap year without us in the background picking up the pieces

'It might help,' Louise's husband, Dave, had said with a hint of bravado, 'show them a bit of the real world. I mean, we do everything for them.'

'That's true,' Nate had agreed.

Louise and I had stared at them both.

'I never did a gap year and I figured out the real world,' I'd said.

This gap year makes me feel sick. Two innocents abroad – it feels like a recipe for disaster.

'It was different when we were teenagers, though,' Dave had said manfully.

'Totally,' Nate had replied. 'It was either get a proper pensionable job or else get a part-time job so you could pay to go to college.'

'Yeah,' Dave had continued, 'no messing in those days.'

'But we don't want to raise our kids like that,' I'd said, 'we want to give them something different.'

'Every generation says that, Marin,' Nate had pointed out. 'You're too soft, that's what you are. They'll cope.'

I remember being really annoyed with him for implying that being soft was somehow a failing, because I'd always tried to be a very different mother to my own mother and nobody could ever call my mother soft. Certainly not my poor father.

I order dinner then go into the sitting room and sit down with a small glass of white wine. I have the room to myself, the TV to myself, and nothing needs to be done in the kitchen. There'd be no washing-up, no cooking, no sweating over the stove: absolute joy. All I have to do is wash up the containers, put the ones that can be recycled into the right bin, easy.

Nate's in a fabulous mood when he gets in.

'Dinner,' he cries, even before he's shut the door behind him. The scent of various meals drifts in with him. I think of Rachel wanting to learn about the culture of the places she'll be visiting, and how much I wish I could go with her. I'd never travelled the way Rachel was going to. I'd gone to college and met Nate and we had married young. I hadn't needed to leave for work like so many other people. And I'd never considered a gap year. But wouldn't it be lovely to take off around the world and see such different places?

Nate and I share the bottle of wine over dinner, me finally letting my shoulders relax, safe in the knowledge no major clear-up job awaits me. Then we find something the whole family can watch, which is almost impossible and, even if it is something a bit action-heroeish for Joey, nobody minds.

'I watch all your soppy girl things,' says Joey, half waiting for Rachel to say, 'Ah do we have to watch this?'

'I know, little bro,' she says, 'you're a really good brother. I'm going to miss you when I'm away.'

'Really?'

'Yeah. You should send me emails, it will help you with your writing. And it will tell you if you spell things wrongly.'

'My spelling is brilliant.' Joey grins.

'Absolutely brilliant, kiddo,' says Nate, ruffling Joey's hair.

'I'll send you all long emails,' Rachel goes on. 'Maybe we can get to China too.'

'I didn't think that was on your itinerary,' I say, but she just rolls her eyes at me.

When both Rachel and Joey have gone to bed, Nate takes me to task about my worries.

'Marin, you need to relax about Rachel's trip,' says Nate to me quietly, firing up my irritation sensors. 'They'll figure it out.'

'I know, but I worry about them figuring it out,' I snap, trying to keep my voice down.

'It will help them grow up a bit,' he says idly and I feel the involuntary shudder that goes through me every time I think about Rachel and Megan on their own going off around the world.

All the things that could go wrong: but Nate seems so calm about it. They'll be fine, end of story.

'But think about the dangers out there, two girls on their own?' I say, annoyed. It's like he doesn't see the gravity of this, like he wants to dismiss it.

I get up and march into the kitchen. He follows me.

'Relax, Marin,' Nate repeats, more angrily this time. 'You've got to let go. You worry over nothing. It drives me mad.'

He reaches for the bottle of wine we opened earlier and pours himself another glass. Not for me, just for him.

Of all the annoying things Nate does, this 'relax, you worry too much' thing is the one that makes my blood boil. And now he's having more wine and hasn't asked if I want some! I want to hit him, hard, and tell him I will worry if I bloody want to, and that if he thinks two teenage girls going off on a gap year is risk-free, then he needs his head examined.

But he's ignoring me now, sitting down at the kitchen table, scrolling through his phone because he's bored with the conversation.

Tiredness hits me in a wave and I snap that I'm going to bed.

I often go to bed before Nate, even though he's up earlier than me, off to do his swimming and his running. He has amazing stamina. But tonight he follows me upstairs, having speedily turned out all the lights and locked the doors. On the stairs I can feel him briefly touch the back of my thighs.

'So?' he whispers. He's tall, so he's already close to my ear, even if he's that far behind me. 'What do you think? End of a long week, a man deserves something . . .'

He has got to be kidding.

And then I stop myself.

Am I turning into my mother? Irritated with my husband at every moment? Look how well that turned out.

So, Nate thinks differently from me about the trip – he doesn't understand the danger out there for girls but I'll make damn sure they both understand it before they get on any plane.

I take a deep breath. I turn around and face him and he grabs me and presses me tight against him and I can feel his erection.

'This is what a man needs,' he says.

It is of course exactly at this moment that Rachel sticks her head out of her bedroom door and goes, 'Ewwee,' at the sight of us and slams the door shut.

'You think we have put her off sex for life?' I say, everything else forgotten.

'Hopefully,' says Nate, unconcerned as he leans in to kiss me.

It's one of the wonderful things about our marriage, how well we fit together sexually, as if just when Nate is ready to explode with wanting, he manages to turn me on so I'm ready too. Equally, when I'm premenstrual and miserable, Nate's always been amazing. Gets a hot water bottle for my belly, tells me to get more rest. It's nice.

He might be useless in the kitchen and thinks I worry too much, but he's amazing at this.

9
Bea

It's Christie's birthday and we decide that a party night out
is vital, even if we're all saving for presents for the kids for
Christmas. We'll combine it with our annual December party
– the Single Mommas' Christmas party. There has been no
news on the jobs front – Laoise at work says she has heard
nothing else about the practice moving and I am praying that
it's just a case of misunderstanding. I cannot let myself worry
about it or I will go mad. I need that job: with that, my widow's
pension and Jean-Luc's insurance settlement, we can manage
– but only just.

'We'll just keep it low key and cheap,' says Shazz, who is
brilliant with money.

All our children go to the same school and each class has
a mothers' party a month before Christmas, an event lovingly
detailed in the class WhatsApp we're all in.

I find the WhatsApp useful but Shazz, who feels that single
mothers are treated differently from the smug marrieds, hates
it.

We've all been to the ordinary mums' party but, for various
reasons, we didn't feel like part of the gang.

'They all sat and bitched about their husbands,' said Shazz,
during the post-mortem of the last one we went to. 'It's like
they haven't even considered that us three don't have a significant other and that it might make us feel a bit left out.'

So, this year, we're having our own night out.

'I think we need a gang name,' says Shazz, as we sit in the
taxi on our way into town for our big night out.

'A gang name,' says Christie, sitting in the middle because she's got the shortest legs. 'Like The Feministas?'

'Not sure,' says Shazz. 'I was thinking something along the lines of the New Normals, something like that.'

'Really?' says Christie.

'Yeah, because we are not like the normals, the women with husbands and partners and fathers for their kids and everything.'

'You've got Zep now,' I point out, wriggling my feet in my high-heeled sandals. I'm already regretting wearing them.

'If we call ourselves the New Normals, then they'll think they are the Abnormals,' says Christie, giggling.

'Yes!' says Shazz delightedly. 'That's it, we're the new normals and they are abnormals. What do you think?' she roars to the taxi driver in front. He's a nice man who appears to be keeping his head down, because all wise taxi drivers know it's more sensible to keep their mouths shut when they've got a cab full of excitable women in it, going out on the town.

'Whatever you say, love,' he says.

'Right answer,' crows Shazz.

First, we're going to get something to eat. Christie was in charge of picking the restaurant, because she has a friend who recently returned to Dublin to open a wildly successful new restaurant off Dawson Street. Usually, it's jam-packed, but thanks to Christie's pal, we're getting a special table in the best location.

'They do cocktails, right?' Shazz asks.

'Lots of cocktails,' says Christie.

'And then we're going clubbing?'

'You know the jury's out on the clubbing,' I say now, 'besides, I'm wearing these stupid shoes.'

'Take them off. I told you they were too high.'

'They're my good high shoes. I don't have loads of pairs of shoes.'

'You could have had my platform ones,' Shazz goes on, 'they

fit you. I know they are a bit dated and everything, but still, you could carry them off, for an old chick,' she adds, naughtily.

'Did you have a cocktail before the taxi?' I ask suspiciously.

'Yeah, Zep mixed me up something Caribbean and it's lighting my fire.'

'Which one of us will be doing the fireman's lift tonight?' I ask Christie, who laughs.

Eventually, we're decanted in front of the restaurant, all dressed up in our birds-of-paradise finery. Shazz's long, artfully curled hair is a lovely combination of blonde with purple tips, mine – rippling brunette – has been blow-dried straight down my back and Christie's got a mop of tousled platinum curls that looks as though she has just come off some Australian beach after doing a bit of surfing.

'We certainly hit all the demographics,' says Shazz looking around. 'I mean, look, we got everything, we've got wild pink, we've got sexy brunette, we've got a platinum modern blonde: there's nobody we can't hook up with.'

'I'm not looking for a man,' I say.

'Me neither,' says Christie. 'I'm woman centric. I'm happy, thank you very much. Plus, you've got Zep.'

'I know,' sighs Shazz happily. 'I'll flirt a bit, that's all. But you should score, Bea.'

Christie and I exchange glances.

'Score? Like round the back of the bike shed? I thought I was going to find hot love on whatever website you've put the tissue of lies on,' I say.

'Bird seed,' she says. 'I didn't tell you but I made it go live before we came out.'

My mouth falls opens. It's live! The stuff about French-speaking, saxophone-playing, who-knows-what-else me . . .

If I was religious, I would say a prayer right now. God, please let someone normal be on the site and like the look of my pic. Then I realise what I've said. Do I want to go on a date?

I feel almost dizzy as we're brought to our tables and I'm not sure if it's the heels or the notion that I'm actually thinking of going on a date. With a man!

Christie's friend has done us proud. Our table is a fabulous spot where we can see all over the restaurant, which is very glamorous and very noisy. Clearly the Christmas spirit is already here even though it's only November, but then, many office parties start early because some companies are far too busy to have December parties. There is mistletoe in tiny silver vases all over the place and Shazz grabs the sprig from our table.

'Now,' she said, 'I'm going to break this up into three bits and when any of us go to the loo, we can bring a bit, and if we see anyone we like, we have to dangle it over their heads.'

'*You* can do that,' I say.

'Spoil sport.'

Despite the noise, we all hear the loud ping of Shazz's phone.

Animal Lover 49 is on the screen.

We lean in as one to examine my first 'I'm interested' single man.

'Photoshopped,' says Christie, staring critically at a very professional photo of a man with greying hair and a big smile.

Shazz shakes her head. ' "Animal Lover". Does this mean he keeps ferrets and bets too much on the dogs?'

Laughing, we decide that he is not for me.

Soon we are deep into starters, finishing a bottle of wine, laughing and joking, discussing our beautiful children and wondering why there's always one Queen Bee who likes to run everything.

'I blame WhatsApp,' says Shazz. 'For some people WhatsApp is like a board room and they can bully everyone on it. No matter what you say back it sounds wrong. So you have to say, "wonderful idea", even if you think it's stupid.'

'Yeah,' I say, 'I hate that thing. When's their Christmas party?'

'Oh, they're having it in January, because they are all too busy with social events.'

I start to laugh. 'We're busy with our wildly exciting social lives too,' I joke.

By the second bottle of wine, I am absolutely convinced that I am not going to any night club under any circumstances. I'm exhausted. My feet hurt and I just want to be at home in my own bed going to sleep.

We have looked at Hot Maaan – 'can't spell,' we all agree; Older But Ready – 'ready for what?' and Hunk of the Year 1968, who gets points for humour but not much else.

'He mentions wine twice,' says Christie. 'Definitely a heavy drinker. Definitely a no.'

'I'm tired, girls,' I say, yawning.

'You can't bail now,' says Shazz, who has had more than her share of the wine. 'This is supposed to be our fun girls' night out.'

'I know, honey,' I say sadly, 'I just don't have the energy, I'm sorry. I'm older, OK, let's have that as the excuse; I'm older, I need to be sitting in front of the box watching reruns of silly films and reading magazines about how to knit sweaters with complicated cable patterns.'

'What's a cable pattern?' asks Shazz.

Christie laughs. 'My mum used to knit too,' she says. And then she pauses, because mentioning her mum always makes her sad.

'Stupid cow,' says Shazz, sounding really drunk now. 'Least you've got your dad.'

We both agree that Christie's mother must have something wrong with her if she's disowned Christie, Daisy and Lily just because Christie's gay.

'Karma's a bitch and it will come and bite her on the ass, because she doesn't realise how precious your girls are,' Shazz goes on. 'None of us had it easy but we are doing this amazing job, we are bringing up four beautiful kids and that means so much. I think maybe that's why the normals or the abnormals get anxious around us, because we can do it. It's not that they think we are going to steal their husbands. It's because we do it all, we're Mum and Dad and every bloody thing. And your mum just hasn't a clue, if she doesn't understand why you love who you love. We have our kids – that's all that matters.'

'Yeah,' says Christie. And suddenly we are taking out our phones and looking at pictures of our children.

All the liquids are making themselves felt, so I head off to the loo and am halfway down the stairs when I hear Shazz squealing with delight. Is this okay. She can't see Shazz only hear her.

Another stud for me, I think, grinning, wondering if any normal man is ever going to appear on the site.

There's no queue for the loo, so I'm speedy and on my way back to our fabulous table when I feel a gentle tap on my arm.

I turn to face a tallish, smiling man with fair hair and an engaging smile who is wearing a beautifully cut suit. Handsome, definitely.

Christie's friend, I think. Not long back from Hong Kong, he's now part-owner of the bistro and is working the room.

'You must be Bea,' he says and I realise he's English, with an exquisite accent that makes me smile far more than the cheesy come-on lines of Hot Man or Older But Ready.

'I'm Sean.'

A little part of me I thought I had lost long ago perks up.

'What do you think of the place?' says Definitely Handsome Sean.

I unperk. He's asking me about his new baby. Just because I have finally decided to get onto the dating scene, doesn't mean the dating scene is keen on me.

'Beautiful,' I say, honestly.

'Really?' His eyes are a pale grey and his face is tanned. Is he looking at me admiringly or wondering why Christie has such a dowdy friend?

At that point, I feel about a hundred.

'Yes, gorgeous. Thank you for the lovely table,' I say politely, excuse myself and leave.

Maybe I'm mad to be thinking of dating. The rules have probably all changed.

Back at the table, while Shazz shows me Good Goods In Small Packages and we giggle at this, Christie gets the bill and divides it up expertly, including the tip.

'I saw Sean talking to you,' Christie says as we leave. 'He'd come over to say hello. Isn't he a darling? So handsome.'

'Yes,' I say, a shade too brightly.

I debate asking if he's involved with someone but then decide he showed me not a hint of interest. It's not him, it's me, I think with a private little laugh.

Outside, Christie, who has mastered the taxi-driver alert whistle, summons one to us in a moment.

'Wish I could do that,' says Shazz. 'You know I used to be able to drink three times this much and now I can't.'

'It's called having a child and a job,' I said. 'You're not twenty-one or in Kansas anymore, Dorothy.'

'Yeah,' says Shazz, as she's helped into the back of the cab.

She falls asleep as we drive home. Christie and I talk quietly over her.

'This was fun.'

'We are lucky to have found each other.'

'Do you think our kids will grow up different because they didn't have what everyone else has?' asks Christie.

'I'm always wondering the same thing myself,' I say. 'But you know they just need one good parent who loves them unconditionally and they've got that. Lots of people have two parents and it doesn't work out. And who knows what goes on in other people's lives? We don't. Look at your mother, pretending everything in the garden is rosy, not telling her neighbours that she has two beautiful granddaughters, all because she doesn't want a lesbian daughter. She doesn't want a daughter who got pregnant with a sperm donor. She wants a son-in-law with a big car, whom she can boast about. What's fabulous about that?'

'Yeah, you're right,' says Christie, sitting back. 'I forget that stuff sometimes.'

As the cab drives into the night, I wonder just who I'm trying to convince.

10

Sid

I'm really sorry I decided that a movie would be too intimate and that a hike was a good idea, because it's November, it's cold up on the mountains and it turns out that people with long legs move faster than those of us with short ones. Funny that.

Finn strides on ahead of me, as if he's got some sort of motor in his butt. I look at the way those long legs move in a fairly smooth motion from his hips. From a panting four feet behind him. I try and concentrate on the way I am striding along the path and realise that I'm not walking the same way; I am walking the way I walk when I am trying to get a bus in a hurry and there is a certain frantic pacing in keeping up. Shit. I'm not doing this right and my hiking boots hurt, which is unsurprising as they are new and cheap. Thoreau was right when he said to beware of any enterprise which required new clothes.

'Why did you buy cheap boots?' says Finn, spotting them the moment I arrived.

'Because you might turn out to be a friend I want to dump because you are really boring, what with all your hiking,' I say, half sarcastically, half humorously to him as we stand in the car park and he looks at my footwear. 'And I can't afford a quarter of a month's mortgage on proper Mount Everest boots.'

'I should have come with you to the shop. I could have got you a discount.'

I don't say that I nearly didn't buy any boots, nearly cancelled full stop. Why did I think I could have men friends now? What madness was this?

'Men should be kept out of shops,' I mutter. 'In fact, I should be kept out of shops, I don't do shops.'

'Really,' he deadpans.

We both laugh and I feel some of the tension leave my body. I was over-reacting: this might be OK after all. If it's not, I'll never see him again.

Finn turns round to check on me and catches me wincing. 'You've really never done anything like this before?' he asks, looking at my hodgepodge outfit. I am not a woman well equipped in the wardrobe department for unusual trekking up the mountains. I go to work, do the occasional weight class and collapse onto the couch. End of.

'I don't hike.'

'What did you and your previous – er, friends, do?' says Finn, gesturing for me to sit down on a rock so he can re-lace my boots.

'We didn't hike,' I say. 'And that's a very datey thing you're doing, trying to fix my boots,' I say, but his presence is calming, not threatening. I like the way he's gentle, as if he senses I can get nervous.

'This is what people who are on a group trek do for each other. They generally don't have to fix boots but if there's a newcomer, they will. They make sure that their backpacks are comfortable and they adjust them on their shoulders, because if they're not right, you're in trouble.'

'What do you mean you're in trouble?' I say, eyes narrowing. 'Is this one of those ultimate-challenge army rangers/SAS survival adventure things, where we hike over the mountains for eight hours and then somebody – with luck – picks us up in a Land Rover? Or, worse, if we miss the pick-up point, we have to throw ourselves in a sleeping bag on the side of a hill for a night of hypothermia?'

'Yes.' Finn grins. 'Second option.'

We laugh again. Must be the briskly cold air, I decide, that's making me laugh so much. And relax. Because the mountain air is relaxing. He's right. Just not about any army ranger shenanigans.

'Hypothermia. For real? Forget it. I'm not doing that, I am good for maybe an hour of hiking and then I was thinking about a pub and nice food: chips, ideally. A cup of coffee, a good stretch and then someone to magically transport me back to the car. Then I'm going to go home, have a bath, put on fluffy PJs and lie down in front of the television. That's what I was thinking.'

He rolls his eyes. 'Boots are finished.' He stands up. 'You're sorted. Now,' he moves behind me to adjust my rucksack, 'that's a useless rucksack. Plus, you've only brought one bottle of water.'

'Should I have brought one of those enormous pig bladder things from the camping shop?' I say.

'Yeah,' he says and then laughs again. 'No, only kidding. That's for really long hikes. Would it lower your stress levels to tell you I've chocolate, too?'

'I didn't know chocolate was allowed in health activities,' I say, delightedly.

'You have so much to learn. When you have done this much walking you are allowed to have chocolate. Now check my rucksack.'

'I don't know how to check your rucksack,' I say. 'What am I checking it for, squirrels?'

'Beginners,' he sighs and starts to demonstrate that everything is in the correct place. There follows a short lecture on how having the straps in the correct place mean his rucksack – which feels like it holds rocks – will be comfortable.

'OK, lead on, McDuff,' I say, once he and his bag of rocks are sorted.

After about fifteen minutes of his leading on, I realise that he is actually getting further and further ahead because of this hip movement thing that I do not have. I call time.

'We've only just started.'

'I'm just asking for a little break; you did say you'd go gently with me.'

He laughs.

'If you were in my hiking team, we'd all be talking about you behind your back,' he said.

'You sound like complete pigs,' I remark.

'How are you not fit?' he said. 'I mean you work in Nurture.'

'There was no room for a gym in the office,' I say with a hint of sarcasm. 'I work in development, which means I am very involved in schools and community projects making sure that people in communities are fit and have correct nutritional advice, plus helping raise funds for facilities within less advantaged regions. I do not go out on hikes at weekends. Although we do have people within the organisation who fundraise and do that sort of thing.'

'And you never have to help?'

'Of course I help, I just don't do any marathoning,' I say.

'And your man Marc, did he help when you were together?'

'If you are trying to find out what Marc was like I will tell you everything,' I say, astonishing myself.

I am telling him nothing, surely?

'But I'm only going to tell you because we are friends, nothing else – so if you are enquiring because, well –' I stop. Suddenly I didn't know where I was going with this. If I was about to say, *because you were trying to fill his position*, that would sound very big headed of me.

So far, Finn hadn't shown the slightest romantic interest in me. Bizarrely, I trusted him. What was not to like?

I make one of what Vilma calls my 'executive decisions'.

Why *not* talk about the past. That's normal behaviour, isn't it?

'Marc and I were very lazy,' I admit. We did canal-bank walks and he once – briefly – was in a gym with a climbing wall, but he fell and fractured his wrist, so it put him off.'

'Poor guy,' says Finn.

'I did karate for a while but I had to leave because I whacked the instructor over the head with a pole when he was showing us how to block blows.'

Finn stops and bends over, he laughs so much. 'Really?'

I nod. 'He wanted me to hit him so he could demonstrate blocking – I'd only started. So I bashed as hard as I could and – well, he wasn't ready.'

I can still remember the man swearing at me as he clutched his head and howled.

'I did point out that the whole point of martial arts is that people don't announce they're going to hit you with a pole.'

Finn is still laughing. 'You are priceless. A tiny ninja.'

'Still a ninja,' I say proudly. 'I never learned karate but I have my own moves.'

And then we're both giggling and it's lovely: up in the clear, fresh mountain air giggling with a nice man who is funny, kind and doesn't make me in the least scared.

'Ivanna, my most recent ex, who came after Mags, was very into the gym, never hiking,' says Finn, when we're back walking. 'I like a bit of gym work but I love swimming, especially wild swimming when I can manage it, but I swim in a pool several mornings a week. This, though, is like meditation. You can see for miles.' He gestures at the broad expanse of the Wicklow mountains around us, strewn with gorse and heather, the odd mountainy sheep still grazing and giving us beady eyes.

We stop and admire the view.

'You liked different things,' I say.

'Yes.'

'Marc and I liked a lot of the same things,' I say. 'We liked cheap restaurants and box sets.'

'Partial to both of them myself. So, what went wrong?'

Given how comfortable I feel with Finn, I answer.

'The things we liked turned out to be different after all,' I say, 'so he moved out. What about you?'

'I'm not sure,' he says. 'She turned out to be tricky. I'm not dissing her. I genuinely thought she was fabulous. But my friends called her Ivanna the Terrible.'

'Were they your male friends?' I say, in an accusatory voice.

'Yes, but also one of my best friend's wives: Marin, who is a real woman's woman, or so people tell me.'

'Another woman dissed her?'

'Yes. I had to push her to say anything. But she said –' his eyes glaze over as if he's remembering –'that she didn't really trust Ivanna. It turned out she had another man at the same time as she was seeing me, which was not part of my master plan.'

'Sounds like Marin has good instincts. And in my experience, master plans don't work out,' I commiserate. 'Still, we've given up all that now – we are happy celibates who have friends.'

'That would make a snappy business card,' says Finn.

'Definitely going to have some printed up,' I deadpan back. Having a friend is nice, I think.

'OK, we have stopped for two minutes.' He's looking at his watch, a manly sort of piece of machinery that was half-divers' watch, half-'I am going to haul a submarine up with one hand, while I'm at it' thing. 'You can't stop too often or you seize up.'

'This is a military exercise, then, is it?' I say, heavy on the irony.

'Nearly.'

We set off again slightly more slowly. He keeps his pace slower so that we're walking together and he talks, explaining about the peaks in the distance, showing areas where his hiker pals go on different days, how it all looks beautiful on a day like today but once the mist comes down and it gets dark, people get lost. Fog can be dreadful, hypothermia can set in. You have to be fully prepared to go out and hike, otherwise you could get the poor rescue helicopter circling the area trying to find you.

'You wouldn't believe the number of people who get lost up here at weekends,' he says.

'Yeah,' I panted, 'I would, I really would. I would never be one of them, though, because I would not be up here in the first place.'

Three hours later, after managing a sit-down on a rock where we ate some sandwiches that Finn supplied, because he figured my jar of peanut butter, two spoons and a flask of coffee was not sufficient, we arrived back at our cars.

Every bit of me aches and I feel exhausted but pleased with myself. I did it. I have hiked, high up on top of the mountains in winter. Colour me achieved.

'Now wasn't that wonderful?' he says, stretching.

'Sure.' I've been dreaming of a hot bath for the past thirty minutes, boiling hot with possibly some Epsom salts in it and lavender and I will lie there for an hour until my limbs melt . . .

'Come again next weekend?'

'Are you mad?' I say. 'It will take me three weeks to get over this.'

'No, it won't,' he says fondly. 'Epsom salts in your bath, you'll be grand.'

I laugh. 'Already there,' I say.

We fist bump and head to our separate cars. He waits until I get in my car and start to drive away, waving me off. He really is very gentlemanly, I think, with a nice warm glow inside me.

II

Marin

It's true: when your children are teenagers, you never sleep at night when they're out until they're home in their beds again. Sleeping implies an inability to leap out of bed and rescue them from the emergency that will surely find them.

Rachel and her best friend, Megan, are out. It's a Friday night and my mama-radar is on high alert.

I've dozed but, suddenly, I am wide awake. Two a.m. The girls insisted they'd be home by one. An hour ago. I grab my phone and dial Rachel's number. Straight to voicemail. I try Megan. No answer.

She's never been out this late without it being an overnight. They are *eighteen*. Kids.

Something's gone wrong; I feel it.

The bed beside me is empty because Nate is at a schmoozing-client event in the city and though he said he'd be late, did he mean this late? Did the client fall asleep in his soup?

My brain sloughs this off as unimportant – what matters is that I feel, *I know*, something's wrong and I need to rescue my daughter.

But who will mind Joey, nine, blissfully asleep in his bedroom, the walls of which are innocently covered with robot posters? I text Rachel, saying that if taxis were a problem, Louise, Megan's mother, would have to pick them up as I couldn't leave Joey.

We don't have a blood pressure machine, but I'm sure I can feel mine increasing silently.

I give up trying to sleep, switch on the light and grab my phone again.

There is still no reply to my text – it just says 'delivered'.

You hear anything? I text Louise. We've been pals since our daughters bonded when they were four. Not best pals or anything, but we're on the same page when it comes to parenting.

Not a dickie bird, texts Louise back at speed.

I stare at the words, feeling utterly powerless.

I never felt like that when they were younger on sleepovers. The Network of Mothers would have got in touch by phone, text in those pre-WhatsApp days, Morse code, if necessary. Discussions about how much children's paracetamol to give, any allergy information, nightmare procedures, etc. would have been had in advance.

'If Megan loses her bear, she will sob and then scream,' Louise told me when Megan and Rachel were eight, on their first sleepover. 'She can lose him in a heartbeat. He must stay in her bed until bedtime. Check. She will try to smuggle him into the cinema. We lost him there once – worst twelve hours of my life.'

That sort of thing. It's our life's work – taking care of our children.

Now Megan is also eighteen, somehow looks twenty-five, and has buttery blonde highlights that go perfectly with her buttery skin (amazing fake-tan application by herself). She and Rachel, also with buttery blonde highlights and a couple of silvery purple hints around the tips, were going to a club tonight.

The club – Les Cloob and no, I am not making this up – admits over twenty-ones only but the girls in their silky vintage dresses look older. Les Cloob likes attractive young women and will not card them. Where gorgeous girls with no money go, less gorgeous men with money will follow. The eternal cycle continues.

Rachel read *The Handmaid's Tale* when she was fourteen. And still, four years later, she wants to go to Les Cloob. A hotbed of men who think a questing hand on a girl's rear end is a compliment. Both girls did Tai Kwan Doh for two years – they can handle a questing hand. But afterwards, tipsy on expensive cocktails, leaving said premises – what then?

A vision of both girls leaving the club, tripping along on ludicrous shoes, pulled into an alley, assails me.

The phone rings.

It's Louise, with the words no mother wants to hear.

'There's a problem.'

'Jesus.' My hand is at my mouth. 'What?'

'They got into the club, were dancing and got separated. Megan has spent the last hour looking for Rachel. She can't find her.'

'An hour . . .'

'I know. I said why didn't she call –'

I'm not even listening.

My flight response doesn't stand a chance – the fight one kicks in instantly. I press the phone's speaker buttons, and am out of the bed, dragging on clothes, trainers, grabbing my bag, while speaking: 'Did Megan tell the doorman, any of the staff, that Rachel had vanished?'

Louise doesn't hesitate. 'Yes and they've looked too.'

'CCTV,' I say. 'Someone's dragged her out of there. We need the police. I'll ring Nate, get him home. Can you get over here and take care of Joey until Nate comes home?'

Louse lives one street away. She doesn't question the plan. My daughter is missing, therefore I have to go into the city.

'I'll be right there,' she says.

Nate's phone goes to voicemail. Sweet Jesus.

'NATE!' I yell into the phone. 'I need you!!! Rachel is missing. Come home to take care of Joey. Please!'

I keep ringing until I've rung three times and still nothing. Voicemail each time. What has he done with the bloody phone?

Damn it, I need him.

Louise meets me at my door and hugs me, her eyes red.

'She's going to be fine,' she says walking in, trying for cheerful. 'You know how dizzy they get when they're excited.'

'They're joined at the hip, Louise,' I say grimly. 'Nothing would make Rachel go off and not come back.'

I watch too many news reports on TV. Far too much. But I know something isn't right.

'Megan's in the back room with the manager,' explains Louise. 'He doesn't want to call the police.'

I bet he doesn't.

I phone the police as I reverse the car out of the drive. It's been five minutes since Louise rang. Five more minutes of Rachel not being attached to her friend.

The police are amazingly helpful. They have a squad car a minute away from the club.

I wish I was a minute away. The drive into the city centre usually takes twenty minutes, but I make it in fourteen. Screw the red lights and God help anyone who tries to stop me. I can find Rachel: nobody but me. I know her, understand her: she came from my body, covered in blood and vernix, she's mine to protect.

I throw the car vaguely at a parking space, leap out and run up the street, noting the ridiculous number of alleys lining it. A couple emerging from the basement entrance of Les Cloob are shoved rudely aside as I two-step-it-at-a-time down metal steps. I push pass the bouncer and something in my face tells him not to bar my way.

Inside, people are dancing, music's playing, but it's all white noise to me. I scan the room for the bar, find it, then shove viciously past a crowd, mostly half-drunk who complain and I shout 'back off' at them with such ferocity that they move back.

'The manager's room, the police? Where are they?' I snarl at a young barman when I get to the counter.

He gestures to a door in a wall and I take the shortest route, pushing roughly through dancers. I don't care who gets flattened. I have to find Rachel. Nothing else matters.

A man in dark blue serge is at the door and I shove past him too, spotting Megan in an armchair and, beside her, sobbing and dishevelled, with vomit on her silky vintage slip dress, is Rachel.

I sink to the floor beside my daughter, looking for signs of assault, hurt.

'What happened?' I ask.

'Oh Mum, I went outside for –' She stops in her shaky confession and starts crying again.

'It was only a cigarette,' says Megan quickly.

'Nobody hurt you?' I demand. I don't care about cigarettes, even though she swore blind she'd never smoke.

'The door got stuck,' my daughter goes on.

'She went out the wrong door into the stores and she couldn't get back in,' adds the manager.

'And nobody hurt you?' I ask again.

Rachel shakes her head. 'I felt sick and I kept banging the door but nobody heard me –'

Uncaring of the vomit, the way I never cared about it when she was little, I pull her close to me and croon her name as I stroke her hair. My girl, safe, unhurt.

Scared but unhurt.

We phone Louise, who's back in her own house, which means Nate must have reared his head at last. I can almost feel the tension flow out of her at the news that Rachel's safe.

Once Megan's in her own home, and both Rachel and I have been hugged by Louise, we drive home, Rachel drunkenly apologising, for the cigarette, for everything.

My hand finds hers in the dark of the car.

'We'll talk in the morning. I love you so much, Rachel,' I say, determined not to cry in front of her. 'You're safe, that's all that matters.'

That's all we care about, us mothers.

At our house, I help her out of the car in those daft shoes but Nate is out the front door in seconds and sweeps her up in his arms, his face white.

'Oh my baby,' he says, half to her, half to me.

I cling on to him, letting myself breathe deeply for the first time in hours. Nate's here – it will be fine.

'I'm so sorry . . .' Rachel is saying brokenly.

He carries her quietly upstairs and lays her on her bed, kneeling beside it, clutching her hand.

'Where were you?' I mouth at Nate.

'Later,' he mouths back, face filled with guilt.

I clean Rachel up, get her into pyjamas, leave water beside her bed and plan to return to sit with her in case she's unwell – six varying cocktails, Megan admitted tearfully in the car, all different, all very strong – in the night.

But first.

Nate's half undressed in our bedroom, sitting on our bed, as if he can't get any further. His shirt is off displaying the admirable physique of someone who swims every second day and does the weight room when not swimming. Nate's hair, like his chest hair, is still dark. I keep finding grey ones in my shoulder-length chestnut curls. Forty-eight to my forty-three and I am not ageing as well.

'Is she going to be all right?' he asks.

I nod, sitting beside him. 'Where were you?'

'We were late but it was only half one and then Anton, he's the main client, says let's go to his hotel and have a cognac in the hotel bar and –'

Nate looks up, his face wracked with remorse. 'I'm so sorry. There was a noisy crew in one end of the hotel bar and I just didn't hear the phone. I had trouble getting a cab – you know what it's like – and when I got a cab and saw your message . . .'

He shudders and looks as if he might cry. Nate never cries, except for when the children were born.

My blood's fired up. I want to rage at someone and he's

sitting there, being nothing like the alpha male I know and love.

Then I think of the bullet we dodged. How Rachel is not sitting mutely in the sexual assault unit, her life changed forever.

We have everything.

'There's nothing I can say, Marin,' Nate says, looking broken as he sits there. 'Rachel needed me, you needed me –'

I stop him by reaching out and taking his hand.

He's the warmest human being I know – never cold, despite his low pulse rate, needing only the lightest duvet, even in winter. His big hand feels warm to my cool one and he grips mine tightly.

Rachel is safe: both my children are safe. I say a gratitude prayer to whoever is listening.

'I'm sorry, so sorry,' he says again.

'I was here, Rachel's OK,' I say and I let myself go, finally crying, as my husband holds me tightly.

12

Bea

I used to take Jean-Luc's anniversary off work but now I don't. I need to be busy. Frantic, actually, as the day after Jean-Luc died is the day Luke was born and each year since he was three, we have a party in the house. Our funds never reach to adventures out but I am getting McDonald's for his five chosen pals this year and Mum has made an amazing cake in the shape of a Formula One car.

'Magic,' says Shazz, when I tell her about McDonald's. 'No cooking!'

'Double figures, Mum!' says Luke at breakfast the day before his birthday, oblivious to the three special anniversary cards on the kitchen window.

There's one I buy every year, an unusual type I have to order off the Internet. It says: *We miss you, Dad!!*

I don't want Luke to forget. I need to keep his father's memory alive but it's getting harder and harder. I never know whether showing Luke pictures of his dead father will help or not. How can one tell? Yes – you have a dad, but he's dead, so this is what he looked like, endlessly. Or simply let Luke know he has me and a wonderful support system. I feel freshly guilty of not pushing contact with Jean-Luc's mother more often – she's a nervy woman – because I'm terrified she'll want Luke to go and stay with her and I couldn't bear that, being alone here. One day, but not yet.

Then, every year on his birthday, I wonder if I've failed Luke somehow in not reminding him enough about his dad.

'It's OK about the dog, Mum,' says Luke, looking at me

with Jean-Luc's eyes, which are blue with startling shards of copper close to the irises.

'Heterochromia,' Jean-Luc told me when I fell in love with his eyes. 'When you have completely different-coloured eyes or a very obvious combination of colours in both.'

'Rare?' I asked him. It was so early in our dating career but even then, everything about him seemed rare.

'Very,' he said, moving in to kiss me so I had to close my eyes and stop staring at his.

Luke is a beautiful mix of his father and I, but I no longer see any of that: I just see Luke. A gangling boy with a warm heart, large hands like his dad, a glorious sense of humour and thick dark hair that defies any comb.

'I know it's not a dog,' Luke goes on. He is so stoic and strong, my little warrior, kindest boy ever. 'I know we can't have one. When I'm a grown up, we'll have a dog.'

'The dog might eat tomorrow's birthday hamster,' I say, deadpan.

'Hamster?'

Luke looks joyous and leaps up to hug me. 'Mum, I'll look after it and –'

'– walk it,' I say, still grave.

He giggles. 'You don't walk hamsters,' he says.

He's so happy at the thought of any living animal to care for. I think of the small bundle of fur I've been waiting several weeks for, ready to be picked up by my mother today. The rescue people Shazz knows are desperate for homes for two lots of puppies rescued from inept puppy farmers trying to make a living from beautiful animals for the Christmas market. It's due to Shazz and the abandoned dog overload that we're getting any puppy this close to the holidays. I can't wait to see Luke's face.

Later in the day, I get two texts from Marin.

The first is: We are thinking of you today.

The second is an invitation to Joey's tenth birthday party to me, to my phone, but written to Luke as if Joey had written it with his mother watching. It's sweet:

Dear Joey, will you come to my party because it will be boring without you? It's the cinema, Joey. p.s. I'm ten and I'm not supposed to ask for presents.

And then I can see absolutely where his mother takes over. 'No presents! Your presence is enough!'

Marin knows that money is tight in our house and that while Joey goes to a private school where kids get things like iPhone ear-buds for Christmas, Luke goes to a school where lots of the kids don't get anything if the Vincent de Paul do not step in.

Honestly, just bring yourselves, is written firmly in Marin's utterly detectable text.

Friendships are strange. They start off one way and twenty years down the line they become something totally different. When I met Nate, Finn and Steve, and later met Marin she was dating Nate, we were all young and full of beans, going to change the world, have fabulous adventures, travel, never be tied down and be friends for ever, obviously. It sort of worked out like that. Marin and Nate fell in love and they were right for each other, absolutely. I was the crazy one for a while, travelling a lot, a variety of jobs, interesting six-month relationships around the world with interesting men. And then I met Jean-Luc and that was it: he was the only man for me.

In those early years, the four of us saw each other all the time. The men clicked and Jean-Luc became part of the Steve/Finn/Nate gang, going to the pub and playing snooker, watching sports together, supporting opposing teams just so they could rib each other.

There was a rivalry between Nate, Steve and Jean-Luc that somehow Finn never took part in – which would wind the others up even more. The secret, I always felt, was that Finn was so fiercely intelligent, a polymath, and utterly confident in his own skin that he never had that need to compete with his friends. We'd meet Finn's girlfriends, and for such a clever man, he had an unerring knack for picking totally the wrong people for him.

Jean-Luc and I wanted a family, but it didn't happen for years. We turned to infertility treatment and, finally, I became pregnant. It was amazing, joyous. Marin was one of the few people who knew about the infertility treatment, and I begged her not to tell Nate. I knew he'd have felt superior to Jean-Luc if he knew: Nate could be childishly macho. If he became aware that we'd needed help to have our baby, then he'd feel superior to my darling husband in the ultimate way.

Marin was delighted. She was pregnant with her second child – due almost the same time as me.

'We can go through it together,' she said, happily.

Afterwards, did it really matter that we had spent three years and so much money trying to have a baby by IVF? Was that important? No.

Nothing was important but looking after my beautiful little baby boy all the time I was grieving. Without Luke, I don't think I could have kept on living because my beloved Jean-Luc wasn't in the world: suddenly he didn't exist, he was gone.

At the time, so many people said the wrong thing. *Everything happens for a reason.* I blocked those helpful souls from my phone. Or worse, 'God has a plan'. What plan was that, precisely? Needless to say, the 'God has a plan' people were immediately blocked.

The people who said, 'I don't know what to say, because I have no idea what you are going through, but I am so sorry, and if I can help,' they could stay.

I culled a lot of friends in those months. But Marin, Nate, Finn and even Steve made the cut.

Finn, dear man, would come round with supermarket groceries when Luke was a tiny baby. He'd bring it all in, put it all carefully in cupboards, tell me just to sit up at the counter and direct him. I got used to it, got used to his calm, gentle presence. He wasn't asking anything of me, he wasn't expecting to be entertained, he just was kind and practical.

In times of tragedy, practical helps.

It meant I didn't have to drag food and boxes of nappies home from the supermarket when my heart hurt so much, I thought I'd cry with the physical pain.

My mother was my birthing partner. My mum had never had it easy, but she was strong. My father used to say there was a rod of steel in my mother's spine and he was right, there was. There was a rod of steel in mine too. And together the two of us got Luke into the world squirming, roaring, a long baby with lungs like a sailor. He was going to be tall like his father, we decided, wiping away tears and sweat. The change-over midwife – because the original had gone off because the labour had lasted twenty-eight hours – said, 'Will we call the dad?'

Mum and I looked at each other and neither of us had cried. We just held on to Luke.

Marin was almost the first person into the hospital with lots of useful things, soft baby onesies and cream for my nipples just in case I decided I was going to breastfeed, because the jury was still out on that one. I cried when I saw her because she was ripe with pregnancy then, nearly nine months gone and her baby was going to have a father.

I felt so bereft and I sobbed when Marin was gone.

'It's the baby blues,' the nurse said kindly, putting an arm around me and a note on my chart simultaneously, probably recommending the psych team come in to assess me.

It wasn't the baby blues – it was the widow's blues, which is a different song altogether, like a long jazz note blown on a sax, wavering into the night. 'My man left me . . .'

It still surprises me now, the word 'widow'. Widows are supposed to be older, having had a lifetime of love, but I'd had so little. I'd imagined us growing old together and once Jean-Luc was gone, that dream died with him. Everyone gets one love story and I'd had mine.

Yet now . . . it must be Shazz and Christie with their pushing me to go on dates because I keep thinking about it now. It could never be what I had with Jean-Luc but could I have happiness again? Just a hint? Someone to hold me, to kiss me, to remind me that I'm a woman in her forties, that there's plenty of life ahead.

There's no time limit on grief – so what if I am ready for someone new?

The day before Luke's birthday, Mum phones about the surprise present and she sounds a bit flustered on the phone.

'Did you get it?' I asked, glad that the puppy code emergency would soon be over and that the little bundle of fur which was allegedly a terrier girl puppy, would be ours.

Mum had gone to pick up the dog and this evening, when we went to Mum's for dinner, his present would be there. I don't know which of us is more excited – me or Mum.

'I did –' says Mum, hesitantly.

'Is she OK? Did she get sick all over the car?' I asked.

We'd had a small poodle when I was little, an adorable bundle of grey who loved eating grass and doing tiny, discreet vomits on the rugs.

'No. Well, the thing is . . . they gave me two,' says Mum rapidly. 'Someone didn't come for the other one and – well, I took her.' She says this last bit in a rush and I laugh. Of course she took two!

'So we have two puppies?' I say, half laughing. In for a penny, in for a pound.

'Yes. I had to, Bea. I couldn't separate them. They snuggled together and cried. I'll send you a picture.'

She didn't really need to send anything. It wasn't just Luke who wanted something fluffy and warm to love: I did too.

'Beautiful,' I sigh. 'We'll be over to you in ten minutes.'

Luke never suspected a thing.

He and I chat about the party the next day, whether he'd get homework from school that night because 'it is my birthday . . .' and he looks at me sideways and says: 'Where will the hamster sleep? They can't sleep outside because they're tiny. I'd like him – or her – to sleep with me but it's fine if he can't, because he might get lost in the bed the way small things get lost in couches, the way Rhianna from my class lost her pet rat. She called it Snowy because it was white and rats are clever but I'd never ask for one, Mum, because I know you're scared . . .'

Inside, I glow with happiness.

The thinking part of my brain is already going over the logistics of having two small dogs in the house. The crate to keep them in for puppy training was certainly big enough: it had fitted a Rottweiler puppy once from someone on the road where Shazz lived. I had soft blankets, puppy food, food and water bowls and even training mats to put on the floor so that the dog would know where to pee. I doubted this would work at first but you've got to try.

My mother is at the door as we drive up. Her cardigan is definitely sporting puppy slobber but her face is alight.

'I've got cake!' she says, fizzing with excitement. 'Special cake.'

'More cake? Not the one for tomorrow?' Luke likes getting things sorted out.

'No, special cake. It's . . . it's in a box.'

The cake box was on the floor of Mum's kitchen and it's making very un-patisserie-like noises. Squealing noises, unhappy squealing noises.

Luke is on his knees in front of it in a flash.

'Mum?' He looks up to me.

'Happy Birthday, darling. It's from me and Granny. Or rather, they're from us. Because we love you so much.'

He opens the box flaps as if opening an organ donor box,

carefully, breath held and then we all saw the two inhabitants: short-haired, fluffy and with their little puppy faces in full moan as if the world was a cruel place and if they had someone to lick, it would all be rosy again.

'Mum! Granny!'

Instinctively, Luke reaches in and gently lifts out the first puppy, who has a patch of dark brown over one naughty eye and an entirely white body. Left alone, the other puppy's wails rise.

Luke scoops the second one out with one hand, this one dappled dark brown, pale brown and white. She looks scared and whimpers to be out of her box, but Luke gently holds the two of them close to his face, and croons at them.

'You're safe, we're going to take care of you. And love you and kiss you and maybe you can sleep on my bed, but you can't fall out in case you get hurt and I am going to love you and love you so much.'

The puppies start licking him ecstatically, as if Luke is what they have been waiting for all their tiny lives.

My mother and I look at each other and the tears in her eyes are reflected by the tears in mine.

Everything doesn't happen for a reason, I know – except, perhaps, two puppies instead of one for a fatherless ten-year-old's birthday.

13

Sid

Another Friday night, and it's sleeting mildly as I hurry across the road from the office into The Fiddler's Elbow to join the rest of the Nurture crowd for our Friday-evening drink. I had some last-minute emails to catch up on, so I'm all on my lonesome as I dodge traffic and arrive in the pub in a panting mess with sleety snow clinging to my hat, which is a very attractive item, being another of my black fluffy much-washed items.

I wriggle through the crowds thronging the pub, all festively celebrating as I make my way to the snug. And suddenly I'm tapped on the arm.

'Thought I'd find you here,' says a familiar voice.

I turn around and there's Finn, standing with two other guys. I can't help it, I beam at him, and say, 'What are you doing here?'

'All his old friends are bored by him so he says he was going off to see his new friend,' says one of the other guys, a slender man with very professorial round glasses and a beard, who is wearing what looks like three jumpers all at the same time. 'We had to come along. Old Finn here needs help from time to time.'

'What sort of help?' I say, grinning.

They're grinning back and the other guy is poking Finn in the ribs.

'Basic conversation,' says Mr Round Glasses.

'Poor thing,' I say, 'so, doesn't have many friends, does he?'

'Well, we're not his friends either, we're colleagues,' says the other man. 'Friends with this fella? Are you mad? I'm Philip

McDonald.' He holds out his hand. 'Modern Irish History.'

'Lovely to meet you.'

Finn is openly amused and watches.

'Michael O'Shaughnessy, Medieval,' says Round Glasses.

'In truth 'tis beautiful to meet with you too,' I say and then laugh. 'That wasn't really medieval, was it?'

'No,' he laughs.

'I didn't know you came in here,' I say to Finn.

'Ah, myself and the lads were getting bored with our usual watering holes, so we thought we'd drop in here for a quick pint before heading home.'

Cue more naughty beaming.

'He told us that he had a new friend who worked in Nurture who came in here.'

'Ah,' I say, and I had to work very hard not to grin. 'And that's cause for excitement, is it?'

'Well, he's got scads of male friends and there are plenty of female colleagues. But apparently he's enjoying your company and he says he's never had a female friend like you before. Probably because you don't know him well enough yet and you haven't got annoyed with him. I mean, we get annoyed with him all the time. He gets very carried away with politics in the 1800s. Drives us nuts.'

'Shut up,' says Finn mildly. 'Don't give away all my secrets.'

He turns to me and his smile is wide, warm, welcoming: 'Can I offer you a drink? We've been here a few minutes and I've been looking around for a group of healthy-looking people all drinking sparkling water.'

I laugh so loud, I'm afraid I might have peed a little bit.

'That,' I say loudly, 'is exactly what myself and my colleagues do.' Then I beckon the men close and begin to whisper. I was going to give away one of Nurture's great secrets. 'We drink in the snug,' I look at Philip and Michael, 'and we try not to be seen necking bottles of wine and eating crisps and snacks and chicken wings in baskets in the pub after work. Because that would look bad, given that we spend a large portion of our work telling people that they should all be following the Mediterranean diet and avoiding trans-fats.'

'All things in moderation,' says Philip.

'Absolutely, but some enterprising young photographer might get a picture of us all sitting there with glasses lined up in front of us and packets of crisps littering the place and . . .' my voice trailed off. 'It's about reputational damage. We have to consider the optics.'

'You're far too clever to be Finn's friend,' says Philip happily. 'Finn's last girlfriend was –'

'I'm not his girlfriend,' I interrupt. Although I couldn't deny a faint frisson at the thought that these men assumed this might be a possibility.

'We're friends, didn't he explain? That's the whole point; friends. Non-dating friends. It can happen in the twenty-first century.'

'Oh we know that,' says Michael quickly.

'Will you stop,' says Finn. 'I just said I was going to come down and say hi to Sid, and you pair tagged along, and now you're making me look like some lunatic.'

'I think the three of you are looking like lunatics with no outside interference,' I say gravely. 'But you're harmless lunatics, so I will go and say hello to my pals in the snug and tell them I'm going to drink with some non-Nurture people outside.'

'Can we not come in?' says Philip, looking excited. 'Only we normally just get to talk with other people from the university and it's nice to meet civilians.'

I laugh loudly at this. 'Civilians?'

'You really know how to insult people,' Michael mutters to Philip. And Finn puts his hand up to his head and closes his eyes.

'Sorry, Sid,' he says, 'I just thought it would be nice to drop in and say hello, that's all; I didn't mean to bring these two eejits with me.'

'No, it's fine,' I say. 'Come on. Let's go in and meet the civilians.'

The three of them pick up their drinks and follow me into the snug, which is already quite jammed with people.

'Friends of mine,' I say, holding up a hand to the assembled company. It wasn't unknown for friends of ours to drop in. The snug couldn't be entirely cut off for Nurture's use. And plenty of people had friends, girlfriends, husbands, wives, drop in.

'What are you having?' says Finn.

'I thought this was my go?' I say.

'No, mine – to make up for ambushing your evening,' he replies.

I accept a glass of red wine, the red being more drinkable than the white in The Fiddler's, and we find ourselves a bit of window to lean against. There is no hope of getting stools, of course, not at this point in the evening. Occasionally, someone goes out into the main bar, steals a stool and drags it back in triumphantly like a Neanderthal belting out of the cave to steal a bit of someone else's woolly mammoth.

Philip is regaling us with stories of the Drama Society Christmas party when he'd been a student, and is on his third hot whiskey – he drinks hot whiskey because, he says, he is always cold – when Adrienne arrives and inserts herself into the group, demanding introductions. The trio of newcomers are delighted to see her and chat away. Not a hint of shyness among them.

Finn turns to me and says quietly, close to my ear, 'I hope this was OK. Should I have rung beforehand, or texted? I just thought it would be nice to drop in and see you. Otherwise we'd be going to the same old dull pub. And I thought it would be nice to say hello. How's your week been?'

'It's fine to do this,' I say, trying to sound blasé, 'absolutely fine. I just come in for a couple of glasses of wine and then I head off.'

'You're not heading off yet,' he says, looking upset in a way

I find deeply flattering and then, instantly, bewildering. What is wrong with me?

Even though it's too early to phone a taxi at this point, ready to hear about Gareth's chugs, Pickle and Kiki, I shake my head.

'No, not heading off yet,' I say and his eyes glitter as he looks at me.

Just then Adrienne appears at my side. 'I like your man,' she whispers into my ear.

'He's not my man,' I hiss back. 'He's a friend.'

'Oh, well, I like your *friend*,' says Adrienne naughtily. 'Can I be his friend too?'

'He has enough friends,' I say primly. 'Besides, I thought you were seeing someone?'

'I'm always seeing someone,' says Adrienne. 'I don't know why. You'd think I'd know better after being married twice.'

'Third time's the charm,' I say.

'And you know this, how?' she asks. We both laugh.

'Isn't romance a triumph of hope over hideous experiences or something like that?' I say.

She gives me a searching look. 'Yeah, right.'

'Nice to meet you,' she says to Finn and wanders off again.

'It's noisy here,' he says. 'Is there a quieter bit of the pub where we can talk?'

The Fiddler's Elbow has no quiet bits. It's like a giant cocktail party on acid on a Friday night, full of revellers, loud stories and, soon, live music, which just means people have to roar their stories at full volume.

'There's a teeny wine bar down the road. I've had lunch there with my boss Adrienne, whom you just met, a few times. I've never been at night but it might be quieter.'

We quietly make our escape from the crowd at The Fiddler's and, ten minutes later, we're installed at a small table in the wine bar and have two glasses of decent wine in front of us, along with menus.

'Oh, mushroom risotto,' says Finn, almost moaning. 'I can never resist it.'

I look up at him. 'That's one of my favourite things to eat.'

'Really?'

'Really. But the portions are huge here. We could –' I pause. 'We could get a big one and share.'

'Excellent plan.'

I used to share meals with Marc but with another man – never. Yet this feels utterly normal. As if I've known him for years. Weird.

We order and chat idly, getting to know each other.

'First pet?' asks Finn.

'A kitten called Miaow when I was three. She was what they call calico – many colours – and she adored me. We had lots of animals, including, once, a cockatoo, but we were only taking care of it. But Miaow was my first baby. You?'

'A wheaten terrier called Lucky. He was a rescue, had only half of one ear, was nearly totally deaf and had a limp. The vet used to laugh every time we went because he said if this was Lucky, he'd hate to see Unlucky. Gorgeous dog, though. Very sweet. Right . . . death row meal?' continues Finn, as if we're about to do a quiz on each other and need to know everything.

I shudder. 'No, not death row. Too sad. Final meal, if I was well enough to eat it.'

He smiles at me. 'You're a softie, despite the biker boots. I knew it.'

'I am sort of soft but I can be tough when required,' I say, attempting hauteur, and failing. 'Don't forget my karate skills.'

We both laugh as the risotto arrives. It's huge, in one bowl and with two forks. The intimacy of the situation hits me but I dismiss it. Finn is good people. He will not read anything into this – unless I want him to. Maybe I do . . . Or maybe not. To cover my confusion, I launch into telling him my final meal.

'A veggie burger with lots of mayonnaise, sweet potato chips and steamed broccoli. Then, for afters, a giant coffee cake, which would make me sick, but I'd be dead, so it wouldn't matter.'

Finn's just looking at me, elbows on the table, staring. At me. Like he's drinking me in and liking it.

'Eat up,' I say, both unnerved and excited. 'We have a trough of food to get through.'

The risotto is delicious and I can't help but moan at my first forkful.

Finn's head shoots up at the sound.

I feel the oddest quiver inside me. What is happening? Stop this, I tell myself sternly.

'Or maybe I'd make this my last meal,' I say, to cover up my blush.

'Are you vegetarian?' he asks.

'Pescatarian,' I say. 'I eat fish. Meat is murder but fish is justifiable homicide,' I quip. 'So, your last meal of choice?'

'You'll hate this but it'd be steak. The French way, almost bleu, which is when they show the steak the pan and for a brief moment, the two are joined.'

I am definitely blushing now. 'Gosh,' I say, 'you are a carnivore. Am I safe?'

As soon as the words are out, I regret them. What is happening to me? It's like careful Sid has been body-snatched by flirty Sid who can't open her mouth without a double entendre emerging. Flirty Sid is a new person, and I have no idea what planet she has come from but she needs to go back there.

'People probably taste like chicken,' I continue weakly, and wonder if I am making it worse. 'Everything unusual is said to taste like chicken.'

'Moving on from the cannibalism, I'd have chips, ordinary ones. Very boring,' Finn adds.

I can't help it. I look up at him, taking in the breadth of his shoulders, the warm, open face, the kind eyes searching mine, and I say: 'You're not boring at all, Finn.'

We both eat some more risotto and he tells me how he read *The Lord of the Rings* at fourteen and scared the hell out of himself, and adores any movie made by Wes Anderson.

'I like any movie with a woman on a revenge kick,' I say before I can help myself and he watches me carefully, saying nothing. 'And *Little Women*. Oh, I loved that book.'

'My sisters do too,' he says.

The risotto is finally finished and it's getting late. Despite the fact that I feel so utterly safe with Finn, I feel I should be getting home. It's hours past my normal Friday evening leaving time.

'I'm tired,' I say apologetically. 'Long day.'

'Of course,' he says. 'I dragged you out, I'm sorry.'

'Don't be,' I say, and feel the dreaded blush again. Quickly, I make my normal phone-call arrangement with my taxi guys. Finn's watching me as I come off the phone.

'You don't use an app?' he says.

'No,' I say, looking at him straight on, 'I don't. There's this lovely company I use and I trust them.'

He seems to be thinking, but he doesn't say anything.

'Good plan,' he says. 'Good plan.'

We split the bill after a verbal struggle of 'me', 'no, me'.

Then my phone pings. My taxi's outside. I grab my coat, shrug myself into it and turn to say goodbye.

'I'm walking you out,' he says.

It's a nice feeling having him at my back. The street is busy, people belting up and down, heads bent against the rain which has replaced the sleet. Plenty of people have started the Twelve Pubs of Christmas early now December is officially here and there is lots of laughter and high jinks in the air.

'I think I'll head off, too,' he says. 'You hiking tomorrow?'

'No,' I say, 'I can't. But maybe next week.'

'Great,' he says, looking pleased.

He opens the cab door for me, waits till I'm inside, then leans in and says, 'Night, hope you get there safely.'

'Don't worry, she will,' says a voice from the front, 'she always does; we take care of her.'

Finn's eyes smile as they meet mine. 'Good to know,' he says, and he shuts the door.

And my heart does a little weird skip.

14

Marin

It's nearly the weekend of Joey's birthday party and today, Thursday, two days before the party, I realise I will have to order a cake. Because work has been so manic, I haven't managed to bake one. I've been trying to sell a lovely cottage in a prime location in Dalkey for a sweet elderly lady who wants to move into an apartment and the sale fell through at the last minute. She's devastated because it means she might miss out on the apartment she wants to buy and I'm devastated because the would-be buyers have been stringing me along for weeks now.

And then Nate ruins everything by mentioning that Steve and Angie might hang around for a drink when they come to pick up Alexandra on Saturday evening after the party.

I don't know why but this sends me into orbit.

'I'll be tired,' I snap.

'It's only a few friends, for God's sake,' he says, irritated.

I'm cleaning up after dinner and even though the kids usually take their turns, this is mine and Nate's evening and yet, somehow, I am scrubbing the frying pan that can't go into the dishwasher or the special coating will come off, and he's sitting at the kitchen table with his phone and the work diary that Rachel says is 'soo old fashioned, Dad!'.

'Once, we didn't have mobile phones, kiddo,' he likes to say back. 'I prefer to make notes and this is how I do it.'

He's using the Mont Blanc pen he's had for years which was the source of one of our rare early rows as money was excruciatingly tight at the time – Rachel was two and I was only working part-time. I like to think I don't hold grudges but clearly I do as, lately, I cannot even see that pen without thinking of that time when we were living on the budget from hell.

Mind you, I think guiltily, I was better at budgets then. Now I am afraid to look at my credit-card bill. I did some online shopping during the week – new winter boots from Acne and some perfume, the exotic Atelier Cologne's Grand Néroli, which I read about in a magazine and then fell in love with. It's so expensive I feel a frisson of guilt every time I spray it on.

I can hardly feel annoyed at Nate's expensive pen when I can't be let near a website without flexing my credit card.

'If you really don't want Steve and Angie coming, I can put them off. It's just drinks and a little something to eat. But if it's too much trouble . . .' he says now, a hint of acid in his voice.

Irritation at having to magic up nibbles as well as drinks ratchets up to rage. How dare he dump Steve and Angie into the mix on the same weekend as Joey's party? It's costing us a fortune – in money, time and energy. Most of which is mine.

'I like our friends coming to have drinks,' I snap, 'but in order to have Alexa at the party, as she is hardly Joey's close pal, I had to invite the whole class, Nate. Twenty-five kids.'

'You didn't have to invite them all,' he says.

'You don't understand school politics,' I reply. 'It's all or nobody.'

I wish it wasn't this way but I can't risk upsetting any of the mothers – and then I think: why not? Why do I always have to please everyone?

This party is genuinely costing a king's ransom in both food and entertainment. As all twenty-five children are coming, it means myself and a few other parents will be ferrying the lot to ours back from the cinema where already I will have forked out shedloads of cash on tickets and nachos and heck knows what bad food groups to keep them happy.

Nate and Rachel will be there, but hopefully some other

kind parental soul will stay to help? Some parents belt off at high speed, delirious to have got shot of their little darlings. Others stay because cinema trips with lots of kids are recipes for disaster. Back at our house, they will have cake and party bags, and be picked up. An entirely plausible plan when it was six boys: one verging on insanity when it's twenty-five.

I'm annoyed with Nate but I say nothing because it occurs to me that this is precisely what my mother would do. I always swore I'd never be like my mother but lately, I have a horrible feeling I'm turning into her.

My mother is the most dreadful martyr – every action has to be accompanied by a diatribe about how she's the only one who can cook dinner/shop/organise the washing. When we were younger and I was there to help with all of this, Ma found other things to be a martyr about. I didn't have a birthday party after my seventh because Ma said it gave her a headache baking a cake. From then on, I made cakes for April and Dom because I liked baking. Am I turning into her? A martyr, the way Dom described it.

A martyr with an added extra: an addiction to shopping.

Friday morning, I'm early to the school for drop off and find myself beside Angie, who gets out of her sleek sports car and runs over to me.

'Anything I can bring to dinner tomorrow night?' she asks.

Dinner? I have that falling-through-a-hole moment when I feel the ground vanish beneath me.

What happened to *drinks*?

After Joey's party, I will be able to manage a drink and a bowl of crisps afterwards but will be found lying on the couch immediately once all guests have gone. Dinner was going to be cereal.

'Er . . .'

'He told you it was just drinks, didn't he?' she says, perfectly volumised blow-dried head at an angle. 'Men!'

'Yeah, men!' I join in, wondering if I am grimacing instead of smiling. Hard to tell. 'Dinner is fine,' I lie.

I don't know why I am doing this but I will not let this woman think I can't handle twenty-five kids all afternoon and a few people round to dinner afterwards. She could probably do it. Mind you, she'd probably have it catered.

'We can have takeaway,' she adds, cheerfully.

'No,' I say immediately, my mustn't-let-the-side-down genes coming to the rescue. Damn, I am my mother. This is a deeply depressing thought. 'I love cooking.'

Angie looks at me oddly but I am not going to break my false smile. If she's coming, if Nate has dropped me in it again, I shall be the perfect wife. If it kills me.

Half an hour and one fabricated dental emergency excuse for the office later, I'm in the nearest shopping centre in the most expensive shop, determinedly ignoring sales assistants watching me rifling through casual T-shirts that run into treble figures and fingering buttery leather biker jackets that cost more than my yearly car insurance.

Sometimes I can ignore the urge, can abstain. The trick is not to go near the posh shops or onto Net à Porter, which raises a lust that sends the neurons in my brain berserk.

The site is effortlessly clever and once you pretend you can afford something on it, it delightedly shows you other beautiful things you might also like.

I like them all. Want them all. With this jacket, that silk blouse, those heels, that mouse-sized handbag – with a handy shopper for holding actual stuff – I will have achieved perfection.

My breathing is definitely faster now as I gather a great armful of clothes and march into a changing room, storming past the assistants who are wondering if a woman with a seven-year-old Coach tote bag and rather tired office flats can afford this or should they call security?

I slide the lock across, in my happy place now.

This stuff is brand new, picked by clever, fashionable people. It's expensive and that means it's good. Every item an investment.

My favourite words.

An investment piece. The words to justify it all.

Today, I will find the one missing piece. I always knew it was out there in the wild. A work/home jacket I can wear forever and people will say 'Marin's so cool, effortlessly so.' A coat for the school gates that screams 'her life is sorted!' The jeans. The ones that make my legs look thinner, longer, that flatten my belly with its overhang of two-baby flesh.

I will look like Angie. I will be able to tell Nate I am not a dogsbody and to stop with the one-armed hugs. I will reclaim my life –

'Do you need any help?' says an assistant outside.

'Uh . . .' I mutter, looking round at my haul.

Boots, I ponder? Or cool-mum-around-town trainers. Like the ones Angie has. With the right footwear and a fabulous jacket/coat/pair of jeans, it doesn't matter where you bought the rest of it.

'Boots,' I say, deep in the throes of it now. Those Acne ones I bought online haven't come yet. I need boots now. 'Like those ones by Balenciaga but not them, obviously. Trainers too. Size 37. White. Not the Veja, as they're too tight. Had to give my last pair away.'

Sometimes my choices are questionable. I nearly once bought a Hermès handbag but when I realised the girl was looking at both my unmanicured nails and the rather battered leather tote that's perfect for all my files and brochures, I was shocked back to reality. Like most ordinary humans, I could not afford the bag. Not under any circumstances, short of selling the car and my body. I'd shuffled away and then almost ran out of the shop.

Not so today. Boxes of boots and trainers appear, and I rip clothes on and off, admiring myself in the special changing-room lighting.

Each piece is perfect but I'm not greedy.
One thing, I tell myself. Just one.

I'm in the car driving back into work when the fever breaks. A rash of hot shame and then the sudden plunge of guilt.

What have I done? Beside me on the seat is a bag holding two items. The black jeans and one of those elusive 'perfect' white T-shirts.

'Those jeans look incredible,' the assistant said.

Clad in my borrowed finery, I step out to look at myself in the big mirror. Transformed.

'The T-shirt is flying out of the shop,' she pointed out gravely. Sensible Me knows this is fabulous upselling. Shopper Me nearly buys two.

Now that the shopping adrenalin rush has left me, the fear and guilt are overwhelming.

I cry as I drive and the precious shopping bag beside me on the passenger seat doesn't help in the least. Shopping is an urge to fill that great gaping wound inside me. The one from my childhood that tells me I'm not anything special and really, once you get to seven, you don't need a birthday party, do you? Some people use alcohol or drugs to numb pain. I buy things.

But still, clothes don't hurt anyone, do they? And all women love to shop. It's what we do, right?

But I know I've gone too far this time. I've spent too much. I don't need to look at the bank statement to know that I won't be able to afford to pay even a quarter of my credit card bill this month. I shudder to think of the interest ratcheting up. Why do I do this? Why?

When I get in to the office the rest of the day stretches ahead, made longer by knowing that the contraband is in my car. Guilt-inducing contraband. Our bank balance has not been good lately but this will push it over the edge. I bought the stuff out of the housekeeping money and I haven't dared look at the balance on my phone. Only if I shop in the low-cost shops for the next month will we be able to manage – which is hardly realistic given Christmas is coming. The guilt ripples through me.

The day is not made any better by a text from April, the oldest of my family and the one whose entire life I have to keep a secret from my mother.

That's me: secret keeper extraordinaire. All weird families have them and my family of origin certainly is weird.

Jared's leaving her! Today!!!!! Phone soonest!!!!

April, I mutter to myself as I tidy up my desk.

My sister is one of life's innocents, so trusting of the world that she sees only what it shows her on the surface. This trait makes her both a genuinely lovely person and a magnet for men attracted to naïve women with shimmering sex appeal.

Essentially, we're alike: short, chestnut-haired and blue eyed. But that's it. I have kindness writ large on my face and April's has a look that says '*You!* I've been waiting for you for a lifetime . . .'

Plus, she's very slim, more hourglass than I am, which means a tiny waist and boobs men speak to. She has full lips and always wears lip gloss, a combination that has an almost mesmeric effect on men. Between the lips and the boobs, she's a walking *Playboy* girl, despite being close to fifty. The trick is that April does not behave as someone who is or who believes she is, in her forties. She is excellent at escaping reality.

If I am the fixer in our family, April is the runner. She left home as soon as she could to escape our mother, and she's still searching for someone to save her, like a fairy-tale princess, and even though I have bought her many self-help books, she does not get that she has to save herself. But then, who am I to talk, shopping myself to happiness?

'Thank goodness you rang,' says April, picking up after the first ring. 'It's happening, it's really happening. Today, finally –'

'April,' I interrupt her as a blast of icy wind hits me on my walk to the car, 'we've talked about this: don't get your hopes up.'

'Please don't say anything negative,' she begs. 'Can't you believe in me for a moment?'

I don't answer. I believe in her. I just don't believe in Jared. Not that I have met him. Jared is either a practised adulterer of enormous skill or can disappear over rooftops like Spiderman. I went through a brief phase of trying to catch him at my sister's apartment, just to size him up for myself. But he must have superhuman powers of evasion. I never managed to meet him.

This, given that their relationship has been going on for two years, makes me think it's highly unlikely it's going to end well for April.

'Darling,' I say, trying a different tack, 'I just don't want you to get hurt. He's said this before. Nothing has changed.' I stop, not wanting to hurt her, but she's my sister, I owe her honesty. 'He lives in a very big beautiful house with his wife and adult daughters, and if he leaves her, he's going to be giving up all of that. So it's going to be ugly.'

Being at the property coalface of divorcing couples is too instructive. Generally, the more money and prestige people have, the more enraged they get when one spouse ups and leaves. People frequently rely on their homes as barometers of their success in the world. *Look at us: big house. Architect-designed extension with floor-to-ceiling windows and a terrace overlooking the sea/mountains/Italianate gardens. We are fabulous!* Until one of them falls in love with another person and packs a suitcase. Or an antique Vuitton steam trunk, whatever.

Jared Quinn and his wife live with their two college-going daughters in an exquisite Georgian house on a whole acre in Killiney. It's a stunning property and hasn't been on the market since they purchased it twenty-five years previously. Jared would be leaving the cachet of his address to move in with my sister in her six-hundred-square-metre apartment with south-facing balcony along the river. About three million euros less cachet. I have no idea of what Mrs Quinn looks like or how lovely his two daughters are, but that house is something special.

'I know all those things,' she says, as I wriggle into the car, 'but this time it's going to be different. He rang first thing this morning. He hadn't slept, poor darling: he'd had a nightmare.'

Other people's nightmares are generally boring, but the nightmares of your sister's married boyfriend are in a class all of their own, particularly during your commute.

Poor April. I know I shouldn't be on the phone in the car but I can't face this at home: better to get it done now, so I half listen as I sit in lines of traffic to my turn off.

'So he's going to tell her tonight and then come over here.'

I tune back in. 'Is he telling her before or after dinner?'

'I, I don't know. Should it matter?'

'Before dinner makes more sense because then he can collect his stuff and leave. But after dinner implies everyone sitting down together and –'

There's a silence and I fervently hope April is seeing the Quinn family sitting around whatever sort of table rich people who live in Georgian mansions eat their dinner on.

Nobody split up during dinner. 'Pass the salt. By the way, I'm leaving you.'

Cue crashing of precious, lead-bottomed wine glasses. There are far too many items to fling at a departing spouse at meal times. No. I just didn't see it.

'Marin, you're so lucky, you have everything but, this time, I'm going to have it too.' She hangs up abruptly.

Given the newly organised dinner tomorrow, I should stop off and get some shopping for it, but I'm too worn out. I'll get up early to shop. I want to go home and hug Joey, Rachel and even Nate, which is a plus, since I was so cross with him this morning.

I can't help April. Not tonight, anyway. Tonight I have to pick up Joey's birthday cake, finally ordered at lunchtime, and get the house balloon-ready for the after-cinema party tomorrow.

I want it all to be *perfect*.

15

Bea

There are so many SUVs crowded in the car park of the small cinema where Joey's birthday will begin, that I think they must be breeding there.

Women with glossy hair, expensive clothes and perfect make-up are dropping off children, while Marin and Rachel stand at the door counting kids off and putting stickers on their tops. There are some fathers too, which always hurts – imagine having a man to bring Luke places, to be a dad to him, to say: 'You rest, honey – Luke and I are going off to discuss manly things while walking the dogs.'

I could have that, I think – have been thinking about it a lot lately. Nobody says I have to be alone forever. Shazz and Christie aren't anymore. But it's such a leap.

'Mum, Mum, park there,' says Luke excitedly, showing me a sliver of a parking space near the door that will fit my small Nissan perfectly and which would never have been big enough for one of the posh cars with their new registrations.

The puppies, Sausage and Doughnut, are in the back of the car, squeaking with the excitement with which they treat every trip out. They're too little to actually go on a walk, not having had their three-month booster shots, but Luke begged me to bring them today, 'so I can show Joey'.

Sure enough, amid the sea of faces and big cars, Marin sees us. I've told her about the dogs and she knows nothing will please Luke more than to show off his birthday present to his friend. Joey races over and is soon in our small car, with Sausage and Doughnut clambering all over him, their little puppy tongues licking as though their life depended upon it. The scent of them fills the car. There's something about the smell of puppies. A smell of joy and happiness.

'You're so lucky,' says Joey, hugging Sausage close and I see Luke's face surge with pride. For once, he has something Joey does not, and I let myself breathe out. Who cares if I am cleaning up puppy poop for time immemorial? My son is happy.

Finally, Joey and Luke get out of the car.

'Can we bring them in, Bea?' begs Joey and he looks just like Nate – he's going to be a heartbreaker for sure. Before Nate went out with me, he'd cut quite a swathe through the college. It was one of the reasons I'd broken up with him all those years ago. I never entirely trusted him, but then Marin came along and the rest is history: Nate finally hung up his bad-boy spurs.

'You can't bring the puppies into the cinema, Luke, lovie,' I say, 'they're too little. It's not safe for them because they haven't had all their vaccinations – the way you had to have measles shots when you were young. And they'd be bored in the cinema –'

'– and do poos. They do them everywhere!' interrupts Luke joyfully. 'Squelch, poop, squelch.'

Both boys erupt into fits of giggles and I laugh. *He* has not been trying to wash the cream fluffy rug from in front of the fireplace. I swear, that puppy poop was green. It's like having two small babies running around *without* nappies. I am not sure how I'm going to manage to take care of them and walk them when they're bigger, but we'll cross that bridge when we come to it. Besides, and the fear hits my heart afresh, what if Laoise is right and there are job losses on the horizon in work? This is not a good hiring economy right now, particularly for lovely part-time jobs where you share your job with a woman who has grown-up children and can help you out if your small son is sick and you can't come in. Where would I get a job like that again?

Trying not to shudder at the thought, I manage to put the puppies back into their little car crate and get out with the boys to go to see my friend at the cinema door.

'Marin,' I say, hugging her.

She's dressed beautifully – in something wonderfully expensive, I think, and she looks happy. I'm glad. Marin does love her clothes but her mother, who can do passive aggressive and plain old aggressive like a veteran boxer, knocks her confidence all the time. It's wonderful to see Marin here today among the glam posh mums, looking confident, although she is a little tired around the eyes, I notice.

'I'll be back at five,' I say, 'to get Luke and anyone else who needs a lift to your place.'

'Yes, thank you,' she says gratefully. She comes closer to whisper. 'Some people literally want to dump the kids and run till six-thirty pick-up at my house. How do they think I'm getting them back to ours? In a bus? On my magic carpet? I do not understand some parents.'

I laugh out loud. 'See you later,' I say. 'I can't arrange the magic carpet but I have room for two more in my car.' I hug her again and look around for Luke, but he's already inside, talking to Rachel, delighted with himself.

My afternoon passes in a blur of life admin and puppy fur. At five-twenty, myself, Luke and two other boys arrive at Marin's house, which is remarkably SUV-free. I park carefully then let everyone out on the side of the footpath.

I always feel anxious when I'm taking care of other people's children; Shazz says it's post-traumatic stress disorder. This is her latest kick – that I have PTSD after Jean-Luc's death and that's why I can't date.

'Don't be ridiculous. I just don't want to lock lips with some of the idiots that put their names into the online dating hat. You saw those guys . . . Would *you* date any of them? No!'

'We'll find the right website,' insists Shazz. 'Give me time.'

Marin and Nate's house is a testament to Marin's perfectionism.

It's large, beautifully decorated in elegant creams and whites, but it's cosy too. That's Marin's touch: dried flowers and wicker hearts hanging from the bannisters, Rachel's tiny old ballet shoes in a framed box beside a miniature pair of Joey's shoes from when he was born and somebody gave him adorable but deeply silly Converse shoes. He couldn't wear them but they look so sweet in their box frame.

The party is in the living room where three other parents, all mums, are trying to calm things. I stay there for fifteen minutes and help out, then, knowing the food is due because there's a bit of moaning going on about people being hungry, I head into the kitchen.

Rachel and Marin are shoving McDonald's, purchased by Nate who has just arrived, onto plates.

Nate is ticking off a list of orders and when he sees me, he puts it to one side for a hug.

'Hi, sweetheart,' he says, planting a kiss on my cheek. 'Now, I think we might have too many packets of fries, but then you can never have too many fries, can you?'

'No,' says Rachel, grabbing a pack and stuffing a few into her mouth.

I laugh and for a moment, myself, Rachel and Nate grab fries, moaning at the taste.

'I love this stuff,' says Nate.

'I don't know why it took you so long to get it,' hisses Marin at him. 'You said you'd have it all laid out when we got home. I thought we'd have to give them the cake next and they'd all be hyped up on sugar.'

'Even more hyped up,' says Rachel. 'You want to see how many sweets they ate at the cinema.'

'I had a work call,' Nate bites back. 'Life doesn't stop for parties. Jesus, it's not exactly hard – amusing twenty-five kids in a house with a giant TV, every cable channel you could ask for and a giant cake.'

I'm caught in the middle of a deeply uncomfortable family scene, so I grab the first three plates and head back into the living room.

'I have chicken nuggets, barbecue sauce and fries,' I announce, slightly shaken by what I've just witnessed.

There's a wild scramble and, luckily, Rachel comes in with more food before the riot starts. For once, I am glad that Luke only has small parties. The very notion of entertaining twenty-five kids is overwhelming. But even more overwhelming is the thought that things are tricky between Nate and Marin, whom I have never once seen bicker like that.

I am very anxious about change. Even if Shazz is right about me having some syndrome as a result of Jean-Luc's death, change is never good.

Not in my experience, anyway.

16

Sid

I always feel the thrill of going home when I reach the crest of the hill into Greystones. Until that point, I've been driving along with only mountains in the distance, but at that crest, suddenly sea is spread in front of me like an iridescent cape of blue, shimmering into the curve of the harbour, reaching out into the distance along the horizon.

Whatever the season, it's beautiful and today, sharply cool with the low winter sunlight dusting the world, it's magical.

The Christmas spirit is probably responsible as every house seems to have a gleam of fairy lights from their windows, even though it's only half two in the afternoon. I know our house will have been given the fairy-light treatment to within an inch of its life. My mother, Giselle, loves Christmas and has never been able to pass a charity shop without searching out any baubles someone else has discarded.

Stefan spends a lot of his December weekends stapling icicle lights to the whole outside of the house and wrapping white fairy lights round the maple trees in the front garden. Even the hen house gets fairy lights, although the hens don't seem in the least put out by the added shininess.

Giselle, wrapped up in her olive-green home-felted coat with her silvery hair hanging in a long plait down her back and looking like a faery person herself, directs it all like the art director on a fantasy movie. Adding in some of the ivy she spray paints silver when it dies and then working out which of the metal artwork she makes will look best in the right spot, is her next job, with Stefan holding the ladder and saying he should do it and then watching her anxiously as she bounces up each rung without fear. With a house called Rivendell, what else can you do? Giselle is a huge *Lord of the Rings* fan and had renamed the house instantly when she moved in. This and the fact that I call her Giselle rather than Mum almost tells you all you need to know about my mother, except that she is utterly special, one of life's truly good people who never sees the bad in anyone.

My Great-Granny McNamara left her the house and apparently, my grandmother, who was not a person to be trifled with, was outraged. But Giselle, already a fully fledged free spirit, pointed out that Great-Granny McNamara had always had second sight and that the house needed her. She was also pregnant at the time and when my father said he was too young to be a dad and maybe after he finished college he'd consider it, she needed a place of sanctuary. Rivendell became that place. My father never returned.

Before long, Giselle installed herself and a few equally free-spirited friends in the house to keep her company. They dallied with New Romanticism, attempted to grow their own vegetables and failed miserably until it became clear that some of them would have to get jobs.

'Jobs.' Giselle smiles dreamily whenever it's brought up today. 'We were so innocent. We thought we could live in the wild and be our own people but it turned out that we still needed money and you can only eat so many turnips.'

Despite the gardening disasters, the turnips grew. They bought lentils. I still hate both.

The garden's fruit trees, hidden behind a tangle of briars, became the Rivendell family's saviour. They learned to make jams. Apple jellies, French apple and almond marmalade à la Madeleine, rhubarb and ginger jam, gooseberry jam. If it stood still long enough, it was made into jam.

The house was an ancient Edwardian wreck which gradually improved as the various shifting inhabitants got better at fixing plumbing and shoring up against the damp for a few more months. I grew up with lots of people and children: artists doing things with tiny canvasses and nearly dried-out paints to sell in the city squares at the weekends; sculptors busily making insane wire sculptures in the huge back shed; one enterprising girl who thought she could start a business by growing cannabis in her bedroom.

The gardeners might have been useless with anything that wasn't a turnip but they could recognise hash plants when they saw one. She'd had to leave. A little recreational smoking was fine – growing with intent to supply was not.

Other kids in school thought I was a bit weird as a child, but they envied me too because it was quite obvious I didn't have to do my homework. If Mum was called into the school for some infraction of rules, she'd trail in happily and tell them that Sidonie was a free-spirited child and that children should be allowed to make their own decisions. Not the big ones, but the ones that called to them. 'One day Sidonie might understand the value of education. And then,' my mother would say happily, 'perhaps she might settle a bit more at maths.'

I never settled a bit more at maths.

Nowadays the house looks a bit better, which is 100 per cent due to Stefan's inhabitation. Stefan and my mother fell in love twenty years ago when he came along with some rather more industrial jam-making equipment he was selling. With him came stability and most of the commune moving out, because for the first time, my mother envisaged a life with just the three of us – and eventually darling baby Vilma in the house. With, of course, the dogs, the cats, the collection of hedgehogs and the two African grey parrots that nobody had known what to do with when their owner, old Mrs Ryan up the road, had died. It was a very happy menagerie.

Giselle was at the kitchen table stirring a giant bowl with Christmas cake mixture in it, watched hungrily by two dogs and one cat, when I arrived. The scent of cinnamon, which I adore, was heady in the air and the sixty-year-old cream range, which had defied all of us until Stefan moved in, was quietly heating the room to a blissful warmth. Blue, the other cat, was curled up on a couch beside the fire, warming his arthritic bones and ignoring the culinary efforts.

'Sidonie!' exclaims my mother, throwing down her wooden spoon to throw her arms around me. 'You're early.'

'We only did a small hike today. Everyone's exhausted: work parties, Christmas madness, etc.,' I said, holding on to her tightly. This had been my third hike with Finn, the second where we'd had company and while it was fun hiking over the mountains, chatting and breathing in fresh mountain air, it was weirdly not as much fun as when we were alone. 'I thought you'd made cakes already.'

'Oh I have,' says my mother, helping me out of my coat, 'but myself and the Romantics are doing a cake run next weekend for ten of our darling older inhabitants who we feel could do with some cheering up. We've got very gentle chilli jam, plum relish, a few tiny bottles of sloe gin because we don't want them all to get sozzled and Rowena's sloe gin is like rocket fuel, and the cakes.'

The Rivendell gang from the early days had nearly all settled nearby. They drove sensible cars, had normal jobs and astonished their children with stories of how they'd lived for several years in the Rivendell house and survived on their pooled resources. Their nickname for themselves was the Romantics as it made them laugh, thinking of the days when they'd thought they could survive outside normal life without rents, mortgages, car loans, pensions and school shoes. Carrie, who was a couple of years younger than I was and had moved out of Rivendell with her mother when she was seven, was an accountant, having watched her mother qualify as an accountant and marry another accountant. Every once in a while Carrie and I met up, normally during the holidays, and Carrie would tell me that she couldn't really remember much about Rivendell, apart from the fun and the menagerie of animals and the first hedgehog. We children called him Hedgy and we went to great lengths to ensure that he was happy and that the dogs, cats and the goose we owned for a brief period left him alone.

Hedgy had eventually shuffled off into someone else's garden one day and we were heartbroken, because he never came back. We used to love his adorable little snout, and how he'd look at us with great intensity when we got down on our knees to gaze into his eyes. Contrary to popular opinion, hedgehogs don't immediately curl up at the first sign of people looking at them. While Hedgy didn't precisely let us stroke him, he was perfectly happy to snuffle around near us when we weren't with the dogs. And whenever we had to lift him out of harm's way, his spikes weren't spiky at all, but were like delicate bristles. I loved that about them.

But our garden's suitability for hedgehogs must have spread among the community because we were always being gifted with ones wandering into tiny gardens or found perilously crossing and re-crossing dangerous roads despite all attempts to put them into fields.

'I wish I could have a hedgehog now,' Carrie once said mistily, 'but we have two Labradors and they'd probably think he was a football.'

I had met her two Labradors, and they were so adorable I couldn't imagine them treating a Hedgy with anything but respect. But perhaps she knew best.

I think about my first beloved cat, the little calico called Miaow, and telling Finn about her. I feel so strange when I think about Finn – feelings I thought I'd never feel again. Different from the way I was with Marc. We had been running away together, from our situations at first and then later from real life. Not the basis for a relationship, as I've found out.

Maybe I was a bit like Hedgy the hedgehog, not quite as spiky as I tried to imply, but gently bristled. To keep people out.

'Tea?' says Giselle now, after I have hugged her. She abandons the cake for a moment to sit down on the couch beside the fire, and I join her and stroke Blue gently. You have to be gentle with Blue, because his poor joints ache so much. But I have discovered a tiny little nodule at the base of his spine, whereupon you can massage gently and he arches his back ever so slightly because it's pleasurable. Hours on the couch on Pinterest can come in handy, it seems. I am not wasting my life.

'No, I'll make the tea,' I say, kissing Blue on the top of his grey furry head, 'then I'll do some stirring.'

Passing, I stick a finger into the bowl and scoop out a squelch of the delicious mixture. 'Oh,' I say as a moan emerges from me. 'I think it's better uncooked.'

'Everyone says that until they've licked three bowls,' Giselle says matter of factly. 'Then they say they are going to be sick. I have made a lot of cakes and a lot of children have passed through this house.'

'I know,' I say, 'I was just thinking about Carrie. I'll have to give her a ring over Christmas and perhaps we can meet up.'

'She has news,' says Giselle, suddenly busying herself with the cat.

'What?'

'She's pregnant.' There's a pause. 'It's twins.'

'Wow,' I say, catching myself and trying not to sound shocked or envious or any of those other emotions that might betray how I feel. I'm not sure how I truly feel, but I do know I'm not ready to feel it now.

'Tony's thrilled but Rowena is delirious,' my mother says to my back as I fill the teapot with boiling water from the stove.

'Course she is,' I say, putting a smile in my voice. 'What mother wouldn't want grandchildren?'

As soon as the words are out, I wish I could put them back in the bottle.

My mother: kind, loving, one of nature's born magnets for children and small animals.

'Yes,' she says, and I can hear the pain in her voice.

It's primeval, that pain: it comes from wanting love and happiness and family for your own children.

She tries to hide it but she can't. I'm very good at hiding my emotions now but my mother never learned.

I can't tell her I never want to bring children into this world because how could I protect them? I won't do it. It's all I can do to protect myself.

I could never tell her what happened, kept away from home for weeks afterwards – the shame stopped me telling, shame that I had done something wrong, coupled with the fear of what it would do to her. Shame reminds me of those pictures of beautiful sea birds covered in oil after an oil spill: it sticks to them, blackly, dangerously, stopping everything. Their wings cannot move, they cannot breathe and only if they are helped is there some hope for their survival. But if the shame goes unnoticed or if people do not recognise the wounded, utterly broken look in the birds' eyes, then they lie down in the shame of the oil and let it encompass them.

My mother tried so hard to take care of me all my childhood and it was all ruined in an instant. I can never tell her the truth now. It would devastate her, truly. She'd tried to protect me and it had gone wrong. I would never break her heart with the truth, that it was all my fault.

A stamping of boots announces Stefan's arrival in the kitchen.

Even in his socked feet he's incredibly tall but has the gentle empathy that a woman like my mother needs. He can sense the tension between us and, in a moment, he goes over to my mother and kisses her against her temple, his long arms encircling her. I see her lean against him, just briefly, their love almost tangible.

Then he comes to me, bends, kisses me on the forehead, before gently putting his arms around me, as if I am something very precious and fragile. It requires no effort to see why Stefan has changed all our lives for the better. He is the most gloriously kind man. My mother, fey, wild at heart, has blossomed with him in her life.

Today, with thoughts of shame in my head and Finn creeping daily into my heart, I wonder if I could ever have what my mother and Stefan have? Love, happiness, the simplicity of a life well lived?

Tea inside us, I stir the cake with my mother assisting, and when it's neatly in the oven in its sheath of baking tin, brown paper and string, I help Stefan with dinner while Giselle drives down to the train station to pick up Vilma who's also home for the weekend.

She comes every few weekends, the way I used to in the early days, apart from that first six weeks when I was twenty-two, when I didn't come home once.

Giselle rang me, Stefan rang me, Vilma rang me and I did a pretty good job of saying I was really busy and the new job was fabulous and the little apartment I was sharing with three girls was just so full of fun, that I couldn't leave but I'd be down soon.

Because I couldn't see them, or I'd have broken down.

Staying away was the only option. I was so wounded and covered in the vicious oil of shame. I could not have pretended to them, the people I loved. I felt complicit, as if I had done something wrong, because I must have, mustn't I? The shame went that deep.

So I stayed in my tiny apartment and drank neat vodka, which I had never done before, because I had to numb the pain and it seemed like the only way. I didn't cry. I merely made myself numb. I could not think of what had happened without wanting to make the cut in my wrists that would end it all.

As if some deity is helping me emerge from my dark thoughts, Stefan puts on music, Nina Simone at her happiest, singing 'I Want a Little Sugar in My Bowl' and I grin.

Finn, I think: he could be the sugar in my bowl . . .

I'm smiling as I slowly heat up the smoky goulash Giselle made earlier, a recipe she had picked up from some of their travels around Europe, while Stefan's in charge of the kibinai, tiny little curded cheese pastries we're going to have as a starter. Stefan has brought so many glorious Lithuanian foods into the house. Although we had to stop getting him to make fried bread because, Vilma said, exactly around the time when she started doing nutrition in Home Economics, it was bad for us.

'It's not bad for you,' Stefan had said, laughing, 'but it's probably not good for you either. Still, we enjoy the simple things in life while we can.'

Which sums up Stefan's motto.

We assemble dinner companionably, with him asking me questions about work and my friends. He's much better than my mother at getting information out of me, but I'm wise to his ways. No matter how much Stefan loves me and wants me to be happy, I don't want anyone looking at my life and seeing what they perceive to be wrong.

I always loved going home to Rivendell and just enjoying myself without any reminders that I wasn't ticking off the boxes for husband, children, super job: all these markers people are supposed to have achieved by the time they get to my age. Is that what life's supposed to be about? Ticking off the boxes?

I wasn't ticking off any boxes, but I'd never hurt my beloved Stefan or Giselle by saying such a thing. But now . . . maybe things were changing. I wouldn't say anything, though. I held the thoughts of Finn close to my heart. I liked him – I could admit that – but it didn't mean he'd love me. I came with so much baggage I could fill a 747's baggage hold. Who'd take that on?

Vilma arrives in a flurry of hugs for everyone and a bottle of wine she's picked up somewhere that was cheap, but 'it's supposed to be really, really good'.

Stefan hugs her. 'Cheap and really, really good, my favourite words,' he says, 'apart from Giselle, Sidonie and Vilma.'

'You forgot the cats and the dogs and the goose,' says Vilma.

'The goose met with an untimely death,' my mother says gravely.

'Not another one.'

We could never keep geese very long; they were always escaping and getting out onto the road and terrorising passers-by. Geese were the untrained attack dogs of the animal world, ferocious fowl with teeth.

Dinner is lovely. We talk and laugh, though the wine is sadly tragic. And Vilma insists we don't drink it, and says she'll bring it back to the shop and make the man in the shop drink a bit of it until he sees that cheap and nice are not the same things.

'No, no, darling,' says Giselle, 'there is no point. But you shouldn't be spending your money on wine for us anyway, you should be spending it on you.'

'I know but I brought home most of my washing,' says Vilma.

'And you can do it yourself,' Giselle laughs.

My phone pings with a text and I see, with a dart of excitement, that it's from Finn. He's asking me to dinner at his friend Marin's. She's the one married to his pal, Nate.

'I'd love you to come,' the text finishes and I feel myself fill with excitement. You didn't invite people you didn't like to dinner with your friends, I think. Then my crazy mind gets involved and reminds me that we said we'd be friends. Just friends.

'Must go to the loo,' I say idly, and rush off to sit alone and examine each word of the text. It's all straightforward except for the last line.

I'd love you to come.

You don't say that to someone who's a friend, do you?

I beam at myself in the foxed old mirror that's been in Rivendell forever.

'Finn,' I whisper into it. 'Finn and Sid. Sid and Finn. Imagine if that came true . . .?'

I'd love that too, I text back and feel a quiver of excitement run through my whole body. I've met Finn for coffee twice since our meal in the wine bar and we've gone for another two walks, which weren't quite as much fun because we weren't alone. His fellow hikers are nice but they're not his real pals.

I feel schoolgirlish at how anxious it makes me that his friends will like me.

Me: biker-boot chick, wanting a guy's friends to like me. I must be going a little nuts.

As I come down from my girlish fantasies about Finn, I tell myself that it's simply nice having a male friend. It doesn't have to go anywhere. We talk about work and sometimes he talks about sport, and I tell him sport is really boring, which makes him laugh. We talk about all sorts of things. Sometimes Finn tries to subtly meander the conversation around to Marc. And I just as subtly shove him off.

I can't go there with him.

He thinks I had a normal relationship with Marc. I can't tell him the truth.

I flush the loo for the sake of noise and return to the kitchen, my phone hidden in my pocket, like something precious.

After dinner we sit in the big old sitting room with the funny purple velvet couch we have had for years, and the old brightly coloured carpets that feel like they have been in Rivendell as long as I have. We love cards and we play all sorts of games and when there are the four of us together, it's so much fun. Vilma's the most competitive, with Stefan being the gentleman banker of all the pennies we keep in a jar so we can place bets. Blue curls up behind me on the couch and it's lovely to feel his gentle feline heat in the small of my back. Soot, who has mixed parentage but is certainly over half dachshund, sits on my mother's lap, eyes closed in blissful contentment because he's with his dearest person in the whole world. There is the faintest hint of fox poo off him and Giselle says she's going to have to wash him properly tomorrow.

With the fire roaring in the grate and the house cosy and happy, outside lit up with its twinkling of fairy lights, I think that Rivendell must be one of the happiest, most magical places in the world, and I'm so lucky to have it, to dip in and out of. If I am really lucky, I think dreamily, slipping into fantasy land, I might even have someone to bring here one day.

17

Marin

It's another Saturday morning when I should be lying in bed with a novel, but instead I'm drinking a strong coffee, figuring out what I'm going to cook for dessert. Tonight, Finn is bringing his new friend who is not, repeat not, his girlfriend.

'Don't treat her like that,' says Finn to me. 'She's –' he pauses, thinking – 'just don't treat her like that. I haven't asked her out or anything. I need to go slow here.'

'Why?' I ask.

'Just because,' he says enigmatically.

So, no pressure. Finn – a gorgeous human being – has, since he split up with Mags some years ago, had the taste in girl-friends of someone who's suffered a lot of concussions. But this sounds different. I hope.

Once, I harboured plans that he'd fall for Bea or even my sister, April, but Bea isn't interested in anything but friendship from Finn and April only likes those men who are permanently unavailable. It's a mystery why Finn – decent, a gentleman, funny, kind to children and animals and good-looking – is still single.

His break-up with Mags seems to have affected his ability to recognise women who are all wrong for him. His last girl-friend Ivanna – whom Steve and Nate cruelly called Ivanna the terrible – was far too cold and humourless for him. And this woman, this Sid? Who knows – time will tell.

'Mum,' says Rachel, moving into the kitchen with speed and snagging a banana from the fruit bowl, 'since you have got people over tonight, could I possibly borrow your car?'

'Where are you going, darling?' I say idly, as if I wasn't checking up on her, but I so am. Since the Les Cloob incident, I am terrified of something happening to Rachel. My motherly fear sensors have edged up a notch because of it. Now, I see, she's truly at the age where she can go off into the world on her own and I cannot be beside her every moment. Another lesson in the painful and lifelong parenting journey, for which there is no damn guidebook.

Louise, Megan's mother, is more sanguine: 'They learned their lesson,' she says.

'No they didn't,' I say. 'They're kids and at that age, the brain tells them to take more risks.'

I feel generally more anxious lately and I don't know it if it's because of what happened with Rachel and Megan or because of how Nate's becoming more and more distant. The one-armed-hug king. Not a single sexy moment on the stairs for weeks. I might as well be invisible. And now, another bloody gang over for drinks and food, which means another family Saturday evening gone. When do we ever get to have time to ourselves?

Despite the Rachel incident, I have to be careful not to imply that this one-off means she is untrustworthy. You can't keep harping on about don't drink and drive, or never get into a car with anyone who is drunk. You have got to let go or they won't tell you anything at all.

'Megan and I were thinking of seeing a band, just a small indie thing with some of the guys,' says Rachel.

'Guys?' I can't help myself using an inflection to imply that I need the names, addresses and photo IDs of these men. As soon as I have said it, I'm sorry because you are not supposed to enquire as to the identity of your eighteen-year-old daughter's friends.

The modern parent is, apparently, supposed to cheerfully say: 'Yeah, fine.'

And the next morning, when the police come round and

say, 'do you know who your daughter was with last night?' you are going to look like you really don't care. How to strike that balance?

Rachel takes pity on me.

'Matt, Lorcan and possibly Cameron.'

'Sounds lovely,' I say, much more enthusiastically. They're nice young men. Responsible. I have had them in my house many times and I have given them fierce looks, analysed them, looked at the way they filled the dishwasher and said, 'thank you, this is lovely, Marin' politely as they ate meals I prepared for them. And basically did my best to frighten them so they will not even dream of hurting my daughter. Nate always laughs at this.

'You are so soft in every other way, Marin,' he'll say. 'But you're like someone with a copy of *Guns 'n' Ammo* under the bed when it comes to those guys, and that's supposed to be my job.'

I agree that he's the one who should be doing the tough dad thing – but Nate is very laid back lately. Honestly, he's being useless.

I want to make sure that Rachel is hanging around with decent young men who get the concept of consent, full stop, and that when they are out they stay together, and they understand that drunk and unable to say no does not mean yes. I want to be sure that she'll be safe. Because I will find those boys and rip them into pieces if she is not.

'Sounds fine,' I say to Rachel now. 'Can you give me a hand for a few minutes and get some eggs in the corner shop? Finn's bringing a new woman who is a friend, and not a date,' I add, 'so all stops are being pulled out.'

'Hope she's better than the last stupid cow,' says Rachel.

'Rachel, we do not diss other women,' I say sternly, even though I had been dissing Ivanna in my own head. 'If you're still around when this Sid comes, drop in and give this nice new girl/woman the once over,' I said. 'Just don't push her up against the wall and ask her too many intense questions.'

Rachel laughs. 'That's your job, Mum,' she says.

Then Joey is at the door, an empty cereal bowl in his hand and a look of hunger on his face. Joey, almost taller than me already at ten, is always hungry. There's something of the monster about him in that he can keep eating the way Godzilla keeps eating things, even when there really can't be any more room for stuff in there. But Godzilla's not lanky, with ruffled hair and that lovely half-little-boy, half-tweenager look of my darling Joey.

Rachel grabs the keys.

'We need Cheerios,' says Joey, as she disappears out the door.

'Sure,' she calls out.

'I'll text you a list,' I add and can hear her groan. 'Pay off for taking the car tonight,' I say.

'Stop having dinner parties, then,' she yells.

Tell your father that, I think grimly. He's the one who keeps organising things for every weekend.

I turn to my darling son.

'There's a box in the corner cupboard up high, Joey. Don't forget to put the bowl in the dishwasher after, honey,' I say, which is half for me and half for him. I have to stop doing everything for him. When he clatters his bowl into the dishwasher, I give him a big hug. He's such a pet. Ten years old, still happy to hug me.

The same age as Bea's Luke. I hope he's still hugging her, I think.

Poor Bea — proof that being beautiful means absolutely nothing in the lottery of life. Bea's stunning, and has the best work ethic of anyone I know — she's had to single parent her son, after all. But we were on the phone this week when I asked her here tonight and she admitted — rather reluctantly — that she was going on a blind date the following week.

'Two of my girlfriends set it up and you probably think I'm crazy –' she begins, but I stop her.

'No! I think it's wonderful!' And I do. The thought of beautiful Bea with someone makes me so happy. If anyone deserves happiness, it's her.

Nate walks into our bedroom and looks at me as if I am stark raving mad as I pull garment after garment out of the wardrobe, put it on and find it wanting.

Clothes litter the bed like the end of an everything-must-go sale day in a posh shop.

He's wearing chinos, a T-shirt and a light sweater, all of which took precisely two moments of effort, but now that he's dressed, he's staring at me.

'Dejunking?' he says mildly.

'Yes, that's exactly it,' I say with heavy irony from under a coral-coloured top that was cheap but somehow draped well. I drag it down. Once clingy, its cheapness means too many washes have shrunk it, so I pull it off.

'Okey doke, I'll go down and open the wine.'

He plants a kiss on my head and leaves, at which point I sit on the bed on my coral top, in just my bra and slimming black jeans and tell myself that crying won't help. I know this is stupid but I can't look bad in front of Finn's new girlfriend/friend. I have to look like my best me.

I don't want her to judge me. It's bad enough to feel so beneath Angie, even though yes, it's not her it's me, but still. I can't have another person in my house making me feel inadequate. Why am I like this anyway? I never used to feel so unsettled.

'Mum?' Joey is at our bedroom door.

I am frozen. Shame floods me. I've been trying to bring up my son and daughter to feel good about themselves and how are they going to do that if they see me rejecting every item I own in case I look fat in it?

'Hi, honey,' I say, trying for breezy. I grab a T-shirt and pull it on. 'Come in.'

'The bed's all junky,' he says.

'I was tidying up,' I lie. 'The wardrobe was untidy.'

'The bed's untidy now,' says Joey. 'You really messed up, Mum.'

He turns and heads off.

I stare at the pile of clothes and my eye catches a black T-shirt thing that was supposed to be either a dress or go over trousers but looked wrong as both.

There's the one I lost the receipt for so I couldn't take it back. A shameful purchase: full price, had us eating very, very carefully for a week because I blew so much of the housekeeping on it. Turns out that silver sequinned blouses are only flattering in the shop's lengthening, low-light dressing-room mirror. The bed is littered with my sartorial disappointments, my dreams as wrinkled and crushed as the cottons and silks.

It's nearly time for everyone to arrive and there's a ring at the doorbell.

My heart sinks but I take a deep breath and put my game face on.

Nate whisks the guests into the kitchen and it turns out to be Angie, who is wearing an entirely wet blouse and holding out the remains of a bouquet of flowers at arm's length.

'We collided because we'd parked round the side and I came round the corner at speed,' says the woman following her. This must be Sid. 'You know how fast I walk, Finn. We were like two wildebeests at the watering hole. Some of my flowers are in a heap in the ground at your front door.'

Steve and Finn follow them, laughing.

Sid puts down the remains of the flowers. 'I wasn't sure about the lilies,' she says, wiping her hands on her black trousers and extending one forward.

'It's fine,' I say. And I'm beaming at her because Sid is as straightforward as they come and her smile is utterly genuine. She is dressed in possibly the least pretentious way I have ever seen and, believe me, I have seen them all. She's wearing a black T-shirt, a black cardigan, black trousers and black trainers. Nothing looks expensive label-y. She has short, messy dark hair, quite a heavy splurge of dark eyeliner and eyeshadow and possibly a swipe of lip balm. That is it, the extent of it. There's no, *I am here and I am fabulous, look at me in my cashmere.*

I have to stop thinking like that, it's not normal.

I immediately let my stomach out. It's fine, so what if the ludicrously expensive jeans I bought recently do not suck the two babies' worth of belly in.

'Will we leave the flowers out there?' I say.

Angie has dumped her flowers in the sink and gone off in search of the loo.

'I'll get scissors and go out,' says Sid thoughtfully. 'Snip off anything that's still salvageable. But all in all, I think we did a really good job of destruction there.'

'Knew you'd get on,' says Finn.

I look at him and I think he's glowing with happiness. They might be friends but I sense it could easily segue into something more. Or has it already . . .? Once, I would have whispered this to Nate as soon as we had a moment alone, but not tonight.

'So, this is Sid,' he says, ready to welcome them now they're in his castle, and I watch my husband go to Sid to kiss her on both cheeks, Continental-style, which is his normal greeting of women in a social setting, even those he doesn't know. But a weird thing happens. Sid moves a step back and extends a hand.

'You must be Nate,' she says, in a low, firm voice, hand further extended than normal.

She doesn't like being touched: it comes to me in a moment. No, she doesn't like being touched by men, because she didn't mind colliding with Angie, seemed to think it was funny, and was relaxed about shaking my hand.

Nate seems taken aback, cross even, and for some reason I can't explain in my rational mind, I decide that she is fabulous. FABULOUS.

Steve and Finn burst out laughing, as if at some private joke.

'The old charm doesn't always work,' says Steve and he digs my husband in the ribs.

Yes, Nate, I think – the old charm doesn't work.

Sid says, 'If you could give me scissors and a compost bag for the flowers?'

I laugh. 'You are kind but, honestly, it's fine.'

'No, really,' she says. 'I hate when there's mess, I like to tidy things up.'

'Right,' I say, knowing determination when I see it. I see it in Joey every day, when he tries to get out of doing his homework. And even though Sid is a lot older than Joey, I can see absolute firm determination written all over her. I hand her scissors and a compost bag.

'Won't be long,' she says. And she's off out.

'She's great, isn't she?' says Finn, leaning against the cooker, which is where he normally stations himself when he comes to our house for dinner parties. 'Knew you'd like her.'

'I love her,' says Angie, coming back into the room having removed her blouse and now clad merely in an elegant camisole with a silky wrap around her shoulders.

'That's because she's normal,' says Steve. 'You were expecting Ivanna the terrible.'

'She wasn't terrible,' says Finn. 'She was just high maintenance.'

'You don't need high maintenance,' says Nate firmly, as if he needs to be top dog again. 'You need someone like Marin, only you can't have her because she's mine.'

'I don't need anyone. I'm off dating, I've told you. Sid and I are pals.'

Yeah, right, I think.

Finn begins lifting lids off saucepans and doing the sort of thing that you only allow a person who is very familiar and adored to do in your kitchen.

'I love that seafood chowder,' he moans. 'Could you make

me up a bucket of it, I'll pay, bring it home and freeze it into little pots, and then I won't have to shop for a week.'

'I promised to show you how to make it,' I tell him sternly, the way I tell him every time. 'Rachel has learned. Teach a man how to fish and all that.'

'I'm unteachable where cooking's concerned,' says Finn.

'Nobody's unteachable,' says Rachel, coming into the room and smiling at everyone.

Finn and Steve hug her.

'Off to break a few hearts, eh,' says Steve.

'No,' says my daughter loftily. 'Off with friends. No hearts involved.'

'Our daughter is going to be running her own accountancy firm before she's forty,' says Nate proudly. 'So none of this breaking-heart stuff, she doesn't have time for men.'

Everyone laughs.

'Enough, proud papa,' I say. I've been a cow, I decide. Nate can be self-absorbed but he adores the kids, loves us all so much. He's just not always brilliant at showing it.

Sid comes back and is introduced to Rachel, who seems to approve.

'Your hair,' Rachel says, awestruck. 'I love it.'

Sid puts a hand up and ruffles it. 'A no-effort hairdo,' she says, grinning.

'It's so *now*,' Rachel goes on.

Now is the best thing of all for Rachel and Megan – encompassing the right clothes, shoes, hair, make-up and views.

'Who does it?' Rachel asks and Sid looks bemused.

'Small place in the city near the office. Nothing fancy,' she says. 'I just wash it, towel dry it and I'm done. Had it for years. Fifteen, actually,' she adds and she sounds different for a moment, a less cheerful tone to her voice.

Who, I think, knows how long they've had their hair cut a certain way? I forget my anniversary, never mind the length I've had certain clothes or hairdos.

'Muum,' interrupts Rachel. 'Earth to Mum. I'm going.'

I abandon the cooking. 'Excuse me,' I say to everyone in the kitchen. 'Nate, fix the drinks, I'm going out to say goodbye to Rachel.'

Rachel is hugged and admired as she makes her way through the kitchen. They have all seen her grow up from a little child to the beautiful girl she is now. She definitely looks more like Nate than me with that incredible streaky blonde hair that's rippling down her back and the brown eyes, although hers are wide apart whilst Nate's are narrower, shrewder.

I wonder is it some strange evolutionary fact that makes mothers think their own children are the most beautiful creatures in the world? And does that in its place make us more protective? It must do. Evolution at work.

'Now you will be careful, won't you, honey?' I say as we get to the front door.

'Mum, I will,' she says with a hint of irritation. 'I'm driving, I'm not drinking, we are going to see a band. End of. I'll park the car somewhere safe, the lads will be with us, you have my phone number, you have their phone numbers, their addresses, probably their social security numbers too.'

I laugh. 'You got me, darling. Have fun,' and I watch her head off to pick up Megan.

All's right in the world.

18

Sid

Rachel seems like a very put-together young woman, a lot more together than lovely dizzy Chloe from my office, I think as I watch her and her mother head out. I really like Marin, even though I wasn't sure if I would from the way Finn was describing her. She just sounded perfect and I've never liked perfect people. Perfect is boring. But she's warm, if a little frazzled, but that's probably just due to an influx of guests.

She likes looking after people, I think, which is lovely. Makes me think of my mother and her collection of artistic strays always littering up our table, and I grin because looking at Marin in her lovely silky shirt and black jeans, I know she's a million miles away from my mother and yet similar. Both part of that decent crew of women who take it upon themselves to take care of people. It's clearly not genetic.

Rachel and Marin head out to pass over the essential wisdom that goes between a mother and her daughter going out for the night.

I accept a glass of juice, grab a handful of nuts from a bowl, and wander over to Finn. Seeing a person with their friends is very instructive, but tonight, I find that I merely want to be close to him. There is nobody I want to impress, not Nate, Steve or Angie. The person I like most apart from Finn is Marin. So I'll whisper to Finn that if we could sit close to her, that would be lovely. It would be too much to say I want to sit close to him . . .

'I'm not used to going out much lately,' I say, knowing this is a huge admission, but I don't care. If he doesn't understand, then he isn't the man I think he is.

One large hand pats my arm.

'Message received. And thank you for coming. I didn't want it to be a baptism of fire.'

'This is nice, they're good people.'

Rachel has just gone when there is a ring on the door, and Nate goes out to answer it. He comes in with a woman I assume is Bea, who's tall, slightly too thin and is dressed in a pretty but old floral dress with a heavy knitted cardigan on over it. She'd be utterly beautiful if it wasn't for that hauntingly sad look in her eyes. In fact, I can imagine her as a model when she was younger. Nate is all over her.

'Let me take your cardigan, are you too hot, too cold, will I throw another log on the fire? Now, did you get a taxi, I told you to get a taxi because you can have a drink. You didn't, I don't know what's wrong with you.'

I steal a look at Marin as this is going on. And even though nobody else appears to see this as a little over the top, Marin is watching Nate with a slightly resigned look. I sense that she is anxious about Angie because Nate seems delighted to talk to Angie and tell her how marvellous she is. But, this is different. This is like he's taking care of Bea, some special command from his royal master and he's doing it to the tee, because Bea is precious and must be looked after. And yet there has been none of that in his conversations with Marin, no thanks for cooking this amazing dinner.

I don't know what it is about Nate, but he rubs me up the wrong way.

It's not Bea's fault. She's not looking for this. She comes in and embraces people, comes to me, holds out her hand formally, says, 'Hello, so nice to meet you.' And sits down quietly. She's compact, neat for a tall, elegant person. And I wonder about this group of friends and how they all fit together, because something just feels a little odd.

*

The food is fabulous. Every time I try to get up and help Marin, she says, 'no, no sit, I can do everything.' Angie offers too, but Marin absolutely insists *she* sits down. The person who does most of the helping is Finn. Nate just sits at the head of the table, holding court, laughing, chatting, making jokes, pulling people into the conversation if he feels they are at a loss. It's like he's taken a course in how to be the centre of attention at every party. It's strange, he's one of Finn's best friends and Finn is such a decent man. But this guy, I don't like him. Don't like the way he tried to touch me when we met. Nor do I like the way he's letting Marin run around like a little creature on batteries while he just sits there. If he's the one who loves giving dinner parties, why isn't *he* killing himself? Eventually, I get up.

'No,' I said calmly, as I walk behind Marin carrying some plates. 'I am going to help, I just cannot sit down, I'm not good at sitting down. I grew up in a house where there were loads of people hanging around looking for food. And the rule of thumb was, bring your own plate back to the kitchen and wash up.'

'You're really kind but –' she says.

'No buts,' I say.

She looks tired. She's an attractive woman, dark hair, beautiful eyes. But she's worn out. And I feel she didn't really want to do this.

'I'm sorry,' I said, suddenly knowing I'm right. 'You had to pull all of this out of a hat because someone decided a dinner party would be a good idea, right?'

'No, no, honestly.' She almost looks panicked. 'I really love having people over.'

'Sure, but sometimes it's nice to sit and hug your couch cushions and watch the box. I mean, I know it's different when you have kids and a husband,' I add, because she might think it's different, but I feel that somehow even if I did have a husband

and kids, I would be very slow to deal out dinner-party invitations the way this nice woman appears to. 'I quite like to couch surf a bit on a Saturday night after a busy week.'

'But I always love it when we have people over,' protests Marin. 'Specially this lot.'

I think of Angie in her beautiful clothes, a very poised and elegant woman, who seems perfectly nice but doesn't have the womanly talk gene thing going for her. Watching Nate fussing over her or Bea wouldn't be my idea of a nice evening at home.

'You haven't known Angie as long, no?'

Marin blinks at me. 'Not as long as the others, no. I love her clothes, don't you?'

I shrug. 'I don't do the clothes thing,' I say. 'I've a nice simple uniform going for me, and I could probably wear the same thing every single day and nobody would know. Although I do have loads of this particular outfit so I can have a new one every day for two weeks.'

Marin laughs and sits down at the table.

'I'm terrible with clothes,' she says. 'I always look at Angie's and I feel like a slob.'

'Well, she's five foot ten, everything hangs well when you're five foot ten and she works out, I can tell.'

'Sometimes I work out too,' says Marin thoughtfully. 'But I don't have a lot of time.'

'Course you don't have a lot of time, you've a big job.'

'Oh, it's not a big job –'

'Who says it's not a big job?' I say and suddenly I feel as if I'm hearing Nate's voice. 'You're an estate agent, which is a big job, and you're a mum, and you run the house and you clearly do all the cooking.'

I don't know why, but I want to shake her and tell her she's incredible. And that good-looking dude in there doesn't deserve her, because all he wants to do is show off his lovely house and his great choice in wine. And she's running around exhausted. I stare at her and I realise I've upset her.

'Oh don't mind me,' I say, 'I shouldn't really be let out to see the general public. I'm a bit eccentric, I think.' I'm exaggerating, but I want to make her feel better.

'Are you seeing Finn?' says Marin hopefully. 'He's gorgeous. I know he says you're not, but I would love to see him happy. I used to long for him to get together with Bea because he's such a darling and so's she, but they're just old pals.'

At that exact moment, I want to say no, that she can't have him because I want him. And then I think, don't be ridiculous, where did that come from?

'No, we're friends,' I say quickly, 'just friends. It's good to have friends, right, you know, like dinner parties: fun.'

'Yeah,' says Marin, 'fun.'

19

Bea

I feel like someone from Hollywood being primped for the Oscars.

I'm standing up in my bedroom with Christie and my mother sitting on the bed, watching, while Shazz fusses over me. I'm wearing a tight black skirt, black nylons and a low-cut top from Shazz's wardrobe that says 'come and get me, baby'. Or so I'm told.

'It's too low,' I say for what feels like the tenth time.

I bend forward. 'Look, if I do this, you can see my bra.'

'But it's a nice bra,' says Shazz, utterly delighted with herself.

We have very different ideas about clothes and while Shazz thinks there is no such thing as 'too tight', I do. The top is satin and I feel I should be standing on a street corner telling people how much I cost.

'I'd fancy you in it,' says Christie.

'You are not my target market,' I reply. 'My target market might think I am asking for it. Imagine what Tom will think.'

Tom is my date for this evening, picked after enormous examination of all the prospective dates and while his looks do not fill me with excitement, although it could just be a bad profile picture, he sounds mild. Mild is what I want for this first date.

'Tom will think all his Christmases have come at once,' says Shazz, trying to decide whether her vermeil heart necklace – which nestles just above my breasts – is better than my own tiny gold and lapis lazuli beads, which circle my neck.

'I wish I could become a lesbian,' I say to Christie, with a sigh as I have often said before. She laughs, as she always does. 'Women are kinder and have much less testosterone,' I add. 'Testosterone is the problem.'

'It doesn't work that way, sweetie,' pipes up Mum, who has never heard this conversation between me and Christie before. 'I don't think you get to choose. You just are what you are.'

Christie leans down and hugs my mother tightly. Her own mother is devoutly religious, thinks any variation of homosexuality or gender issues is bad and has never even seen Christie's two beautiful daughters because they weren't born in a straight family. Her predjudice is her loss, Shazz and I always say when Christie gets sad.

'I know that, Mum,' I say. 'It's a joke between us but it would be easier.'

Shazz has been ignoring us. 'Tom is going to love this,' she says thoughtfully, deciding – to my relief – on my own beads. Her necklace would be like a sign pointing down to my bosoms.

'I still feel like I'm hooking in this outfit,' I say.

'You're too classy, Bea,' says Shazz and both Christie and my mother agree.

'You look elegant,' Mum says. 'Now have fun.'

Tom and I are meeting for drinks in a pub not too far from my home.

'Dinner's too risky,' says Shazz. 'If he turns out to be a total weirdo, you're stuck.'

I park the car, because I plan to drink mineral water, and enter the pub, keeping a wary eye out for a 'tall man wearing a navy cashmere sweater and with blond hair.'

That's Tom's personal description and it fits with the profile picture. If he is everything he says he is, he sounds lovely. A lawyer, divorced, with two daughters and heavily involved in his local sports club. What's not to like.

But there is no sign of a tall man in navy cashmere. I stand, like a flamingo, on one leg because when I'm nervous, I tend to do this. The lounge part of the pub is small. Unless there is another bit, Tom is hiding. Everyone is in groups or couples, apart from one guy . . .

'Bea! I knew it was you. You're beautiful!'

A distinctly short man stands on tippytoes to kiss my cheek and I think that someone with a legal background must know that it's illegal to pass oneself off as something else. But then, probably not on dating websites.

I'm five eight, tall for a woman, and there is no way Tom is over five foot six. Which is fine. But he's lied.

He grabs my hand and leads me over to a table, where he's clearly already downed one pint and a packet of peanuts, and is half-way into another one.

'I'm nervous, so I got here early,' he says and smiles. Truthfully, he has a sweet smile but there's a bit of peanut stuck in his teeth and the hair – the blond hair that looked outwardly tousled in his profile picture – is almost definitely a wig.

He's also older than he said he was. Tom fifty-four is more like Tom sixty-three or older.

'You're even more beautiful than your picture,' he gabbles on.

'Thank you,' I say because I don't know what else to say.

Am I so shallow that I can't allow myself to like a shorter, older man with a wig? Who knows what sort of wonderful person Tom is?

Except, I think, as he energetically waves at the barman for drinks, he lied. My profile told the truth, even though Shazz says this is the kiss of death.

I order my mineral water and sit back against the banquette. I soon realise that sitting beside Tom is a mistake. He's very close to me, saying he's been looking forward to this ever since I messaged him back and that he doesn't mind that I'm a widow.

'No competition, eh?' he says jovially.

'That's one way of putting it,' I say, bristling.

'My girls are thrilled I'm seeing someone else,' he goes on. 'The ex has found herself some bit on the side. "Dad," they said to me, "you need someone to love, someone to enjoy the rest of your life with".'

'How old are your girls?' I ask politely.

Next second, his phone is out and he's scrolling through pictures, showing me two women who are either very late twenties or early thirties.

'You must have married young,' I say, thinking that maybe I'm wrong and he's younger than he looks, that divorce must have shattered him so much he's aged.

'No, had Lara when we were just thirty. Right little chip off the old block. Got into law first try. Doesn't work in my firm, though.'

And he's off, showing me old pictures on his phone that he must have transferred from actual hard copies. Tom is a doting dad, for sure. But the sight of him and a woman with a very 1970s haircut and their two small children clarify the fact that he's lied about his age.

He manages to drink his second pint too and is soon ordering another one. He's chatting garrulously about his life, not asking me anything about mine, and I can see that for Tom, this date is going swimmingly. I feel as if I am floating above myself - witnessing it all with the mild disinterest of a television camera person.

'Have a real drink, love,' he says. 'It'll loosen you up. You're stiff as a board,' he adds, running one finger down my back against the silky top and pinging my bra strap as he does so.

I jerk away.

'Tom, we have only just met and that was entirely inappropriate,' I say, trying not to sound harsh. But real anger has sprung up in me.

'Oh honey, look at you – you came here all dressed up and

you can't just drink bottled water and expect a man to just look. This is one helluva sexy outfit.'

His other hand touches my tight skirt and begins to slide it up my thigh.

The last bit of calm snaps inside me. Tom is lucky I keep the snapping internal or else he'd have broken fingers. I am stronger than I look.

I grab my handbag and push myself out of the banquette.

'Thank you, Tom, for the water. I don't think we're suited,' I say icily.

'Don't tease, honey,' he says and, unbelievably, he's still smiling, still convinced this is salvageable. 'With no man at home, you must be lonely . . .'

'I have my husband's old double-barrelled shotgun,' I lie. 'It keeps people away and I'm never lonely.' I stare full-on at Tom: 'I'm an excellent shot,' I say. The whole thing is a lie: there is no gun but I am suddenly furious that this complete stranger has invaded my personal space, touched me inappropriately and lied solidly to get me here.

Holding my head high, I march out to the car, daring him to come after me. I swear, I will kick him in the nuts if he attempts it.

I'm halfway home before I stop shaking and I realise that this was a horrible encounter. Liars cannot be trusted, no matter how smiley-faced they are.

Mum reaches the hall as soon as she hears me unlock the front door. She takes in my face, which I know has two bright red patches on my cheeks – I always get red in the face when I'm shocked or angry.

'Not so good?' she asks tentatively.

I lean down to hug her.

'Oh Mum, it was awful. He lied about his age, looked nothing like his photo, had a wig . . . And he ran his hand down my back and up my leg, *and* pinged my bloody bra strap. One minute we were talking, the next: ping!'

'Bastard!' she says, shocking me. Mum never swears.

'Why did I let Shazz and Christie convince me to do this?' I say into the warmth of her shoulder.

'Because you're ready,' Mum says softly. 'You've grieved for long enough. There's no time limit on grief and you had so much to grieve, but you are ready for someone else in your life, someone to hug, someone to hold you and make you feel like a woman again. Though this Internet thing might not be the way . . .'

'No, it isn't,' I say, shuddering.

She leads me into the kitchen where the puppies are in their bed but come awake and waddle out of the cage to see me.

I sink onto the floor and Sausage tries to climb my leg, ripping the hated slinky tights as she does so.

'You little darlings,' I croon and they lick every bit of my face they can reach, making their happy little puppy noises. 'I don't think I am ready, Mum,' I say. 'This is enough – Luke, me, you, my friends and these little angels.'

'No, you are ready,' Mum repeats. 'Let's try the old-fashioned way of finding someone.'

'Blind dates? Remember crazy Ed and the man who was married who thought I was his?'

'They were disasters,' Mum says, boiling the kettle. 'No, there must be nice men out there somewhere and I have plenty of women friends with sons and nephews and contacts who will know someone.'

'What are you going to say?' I ask. 'My daughter is desperate –'

'No,' Mum interrupts firmly. 'I'm going to say that my beautiful daughter, whom many have admired, has finally finished grieving her husband and that she might welcome a lovely man to take her to dinner.'

'I draw the line at wigs,' I say. 'I'd far prefer someone who was bald and honest than someone with a bad wig. I'm too old to be in a relationship with someone who can't be honest with himself, never mind with me.'

'Good thought to start with,' says Mum, making tea and smiling her Cheshire Cat smile, which only comes out when she's got a plan. 'Leave it to me, darling. Just leave it to me.'

PART TWO

Christmas Lights Sparkling

20

Marin

Ma has a task for me. She wants me to phone Dom's beleaguered wife, Sue.

'Talk to Sue and tell her we want her here for Christmas,' commands my mother early one morning, as I'm shaking off my coat after arriving into work. It's freezing, the week before Christmas and I don't want to be here and I don't want to be in the middle of my mother's nefarious plan.

I nearly hadn't answered the call, but some Pavlovian response made me.

'Ma, she's probably going to her own family for dinner, you know how it is.' I'm thinking of Nate's vast plans for Christmas. The party he wants to give just before Christmas. The flying visit we'll make to my home, the equally flying visit we'll make to his. And then the supposedly grand dinner in our own house where he'll want to somehow round up a few of his random friends to come in and enjoy his largesse. I'm going off parties. Seriously. I did try looking up if irritability was one of the signs of the perimenopause, but there are so many signs that any normal woman could have them all. Sadly, there is no special mention of disliking parties.

'I don't see why she's not coming here, she's still married to Dominic,' Ma bleats, 'and he'd love her here, I know he would. I have no idea what April is up to, she doesn't tell me anything.'

There's a very good reason April doesn't tell my mother anything. Most of April's Christmases are spent waiting for phone calls from her married lovers, or occasionally the odd torrid session out when one escapes the marital fold for half an hour, to get over to April's to hug her, kiss her, bring her some ludicrous present and then disappear, leaving her that strange combination of happy and sad. Only *then* can she actually go anywhere for Christmas. This Christmas, there'll be no waiting-for-Jared time as he, predictably, didn't leave his wife or his house.

I realise Ma is still talking about Dom and how Sue is being so tricky.

'Why isn't Dominic ringing Sue?' I ask suddenly.

Big mistake. There's something about being in the office that brings out the professional woman in me, and I come over all direct, which is not something I normally do with my mother. In our house, you kept your mouth shut and let Ma run things her way. If you did anything she didn't like, she would deploy the silent treatment. Which I feel sure has already been banned under the Geneva Convention.

'Of course he's not going to ring her, because she's not answering his calls,' snaps my mother as if it's all perfectly plain and I must be an absolute cretin not to have thought of this.

Why does she talk to me like this? I think.

'She'll listen to you. You need to do this, Marin.' I know this move, it's like one of those marvellous chess games that have names. The Immortal Game. I am the pawn and my mother is the Grand Master. 'It's not as if I'm asking for much!' Ma says in a more heated voice.

Ah yes, the 'I'm only asking this one little thing of you' gambit.

Like the good little girl I am, I slip back into my role.

'Of course, I'll ring her later. Ma, I'm just at the office, I'd better go.'

'Fine, fine, busy busy, I know, bye,' she huffs, as if my having a job is something I do purely to annoy her.

I sit at my desk and tap out a text to Sue. I don't really feel up to ringing her just yet. But I know I can be honest with her.

Hi, Sue, Ma has been on because Dominic apparently
wants you to see him on Christmas. I know – he should
be texting or phoning. I apologise for my family in general.
Can we talk, so I can say I've done my best? xx Marin

Sue and I have always got on. She's normal, far more normal
than anyone else in my family, so I have absolutely no idea how
she managed to get married to Dom. But I can only assume
that his good looks, and he *is* very good looking, somehow
blinded her to his ability to seem like a grown-up but act like
a teenager.

What's your day like? she texts back quickly.

I scan down my calendar. Sue works about a mile away in an
office in the city.

I could manage a coffee at about twelve, I say, I can come
close to you. But I've literally got half an hour.

Great, she says, let's do it.

The city is no fun this time of the year. There's a wild Christmas frenzy in the air as if people will actually implode if they
do not wave their credit cards enough. Nobody looks happy,
just harassed, belting along the streets, going to meetings and
fitting in a bit of Christmas shopping along the way. Or just
in town to buy the perfect gift, which, of course, doesn't exist.

Sue and I arrive exactly at the same time in front of the
coffee shop.

'Good timing,' she says. She's taller than me, younger, fair,
athletic. Could have had her pick of any number of men. I
remember their wedding day, and she looked like a goddess
in a long cream sheath. Dominic had the faint air of a young
Hugh Jackman: the shoulders, the face, everything. He's even
nice. But being married to him must be like being married to
a large child who wants amusing all the time.

We hug, grab two coffees and find a corner.

'I knew you'd draw the short straw,' says Sue, drinking her

coffee black. This is obviously the secret to the athletic thing. I have milk and sugar.

'I'm sorry,' I say, 'I really am. I wish it had worked out, honey, but you know, you've got to do what's right for you. I adore Dom but he hasn't quite grown up yet.'

Her eyes are sad as she looks at me.

'I love him,' she says, resignedly. 'But I can't live with him, I can't stay married to him. He's useless around the house, even though I work longer hours than he does. He honestly can't even work the washing machine.'

I feel a faint stab of recognition. Nate claims that only women understand laundry equipment. He always says it as a joke but it's not, I realise. He never does the laundry. He can put things in the basket all right, but he never carries the damned thing downstairs or puts on a wash.

Sue's still talking: 'And the lads, those idiots he's in "the band" with. They're all adults but they still harbour this belief that they could make it big. Every damn weekend, he wants them round so they can pluck their bloody guitars and I'm supposed to provide food.'

Another stab. Nate may not be in a band but he's obsessed with having people in our house. It's very similar.

'Plus, your mother's always on the phone to me these days, blaming me. Drives me nuts. I just wanted a quiet life, and kids. I want kids.'

I stare at Sue and grab her hand across the table.

I suddenly realise that I have been a hopeless sister-in-law: there was lovely Sue, married for years, and not a sign of a child and I had never noticed, never wondered if it was choice or circumstance. I bet my mother noticed. Bet she mentioned it to poor Sue too.

'My darling: infertility?'

'No.' She sounds weary now, as if she has thought about this so often, it's imprinted in her brain and she can speak without engaging anything but the most limited mental circuits:

'Dom's "not ready for kids". He wants us to do fun stuff first before we settle down. I'm thirty-three. My body's about to hit the downhill slope and he doesn't care, never thinks about that. Just wants to have fun . . .'

There it is: the bitterness of pain long kept inside.

Something in me reacts to it. Dom doesn't really care what Sue wants. Not because he's a horrible person but because what he wants comes first: it always has. Ma adored him and he could do no wrong.

Nate is the same. We do what he wants all the time. Case in point: endless entertaining when I am so tired working and rushing around after Joey and even Rachel, who always wonders where her new sweater/skirt/jeans are.

There's no comparison, of course. Sue is in deep pain and I'm merely irritated. Isn't that all it is?

'He does want children but not yet and he never thought to mention that to me. Because you don't talk about that stuff in advance. Why the hell not? Why do you need to have the wedding dress booked months in advance, spend hours discussing invitations, all that superfluous stuff and never sit down and have a serious conversation? Let's discuss these important things – like how do we feel about money, where will we live, do we both want children and when? What do we want out of our lives? Would we like to retire and live in the country when we hit fifty? Are we going to argue about how to bring the kids up? Are we going to try and live like vegans and have no TVs?' Sue sighs. 'Stupidly, I thought we were on the same page planwise but Dominic doesn't have any plan. He thinks planning is boring. And he sulks if I bring anything serious up now. He could sulk for Ireland, but I guess you know that?'

'Yeah,' I say, 'I thought you knew that and got it?'

'No, I didn't know it. He hid it. He hid it until we were married. It's like he's hardwired to sulk. Then I realised it's just the family hardwiring – no offence, my family has its own hardwiring but with yours, April is hardwired to try to have what she can't, Dom is hardwired to be a child and sulk, and you're hardwired to try to keep everyone happy and take care of them all.'

I look at her, and my eyes fill with tears.

'Yeah,' I say, suddenly sad. 'I am. I'm hardwired to keep everyone happy, because you know Ma, you know what it's like.' I'm half-processing this statement but Sue has rushed on with the conversation.

'When I married Dom, I didn't know it was going to be like that. I want a family and a life and I can't have that with your brother because he's totally messed up. Dom hates plans but I've got a plan, Marin, a plan to have a good life. And I'm never going to have that with Dom. That's why I want to get divorced so I can start again. Your holier-than-God mother is going to have to deal with it, because it's her bloody fault.'

'I know,' I say sadly.

This time Sue grabs my hand.

'It's not your fault, Marin,' she says. 'You've always been so amazing to me. I love you, you take care of Dom, you've done everything for everyone, even April, and her problems are pretty unsolvable.'

I smile sadly. April has that effect on me.

'I don't think I'm doing very well there.'

'You can't fix April because the fact is, nobody can fix anyone else. The fixing up is an inside job.'

'Did you mean it when you said you had a plan?' I say suddenly.

'Yeah sure,' says Sue. And I'm struck again by the fact that she is thirty-three and that thirty-three-year-olds might have plans. Whereas people like me never had a plan. Nate came into my life and there was no need for a plan. He was the prince on the charger. I always thought April wanted the prince on the charger who was going to rescue her, but now it hits me. April wants the unavailable, because that's what she knows, has read about since she was young. It's me who wanted rescuing. And instead I'm still trying to fix everything for everyone and it turns out that nobody is rescuing me at all.

'I've upset you, I'm really sorry,' says Sue shrewdly. 'I just can't deal with your mother at Christmas or Dom. I'm not going to be around for Christmas, I'm going away with my sister; we're going to go skiing. I thought it would be fun. I have only done it once and it's horrendously expensive, but whatever.'

'New beginnings,' I say, pulling myself together. 'If you don't go, we'll be having a big party at my house and I will control Ma.'

She laughs so loudly that the other people in the coffee shop look around.

'Marin, honey: nobody can control your mother. Have a good party.'

I feel suddenly sick at the thought of Nate's big party. He's obsessed with a big Christmas bash, has already bought the wine, discussed canapes with me. I haven't had a chance to get my roots dyed and yet I already know I'm making asparagus wrapped in filo pastry because Nate loves it.

'I will,' I say, forcing a smile. 'Enjoy skiing.'

'I can't wait,' she says, beaming, and I'm struck by her fresh youth and the fact that she's prepared to let my poor brother and all his baggage go and move on. At that moment I want to slap Dominic and my mother. Although I think my mother might get the biggest slap.

'I'd better get back to the office,' I say.

She stands up and hugs me. 'I'll pay for this, go on. We'll talk after Christmas, OK?'

'Yes, right. If you need me to intervene in the whole legal thing talk to me.'

'No, I don't,' says Sue firmly. 'You're not fixing this, you are not helping me, you are taking care of yourself. Hey, maybe that can be your Christmas present to yourself, Marin, you taking care of you. Your mother shouldn't have sent you here. It's none of her business.'

She gives me an extra tight hug and releases me.

I walk down the street and I feel shaky, as if someone has just ripped a veil from in front of me and shown me something I didn't know. People have plans and they can choose what they want, they don't have to get tied up in the past, they don't have to follow the old message. And I thought, I really thought, that April was the one searching for the prince, but it was me, and Nate's the prince and I'm always trying to do the right thing for my prince in case he goes off me. I don't want a Christmas party. I don't want to go to my parents' house for Christmas – well, I do to see Dad. But Ma, I could give her a miss and it wouldn't bother me.

And I don't want to go to Nate's mother's house on Christmas Day, because Nate's mother always looks at me as though I'm some consolation prize he was made to marry. I want to be at home in my own house with maybe April coming over whenever she's freed from waiting for the current married lover. I want to have simple food I haven't spent four hours preparing and play Monopoly or cards with the kids, watch a Disney movie, and just have fun.

That's my plan. It may not be a five-year one, but it's a plan all right.

21

Bea

Antoinette is sick so I have to do her shift and stay for the full day in work, which means Mum picks Luke up from school. I'm tired and anxious by the time I drive in her gate to pick him up, and I hope she's fed him because I am literally too shattered to even think of heating up the mac and cheese I made at the weekend in one of my ultra-organised cook-and-freeze days.

At work, Laoise was muttering about the practice being halved although she has no more evidence than she had last month.

'Why don't we just ask Dr Franklin?' I say to her.

Laoise goggles at me. 'Ask?' she says, as if I have suggested a day trip to Mars.

'Yes, ask. This is our job security we're talking about.'

Laoise deflates. 'I don't know anything else. I was just worrying out loud.'

'I wish you wouldn't,' I say, 'because when you worry, I worry and the week before Christmas is not the time to think about possible job losses.'

I'm thinking of this as I let myself into Mum's and feel the huge relief I always feel when I'm there. I'd never have managed without her all these years. She's had my back in every way: I am so lucky to have her.

This whole week, I feel as though somebody has got a giant Christmas tree and bashed me over the head with it. The practice is madly busy with people determined to have doctor's visits for random complaints because they know we'll be closed over the holidays.

I've also been working hard the way I do every year to make everything Christmassy for Luke. We're going to have Christmas in Mum's house this year. And she's very excited because a new neighbour moved in next door, a very charming sixty-something gentleman with rippling silver hair, who was apparently something big in the boat-building industry.

'I think they're boats but they might be yachts,' says Mum. 'Maybe you could ask, because I have sort of forgotten and I don't want to let on. His name is Cliff and he's coming in for a pre-lunch drink. I did think of asking him for lunch but . . .' Her voice trails off. And I realise she's anxious about what I will think.

'He's a widower. I told him all about you and Luke and he says this is a very precious time with your daughter and your grandson. Is there anything I can bring? Imagine, he thought of bringing something. You do think it's all right, darling, don't you?'

I beam at her. I'm genuinely so thrilled for Mum, it's completely wonderful. But it makes me feel everything is changing. Mum is looking at a man in a romantic way and it's startling. I never thought there'd be anyone for her but Dad. And, Lord, I hate those kids who expect their parents to remain surgically attached to a corpse for the rest of their lives. But it's just so unusual. For so long it's been her and me and Luke. And then Shazz and Raffie and Norma and Christie and Vincent; it's our little gang, and Mum's changing it.

'You don't mind, darling, do you?' she says, still anxious. 'Do you feel I'm being unfaithful to Dad?'

'Mum, you loved Dad so much and he loved you, but I want you to be happy. For goodness' sake, you do realise that people who have happy marriages often get married again really quickly if something happens to their spouse? It's proof of how wonderful marriage was for them.'

'Well, yes,' she says, flustered. 'I'm not going to marry Cliff; he's only coming in for a drink.'

'Why doesn't he join us for dinner?' I hear myself say.

Imagine – darling Mum thinking of falling in love again.

She chatters happily as she makes us both tea and I think idly of Nate and Marin's annual Christmas party and how I'm dreading it. I'm tired of these parties. I'm tired of being the single woman like a splinter in a thumb. The person who used to be part of their gang and is now the pity element. Not that Marin thinks like that, or Finn. But sometimes I think I'm stuck and I'll never get out of being stuck. Yet, if I move away from everything that Jean-Luc and I had together, then maybe I'll be nothing. I'm stuck in limbo – unable to get a decent date, destined to be alone until I'm Mum's age and meet a sweet widower from next door.

Myself, Luke and the puppies drive home, Luke chattering excitedly about the Christmas play where he is playing a Christmas pirate, which makes no sense but then, Christmas plays aren't supposed to, I think, being a veteran of so many of them. He was a rainbow fairy angel once and I made his costume out of an old sheet, glitter and lots of stick-on rainbows. We still have it.

Our house is almost the most Christmassy house imaginable – with the possible exception of Number Twenty-six on our road, where they have practically wiped out the national grid system with twinkling lights, a giant Santa and a complete herd of reindeers perilously perched on the roof. My Christmas extravaganza is confined to inside and our indoor lights are so pretty. I've always wanted the holidays to be incredible for Luke. When I was a child, I loved Christmas. And just because his dad isn't here, it doesn't mean he's going to miss out.

'They definitely know,' Shazz says to me the day before the Christmas play.

'You think?' I say miserably.

'Oh come on, kids know about Santa younger and younger; we're kidding ourselves.'

'But Luke hasn't said anything, I so want him to believe, it's part of the magic. And if the magic is gone, I feel he's growing up and moving away from me, and everything is changing and I can't cope with change. I don't know, when did I get so weak and frail and frightened?'

'I don't care,' says Shazz, 'if Raffie doesn't believe – well, that's fair enough. I mean, we don't want them getting on for eleven and having kids in class slag them because they don't know. And there is always some little gutter snipe whose mother or father or big brother told them. Don't know why that isn't on the mothers' WhatsApp,' she says, grimly. 'But I'm going to say to Raffie, if you don't believe, you don't receive. So he knows but we still have the fun. It's a win-win situation.'

'Yes, you're right,' I say. 'If you don't believe, you don't receive.' I think of the presents, even presents for the dogs. They've got special dog-food stockings and a fluffy teddy for each of them. Even though I know said fluffy teddies will be disembowelled really quickly. Sausage knows how to de-squeak a teddy faster than you would think possible.

Luke and I have just got inside when Luke, instead of racing into the kitchen with the puppies, who head for their bowls expectantly every time they get home, stops and gives me his serious look.

'Mum,' he says, slowly. 'The thing is –' He pauses. He's such a fast thinker, and normally, he talks quickly and excitedly but now he's slow, thoughtful. 'After Christmas we're doing this thing and it's, um –' Another pause.

I smile but I feel my heart sink.

'Yes, lovie,' I say cheerfully, implying in my best motherly way that whatever happens, we will manage it gloriously.

'We've got to do a Family Tree project. We've got to put pictures of people in it, like our families and –'

'That'll be great fun,' I lie, managing to look as if I mean it. I put an arm around him. 'We're so lucky to have such lovely family and friends. Can we put the puppies in too, do you think?'

He smiles and I know he's relieved, that he was hating having to tell me this. 'Yes! Christie has ink in her printer and we can print them there. I want colour ones so everyone can see how adorable they are.'

'I bet nobody has puppies like them,' I say, continuing to squeeze him as we walk into the kitchen.

The girls are looking up at me expectantly, then back down at their bowls. They think food should be a 24/7 sort of experience.

'I love you,' says Luke, launching himself onto the ground and grabbing them both.

They squeal delightedly and I think that Luke's birthday dogs were simply the best present he's ever had. What a pity dads can't be put on Christmas lists.

22

Sid

'Going to a pre-Christmas dinner with his best friends sounds more than "just friends" to me,' says Vilma slyly as we meander through the food market in the city and try free samples of juicy olives and just-baked bread with a new type of goat's cheese smeared on top.

'We are just friends,' I mutter with my mouth full.

Vilma pokes me gleefully in the ribs.

'Don't believe you!' she says. 'You like him! It's about time. Are you going to buy him a present? Or is he getting you one? Because if you get him one and he hasn't got you one, then that's awkward. Maybe he's in the Brown Thomas lingerie department as we speak, standing in front of a sales lady, cupping his hands and saying "she's about this size"!'

Vilma goes off into peals of laughter at this notion and I feel myself turn pink.

'Course he's not,' I say, although I wish he was.

Finn is haunting my dreams now and my favourite fantasy is of us together in bed, curled up, looking into each other's eyes as he gently touches my body, running his fingers over my skin as if I'm a precious gift.

'You bought bloody Marc that cashmere sweater for Christmas and then he dumped you. OK, it was TK Maxx and only cost forty-five quid, but still. Cashmere!' Vilma has moved on at speed. Marc still rankles with her. I wish I could tell her that poor Marc had to leave me, really. I was too broken. We'd tried intimacy and, eventually, it had petered out. He deserved a woman who'd make love to him.

And as for Finn . . . *he* makes me think of making love. I stop by the Christmas gift area and see a body butter in a jolly jar, something chocolatey designed to be spread on a lover's body and licked slowly off. I have never licked *anything* off *anyone's* body but I have the fiercest desire to buy this for Finn and to tell him what I want to do with it.

'Can I phone Marc up and say Happy Christmas?' asks Vilma, suddenly at my side. She looks younger than her nineteen years.

I forget how young she is. Marc was like a big brother. I vow to phone him and make sure he talks to her.

'I'd love if you did,' I say. 'It hurt me so much when he left, honey, but we had moved apart.'

It's the only way I can explain it to her.

My sense of betrayal at his leaving had far less to do with him than with my past – Marc's leaving meant I was on my own and he had been my security blanket. But perhaps he had to leave to free us both to move on? Of course, I can never tell Vilma any of this. I want her to believe in romance.

'I still think Finn must fancy you,' Vilma says now. 'Go on, get him a pressie.'

My eyes swivel to the chocolate body sauce and I gulp at the thought of his beautiful head bent over my body, licking it off *me*.

I'd love to be able to tell Vilma how groundbreaking this feels but again, I can't.

'Something funny,' she suggests, mistaking my silence. 'Or foodie things. Something from here. Like cherries dipped in dark chocolate? I love cherries.'

I imagine Finn dangling one over my mouth, feeding me.

'Biscuits,' I say quickly. Nobody can feel erotic over biscuits. This madness has to stop. Body butter, indeed. 'Really special shortbread.'

Which he might ask me to his place to eat . . .

*

One of the many things working at Nurture has given me is the ability to put together a wonderful healthy food package. After all, we do tell people how to eat healthily and if I can't get it together to put a Christmas package of glorious and sugar-free goodies together, then nobody can. So after my shopping trip with Vilma, my basket of gifts for Marin and Nate's big Christmas party is a combination of semi-naughty, but nice. There are the delicious home-made beetroot chocolate brownies – I know that sounds like an oxymoron, using the words beetroot and delicious in the one sentence, but it's true. Also, I didn't home-make them myself, obviously. Somebody else home-made them for the beautiful deli and I just bought them and made them look a bit home-made, because I tied them up in the tissue paper and added the ribbon. That has to mean something, doesn't it? I have also put in Fairtrade chocolates – dark, naturally, because it's healthier for you – and some really beautiful olive oil. I controlled myself from adding the special booklet on the correct sort of oils because I suspect that everyone in their house already knows that. There is loads of other stuff, including the decidedly unhealthy two bottles of wine I drop in at the last minute. I also stick in some of the grapefruit juice I love, because I have absolutely no plans to be standing on the side of the road trying to hail a taxi on Christmas Eve evening, because I have had a couple of glasses of wine.

'I can drive you there and back,' Finn says when he phones later to chat and check if I'm still coming, sounding slightly put out that I didn't already expect this.

'Don't be daft,' I reply. 'I'm just dropping in for a couple of hours. You'll definitely be there longer than me. So don't drink and drive is my motto. And besides, I might head down to Giselle's and Stefan's earlier than I had planned.'

'Fine, your choice, Sid,' he says and I feel crushed.

After all my fantasising earlier, Finn hasn't said a word to me about us doing anything special over Christmas in our conversation.

I feel very stupid for having indulged in chocolate-based fantasies about him now. I am clearly just a friend. I bet he's found a girlfriend now; he's too handsome and lovely not to. Biker-boot Sid will just be one of his old pals he occasionally hikes with and if I was said girlfriend, I'd make him ditch all extraneous female friends instantly.

This thought makes me laugh to myself: he isn't interested in me and yet I still know that if he was, I'd be possessive about him because – well, just because. I think that if Finn was really in my life, I'd never let him go.

But that's not happening, is it? I mentally let go of the chocolate sauce.

'There are so many crazy drivers on the road at Christmas,' I add, putting on my cheerful act. 'I'd prefer to drive off earlier and avoid the madness.'

The official story – I love having an official story, which means I can hide the real story – is that I'm spending Christmas week with my mother, Vilma and my dear stepfather Stefan and whoever else they decide to invite. The reality is I think I might just do one overnight there, because it seems that Giselle has a load of nearly homeless sculptors and potters who are a bit stuck for somewhere to stay over Christmas. Because Mum has a sprawling back garden with the big shed that's housed both humans and every sort of art medium going over the years, I'm quite sure she can fit in a couple of potters, but sculptors . . . I'm not so sure. They need spaaace. Either way, I'm not entirely sure that Mum will not have loaned out my bed to one of these people and I'm not bunking in with Vilma because she wriggles.

Our work party was two nights ago and some of the office are still nursing hangovers because Adrienne put money behind the till in the little Argentinian steakhouse we went to and copious bottles of red wine appeared on the tables.

'I am never drinking again,' was the most repeated phrase the next day, apart from 'Does anyone have any paracetamol left?'

Adrienne sent most of them home at lunch.

'It's my fault,' she said ruefully. 'I didn't expect everyone to go quite so wild.'

'The owner did play all that tango music after twelve,' I reminded her. I had no idea there were so many different types of tango music and after a while, everyone – well, obviously not me – was up swinging their legs as if they were on *Strictly* and kicking their partners in the shins.

'Painful sort of dance when performed by amateurs,' said Adrienne. 'I always wanted to be good at the tango. I'm very disappointed in myself.'

'Freddie could hardly walk in a straight line by the time you and he got up,' I reminded her. 'You can't gauge your fleckles, or whatever they're called, when your partner has to be held up.'

'True.'

Nobody brought partners to the Nurture party – it had always been just for staff – but as I watched people giggling as they tried to dance, I'd found myself wishing I could try a little dance in someone's arms. Finn's.

In honour of tonight's party at Marin and Nate's I apply my party make-up, which is a good, heavy brown eyeshadow with hints of bronze to liven it up and a nice nude lip. Vilma and her friends love this look. They think I look like a goth French lady. For total excitement, I wear my newest black jeans and a black shirt with a hint of silver in it. Wild, huh? That's me.

I can't help but close my eyes and wish, just a teeny bit, that Finn would see me as more than just a friend tonight, but I can hardly make the first move. I'd pushed us into the friend zone – and now I was stuck there.

23

Marin

On the afternoon of the Christmas party, Nate walks into the kitchen looking both casual yet dressed up in a shirt I am convinced I have never seen before, in a wonderful cornflower-blue colour, which looks marvellous on him.

'Have you been shopping?' I say, astonished.

'Yes,' he says, like a delighted small boy. 'Couldn't resist it, everyone slags me off for wearing boring old business shirts, so here, look at me.' He holds out his arms and does a full rotation. 'Treated myself to a new shirt for Christmas.'

'Oh darling, you should have said and I'd have bought you one.'

'No, sweetheart, it's fine.' He comes over and kisses me lightly on the forehead. 'You have quite enough to do, what with catering for the hordes. How are we getting on?'

'Food for the hordes, all made, present and correct,' I say opening the fridge and then the oven, to stuff in some filo pastry things. 'You said you saw Louise yesterday – did she say she was coming to the party?' I ask. 'She hasn't replied.'

'No.' He hesitated there for a moment and I don't miss it.

'What do you mean, "no"? She's not coming or you didn't ask?'

'Er . . . didn't ask,' he says.

'But you hesitated. Has she said something, is there something wrong with the girls, do you think I – I don't like to ask Rachel, because who knows what madcap plan they've come up with now . . .'

Lately, I feel as if Louise and I are no longer on the same

page. She's so much more relaxed about the girls' gap-year trip and it's stressing me out.

'You worry too much, Marin,' says my husband.

And I think this is possibly one of the most dangerous statements in the entire world.

'You worry too much, dear.'

Probably every police report where a woman killed her husband, starts with, 'Well, then he said to me, you worry/talk/drive me nuts too much and then I picked up the shotgun.'

I have never been a sulker, but I decide that Nate could do without my attention for a while. I dump the wiping-down cloth into the special washing basket I keep for dishcloths, extract a new folded one from the cupboard, slam it down on the counter and leave the room.

Nate is not even aware of this, does not even say, *Did I say something?* Nothing, I think with irritation, absolutely nothing.

He's accused me of being a worry wart and we have a teenage daughter who is going away soon with her friend, across the world, for months, and of course I'm worried. I'm worried sick!

Right now, I'm filled with an intense rage against Nate. Is it the menopause or the perimenopause or one of the bloody pauses? Please don't tell me it's happening now. There has got to be a reason I'm this irritable, it's not normal. Normal people don't feel irritable like this, do they?

Then I try to rationalise: it's the day before Christmas and we are doing what we do every year, which is to have a massive party with friends and family. It is stressful enough to drive a lesser woman to drink.

Of course I'm stressed and irritable. My husband has just marched downstairs, having done practically nothing except buying in wine and arranging it lovingly, and then has accused me of being someone who worries all the time.

Plus he's wearing a new shirt and he hates shopping. I'm stung that he's gone without me. We always head into the sales together and he finds some good work clothes, while I look longingly at nice things at 50 per cent off and dream about how they'll change my life.

I hope he felt in just enough of a shopping mood to buy me something nice for Christmas, I think mutinously. Nate is a terrible shopper. He goes into the pharmacy and asks them what the most fabulous perfume is at the moment and buys that for me. It is one of his grander flaws as a husband, I must admit. He is brilliant in so many other ways, and I do love him, but that man can't shop – unless it's for beautiful party shirts, it seems. I feel like I'm being a bitch but at the same time all my anger feels entirely, totally justifiable.

I go upstairs into our room, shut the door, thankful that my two offspring are both doing other things in their rooms and I practise some deep breathing. This party will be lovely, I will be calm. I breathe and count to ten. Is it breathe in for six, hold for seven, out for eight or the other way round? Oh hell, I just breathe a bit. In, out, in out. Breathing is supposed to come naturally but it doesn't feel natural right now. I'll be OK, I tell myself, when the party has started and everyone is here: then I can relax.

I open my wardrobe and take out tonight's outfit. I know I shouldn't have bought it but it's a very sexy velvet dress in midnight-blue with some magical properties that make me look both taller and thinner. If Nate's been buying things for himself, then I'm allowed a treat, I reason? His shirt *probably* cost as much as my dress . . .

With this happy thought in mind, I race to his drawer where he neatly stores all receipts. He's so anal about things like that, whereas I just dump everything into a big box and try not to look at it again because of how guilty my shopping receipts make me feel.

Finally, I find the receipt for his shirt – except it's not a proper receipt. It's a gift receipt. From an expensive store – the kind Nate would never visit without me dragging him in there.

This time, I'm not the one who has something to feel guilty about. Why would he lie to me?

24

Bea

Luke is staying with Mum tonight, along with the puppies. When she heard that Nate and Marin's party was today, she insisted on a sleepover. 'Just in case you meet someone, darling, and end up staying later, having a drink and getting a taxi. Christmas parties are very good for that, you know.' Unlikely, since I'll know everyone there, but I'll welcome a sleep in.

When I arrive with Luke and the puppies, who go everywhere with Luke now, an elegant older gentleman with white hair and a sailing tan is busily doing something to the hinges on Mum's cloakroom door, which has been hanging badly lately.

'I'm sure you could do it yourself, Mabel,' he's saying. 'You're so very competent but you need the right tools.'

I think he might be a tad deaf as he doesn't hear us at first but then Luke and the puppies make themselves known.

'Hello, there,' he says and I instantly like him. He could be a model for an attractive older gentleman in a knitting catalogue with twinkling eyes and an engaging smile.

'I'm Cliff and you must be Bea. And this young man must be Luke – how lovely to meet you all.'

The dogs, whom I believe are great judges of humanity, fling themselves on him and he instantly crouches down, which pleases Luke no end.

'This is Sausage and this is Doughnut,' he says. 'Sausage is not allowed to eat sausages. The vet said so.'

Within moments, Cliff has shaken my hand and he and

Luke are on the floor with the puppies, engaged in conversations about what dogs cannot eat – grapes particularly bad, they both agree, and Cliff is talking about his first dog, a small Labrador. Mum comes through from the kitchen, a big smile already on her face.

'That dog was so very lovely to cuddle, just like Sausage and Doughnut are,' he says and I have a vision of him being wonderful with grandchildren.

Mum must have read my mind.

'Cliff has three grandchildren but they live in Japan, which means he doesn't get to see them all the time.'

'We Zoom,' says Cliff proudly.

Nothing wrong with his hearing, then.

By the time I leave, I can see that Mum is nearly as besotted as Luke and the dogs, who are now sprawled on Cliff on the floor and Cliff is telling Luke how his youngest granddaughter wants a kitten for her birthday.

'He won't stay long and don't worry, I won't leave them alone for a moment. I know Cliff is still a stranger to us all,' she says to me quietly.

I smile gratefully. I'm fearfully protective of Luke.

As I drive away, I'm still smiling because I can see how Mum's face lights up at the sight of Cliff. But if she moves on, everyone in my little circle of love will have found someone. Everyone but me.

As I near Marin and Nate's house, I have reached that surge of emotion I haven't felt in years: a swell of pure loneliness. It's not fair, I want to wail out loud as I drive along the Christmassy streets. Everyone has someone, except me.

I park on the street, make a vague attempt at wiping my eyes, but decide that I'll fix myself up when I get in. I can race upstairs to Marin's bathroom and do a make-up repair job before entering the fray. Hopefully, Marin or Rachel will open the door. But they don't – Nate does and he takes one look at my tear-stained face and puts his arms around me.

'Bea, honey,' he croons, and I'm held against him, feeling the strength of his body as he hugs me tightly.

It feels so long since anyone did this – so very long – and I let out a sob.

He leads me into the cloakroom in the hall, shuts the door and goes back to hugging me.

'I'm really sorry,' I mutter. 'It's just . . .' I can't continue the sentence, can't explain how lonely I feel.

So we stand there, hugging, and it begins to feel better.

'Everyone thinks ten years is forever but it's not, it's the blink of an eye and I still remember him.'

'Shush, I know,' he says gently.

The door rattles and suddenly it's opened and there, looking astonished at the sight of the two of us hugging, is Angie.

'Hi, Angie,' says Nate urbanely, as if he's always being caught in tiny cloakrooms with women other than his wife, 'poor Bea was upset.'

'Really?' says Angie, staring at both of us in a blast of ice-cold disapproval.

Mortified, I push out past her. 'Sorry, Nate. Sorry, Angie,' I say, and rush out the front door. I can't stay. What will this look like?

25

Sid

I rock up at Nate's and Marin's to find it's a winter wonderland. There are people all over the house. Marin and Rachel have obviously been working incredibly hard decorating, because everywhere is festive in a pretty and warm way. There are no expensive decorations, just nicely thought-out ones. A tree in a pot so you can plant it again, which I approve of, all sorts of elderly decorations, including lots of rather battered children's ones, presents under the tree. In one corner there is a table set up and several people are playing cards with much squawking and giggling. Holding my juice, I wriggle into the room and begin to circulate with Rachel introducing me. There are lots of little groups of people here and children running around. I don't know many people but that's one of the benefits of growing up in any communal sort of living: you get used to fitting in. I look at the party of card players, one of whom turns out to be Marin's mother, who looks fearsome and is crammed into a fire-engine-red dress.

'Granny's very into her cards,' whispers Rachel, who has shown me in. 'Likes to win.'

There's Marin's father, who is sitting quietly talking to a glamorous-looking blonde who might be Marin's sister, and he's eating chocolates out of a box as if someone is about to come over and wrench them out of his hand. Steve's mother and Angie's father are there, Rachel points out, along with another lady who lives next door, who is clearly thrashing them all at poker.

'Aha,' says this lady, who looks by far the oldest person in the room and is already wearing a gold hat from a cracker. 'I win.' And she hauls the coins across the table, starts gleefully piling them up. They are only copper coins and I suspect none of the people playing would care if they were playing for matchsticks or buttons, because it's the joy of winning with this lot.

'Beryl, I am sure you have several cards stuffed up your jumper,' says one of the women.

Beryl, the older lady, laughs uproariously. 'You are a terrible tease, Millie. You say that every year. Just because I beat you every year.'

Great roars of laughter come from the table and it's clear that this is not some serious accusation of cheating, but more an enjoyable tradition that goes on every Christmas.

Granny in Fire-Engine-Red looks up. 'Hello,' she says, with very unfriendly eyes, 'you're new.'

'Sid,' I say. I hold out my hand, amused.

No surprise as to how Marin is always racing around doing things for other people if this gorgon is her mother.

'Sid – that's a strange name. I'm Eithne, Marin's mother. You're with Finn now?' The woman looks at me shrewdly. With interrogation techniques like that, she could work for any of the Interpol-related agencies.

'He's just my friend,' I say, which is an understatement, 'and he's not here yet, is he?'

I looked very hard when I came in but there was no sign of him.

Rachel, who is obviously trained at rescuing people from her grandmother, appears beside me. 'Now, ladies and gentlemen, can I get you anything else? I know you already have some punch but I am also serving teas and coffees, because we don't want anyone staggering.'

'Are you talking to me, young lady?' says Beryl in a pretend annoyed voice. 'I can hold my liquor.'

The others start laughing again. Clearly this is some joke and Rachel and I look at each other.

'They are like this every year,' she says. 'Respect your elders, I'm told.' The giggling goes on, except that, clearly, Eithne is not a giggler.

I help Rachel distribute tea, coffee and what are undoubtedly home-made mince pies to the card players, who nibble and drink and then shove it all to one side, so they can get back to the game.

'Who,' I whisper to Rachel, 'is the lady beside your father?'

Rachel whispers back: 'My aunt, April.'

At this precise moment, April bursts into tears and Nate hugs her.

'I thought she might be,' I say. 'Should we do something?'

Rachel stares at her aunt, who's still crying.

'I know you think you can help,' she says, 'but you can't really. April has always got a drama going on and you just have to let her get on with it. That's what Mum says. I love her, but, you know, some men are unobtainable. And April loves them.'

'Ah,' I say, understanding. 'Is this one of those, he's with his family at Christmas and she's here alone without him feeling neglected?'

'Got it in one,' says Rachel. 'Poor April, she doesn't know how to be happy on her own, she has to have some complication connected to her. I don't understand it. Feminism passed her by.'

I look at Rachel thoughtfully. 'You really do remind me of my sister, Vilma,' I say. 'Girls don't rule the world. Not yet, anyway. We're trying, but it's not an even fight. Don't think we've won because then you underestimate them. Feminism 2.0.'

'Oh I know,' she says grimly. 'I had an – er . . . little incident one evening my friend Megan and I were out. Some guy did his best to put his hand up my skirt and I literally had to run. Got stuck outside the back of the club and Mum ended up racing in because Megan couldn't find me. I never told her about the guy, by the way,' Rachel adds, looking panicked. 'I mean, it was nothing.'

'It's rarely nothing,' I say carefully. 'It leaves a mark.'

'Yeah, taught me not to wear short skirts,' says Rachel cynically. 'But that's wrong, isn't it? Why can't I wear what I want without some dude thinking he has the right to stick his hand up it?'

'There's what *should* happen and what does,' I say. 'The two are often different. In an ideal world, you should wear what you want and be alone with anyone you feel like, but in the real world, the rules of the jungle apply.'

She nods and looks at me thoughtfully.

Just then, I see Finn arriving. Our eyes meet and he strides straight over to me, which makes me light up inside.

'Hi,' I say breathlessly.

'See ya,' whispers Rachel, and she's gone.

'Sorry I'm late,' he says. 'Traffic.'

I have this overpowering urge to reach up and pull his head down to mine, to kiss him, but at that moment, Marin whizzes past, says 'Hello all!' and the moment is gone.

I let out a shaky breath and watch as Finn hugs Marin hello and thanks her for inviting him.

He didn't hug me, I think, suddenly hit with the realisation. He has never really touched me.

All this fantasy is on one side because if he liked me, really liked me, he'd have put his arms around me and given me a friendly hug, one that could gently segue into something else, but he hasn't.

My silly head, my crazy heart, has invented this great romance.

Stung, I lower my head and remember his present. I'll give it to him but then he needs to be out of my life because I like him too much. And it's not reciprocated.

'I got you some nice chocolate today when I was out with Vilma,' I say, offhandedly.

His eyes stare into mine.

I can't read the look in them: guilt that he hasn't bought me anything? Horror that I'm overstepping the friend thing with a Christmas present?

Bloody women, that's probably what he's thinking.

I shove the gift into his hands and stalk off towards the kitchen. I'll help Marin out and then I'm gone. Rachel is still on service duty and seems to welcome the help. I'm doing one last run of goodies with Rachel and we end up in the kitchen again where, miraculously, Marin is not racing around.

Rachel's intelligent young gaze turns to me. 'Are you dating Finn?'

I am used to this utter honesty from young women, seeing as I have Vilma doing it to me all the time.

'Don't forget I have a sister around your age,' I say, 'so I am immune to being interrogated,' and I manage a brave grin at her.

She grins back.

'It was worth a try. We are just friends,' I say, over-brightly. 'It's a great thing to have male friends. You probably have some?'

'Yes,' she says thoughtfully, 'but I look at them as guys I have decided I won't go out with, so then they can be my friends. It doesn't work otherwise. Is that what happened to you and Finn, you met him and decided he was nice but you wouldn't be interested in going out with him, so then he can be your friend? Or do you actually want to go out with him?'

This takes me aback.

'Eh, no, well,' I stutter, trying to buy time. I can only do this for so long. I just might cry soon. Finn hasn't come searching for me. I embarrassed him with the present. I need to get out of here, soon. 'My sister keeps trying to bring me out with her friends because she thinks I'm going to moulder away in my apartment with no cat and turn into an elderly spinster lady who never has any fun. But it's all right, I don't see it that way, I'm happy.'

'I didn't mean to offend you,' says Rachel. 'Honestly, did I offend you? If so, I'm sorry.'

'Course you didn't offend me,' I add quickly.

'Because Mum thinks you're brilliant and she'd kill me if she knew I said that to you. It's just – well, you are younger than all the other grown-up people, and I felt I could say that to you.'

'It's fine,' I say. 'Lots of women are alone, and might stay alone, a changing world and all that. You get to choose how to live your life. '

'Yeah,' Rachel nods, 'as long as you are happy.'

'Exactly,' I say, 'as long as you are happy.'

26

Marin

Both ovens are going full pelt and for some reason the air extractor is not working terribly well. The place is hot, steamy and I can feel my hair that I carefully set with my heated rollers early this morning drooping. The playing of carols has been taken over by something totally else and I suspect that Megan and Rachel are now in charge of the music. There was no more George Michael's 'Last Christmas' or even Mariah Carey belting out, 'All I Want for Christmas Is You' – no. We had moved on to all sorts of songs that had no Christmas relevance at all, and I wasn't sure that the varying ages of guests would appreciate it, but oh, whatever.

I'm alone in the kitchen because everyone else has decided that they do not want to be hot and bothered and it is much more fun being in the open-plan living area, sitting down, standing up, laughing, talking, drinking, eating nibbles or mince pies. The children are probably close to requiring their second batch of food of the day so I shove a load of home-made sausage rolls into the oven.

Then Sid comes into the kitchen.

'Can I help?' she says. 'I'm pretty useless at cooking, to be absolutely frank, but it's getting crazy and noisy in there and I just thought you might need a bit of a hand.'

'Oh Sid,' I said, thinking I could have hugged her. 'That is so nice of you, but you don't have to.'

She cuts me off. 'I know I don't have to, but I'm here. So, what can I do, why don't you sit down and instruct me. I have an office job, I take instruction extremely well, I can open the oven and close the oven and put things on plates and open bottles and make tea.'

Somehow her voice has a calm commanding air to it.

'Are you in charge of many people in the office?' I say, sitting down on one of the kitchen chairs, realising that I haven't sat down for ages and my lower back is starting to ache.

'I am in charge of a department, but I run it with a very light hand,' Sid says, 'I'm not cut out for bossing people around. But when I see another woman who needs a helping hand, I like to be there.'

'Thank you,' I say, knowing I sound tearful and not even slightly like myself. This is not me, nobody in my own office would recognise this version of Marin, but it's Christmas and I'm tired and maybe having these parties is just too much . . .

'Are you teetotalling or do you want tea or a drink or what?' says Sid, standing midway between the fridge and the kettle.

'Coffee,' I say. 'I know I shouldn't or I won't sleep well, but I don't care. I'm just tired, that will perk me up.'

'Coffee coming up,' says Sid, and she goes and stares at our complicated machine, finds a cup and works it expertly.

'I love practical people,' I say to her back. 'You're very practical. That's nice, it helps.'

'Well,' says Sid without turning around, 'my mother is a glorious woman but she has never been practical and one of us had to be. So I pretty soon learned how to do everything. This coffee machine is easy – we have one quite similar in the office. I look at things and I figure it out. Now, the stuff in the oven – does that need to come out soon? I do not have the cooking gene so have no clue. Give me timings.'

'No, it's got at least seven more minutes,' I say, 'but we could probably heat up some more mince pies and get the shortbreads out.'

I direct her to where the spare mince pies are sealed away and she takes them out and looks at them.

'Did you make these?' she asks, astonished.

I nod.

'So you have a full-time job, a family and you still made all these mince pies?'

'Yeah,' I sigh. 'Am I nuts?'

'No, each to her own,' says Sid. 'You will find no judgement here. I'm just in awe of you. I was thinking of getting a cat but what if I have to make special dinners for the cat if it was sick?'

'I think they have special sicky-cat, cat food,' I say.

'My mother always looked after the cats at home, we had loads. My mother takes in strays, you see, stray animals and stray people. And I like to look after her.'

She sits down beside me.

'She sounds wonderful,' I say, 'tell me more.'

'We lived in a big but absolutely shattered run-down house when I was a child. There was no heating, so if there was a room that didn't have a fireplace in it you were in terrible trouble. We went through a lot of hot water bottles and blankets: you needed blankets. I still don't like being cold,' she admits. 'People would turn up at the house with kittens and puppies because they knew that Mum would take them in. Maybe because lots of women stayed with us over the years, the locals thought she was gay, so random strangers would turn up at the door and say, "we were told that the lesbian lady would look after the cats/puppies/whatever".'

I laugh.

'That's so funny,' I say and then realise I might have just insulted her mother if she is gay.

'She's not a lesbian, but two of the women living there for a few years were, so people assumed any woman in our house was a lesbian until my stepfather came to stay. Where we lived, if you didn't have a family and two point five children, you were weird. Mum's different, lovely and kind. She likes having a lot of people around, likes rescuing people. So she rescues cats, dogs, a hedgehog, several hamsters, a very aggressive rabbit and lots of people. Somewhere along the way she rescued Stefan, my stepfather, although really Stefan rescued my mother and turned things around. There were less people coming in and it was all less chaotic after he arrived.'

'Sounds wonderful,' I say wistfully, thinking it does. This marvellous bohemian lifestyle seems gloriously different and at odds from our very ordinary world where we have a party every year and invite the same people.

I am fed up with doing this, I realise. And Nate knows I'm fed up. But he's just not listening to me.

'Yeah,' she says wistfully. 'It is. They're very in love, my mother and Stefan. Makes you almost believe in love.'

I look at her because I swear I can see the glint of tears in her eyes.

'You OK?' I ask. 'Things all right with Finn?'

'Oh we're not going out,' she says almost harshly. 'We're friends. I'm not exactly girlfriend material.'

Strange, but she sounds almost childlike for such a practical, grown-up person. I get the sense she's been badly hurt somehow in the past. And I don't believe for a second that Finn isn't interested in her. He's never brought a female friend to our house before if he wasn't interested in them romantically. Never.

I decide that some matchmaking is in order.

'Just nipping out to the hall to er . . . check something,' I say.

The mistletoe is in the hall. I'm going to hand it to Finn and tell him he's going to lose this lovely woman if he doesn't do something. Delighted with my plan, I rush out only to see Nate and Angie coming back into the house, clearly after being outside, both looking as if something has just gone on.

They don't see me in the dimly lit hall and I step back into the doorway, shaken.

Nate and Angie? What were they doing outside? Kissing? What other explanation could there be? I knew there was something wrong. Knew it.

She's the difference. He's having an affair with her. Is he?

She bought him that damned shirt. Or am I imagining it? I've always felt so anxious around her – now my insecurities are rushing through me and I can't think straight.

I wait for them to join the others in the living room and then slip upstairs, locking myself in our bathroom. I can't cry when we've a houseful of guests but I feel as if my world has just ended. If I'm right, it just has.

After a moment, I sit up, dab away the tears under my eyes and determine that I can't be right. I just can't. I must have misunderstood.

I've left my phone up here on the dressing table out of the way and I have a quick check now, several notifications flashing up on the screen. One is a message from Bea:

Sorry, Marin, I got held up and won't make it after all.
Happy Christmas xx

I deflate a little – it would have been lovely to have Bea's warm, calm influence here right now. I hope she's OK.

Heading back downstairs to the party, I make my way into the room where all the guests are. Nate and Angie are at the opposite ends of the room and I'd swear there's a tension between them, almost as if they were arguing.

I look around for Finn and Sid, determined to do one thing right tonight but Finn is Sid-less.

'Where's Sid?' I ask.

'She gave me a lovely present and then disappeared into the kitchen,' he says, running his long fingers through his hair distractedly.

'There! She's feeding the masses with Rachel.'

I call Sid over and she gives both of us a forced smile.

Finn's body language is so obvious, I don't know how she can't see it or feel it. But she puts down her plate of mince pies, pats him on the sweatered arm, hugs me quickly and says: 'Sorry, have to head off now. Have a lovely Christmas.'

And like a little runner, she turns and dashes through the party and is gone.

Finn's face is stunned. 'I wanted to say thank you . . .' he begins.

I look at him sadly. Earlier, I might have said something wise to him but now . . . I have nothing wise left to say. Nothing.

27

Sid

I continue to stare at Finn's WhatsApp as if it's an unexploded bomb.

My cinema mates are all busy, but there is an old showing of Casablanca on in the Stella next week, do you fancy it? Totally non-date, fellow hiker. Say no if you don't want to, but there's something relaxing about old movies. Finn.

I have never been to the Stella in Rathmines, an old cinema that, legend had it, had been a bit of a flea pit in its time. In recent years, however, it's been updated into a 1920s centre of glamour, where the modern world stops at the door outside. Apparently, cinemagoers sit in beautiful and glorious comfy seats in a perfectly recreated twenties setting and have drinks and nibbles brought to them. There were possibly even girls going around in mad little 1920s outfits selling cigarettes like in the old movies.

But it was very datey, wasn't it?

Vilma has been asking about Finn since our shopping trip when I bought his Christmas present but I've been deliberately vague. I don't want her thinking I've had my heart broken. Because it's not. No. Course not.

Vilma wants me to fall in love again – she still believes in the fairy tale and that, after Marc, I will find another prince and can be a princess again. I didn't want to go into that.

I can't ruin fairy tales for her. Maybe she'll have one, after all. One sister learning that life is more Grimm's fairy tale than Disney is enough for any family.

Adrienne, who runs Nurture and is not much older than me, is my go-to person for lots of things. We can talk but we don't have girlie drinks or dinners. We work together, we share problems occasionally: end of. It works for both of us. As I've said before, I do not have a vast circle of friends, but if I'd met Adrienne outside of Nurture she might have become one of them.

First up, Adrienne is not a girlie woman. She owns no lipstick and her haircut is also done in the same tiny local salon as mine, where shampoos and sets make up 90 per cent of the business. A shade under forty, she runs an average of sixty kilometres a week and unless she has an actual meeting in government buildings, lives in jeans. Even on those government-buildings days, she often wears her newest jeans with a smart jacket.

'I do the work, I don't model,' she told one reporter dumb enough to ask her about her 'casual style'. 'Would you ask a man about his choice of clothing?'

Said reporter disappeared, tail between legs, but there followed a raft of predictable articles on 'why women were judged on what they wore rather than on what they achieved'.

Adrienne had refused to comment. We had a book on it in the office. Long-time Nurture workers, like myself, put our money on her not commenting. Newbies were sure Adrienne would make a stand. They didn't get that by saying nothing, the stand was made. 'I don't comment on my clothes.' QED.

Today, I run the boss to ground in her office where she's staring out of the window and drumming short fingernails upon a window ledge which has already been drummed to bits, if the peeling paint is anything to go by. The Nurture offices are not establishments of glamour like the Stella Cinema.

Yeah, subconscious, I hear you. Now shut up.

'Oh, sorry, you're on the phone,' I say, as she turns and I see she's got the phone clamped to one ear.

'No, on hold,' she mutters, eyeballs rolling. 'What is it?'

'Nah, this isn't the time.'

'Please. Come in and sit down. I've been on hold for twenty minutes. I'm giving them five more minutes before I'm going to send them a strongly worded email with the words "off" and "fuck" in it.'

I grin. When Adrienne says stuff like that, you know she means it.

'Just a real quickie, OK. Non-work.'

She looks at her phone. 'OK, that's twenty-two minutes I'm on hold, that's just too long.' She pokes at the phone screen as if she's poking someone's eye out in person, throws it onto the desk with a clatter, sits back in her chair and puts her cowboy-booted feet up on the desk. 'Oh wow, what a day. So, problem?'

'The circular argument of hell.'

'My speciality,' she says with a grin. 'Spill.'

'There's this guy, Finn – the one you met at the pub,' I say, 'and he's nice, but we were supposed to be friends, platonic. And now he's asked me on a date but . . .'

'Is he hassling you?' says Adrienne, giving me a fierce look. She's ready with the 'do we need to kill him?' face. She's tough for the boss of a charity.

'No, he's not hassling me, he's –' I search for the word – 'lovely. But I don't know if I'm ready. We're in the friend zone.'

She snorts. 'Friend zone. So he's friend-zoned you?'

'No, no,' I say, 'I friend-zoned *him*. I wanted him to stay there because, you know – what with Marc . . .'

For a second Adrienne's eyes, shrewd enough to see through every possible lie on the planet, laser me with intensity.

'Tell me if I'm getting any of this wrong. You put him in the friend zone because you're not ready but now you're in here discussing him with me? I'm calling bullshit. You want to go on this date and you're looking for permission to do it.'

'Look, it's just –' I stalled – 'I'm not over Marc. I'm not ready to date.'

'Sid, stop with the you-and-Marc thing. It's so old. Marc was nice, but you and him, really!'

'OK, I'm sorry I came in without senior counsel,' I say crossly. Adrienne knew me so well. I'd never told her the truth of my relationship with Marc but she'd obviously figured it out.

'Don't shoot the messenger,' she says.

'I thought you'd understand.'

'Because I'm divorced?'

'Yeah, you get men.'

'If I got men I wouldn't be divorced,' she reminds me.

'OK, you get men better than I get men,' I say.

'True. I would not ever say that you *get men*. But maybe you are getting men now. Progress, right?'

'Adrienne, you're really annoying, you know that?'

She beams back at me.

'People tell me that all the time. My ex certainly did. So where does he want to take you?'

'The Stella.'

'The Stella! If you said he was booking the Presidential Suite in a swanky hotel and had the pink furry handcuffs lined up and a bucket of oysters so you two could keep going all night, I might say yeah, he's moving a bit fast, but the Stella? It's not exactly Ferrari speed yet, is it? It's a definite sign of intent but he could be a metropolitan man who likes classy spots and old movies.'

Finn is not a metropolitan man, I think. He's kind. Gentle. Sexy . . . Oh hell, this is killing me. I'd made up my mind not to see him again after Christmas. I'd felt so hurt because it was obvious he wasn't into me the way I was into him, but now he's asking me out on what is clearly a date. My brain feels like it's going to explode.

'Sid?' Adrienne is looking at me.

'Should I go?'

'You like him, don't you?'

'Yeah, I like him.' It stung that I was finally admitting it out loud and not just to myself. And I do like him. I like him a lot. Maybe I do want to date him. Dammit – this was *impossible*.

'Go. State your parameters. Bring your highly illegal pepper spray. But you're a good judge of character, Sid. The best. If *you* like him with all your antennae up like you're looking for life in outer space, then he's good stuff.'

I let the crack about my antennae go.

'What if it hurts, emotionally?'

'Life is a risk,' said Adrienne, picking up her pen and her phone at the same time. 'Everything we do is a risk, so take some of your own. Marc's gone. He flew the nest. You can fly too. Now I'm going to ring those people again. No, I'm not, I'm going to ring the press office. That normally scares the shit out of them. Should have done that in the first place.'

Delighted with herself, she scrolls through her contacts and I leave.

I think about what she'd said – life is a risk. I knew that. I'd once blindly stumbled into a risk and it had ripped me in half so badly that I'd been hiding from any risk at all for fifteen years. Dare I risk anything again?

28

Marin

I'm not a fan of January – January means cold weather, rain, grey skies and if a bit of low winter sun manages to pierce through the clouds, it only stays for a moment and then it's gone. The plus about January is that it's sale time. Normally, I go shopping to fill the hole in my wardrobe and my psyche – now, I'm going shopping because I feel so empty and alone.

Nate seems the same as ever but I'm not. I can't unsee what I saw at Christmas: him and Angie coming back into the house. I should ask him about it all but I'm afraid he'll have some glib explanation for it, which would be worse because I'd know if he was lying.

This year, I'd had so many plans for New Year resolutions involving things like doing more exercise, cooking more nutritious food (too much cheese is creeping into everything!) and, most importantly, staying out of the shops. Pre-Christmas, I'd been doing very well at this. I felt like a junkie looking for a fix every time I passed one of the little boutiques I love and saw the word 'Christmas party sale' winking at me from the window, like it was covered in glorious diamonds and it was calling just to me. *'Marin, we have the perfect outfit for you, this will change your life, this will let you be the person you were always meant to be . . .'*

The new me is supposed to be walking firmly past, nose in the air, ignoring the siren call of the sale rail. I've been caught that way so often before. I could show you the pink satin opera coat thing I bought once, that looked spectacular in the shop and was down to fifty euros and was a bargain, if, for example, you were a bit taller and went to the opera, whereupon you might *need* an opera coat.

However, not being an opera-going person and not being tall enough to wear it, I just looked like a meringue in a tightly belted coat, who'd never be knocked down because she was almost luminous. I never did manage to sell that one, the charity shops got it. Now, however, I'm buying like the end of the world is nigh and the only way to save us all is for me to shop.

But, and this is the really scary thing, something that would worry me senseless if I wasn't so anxious anyway, we seem to be running low on money. And I can't figure out why.

Nate and I rarely talk about money. Why is money such a tricky subject with couples? We can go to bed and kiss and exchange bodily fluids and lie there bathed in each other's sweat. But we can't say, you know we are about four hundred quid down, what's happening there, was there some bill I didn't know about? Did you buy something for some woman? And I can't tell anyone, certainly not April, whom I'm rushing to meet through the horrible rain. I've got an hour for lunch today and then I have to drive out to a beautiful house in Shankill that I'm showing.

January is not a prime time for selling houses, but needs must. April has been in a very sad, depressed mood since Christmas, when Jared inevitably did not leave his wife. I have not said, "I told you so", because it would be cruel and I love her to bits. She needs support from the only member of her family who knows about her life. Ma would stab her with a sharpened crucifix if she knew about April's fondness for married men.

We have arranged to meet in a small café around the corner from my work, so I can belt back to the office, grab my car and change into my nice showing-house jacket.

She's sitting in the corner of the restaurant and I go over to her and give her a hug. Even miserable, her eyes swollen with tears and her lips quivering, she manages to look desirable. Poor, poor April.

'Do you want anything else?' I say, looking down at her cup of coffee and sandwich barely nibbled, which is how she has always kept so thin. She doesn't do that 'leave half of what's on your plate' thing. No, April does the 'leave three quarters of what's on your plate' thing. When she was younger, April was a more rounded girl and Ma never let the opportunity to tell her so pass by. It's meant a lifelong aversion to eating for any reason other than pure sustenance.

'No, this is enough,' she waves an airy hand, 'maybe a water. Still, bottled.'

'Of course,' I say, determined not to transform into my mother and say, *It's far from bottled water you were reared, what's wrong with tap water?* Instead, I go up to the counter, order a sandwich, a cup of tea, bottled water and wilfully add a chocolate muffin to my order.

Then, I sit down beside April, reach over and grasp one long elegant hand with its beautifully manicured nails. April so often works in terrible jobs because she's never found any great ambition for her own career, so she never has the funds to get her nails done professionally. She's brilliant at doing them herself though. Today, they're a delicious rich espresso brown.

'So, how are you?' I ask. I haven't seen her since our Christmas party.

'How am I? How do you think I am?' she says, and tears well up in those huge beautiful eyes and it's easy to see how so many men have fallen into their depths. However, the men always seem to scramble out at some point and go back to their wives.

'Is there any word from Jared?' I say. Jared went long before Christmas but she's still been holding out hope that he'd come back to her.

'Don't speak his name,' she says brokenly. 'He was full of lies, why did he tell me he wanted to be with me, why did he say that I was his immortal beloved?'

The part of me that knows how to placate and the part of

me that really, really wants to tell the absolute truth, battle for supremacy in my head. Absolute truth wins. I poke my teabag around in the little teapot until it's nice and strong, pour it, add milk and begin.

'April, you know I love you.'

'I don't want a lecture,' she interrupts.

'This isn't a lecture, it's your life, you can do exactly what you want to do with it.'

'I didn't ask you for lunch just to be told where I'm going wrong.'

'We all go wrong,' I say in exasperation, 'every single one of us. Do you think I'm perfect?'

'Yes,' she says, pain evident in every angle of her face, 'you have everything, you have Nate and he's so handsome and attractive and you know other women love him and look at him. And then you have Rachel and Joey and you have your job and friends and everything. And what do I have?'

Inside, I feel a little nauseous. I have Nate, have I? I wish I knew if I did.

'You have what any of us have,' I say, ignoring the inner me. 'We have ourselves and you keep giving yourself and your power away to men who are not worthy of you.'

The anger fades from her face. She still looks beautiful and I wonder idly what it must be like to have that power and still for it not to bring happiness.

I'd always wanted to look like April when I was younger. Once she'd conquered the puppy-fat stage, she was so sexy and glamorous, capable of making men watch her as she walked past. People didn't watch me as I walked past and yet my life had worked out better. I had my children, my work, I had Nate . . . it kept coming back to Nate. Was he my sum total?

'I don't feel like I have any power,' she says, 'I just wanted someone to take care of me. Do you know, I never pursued any of the married men I've been with?'

I stop drinking my tea and shake my head. There's nothing

predatory about April – she is no femme fatale. I always knew this and yet I never fully put it into thoughts.

'They asked me out and I –' she pauses – 'I never asked them to leave any woman for me. I never said: "leave her and live with me". Not once, never. I didn't think I was worth it. I've never thought I was worth it. I thought I was lucky to get just a piece of pure love. If life was different, then maybe these men would have met me first and I'd be married to them. But it didn't work that way because I am unlovable. I need to see myself reflected in their eyes because they love me – for a while, anyway.'

'April, that's not true,' I say kindly. 'I love you, my children do, Dom does, Dad adores you.' I leave Ma out, another irredeemably sad omission.

'Thanks, sis.'

'You really never asked Jared to leave?' I am truly astonished. She shakes her head. 'He kept saying he couldn't live without me and I believed him. He hurt me more than anyone else because I thought he loved me but he said –' she's crying now – 'he said I'd be fine on my own and he didn't want to regret leaving and he would: regret it.'

Regret leaving that lovely big house, more like.

'Oh April,' I say.

At this point, big tears began to slide down my sister's perfect face.

'Oh darling, I'm sorry, I'm sorry.' I shove the chocolate muffin over to her side and she begins to eat it mechanically.

I can almost see her thought processes because I understand them: *I'm going to eat this because it's bad for me and it will stop me being beautiful, and then men will have more reasons not to want to be with me.*

I thought of all the ways April had learned to dislike herself. Our home had never been an easy one in which to grow up. Dominic had stayed an eternal teenager because it was the only way he could cope with our family's dysfunction. As for me,

I'd read the mood of the family and tried to keep the peace, and Dad had hidden in his allotment. Finally, April had retreated into the fantasy world of the princess being rescued by the prince. And the princess must be thin, of course, because that was what fashion dictated. Princesses did not wear a size-fourteen dress, therefore neither would April. It was all cruel, wrong and ultimately destructive.

'I just want what you have,' April says, between mouthfuls of chocolate muffin, 'just happiness, someone to come home to, someone who can cook dinner.'

'Nate can't cook dinner,' I say, 'he's useless at it – in fact, I think he's getting worse. Once upon a time he'd heat up some soup or something, but now he comes home and he's exhausted, between the gym and work.'

The gym – that's a sign, isn't it? Men who have affairs are always going to the gym. But then, Finn, Steve and he have always swum and gone to the gym.

'But men are different,' says April, as if this is self-explanatory. 'We're supposed to look after them.'

'No, we're not, we're equal.'

'Ha! If we were equal, men would be buying lipsticks and suck-it-all-in knickers and having their legs shaved. So it's not equal at all. We're supposed to make ourselves desirable for them. And not earn too much or be too successful. I just want someone to take care of me the way Nate takes care of you.'

'He doesn't take care of me,' I say a little dully, because as I say it, I realise he doesn't. If anything, I take care of him. And look where it's got us now – me wondering if he's being faithful, too scared to ask in case I find out.

'Marriage is never what it looks like, April,' I say, 'it's hard, you get annoyed with the other person. But you stick it out.'

'I made a New Year's resolution.' She laughs and there's no humour in her voice. 'I'm going to give up men for six months, totally. I'm not even going to speak to a man unless he's someone I work with. Don't tell me that I need friends and that if you have lots of friends, then you will find someone to date, because it doesn't work that way. I'm nearly forty-six, no matter how good I look, I'm still nearly forty-six. Men want a younger model.'

'Oh April,' I say, taking both her hands in mine. 'So what exactly are you going to do?'

'I'm going to concentrate on work,' she says, 'I'm going to stop going part-time, if I can, and I'm going to get some hobbies. I'm going to stop waiting. I'm going to get some rescue puppies. This year is going to be different.' She looks defiant.

Ma never allowed us to have dogs in the house. 'Dirty smelly things,' she called dogs.

'Good for you,' I say.

'And if a man invites me out in that six months, I'll tell him no. And if at the end of it he's still there, well, we might give it a try. But I will be looking for upfront disclosure. If he's married or *about to be divorced*, and that happens more often than you think, then no. Or is *living separate lives* with his wife, that's another big no-no. If only you knew all the stories they tell . . .'

I don't want a story from Nate. I'm going to find out myself what's really going on: no excuses from him, the actual truth. And if he has been cheating, then he'll be sorry.

29

Bea

Mum's been very busy finding me dates. New Year, new love life, apparently.

'It's my new mission,' she says cheerfully, as she lists her friends' relatives, who generally sound as if they should be attending some sort of group therapy after tricky divorces/relationship break-ups.

I have had coffee with some of them and I think that if work goes belly up, I could always retrain as a counsellor with a view to working with the recently divorced.

There's Jim, who married a Brazilian lady, who ended our two-hour coffee session in a local Starbucks by saying he was very dull, which was why the love of his life had left.

He told me all about her during our 'date'. Two hours is a long time for a blind date but I felt so sorry for poor Jim and it ended up with me almost counselling him about how he might get help so he could recover some of his lost confidence.

There's Leon, who has three daughters, has been though an epic divorce battle and cheerfully told me he'd never have a bean again.

'Cleaned me out,' he said. 'Still, I want the girls to have a good life. The flat's fine, although they have to share the second bedroom when they come to stay. Mea culpa,' he added. 'I had the fling, it was my fault.'

I said I didn't know this and Leon looked a tad annoyed. 'I was sure Aunt Josie would have said that, just to warn you. She says you went through a hard time, what with your husband being killed and all that.'

'Yeah, hard time,' I agreed. Leon is too much of a player for me to want to say any more.

Mum is sorry that Leon and Jim weren't keepers but she's still hoping and it keeps her amused. Plus, it's keeping my mind off the absence of news at work about our impending doom. Dr Ryan discussed it but now isn't going anywhere after all, says Laoise, who has taken it upon herself to be the bringer of news on the office front. 'I think the move is off.'

Myself and Antoinette, with whom I job share, discuss that we now get anxious whenever Laoise approaches either of us on our shifts in case she has newly gleaned bad news about the doctors' plans to downsize.

'I need this job,' says Antoinette.

'Join the club,' I agree.

So I'm kept busy until, suddenly, the day the Family Tree project hits Luke and I, and it blows our lives out of the water.

To families with two parents living with their child, it must be easy, I think.

But not for us.

Worse, I didn't think it would hurt us and I had advance warning.

'That family tree bullshit – it's coming up,' Shazz says to me one week. We both knew it was coming, had been waiting since before Christmas.

'Lori reminded me,' Shazz went on. 'It's part of the New Year curriculum, always is in fourth class.'

Shazz has a friend with an older girl in the boys' school and she's like us, a single mother. She's very helpful for filling us in on issues in senior classes, so we're ready for them when they occur.

'Kids want both parents,' Shazz said to me one night while we're discussing the issue of being single parents. 'Why? Why aren't we enough? We give them everything.'

I swirl the wine around in my glass.

'They want to be like everyone else,' I say. 'We talk about

Jean-Luc, maybe not a lot, it's a long time ago now, so I try and keep his memory alive and say things like, *your dad would be so proud of you, Luke*. I mean he never asks anymore, which is odd. He used to wonder if he was like his dad but he literally never does these days.'

'No, Raffie doesn't do that either,' says Shazz, 'although he's nothing like that bastard.'

'One day he'll hear you, you know,' I say to her. 'You just can't call him that.'

'Yeah, you're right,' she said. 'I just get so angry, the fact that he just left, couldn't cope with it. Why can men father children if they are not going to go through with it properly? It's about more than just producing sperm, it's about being there, being a parent. Evolution got it all wrong.'

'Well,' I say, shrugging, 'Jean-Luc wanted to be a parent and he never got his chance, so I guess life doesn't work out the way we want it to, evolution or not.'

The school has always been pretty good when it came to looking after the kids who were in single-parent households. But there were still parents' evenings and teachers would forget and say things like, *Oh, maybe ask your dad about that*. The first time that had happened, the first time it had actually penetrated Luke's brain that he didn't have a dad, he'd been six years old, and when I picked him up from school he was crying.

'Mr McManus said I have to ask Dad something, but I can't and Raffie can't and we don't understand, and you have to make Mr McManus understand.'

Mr McManus was the boys' teacher at the time and he wasn't long out of teacher training college.

We'd got through that and when Lori had told us about the Family Tree project, we hoped we'd be ready and now it was here.

I tried discussing it with him in advance.

'Honey, I think the Family Tree project is coming up soon. We must get photos of the puppies for it,' I said brightly.

'Sausage and Doughnut will look beautiful. And maybe one of your dad? We can look through the box of photos together.'

I had photos of Jean-Luc in the house but somehow, they'd become part of the place rather than objects that stood out anymore. I'm not sure how that happened – maybe I was trying to protect Luke by not highlighting what he didn't have.

Luke didn't tell me the day they were given the project to start at home, but I knew. Shazz texts me that afternoon, when Luke had stomped upstairs to his room.

They got it, she says. Raffie is miserable and is sulking in his room. I didn't know what was wrong and he said, he's not going to school tomorrow, he's not doing his homework. I thought what the heck? Then I remembered, family-bloody-tree.

I think of Luke's pale little face as he sat in the back of the car coming home from school earlier, because he still isn't quite tall enough to sit in the front yet.

I go upstairs and he's sitting on his bed, not doing anything, not looking at a book or messing around, just sitting there.

'Mum,' he says, his little face serious, 'is my dad dead or did he just go? I know Raffie's dad is gone. But you have just been saying that, haven't you? Dad's not dead. All that stuff about how he'd have been proud of me doing stuff, you're making that up. He just ran away like Raffie's dad, didn't he?' I think my heart is going to shatter into a million shards. All these years I thought I was being a good mother, and I was holding it together and instead, I've ruined everything. I didn't want Luke to feel he was missing out by not having a father, so I tried to be Mum and Dad. And I'd mistakenly let his father figure drift into the background, because I didn't want Luke to know he'd lost so much. My son is ten and he thinks his father is a waster who ran away and left us, left *him*.

'Darling,' I stammer, 'I . . .' It's like the words are stuck in my throat; I don't know what to say. 'He's dead, your dad is dead, he died. I never showed you the piece from the newspaper but it was an accident. You have to believe me. Ask Granny.'

I sit down on the bed beside him, and then I slide onto the floor because I'm not sure what to say. I don't feel like the calm mother anymore. I feel like someone who has failed utterly. I turn around so that I'm facing him and I say, 'Luke, your dad and I were so in love and I was pregnant and none of this is a lie. A driver who had been drinking smashed into his car and he was gone.'

His little face stares at me, those eyes so like Jean-Luc's, and I think of all the things I have done wrong. Like nails shattering down out of the sky, piercing every part of me.

'I'm sorry, I'm sorry, Luke.'

Luke stares at me and I start to cry. I always swore I wouldn't cry in front of Luke, not letting him have to be my protector. He was a child and blast it all to hell, he would be allowed to be a child, not have to comfort his grieving mother.

He wouldn't have to be the man of the house, I could be both the mother and the father.

Or I thought I could.

He's staring at me, his face white.

'You still don't believe me, do you?' I say, shocked.

He shrugs, doesn't say anything. I can see the shimmer of a film of tears on his eyes. I get back up on the bed to try and get close to him, but he moves further away. 'Please let me hold you, let me hug you, please darling,' I say, begging.

'I just want a dad, like everyone else. Raffie wants a dad and he's got Zep now. I don't have anyone. Even the ones who live with their mums, they still see their dads at weekends, but I don't. What did we do wrong?'

'Nothing! We did nothing wrong. He died. Oh Luke, please believe me! I'm sorry, I'm so sorry,' I say. 'Will we look at his photographs?'

'I don't want photographs,' he says angrily.

'I'll ring Granny, get her over here and she can tell you.'

'She'll lie too!' he yells.

And it's like my beautiful, gentle son has turned against me.

233

He's angry because I have hurt him. In trying to protect him, I did it all wrong.

Then all my plans not to fall apart disintegrate.

'I love your dad, still love him, actually,' I say, and now I'm really crying. 'I love him for himself and I love him because he gave me you, but he died.'

'You just say that,' Luke shrieks at me.

'Oh Luke,' and I pull him to me. He's in my arms crying like he used to when he was smaller. I suddenly feel so angry with Jean-Luc because if only he was here, we wouldn't be going through this. I'd be happy and Luke would be happy and he wouldn't think he'd been abandoned.

'We need help with this, Lukie. Some clever person who can talk to us and will talk about how it's different when your dad dies instead of when he leaves.'

'I don't want to talk to anyone,' he says mulishly.

'We need to, darling. I've messed this up and we're going to do it right. Plus, we're going to talk more about your dad and you are going to tell me about how you feel, because you don't talk about this anymore.'

'Didn't want to hurt you,' he mutters, 'because I knew Dad made you sad. I hated him for that.'

So I do the thing I haven't done for a couple of years. I get down the big box of photos of pictures of myself and Jean-Luc when we were younger and I go through it slowly, pointing out places we went, things we did.

'See the way you are just like your dad there?'

'Yeah,' he says and he's smiling again. It's like he was afraid to ask, afraid of hurting me by bringing up his dad.

The pain nearly kills me. 'Do you feel different in school?' I say delicately, thinking of the Family Tree project. Why had I not been more ready for it?

'Yeah, there are kids like me and Raffie, but most of them have two parents, even if they are divorced, they've got two. Some of them have stepmums and dads and that's good and that's bad. Henry hates his stepmum. Says she's grumpy in the morning. But we just have you guys and the grannies and you know that's different. The other kids have dads that take them places and play football with them and . . . I don't have that.'

'You lost something precious, Luke, and so did I. And I thought it would be better if we just kept going, just you, me, Granny, Shazz, Norma and Raffie, and I thought we were family enough.'

'You are, you are,' my strong little boy says, 'but just some-times it's – you know –' he can't find the words and I understand because I can't find the words either.

'OK, let's talk about Dad more. We'll go to France on holi-days, see your granny and granddad there. Let's write them an email now, OK?'

'Why don't they come over here?' He's still suspicious.

'They did a little bit when you were younger, but it's been sad for them too. They weren't like Granny –' I pause – 'they didn't want to travel too much.'

'Why didn't we travel to see them?'

The truth was I'd always feared that Geneviève, Jean-Luc's mum, blamed me in some way. If Jean-Luc hadn't been living in another country with me, he'd never have been killed. 'I made a mistake and we are going to change that,' I say firmly.

I turn a few more pages of the album. There's the funny ones Jean-Luc took of my belly as I was getting bigger. The ones he took of both of us with him on the timer and him kneeling down and kissing my growing bump.

'See,' I say, 'he wanted you so much, darling. But your dad was very strong. He'd want us to miss him, because he was a super person and he'd want us to talk about him. But he would hate you to think that he didn't want you or that he left you.'

'No, I didn't think that,' Luke says suddenly, taking a deep breath, 'it was just this family-tree thing made me sad, and we have to bring in pictures.'

He's being brave, my strong darling son.

235

'How about we make it the best family tree in the class,' I say fiercely, 'the very best. We're going to email *Grandmère* right now and see what wonderful pictures she can come up with, ones I don't have.'

'Maybe we could Skype her?'

'Sure,' I say. We'd tried Skyping when he was little and Geneviève, found it very painful to look at the little boy who looked so like her lost son. I should have pushed it. I shouldn't have let the contact slip away. She's his grandmother. I have to make this right.

Finally, Luke's in bed asleep and I sit in the kitchen and cry. I have failed him so badly. I kept all men away thinking it was the right thing to do, but now it feels like I was wrong.

I find a bottle of white wine in a cupboard and open it, not caring that it's not the right temperature – the sort of thing Jean-Luc used to worry about. I've been holding on to the pain from the past too much. It's time to think about the future.

30

Sid

Friday evening and the January rain is coming down as if every cloud in the sky got an urgent memo to dump all supplies, now. I'm getting soaked as I run through the puddles, wondering why I'd got a bus rather than a taxi and was wearing a skirt and not my combat trousers.

Yet, I know why. Because I don't want to talk to one of my nice taxi drivers who know me well and will wonder about my outfit – very un-me – or why I'm quivering with weirdly excited nerves. I feel incredibly first datish, which is ludicrous because I genuinely can't think of the last time I went on a first date.

Head down, I make it to the Stella and Finn is there, waiting for me with a big umbrella, and I hurry and stand under it because, naturally, I have not brought mine.

'It wasn't raining when I left,' I say, and he smiles down at me. I've forgotten how tall he is, six something, Stefan's height. I'm useless at height. Most short people are. For the first time since I've met him, Finn is not in casual, where's-the-mountain clothes. He's wearing dark trousers, a very non-casual grey woollen jacket, white shirt and a fine grey sweater. He's dressed up. For this non-date involving two just-friends meeting to see a movie.

'Should we go in?' he says, his eyes never leaving my face and yet I feel he's taken in the skirt of my dress, my sheeny-hosiery legs in the neat little pumps I break out for important meetings.

And against some of my better judgement I nod, and with

one long arm he pushes the doors open and I brush past him into the heat.

I had gone online to look up the Stella. An old 1923 cinema, it's been refurbished to look like it might have done in more glamorous 1920s style, complete with a ritzy cocktail bar. It's an elegant cinema with lots of little table lamps and fabulous seating. He takes off my coat and gives it a little shake, because it's now just a soggy mess, and reaches out to touch my shoulders to see if I'm dry. Normally, I don't let people touch me, but this is OK, this is Finn checking whether I'm dry or not, the same way he needed to check if my rucksack was on correctly.

The cocktail bar is glorious with a chandelier and an air of utter excitement and glamour to it.

'This is beautiful,' I say.

'Yes, isn't it. The photos don't do it justice,' he says, looking around.

'You mean you haven't been here before?'

'No,' he says, 'not the sort of place I normally go.' He smiles at me, a smile that crinkles up his eyes and sucks all the oxygen from the room.

'But, you know, on other dates,' I ask, shocked to find that I'm actually angling for information about other women he might have taken out. Like Mags, or Ivanna the Terrible – was she tall and beautiful? I want to know. And what was so high-maintenance about her?

'You're the first person I thought of to bring here,' he says, 'because it's different, special, like something out of another age. And that seemed to sum up you.'

I keep my head down until we find a banquette, not wanting him to see that I'm blushing. We sit down and a waitress comes by and definitely shoots Finn an admiring glance. Hey, sister, hands off, he's mine, I want to say.

I recklessly order a Martini, while Finn sticks to sparkling water.

'I brought the car,' he says, 'so I could drive you home.'

We sit there for a minute in silence while I look around and I shiver because my cardigan is damp. Despite the heating, I'm cold, but I'll wait to take off my black cardigan when it's dark and he can't see.

'Take my jacket,' says Finn.

I look at him and his face is a little set, different to the way it normally is.

'Please,' he says, 'take off your cardigan and I won't look.'

I'm touched he's picked up on my shyness. Underneath I'm wearing a sleeveless dress, which is probably not the right thing to wear in Ireland in icy, wet January, but it was the most date-like thing in my wardrobe. I put his jacket on over me. It's huge and the soft silkiness of the lining is like a living thing draped around me, like his arms, and it feels wonderful. I fold it around me.

'Thank you,' I say.

'No problem,' he says.

'Gentlemen used to always provide ladies with their jackets when they were cold, didn't you ever see it in movies? And I used to wonder why the guys would sit there and not shiver?'

'Because it was the correct thing to do and gentlemen in those movies were not allowed to shiver; it was written into the contract: no shivering. Ruins the effect,' he quips, deadpan.

The film is starting, according to an announcement, and we get up. Me, bringing my wet cardigan with me.

'We can spread it out somewhere and it will dry,' he says. 'Here, give it to me.'

And he takes my cardigan and offers me his arm as we go towards the cinema.

'Is it this place?' I ask. 'Or have we slipped back in time to the nineteen twenties?'

Finn looks down at me.

'I think it's you,' he says and I feel that quiver inside.

He has got us an amazing seat to the back. Not the single luxurious seats further up, but curved, soft bench seats. The

sort of ones all cinemas once came with, where courting couples could sit together, wrap their arms around each other and
basically do things that did not involve looking at the screen.
But I don't mind, I don't mind at all.

'It's a great place for a date, isn't it?' I say.

For a second his face is conflicted and he says, 'Sid, I didn't
want to trick you but I thought you'd like this place and these
seats were all they had. There was a cancellation.' He looks
forlorn. 'We don't have to do this, we can go, we can find some
pub where there's mad, loud music and people are getting
happy and where we'll have to shout all evening to be heard
above the noise. I'm sorry, I didn't mean to do this, it just fell
into place and –'

I thought of Adrienne, 'life is full of risk'.

I haven't risked anything for fifteen bloody years.

'It's perfect,' I say. And I reach out and I take his hand. 'Let's
go.'

And then we're sitting in this beautiful cosy seat. The space
means we naturally sit quite close to each other and Finn turns
and says to me gravely, gesturing with those large hands.

'I honestly didn't mean to do this to you, this wasn't my
plan.'

'So you don't want a date?' I say. Whatever happens, I can
take it. Just because I've built myself up into a state of excitement doesn't mean I'm going to crumble if he just wants to be
friends.

'I'd love this to be a date,' he says slowly. 'I just didn't mean
to bulldoze you.'

For the first time in forever, I reach up and touch his face
and say 'No, this is lovely, perfectly lovely.'

He smiles and I allow myself to breathe out.

'Where is Sid and what have you done with her?'

'Still here,' I say lightly. 'Settle up there. Don't get any ideas
but I want to lean back against you so I can stop shivering.
Let's watch the film.'

I hear him sigh with contentment as I lean back against his big body and feel his warmth. I am not afraid. If this feeling of happiness is a risk, then it has to be risked. Just for this.

The film is wonderful, I'd forgotten how wonderful. I can remember watching it when I was a kid on our old, tiny, hopeless black-and-white television as Mum had never gone in for proper colour TVs or anything along those lines. But on some Saturday afternoons when Vilma was little and Mum would go back to bed for a rest, Stefan would take Vilma off to the park to wear her out, and I'd lie down on the squashy old couch in the big room and watch old movies, let myself fall into that romantic world where love conquered all. I thought that was the way life was supposed to be. I don't know how my father had left my mother when I was only little. But there had always been so much love to go around and I don't think I ever missed him. Stefan loved us all, we were his family, he would protect us, and I saw the way he and Mum were. I could believe in true love back then.

'They don't make them like that anymore,' says Finn, when it's over, as he unfolds his length and stands up in the cinema and stretches.

'No,' I say, 'they don't. That was wonderful, thank you. Can I go Dutch with you on the tickets?'

He looks at me assessingly.

'Well, it wasn't supposed to be a date, and it cost more than it should have cost for a non-date friend-zone thing, so just let me deal with this one.'

'I'll do the next one,' I say.

He beams. 'Perfect.'

Outside, the rain has stopped but Finn insists I wear his jacket as mine is still wet through.

'You'll freeze,' he says.

'And you won't?'

'I'm a big strong man,' he says jokily, walking along beside me, hovering protectively.

I feel strangely safe and I *never* feel safe. Not really. And then I check myself, because safe isn't always safe. My brain runs its circuit of checks and it still comes back to the same answer, this is OK. Finn is good, he isn't going to hurt me, I can tell.

'*This* is your car, really?'

We stand in front of a rather old, battered Mini. It's small and he's tall. A vision of getting a certain number of clowns into a Mini comes to mind.

'How do you even get into it?'

'With the seat pushed all the way back,' he says. 'I think I have made a sort of bump in the ceiling where my head is,' he adds gravely. 'It is not the ideal car for someone of six foot three, but I have the motorbike, and I couldn't exactly drive you home on that.'

'You didn't know you were going to be driving me home?' I counter.

'I sort of hoped I would be. Have I messed up with the friend thing?' he says, looking me straight in the eye when we are both in the car, and I have stopped laughing at how amusing it is, watching a man of his size folded up into a Mini.

I look down at my lap.

'No, you haven't messed things up,' I say, 'not one bit.'

I direct him to my apartment, and I know absolutely that I could invite him in, but I'm not going to. I'm not ready, not yet.

Gallantly, after unfolding himself from the car, he helps me out. He then walks me up the steps to the apartment-building door.

'You're still in nineteen-twenties mode,' I say.

'It's you,' he says, 'you do that to me.'

'Really? A nineteen-twenties gentleman would not have made a lady go on a twenty-kilometre hike,' I point out, and he laughs.

'It wasn't twenty kilometres.'

'It felt like it.'

I slip the jacket off my shoulders and reach up to him, put it around his, but I can't quite make it. Instead, he balances his jacket over one arm and then two hands with their long fingers catch my face.

'Thank you,' he says. 'Thank you, Sid. Tonight was lovely.'

His lips come down on mine, warm and soft. I'm not afraid. It just feels right. I feel a pooling of warmth deep in me, and I think, oh right, yes. Then the heat of his lips is gone and he's standing up.

'Go in,' he says, 'you'll get cold. Is it safe in there?'

'Security cameras all over the place,' I say.

'Text me when you're in your apartment.'

I nod.

'I'm not saying that in a crazy, possessive stalkery way,' he adds, as he shrugs back into his jacket. 'But just text me.'

I nod and I slip in. As the lift doors close on me, he's still standing outside watching, like a knight.

After I bolt the third lock on my apartment, I send him a text. Thanks for a beautiful night, I'm home, Sid. I don't add a kiss or a funny emoji, I'm not a funny-emoji sort of person, except for Vilma and Mum.

The lovely glow inside me continues, something I don't know if I've ever felt before, something soft. But I do know I don't want it to go away.

31

Marin

Louise phones me up so we can talk about our beloved daughters going off on their six-month trip around the world.

'Hello, stranger,' I say, and I know there's an edge to my voice. I feel as if there's a permanent edge to my voice these days. Even Bernie in work has mentioned it.

'You doing all right, Marin love?' she's asked more than once when I've been sitting at my desk, knowing I look glum and not being able to change my face. Not even having bulging shopping bags in my car boot can cheer me up. I'm spending worse than ever and Nate seems to think I'm in perimenopausal hell as he's giving me a wide berth.

I still haven't asked him if he's having an affair: instead, I'm buying the world.

'I can't believe they'll be gone in a few weeks,' sighs Louise on the phone, ignoring my edgy tone.

At the thought of Rachel being gone away with Megan, I burst into tears.

Bernie looks up from her notepad where she's been writing something about a showing in Shankill that's been cancelled.

'Marin,' says Louise in surprise, 'what's wrong?'

'Nothing,' I lie.

'Are you in work?'

'Yes.'

'Can you escape for an hour?'

I look at my desk with all the things I have yet to do, think of the house I have to show this evening at seven-thirty, and tell her I can't.

'Tomorrow, after school drop off. Come for a ten-minute coffee in mine,' she says. 'I'm working from home and you won't be late – you'll speed into work because you'll miss the worst of the traffic.'

'Yes,' I mutter. 'See you then.'

The next morning, I arrive at Louise's house and think that it is simply months since I've been here. With Megan and Rachel so close, I used to spend hours here. Louise and I became firm friends and it's only in the past few months that she's more or less vanished.

Louise is dressed in her at-home gear of jeans and blouse, in case she has to do a Zoom call. She's a banking executive and has one day a week working from home, which she says she loves. 'I get far more done on those days than when I'm in the office.'

She hugs me. Louise is such an affectionate person and as she holds me, I feel as if we're connecting suddenly in the way I've missed for so long.

'Now, in case you're worried about the girls' trip, I've been making lists for them – calendar reminders of when they're to email and WhatsApp us, notes on the consulates in every place they're going. Even a book on customs for single-female travellers!' She waves the book at me. 'But Marin, is that what's wrong? Is it the girls' trip, or is it something else?'

I want to bleat that she's been avoiding me, that we haven't had a heart-to-heart talk for ages, but I don't.

Instead I say: 'It's Nate and me . . .'

In a quieter voice, she says: 'Come on in, I've got coffee on.'

We sit in her kitchen and she finally tells me.

'I'm sorry, Marin – I didn't know what to do. If I told you and I was wrong, you'd never forgive me. The messenger is always the one in trouble . . .'

'If you told me what?'

She hesitates, then says: 'I saw Nate coming out of a hotel

in town one afternoon, with a tall blonde woman. I didn't see her face because she was facing the other way, but he kissed her goodbye.'

My heart doesn't sink: it plummets. I've been kidding myself that I was imagining things. But here are two riddles solved: the one about why Louise hasn't been able to talk to me and the one about Nate.

'Do you think it could be Angie, Steve's wife?'

She considers this and shrugs. 'I can't say. Honestly. But I'm really sorry for telling you, Marin. And for not telling you. It could be totally innocent –'

'Hardly,' I say, and I fill her in on what I saw at Christmas.

With a willing listener, it all comes tumbling out. The gift receipt, his cornflower-blue shirt, all my fears.

'I didn't want to believe, but I knew something was wrong,' I say, 'and I kept hoping I was imagining it, that he was going through a mid-life crisis or something. But it's not just me who's seen something, you have too –'

'Nate loves you, though,' Louise says. 'Men – men are different. We love with all our hearts but they're not the same. They can honestly have sex and it can mean nothing to them. For us, it does.'

'So it meant something to the blonde woman and nothing to him? I don't care!' I cry. 'It matters to me. I love him and he's slept with another woman.'

'I didn't see that –' she begins, but I stop her.

'What else would he be coming out of a hotel with another woman for?' I say. 'It's got to be that. He's got someone else.'

I feel like I'm crumbling from the inside: my security blanket was that I was loved. Without that belief, I am nothing.

I sit at Louise's kitchen table and sob. My breathing is laboured and I think, brokenly, of how Rachel and Joey argued about people breathing properly, and how I was happy then. Or maybe I wasn't really happy – I simply didn't know all the facts. I was unhappiness in waiting. Now it's arrived in all its painful glory. I try to work out was I better when I'd just wondered if Nate was unhappy – or if the proof is the rock falling onto me, crushing me. I don't know the answer. But I feel crushed, all right. Crushed into pieces.

32

Bea

I walk through the front door and begin texting Mum to let her know how it went.

'Piers was lovely, Mum, but no romance. Sorry!'

Mum has almost given up the blind-date thing because it's been so bad, but finally she's met one of her friends' nephews and says, 'He's good-looking and funny. I think dinner wouldn't be a hardship.'

It's not a hardship at all, even though Piers and myself know within five minutes that there's not a spark between us, but he's truly entertaining. Luke and the puppies are staying over at Mum's, so we linger over coffee and tell stories about our blind dates from hell.

'If you ever need a fun night out,' he says to me as we leave the restaurant, 'give me a buzz.'

'Right back at you,' I say, cheerfully, thinking that if only all the dates were like this funny, non-date one, then who needed a man in their life?

I'll fill Mum in on the details in the morning but now, I angle my head as I hear something odd.

Water, water dripping from somewhere. It's coming from the kitchen.

I race in to find the floor near the sink awash with water. Something is leaking and, after ten minutes, I still can't stop the leaking or figure out what to do. The pool of water is growing slowly, so I've thrown towels on it. I'm worrying about the cost of getting a plumber out at half nine on a Saturday evening when the phone rings: Marin.

Briefly, I consider not answering because I have this crisis to figure out, but autopilot kicks in and I pick up.

We haven't talked since Christmas and she's ringing for a chat.

'Nate has had some work thing on,' she says brightly, and I'm not sure why, but she sounds a little off.

'Myself, Rachel and Joey are here and we've had a takeaway – bliss not to cook. They're arguing over what Disney movie to watch.

'*Frozen Two*,' I manage to joke, because Joey's true adoration for this movie shows no sign of abating. Nate hates this, he doesn't understand why Joey doesn't want to watch some macho little boy movie. But, no, he's a *Frozen* boy. And Marin, normally so yielding with Nate, takes no crap when it comes to Joey's obsession with the Disney princesses.

'Possibly,' says Marin, and I'm distracted from her odd tone by the continual leaking of whatever it is under the sink.

'Ah, that sounds lovely,' I say, 'but you know what, I'm going to have to hang up. I'm going to try Finn and see if he's around because I've got a leak in the kitchen and if he's not there, it's time to call the emergency plumber.'

I'd had to ring the emergency plumber before. And when he left, I was quite surprised he wasn't driving off in an S-Class Mercedes because of the amount he charged me just for the pleasure of coming out to my house on a Friday evening.

'Finn's out with Sid,' says Marin. 'I'll phone Nate,' she offers.

'That's so kind of you, Marin,' I say, mentally shelving the option of phoning Finn, 'but if Nate is at a business thing, you can hardly get him out on the grounds that his wife's friend is having a problem with a leak.'

'Just let me ring him, OK? He said he wouldn't be late, would just be out for a couple of hours. So you never know.'

She rings back to say he's coming, so I make tea and wait. Twenty minutes later, a taxi deposits Nate at my door. He's been drinking and he looks even more piratical than normal, dark hair ruffled, smelling of strong woody eau de cologne and brandy. He's wearing a suit too, although he's loosened the tie. These are clearly important clients, which is why he's dressed up so much.

'You're home early,' I say. I haven't any energy for conversation. The buzz of the evening out with Piers has worn off. I wish I'd made it just drinks so I could pick up Luke instead of letting him sleep at my mother's. The house feels so lonely without him.

'Oh, I managed to pawn them off,' he says. 'Some of these people would wreck your head, Bea, do you know that?'

'No,' I say. 'Listen, Nate, far be it for me to refuse an offer of you coming to help me with my plumbing but you're plastered. What good are you going to be? Really kind of you and everything, but let me call you a taxi and send you home, OK? We'll manage tonight and I'll send Finn a text in the morning, he's normally up early on Sundays.'

'I can handle a boiler just as well as Finn, drunk or not.'

Nate is always the most competitive person in the room. He has macho running through his body like whorls of writing through a seaside stick of rock.

'Come in,' I mutter, 'and let's get you a cup of coffee while I call the cab.'

I need this like I need a hole in the head. It's time for the emergency plumber.

'No,' he says, taking off his suit jacket and hanging it on the newel post. He loosens his tie and undoes the top three buttons. 'You just need to shut the water off, silly, and yes, coffee would be good. They were throwing wine into us earlier.'

He follows me into the kitchen. My cottage kitchen is big enough for possibly three people at a stretch, but only if they're small people. I'm tall and Nate is altogether too big for my kitchen. I try to think of the last time he's actually been here alone without Marin, and I can't. It was the way it was. My friendship was with Marin now, and when I saw them, it was as a couple. Finn drops over from time to time, but that's different. Finn's a friend, but Nate, leaning against the door jamb watching me intensely, feels weird tonight.

'Show me your tool bag,' he says.

'How'd you know I have a tool bag?' I ask.

'Because Marin told me. She says you are brilliant, you can do everything. Except think to turn off the water.'

I open the cupboard under the stairs, where I keep the tools along with the vacuum cleaner, the ironing board, ancient bits of discarded sports equipment of Luke's. And all sorts of other odds and ends that I'm always meaning to tidy out but never get round to.

Nate pulls the bag out.

'All right,' he says, examining it all like a surgeon looking at new theatre equipment. 'I can fix whatever's wrong. I'm pretty handy around the house, you know.'

'Have your coffee,' I say, handing it to him, 'and forget about the leak. I'll cope till tomorrow.'

But Nate's already pulled off his suit jacket and is under the sink, strong shoulders and arms reaching in and doing whatever it is that men do when faced with plumbing problems.

'Look, just leave it, will you, you're plastered.'

'I think it's nothing more serious than a burst pipe,' he says.

'Really?'

'Yeah, it's obvious.'

I stifle the urge to slap the back of his head.

'Bet you I figured it out quicker than Finn.'

'God, you're so competitive,' I say, laughing at him, because it reminds me of him all those years ago.

'What's wrong with that?' he demands. 'Men are competitive, Bea: it's testosterone. Evolution, etc., etc.'

He takes a slurp of coffee and grins suddenly.

'Can you stick a bit of whiskey in it?' he asks. 'And a dollop of cream?'

I raise my eyes to heaven but give in. As he fills a couple of big saucepans with water and then searches for the stopcock to turn it off until the morning, I make two Irish coffees. It's probably last Christmas since the bottle of whiskey came out in this house, I think, as I take a sip of mine.

'I won't send a bill,' he says, standing up to take his.

We sit at the kitchen table drinking slowly, not talking, and I enjoy the subtle sweetness of the Irish coffee. I used to have a drinks measure, I think. This is definitely a double but I know I'll sleep after it.

'Another one would be lovely but a mistake,' says Nate, finishing his and getting to his feet. I finish mine too and stand up. He'll need a taxi now, I think, and wonder where I put my phone so I can check the taxi app.

But suddenly, Nate smiles that lazy smile, pulls me towards him as if we were still going out like crazy twenty-year-olds, and I'm held in Nate's arms, my whole body pressed up against his body. He's lowering his mouth to mine. The first flare of wrongness disappears.

It's the first time I've been held like this since Jean-Luc died.

And, oh forgive me, I don't push him away.

It's like some ancient body memory, this being held.

You've missed this, my body is saying and I lean into him and as if I have no control, I kiss him back. My hands go round to hold him and he fixes his on my waist, large hands, then splaying down to cup my buttocks and pull them closer.

I know this is wrong, wrong on every level, wrong because he's Marin's husband. Marin, my friend! Wrong because me and Nate were in the past when we were kids.

But then his hands are in my hair and he's whispering to me, and even though I know it's utterly wrong, I don't stop him.

I'm held against his chest and he's murmuring into my ear about how beautiful I am.

'Fragile and elegant,' he murmurs.

When his fingers reach up under my silky sweater, I moan. It's like having somebody point something out to you that you had never known you'd missed and I am lost. I kiss him back, just one kiss, I think, letting my body press even more closely against his and it feels so lovely just for once to have this closeness, this tenderness, in my life.

It's dark. I wake up and sit bolt upright in the bed. There's something wrong. And I can't think what it is and then I realise; there's a strange smell of alcohol and beside me in the bed is Nate. Nate is in bed beside me and he's naked and snoring. I'm in bed with him. Naked. Oh Jesus. We had sex. Actual sex. I can't believe this, I cannot believe I did this. I know I was at a low ebb with the sense of a sweet date that would never mean anything behind me, and no sign of true love ahead of me, and he was there. I just wanted to feel held and not the person who was always in charge . . . but how could I let this happen?

What have I done?

I have to get Nate out of the house and nobody must know. But I know.

I know, oh God, I know.

I close my eyes and I cry, great heaving sobs. I wriggle out of the bed, because I don't want to be beside him.

I'll have to burn the bed. I can't have him in it. I can't have his memory in it. This was the bed I shared with Jean-Luc and it's old and needs a new mattress and now it's tainted for good.

I reach for my phone. Half two in the morning. I've got to get him out of here. Now.

I go into the bathroom and stare at myself in the mirror and I look the way I always look: pale, my hair dark, grey bits, my eyes shadowed.

Why now, why now? Look at all those stupid men people have been pushing towards me at parties for years, people's nephews and friends and 'oh he'll be perfect for you'. Men like the Teds of this world who are never going to be perfect for anyone. And I said no, because I didn't need them. I didn't want them.

Me and Luke are perfect together and now in this moment of weakness, not long after the pain from that bloody Family Tree project, just because I was lonely, I have fallen into this hole of disaster.

Just then, a thought occurs to me. Maybe he's done this before. Marin had told me about Rachel and that horrible night when she was missing in town for an hour. Nate was supposedly off with colleagues and his phone wasn't working, or he didn't hear it or some ludicrous excuse. Is this what he's been doing with other women? And now I'm just as bad, worse even, because I'm her friend.

I can't ever be her friend again. The thought makes my heart ache.

I run back into the bedroom, grab a pair of jeans, boots and pull on a sweater. Downstairs I make some very strong coffee and order him a taxi.

I bring up the coffee and I shake him hard.

'Drink this,' I say loudly. He wakes up blearily and looks at me.

'Hi, baby, that was sexy, you were always sexy.'

'Nate!' I say, horrified the way I wasn't horrified a while ago. 'Don't. We've done a dreadful thing.' I hand him the coffee and try not to cry.

Two-shot espresso, no sugar, no milk, straight-into-the-vein caffeine. If I had a syringe I would stick it straight into him.

'Drink that, throw on your clothes, you're getting out of here. You've got to go home.'

'No rush,' he says reasonably, 'maybe we can do it again . . .'

'No we cannot! I was weak, weak! We cannot ever let Marin know or it will destroy her. I haven't had a man since Jean-Luc. I now realise you might do this routinely, but I do not.'

'Shit, Really?' He looks horrified at the idea of no sex for over ten years.

'Yes, really. And I would not have chosen you if I had been in my right mind. I do not mess with married men.'

Saying the words makes me feel how much I've betrayed Marin. This is her husband, not mine. Why didn't I send him away, why didn't I push him away earlier?

'Nate,' I say in desperation, 'get up, get out and be quiet. I don't want my neighbours seeing you leaving.'

Dublin is a village and word spreads. I can't bear the thought of how this will hurt Marin.

I send him outside as the lights of the taxi appear in the dark and lean against the door, locking the big lock. I can feel the fear in me, making my body vibrate with fear and anxiety. Then I go back upstairs, strip the bed. Stuff everything in the washing machine. Have the hottest shower I can bear, put on different clothes. Make my bed again after turning the mattress over.

I lie in an uneasy sleep until dawn comes. I wake up every half an hour, shaking, anxious, aware that some fabric of my life has shifted and there is nothing I can do about it.

33

Sid

The poster for the Rape Crisis Centre parachute jump practically leaps out at me. It's synchronicity at work, I think, as I stare at it. The traffic has stalled on my route into the office and because the car simply isn't moving, I have time to look carefully and note the website.

At work, I check the site and see that if I can raise two thousand euros, I can do a tandem jump in ten days and all but two hundred euros of the money goes to the charity.

There's a fundraising page and I join it, looking at all the eager faces who've already posed excitedly online about how much money they've raised. I'm coming late to the party when it comes to fundraising. But without even considering how much I don't like heights, I know that this is something I've got to do.

Fear keeps you in your little cage so that you can see the outside world but not get out.

Not anymore, I think. Time to fly.

You're doing what? Finn replies to my text.

You read it right, I answer back happily. Can you forward this to anyone who might donate a fiver or a tenner?

Of course. But can I come?

I don't have a lot of time to raise the money but Mum, Stefan and Vilma come to my rescue, along with what must be everyone in Finn's college.

With four days to spare, I've raised more than two thousand euros.

On the Friday evening before the jump, Adrienne and I are last in the office.

'I'm skipping the drinks this evening,' I say, as we walk out the door, with us both saying bye to Imelda, who has nearly finished the evening clean.

'No Dutch courage,' she says.

I glance at her.

'Tea,' I say. 'Lots of herbal tea to help me sleep. The last thing I want to do is drink too much to blot out the impending fear, then wake up with a dreadful hangover and not be able to do it,' I reply.

Adrienne nods. 'It does sound scary but anyone who's jumped always says it's amazing. One friend's mother is still sky diving at seventy.'

'I'd say this will be my only jump,' I say with total confidence. 'I'm terrified of heights.'

'What?'

I realise that I have actually shocked Adrienne. Which I'd thought was impossible up until this point.

'*Now* you're shocked?' I demand. 'I thought you belonged to the "do what scares you" school of thought?'

'What scares you in a metaphorical sense,' she says. 'Not what bloody terrifies you. Why put yourself through that?'

I don't answer straight off. Instead I explain about Vilma's roof climbing: 'When she was about ten, Vilma used to climb onto the kitchen roof from her bedroom, and I was terrified the first time I saw her do it.'

I can still see it in my mind.

'It's safe,' Vilma had said airily.

'Get in!' I'd shrieked.

'You get out,' she said.

I hadn't. I'd run downstairs to find Stefan.

'Fear is what terrifies me,' I tell Adrienne. 'I can guarantee you that I won't jump again but I'm jumping tomorrow.'

*

Finn is driving me down to the Kildare parachutists' club where the gang of Rape Crisis Centre charity jumpers are to gather. It's a cool morning and I'm nervous but Finn drives most of the way with his left hand holding on to my right one, only taking it off to change gear.

We don't talk and it's strangely peaceful in the early morning light. Because the weather is changeable, we have to be there at half eight, so we can complete our training and be jumping by lunch.

I'm jumping out of a plane in a few hours, I think, watching the landscape pass by in a blur. But it's going to be all right, I know. I hold on to Finn's hand and I know this is the right thing to do.

He hasn't asked me why I'm doing it: he's simply there with me, supporting me. I haven't explained a thing. I don't need to.

Only jumpers are allowed into the training area and once we're in our flight suits, all twenty-four of us, twenty women and four men, are brought through the training technique over and over again: how to exit the plane, how to use our emergency chute if we need to and how to land, which is a tricky manoeuvre unless you fancy breaking your legs.

'Just because it's a tandem jump, don't think you can coast,' says the instructor, 'no puns intended.'

We have coffee before it's jump-off time and I'm happy to be in the second group of four going up. The clouds are moving in and if they do, the jumping will stop till tomorrow. I'm ready now – I might have become properly frightened by tomorrow.

Finn's sitting in a cosy room with some other drivers and one half-asleep father who has brought twin daughters for a twenty-first birthday jump.

I go straight to Finn and hug him.

'I'm scared,' I whisper, now that it's almost time. I can hear the whine of the plane taking off with the first team. I have ten minutes to be out there for my turn.

'You'll be safe,' he whispers into my hair. 'I'll be waiting for you.'

On the plane, it's so loud that I can't hear my teeth chattering with fear. The other jumpers are grinning, and the tandem instructors are so relaxed, I almost can't bear it.

'You OK, Sid?' says Carla, the female instructor jumping with me. 'It's a blast but you don't have to. There's no shame in admitting that it's not for you.'

It's that word again. I can feel my spine strengthen as the steel comes back into it.

'Oh, I'm jumping.'

I must have spoken out loud.

Carla grins at me.

She expertly hooks us together and when the small plane's engine is shut off and we're flying on the wind, coasting like a bird of prey riding a thermal, Carla and I make our way over to the fuselage door which has been pulled open.

Beneath us, two thousand feet below, everything looks like a child's toy farm, with fields spread out around us and the parachute centre nothing but a tiny little collection of buildings.

I know the statistics: two minutes for me and Carla to land, if all goes to plan. Thirty-seven seconds to drop to earth if not.

I'm frightened but I've been far more frightened and that fear has held me in its grip for too long. Not anymore, I think.

'Ready? Three, two, one –'

And we're gone, into the air speeding down until Carla pulls – I mean, she must – the rip cord and we jerk up.

'Look up,' she yells and I look to see the beautiful sight of an opened chute above me. I breathe in, letting the glorious air fill my lungs.

'See?' she says joyously. 'Isn't it amazing!'

I exhale slowly and yell back. 'Yes. Amazing.'

Some fears are meant to be faced after all.

PART THREE

Witch Hazel Blossoming

34
Marin

I wake up in the morning and I'm in bed alone. There's no sign of Nate and I'm feeling ripples of fear run through me. It's a combination of everything I've been feeling and thinking for so long. I get out of bed, race into the shower and let water stream over me. I don't just want to wash him out of my hair, I want to wash him out of my life. I get dressed quickly. It's half six; normally I'm not awake or dressed this early on a Sunday morning. But I get myself ready, because I feel I have something to face.

It's an instinct. Ancient.

I refuse to sit in bed waiting for him to come home on a Sunday morning, smiling and saying: 'Oh babe, how are you, you were out all night?' I've just had it up to here. I go downstairs and make the strongest coffee I can cope with and some toast. But I can't eat the toast. Who can I ring? I need to talk to someone.

April, who warned me, of all the people to warn me. That it should be April, still astonishes me. I dial her number.

'What's wrong, Marin?' she says, answering instantly. 'Has something happened? Is it Ma, Dad? Tell me.'

'It's Nate,' I say. 'He didn't come home last night. And you know what, he's been late home so often and I couldn't tell you. I think he's having an affair with Angie.'

'Angie?'

'Yeah, Louise saw him with a blonde woman, although she couldn't see who it was, and then I saw them having a weird moment at the Christmas party. It has to be Angie. I haven't had the courage to confront him. I thought he'd leave me . . .' There: I've admitted it.

'I'm so sorry, lovie,' she says. It doesn't escape me that April, who is always the other woman, is feeling sorry for me because my husband is cheating on me. 'But how do you *know*?'

'I just know,' I say.

'Well, you can't put up with that, I mean, he's got –' she stops. 'No I'm not going to tell you what he's got to do. What do *you* think he's got to do?'

'I don't know,' I say and suddenly I want to cry. 'We've got two children, we've got a life. What do I do? Just say get out of here now and let's sell the house and I'm going to try and make it on my own. I don't know what to do.'

And then I hear a noise downstairs.

He can't have been here all along? His side of the bed wasn't slept in. But –

'I think he's home,' I say suddenly. 'I'll ring you later.'

I stalk downstairs and he's in the kitchen, in underpants, socks and a T-shirt he must have found in the laundry basket.

He's clearly just woken up, so he must have been here.

'When did you get home?' I demand.

'Too late. I didn't want to wake you,' he mutters. 'I slept on the couch, which is bloody uncomfortable and oh hell, have we got any of the strong ibuprofen because my head is splitting?'

In his half-dressed state, smelling of alcohol and looking unshaven, he looks precisely like he slept on the couch.

'I'm really sorry, Marin,' he said. 'I just got pissed and when I got home, I made it into the kitchen and some bit of brain came alive. I couldn't crawl into bed with you like that . . .'

And he falls into my arms and somehow my arms go around him.

'You weren't with anyone,' I say, my voice shrill.

'Jesus, don't shout so close to my head,' he says. 'You know, Marin, stop imagining shit. I went out, I got pissed, and I am a moron. At least I didn't wake you at whenever time it was when I got here.'

'I didn't think you'd come home,' I said and I don't know how, but normality is restored. And I'm not thinking he's cheating or that he's cheated. He couldn't come in and be like this, be normal. Nobody can lie like this, surely? No, I'm imagining it.

'Get upstairs and have a shower and get into bed,' I say, 'and just try to do dry spring. There's far too much drinking in your job.'

'I'm not an alcoholic.'

'I don't think you're an alcoholic, I think you're a moron,' I say.

'Why are you up so early anyway?' he says, his eyes bleary.

'I woke up and you weren't here and I was worried.'

'Oh baby, you thought I was in hospital or somewhere, I'm so sorry.'

He hugs me. I don't smell anything on him, I don't smell any perfume or any woman or anything, it's just unshaven man. His teeth aren't brushed, surely if he was sleeping with someone else he'd have made a bit of a better effort?

'Go to bed,' I say.

It's like a weight has been lifted. How could I think the worse of him. Sure, he's a selfish bastard sometimes but I don't get him doing enough around the house and with the kids. That's my fault for needing to do everything. Things are going to change around here. First, I'm going to cut up all my credit cards. That would be a wonderful start. Yes, that's it. That's a big part of the problem.

35
Bea

How do you measure the worst week of your life?

On Monday I can't go into work.

'Mum, what's wrong?' says Luke.

'Just feel sick,' I say, 'I don't know what it is, it's a bug.'

It's not a bug, but I am sick, I literally haven't been able to keep any food in my stomach since I got Nate out of the house and I feel so weak. I'm drinking those replacement salts because I'm afraid I will actually get sick. But all I can think of is, what have I done, what have I done? Just for a moment of not thinking. And I've hurt Luke, because he's so precious and to think that I'm his mother and I've done something like this. And Marin, and I love Marin . . .

How I've betrayed her. I think of the time she came to me when Luke was a newborn and she was so heavily pregnant with Joey and she waddled in the door with another gift, with some food, with something, *anything* to help me.

'What's up with you?' says Shazz when she comes to pick up Luke to bring him to school.

'Just feel like shit,' I say.

'You look like shit,' she says.

'I must have some sort of bug or something, I can't eat.'

'But Luke's OK?'

'Luke's fine.'

'You sure you don't need to go to the doctor, get a – I don't know, injection or something?'

There's no injection for this, I think, absolutely no medication whatsoever.

I take the week off work. I'm so reliable, nobody suspects a thing. I literally cannot face people. In the day time, I sit with the puppies and I hold them and pet them. And Mum and Cliff, who's been partnering her in bridge recently, come and walk them for me.

'You poor darling,' says Mum. 'Now, I've brought you some chicken soup. You know it's the best thing.'

'Penicillin,' says Cliff, smiling in that lovely paternal way he has. He'd be a lovely granddaddy for Luke, I think. What sort of person would he think I am if he knew what I'd done? Mum won't judge me because she loves me and she loves Luke. But how can any other normal person think I'm anything but dirt? One of those other women. Before, I just thought of other women as Shazz and Christie, women who held me together, who were my family. Now I realise there can be many types of other women.

Somehow the week passes and it's Thursday. Shazz calls me first thing, before Luke has left for school.

'Why doesn't Luke come and spend the night with us and we'll bring him to school in the morning? It will be sort of a bit of fun, you've had a low week. And it's been hard on him too. Send him in with an overnight bag, your mum can mind the dogs and you can just sleep and do absolutely nothing.'

I'm beginning to feel marginally better. I can eat a little. The chicken soup does work. And the thought of being on my own in the house, even without the beautiful dogs, helps; it would be peaceful. I can exorcise the memory of Nate in here. I could pray in each room, pray for forgiveness, even though I'm not religious.

'That would be lovely.'

Shazz is off organising it in a flash.

That evening I fall asleep in front of the TV. I started watching a thriller and then the tiredness pulled me under, and suddenly I'm awake. I hear a tapping noise on the window and I get an awful fright. I look at my phone quickly, it's ten-forty.

Only Shazz would do this – but she has keys . . .? Something must have happened to Luke. I run to the door and unlock it and wrench it open. And there is Nate.

'Hey, babe,' he says, and he's smiling at me like it's over twenty years ago and we're dating.

'Nate?' I say in disbelief. 'You can't come in. Not now, not ever again.'

'Oh, honey, don't be like that. I've thought about nothing but you all week,' he says, and before I know it, he's in the house.

'Get out,' I say.

'Babe, don't be like that,' he says. 'Look, last week was such a wake-up call for me. I've always been crazy about you, Bea. You must know that.'

I can't think of a thing to say for a full minute.

'No, I don't know that,' I hiss. 'You're married to Marin, we're friends, remember?'

He's back in the kitchen and he looks, in some automatic male way, under the sink. 'You got this fixed, right?'

'Yes and don't change the subject.'

'I can do things for you like that now,' he says, going for the kettle.

'Nate, what are you talking about?'

'Now we're together. Where do you keep the glasses? I'll have a straight one of those whiskeys from last week.'

'We're not together.'

'Bea, last weekend in bed, it was amazing. I know you felt it too. Then, your mum was talking to Marin and said you weren't well, needed a little time on your own. I can pick up the hints, you know. Of course it would have been easier if you had rung me yourself.'

I feel something akin to panic. This cannot be happening. Nate is a good man – dumb, for sure, because how can he not be reading my reactions, but a good man. Has he lost the run of himself entirely? He's had a few drinks, I can tell. He likes good wine. How am I going to get him out of here?

'We are not a thing,' I say. 'Last week was a mistake.'

'You don't mean that,' he says, eyes glittering.

Yes, definitely a bit drunk.

'Darling Bea, I can't stop thinking about you, how lonely you've been. I'm not leaving Marin, I love her, but I hate to think of you being so lonely.'

'I'm not,' I say. 'And marriages don't work like that – you don't come round to your old girlfriend's every weekend and then play house with your wife the rest of the time, Nate!'

I am so angry, I think I am going to hit him.

He honestly thinks this is a helpful plan.

'There's always been something between us. And who's to know? It's not going to do anyone any harm. You don't want anything serious, you still love Jean-Luc, we all know that. But everyone needs love in their lives, Bea, and you're so lovely. Jean-Luc would hate to see you so lonely.'

I stop backing away at this ludicrous statement.

'You want to have sex with me because Jean-Luc would want it? Seriously?'

'Well . . .'

I have to get him out of the house. I left my own phone on the couch in the living room, which makes me furious because it's far easier to ring the emergency services from a mobile than it is from a house phone. Mobiles are easier to tap out numbers on.

'Why don't you take your coat off,' I say, stalling for time. If he's preoccupied, I can run to the living room and phone someone – but who? Finn? How would I explain this? My mother and Cliff? Worse. The police. Say he's drunk, an old friend, can they get him home . . .?

'Aha!' He's found the whiskey and he's got two glasses. 'I believe we have the house to ourselves.' While he's taking his coat off, I run into the other room, grab the phone and I dial 999. I'm just about to press the green button and he appears at the kitchen door and says, 'What are you doing?'

'I'm ringing the police,' I say. 'You've got to get out of here.'

'You can't do that, you can't ring the police. I mean Jesus, stop it.' And he lurches towards me.

I run away into the kitchen and slam the door and shove the kitchen table in front of it, which is absolutely no good because Nate is strong, he's like a bull, he'll get through anything.

'I am going to ring the police,' I shout. 'Or would you like it if I rang Marin first? Your call.'

Please let him just go home and leave me alone. I am not able for this.

'Don't ring Marin,' he says. It's the first time he doesn't sound like Mr In Control.

'I'll ring Marin,' I warn. 'She is my friend.'

'You weren't thinking of that last week.'

'Last week you caught me at a weak moment and I did something so stupid and shameful. But you – you put your arms around a woman who was vulnerable and we hurt Marin . . .'

Suddenly there's this weird, lightly strangled noise outside the door. I hear the door creak, like something has just banged into it and an odd noise like someone being kicked.

'Nate, Nate?'

I run around the other door of the kitchen, the one that leads from the dining room to the living room back into the hall. Nate is lying on the ground crumpled up, holding his left arm. His jaw constricted, his face white.

I click the green button on the phone. 'I need an ambulance,' I say. 'I think he's having a heart attack.' And I give them my address.

36

Sid

Stefan has just cooked us the most incredible dinner and myself and Mum are sitting in front of a roaring fire, with the kittens playing on the rag rug in front of us. Mum has been telling us all about one of the old gang who's getting married in Hawaii and we're all invited.

'Hawaii,' I say dreamily. 'I love the sound of that. Is it true that the word for hello and goodbye is the same?'

'No idea,' says Mum, smiling at me. 'Probably a crazy rumour the way people think Ireland is full of weird little men with pots of gold.'

'Yeuch, the whole leprechaun thing,' I say, shuddering. 'We have so many lovely legends, so many ancient stories. How have horrible little green men with pots of gold come to be an actual symbol people associate with this country? Where are the tourist statues of powerful Morrigan or the Tuatha de Danann?'

'All countries have their burdens,' says Stefan gravely. 'You know nobody can talk about Lithuania without discussing the kaukas, same as the leprechauns. Evil spirits. Nobody is talking about the higher beings, the gods and goddesses. My mother was called Laima, named after the goddess of Fate and women bearing children.'

'I prefer Vilma to Laima,' Mum says to him grinning. 'Stefan wanted your sister to be Laima but Vilma, truth, has such purity to it.'

They share another glance with such love in it that I'm smiling at them both, and then Mum turns her eyes to me. This time, she's beaming at me.

'So, truth, my darling. Tell us about this man.'

'What man?' I ask, blushing so much that Stefan laughs.

'The man who makes you so happy, of course. Why have you not brought him to see us?'

I laugh then. How do mothers know these things?

I tell them how wonderful Finn is, how we've gone walking together, how he came to my charity parachute jump, how I had to meet his friends, how gentle he is with me, how gentlemanly, and how I'm going to his house soon for dinner.

'He's been learning to cook,' I tell them, grinning like a loon, because it is adorable. ' "I want to cook things for you, feed you up, look after you," he says.' Just thinking about this and telling them makes me feel full of joy. I never dreamed there could be such happiness. All those years with Marc, thinking that I was safe because I had a man living with me, a man who was more of a brother than anything, a friend who shared my bed but never touched me because I couldn't face the intimacy.

And then I tell them how it was all down to Vilma and her friends insisting that I go out with them one night.

'I'd met him in the queue and she could just tell he was special,' I recount. 'You want to have heard her when I came back to the table with the food and drinks and hadn't agreed to be friends with him.'

'I knew Vilma had something to do with it,' Mum crows. 'She's been keeping the secret very badly, you know. No talent for keeping things to herself, your sister.'

'It is why she is called truth,' says Stefan.

'She told you?' I ask.

Mum laughs. 'She may have said something. But I can see it in you, Sid. You look –' she pauses – 'you look like you haven't looked for years. You look like you did all those years ago before you went to the city.'

I stare into the fire. I never wanted to tell them because it would hurt them, but now that I am happy, now that I am healing, I can. So I do.

37
Marin

The phone rings, jerking me awake and I sit bolt upright in the bed. What was the noise? Then it clicks into my brain.

The house phone, Nate's side of the bed. He's not there, working late. Again.

I'd gone to bed early because I have an early meeting in the morning and was in a deep, heavy sleep – I feel like I'm underwater. I lunge across Nate's side of the bed and drag the phone out of its cradle.

'Yes,' I hiss.

'I'm looking for Mrs Marin Stanley,' says the voice.

'This is me, Marin, she, whatever.'

'My name is Dr Luther, and I'm calling from the Emergency Department in St Vincent's Hospital. Your husband Nate is here. He's had a cardiac event.'

'Is he all right, is he dead? Tell me.' The words just keep tumbling out of my mouth.

'No, he's OK, stable for now. Do you have someone to drive you, to be with you?'

'Yes,' I say, 'but, but what happened?'

'That's really all I can tell you over the phone.'

'And what do I do when I get there?' It's like all my synapses are fried and I can't think straight.

'Just come to reception, ask for me, Dr Luther, or say who you are and you'll be led in. You'll be able to see your husband.'

'But is he going to be all right?'

'He's in good hands.' It's the voice of a woman used to saying things like that to people, I think blankly and then she's gone.

I'm left holding the phone, sitting on the edge of the bed, feeling the blood pumping through my skull and my chest as if I'm the one having a heart attack.

I stuff the phone back down and race into Rachel's room. She's there, in bed asleep, looking younger than ever, her long dark hair spread over the pillow. I can't wake her, but somebody needs to be here for Joey. I run to Joey's room and look at him, slipping in to stroke his face because he won't wake up. Nothing short of an earthquake wakes Joey when he goes to sleep.

I race back into our bedroom and grab a bit of paper and scrabble among the detritus of the dressing table for a pen.

Your dad not well, in Vincent's Hospital, gone to see him, stay here with Joey. I'll call you if I need you, it's . . .

I realise I don't even know what time it is, so I look at my watch and it's 1.05 a.m.

I grab my handbag, throw my phone and charger into it trying to think sensibly but it's impossible. Then I strip off my clothes and pull on leggings, a bra and a sweatshirt, all of which I was wearing around the house yesterday evening. I don't care. Socks, runners, I don't even pull a brush through my hair – it's not important. And then I'm out and in the car, shaking as I grab the steering wheel.

I turn the radio off, I don't want to listen to any music. I drive quickly, thinking of the last time I sped out of our suburban village towards the city, the night I thought Rachel was in trouble and I knew that if I had met any police car that night I'd just tell them and they'd help me, bring me, and now they'd do the same, wouldn't they? But I can't crash, so I slow down and try to breathe. He was OK, he was in good hands, he was stable, those were the words she said. They are good words, good news.

I park the car on a grass verge at the hospital, ignoring all the signs warning me that it will be clamped.

I don't care about clamping. I have to get to the emergency department. What does a car matter?

I half run, because the heaviness in my chest since I got the phone call from the hospital won't allow me to run properly. Or breathe. I need deep calming breaths.

Screw deep, calming breaths.

I need to be with him.

Now. Sooner.

I can keep him alive. No doctor can do it: he needs me, holding his hand, willing him back to life.

I don't have time for the information desk – I know this hospital, see the double doors leading into the actual A & E itself, see a man pushing out of them and I race, grabbing one swing door just before it shuts.

I'm in.

Scanning. Peering in past half-drawn cubicle curtains. A man throwing up vile black stuff.

Two cops standing outside another cubicle. A woman on a heart monitor.

And then there he is.

I see his hand lying limply. A hand that's caressed me so many times.

I stand at the edge of the already-full cubicle, about to speak when a doctor hangs her stethoscope round her neck and says: 'I'll talk to the wife.'

She's gone instantly and I follow her, see her approach another woman. The doctor puts a comforting hand on the woman's forearm.

'I'm the wife!' I say, my voice frantic.

And then, as the doctor spins around, I see the other woman, recognise her, see the horror on her face.

'I'm his wife,' I say, 'not her.'

She looks white and, at first, she runs to me, then stops dead, her hands flying to her mouth.

Bea.

Nate has been with her? In all my horrible imaginings about other women, I never thought it could be Bea.

'I'm his wife,' I repeat to the doctor, who looks startled and then immediately a blankness falls over her features.

'Right,' she says. 'Do we need to sort out some identification?' she asks.

'I was just with Nate when he collapsed,' Bea says. 'Marin is his wife. I'll leave now that she's here.'

I don't give her a second look, I only want to see Nate.

'He is under sedation,' the doctor tells me, matter of factly, as we walk back to the cubicle. I take Nate's hand and hold it. None of this seems real. He's hooked up to machines with the reassuring beep of the pulse, his chest a tangle of wires ready to connect him to the ECG machine. But there is nothing reassuring about this scene.

I can't speak. My fingers keep stroking the cold part of Nate's hand encumbered by oxygen monitors and wires.

'I'll get the cardiac consultant to talk to you in a little while, but we are slammed tonight, big traffic accident.'

I nod.

'Is there anything more you can tell me?' I find my voice.

'No. Your husband is stable for now. It's important we get him upstairs to the cath lab.'

'OK.' I take the news and nod, as if I'm used to hearing this every day. And then she's gone, whisking out, pulling the curtain back into place. Bea has followed me in, and now the three of us are in the tiny narrow cubicle, Nate's breathing even, the beep of the machines the only sound I'm taking in, although it's chaotic outside.

She doesn't leap in with excuses or lies. Instead she says, 'Marin, there's a chair, please sit.'

I don't sit. 'Get out.'

I can see her eyes fill with tears but I feel no pity.

I cannot work out which of them I hate most at this moment.

She slips quietly away and I'm alone in the cubicle with my husband, who isn't really my husband, who's only been pretending to be my husband. I look at his face, touch his brow, his nose, his lips and I lean over to kiss him on the forehead because I love him, he's the father of my children. And then I allow myself to cry.

After a little while, an older doctor arrives along with the porters.

'Mrs Stanley?' I can tell that he knows Nate has come in with another woman: the look he gives me is pitying. 'I'm Dr O'Donnell. We are moving your husband up to cardiac care where we'll perform more tests. He may need an angiogram to see what the problem was; we need to keep him stable and you probably won't be in with him for a little while. Do you want to go home?'

'No, I'm going to stay.'

'OK, go back out and someone will show you how to get up to coronary care and wait near the nurses' station, and we can talk to you up there.'

'Is he going to survive?' I only have one question I need answered. 'Is he going to be all right?'

'I can't say right now, we are doing our best. You have got to trust us.'

And, with that, the nurses and the porters organise my husband so his trolley can be wheeled away from me and I am led to the doors out of the emergency department.

I find coronary care on the fourth floor, although I am feeling weaker with every step closer to it.

Nate has had a heart attack. The words sound too serious, too dangerous, to apply to Nate.

And he'd been with Bea.

How could he do that? He loved me, he loved our children; none of it made any sense. I'd suspected Angie, had on-and-off conversations in my head about confronting him, kept putting it off because I wanted to believe that Nate would never risk what we had. Would never have an affair, certainly not with his friend's wife.

And all along, he had been doing just that. Except that the friend was Jean-Luc and the wife was Bea.

I have to sit in a little ante-room beside coronary care. I hold my phone in my hand, wondering who I can text to say, you won't believe what's happened. In hospitals, people ring family and friends so that these loved ones tell them it will all be OK. How can that happen here? Who could I ring?

April, who probably knew women who'd accompanied men who weren't their husbands to all sorts of places, if not hospitals. No, I'd talk to her in the morning. I thought of Rachel, happily asleep in her own bed with the alarms on and Joey tucked up in his room. How could I ever tell them? Did I have to? I couldn't.

There was nobody I could phone and tell, nobody to cry to.

38

Bea

Outside the hospital, there is one lonely taxi. I get into it and give the driver my address. I don't look at him. I don't want to look at anyone. I'm still shaking from the combination of shock and grief. I slept with another woman's husband, not just another woman, but Marin's husband, and that single act of selfishness has brought us here to the hospital. I could have just left, but that would be the coward's way out. No, I had to stay and make sure he was all right and greet her.

'You all right, love?' says the taxi driver. He can see my undoubtedly white face in his rear-view mirror.

'Not really,' I whisper.

'Sorry, love,' is all he says.

Even he can see that I am not to be spoken to.

The driver takes me to Shazz's house because Luke was staying over with her and Raffie last night so I could rest, all of which seems like a million years ago.

I wish I'd told Shazz before what had happened last week; I can't have her thinking I planned for Nate to come, that I made them all complicit in a lie. What happened tonight was all because of one weak moment, for the momentary sense of comfort of having another human body wrapped around me. Because that's all it was. It's like my brain had deserted me and all I needed was the comfort of someone to hold me and love me. All these years of saying I didn't want anyone and then these stupid dates, all culminating in me having sex with the very last person I should ever be intimate with.

I've got Shazz's keys in the same way she's got my keys. So I let myself in, turn off the alarm, turn it on again and realise it's four in the morning now. There's no way I could sleep, although Shazz has a very comfortable couch in her kitchen. I take off my coat, throw my handbag on the floor and make myself a cup of herbal tea. Chamomile, although it will take more than that to make me sleep. It's closer to morning than night – how can I sleep now? I sit on the couch, pull a throw around myself and wonder what the hell I can possibly say to my friend about this. How am I going to live with this knowledge forever? That one act of stupidity brought Nate back to my door and now look where we are.

'Jesus, you frightened the shit out of me,' says a voice. It's Shazz, standing at the door to the kitchen with a baseball bat in her hand, dressed in her woolly pyjamas. 'What are you doing here?'

I look at her and no words come, only tears.

'Are you OK?' She's by my side in an instant kneeling on the floor. Putting down the chamomile tea and taking my hands in hers. 'Did something happen?'

I shake my head.

'No, Shazz, no; I've done the stupidest thing, I can't explain.' It all started with that horrible family-tree thing and you know how that threw me, how Luke thought I was lying to him about his dad. And I felt I'd failed, I felt so lonely. And then, I went out with Piers last week, which was fun but would never amount to anything and then Nate turned up when I had a leak in my kitchen.' I let the tears fall onto the blanket.

'Last weekend?'

I nod.

'I knew you were freaked by something.'

'He put his arms around me. You know how that feels when you've been lonely for so long. But I could have said no, I could have hit him over the head, I could have rung Marin up and told her.'

I start to cry properly. Shazz goes to a cupboard high up and takes out a bottle of brandy. She pours two glasses.

'This is my medicinal brandy,' she says, 'it's actually not bad, not that I like brandy, but it has a bit of a kick in it and reminds your body that it's still alive. I think possibly because it makes your heartbeat go up, but you look like you are going to pass out, so maybe having your heartbeat go up is a plus.'

'I can't drink brandy,' I say, shuddering at the look of the glass.

'You can and you will; get it down you. The kids sleep well but you never know, any minute now they'll suddenly erupt downstairs and want to know what's going on. So let's get our plan organised and sort things out.'

'There's no sorting out,' I say. 'He turned up out of the blue tonight and I told him to go or I'd phone Marin or the police. I began to and he had a heart attack with fear, so I called an ambulance and I brought him to hospital.' Shazz's mouth falls open. 'And I gave them Marin's number and they rang her and I stayed until she got there.'

'Jesus wept,' says Shazz.

'And they were carrying on as if I was his wife, although I kept telling them I wasn't and that his wife would be there. But I mean they all must have known. And then she came in, and her face, oh Shazz, her face. She looked so heartbroken.'

'Yeah, well, I'd look heartbroken if I was married to that bollix, I never liked Nate.'

'You know Finn's new girlfriend? She doesn't like Nate either.'

'Smart woman.'

'The first time she met him he went to do the kiss on both cheeks.'

'Yeah, pretentious wanker,' interrupts Shazz.

'No, but she pulled back instantly, it's like she knew.'

'Clever chick must have met his type before. It's nice that Finn has got someone with a bit of sense. If Marin had any sense, she'd dump Nate. I know you're feeling like shit right now, Bea, because you have never done anything like this before in your life. But you have some sort of excuse. Nate hit on you when you were really, really low and he did the hugging and the minding and the *I'm always here for you*. And then suddenly he's kissing you and it feels nice to be held. Guys like him, it doesn't just happen once. I bet there's a trail of women. I bet he has his own football team of them.'

'You could be right,' I say. 'But that doesn't take away from the fact that the football team are not friends of his wife, part of his circle. I've just destroyed that.'

'If you've destroyed it, he's destroyed it too. Now you're going to get over this and you're going to stop beating yourself up. People are complicated, and life's mental. That's my mantra, babes. Drink your brandy, one gulp, go.'

We drained our glasses together. The brandy burns the back of my throat and I start to cough.

'I thought you said this was good stuff?'

'It's all relative,' says Shazz, pouring us each a smaller shot. 'It's good stuff to me, Lady Muck. OK, one, two, three, shot!'

With two brandies inside me, I'm slightly stabilised, although I doubt if the hospital advise brandy for helping people with shock. We sit together quietly and I myself relax as much as I possibly can. Finally, Shazz looks at her watch.

'Now, you've got to get back to your house, lie down for an hour, get up early, wash your hair, do your make-up, have a lot of strong coffee and face the day as normal. I'll bring Luke to school. You go into work and don't answer any phone calls, except if they are from me or your mum. Marin might ring you from a different phone, you don't want that, you're not ready for it now, OK?'

'OK,' I say. 'OK.'

As I start the short walk home along the totally deserted streets that separate our houses, I think about how grateful I am for Shazz's friendship.

But mine and Marin's will never be the same ever again. I've broken it.

39

Marin

They won't let me into cardiac care but a nurse suggests I have a tea or coffee from the machine down the hall.

'It's working at the moment,' she says, as if this is an unusual occurrence, 'do you have change?'

'I think so,' I say, looking around in my purse, 'yes.'

'Come back and hopefully in the next fifteen minutes you'll be able to come in, OK?'

'Thank you,' I say.

It's now half four, and I feel as if I'm starring in a nightmare, somebody else's nightmare. The machine coffee is horrible, but it's strong and it wakes me up. Nate has had a heart attack and he was with another woman, one of our friends, one of my friends.

I want to kill him and I want him to live. I didn't know my mind could hold two such opposing views, but it can. I sit in the little lounge just outside the coronary care, where the television is turned on and where another man sits staring blindly at the box. It's a grainy TV, not a thing of hi-definition beauty and *Murder, She Wrote* is playing. The man and I don't speak. He's staring into the middle distance, his eyes wet. I haven't cried a single tear: shock, I think.

Shock, horror and betrayal. I gulp down my hideous coffee and think that I have to be strong. Strong for Rachel and Joey, strong for myself, and perhaps strong for Nate. All I know is that I love the man on the other side of the perspex doors. And now I hate him too.

'You can come in now,' says the nurse, popping her head

around the door and looking at me. I gulp down the rest of my coffee, throw the cup in the bin and follow her. Cardiac care is utterly frightening, a land of machines with nurses and doctors walking slowly around. In the middle of the beeping and winking and many corded machines, lies my husband.

'We think he's too weak for an angiogram, therefore we are going to do some imaging on his heart and the arteries surrounding it. We need to get a vision of whether he has blockages or not. But we don't want to push him until he's out of danger.'

I nod.

A nurse gave me a number for the ward. 'We don't let people sit in coronary care overnight,' she says, 'it's too difficult for them and us. So if you want, you can sit with him for ten minutes. We will call you if anything changes or you can call the unit directly. We will need some forms filled in as well, so you could do that on the way out, so we have your phone number. The next-of-kin number,' she says. And the way she says it made me think that news of my husband's arrival with one woman and subsequent movement up to the cardiac care unit with another has not bypassed the hospital bush telegraph.

I sit with him and hold his hand again.

Nate, I want to say, why did you do it, why did you risk what we had? But instead I said, 'I love you, Nate, please be strong, please fight this, so that Rachel and Joey can come in and hug you and you can get out of hospital and we can begin again. We don't have to talk about any of this,' I whisper, stroking his forehead and his cheek, 'I just want you well, please understand that, please be well.'

After ten minutes, I am gently extracted from Nate's bedside and brought out into the corridor where a clipboard awaits me to fill in all his and my details.

'You'll ring me if anything happens?'

'Yes, we'll ring you. But this will not be a quick process, so you need sleep,' said an older nurse. 'Go home. We'll phone you after the new shift takes over about half eight, quarter to nine, we'll have a good vision of how he passed the night and that's a good litmus test for his strength. He's young, he has that on his side.'

'Forty-six,' I say.

'We need to take care of him now, you need to let him go into our hands.'

'OK,' I say.

I'm not sure how I leave the hospital or even make it to the car. I drive home feeling both dizzy with tiredness and wide awake at the same time. What am I going to tell the children?

Your father has had a heart attack and he's in hospital, and I wasn't with him because he wasn't home, he was with someone else . . .?

There's no way of saying any of these things, no way at all. I close my eyes. I'll try to figure out the right thing to do. But right now, I just have to survive this. I just have to exist, that's all.

Everything looks different, the roads seem unfamiliar. Maybe it's the fact that I'm driving in the early morning and dawn is thinking about creeping over the horizon. It's a cold morning and a few early-bird workers are on their morning commute. I'm going in the other direction, home. *Home.*

Even the words seem strange. Home implies a place where you are safe and you live with your loved ones. But, my husband is lying in coronary care after having a heart attack when he was with his mistress, who is also my friend, *was* my friend. I practise saying this out loud and it sounds stranger, every time I say it.

What am I going to tell Rachel? With Joey, I can fib a bit, he's still young enough not to see through a lie, so I can say he was out with friends. But Rachel, she's an adult, I don't want to lie to her.

I'm not ready to tell my mother, she'd have a story printed in the local free sheet newspaper, castigating Nate and with pictures of him saying, 'cheater' if she could possibly get away with it. And if she couldn't, she'd be handing out leaflets. Dominic will hug me. And that's when I do cry, thinking of being hugged by someone whom I know loves me. All the pain of thinking that Nate didn't, all the worry that's been bubbling inside me for months now, breaks. I cry for much of the journey home.

And to think I worried about Angie. Or maybe it was Angie too. Maybe Nate has lots of women.

I get home at half six and I make strong tea, which then makes me feel nauseous. I run to the bathroom and throw it all up.

In half an hour, I have to wake Joey, make him breakfast, pretend this is a normal day. Do the same with Rachel. Or do I? Normality has gone out the window. I have a showing this afternoon but I'm not going into work, no way.

Instead of our usual Friday routine, I sit and wait for everyone to get up.

Even though it's too early, I still ring the hospital, get put through to the coronary care ward. And a nurse tells me that he's doing well but that the cardiology team will be on their rounds later. Soon but still later.

'Can I talk to the cardiologist?' I say.

'Possibly this afternoon we'll have some news for you, because they'll have to have a team meeting to decide what to do.'

'OK, but he's stable?'

'Stable, absolutely, passed a good night. We'll call you if there is anything else we need to tell you, Mrs Stanley,' said the nurse. Even her saying my name makes a flush of pain rise inside me. I'm the woman whose husband was brought in with someone else.

'Mum?'

I turn swiftly and Rachel is standing at the door to the

286

kitchen, still in her pyjamas. She looks me up and down. I always shower and dress after breakfast. Now, I'm wearing my boots and proper clothes, not my slippers and comfortable fleecy dressing gown. 'What are you doing up so early, Mum?'

The note must have fallen off her bed, I think, and she didn't see it.

'I haven't been to bed actually,' I say.

'Why, what's wrong?'

She's beside me in a flash, slender fingers clutching one arm. And suddenly she is not grown-up Rachel who's ready to travel around the world: she's my idealistic daughter, who idolises her father, who thinks everything is normal and simple in life and that things will work out the way she wants them to work out.

'It's your dad,' I say, and years of training kick in. I cannot tell her the truth. 'He's going to be fine, but he had a heart attack, a cardiac episode.' I fumble around a bit trying to find the correct words, words that won't frighten her. 'He's in hospital and he's OK. I was with him last night for a little while, but they sent me home.'

'Why didn't you wake me?'

'I didn't want to worry you, darling,' I said, thinking back to that moment when I was leaving the house and I really wanted to wake her. Just to hug her and hold her. 'You needed to sleep and there was nothing you could do. I didn't want to put you through that. Now he's fine, I've just been on to the hospital, he's stable. And they are going to decide what to do later. He might need some surgery after this, who knows. But your dad is young and strong and fit.'

'Poor Dad,' she says and she starts crying, rubbing at her eyes, making the mascara she hadn't quite taken off properly smudge across them. 'He's very fit, but will he be all right? Did they say that, did they promise?'

'They don't promise things like that, darling, but he's in the right place.'

I'm not sure the message is coming across very well right

now, but I'm doing my best. No matter what has gone on in the night, I am still Marin, mother, mother lioness and I'm going to take care of things.

'It's all right, darling, he's going to be all right.'

'You don't know that,' she says, with unerring accuracy.

'I do,' I said, 'they told me so.'

I wonder how many more lies I'll have to tell. There's no way Rachel can ever find out how her father got into hospital. It would destroy her. And suddenly I want to be beside Nate in the hospital so I can slap him hard across the face. He hasn't just betrayed me, he's betrayed Rachel too.

Rachel goes up to get dressed and I am so angry with Nate, that I want to tell someone.

Finn, I think, I'll ring Finn, because he knew, he must have known, he is so close to Nate. And if he knew and he didn't tell me, he's never coming near my house again, our friendship is over. I know I might be a little unhinged right now, but I dial Finn's number and he answers on about the fourth ring.

'Yes?'

'It's Marin,' I snap. 'I've been at the hospital. Nate's had a heart attack.'

'Oh, Marin, I'm so sorry, I'll come right over.'

'There's no need,' I say. 'Somebody brought him in.'

'Well that's good,' says Finn, a hint of confusion in his voice. 'Somebody . . .? Where did it happen?'

'Bea brought him in, because he was with Bea, you know, our friend. Overnight.'

'Bea?'

Nobody can sound so astonished on purpose. Nobody who hasn't graduated from acting school and got a few Oscar nominations along the way.

'Our Bea? Are you sure, like how do you know he was with her?'

'They thought she was his wife and she travelled with him

288

in the ambulance. They got in at two o'clock in the morning. It was written all over her face, Finn,' I say, coolly, 'just tell me one thing, did you know about this?'

'About Bea and Nate? No, I hadn't a clue. I can't believe it, Marin, honestly –'

'You swear?'

'I swear.'

'Would Steve have known?'

'Steve? Steve isn't interested in other people in that way,' says Finn. 'Love him like a brother, but he's – you know, pretty self-obsessed.'

'Has Nate ever done this before?' I waited for a pause but there was none.

'Marin, I've been Nate's friend for a very long time and I have never seen or heard of him being involved with any other women. I can't believe this, there must be some explanation. Bea would never do this to you, either. She's been trying to date these past few months and I'm pretty sure none of the dates have gone beyond a first one. There has been literally nobody since Jean-Luc died.'

'OK, well, if you can come up with an explanation as to why Bea was with my husband at two o'clock in the morning, and was the one who accompanied him to the hospital in the ambulance and sat by his bed until I got there, and then said sorry and left . . . If you have any other way that explains those facts, please tell me, because I'm home now and I've just avoided telling our daughter that her dad's a cheat and it was very hard, let me tell you.'

I hang up, with a mild pang for Finn but really, I don't care. I just need to be angry with somebody.

It turns out that her somewhat chaotic life means April does trauma and disaster marvellously.

'Marin, you need a hug,' she says when I open the door to her. She was the second person I phoned.

There are two carrier bags on the step behind her, full of food with flowers and a blanket for some reason which escapes me, and the latest magazines. April, dear April, is coming to take care of us. I think I might cry. But I cried enough last night and I have certainly dried out my entire tear duct supply already and it's going to take quite a lot of water and coffee to get them working again.

'Thank you, darling, you're a lifesaver, I couldn't call Ma.'

'Only if you were having a psychotic breakdown,' says April cheerfully. 'And if you call Dad, well, she'd know, she'd want to be here. It would be your fault, either way.'

'That's true,' I say.

I look at April with renewed respect. Normally, she doesn't want to talk about our family and gets upset if she has to discuss Ma at all, because Ma is such a judgemental, angry character. In fact, I was under the impression that April prefers to pretend she doesn't exist. A bit in the same way she pretends to imagine that her prince will come. But this no-men-for-six-months thing is clearly changing her.

'Have you told Rachel anything?' says April quietly.

'No, not going to yet, maybe not ever.'

'It's your call,' says April more decisively than she ever normally says anything. 'But if you ask him to leave, then you'll have to tell her. It's your secret in one way but in another, it's Nate's. He's the one who got caught with Bea. Bea! I am astonished, I have to tell you. Joey and I will have a lovely day here. I've got supplies,' she displays many supermarket cartons of ready-made food, 'so that whenever you come back we'll have food and we can watch nice movies and play games and do whatever.'

'You're wonderful,' I say.

'Oh, Aunt April.' Rachel has suddenly appeared in the room and throws herself into my sister's arms.

What did she hear? I think in horror. But her next words prove that she didn't hear any painful truths.

'Poor Dad, I don't want to cry, I shouldn't cry in front of him, should I?'

'Your dad loves you, he'll be fine. And I'm sure he's going to be all right,' says April.

I look at her thinking, where is my sister and what have you done with her? But then maybe I never needed April before. Maybe being needed is what *she* needs.

I don't have time to think about that now. It's time to go into hospital and see my husband and pretend that he was not brought in with another woman. I kiss Joey goodbye.

'We'll ring you with Dad when we get in, OK? But it's probably better if you don't come in today, just until later and we know how he is and he's out of the intensive care place, which he's going to be out of later today, OK?'

I am lying again. I know nothing. I merely want to make him feel that everything is under control.

'I want to come, Mum,' says Joey tearfully.

'Well, you know younger people bring in lots of germs, so I think probably the best thing is, if you don't come in now. But we can go in again later.'

'He's going to be fine,' says April. 'Your dad's so strong. Doesn't do all that swimming and weightlifting and all those running things for nothing, you know. This will be nothing for him, Joey. I dare say he'll be doing next year's marathon in aid of people who have had heart attacks.'

Joey grins. 'That's Dad,' he says, looking cheered up.

'Now, Rachel, it's perfectly fine to cry when you see Dad,' I say to Rachel, as we park in the hospital car park. 'Hospitals scare all of us.'

I'm saying this because I want her to feel strong. I don't want her to be undone by seeing her father in the hospital bed. I've no idea what I'm going to do. Hit him, hug him, tell him he's not coming back to our house? None of those things.

I can't tell my husband he's being thrown out of our house and our marriage while he's in coronary care. There's probably a law against it. I realise that the trauma seems to have brought out my funny side. Not suitable right now, Marin, I tell myself.

'Are you all right, Mum?' Rachel squeezes my hand. 'You look scared.'

'Yes I'm fine, I'm fine. We're going to get through this. Just got to be calm and let the doctors and nurses do their jobs,' I say, and silently add, and not let on that my husband came in with another woman.

The nurse on the desk outside coronary care tells us Nate had a good night, which I already knew, and says we can both go in and see him. 'He can tell you himself what the doctors have been saying. It's going to be a slow recovery, but he's doing well.'

There's still no let up on the numbers of machines surrounding Nate in the bed. And in the way hospital beds always diminish even the strongest people, he does look smaller, paler against the snowy white sheets.

'Dad,' says Rachel, throwing her arms around him.

'Oh Rach, sweetie,' he says and his face crumbles in a way I've never seen it crumble before. This is Nate, my alpha male husband, and he's crying, actually crying. He cried when both children were born, but I don't think I've ever seen this before, not since.

Then he turns and looks at me.

'Marin,' he says, and he knows I know. And at that moment I have to choose, because there's a choice: I can turn around and walk away, or I can walk over to him and try to fix this for Rachel and Joey and our family. And there's no choice. Strangely, weirdly, there's no choice. I thought I'd go in first and shout at him if he was awake and I knew I couldn't. Now seeing him with Rachel crying into his shoulder, I can't. I lean over and kiss him on the lips.

'Gave us all quite a fright.'

'Oh Marin,' he says and he pulls me closer. 'I'm sorry, I'm so sorry,' he says.

'It's not your fault, Dad,' says Rachel, 'people have heart attacks.'

'Exactly,' I say.

Who knows what kind of stabilising, calming, tranquillising medication he's on? I don't want him saying, I'm sorry I was with Bea last night when I was brought in. One of us is going to have to be strong here, and it's going to be me.

'There's nothing to be sorry for,' I say. 'Tell us what the doctors have said to you?'

'I'm having an angiogram this afternoon and then, depending on what they see, stents inserted in two places.'

'Whatever happens you're going to be fine,' I say, sounding weirdly like my mother, who makes pronouncements.

'I love you, both of you, both my girls,' he says, tearful again. 'Where's Joey?'

'We thought we'd wait until we saw you were OK.'

'Oh I want to see him.'

'I'll ring April, bring him in, just for a moment, we don't want to tire you out.'

'OK.'

And as I look at him there in bed I think, it's going to be OK, we're going to get through this. I'm going to make sure we are going to get through this. I'm not letting my family fall apart.

40
Bea

Luke is delighted when I pick him up that afternoon.

'Sausage did a poop outside,' he tells me happily as I drive him home from school.

'On the grass and everything! Shazz doesn't mind. She says she's cleaned up lots of my and Raffie's poop when we were small. I said yuck!!!!'

I am exhausted and shaking, so shaky, in fact, that I am probably a danger in the car but still, we drive home slowly and as Luke chatters, I think about everything that's happened.

I, Bea, have cheated on my dear friend, Marin, with her husband, and I have destroyed her. What sort of a person am I?

'Mum, are you OK? You look sad,' says Luke suddenly.

I almost haven't the energy to skip into Mummy mode and lie, but I do: it's my instinct. Protect my child. Keep him safe by making him the focus of my life and in the process, make him fatherless because he's never had a chance to have another father figure and also, make myself so lonely I actually sleep with the first man who really holds me in a loving way since Jean-Luc died.

What sort of evil person am I?

'I'm sleepy,' I say, faking a giant yawn.

Finn's Mini is parked outside ours when we get there and instantly I know that Marin has phoned him.

'Finn!!!' yells Luke, delighted to see his favourite uncle.

Will Finn still be a part of our lives now that he knows what I've done? He knows me, surely?

I get out warily.

'Afternoon,' I say.

'Hello, Bea,' he says gently. 'Just thought I'd pop around, see how the two little biscuit monsters were.'

'They're not biscuit monsters,' says Luke happily as the two of them extract the dogs from the car, a tricky task at the best of times. 'They do like biscuits, though.'

I open up and let us inside. Nate's jacket is not lying on the floor because I remembered to bring it in the ambulance. If only I'd let them take him on his own but I couldn't. If something happened, he needed to have someone he knew with him and despite knowing exactly what it would mean, I'd chosen to go with him in the ambulance.

'Bring the girls out the back and see if they poo in our garden too,' I say in a faux cheery voice to Luke.

Once I've let him and the girls into the garden, I boil the kettle and face the window, looking at my son, waiting for judgement. But I've been so busy castigating myself, I've forgotten I am with Finn. He is not a man who judges.

'Talk to me, Bea,' he says. 'Marin thinks you spent the night with Nate, have been spending lots of nights with Nate, because you were with him in the hospital . . .'

I sigh.

'I wish I could tell you she was wrong but I can't,' I say. 'I was with Nate last night but –' this sounds so hollow and lame – 'he'd come in the week before to fix a leak in the kitchen, and I was feeling vulnerable and he –'

'He moved in,' he finishes.

I nod. I still can't look at him.

'Last night he just turned up. Shazz had taken Luke because I was sick with guilt and self-hate all week. I wasn't sleeping, was sick, so she said – she didn't know what had happened – that I needed a rest.' I laugh without humour. 'She had Luke on a sleepover so I could sleep and Nate turned up here unannounced, ready to rock and roll again. I said no, Finn.'

I finally turn away from the window. 'I said no. I told him to leave or I'd call the police and that's when he had the attack.'

Finn looks as if the whole of mankind has let him down. That's two beautiful people whom I love that I've managed to hurt.

'I had to accompany him to the hospital. What if he –'

'Died?'

I nod.

Finn shrugs. 'You did what you thought was right.'

'But it didn't turn out to be right, did it?' I say. Then I ask the question I've wanted to ask, the one which is ludicrous because I know the answer in my heart.

'How's Marin?'

Finn, who danced at my wedding, whom I would call one of my closest friends, looks at me sadly: 'How do you think?' he says.

I start to cry. I feel so hopeless and now I'm losing Finn too. One night lost me Marin and now Finn will join her in the list of people who will cross the road if they see me coming.

But Finn hugs me like the brother I've always felt him to be.

'It's OK, Bea,' he says, holding me tight.

I sob into his shoulder. 'I never meant it to happen,' I sob.

'Of course you didn't,' he says. 'You wouldn't think of it, but men are different, Bea, and Nate –' He pauses. 'I hate what he did,' he says. 'He messed you and Marin up. I can't forgive him for that.'

'I can't forgive me,' I say tearfully.

'Nonsense. You've been alone a long time. You were vulnerable, the stupid moron just picked up on it. You'll always be my friend, Bea.'

'What about Marin and Nate?'

'Marin's my friend too but Nate, well, I'm not sure I want to be his friend anymore. I know you and I know Nate. I know which one carries the can for this one, Bea. And it's not the one who's been alone for ten years bringing up her son, being a proper friend to us all.'

I lean against him, weak with relief. He's not judging me. I might survive this after all, I think, if I still have some people who believe in me.

41
Sid

I have just settled myself perfectly on the couch with the cushions just so to rest my neck on, a cup of tea, my Saturday-morning toast and the various remotes within easy distance. My perfect Saturday morning at home. I'm still in my PJs and fluffy socks because I get cold feet. Giselle is the same, runs in the family, she said, your grandmother was exactly the same. I have only a faint memory of my grandmother because she and my mother didn't get on; the whole happy commune-living style of life didn't go down too well in the leafy suburb my mother came from, but that's OK. If Granny Harrington had wanted to know me, she would have known me. So here I am: feet warm, ready to dive into a new episode of— The doorbell rings. I jerk so quickly that I spill my tea. I really do have a very intense startle reflex. Sometimes people notice it but most of the time they don't. Cursing a little bit I put the tea on the coffee table, wipe myself down, aware that I am now drenched with warm tea and go to the door, muttering that if it's some member of the residence committee with the newsletter about moving the bins a quarter of a centimetre to the right, then there is a very good possibility I will whack them over the head with the pottery vase in the hall. This is a Saturday morning and it's sacrosanct. I peer through my peephole to see who is on the other side. I have to stand on my tippy-toes to do it because those little holes are made for really tall people. At this point all I can see is a bit of a neck and then I see a zipped-up fleece and realise it's Finn.

What's Finn doing here? He's never been in my apartment,

we haven't got that far yet, although I've asked him, and he's going to cook me dinner in his tonight. What's he doing here hours earlier when he's due to pick me up at seven?

I open the door. 'Hello. You're a bit early.'

'Can I come in? Sorry for turning up unannounced but I need someone to talk to.'

In all the time I have known Finn, which, admittedly, is not very long, he's never looked like this, upset, anxious, distressed.

'Sure,' I say, letting him in, thinking, maybe he is slightly mentally unstable and is off his meds and is now going to produce a hatchet from behind his back. I really must stop watching the true-crime stuff. Too many people kill other people with hatchets, who'd have known? I follow him carefully into the sitting room and note that unless he has the hatchet stuffed down his trousers, he's hiding it very well.

'Really sorry to barge in on you like this,' he says, and plonks himself down on the armchair, not even looking around or commenting upon the semi-bare state of the apartment. Marc did take a fair amount of the furniture with him.

'Do you want a cup of tea?' I say, scooping up my cup.

'Tea, that would be lovely,' he says distractedly.

I'm not really sure what to do with this new distressed Finn, so I hide in the kitchen peering around the wall to see what he's doing now. He's sitting back staring into space and I think that this would be the time when a companion animal, preferably a cat, would be very beneficial, because the cat could go and sit on Finn and calm him. Maybe I should get one of those TV cats that you can turn on and look at. I must look into that. I return with tea and sugar, because even though he doesn't take sugar in his coffee, which I know from having multiple coffees with him, he might with tea. He eschews the sugar, pours milk carefully into the tea and looks up at me.

'Biscuits,' I say, 'biscuits.' The one thing I'm fully supplied with at all times is biscuits, because box sets and chocolate and wine or tea and sitting on your own a lot, means biscuits. So far none of this has told on my waist but I feel sure from listening to other people around the office that there will come a point in my life when everything I have ever eaten decides to lodge itself around my belly. Still, hasn't happened yet: onwards with the biscuits. I bring another, more chocolatey pack in and sit at the other end of the couch just in case.

'So what's up?' I say.

'It's Nate, he has had a heart attack.'

'Oh, oh I'm so sorry, Finn,' and suddenly I understand. Nate, Finn and Steve have been friends since college, which is a long time ago. They are very close friends.

'I'm really sorry, how is he, was it a serious attack? How's Marin?'

It's then that Finn looks at me and I see he has got a haunted cast to his face.

'Marin is in bits,' he says, 'Nate is still in cardiac care and there's more to this story.'

'Spit it out,' I say.

'He was with Bea when it happened. I was round with her yesterday and apparently they had a one-night thing. It sounds like Nate tried it on when Bea was vulnerable, and she's devastated. I mean, she is so not that person –'

'If she's been on her own since her son was a baby, she's lonely, Finn,' I said.

'I know she is. So Nate turns up and hugs her –'

'And gets her into bed because, God forbid, if Nate doesn't get what he wants –' I say harshly.

Finn is a little astonished at my tone but says nothing. 'So he goes over there again on Thursday night and when Bea tried to throw him out, he had a heart attack. Bea brought him in the ambulance. The middle of the night.'

To my credit I don't blink or gasp or do any of those things. In fact, I don't know if I'm that surprised. But the feeling sends a shiver up me. I knew I was right about Nate. He went back again and Bea had to threaten to call the police.

300

'When the hospital phoned Marin, she turned up and Bea was there.'

'Very brave to wait it out,' I say. 'She knew that, somehow, it would come out that she was with Nate, so she stayed to face the music. That's brave.' I move and sit closer to Finn and pat him gently on the hand.

'I'm really sorry,' I say. 'How's Marin, have you been to see her?'

He shakes his head. 'Not yet. I will. She's angry but she hasn't been angry with him, and she can't tell the kids. I wish I could help but I can't. And the thing is,' he looks at me with anguished eyes now, 'I had no idea. I see Nate all the time. We swim, we used to cycle but not anymore, we talk in the sauna – I know this man, he's like my brother. And yet I didn't know that he had this double life, I didn't know he could do this to Marin. He's very flirty, you know. He must have done this before. Jean-Luc was our friend. If he can seduce his widow, then I don't know what sort of person he is.'

I can tell he's getting angry now.

'Sometimes people surprise you, shock you,' I say, calmly. I know all this for a fact.

'Did you suspect?' Finn looks at me quickly.

'I'm not sure I liked Nate that much. I'm good at reading people and I think he left Marin to do all the work. He was very keen on Angie, too, which wasn't nice. He kept talking to her and at worst it was a type of emotional infidelity, ignoring poor Marin slaving away, and, who knows where that can lead to. If I was Marin,' I considered, 'I'd probably go into the hospital and pull out all Nate's leads.'

Finn looks at me and for the first time he laughs.

'You would, wouldn't you.'

'Yep, every single one of them. I mean, that's probably technically murder or attempted murder, depending how fast the doctors and nurses got there, but, you know, I would want to get my point across.'

'You're amazing,' says Finn, and he looks relaxed for the first time since he arrived. 'Seriously, what would you do really if you were Marin, not just go into the hospital and pull out all the plugs?'

I look at him and answer honestly.

'I think all my neuro-pathways would be standing in a corner chain-smoking and having anxiety attacks, and I'd be wondering what I had done wrong.'

He looks at me. 'You wouldn't have done anything wrong.'

I take a breath. He sees me, I think.

'Sorry for barging in on a Saturday morning but I've been thinking about it all day yesterday, couldn't sleep last night, and I just needed to talk to someone about this. Steve is trying to take care of Angie who's taking it really badly.'

'It's upsetting,' I say, 'when people you have known forever and are close to you suddenly do something that's abhorrent to you. It changes how you feel about them, changes how you feel about everyone, about life in general. Pulls the rug from under your feet.' I was speaking from experience now. 'Marin is going to need all the friends she can get. And even though you started off as Nate's friend, you are her friend too, so be there for her and the kids. Be there for Steve, because it's tricky, he'll probably be rethinking Nate and Angie now.'

I make Finn eat a few biscuits.

'What are you going to do next?' I say.

'I don't know – go into the hospital and rage at Nate. I don't blame Bea. I honestly don't. I have never seen a sign of this with her. She's so dedicated to Luke, it's like she won't allow herself to have a life. To mess with that . . . she's had enough pain. I'm so angry with Nate.'

'Good,' I say, 'rage you can work with.'

I hand him the whole packet of biscuits.

'I know this is not good swimmer-cycling-person food, but it will help. You need sugar.'

I was about to stand up, give him the signal that it was OK,

that he could go and be with his friends. And suddenly I realise I don't want him to go. I want to comfort him, I want him
to stay with me. I want him to comfort me, and it's really hard
to get my brain to process this. Because my body has already
processed it and worked it out, but my brain hasn't quite caught
up yet. But if the body can remember trauma, it can let it go
too, slowly. I've been healing for a while and Finn's been a big
part of that.

Despite hearing about poor Marin and Bea, and scuzzy
Nate, I have this lovely man in my flat. I'm in my pyjamas and
he's having the effect on me that he always has on me. The one
I can't quite believe I am capable of. The feeling of wanting
him to hold me naked and kiss me and I want to kiss him back.
I want us to be in bed together. I want to feel him, touch him,
let him touch me, kiss him. And I stop thinking, because he's
staring at me as if he can see right into my brain.

'Are you OK?' says Finn.

'Fine,' I say. 'I'm thinking of tonight and how much I've
been looking forward to it. And now, instead of having to wait
for tonight, I don't have to.' And before I know what I'm doing
I say, 'I want you to kiss me.'

'Are you sure?' His voice is low. And I know absolutely
without being told, without going through my brain, but with
purely going through what I sense, that he knows I've been
hurt.

And that he's asking my permission.

I nod.

He reaches out with one big hand and strokes my cheek and
then his hand is gently around the back of my neck and he's
leaning towards me. His fingers are so soft, and his mouth is
close to mine, but he's hesitating.

'Just kiss me,' I say.

And he is kissing me and it's like I've never been kissed
before, I haven't been kissed for so long. It's wonderful, this
beautiful man, holding me, taking care of me and I shift and

suddenly we're jammed close together. He gently angles me so that I'm sitting on his lap and my arms are around his neck, my fingers tangling in his hair, his arms wrapped around me.

'Oh Sid,' he says. 'We can't rush this, I don't want to rush this.'

He's kissing near my ear now. His lips soft around my neck, nibbling, and I'm arching my head backwards, as his mouth moves down towards my throat, lazily kissing my collar bone. And his hand is stroking my shoulder which is suddenly the most erogenous spot in the world. His fingers are soft on my body.

'I've been hurt,' I say, 'long ago and I haven't done this for so long, but I want to, I want to do it now with you.'

He moves away, slowly.

'Was it Marc?'

'Marc and I were friends,' I say, 'we ran away together, it's that simple. He was my boyfriend for a time but I wasn't really ready, and we just stayed with each other out of habit. By then it was easier to let everyone think we were together, but we weren't. We were like brother and sister.'

'You ran away? But you love your home,' he says, confused. 'Who hurt you, my darling Sid, what did they do?'

'No.' I put a finger against his lips. 'No. That was then and this is now. I let that define me for so long, not anymore. You've smoothed away the hurt piece.'

And I climb off him and take his hand and he gets up off the couch.

'Come on, we'll go into my bedroom.'

It's sort of girlish, a bit like the bedroom I used to live in at Rivendell.

'Marc never slept in here with me after the first few months, because he had his own bedroom, where he had all his super-hero stuff and his TV for the computer games he used to play. Whenever Vilma came up, she'd sleep on the couch and I'd say that Marc snored so much he had to have his own bedroom, it was the only way. And she believed me, poor darling. I owe it to her to tell her, but not now.'

The room is smaller with Finn inside it. He fills the space.

'Say no at any point,' he tells me. 'Understand?'

'You don't want to do this?' I say, suddenly vulnerable.

'Oh no.' His eyes are dark with desire. 'I want to do this, I think I've wanted to do this since the day we went hiking and you asked me what I had in my rucksack and I just loved you then. You're so funny and clever and beautiful and spiky, like the hedgehog pet you told me about. A little bit bristly but soft. And lovely when one opens up to you.'

'You don't get to give me a nickname now, I'm not going to be hedgehog.'

'Oh no, you are going to be my own beautiful Sid.' And then he bends down and wraps his arms around me and carries me over to my own bed.

I wake up later in the afternoon to this incredible feeling of another naked body warm beside mine and it's glorious. I move, feeling the softness of the sheets, the comfort of the bed, the smoothness of the skin, warmness spooned against me and then one big arm reaches round and tucks me in closer. I feel his face burrowing into the soft place behind my ear and he's whispering. 'Good afternoon, gorgeous.'

'Good afternoon, gorgeous yourself,' I say, 'this is a lovely way to wake up.'

'We could wake up this way all the time,' says Finn. And I can feel the smile in his voice, so I wriggle onto my back and turn to face him. He's supporting his head on one big hand, leaning on his elbow, and I reach up and kiss him and then suddenly I'm lying on top of him and his arms are around me. And I feel so happy.

'Would you like some Saturday very late brunch, madam, or slow, passionate love?' He reaches up and sucks one of my breasts and I arch my back against the exquisite sensation of it.

'Brunch can wait.'

'Perfect,' he murmurs, taking his mouth off my nipple for one brief moment. 'That's the answer I was hoping for.'

An hour later, I feel heavy limbed and indolent. But Finn gets out of bed and says, 'I have to cook for you. I'm not a cook by any means but I've become competent at morning stuff like pancakes.'

'Really? I know you're very good at other things,' I say.

And he smiles, 'So are you.'

'I have no practice, well very little practice.'

'We'll have to do something about that. We could draw up a schedule.'

'Do you have a calendar in the kitchen?'

'We'll mark in the dates: every morning and at the weekends, twice, maybe . . .?' he says, 'so we'll get you all practised again.' And then he smiles, strokes my hair and kisses my forehead, takes my face in his hands and says, 'You're perfect, never change anything. I'm going to throw myself in the shower and I'm going to make you something wonderful for breakfast. What do you want?'

'Well, that depends what's in the fridge,' I say. And I don't really care what's in the fridge. Normally people aren't over in my house – except Vilma, and she generally gives out about the contents in my fridge, but I don't care about Finn seeing it, because Finn likes me for me. I don't have to be anything I'm not. With Finn, I feel good enough just the way I am.

Five minutes later he's out of the shower, hair slicked back, wearing his jeans and a T-shirt.

'Right,' he says, and stalks off to the kitchen.

I throw on a T-shirt and go and follow him. I brush my teeth but don't stop to comb my hair: I don't care, this is me. Finn likes me for me. Imagine!

He's in the kitchen making coffee and I walk up behind him, put my arms around his waist and lean into him, my head barely comes up to his shoulder blades.

'You feel good there,' he says but he turns to face me, still with us enmeshed. 'Are you still feeling good, Sid, happy?' He really has the most beautiful eyes and they are looking at me with such understanding and concern.

'Why might I not be happy?' I say, looking up at him.

He keeps staring down at my face and says: 'You're so strong and feisty but underneath it all you're fragile. I don't want to hurt you. Please tell me I haven't hurt you or scared you.'

'Stop,' I say, 'I don't know what miracle this is, I honestly don't know, because for almost fifteen years, apart from a brief time with Marc, I haven't been with anyone.'

'Really?'

'Really,' I say. 'You're on the money – something happened to me and it made me really scared. Scared, guilty and ashamed. I ran away and hid behind funny remarks and black clothes. And then you came into my life and I stopped wanting to run away. I stopped feeling ashamed.'

'Whoever hurt you is the one who should be ashamed,' he said. And there's something in his voice I've never heard before, anger.

'I've been angry,' I say, 'I've been angry for a very long time. But anger doesn't work. Or rage, sometimes the rage comes and gets me. When I'm in the rage place, I think if anyone banged into me in a pub or a club, I'd explode with anger, which would not be good.

'But now –' I smile at him. 'I feel happy. You make me happy.'

'Will you tell me what happened?'

For a moment I don't want to ruin what we have, this glorious happiness. Him standing there, in T-shirt and jeans with his feet bare; me in a T-shirt, more undressed than I've been with another human for years, my hair all bed messed, the scent of him on my skin.

'How about we have coffee and breakfast, go back to bed?'

'One cup,' he says, 'I think that's all I can cope with before I do this again.' And he sits me up on the counter, puts his hands around my face and kisses me deep. 'You can open up to me, Sid. I'm not going anywhere.'

I take a deep breath. 'OK. I'll tell you.'

42

Sid

Fifteen years ago . . .

It's hard to know which one of us is more excited about my new job: Me or my mother.

We're in my bedroom and she is eyeing the sedate clothes I've bought to impress all in Lowther & Quinn, the legal firm I'm interning in. I want to get into family law but the only company I can get any work in is a company offering four-month internships for minuscule pay. Lowther & Quinn specialise in commercial law and I know it will be scut work but it's a foot in the door.

'It's all very . . . grey,' Giselle says doubtfully. My mother thinks grey is an absence of colour and has no place in clothing.

'I need to blend in until I can make my mark and then, mix it up a bit,' I say, closing the wardrobe on my college clothes which were funkier.

On my college work placement, I realised that my version of sedate was not quite sedate enough, so this time, with my first real job since college, I want to nail it. There will be two interns in the company and I am determined to be the one who gets even a quarter of a job.

White shirts, a plain woollen coat that cost half of my savings, two skirts, a silky blouse and a couple of cheap dark grey suits from Marks and Spencer's. Personally, I think it's all hideous but societal mores insist on a certain kind of dressing for junior business people.

The sort of dressing mum and I abhor.

She fingers a light-grey suit jacket and shudders.

'You'll blend into the walls, lovie.'

Mum is wearing her standard uniform of a floral quilted kaftan (patchwork purple today), belted with a crocheted Obi, olive-green cargo pants and heavy socks because her boots for working in the polytunnels are just inside the back door. The restaurateurs who buy her heritage tomatoes and tiny aubergines and edible flowers think she could wear a bin liner and they wouldn't care.

'I'll stand out when they all think I'm fabulous, but not before,' I say. 'I want them to notice me for the right reasons.'

'Why does what you wear matter?'

'It shouldn't,' I mutter, following her out of the room.

Giselle goes gracefully downstairs in our small farmhouse with me in tow. My mother is graceful, with tiny wrists, sleek limbs and stands at five two in her socks. I am precisely the same, only twenty-two to her thirty-eight. With our Matrioska doll caps of shining dark hair and Giselle's remarkably unlined and perpetually smiling face, we do resemble sisters more than mother and daughter, but then she was sixteen when I was born, and she fought fiercely to keep me.

Our kitchen is chaotic but beautifully so. Gertrude, our sheepdog, is on the couch near the stove, smiling, wagging her tail and shedding black and white fur everywhere. Vilma, my little sister, four and three quarters, and gravely kneeling at the kitchen table making a very long necklace out of pasta shapes, doesn't even look up when we come in.

'It's six foot tall,' she announces. 'As tall as Daddy. I want to be as tall as Daddy. He's hidden the chocolate biscuits up in the high cupboard.'

The adorable little face, with those keen dark eyes, is raised to us as though to say that if being tall gives a person an unfair advantage, then Vilma wants it too.

Stefan walks into the kitchen at that precise moment. He has to bend his head to enter the door and, as ever, he beams to see us. He really is very tall, six foot five or thereabouts like all his family, a glorious melting pot of Lithuanians who are all carpenters, like Stefan. Some people bring happiness to the world – the combination of my mother, my stepfather and little Vilma brings utter happiness to mind.

I quash down the anxiety about starting a new job in my grey dressing-up clothes on Monday. I have tonight and to-morrow afternoon left of the weekend to bask in their presence before I head to the city and my rented box room in a shared house where my new life begins.

By day three of working in Lowther & Quinn in the city, I've been in Dublin for a week and I feel I've got a routine.

First, I'm adding to my grey wardrobe: a dotted silk scarf I picked up in a second-hand shop, my Sarah-Janes that look so much better than shoes with a little heel. A flower brooch that Daisy, who also lives in the shared house, made with pale turquoise tulle and silk.

Second, I get up early and have a coffee in a cute café near the office, where I can watch the city walk past and make my list for the day.

Me: country girl at heart is now city slicker and I like it.

I feel like one of the *Sex and the City* girls – myself and Lois, also new in the firm and from my year in college, better ward-robe though, and I discuss which character we are. As it's our second week and we've actually got some money now, we go out to lunch.

'Samantha,' says Lois, admiring her nails for the nth time. Her second manicure ever. Lois is ignoring the fitting-in con-cept and her nails are too. They're Rouge Noir, a sexy midnight burgundy. They look like they're made for ripping things.

'How many guys have you slept with, then?' I ask daringly. Lois is the sort of person who won't hit you if you ask her this. She wears her utter ease with herself with such glorious pride.

'Five and a half,' she replies, after a moment ticking on her fingers.

'A half?' We both giggle.

'He fell asleep,' Lois explains.

'Which half?'

We snort into our sandwiches and it takes a while before we can eat again.

'You next,' she says.

I flush a little, wishing for some of Lois' easy sensuality.

'One,' I say, 'a long term thing. We were together for a whole year. Since then, I obviously have my boyfriend-repellant on.' I'm only half-joking.

'Guys are unsure of you,' Lois says. 'That kooky arty look scares them off. Plus, there's the black nail varnish.'

'True. I had to get rid of it for here.' I gaze at my nails with their badly applied layer of see-through pink. With black, you just slop it on and it always looks right.

'If you want a job, look like the person they'd want to hire,' we parrot, courtesy of one of the Getting A Job seminars we went to.

'It worked, though,' says Lois. 'I'm wearing a blouse instead of a Doors T-shirt and you've cornered the market on white shirts and skirts. Skirts! You're Charlotte.'

'Am not!'

'Yes, you are. You want one lovely man, not a string of lovers. And you look Charlotte-y in those on-the-knee numbers.'

Like Mum, I've always seen myself as a free spirit in the world and I have to fit into the legal world with my conservative clothes. But one day, in a smaller firm and with my own clients, I can be myself.

When we get back to the office there's a buzz in the air. Alex Quinn, one of the company directors, has been on holiday, somewhere hot and expensive, and he's just returned to the office, the reek of Chanel's Eau Sauvage and a hint of After Sun flood the place. I sneak a peek from behind my partition and see a middle-aged guy with white-blond hair, a handsome face, and a tan that looks as if only rich people can buy it.

'Hello, team,' he says loudly.

Even his voice is rich and Michelle, second year there, rolls her eyes and yet stands up and says, 'Hello, Alex, welcome back.'

Like a celebrity visiting a disaster site, he tours the office, a laughing comment here, a pat on the shoulder there, a shake of Lois' hand when he reaches her corner.

I notice him looking her up and down appraisingly, but Lois doesn't smile at him.

Some Samantha, I'll tease her later.

'And you must be Sidonie, our other new intern.'

Suddenly he's standing in front of me, and I feel something sparkle inside me: this man, he's one of the company's partners and he's noticing me, an intern. Maybe he's heard I'm good at what I do!

'Yes,' I say, beaming. 'It's really lovely here, Mr Quinn, everyone has been so nice.'

'Oh, call me Alex,' he says, and he smiles. He's forty, definitely. Which is like miles older, even Stefan isn't forty, Mum isn't quite forty. But this guy, forty seems younger. He's got this vibrant energy and something else, I can't put my finger on it . . . charisma, that's what it is.

He comes around behind the partition and leans against it, one long leg crossing the other.

'So,' he said, 'how do you like it here?' He's got a low deep voice. And I feel very flustered by all this attention. So far I've been treated like a normal young member of staff and there has been a lot of coffee runs, shouted commands to get files, boring document searches, and 'Can somebody work out where my phone charger went?' Stuff like that. The sort of thing you get to do as an intern.

Lois, somehow, doesn't do most of those jobs.

'If you do those jobs, people will think that is all you are capable of,' she's told me, firmly. 'You've got to show them you are here to work, not to be a run around. You didn't go to law school to find that bitch Michelle's phone charger.'

'I know,' I say, but there's a part of me that's always been built in to what I'm supposed to do, helping out. I help people, that's what I do. That's how I got on in school, I worked hard and made Mum proud of me and then Vilma and Stefan. I've always been a good girl.

'Good girls finish last,' Lois said.

'That's just wrong, the world doesn't work like that,' I pointed out.

And now here's Alex Quinn, smiling down at me like I'm the only person in the world. It's a heady feeling. I think he must have heard that I've been working really hard and he's come over to say thank you. And I know I've done the right thing. I'm proving myself an important part of the business and that's what I want to do.

'It's been lovely working here, and I'm really here to learn and I'm so grateful for the opportunity,' I stammer.

'Well, that's good to hear,' he said. 'I'll have to bring you out to lunch to talk to you about this; I like to bring all the interns out to lunch. I think you lovely girls need to get out of the office and see the real world we are dealing with.'

'Oh, well, I do lunch from half twelve to a quarter past one, so I don't know how we could do that. But I'll ask Michelle.' Michelle is in charge of myself and Lois.

'Oh it will be fine with Michelle,' says Alex. 'Anyway, we'll work it out, put it in our diaries. Anyway, nice meeting you.' And he pats me on the shoulder, his hand for a moment touching my hair. And I feel that frisson of excitement at having been noticed by this demigod of a person. Oh wow. I sit there for a minute in silence staring at my computer. And then Lois pokes her head around the partition.

'What is he like? He really loves himself that guy.'

'Shush,' I say, 'he'll hear you.'

'Don't care if he hears me,' she says.

'No, he's lovely, he was welcoming us in.'

'Yeah, right,' says Lois.

She shuffles off and before I can think about it any longer, Michelle appears with a mission for me to deliver some papers to an office up the street.

'Course,' I say, bright, shiny. 'That's what I'm here for.'

'Yup,' says Michelle.

I don't really think she likes me and I don't know why. But as Mum always says, strangers are just friends you haven't met and Michelle and I haven't made friends properly yet, that's going to take time, maybe. But we'll get there, I know.

It's Friday night and normally the partners are gone a bit earlier than us. They have dinners to go to, wives to go to. It's a very male practice, with the exception of people like Michelle and ourselves and the accounts and legal secretaries. There's not much of an after-work culture. I'm sitting at my desk tidying up some loose ends, still determined to be the best employee ever. I'm going home tomorrow morning to Rivendell and I can't wait, because it's just been such an amazing two weeks and I have been telling Mum and Stefan all about it. And I've told Vilma I'll bring her a lovely present. I've got her a really pretty little zippy rucksack with sparkles on it, and I know she's going to love it. I'll have money, wages, it's really exciting. I'm trying to think what I'll get, maybe some wine, although Mum is not much into wine. Stefan really likes beer, but wine seems like the sort of thing you bring home after your successful first two weeks as a woman with an actual job. Oh and chocolates, I might bring chocolates – some of those fancy ones that are handmade and have cream in them. I'm thinking this, as I'm tidying up my desk and pretty much everyone is gone. There's a guy cleaning the offices, pulling along the big red Henry Hoover. He's nice and we nod, but don't talk and I smile in a sort of, 'Hi, how you doing' way, and he smiles in a 'Hi, I'm doing OK' way, but we haven't got as far as actual conversation yet. I know I'm shy, I'm really trying. Nobody ever thinks I'm shy. Everyone assumes that if you are brought up in a place like Rivendell, you must have loads of friends and be marvellous at talking to people.

'Hello, Sidonie, you're working late,' says a charming urbane voice.

I look up and there's Alex.

'Oh, hi, hi,' I say, and I know I sound like some idiot kid with a crush on a movie star or something. But he seems so glamorous, like someone from another world. He's the big boss and he knows my name.

'Lovely name, Sidonie,' he says. 'You must come from an interesting family, I think?'

'Yes,' I say, all bursting enthusiasm and then wish I hadn't sounded like such a moron. I have to try to appear cool. 'I'm just getting ready to go,' I say. 'I thought I was the last one here?'

'No, just you and me, that's all.'

He doesn't appear to count the guy dragging the hoover around. For a second I feel shocked by Alex Quinn. He doesn't count the man cleaning. But maybe the Alex Quinns in the world don't notice someone who does the cleaning, and I don't like that. Still, as Mum always says, 'People are strange, not everyone thinks the way we do.'

'I am just about ready to finish up,' he says, 'but I finished a big case today and it's all gone very well. Litigation is the toughest, you have got to be able to fight,' he says. And I swear I can see his canines as he says it. Beautiful canines too, it has to be said. Lois thinks he's too full of himself and says he's got veneers and probably a sunbed tan.

When she said this, I replied: 'No, no, I've heard from Glenda that he's got a boat, and people with boats are always tanned, aren't they?'

'I was just about to open a bottle of wine to celebrate,' he says now. 'But you can't open a bottle of wine on your own, can you?'

I don't know how to answer this.

Myself and Daisy only open bottles of wine together in the teeny apartment, and even then they are really cheap, screw-top ones.

'I'm sure you can't,' I say and, astonished at my daring: 'you could bring it home and have it with your wife to celebrate?'

'She's got a committee meeting this evening, Lady Captain stuff.'

'Golf?' I question.

'Yes.' He seems amused by the question. 'You don't play golf, do you?'

I shake my head. All I know about golf is that people who play golf have bigger cars and kids who go to private school, because that's how it was in Greystones and I personally don't know anyone who plays golf. I mean, there were lots of people who played pitch and putt, but that's different. I don't think they have lady captains in pitch and putt. But I could be wrong.

'Could you do me a favour, lovely Sidonie?'

'Yes,' I say, sitting up perkily. Work, I can do more work, I am a working machine.

'Come into my office and share a glass with me and then I will have laid this case to rest. I can go off for the weekend feeling it is put to bed.'

'O-kay,' I say, and I don't know if this is the right or wrong answer, because it seems really weird. I mean, why does he want me to come in with him? But, he's the boss and you do what you are told. Same way as when Mr Kinnehan, the vice principal at school, asked people to stay behind and do the litter pick-up in the playing fields, we all stayed behind and did the litter pick-up in the playing fields – except for the people who put the litter there in the first place, who really couldn't care less and were truanting from school.

'Of course, I'll just tidy up here.'

I run into the bathroom first, because I know I pull my hair out of my ponytail when I'm concentrating and I want to look perfectly professional. I sweep the brush through and retie it up: there, the picture of a professional young woman.

Daisy said I looked really nice today when I went out.

'You're finally moving away from the waitress uniform,' she said approvingly.

I felt the little cardigan with the embroidered flowers around the top was really nice. The little flowers sat just above my collarbone, so it's both work-like, lady-like and suitable for a legal office. My skirt is a little bit below the knee because I can't afford to get it turned up, and I'm wearing black fifteen denier tights. A lot of the women in the office wear ten deniers, but I can't really afford them yet because they rip so easily. So, I'm still on the fifteen deniers. Cheap ones, too. With my hair freshly brushed, I grab my bag, turn off my computer and pick up my extra bits and bobs, and my coat in case it's cooler on the way home. I walk in the direction of Alex Quinn's office. The man with the Henry the Hoover is obviously in another part of the offices, because I can hear the drone, but I can't see him. The partners' offices are richly glamorous in a different area to where us newbies and the secretarial staff work. Our part of the office is very boring, but theirs is full of nice wood, big doors, high ceilings and huge windows looking out onto busy streets. They reek of money, entitlement and knowledge. Huge legal books line the wall. And I think that maybe one day I'll have an office like this. I think of all the sorts of law I want to practise and I think, I could get there, I just need to find my way up the ladder, that's all.

There's a large desk, what I believe they call a partner's desk and it's bare of practically everything, except one of those Lucite lamps that look intelligent, as if having one on your desk raises your IQ by about 25 per cent. All the files are neatly locked away. And there's a picture of a very attractive woman of Alex's age, blonde, lovely, with two young children in the background.

'Your family look nice,' I say and I think that's cheeky, I shouldn't have said that. Personal comments shouldn't be made.

'They are,' he says, 'they're wonderful, busy lives, of course. You know, when you are in this business you spend a lot of time in the office.'

'Of course,' I say, making a note to self: have to spend a lot of time in the office. Well, I do spend a lot of time in the office. It's a Friday night and I'm the last one here, except him and the lovely cleaning man.

There's a round antique desk with antique chairs set around it. And then there's an area with a couch and two armchairs and a coffee table in front of it. It's a huge office, absolutely enormous. The tiny little apartment that Daisy and I share could fit in here three times over.

'Sit down.' He gestures in the direction of the couch, and I sit. Knees primly together. Maybe he's going to talk to me about mentoring me, I think.

He opens the bottle easily. My hands take a very full delicate wine glass, full to the brim of red wine.

'Gosh,' I say, 'it's a big glass.'

'Oh, we're celebrating,' he says.

He takes an equally full glass and sits down on the chair opposite me.

'So tell me about yourself, Sidonie, I want to hear everything.'

'OK.' I take a sip of wine. It's lovely, not that I know anything about wine but. Still, I'm sure it is.

'What made you decide to study law?'

This I can talk about.

'I grew up with a lot of people who didn't have a lot of money and I felt that it would be wonderful to know how to help them when they got into trouble.'

'And yet you're here. We don't do much pro bono work,' he says. 'Commercial law might not be your arena.'

'I know, oh I know, I need to know all about the law. I mean, you know, you have an idea in the beginning and then maybe find the right thing for you. But I like how the law makes things right, sorts things out, it's so important, isn't it?'

'You're very young,' he says, paternalistically. 'Have some more wine.' He shoves over a little dish of cashew nuts and I start nibbling. They're lovely but dry, so I have to keep drinking the wine to stop my throat from tickling. And it's ages since I had lunch and that was a very quick three quarters of a cheese sandwich, because I was late.

Before long, I'm somehow drinking a second glass of wine and he's regaling me with stories of his early career and ideas he had for the law and what he was going to do. His father was a lawyer and his father before him.

'It's in the family,' says Alex, one long arm encompassing the beautiful office. His watch is some gold expensive thing and I know I should recognise it. I think that Lois would definitely recognise it, but I haven't a clue what it is. I've always been terrible at expensive stuff.

'You're from Wicklow but you're living in Dublin? With whom?'

'With my friend Daisy; we grew up together in Greystones and we thought it would be good to have an apartment in town. Well, it's really a flat,' I slur, realising I'm definitely on the way to being drunk. 'You know, an apartment is bigger and better and a flat is just like small and a bit messy. We can't get the bath clean. We've tried everything, scrubbing and more scrubbing. So we just have showers. I'm going home this weekend and I can't wait to have a bath.'

He leans back against the couch. I know at this point that I am drunk, because two huge glasses of wine, very little lunch and a few cashew nuts are not really enough for a person of my size. And I've just told my boss I want a bath at the weekend.

'And is it pretty, this little flat?'

'We try and make it pretty. My mum is very into crafts and she sent up lots of hangings for the walls and we have got posters, of course, film posters. Daisy's mum gave us a really beautiful old couch. I mean, it's lots of different colours, so we got some throws on it, white ones to make it nice.'

'And boyfriends?'

He was filling my glass again and I protested and said, 'No, not for me.'

'We have to finish the bottle,' he says.

I can't imagine that any bottle can have that much in it. But I think I can't be rude and say no. So I'll just let him fill it and not drink it.

'Boyfriends, well, not now. Work is too important. I did have a boyfriend.'

'What was his name?'

'Daniel, we grew up together.'

'That's lovely. And you're still seeing him?'

'No, not now.'

'Fancy free,' says Alex. 'You're footloose and fancy free.'

And then he's suddenly closer to me, beside me on the couch. And I know he shouldn't be closer to me. But I don't know what to say. Why is he closer to me? So I move just a little bit, but his hand reaches my knee.

'No, don't go, you're such a lovely girl, this is great. We should talk more often like this; it's important, you know, for me to get to know the staff, to be able to help them make good life choices later, you know. Understand the business, and where you fit within it.'

'Right,' I say trying to concentrate, because I definitely feel dizzy.

'And you have a stepfather, you were saying?'

'Yes, Stefan, he's lovely, he's Lithuanian.'

'Oh how nice, very nice. And a little sister?'

'Yes . . .'

His hand is moving up past my knee. I don't know what to say: get your hand off my knee? He's my boss. He's older. This can't be right?

'I don't think we should be doing this, Alex, Mr Quinn.'

'Nonsense,' he says, 'nonsense. There's nothing wrong with this, just a little drinkie after work, way of winding down after the week. People do it all the time. It's business. There has to be a little fun in life, doesn't there?'

Suddenly he's pushing me back onto the couch and he's actually lying on me. His mouth is pressed up against mine, and his tongue is forcing its way into my mouth. And I'm saying, 'No, no, no, Mr Quinn, stop.'

But he doesn't care and he's holding my ponytail tightly with one hand, holding my head back. It hurts, I feel trapped. He's moved away from my mouth and I'm saying 'No!' and his head's down at my collarbone which is hidden by my little frilled cardigan. And he rips it. Just rips it viciously.

'Oh, that's nice, little lady. You like that, don't you?'

'No, I don't like that,' I beg. 'This is wrong, Mr Quinn. Please stop, please.' I'm crying but it's coming out as whispering because I'm so scared. How is this happening? How did we go from us having a chat in his office to him kissing me, lying on top of me? How?

What did I do wrong? I must have done something for this to happen. Wine, I had wine and I talked and told him about the bath and . . .

'Come on, don't be a tease, you knew what this was about. Stay late, look at me, smile up at me, hello, Mr Quinn. I know your type.'

'No, I don't do that,' and I go to scream and his hand is suddenly clamped over my mouth so I can barely breathe and I feel paralysed with fear, because I know exactly what's going to happen now and the fear does something to my body. Every muscle tenses up and vibrates, the fear radiating out like a pulse, a physical Morse code sign of distress. Ancient knowledge takes over. I feel like a small animal where everything is shutting down to cope with an ongoing threat and my voice has receded along with my understanding because I know what's coming. I know and it's my fault for not seeing, for not understanding. He's so much bigger than me, stronger, and his hand's still pulling my ponytail back, so I'm pulled backwards, arched towards him.

I'm five foot two, he's six foot, and all the urbane clothes mean nothing because under them all he's a bigger animal than I am and he can fight me and win. He's pressing his body weight against me and he's pulling at my cardigan and he's got it open and he scrapes me as he rips it. But even though I'm aware of the rip of skin, I almost can't feel it. My mind is aware but my body has gone somewhere else with the fear.

His hands are pulling up my bra and he's got one of my breasts out. He's biting me.

'No, stop! Don't, please don't do that.'

My voice is so weak now. A hopeless whisper.

'You want it, you know you want it. You've been smiling up at me ever since I came in. Hello, Mr Quinn, hello, Mr Quinn. Yeah, I know girls like you.' And then his other hand is up under my skirt and he's pulling at my tights, ripping them. He tears them away and his hands are in my knickers and now he's touching me –

I can't move at all then: all I can feel is my heart beating to the vibrations of fear in my body and my eyes are closed, but tears are leaking out of the corners. His hands are hurting me, abrading me. Like a pulse in my brain, I think if only someone can come and rescue me.

'Touch me,' he says.

I shake my head and he slaps my face and again, the pain almost doesn't register. I don't know how he manages it but somehow his trousers are open, he's forcing himself inside me and then, I feel pain that makes the earlier handling like nothing.

I keep my eyes closed, let myself fall entirely numb because I can't allow myself to think. If I think, my mind will drop into some place it can never come back from. I'm fully animal now – prey gone silent with fear.

I can only scream silently in my head until I feel his strain. He groans and collapses onto me.

'You're a good girl,' he says.

He's panting and he pulls himself off and away from me. He gets up, adjusts himself. I'm lying there splayed, clothes ripped obscenely and my hands pull my skirt over my body. I drag myself into the corner of the couch and I'm shaking. It's like I'm there and I'm not there. Still the animal knowing the predator is watching, waiting. Still not safe.

'Clean yourself up,' he says, looking at me. 'Maybe next week, a little more wine, be nice.' And he leans down to kiss me and I fall off the couch, moving away.

'No, get away from me.'

'Oh no, you're not going to do something silly now, are you?' he says. There's menace in his voice. How had I ever thought he sounded charming? 'You wanted it. Don't tell anyone otherwise. I'm going, and you need to get out of here before me. Fix yourself up.'

My fingers are shaking as I pull my coat on and gather my belongings together. My clothes feel tattered under the coat, so I do up my coat buttons.

'This is between you and me, right?' he growls.

I leave the room and then I'm out on the street, shaking.

I run.

43

Sid

Coming out of remembering is like entering back into a new world and I'm enclosed in Finn's arms and he's holding me so tightly and he's shaking. I'm shaking too.

'I'm going to kill him,' he says. 'I want to kill him, for what he did to you.'

'My mum always thought people were good,' I say. 'And people think rapists are strangers, stranger danger. You know, when you get off the bus and walk strong on the street and things like that. You don't think it happens where you work, you don't expect that. And I've had a lot of time to think about it and a lot of time not to think about it. And I was just there. I was ready for a predator. He saw me, he marked me off.'

'But what did you do?'

'I gathered my stuff and I never went back. I left a note on Lois phone. Said there was a family emergency and I wouldn't be back. Daisy wasn't there in our flat when I got home. She'd gone out for the night with some friends. I got into the shower and I scrubbed everything I could. I had a loofah, I was very proud of that loofah, because they were dear and I scrubbed myself till I was raw, till I bled. In the morning I went to the Family Planning Clinic and I got the Morning After Pill, which made me really sick. They begged me to report it but I said no. I'd studied law. I knew how it worked.'

'How?' he says and he's genuinely confused. Finn thinks fair should work all the time but it doesn't, not with rape cases. The number of known reported rape cases and the number of actual rape cases are always vastly different, all over the world.

The number of convictions is always a tiny number. I knew this fifteen years ago. How could I have known that and not known how to avoid someone like Alex Quinn? But book knowledge and actual inherent, body memory knowledge are two very different things. I'd known nothing, as it turned out, for all my years in college. So clever and yet so dumb all at the same time.

'Can you imagine trying to get him on the stand?' I asked. 'A big shot lawyer and me, just a little girl who'd come to work in his office. They'd rip me to shreds in court. I didn't want to be exploited a second time. Now, I'd do it. Now, I'd tell everyone.

'But I told nobody. Not my flatmate, my family –'

'Why not your family?'

'The shame,' I whispered. Shame was the hardest thing to explain to someone who didn't understand. 'The sense that it was my fault too, that if I'd been smarter, if I'd known more, I could have avoided it. If I'd cried out, if I'd hit him . . . if I hadn't gone into his office. All the ifs you go through. That's shame. That you are culpable.'

Finn is silent but his eyes stay on mine, warm with love.

'I stayed in bed for a week. I cried and I couldn't eat, and this is going to sound really stupid but I cut up that cardigan, I cut it up into pieces and I burnt it in the fire. Wool really smells when it burns. Then I cut my hair off, because it was always pretty. I was pretty. Pretty, naive and stupid. I didn't know what happens because nobody had ever told me.'

Finn runs gentle fingers through my hair.

'Didn't look much different from the way it looks today,' I say. 'I wanted to be invisible, I didn't want anyone to ever look at me and see anything different because, being naive, thinking the best of people, had got me raped and I didn't think I'd ever get over it.'

By now, he's rocking me and I can feel his heart beating fast and furious through his T-shirt.

'I stayed in bed all week. Mum rang and Stefan rang and I said I'd got some terrible bug. The office rang and I pretended to be Daisy and I said that Sidonie was really sick and wouldn't be back. I got a job waitressing, so I could pay the rent, but I couldn't go home. I told Daisy something had happened, but not all of it. I think she guessed, but I told her she was never to tell anyone. I told her my boss had tried it on and it scared me.'

'He raped you, he didn't try it on. He deserves to pay. I want him to pay for what he did.'

'That was fifteen years ago,' I said flatly. 'It's too late and Finn, I can't go through that and I won't. He victimised me once and he won't do it again. It's just my word against his word. And you know, I sat in his room and I drank his wine; it doesn't help me.'

'He was your boss. You were twenty-one, he was what? Forty something. That's, oh Jesus, I want to kill him.'

'No.' I had to make Finn understand this. 'I need you to listen to me,' I say. 'Not avenge me or fix me. I moved away from Daisy, because I couldn't deal with that. And eventually I went back to Rivendell. Started wearing black clothes and never going out. Both Mum and Stefan knew something was wrong but I wouldn't tell them, I wasn't going to tell them. I rang the Rape Crisis Centre, but I told them I wasn't going to report it. I just needed to talk to someone. They were so amazing and they told me it wasn't my fault. But I knew it was my fault, I believed it was my fault. I should have known better. And it took years, years and years and years to let go of that. And I had lots of therapy, healing. Marc was from near me at home and his dad used to beat him up. He wanted to move out and I wanted a man with me so I felt safer. Because I never felt safe from then on. So we moved in together. We let people think that we were together because it was easier, you know. We were broken and we tried to love each other that way, but we were too messed up. Still, we were happy, you know, we had each other.'

Finn kisses me as if I might break.

'I'm so terrified of hurting you now. I wish you'd told me before we . . .'

'If I'd told you before, you would have seen me differently. I needed you to see *me*, to want *me*. I'm sorry I used you.'

He looked at me, his eyes heartbroken, and I smiled.

'No really, I'm making a joke. I know you think I can't make a joke right now. But I've had fifteen years of living with this, Finn. So I can make a joke about it, because I know what is mine, I own it.'

'But that bastard is still running around?'

'I did one thing, one right thing, that I think helped. I told Lois from the law office. She came round after three weeks. I was sitting there and rocking my new goth look, you know, all black: black eyeliner, black eye-shadow, black nails. We were talking and she just knew it was something to do with Quinn. She was adamant I had to do something about it. I said no, I don't have to do anything, I told her.

'Someone needs to know.'

'Well, you can figure out how to tell them,' I said. 'But I'll explain it to you really simply, don't bring me into it. Because if you do, I will deny everything. But they won't listen to you anyway.'

'My father will listen to me,' said Lois.

'Your father who got you the job?'

'Yeah,' says Lois, 'he'll listen to me.'

'OK, good,' I said. 'Don't keep me informed, I don't want to know.'

Lois wasn't exactly touchy feely, but she tried to reach out and touch me, but I wasn't touching, you know. I'm not so good at touching. That's why I hated Nate when I first met him, because he was so handsy.'

'I know, I saw.'

'And I don't know what happened, where he is, what he's doing. But the name Quinn isn't on the company branding anymore. I used to dream about killing him. The rage is very fierce but most of the time, I can deal with it.'

'I love you, you're so brave, so brave. But I do still want to kill him.'

'No,' I say, 'hold me, Finn, just hold me and love me and be you. And let's just talk about this some other time, because for you now this is a huge thing. But for me, I've lived with it for a very long time and I have come to terms with it in my own way. And you unlocked me, like I don't know, Sleeping Beauty, Cinderella, whichever one of them was locked up. Not that I'm a princess who needed to be saved no, but –'

'Nobody needed to save you, you saved yourself,' he says instantly. And he pulls me to him and I can feel him rocking backwards and forwards, as if he's in absolute pain.

'I told you this, so we can have a future, OK?'

'A future.' He looks at me and his eyes are wet.

'Yes, a future. Now either you can deal with me having been raped, and you might not be able to, or you can't, but, either way, what we have just had is amazing.'

'Of course I can . . . I've the most amazingly strong warrior woman ever here. I'm not going anywhere. You've got me for good.'

'OK,' I say. 'That's wonderful.' And I reach forward and I kiss him. Kiss this beautiful man who has given me back something I never thought I'd have again. And I have it because I was finally ready, I managed to let go.

I loved Marc, but we had held each other back. Together, we'd just stayed in our little cosy prison cell. And his leaving had allowed me out. He'd unlocked the door and now I was in the world again and I'd found Finn. I was free.

44

Marin

The person who has helped me most while Nate has been in hospital is April. I never ever thought she could help me through something like this. Help me through anything. My whole life, I've been helping April, being her confidante, cheering her up when she's been dumped, hiding what's going on in her life from Ma's prying ears, rescuing her. Now she's rescuing me. It's quite astonishing.

'What's different, April?' I say, in the morning as we are changing the bed in the spare room, getting it ready for Nate. Ostensibly, the reason he's going to be sleeping in the spare room is because he's had stents delivered via the angiogram and he must not have the groin area banged into. So this is our excuse to keep him safe. In reality, it's because I cannot have him back in my bed. But to everyone, to Rachel and Joey, who are so excited and thrilled he's coming home; to his mother, who has been on the phone three times already; even to Steve, Nate's return is the most wonderful thing ever. Steve has already discussed a party. Unfortunately, he said it to Rachel on the phone, who ran upstairs, her eyes shining, saying 'Mum, wouldn't that be wonderful, you know how much Dad loves parties and we could welcome him home with something fantastic like that, it would be brilliant.'

She's grown up so much in the last few months of working. I'm going to miss her when she goes off on her six-month round-the-world trip with Megan, which is happening in just a few weeks' time. And then I think how young she still is, because I'm still fooling her by not saying, *He was with Bea, the person you consider your auntie, the night he was in hospital.*

'Oh a party is not a good idea,' says April swiftly.

I beam at her.

'No,' April goes on, 'he needs time to rest and recuperate and then maybe a wonderful big party sometime in the summer,' she says. 'Have the family and a few friends over when he comes home, that's all, just for a pot of tea and then off again. Your father will need to rest.'

'Dad would love a big party and I won't be here in the summer,' says Rachel, suddenly forlorn.

'We'll wait till you have come home and you are ready to start college,' says April. 'Your father will love that and he'll be strong by then, because he has to take care and do exercises and things.'

'Yes, you're right,' says Rachel thoughtfully. And April shoots me a side eye that gives me the message that the only exercising Nate will be doing if she has her way will be trying to pull a knife out of his heart; she has said as much. And I laugh. I think I might be going nuts. I was given twenty Xanax by my doctor and I am eking them out, to make sure I don't completely lose the run of myself and giggle at some inopportune moment. Because everyone else is treating Nate getting out of hospital like the return of the king, when to me it's the return of the lying, cheating scumbag. Now that he's getting better, the fear of losing him has subsided and the rage over what he did has reared its head.

'Now, are we all ready to go to the hospital?' says April. She's coming, even though it will be a bit of a squash, even in Nate's big super-duper car. She knows I can't bear to be on my own with him. Not yet, I have to build myself up to it. I know this is the right thing to do, it's the right thing to do for our family. I need to hear him explain what happened and tell me how he came to be with Bea, and we can hardly get into that in the hospital. April bustles us out, managing us all.

Finn has been there for me too. Darling Finn, I believe him

that he had no idea. But he's talking to Bea as well, and I can't hear about her yet. We came close to falling out when he tried to explain it all to me.

'Marin, I've talked to Bea and it was one night when she was at an emotional low. He had the heart attack because he came around again and she threatened to call the police if he didn't go, and that set him off . . .'

'Stop,' I said, 'I don't want to hear it. Not now. Not yet. I don't want to know, Finn, and if that's the message you're bringing from her, well, then, bring it right back.'

'I'm not bringing any message from her,' he says. 'It's just the way it is. And you need to talk to her.'

'I don't need to talk to anyone. I'm just trying to get through every day as it comes. The man I loved has betrayed me. Do you understand that?'

'I understand,' he says. 'And I'm so sorry. But it's not what you think.'

'I know exactly what it is,' I say to Finn, 'don't try and dress it up. I know you are trying to make it better because you're his friend, and Bea's too. But I don't want to hear it.'

And now I'm bringing him home for the first time in weeks.

It's amazing how, after having three stents put in and being told he'll have to be monitored and be on aspirin and all sorts of cholesterol drugs for the rest of his life, Nate still looks sickeningly healthy. Paler, yes, but that's just because he's been trapped inside.

'Oh Dad, you look tired,' says Rachel, holding on to her dad. Then there's Joey's delighted face, as he hangs off his father's other side. And I know I have got to keep doing this for my kids.

Within half an hour, we're home. And despite all plans not to have even the smallest party, everyone, it seems, has turned up to greet us.

There's my mother, who throws herself at Nate, even though

I have never really thought she liked him. Dominic hugs him tightly. Dear Dom hasn't a clue but his heart is in the right place.

Dad is gentle. 'Good man, Nate,' he says, 'good man. Bit of gardening, that's what you need. It's very good for the heart. If you look at all the head gardeners at all the big gardens around the country, you will see that they all live forty-five years from when they're made head gardener. This is the interesting bit,' Dad goes on, 'they are all made head gardener when they are fifty. So, you see, it's a real area of work where people live a long time. Gardening: it's the way forward.'

'Oh Denis, shut up. Nobody wants to hear about head gardeners,' says Ma, rudely.

Something growls inside me.

'I want to hear about head gardeners,' I say, and I turn and give her a gaze that would do Maleficent proud. My mother takes a step backwards.

'All I was saying was –'

'You're always interrupting people,' I say, 'stop.'

From the corner of the room, April giggles. Dominic opens his mouth and stares in total silence. Ma stalks off, indignant.

'Thanks, lovie,' says Dad. And then he whispers, 'She's going to kill me later.'

'No, she's not, because I'm not going to let her,' I say.

'Is everything all right, pet?'

'Yes, Dad,' I say, 'just, you know, the whole near-death thing. Makes you really think of life,' I say. I hate lying to poor darling Dad. But he shouldn't have to put up with my mother, any more than I should have to put up with bloody Nate.

Steve and Angie are here, and they brought some catered sandwiches and nibbles. It's all laid out on the dining-room table. There's no sign of Finn or of Sid or, luckily, Bea. Bea is not welcome here. Not that I've told her that but she's not stupid: she knows.

'Where's Finn?' says Nate.

I look him straight in the eye, probably the first time since he has come into the house.

'He couldn't come,' I say.

'Oh, OK,' says my husband, sounding very much not like my husband.

I'm coming downstairs after having taken a moment upstairs, because the general laughing and hilarity and everything being wonderful is getting to me a bit. And I meet Angie in the hall.

'Can I talk to you for a minute?' she says.

She looks different, although I can't quite put my finger on what it is. Her clothes are still perfect and she looks like she should be on the *just seen at a fashion show* part of a glossy magazine. But it doesn't affect me in the same way. Filling the gaping emotional hole with clothes has done absolutely nothing for me. All it has done has made me ignore what was going on around me.

'Of course,' I say, a clammy feeling in my stomach. What's she going to say? Is she going to say she's been seeing Nate too and she's declaring herself? I'm not able for this.

'Come on out, into the garden, it's a bit cool.' She guides me out by the shoulder. 'I've got wine and two glasses because I'm not driving home and you don't have to do anything. I'll tidy up all the catering stuff and then you can sit down and relax.'

I note that she doesn't say, 'and look after Nate for the rest of the evening' and that cheers me up a bit. Because so far all the conversations have been about how wonderfully I'm going to be looking after my husband and the amazingly low-cholesterol meals I'll be cooking for him and how I'll be helping him get back to full fitness. As if minding my darling Nate is going to be the most important thing in my life.

The garden is a bit of a wreck beyond the pergola. We've got nice back-garden furniture, a dark rattan sort of colour that doesn't change come winter or summer. In the good weather you can stick a few cushions on it and it all looks very nice. We've got a state-of-the-art barbecue, naturally, because Nate loves barbecuing. But Angie has set up a little spot near a wall where I keep my beloved sedums. Nate has no time for these lovely succulent plants, lovely joyous fat little creatures that fall over each other like puppies as they grow, happy and smiling and really needing so little work.

Angie pops the cork out of the wine. I haven't had anything to drink since I came in apart from a strong coffee because I'm not sleeping well, and I need the coffee to keep me awake.

'You will have a glass?' she says. 'I noticed you drinking the coffee earlier. Is it because you want to stay up at night and keep an eye on him?'

I look at her full on. She has an amazingly steady gaze. There's no side to Angie, I realise. I don't know why I thought there was before. I don't know why I thought she talked to the men and ignored the women. That was my own prejudice.

In fact, she has often tried to be there for me. Tried to help at the dinner parties, said things like, 'I wouldn't do it, Steve knows better than to expect me to drum up a party after a hard day at the office.' And I'd always taken it to mean that her work was so much more important than mine, that she couldn't possibly do something like this, because it was beneath her. But now I think she wasn't saying that: she was standing up for me.

'It's about Nate, isn't it?' I say, looking at her.

She nods.

'He, didn't . . .?'

I look at her and I think, *prepare yourself for this body blow.* She hands me half a glass of wine.

'He tried.'

'He tried. Why am I not surprised. At the Christmas party? I knew something was off,' I say. She nods back at me. 'Why are you telling me this now?'

'Because Steve knows about Bea.'

I feel as if someone punched me in the solar plexus. I manage to squash a couple of my little succulents as I collapse down onto the little wall.

'I'm sorry, I didn't mean to upset you. I just wanted to be honest. And I wanted to talk to you about Bea. She's very proud, she wouldn't ever say this to you herself. Nate really took advantage of her at a very weak moment, just after something had happened with Luke,' she says.

'What?'

'It's true. I know because Finn and Steve have talked. Now Finn is different to Steve. Steve idolises Nate, he thinks he is wonderful. Mind you, if Steve ever tried to emulate Nate, I'd be gone so fast, he wouldn't know what had hit him. Now about the other women, I don't know much – but Bea was a one-off.'

'A one-off that got him in hospital,' I say, my voice rising. So there had been others.

'She was shocked the first time, but she was at a very weak moment and he totally took advantage of her. But he went back for more and she screamed at him, called the cops. And then he had a heart attack. Which serves him right,' she says.

'I doubt he's learned his lesson.'

'Are you keeping him?' It was like she was talking about a dog who'd just peed on the rug. But you can also train a dog not to pee on the rug. You shouldn't have to train a person who's supposed to love you not to cheat on you. Humans are who they are. They act their better selves if they really want to. Nate just didn't want to.

'How do you know about the other women?' I say.

'I saw him once, with another woman, not Bea.' She looks down. 'I am so sorry, Marin. I didn't know how to tell you. I should have. She was blonde, they were walking out of a hotel in town together which, in itself, means nothing but –'

In the pause, we both think of the 'but'.

'Did Finn know?'

'No. Finn's a straight arrow. I told Steve but Steve never told him.'

'So how do I find out about the other women?' I say.

'You could ask him but I'd say he'll lie. So check the bank statements,' says Angie. 'You need a forensic accountant and a decent lawyer for the divorce.'

'I wasn't going to divorce him,' I say. 'I thought if he was going to leave, he'd have left.'

'Yeah,' Angie gets up and pats my hand, 'I wouldn't bet on it. You deserve so much more, Marin. I don't want you to think I'm experiencing any happiness telling you this, I just wanted you to know. I've always hated the way he treated you and you're a good woman, Marin. And I'd like it if we could be friends. Somehow we haven't really managed that in all these years.'

'I felt intimidated by you,' I say, 'your make-up, your hair, your clothes, you always look so amazing.'

'Clothes are nothing,' laughs Angie, astonished.

'No, no they're not; clothes are fabulous. I love clothes. Clothes are armour and they're the armour I just can't get right.'

'You're so much more than clothes, Marin. I don't see your clothes when I see you, not like with some women. On some women, all I see are the jeans or the shoes or the handbag. With you, I see you. We give clothes too much power. *We* have the power – they just emphasise it if we're in the mood.'

I'm considering this when Angie gets up to go. She's right – clothes have too much power. *We* have it.

'I'll leave you and please, let's do that coffee. Oh, I meant to say, your sister, April, she's changed, hasn't she? I love her. She was telling me that Nate is sleeping in a separate room in case he hurts his groin.' Angie has a slightly wicked look on her face. 'If he was my husband, I'd hurt his groin.'

I laugh and it feels good. I'm so lucky to have all these other women in my life.

45

Bea

Three months later . . .

The introduction to Sean comes by stealth. Not an attack by
Shazz from her how-to-find-a-hot-man dating app, which was
a small mercy. No, Mum organised this one, although, as she
insists, it's just by total accident that he happened to be there
when I was.

Once every three weeks her book club meet, having actually
read the book, and then they talk for hours, laugh, discuss
things and drink too much gin. There are a few fantastic cooks
among them, so there are always lots of delicious nibbles, and
it's pretty much one of the few events where Mum actually
drinks. She's not a big wine drinker but she loves a little glass
of sherry or a gin and tonic made by a light hand. Elma, the
friend, whose house they are in tonight, has a heavy hand with
the sherry. So every three weeks on a Friday I drop her to one
of her friend's houses, or help her host the evening. It's the least
I can do given how utterly amazing she is to me and Luke.

'I'm not amazing,' she always says, batting me away with
one delicate hand. 'I love you both, what else would I do but
mind you.'

'Oh Mum,' I say, 'you do so much more than mind us. You
love us, you give us so much of your time, this is the least I can
do.'

On the book-club evenings, Luke spends the night with
Shazz or Christie and her twins. Tonight it's Elma's and I know
Mum, with her very weak head for the sherry, will be happy

and chatty in the car coming home, the signs of someone quite unaccustomed to three glasses of sherry, chatting and laughing, enjoying being with her friends. It's the best medicine for everything in life: sharing stories, talking of the book they had read, what they were going to read next, whether they liked the last book.

Today, I know it's almost three months since Nate got home from hospital and I can't stop thinking about how much I want to see Marin and cry my eyes out to her. I can't, of course. No matter that Finn has pleaded my case with her, even though I told him not to, Marin has not appeared to tell me how much she hates me. I'd prefer that. It might make up for how much I hate myself right now.

The only joy is the fact that in a month, myself and Luke are flying to the Auvergne for the weekend with Jean-Luc's mother. He's so excited that he tries to speak French at every meal.

I'm seeing a therapist now. The pain of everything from the Family Tree to the disastrous encounter with Nate has made me see that I can't wither away trying to keep everyone happy while I fall apart myself.

Or, as Shazz puts it, 'You've got to forgive yourself, you daft mare.'

It's been a long week at work. Two of the doctors have retired but the practice is busier than ever because two much younger GPs have bought in.

However, today it wasn't too manic and I managed to get a hair cancellation in the afternoon.

'Do you think you should do something about that grey?' Shazz had pointed out to me one day, with her customary bluntness.

'Ah no, I'm letting it go grey because I think, you know, younger guys really fancy older grey women,' I deadpanned.

'Yeah, Mrs Robinson, I'm sure they do,' she says. 'But it's not working on you. Before you know it, you'll have grey pubes.'

'Ah Shazz,' I groan, 'don't go there.'

Christie had laughed. 'She'll be telling you to get it all shaved into a sexy topiary love heart next.'

I groaned again. 'Forget it, girls. I'm au natural all the way and if the guy doesn't like it, he's toast.'

Still, Shazz was right about the grey hairs near my temples. And something the therapist said has stayed with me: 'Luke will see how you live and think that's the way to live. If you never take care of yourself, how can he learn how to take care of himself?' So I take myself to a salon in Blackrock where a lovely colourist put a semi-permanent rinse through my hair to see if I liked it.

'It's really your own mahogany colour,' she says, 'perhaps a little lighter. But as we age, our skin goes paler and so does the skin on our scalp, so it's hard to keep up the same level of darkness, the same depth. You might want to think about getting some paler low-lights in later.'

'OK,' I said, taking it all in, 'it looks amazing.'

'I have a great canvas to work with,' she says, smiling.

Luke, being ten, didn't notice. But Christie said it was gorgeous.

'About time,' she said, as I brought Luke and his overnight bag to hers.

'Are you two having conferences about how bad my hair is getting?' I said dryly, referring to her and Shazz.

'Do I look like I have conferences with people about other people's hair?' said Christie with a laugh.

Her own hair was platinum blonde and cut pretty short in a sexy style. She dyed it herself.

'I like the wash-and-go sort of method with a blast of home dye every month. I've never seen you get your hair dyed – ever. You look amazing, Bea, stunning.'

'Thanks,' I say.

As I drive over to Elma's to pick up Mum that evening, I think how nice it was to make an effort with my hair and it flickers into my head that Jean-Luc, wherever he was, might appreciate that I was no longer letting myself wither away.

There's plenty of parking outside Elma's, because most of the ladies have taken taxis or have been dropped off. Elma herself opens the door.

'Oh, look at you,' she said delightedly. 'Did you get your hair done?' she says.

There are no flies on Elma. Before she retired she was a teacher. And it's obvious in every part of her warm, clever face that she spots absolutely everything.

'Yes, it is. Thank you, Elma,' I say, kissing her on both cheeks, French style.

'Really suits you,' she says. 'Come on in. I know you won't drink because you are driving, but you can have some herbal tea. We are not quite wrapped up yet. I don't know, this book just took ages to talk about.'

I follow her in and find the usual eight ladies sitting around Elma's dining-room table, nibbling cheese, crackers and grapes, all with full glasses. They're clearly long beyond the book stage of the conversation. Interspersed between them are the drivers, two husbands and one man who's going around the table with what is unmistakably a green tea teapot. He looks up as I come in, and at that same moment I catch sight of my mother, who positively beams at me.

'Bea,' she says, 'you're here. You must meet Sean. We're lucky he's gracing our company tonight.'

I look up and there he is: the man from the trendy new restaurant in the city, the guy Christie knew where we'd had a lovely night out with Shazz. I'd seen him then as I was coming back from the ladies' and he, busy running his restaurant, had barely noticed me and I'd felt horribly invisible.

Tonight, it's different. Tonight, he looks at me admiringly.

The entire tableful beams at us en masse, and I'm struck by the impression that if Sean had dragged me upstairs

341

caveman-style, they'd all wave to see us go and say, 'Have fun, lots of love, we'll come up in the morning.'

My mother played a part in this, I think darkly, watching her. Shazz's 'find a man for Bea' campaign has clearly gone viral.

'Sean moved back from Hong Kong to set up the restaurant and it's doing brilliantly, and he's home for good,' says Elma firmly. Just in case Sean had any ideas about what he might want to do with his own life.

He grins. 'Hello, Bea,' he says, with a faint bow, 'would you like some green tea and an apology for the matchmaking?'

I laugh and decide to give in gracefully to a cup of green tea. The eight ladies around the table have not got the combined ages of about five centuries for nothing. At speed, everyone moves and Sean and I are sitting right beside each other, two cups of green tea in front of us. Everyone else has most ostentatiously moved away to talk about other things.

'Does this feel like a set-up to you?' I say, looking down at my cup and not at Sean, who, close up, is definitely several years younger than me. He's late thirties, while I'm like the conveyor belt at Dublin Airport: full of baggage and a bit creaky with a complicated history.

'Sorry,' he says. 'This is a crazy night for us in the restaurant but she begged me to come tonight and meet some of her friends and as I'm so busy and feel guilty, I said yes . . .' His voice trails off a little bit and I laugh.

'Women who want to be grandmothers rule the world, you know, or at least they should,' I say. 'We were both walked into this.'

'Oh I don't know,' he says admiringly. 'Mum has been telling me about you for the past week.'

'Telling you what exactly?' I say, anxiously. And then I stop myself. Elma is a lovely person and she only would have wanted the best for me, like Mum. She won't have said anything negative.

'You OK?' says Sean. I've spaced out on him.

'I'm fine,' I say, 'let's start this again. I just felt a bit thrown because I had an uncomfortable situation with an old boyfriend recently, and I didn't realise I was being set up tonight.'

'You do know that the Chinese characters for crisis also say danger – and opportunity.' He gives me another admiring look and I raise an eyebrow.

'Really?'

'I feel as if I've met you before,' he adds. 'Have we –? I honestly wouldn't forget someone like you.'

'Is that a line that usually works?' I ask.

'Not a line,' he says, shaking his head ruefully. 'I've been too busy to have lines. But for you –' He breaks off and he's doing that admiring thing again. 'I might manage to think up a line or two.'

'We have met before,' I say. 'In your restaurant.'

He looks genuinely sorry. 'I'm really sorry – that's unforgive-able in my trade. You'll have to let me buy you dinner to make up for it.'

'Now that *is* a line –' I begin.

'No,' he interrupts. 'Just a thought. A very, very nice thought.'

In the car going home, Mum looks like the cat who's got the cream.

'You liked Sean,' she says, even her tone blissful. 'He is handsome. Charming and decent. Elma's good stuff and so's her husband.'

'Mum, he's six years younger than me. And when a woman is older it's counted in dog years. People have no trouble with the whole older-man-younger-woman dynamic but they're very cruel when it's reversed.'

'But you don't care what people think,' says Mum, happily.

'No, I don't care what people think, but Sean is thirty-seven. Thirty-seven-year-old young guys want women who can have kids with them. I don't want any more children and I don't know if I could have one even if I started now. I'm happy with Luke.'

'I just want to see you settled.'

I think of Nate and Marin and everything that has gone on. How can any relationship be settled? They were together for so long.

'Mum, I don't think I can date anyone, not after what happened with Marin and Nate.'

'That wasn't your fault.' My mother play slaps my knee which is the only safe bit to touch when I'm driving. 'Stop this,' she says, 'stop punishing yourself. One day, darling Luke is going to go off and have a life and you are going to be sitting there with nothing. Because you gave everything to him. And you can't do that. Whatever you believe in, Bea, you must believe that there can be happiness again. Maybe you won't find someone forever, but you might have ten beautiful years with a new man. Or maybe you'll have a few years before you grind up some glass and put it in his porridge.'

I burst out laughing at the thought that my mother even knows such a thing.

'Don't laugh,' she says, 'we read lots of different types of books in the book club. So what's wrong with going out with Sean? I know you're going to be terribly shocked with me when I say this – go to bed with him, sleep with him. Let Luke see that his mother can have relationships. Don't drag him home by his hair and say, Luke, go and play your Xbox. Do it gently, slowly. Lord knows, you haven't introduced anyone to him up to now, so it's not as if Luke has had a litany of "uncles" coming into his life. So why not go out for a drink with Sean and eventually drag him up to your lair.'

'I did get rid of the mattress.'

'Well, that was a very good idea,' says my mother, in a matter-of-fact tone.

'Mum, you are surprising me tonight, you really can't hold your alcohol.'

We pull into her driveway where the light above the door is on, shining a warm amber, lighting up the pots underneath it. I stop the car and turn off the engine.

'I know, dear. Your father always said that.'

I reach over and give her the biggest hug possible in a small car. 'I've been mean to you – Sean's already asked me out and I said yes.'

'Brat,' she says, laughing. 'I'm so thrilled. You've waited far too long. Sean might show you some fun and it'll get you used to going out at night. And stop beating yourself over the head because of Nate.'

'It's Marin,' I think, 'it's Marin I feel so bad about.'

'Maybe one day you'll be able to talk to her, I don't know. But life moves on, darling, and if anyone knows that, you do.'

She's right. It's true for both me and Luke. It's time to move on.

46

Sid

Finn has been renovating his apartment and he's asked me to move in with him when it's finished. I'm dithering but, secretly, I want to. When I first saw it, I loved it because it's in an old Georgian building and it's so elegant and unusual.

It's so lived in. It's full of stuff and it's not dusty.

'Do you have OCD?' I ask, as I wander around picking up odd things and looking at them and saying: 'What is this?'

'It's an astrolabe,' he says.

'It's very nicely polished, anyway; you must be a very good housekeeper.'

'Someone has to come in and do it,' he says, grinning.

He shows me how to use it.

'I love this sort of stuff,' he says happily, one hand on my waist as he puts it back.

I love the way he touches me as if he can't bear to let me out of reach. In fact, I adore it. 'Must be a nightmare to polish.'

'It is, I have polished it myself, I admit, although it's fiddly. When you live on your own and you get to my age, you've got to be tidy, or else you are just living surrounded by tins of baked beans and growing experiments that Alexander Fleming would be delighted with.'

'Yes, I often wonder why gone-off bread tastes so weird, when I tried to convince myself that it must be good for me,' I say.

I open his breadbin, 'No gone-off bread here, look at you, you are a proper caretaker man.'

'Not only am I a proper caretaker man, I can open tins and

order takeaways and Marin is one day going to teach me how to cook.'

We are both silent for a moment, the music playing in the background, some soft jazzy thing he'd put on that I didn't recognise, but it was beautifully calming and comforting.

'If I show you the rest of the apartment, I'll be showing you the bedroom and then, when the delivery person comes, we'll be in bed.'

'So, you'll just have to go and open the door with no clothes on,' I say, giving him my best winning grin.

'Not a problem.'

Tonight, we wander around the nearly finished apartment and I think that I'm going to tell Finn I'm taking him up on his offer. I want to move in with him. He's the kindest, most gentle man I've ever met. He understands me sexually, gets that a woman who's been violated needs tenderness and love. He's just marvellous at tenderness and love.

Vilma is taking all the credit for our being together, and when Stefan and Mum met Finn for the first time, Stefan grabbed my sister in a bear hug and whispered to her in Lithuanian, which she only understands a little.

When he puts her down, he turns to Finn: 'I want to welcome you and say thank you for bringing our Sidonie home. She was lost for a time.'

'It's an honour. I will take care of her.'

'I don't need –' I begin but Stefan shushes me.

'I know you are a warrior woman, my Sidonie,' he says, 'but sometimes, let us men take care of you? Just sometimes – and this one, he adores you.'

Mum laughs and hugs me.

'He's a keeper,' she whispers. 'And tall. There's something lovely about a tall man.'

I blush. My mother is talking to me about tall men and I think about how when Finn and I are in bed, it doesn't matter that he's taller than me. I blush some more.

If Mum, notices, she says nothing.

The more she knows Finn, the more she adores him and makes him stews, so I complain that he's never going to learn to cook and look after me.

Adrienne particularly approves of him.

'Well done with Mr Stella,' she said the first time she met him. 'Any more like him at home?' she asked.

'He's a one-off,' I said.

'Just my luck.'

Tonight, we finally make it into the bedroom where there are high ceilings.

'Oh,' I say, pretending my phone has just pinged with a news alert. 'Look!'

He obligingly looks down at it and I pull his head lower so I can whisper into his ear.

'You still want a roommate? A small one, lots of black clothes, biker boots, has furry pyjamas?'

His response is to grab me, lift me up and whirl me round.

'Like it? I love that idea,' says Finn, and, still holding me up, he kisses me. This, I think, is my reward for all the pain, this glorious man. I am so lucky.

47
Marin

The day Rachel is leaving for her travels, I'm up early. I have so much to do before she goes, so many plans. I want it all to go off like clockwork and I'm excited.

I dress quickly because I've sold off all my excess clothes, cut up my credit cards and am part of an online group of shopaholics who keep in touch to discuss how we are coping with the 'no shopping for three months' rule. It's getting easier, plus getting dressed in the morning is a doddle.

First up, Finn and Sid want to come over to say goodbye to Rachel, before she goes off on her travels.

'That's brilliant,' I say, 'she's going to love that.'

Sid is a revelation, a complete revelation. I knew there was something nervy about her when I met her first. But since she and Finn have got together it's like watching a beautiful flower blossom. She's still fiery and funny and oh, quirky with knobs on. But she laughs a lot, touches Finn all the time. Mind you, he can't keep his hands off her either.

She had a pretty intense talk with Rachel as well about travelling with Megan. Both girls told us in confidence – because Sid told them to – that she had been raped by someone she knew, a boss.

Somehow, Sid has managed to talk to Rachel about being careful on her travels in a way I couldn't manage to.

'It can be stranger danger but it's much more likely to be someone you know,' Sid has told them.

Louise is grateful at this advice for Megan.

I'm still in the angry stage because of Nate and growl to

Louise that someone needed to teach the girls that 'it's rarely the strangers who hurt us.'

'Great for you that you are going to make it work with Nate,' Louise says cautiously, ignoring the outburst. I told her about Bea because, in the early days, I was so desperate to vent, that I rang her up and blurted it all out.

'Throw his ass out!' she said.

'I'm not going to,' I said quickly and she was silent.

It's been a bit tense between us since then but things might lighten up, I hope.

'So you got those moves,' says Sid, hugging Rachel goodbye.

'I've got those moves.'

'And it's your body, your choice, consent, no crap. And remember, when you're physically weaker, you have to be clever, work with other women, work as a team. Remember: not everyone is good.'

'Don't scare the hell out of her,' says Nate. And I glare at him, not that he notices. Nate thinks everything is back to normal.

He's been out of hospital nearly two months and his recovery is excellent. Although, he's still not cycling or swimming. His regimen is cardiac care, walking and light weights till his next check-up.

He wants to come back into our bed.

'Let's just leave things the way they are,' I said the last time he asked.

He had to make do with that, for the moment.

'I'm going to miss you,' says Joey to his sister.

'I'll be home before you know it,' says Rachel.

'She will, you know. You could probably take over her bedroom,' I say to Joey naughtily, to break the tension.

'Mum!' says Rachel. 'You wouldn't.'

I laugh: 'I promise I won't let him.'

'But we can think about doing interesting things with your bedroom,' I say to Joey.

'Yeah,' he says, 'but just you and me and Dad now, we're going to have loads of fun.'

Finn and Sid are arm in arm and about to leave.

'Good luck,' Sid mouths as she hugs me goodbye.

'I don't know, I really think that woman has something psychic going on, because it's like she can see into my head,' I say to Finn.

'She's good at watching people, she picks things up that other people don't. Fabulous, isn't she?' he says, love in his eyes.

'Yes,' I say, 'fabulous.'

Bea has sent money to Rachel. I still haven't been able to see her. But I think I will afterwards, because I understand better now: human vulnerability, how complicated life is. It's harder to get my head round the notion that one person can be our *everything*, while that one person doesn't feel the same way. When that person needs more. Much more, so much more that it tears you apart.

We pile into the car. We are driving in convoy. At the airport we hug and even though I really meant not to cry, I do.

'I'm going to miss you, honey,' I say, 'but this is going to be so good for you. Just be careful. I want you to come back safe, strong, having used your brains to take care of yourselves. It's a big adventure, everyone deserves a big adventure.'

'I know.' My girl is grown.

The two families stand there as the girls go off. We turn to walk back to the car park. And Louise and I fall into walking beside each other.

'It just feels awful having them gone,' says Louise.

'I know,' I say. 'But we always knew they were going to go at some point and this is just the first little going.'

'I suppose,' says Louise tearfully. 'Do you think you guys would come over to us for takeaway dinner tonight, maybe fill the gap, make this all feel not so lonely?'

'No,' I say, 'sorry, just something I've got to do.'

'OK,' says Louise, 'maybe another time.'

'Another time.'

We drive home and on the way drop Joey at his best friend's house.

'I'll be back in two hours,' I say, as I watch him go the front door and ring the doorbell and see him ushered inside.

'It'll take his mind off his big sister,' Nate says. He doesn't know my real plan.

Nate sits down at the kitchen table when we get home. 'Nothing feels quite the same, does it?'

'No,' I say.

All the way home I'd been going over what I was about to say. I've been thinking about it for a month, actually. I decided I'd wait until Rachel was gone. Because that way she'd be away having fun when her father left. It's going to be tricky with Joey and I hate putting him through the pain but having parents living a lie is not going to do him any favours. He'll grow up thinking it's fine to cheat on your wife, the way Dom has grown up thinking it's fine to be a perpetual teenager. At least he's got his own place now and has learned – Sue would be pleased – that there is no laundry fairy.

'So Nate, you and I: the future.'

He looks at me cautiously. 'What do you mean *the future*?'

'Our future,' I say brightly. 'Or rather, our lack of future.'

'Course we have a future, we have everything, we've kids, we've family, we've a mortgage,' he says, his usual bullish self.

'What we have is a very loyal wife, two beautiful kids, one an adult and one a child. And one husband who doesn't take anything seriously. Who thinks we are all at his beck and call. Who takes me for granted, who's clearly been spending our money on someone else.'

His face flushes.

'I've found I'm really talented at forensic accountancy,' I say. 'It's amazing. Sid has a friend who helped me with that.'

He's still brazening it out. 'Sid! You brought Sid into this? She'll tell Finn.'

'Oh Finn knows,' I say.

Nate's face is a picture.

'It transpires that you spent a lot of money on dinners for two, jewellery I've never seen and lingerie. Some of the shops you've gone to, Nate, they're way kinkier than I gave you credit for. But of course, if I'd looked properly a long time ago, I'd have realised you have another credit card. But I didn't, because I trusted you. Trust is a lovely concept, but the person has to be trustworthy in the first place.'

'I am trustworthy.'

'No, you're not,' I say.

'Oh come on, come on,' he says, 'you're just over-wrought because Rachel's gone.'

'It's over, Nate, so I'd advise you to go upstairs and pack your bags and move out.'

'What?' I think it's hitting him now. 'What – what about Joey?'

'I'm going to tell Joey that you are working away for a while and frankly I don't care where you go. But you are going to go. And you are not going to talk to our daughter and tell her what's happening until I'm ready to. Nothing much is going to change with Joey anyway, because I bring him to school and I pick him up from school and I bring him to his football matches, because you don't do that sort of stuff.'

'I do.'

'No, you don't, you do your own thing and then you go off with your girlfriends.'

'I don't have girlfriends.'

'Don't bullshit me.' I think of the blonde Louise saw him with. How did I ever suspect lovely Angie, who has been a tower of strength for me.

'I was worried about you, Marin,' she'd said one day. 'He was all over Bea that night of the party – I was giving him a dressing down and he didn't like that.'

Nate stands up and suddenly he doesn't look so big or strong anymore. He's just a guy whom I trusted and I believed was a good person. Probably the way Sid believed the guy she worked for all those years ago was a good person, until she found out he wasn't.

'Just go, Nate,' I say.

I pour myself a glass of wine and after half an hour I hear him dragging two big suitcases downstairs.

'You're going to regret this,' he says, a little flush on his face now he's angry.

'Have you got your meds?' I say, last act of a kind wife. But he's a big boy, he can look after himself at whichever girlfriend's house he's going to. He's not my problem anymore.

'Yes,' he says.

'All right,' I say, 'don't let the door hit you on the way out. Oh yeah, you can leave your keys.'

'You've no right to ask me for the keys.'

'You want a bet?' I say.

He throws his keys down on the table. Then he's gone.

I sit there for a minute, breathing heavily, and then I ring April.

'You can come round now,' I say, 'he's gone.'

'Oh goody,' says April. 'Maybe we should have a party.'

And we both laugh.

Credits

Cathy Kelly and Orion Fiction would like to thank everyone at Orion who worked on the publication of *Other Women* in the UK.

Editorial
Harriet Bourton
Olivia Barber

Copy editor
Marian Reid

Proof reader
Linda Joyce

Audio
Paul Stark
Amber Bates

Contracts
Anne Goddard
Paul Bulos
Jake Alderson

Publicity
Leanne Oliver

Design
Rachael Lancaster
Joanna Ridley
Nick May
Helen Ewing

Editorial Management
Charlie Panayiotou
Jane Hughes
Alice Davis

Finance
Jasdip Nandra
Afeera Ahmed
Elizabeth Beaumont
Sue Baker

Marketing
Helena Fouracre

Production
Ruth Sharvell

Sales
Jen Wilson
Esther Waters
Victoria Laws
Rachael Hum
Ellie Kyrke-Smith
Frances Doyle
Georgina Cutler

Operations
Jo Jacobs
Sharon Willis
Lisa Pryde
Lucy Brem

About the Author

Cathy Kelly is published around the world with millions of books in print. Cathy is the bestselling author of *The Honey Queen*, *Once in a Lifetime* and *Between Sisters* among many others, and is a No.1 bestseller in the UK, Ireland and Australia. She lives with her sons and their three dogs in County Wicklow, Ireland. She is also an Ambassador for UNICEF Ireland, raising funds and awareness for children orphaned by or living with HIV/AIDS. Cathy likes starting craft projects she doesn't finish and snuggling on the couch with her dogs watching other dogs do cute stuff on Pinterest.

Cathy loves to hear from her readers. You can chat with her here:

🐦 @cathykellybooks
❑ cathykellybooks
❑ cathykellybooks

If you loved *Other Women*, discover Cathy Kelly's other
bestselling stories, told with her trademark sparkling
warmth, humour and honesty

The
Family
Gift

'Honest, funny, clever, it sparkled with witty wry
observations on modern life'
Marian Keyes

Freya Abalone has a big, messy, wonderful family. She has
an exciting career as a celebrity chef. She has a
new home that makes her feel safe.

But behind the happy front, Freya feels pulled in a
hundred directions. Life has thrown Freya some
lemons – and she's learned how to juggle! But she's
keeping a secret from her family, and soon
something is going to crashing down . . .

All families have their struggles and strengths.
So can Freya pull everyone – and herself – together
when they need it most?

The Year that Changed Everything

**Three women. Three birthdays.
One year that will change everything . . .**

Ginger isn't spending her thirtieth the way she would have planned. Tonight might be the first night of the rest of her life - or a total disaster.

Sam is finally pregnant after years of trying. When her waters break on the morning of her fortieth birthday, she panics: forget labour, how is she going to be a mother?

Callie is celebrating her fiftieth at a big party in her Dublin home. Then a knock at the door mid-party changes everything . . .

Help us make the next generation of readers

We – both author and publisher – hope you enjoyed this book. We believe that you can become a reader at any time in your life, but we'd love your help to give the next generation a head start.

Did you know that 9 per cent of children don't have a book of their own in their home, rising to 13 per cent in disadvantaged families*? We'd like to try to change that by asking you to consider the role you could play in helping to build readers of the future.

We'd love you to think of sharing, borrowing, reading, buying or talking about a book with a child in your life and spreading the love of reading. We want to make sure the next generation continue to have access to books, wherever they come from.

And if you would like to consider donating to charities that help fund literacy projects, find out more at **www.literacytrust.org.uk** and **www.booktrust.org.uk**.

THANK YOU

*As reported by the National Literacy Trust

THE IMPORTANCE OF
BEING URNEST

THE IMPORTANCE OF BEING URNEST
Sandra Balzo

Severn House Large Print
London & New York

This first large print edition published 2018
in Great Britain and the USA by
SEVERN HOUSE PUBLISHERS LTD of
Eardley House, 4 Uxbridge Street, London W8 7SY.
First world regular print edition published 2017 by
Severn House Publishers Ltd.

British Library Cataloguing in Publication Data
A CIP catalogue record for this title is available from the British Library.

ISBN-13: 9780727893628

Severn House Publishers support the Forest Stewardship Council™
[FSC™], the leading international forest certification organisation. All
our titles that are printed on FSC certified paper carry the FSC logo.

Typeset by Palimpsest Book Production Ltd.,
Falkirk, Stirlingshire, Scotland.
Printed and bound in Great Britain by
T J International, Padstow, Cornwall.

To Jim and Shilow,
for welcoming me home.

One

'You can't keep a man dangling – and I do mean dangling,' Sarah Kingston crooked her little finger and then let it go limp, 'forever. What are you so afraid of?'

My partner and I were alone on the front porch of our coffeehouse, or so I'd presumed until a nice-looking older gentleman rounded the corner and hesitated. He was holding a to-go cup and must have exited through the trackside door of the historic Brookhills Junction train station that housed Uncommon Grounds.

And, judging by the red tinge of his unlined face, had been just in time to witness both Sarah's dangling pinkie and preposition.

'I'm sorry,' I said. 'My partner meant—'

'I'm sure whatever it is, it's none of my business.' With a grin, he hurried past us and down the porch steps, keys jingling in his pocket.

'Please watch what you say,' I said, watching him continue down the sidewalk. 'You're chasing away customers.'

'Chasing away, how? He'd already bought the coffee.'

'And probably will never buy another.'

'Not everybody is as touchy as you are, you little weenie.' She waggled the finger at me.

'Enough.' I nodded toward a well-coiffed blonde

1

woman approaching from the other direction with a young boy in tow.

'Morning, Monica,' Sarah called, apparently deciding to censor herself for the kid's sake, at least.

'Good morning.' Holding up a hand, the woman took the steps up toward our coffeehouse two at a time, the kid flapping behind her like a kite that couldn't quite get airborne.

'She's in a hurry,' I said as the door closed behind her. 'Regular customer?'

In the early days of owning Uncommon Grounds, I'd beaten myself up for not remembering names and faces. Then Sarah pointed out that it wasn't so much that my memory was failing me as I just didn't give a shit. A fact that would have bothered me, if . . . well, I gave a shit.

'You know Monica,' Sarah said. 'Always in a hurry, comes in about this time and orders "just my black coffee, please" and a juice for her son.'

'Oh, yeah.' It was all coming back. 'If the kid looks at a cookie or something else in the pastry case, she says, "No, darling. You know we don't eat sweets," in the same tone people use when they say they don't watch TV. Or read fiction.'

Sarah was nodding. 'Plays holier than the rest of us but never leaves without a sticky bun.'

That, in itself, wasn't unusual. Chef and baker Tien Romano was gaining an almost cult-like following for her gooey pecan breakfast rolls, produced hot out of the oven early each morning.

But while I hadn't recognized this bun-lover's face, her shtick was coming back to me. 'She

2

remembers the bun just as you're ringing up, right? Always an apparent after-thought.'

'More *trans*parent than apparent,' Sarah said. 'Sends the kid off to the condiment cart to get a straw for his juice, then buys the bun and stashes it in her purse. Probably stashes herself in the bathroom later while she gags it back up.'

'She does look trim,' I admitted.

'Too trim for a sticky-bun-a-day habit, in my opinion.'

Mainlining breakfast pastry.

'Not sure there's a bun left for her to slurp and urp today, though,' Sarah continued. 'The gang from Goddard's has pretty much cleaned us out of pastry this morning.'

Until last year, Goddard's Pharmacy anchored the opposite end of the strip mall that had also housed the original Uncommon Grounds. We all were sad the pharmacy was gone, and not just because the same freak snowstorm that took down Goddard's had also leveled the rest of the mall, including Uncommon Grounds. Goddard's Pharmacy had been a slice of Brookhills history. A reminder of when drug stores had lunch counters and comic-book stands instead of grocery sections and computer supplies. The old pharmacy was sorely missed.

As had been its owner, until this morning. Gloria Goddard had suffered a stroke in January and been confined first to the hospital and then the rehabilitation facility at Brookhills Manor senior home. 'It's good to see Mrs G.'

'Ornery though she might be. Oliver has his hands full.'

3

For years, Gloria Goddard had been a sort of surrogate mom to Oliver Benson, whose father had owned the strip mall. When both Oliver's mom and dad were killed, the two had formed an impromptu family. Oliver went to school at the University of Wisconsin-LaCrosse but was home for semester break.

'I don't think she likes Oliver seeing her like this.'

'Or the gang seeing it, either,' Sarah said. 'She's known some of these people for a long time.'

It was true that the group had frequented the pharmacy on Sunday mornings for the better part of the last two decades. The lunch counter had featured good diner-type food and bottomless cups of coffee, meaning free refills for as long as people stayed. We had a one-refill policy, but bent that rule to breaking each Sunday morning for what had become known as the Goddard Gang.

The front door flew open with a jangle of bells and a woman – maybe forty – with long brown hair just starting to streak with gray burst out with two older women. One had a fresh-scrubbed face and was wearing a long, bohemian-style skirt and loose cotton jacket. The other was in full-on Sunday finery – silk dress, hat and heels – all topped by blonde hair, a more than generous spackling of makeup and a dousing of flowery perfume.

'I'm so sorry,' the brunette said when she saw us.

'Sorry for what?' My hand had flown reflexively to cover my nose and mouth against the assault

4

of the perfume and I forced myself to bring it down.

'I'm afraid Nancy,' she nodded toward the woman in the skirt, 'had a bit of an accident.'

Sarah sneezed from the perfume.

'Bless you,' I said, then tried again. 'What kind of accident?'

'I just couldn't control it,' the old woman said hoarsely.

That gave me a hint of what we were talking about, at least. We'd pretty much had every type of accident in the shop, including a car landing on the porch where we were now standing. 'Don't worry about a thing. We'll take care of it.' Or, with luck, our barista, Amy, would have by the time we got inside.

'Thank you,' the younger woman said, helping the ladies down the steps and toward a Porsche Cayenne parked on the street. 'I'll settle them at home and then come back and pay the bill. And any damages, of course.'

'No need to—'

Sarah elbowed me in the ribs. 'You don't know there's no need,' she hissed. 'Maybe the old coot flooded the place.'

Happily, the threesome was out of ear range of the coot comment, though a couple coming up the steps didn't miss it. Not being coots they didn't seem offended, though they did open the door and peer in cautiously before stepping through it.

So far as I could see, there was no common denominator among the Goddard Gang members other than a love of coffee and the fact they'd all shown up on Sunday mornings long enough to form a bond. Gloria told me that one of the things she found most interesting was that she'd never heard anybody ask what somebody did for a living, a normal conversational starting point. Instead, they talked about whatever was the news of the day and then parted to go about their business. People came. People went. And came again. There were marriages and divorces. And remarriages – sometimes to the same person.

With Goddard's no more, the group had been like bees without a Sunday-morning hive. Buzzing from place to place, they'd finally alighted on our new location in the train station.

One of the challenges for the gang had been finding a restaurant or coffee shop with enough space so they didn't have to fight for tables every Sunday morning and enough tolerance to let them hang out for hours. The chosen venue's parallel challenge was not ticking off their regular customers when the gang descended on the shop en masse.

No problem on either front for Uncommon Grounds.

Riders of the new commuter train in and out of Milwaukee were our bread and butter – or coffee and cream – during the week, with seniors, soccer moms, students and the occasional business meeting filling in the middle hours. Saturday mornings were also busy, with people heading to the shops or the farmers' market or whatever organized sport they were ferrying their kids to.

But Sundays?

Let's just say coffee can't compete with God. Or Green Bay Packer football.

We'd considered closing on Sundays, but the arrival of the Goddard Gang had made it profitable enough for us to open from eight to three. And now even some of our weekday regulars had started to pop in to join them.

'I suppose we should go in and see what the "accident" was,' Sarah said, glancing at the door with trepidation.

'We have to finish this.' My hair-trigger gag reflex had barely made it through Eric's childhood.

A BMW convertible – top down – pulled up in front as I turned the key in the padlock and slipped the chain from around the leg of a wrought-iron patio table. The temperature the last few days had been so unseasonably mild for March in Wisconsin that iced-drink sales had picked up and the occasional customer even asked to sit outside on the wraparound porch.

Sarah stopped folding the tarp we'd used to cover the tables and chairs to look up as the driver of the BMW hopped out of the car. 'Morning, Mort.'

Now this one I knew. Mort was the unofficial ringleader of the Goddard Gang. Late fifties, he had a thick head of springy white hair you wanted to tug on to see if it was real.

'Morning, Mort,' I parroted as he mounted the steps toward us. When I actually tipped to a name, I tried to use it. Supposedly the repetition helped you to remember the person. The jury was still out on that one, at least for me.

'Good morning. Spring has sprung early, hasn't it?'

7

'It certainly has,' I agreed.

'May I hope the gang's all here?' Mort smiled at the small joke, which he made – and smiled at – every Sunday.

'Sophie and Henry are inside, along with six or seven of your regular group,' whose names, of course, I didn't know. 'Oh, and Gloria, of course!'

'Oliver did convince Gloria, after all?' Mort asked, pausing at the door. 'She seemed to think it would be too much trouble leaving the manor just for coffee.'

After being released from the hospital, Gloria had gone to the manor for rehabilitation and physical therapy and hadn't left since, as far as I knew. Until now.

'The kid seems to be managing fine,' Sarah said. 'His SUV was too high, so they're using Gloria's Chrysler. I guess somebody in the manor parking lot helped him with the transfer into the car, but he managed to get her out and into wheel-chair here by himself. I just helped guide them up the ramp to the train platform door and into the shop.'

'I'm sure Gloria was grateful.'

'Actually, she told me I stank,' Sarah said.

Mort cracked a small smile. 'Language confusion, or so we might hope.'

'Language confusion from the stroke?' I asked.

'Yes, I noticed it when I visited. She seems to swap words. For example, Gloria might very well have meant to say "thank you" but it came out "you stank."'

'How frustrating for her,' I said.

Sarah was looking sheepish. 'I answered her,

8

"You're welcome," though I wish now that I'd taken some of the attitude out of it.' The attitude most likely being sarcasm. It was Sarah's thing and she did it well.

'It was probably a safe answer, since Gloria could just as easily have meant the insult.' Mort grinned full-on now. 'I'm certain she's frustrated. The woman is not one to sit still, especially in a wheelchair.'

'No, she's not.' I returned the smile. 'Why don't you go in and say hi. Amy is behind the counter.'

'Ah, our multihued barista.' Mort pulled open the door. 'Wonderful.'

As the door closed behind him, I got a whiff of coconut butter. 'Sixty degrees and Mort's pulling out the sunscreen. And this is just March. You'd think people would remember what happened on May first last year.'

Over a foot of snow was what happened. Not to mention a death or two.

'That freakishly long winter is exactly why everybody's enjoying the warmth.' Sarah took the end of the chain from me to unwrap it from around the next chair's legs. 'You know, *carpe diem* or . . . what's that other expression?'

'Make hay while the sun shines?'

'I was thinking more "eat, drink and be merry, for tomorrow we die." Which brings me back to Pavlik. Aren't you afraid that if you wait too long to answer him he'll change his mind?' She straightened with a handful of chain and a smirk. 'Again?'

I ignored the smirk and took the chain from her to unwrap the next chair in the rotation.

9

It was kind of like taking the lights off the Christmas tree.

And about as festive, given the company.

But Sarah was right that Brookhills County Sheriff Jake Pavlik had broken up with me shortly before he'd reversed course and unexpectedly asked me to marry him. Taken by surprise, I'd yet to give him an answer. 'Better that he changes his mind now, I guess.'

'Rather than after you're married, you mean?' My partner cocked her head, studying me. 'If you're having flashbacks of your cheating ex-husband, don't. I have a feeling that Dr T would never have strayed if he hadn't hired that bimbo Rachel as his hygienist.'

'That's kind of the definition of cheating, isn't it? Having somebody to cheat with?' A link snagged on the foot of the chair and I yanked.

The chain caught and then swung up, but Sarah one-handed it neatly before it could take out her eye. 'I was trying to be nice, Maggy. Supportive, even, of both you and Ted. And you wonder why I don't do it more often.'

I felt ashamed, which was exactly Sarah's aim. Now she could put 'nice' on the backburner for another year. 'I do appreciate the support. And I truly don't worry about Pavlik being another Ted. I just don't know if I . . .' I let it drift off.

'Want to marry Pavlik? You're crazy about him. Do you remember what kind of hell you put us through when he broke it off? The whining, the sniffling, the howling?'

'The howling was Frank.' My sheepdog was also quite fond of the sheriff. 'And, yes, I'm crazy about Pavlik, and, no, I don't want to lose him.' Before she could do it, I added, 'Yes, I know. Lose him *again*. I just don't know if I want be married right now. To anybody.'

With our son Eric having just left for college, my stunned reaction to Ted's announcement that he was leaving had been anger followed by terror and then loneliness. For the first time in my life, I was truly on my own.

Over the last two years, I'd adjusted to single life and even come to value my independence. I'd taken Eric's dog to live with me when Ted and I split and, though Frank might not be much of a conversationalist, I was grateful to have him overstuffing my tiny post-divorce house.

And . . . while I cared about Pavlik and certainly had fantasized about a future with him, suddenly the thought of starting life all over again was throwing me into a panic. 'I don't know why we can't just leave things as they are.'

'Maybe Pavlik figures if he's going to put up with your stumbling over bodies every few months, he'd like to know it's for more than the occasional booty call.'

'Isn't that supposed to be every guy's fantasy?' I snapped. 'No-strings-attached booty calls?'

'There are always strings.' Sarah's expression changed. 'But then maybe, flip side, he imagines that once you're married you'll stop the cavalcade of hot- and cold-running corpses.'

My head jerked up. 'You make it sound like I generate them. Or go out looking. They find me. Besides, Pavlik knows me better than to think he can control that. Hell, *I* can't con—'

11

'Morning, ladies.' Another cheery greeting, this time from a female voice and accompanied by a yellow-gloved wave from across the street.

'Morning, Christy,' I called back to our neighbor, just as happy to put the discussion with Sarah on the backburner for now. 'We haven't seen you for a while. Have you been out of town?'

'No, I've been here.' Piano teacher Christy Wrigley had crossed from her driveway to our side of the street, stripping off the rubber gloves as she came. 'I've been working a lot lately, though. And, before that, I was at Ronny's house, first getting it spic and span and then putting it on the market. So much so that I'm afraid I've neglected my own house.'

Fat chance of that. Christy made Mr Clean look like a slacker. Once I'd caught her scrubbing the wheels of our condiment cart with a toothbrush. And, no, she wasn't an employee. Just one crazy-ass customer.

As for Ronny, that was Ronny Eisvogel, Sarah's cousin by marriage and Christy's new boyfriend, at least on visitors' days. Currently, Ronny's room and board was provided by the state prison system.

'Ronny's selling his place?' Sarah asked before I could.

'Why not? He won't be home for years, thanks to you two.' Christy said it without malice.

Ronny was an incarcerated nutcase and Christy a naive germaphobe. I figured it had worked because visits at the jail were conducted by video feed and, as far as I knew, the two lovebirds had never so much as touched. But the thought of them living together? Well, the gloves would be off. Or maybe not, in Christy's case.

'You've already listed the house?' Sarah's Kingston Realty had taken a back seat to the coffeehouse in the months since she'd partnered with me in Uncommon Grounds, but she still seemed miffed she'd missed a new listing.

'We had an offer within the week and closed less than a month later.'

I noticed Christie hadn't said who the listing agent was. Probably didn't have the nerve.

'When was this?' Sarah asked, probing further.

She reminded me of a dentist making chit-chat so you don't notice he's drilling into the nerve. But then maybe I just had my dentist ex on my mind. Could Sarah be right and my failed marriage had more to do with my non-answer to Pavlik than I wanted to admit?

'I must have missed the listing on MLS,' my partner was saying casually.

'We closed mid-December, but—'

'December.' My partner's eyes flickered in what might have been reluctant admiration. 'The holidays are a tough time to sell a house. Your agent was either lucky or good.'

'Well, thank you,' Christy said, pink tinging her face. 'I used Craigslist.'

Sarah's own face darkened at the mention of the ad website that allows sellers to bypass the traditional real estate agent and the multiple-listing service databank. And the associated fees, as well. 'I hope you had a good lawyer do the closing, because—'

I cut in before we could be treated to a Real

13

Estate 101 lecture. 'So the new buyer has already moved in, then?'

Christy glanced uncertainly at Sarah's face before pivoting to answer my question.

'Yes. In fact, she's meeting me here. Hannah has been a bit housebound since she cares for both her mother and another elderly woman. I'm trying to get her out and meeting new people.'

'Not only a broker, but you're a regular Welcome Wagon, aren't you?' Sarah sniffed, her nose apparently still out of joint.

'I think it's nice of you to take an interest, Christy,' I said to counter my partner's snit.

'Hannah is a lovely woman. Besides,' Christy dipped her head, 'I kind of owe her my job. Along with Vickie, of course.'

I was confused. 'So, you knew her?'

'Of course. Vickie was one of my students when I taught piano.'

I wasn't sure what Vickie she was talking about, but, 'I meant your buyer. The person who moved into Ronny's house.'

'Oh, no. Like I told you, Hannah just moved here in December.' Our neighbor was squinting at me like she thought I was losing it.

'But you also said you owed her your job. I thought—' I stopped.

Christy had a habit of sprinkling a conversation with names and facts, as if you should know these things. I, for one, did not. Not about Hannah, nor about the other factoid I realized she'd just dropped.

So I switched on the back-up beepers and rewound the conversation. 'Wait. You said when

14

you *taught* piano, past tense?' I went to gesture at the piano lessons placard in the window across the street and realized it was missing. 'What happened to your sign?'

'Heavens, that sign's been down since January. You really should pay more attention to your surroundings, Maggy.'

'*Yeah*, Maggy,' Sarah said, spirits apparently on the rise.

I ignored her. 'But I thought you loved teaching piano, Christy. Was it not going well?'

'Oh, it was going fine, money-wise.' She looked first to the right and then to the left and lowered her voice. 'Though seeing some of Ronny's prison mates did give me pause.'

'Because . . .' I would have continued, but I didn't have the faintest idea where she was going.

'Convicts hate piano music?' Sarah guessed. 'Did they threaten you with a beat-down? Or Ronny with a shiv?'

'Of course not,' Christy said. 'In fact, I've been asked to play at the prison and received a standing ovation each time.'

'As the convicts got up to shuffle off in their leg-irons?' Sarah again, naturally.

Christy wrinkled her nose. 'Oh, they don't wear leg irons inside. Besides, there are white-collar criminals, too – fraud and such. Some are quite refined.'

As they're stealing your money.

Sarah raised her eyebrows. 'My dear cousin is a killer. What's he doing in with white-collar criminals?'

Christy's chin went up to match. 'Ronny is

15

not your normal killer and you know it, Sarah Kingston. There were mitigating circumstances.'

'I'll give you he's not normal,' Sarah said. 'And the mitigating circumstances are he's bat-shit nuts.'

Christy's mouth dropped open.

Before she could retaliate, which would only egg Sarah on, I asked, 'You said seeing some of these prisoners gave you pause?' I couldn't paraphrase because I didn't have the faintest idea what she meant.

'Yes, about the cash.'

'Cash.' I was giving parroting, a technique Pavlik used when interviewing witnesses, a try.

It worked. To an extent. 'Yes, I certainly didn't want to end up like them.'

'In prison?'

She nodded and I put together the pieces of the puzzle. Prison, white-collar crime, cash. 'You weren't paying taxes on your income?'

'Yes, I was.' Christy's bottom lip went out. 'Most of it, at least. Or maybe some.'

'Lay off, Maggy,' Sarah said. 'Piano teaching is probably a cash business. Who'd know?'

'The coffeehouse is a cash business, too, at least partly.' I felt my own eyes widen. 'Please tell me you haven't been skimming—'

'Of course not,' Sarah said, looking hurt. 'How can you ask me that?'

'Perhaps because you don't seem to think tax evasion is a crime,' I said. 'Did you know that's how they finally convicted Al Capone? The guy ordered the St Valentine's Day massacre and it was tax evasion that finally brought him down.'

16

'Isn't that what bit the bad guy in *The Firm* in the butt, too?' Sarah asked.

'Among other things,' I said. 'I was reading an article the other day that claimed the Cayman Islands bankers still can't forgive John Grisham for bringing attention to them as a tax haven.'

'It was a good book,' Sarah said. 'And movie, too.'

'Which isn't always the case.'

Christy cleared her throat.

'I'm sorry.' I decided to leave movies, books and tax evasion behind. What Christy did was her business and Sarah's views on what was OK in a cash business was going to be a private conversation between the two of us. 'You were saying you're not teaching piano anymore.'

Christy nodded. 'Happily, I've found where my real passion lies, and it doesn't require having grubby little fingers all over my piano keys every day.'

Passion wasn't something I associated with Christy.

'Thoooough . . .' Christy seemed to be giving it some further thought, too. 'Maybe passion doesn't quite capture this feeling. It's almost more a higher calling.'

'You're becoming a nun.' Sarah was coiling the chain.

'Heavens, no, although I did consider joining Angel of Mercy a couple years back. Did I tell you that?'

Angel of Mercy Catholic Church was one of two churches in Brookhills, the other being

Christ Christian just down the street from me. 'I didn't know you're Catholic.'

'I'm not. But Father Jim was looking for an office administrator who could also serve as an organist on Sundays. If I'd taken the job, I thought it only right that I join.'

I frowned, trying to remember. 'Aren't you musical director at Christ Christian?'

'Not any more. Not only did Pastor Shepherd not want to pay me, but every time I introduced myself as "Christy from Christ Christian," I cringed.'

'Too matchy-matchy?' I asked the woman whose yellow rubber gloves matched . . . well, nothing.

'Definitely. Besides, it turns out I'm an omnist. Who knew?'

Not me. 'Is that like an atheist?'

'Heavens, no,' Christy said again. 'An omnist respects all religions.'

Sarah frowned. 'You made that up.'

'Did not,' Christy said, settling into her subject. 'It's a real word that goes all the way back to 1839. Ronny says it fits me perfectly because I'm so open.'

Sarah started to say something but I shot her a warning look. 'Be nice.'

She raised her eyebrows. 'If you'll recall, I told you I was done with being nice.'

'To me, fine. But the rest of the world deserves better.'

'I'm not sure what your problem with Ronny is, Sarah.' Christy's eyes were scrunched in what she probably imagined was a glare but she looked more like a near-sighted squirrel.

Sarah sighed, apparently deciding it wasn't

18

sporting to take aim. 'You know me, Christy. I just like to kid around. I think Ronny is just . . . fine.'

'Well, that's good,' Christy said, unscrunching her eyes. 'Because he has only the nicest things to say about you.'

'I bet,' Sarah said under her breath. And then added, more audibly and with a different inflection, 'I bet! We were always like this as kids.' She held up crossed fingers.

Knowing Sarah, I assumed the gesture was to ward off a lie, not to show the two cousins-by-marriage were peas in a pod. Sarah and Ronny hadn't even known each other as kids, her aunt and Ronny's father having married later in life.

Still, Sarah had made an effort and she deserved props for that. 'That's so sweet.'

My partner threw me a look and I held up my hand, fingers crossed to match hers.

'It *is* sweet,' Christy echoed.

'Thanks,' Sarah said. 'Ronny's right. You *are* very accepting and open.'

If Sarah meant 'gullible,' I had to disagree. Our neighbor might be quirky and sometimes downright peculiar but she wasn't dumb. And she had me curious about this non-religion. Or maybe it was an ultra-religion. All things to all people. 'So, do omnists have churches? Is it like being a Unitarian or something?'

Christy tilted her head to think. 'I'm not sure, really. I just officially became one in January.'

'Did you take an oath of omniscience?' Sarah couldn't restrain herself.

19

'If I had, I would have known you were going to ask that,' Christy pointed out primly.

Point to Christy.

'I guess what I mean,' she continued, 'is that I may have been an omnist all my life but it's only recently that I realized the belief has a name.'

'Found it on Google?' Sarah asked.

'No, Brookhills Mortuary and Cremation. It's how we describe our chapel in the brochure. So much more positive and inclusive than non-denominational, don't you think?'

'I suppose so.' Assuming anybody knew what omnist meant. But she'd dropped another tidbit. 'You said "our chapel." Are you—?'

'Working at the mortuary, of course!'

Two

'I've been with Brookhills Mortuary and Cremation for nearly three months now,' our neighbor told us proudly. 'I'm surprised you haven't heard.'

I was too, quite honestly. Brookhills was a small town and Christy – even without the yellow rubber gloves – one of its most colorful characters.

'What are *you*, of all people, doing at a mortuary?' Sarah tossed the rolled chain toward the corrugated cardboard box already containing the tarps that we'd pulled off the furniture. The chain uncoiled mid-flight and landed at my feet.

'I'm doing what I do best.' Christy stuck out

20

her chin, which wasn't much chin at all. 'Cleaning. It was Ronny's idea.'

I'd leaned down to gather up the chain and now I swiveled my head toward our neighbor. 'I'm confused. Didn't you say a Vickie and this woman who bought the house—'

'Hannah Bouchard,' Christy supplied. 'She's wonderful. And you know Vickie. She's Sophie's friend?'

'Oh, Botox Vickie.' A fan of 'looking your best at any age,' Vickie LaTour was in her seventies, a member of the Red Hat Society and hosted Botox and collagen parties the way my mom did Tupperware parties in our neighborhood.

'But it was Ronny who inspired me, yet again,' Christy explained. 'He said I needed to play to my strength.'

'Which means cleaning a funeral home.' I still couldn't quite believe it.

'Oh, he wasn't as specific as that,' Christy said, her pale skin taking on a pink tinge again. 'Ronny was speaking more big picture.'

'From his small cell,' Sarah muttered.

Christy shook a finger at her. 'You can laugh, Sarah, but give your cousin credit. He sounds just like one of those motivational speakers when he waxes philosophical.'

Ronny was waxing philosophically while sitting on his butt in prison, while Christy would be waxing literally. And dusting. And vacuuming. 'But a funeral home?'

Christy frowned. 'Ronny says it's important to recognize what makes us different.'

'However does one choose?' I heard Sarah mutter.

'Cleanliness,' Christy continued, 'is obviously something I value. And I'm extraordinarily good at achieving it. The question that Ronny posed was how I could best use my talent. Find my niche, so to speak.'

'And you believe your niche is at the funeral home?' Between regular visits to prison and a job among the dead and the mourning, our neighbor seemed to be veering off her neatly cultivated garden path to take a walk on the dark side.

'As it turns out, yes. When both Hannah and Vickie mentioned – the same day, mind you – that the mortuary was looking for somebody to clean, I realized it was a sign.'

'Prescient *and* omniscient,' Sarah said. 'Too bad you didn't know you were going to get the job *before* you sold the house. Short commute.'

'Why? Where's Ronny's house?' The funeral home was just a few blocks north of me on Poplar Creek Road. Given that Ronny kind of tried to kill me, it might have been nice to know he had been a neighbor.

'Right next door to the funeral home,' Sarah said and then sneezed again.

'Bless you.' I wrinkled my own nose as I thought. 'But Christ Christian is on one side of the funeral home and there's nothing but a rutted dirt path leading to the Poplar Creek woods on the other.'

'Thank you.' Sarah swiped at her nose with an Uncommon Grounds napkin. 'And that rutted dirt path is what the Eisvogel clan calls a driveway. The house itself is set back behind the funeral home.'

Christy held out a tissue to Sarah, dangling it between thumb and index finger so as not to accidentally touch Sarah's fingers. 'You're not technically incorrect in calling BM&C a "funeral home" but it's really much more than that. It's a full-service mortuary and crematorium.'

I had a feeling that Christy was quoting the afore-mentioned brochure. But yet another fact had been dropped, this one something that I probably should have known. 'It's a crematorium? Do you—'

Christy raised her hand to stop me. 'I know what you're going to say, Maggy. That for some-body like me, a crematorium would be . . .' She was searching for a term.

'Icky?' I supplied. 'Horrific' and 'morbidly depressing' came to mind as well. But that wasn't what I'd been about to ask. 'They don't actually do the cremations there, do they?'

'Of course. What did you think?'

'I guess I assumed that sort of thing was . . . outsourced.' Preferably to some big anonymous building far, far away from my house. 'And the funeral home – or mortuary – got the ashes back and maybe packaged them for the family to pick up.'

I saw Sarah grin, and God forbid she should keep her mouth shut.

'Oh, I get it. You thought it was like my dry cleaner.' She turned to Christy. 'All this time I thought they were cleaning the stuff right there but turns out they ship it out and then just put it in plastic bags for me to pick up.'

'Exactly,' Christy said. 'That's how things get lost, you know.'

I wasn't sure if we were talking about corpses or clothes now. 'But at Brookhills Mortuary and Cremation you do it all right there?'

'One hundred percent in-house,' Christy said proudly. 'Our pledge is that we will walk your loved ones through every step of the journey to their final resting place, whether that be a dignified casket or lovely – and life-appropriate – urn. Mort,' she nodded to the convertible, 'is quite inspiring. Did you see the article about him in last week's *Observer*?'

'Mort of the Goddard Gang?' I asked.

'Yes,' Christy said. 'He's my new boss.'

'Wait,' Sarah said. '*Mort* is a mortician?'

'Yes,' Christy said. 'Mortician, funeral director and owner of Brookhills Mortuary and Cremation. You didn't know that?'

Again, I probably should have. But I didn't. 'Mort is a nickname, then?'

'I'd assume so.' With her green eyes wide in the heart-shaped face, now Christy resembled an owl. 'Why?'

'I don't know – it just seems a little flippant,' I said, and then shrugged. 'Though I suppose it's one of those fields where black humor is necessary to survive. Like being a cop or a coroner.'

'Humor?' Christy seemed completely lost. 'I don't understand what you mean. Mort is short for Morton. Morton Ashbury.'

'Wait, wait.' I thought Sarah was going to wet herself. 'Mort Ashbury owns Brookhills Mortuary?'

'And Cremation. Yes, I—'

But my partner had turned to me. 'You have

24

the marketing background. He has to have made that up, don't you think?'

I shrugged. 'I suppose it could be a matter of what came first, the name or the profession. Maybe Mort went into the business because of his name.'

'Then why not take full advantage of it? If I were Mort, I'd make hay where the sun *don't* shine, in this case.'

'Where's that?' Christy asked before I could shake my head in warning not to encourage Sarah.

Who was breaking herself up, at least. 'In the grave, of course. Remember the song "Ain't no sunshine when she's gone"? Which would be a great theme for Mr Mort Ash & Bury, come to think of it.'

'Bill Withers might disagree,' I said as evenly as I could. 'Are you off your meds?'

My partner was bipolar, and I had a hunch which of the two caps we were visiting today.

But Sarah just looked offended. 'I'm not manic, if that's what you're insinuating.'

'I'm not insinuating anything,' I said.

'Which is your passive-aggressive way of saying you're coming right out and saying it.'

'I am not passive-aggressive,' I snapped.

'And I'm not manic. Just—'

'High on life?' I suggested.

'I was going to say "clever." Not that you would know anything about that.'

I felt my eyes narrow. 'I'm clever, too. Just not—'

As the door into Uncommon Grounds opened behind me, I heard a loud *snap* and something sailed over my head. Monica Goodwin, busy stashing a napkin-wrapped sticky bun in her purse, didn't notice as a yellow rubber glove splatted on the floor in front of her.

Her son looked down at the glove. 'Can I have it?'

Monica glanced up from her purse guiltily. 'No, dear. It's for Grandma. You know how she likes pastry.'

I had a hunch the boy, who appeared to be six or seven, sensed there was a sweeter score to be had than a rubber glove. 'I like it, too.'

'But you know we don't eat sweets, Timmy. Grandma—'

'Is old enough to decide what she wants to eat.' He seemed to be parroting what he'd been told. 'Is that because she's old and going to die soon anyway?'

'Heavens, no.' Monica zipped up her purse, bun safely stowed. 'At least I hope Grandma's not going to die soon. Whatever gave you that idea?'

'Because Daddy says Grandma's a diabetic and sweet stuff will *kill* her.' The kid was transforming into a devil child before my eyes. Apparently the cumulative result of systematically being denied pastry. 'You're not trying to kill Grandma, are you, Mommy?'

'Mommy' was appropriately mortified that we were watching. And listening. 'No, of course not, Timmy. I wouldn't—'

'So why are you giving her sticky buns then?' The kid's eyes were an innocent blue, but I wouldn't have been surprised if pea soup had started spurting out of the mouth of his rotating

26

head. In fact, I'd have applauded it. Who needed television when you had this kind of reality playing out on your front porch?

Mom was trying to pull Timmy toward the sidewalk but his feet were planted wide on the bottom step. 'Daddy says you never liked his mother.' He cocked his head and looked at her cherubically. 'That's Grandma, right?'

'Well, I . . . She . . .' She was looking wildly around, as if for help.

So Sarah gave it to her. 'Maybe, kid. Or she could be your mom's mom.'

'Nope.' Timmy shook his head decisively. 'She's dead already.'

'Well, then, yeah. The grandma that Mommy is feeding sticky buns to is probably your dad's mom.'

'I'm not feeding her sticky buns!' Monica exploded. 'I'm eating them myself, all right? Are you satisfied?'

The surprise admission must have startled Timmy because his mother was able to pull him away down the sidewalk.

The last words we heard were, 'But Mommy, you know we don't eat sweeeee—'

'Perfect imitation,' Sarah said. 'The kid has a gift.'

I shivered. 'Kind of spooky the way he handled her. It was like he was a six-year-old adult.'

'A malevolent six-year-old adult.'

'His father is a lawyer,' Christy offered.

'Oh,' Sarah said, like that explained everything. And speaking of explanations . . . 'Christy, what in the world made you snap your rubber glove like that and send it flying?'

'I was just trying to get your attention,' Christy said, crossing her arms in front of her.

'You could have hurt somebody,' I said.

But Christy was the one who looked hurt. 'One minute we were talking about my job and the next you were arguing about something. I'm not sure even sure about what.'

Bill Withers' song, Sarah's sense of humor, my passive-aggressiveness – take your pick. So I just settled for, 'I'm sorry, Christy. You know we couldn't be happier that you've found something that you love to do.'

She didn't look so sure. 'Then what was all that about Mr Ashbury's name and marketing and songs and such?'

'Sarah was just,' I glanced at my partner, 'brainstorming.'

In truth, I was feeling ashamed I'd brought up Sarah's bipolarity in front of Christy. Not that my partner made any secret of it. But still, it wasn't my place to talk about it.

Sarah seemed grateful to drop the quarrel as well. 'It's what we do to come up with new ways of marketing the store.'

'Well, then,' Christy said, cocking her head. 'Tell me again. Maybe it's something I could suggest to Mort and impress him.'

Or tick him off. Sarah wouldn't be the first to find the convergence of name and occupation hilarious. 'When you brainstorm, you throw out all sorts of ideas, good and bad. I barely remember what we said, do you, Sarah?'

28

Sarah hesitated and then mumbled, 'Barely.' Breaking up with a good theme song is hard to do.

I turned back to our neighbor. 'But tell us more about this new job. You were saying cremations are done right there at the funeral home? I had no idea.' An understatement.

'Oh, you wouldn't notice anything,' Christy assured me. 'Perhaps a little puff of smoke when the cremator starts up. But there's no smell or black smoke, unless there's some problem with the cremator or the person is . . .' She let it drift off.

But now that I realized the so-called cremator was in my neighborhood, I had to know more. 'Or what?'

Christy squirmed. 'Well, I heard that if the load is very large,' she spread her hands wide, 'it can cause more smoke momentarily—'

'Wait a minute,' Sarah interrupted. 'Load? You mean the body?'

'Yes,' Christy said. 'Apparently if there's a very high percentage of body fat it can cause problems.'

'Oh.' I wasn't sure what else to say.

'That's assuming the retort – that's the chamber inside the cremator – is large enough. At our mortuary, we have—'

I waved surrender. 'No more. But are you sure the mortuary is your' – ugh – 'niche, Christy? You've been amazing, visiting Ronny in jail, which is enough of a challenge. Don't you think you might be pushing your cleanliness boundaries a little too—'

29

'Oh, heavens, Maggy. A crematorium is a picnic,' she seemed to brush an imaginary ant off her arm, 'compared to either county jail or state prison. And cremains – or cremated remains, as Mort prefers we call them – are totally sanitary.'

'Not surprising, after toasting in a thousand-degree furnace,' Sarah said.

'Cremator,' Christy corrected. 'And they get much hotter than that – even twice as hot.'

'So you see my point.' Sarah reached for the chain we'd all but forgotten during our wide-ranging exchange.

I nudged it nearer to her with my foot. 'But surely you're not cleaning out the actual cremator, are you?'

Christy looked pleased at my retention. Me, I was afraid I'd never forget.

'Not yet,' Christy said, putting her hand over her heart. 'I'll consider the process a sacred trust when Mort decides I'm finally ready. It's not just sweeping out the ash and bone frag-ments for packaging, you know. You have to go over them with a magnet to remove metals like surgical screws and such, so the rest can be pulverized, bagged, tagged and given to the family.'

Bagged and tagged. Better and better. 'I'm sure the families are grateful for the attention to . . . detail.'

'What happens to things like gold fillings?' Sarah asked curiously. 'I've always wondered.'

'Gold isn't magnetic, so I think anything left after the cremation would have to be sifted out. The dental gold used for fillings now doesn't have much value, though. Especially after . . . well, you know.'

Now she chooses to mince words?

'The family can also request the teeth be pulled prior to cremation.'

I must have made a noise because Christy turned to me. 'Removing teeth is optional, of course. But things like pacemakers *have* to be removed because they can blow up in the chamber. And I understand silicone implants,' she shivered, 'make a terrible mess.'

I wasn't sure if the shiver was for the implants or the mess. I was betting the latter.

'But the point is,' Christy continued, 'that it's essential the retort be spic and span for the next person.'

Having coiled the chain, Sarah aimed for the box again and this time made it. 'Assuming they're deader than the not-quite-dead guy in Monty Python, why would they care? It's not like they're going to catch something.'

I restrained a grin. The 'bring out your dead' scene from *Monty Python and the Holy Grail* was one of my favorites.

But our Christy seemed less amused. 'It's for the families. The cremated remains mustn't be blended.'

'Like frozen custard,' Sarah said.

First the dry cleaner, now this, God help us.

Visit a 'custard stand' in southeastern Wisconsin and you'll be treated to one of the flavors of the day, scooped just as the rich, egg-based ice cream worms its way out of the machine that churns and freezes it.

31

'Making frozen custard is about as far removed as you can get from cremating bodies, I would think.' Ugh. Double ugh.

'I didn't mean the process itself,' Sarah said. 'Just the idea of cleaning out the chamber for the next person.'

'Or flavor, in keeping with your analogy.' Christy was nodding. 'I worked at a stand and we had to thoroughly flush the frozen custard maker before the next flavor was put in to freeze. After all, who wants leftover Death by Chocolate mixed with their Peach Melba?'

'Or George down the street mixed with Aunt Edith?' Sarah was nodding back.

Before they could descend further into the dead rabbit hole – not to mention ruin the remainder of the flavor of the day list for me forever – I cleared my throat. 'So, Christy, any idea how Clare's Antiques and Floral next door is doing?'

The building was owned by Ronny and had been sitting empty. Now, with Christy in charge, the place had been speedily rehabbed and then leased to Clare Twohig. Probably also through Craigslist.

'The shop is doing well, I think,' Christy said. 'And Clare is ever so clever. Have you seen how she's displayed the coffee and tea services?'

'I have,' I said, hefting the box. 'Using the steps of that wrought-iron staircase is genius. Made me wonder if we shouldn't do some kind of history of coffee with—'

'We're already surrounded by history,' Sarah interrupted. 'The depot dates back to the 1880s, which means nothing to me except that not a day goes by when we don't have to fix something. And now you want to add more old crap?'

The depot with its graceful wraparound deck and vintage ticket windows – now used for serving coffee – was gorgeous and Sarah knew it. She also owned it. In fact, she had been the one who'd suggested re-opening Uncommon Grounds in the depot with herself as my new partner.

It was a package deal and had worked out amazingly well to date. Like any relationship, of course, it required acceptance and respect. I accepted that Sarah was going to be her smart-ass self and she respected my ability to ignore ninety percent of what she said.

Now, balancing the heavy box of tarps on my hip, I opened the shop door. 'There's a difference between old crap and antiques.'

'Yeah, if crap is old enough, it becomes antique. Still old, though, and still—'

The door, blessedly, closed behind me.

Three

Unfortunately, moments later Sarah and Christy opened it again and followed me into Uncommon Grounds.

'Everything all right?' I asked Amy as I set down the box. 'I heard there was an accident.'

'Just a wet chair. All taken care of.' Only Amy could be so perky about a piddle puddle, especially one she'd had to clean up. But that's why we loved her.

She went where neither Sarah nor I dared to go. Consider her our Starship Enterprise.

As the door closed again behind Sarah and Christy, a manicured hand caught it. The tall woman who'd gone running out with the two elderly ladies poked her head in.

Christy clapped her hands. 'Hannah! I was afraid you weren't going to make it.'

The Goddard Gangers, who took up four of our six tables, turned en masse to look as the brown-haired woman stepped in.

'Who's rat?' Gloria Goddard demanded from her wheelchair.

'Rat?' Already seeming on edge from earlier events, Hannah glanced around nervously as the door closed behind her.

Oliver grinned and shook his head. 'Sometimes Mrs G's words don't come out quite right. But you're getting better at the manor, right, Mrs G?'

'Better? Better to die.'

Oliver's face dropped.

'I'm sure she didn't mean that either,' I said.

'My mother gets confused sometimes, too,' Hannah added gently.

He tried to smile and I patted his shoulder. 'Wow, Oliver, you've got guns!'

Now the young man blushed with pleasure while still managing to flex his new bicep muscles. He was wearing a T-shirt on this March day and I had a feeling it was more to show off his arms than beat the heat. 'Can't major in

Exercise and Sports Science without looking the part. Who'd listen to me?'

'Practice what you eat,' Gloria said, patting his cheek.

'You tell him, Gloria,' I said and turned to Hannah. 'You must be Hannah Bouchard. I didn't get a chance to introduce myself earlier. I'm Maggy Thorsen.'

'Oh, Maggy. I'm sorry about what happened. I think Nancy must be getting the flu or something. She was complaining of a headache last night and now it's aches and pains and a scratchy throat. But incontinence has never been a problem before. I suppose a cough or a sneeze might cause her to . . .' Her face was bright red as she trailed off.

I thought we should change the subject. 'I understand you just moved to Brookhills.'

'Yes, with Nancy and my mother, Celeste.'

'Your mother cut quite the figure in that hat.' I skipped past the makeup and suffocating perfume.

A wan smile. 'Mother won't leave the house without being fully decked out and with "her face on."'

'Celeste owned a string of boutiques out east,' Christy told me and then turned to Hannah. 'I'm so sorry I didn't get to meet her today.'

'With Nancy feeling ill, I thought it best to take them both home to rest. It's such an effort to get everybody up and out – I'm afraid we don't do it as much as we should.'

'That's certainly not your fault,' Christy said.

35

'Taking care of both your mother and her friend – you're a saint in my book.'

'What book would that be?' Sarah asked, joining us. 'You're an unbeliever.'

Christy's bottom lip jutted out again. 'I told you, I believe *everything*.'

'And that *I* believe.'

'This is my partner, Sarah Kingston,' I told Hannah.

She smiled a greeting. 'Christy exaggerates. I'm just doing what anybody of good conscience would.'

'Well, aren't we holier than—' Sarah stopped as I elbowed her in the ribs.

'Not at all, I'm afraid,' Hannah said with a patient smile. 'My mother doesn't have anybody else and Nancy is my mother's longtime companion. Almost a second mother to me.'

'Companion? You mean—'

I elbowed Sarah in the ribs a second time. 'Can we make you a drink, Hannah?'

Sarah threw me a dirty look, but the newcomer didn't seem at all put out at my partner's cross-examination. 'I would love a non-fat latte. I didn't get to drink mine earlier.'

'One non-fat latte coming up,' Amy called from behind the counter. 'And it's our treat.'

I sensed Sarah's scowl.

And ignored it. Giving away a drink or two wouldn't kill us. 'Hannah, have you met Amy Caprese?'

'Not formally. Good to meet you, Amy.'

'Hannah bought the house next to Christ Christian.'

'Oh, up that little lane,' Amy said, confirming my hunch that I was the only one who didn't know there was a house there. 'Welcome. Have you met Langdon Shepherd, the pastor of Christ Christian yet? He should be here this morning.'

'He stopped by the house to say hello just after we moved in,' Hannah said. 'Such a nice man. I was sorry to have to tell him I'm Catholic.'

'Not to worry.' Amy twisted the portafilter onto the espresso machine as the sleigh bells on the front door jangled, signaling a new customer. 'Father Jim will be here today, too.'

Langdon was the kind of guy who loved to say that recruiting members was his 'soul mission.' And then spell out s-o-u-l. Father Jim thought that was corny but wouldn't hurt Langdon's feelings by telling him that. The two facts pretty much summed up the respective pitchers in this friendly theological rivalry.

'Oh, good. I have a message for him from Nancy. She— Vickie!'

Vickie LaTour had come in and was looking around expectantly. Her bright burgundy hair was a color that did not appear in nature but she looked remarkably good for her seventy-seven years. It might be worth asking about those 'treatments' she was always talking about.

'Well, look who's here!' Vickie said, giving the younger woman a quick hug. 'Maggy, I assume you've met Hannah? We're so happy to have her – and her ladies, of course – at Angel of Mercy.'

Christy joined us. 'I didn't finish telling you,

Maggy. Vickie took that job I was considering at Angel of Mercy.'

Vickie grinned, though nothing on her face budged but her lips. 'I'm Catholic – we decided it was a better fit.'

I said, 'Christy says you were a student of hers. I had no idea you played the piano.'

'There are many things people don't know,' Vickie said, waving her hand. 'Some of which I'm just fine about keeping hidden. For example, I played the accordion when I was young. But an accordion is just a keyboard attached to a big bag of air, when you think of it. Christy helped me brush up to move on to the piano and organ.'

Sarah, who'd been listening to the goings-on in silence, raised her eyebrows. 'And now, in Christy's new job, she'll be helping even more people move on.' Whistling the *X-Files* theme, Sarah slipped away into the back of the store.

'. . . Think Father Jim will be here,' Vickie was saying to Hannah. 'Do you know if there's anything else I can help with? We were trying to balance the church books but she said trying to find the discrepancy was giving her a headache so we decided to call it a night.'

'Oh, dear. When Nancy sets aside a balance sheet you know she's not feeling well. In fact, she's come down with the flu. I hope you don't get sick.'

'Oh, heavens, don't worry about that,' Vickie said. 'With the people I come into contact with at the manor and the church, I'm constantly being sneezed or coughed on. I have the constitution of a horse.'

I thought I heard a whinny from in the back. Sarah might have snuck away, but not far enough.

'. . . Didn't mention anything,' Hannah said. 'Though she did say I should tell Father Jim in no uncertain terms that he needs to check his messages.'

Vickie laughed. 'I've been telling the man the same thing ever since I took over the office job. After meeting Nancy, I have a feeling she could shape him up in no time if she was able to get out of that house and into the office.'

'She is a force to be reckoned with – or was, when she was managing my mother's chain of boutiques.' Hannah laid her hand on Vickie's shoulder. 'And thank you for coming to the house last night. It's been months since I've been able to go out on a Saturday night. Especially without worrying.' She glanced my way. 'I run errands for an hour or two during the day. But late afternoon into evening are difficult for both my mom and Nancy, so I don't like to leave them alone if I can help it. And since we're new to town . . .' She shrugged.

'Well, I was just happy to help,' Vickie said. 'And even happier to have her help with the books and the committee reports. The least I could do was drive over with what she'd asked for and try to answer any questions she might have.'

'It's good that she has something to occupy her mind,' Hannah said. 'Nancy's as sharp as a tack. Sharper, even, with a tongue to match sometimes. She ran my mother's company *and* my mother, most days.'

Vickie chuckled. 'I saw your mother in the living room last night as I was waiting. I think she was dozing so I didn't say hello, but what a beautiful woman.'

'Even now,' Hannah said a little wistfully.

'And quite the fashionista, too, in her silk evening pajamas. Not a blonde hair out of place.'

'Wigs. She has a half-dozen that she rotates and she'd have more if I let her. They are easy, I must say.'

Vickie patted her own perhaps too thick and certainly too red hair. 'Nothing wrong with wigs or anything else we do to keep ourselves looking good.'

'You know, you should throw one of your make-over parties at our house,' Hannah said. 'Nancy would make fun but Mother would love it.'

Vickie pulled out her cell phone, likely to send out the invitations on the spot. 'Collagen, Botox and maybe makeup?'

'What, no boob jobs?' I was kidding.

'My mother already has better boobs than I have,' Hannah said with a grin. 'Or, at least, newer ones.'

Amy laughed as she set Hannah's latte on the counter. 'Brew of the day, Vickie?'

'Please.'

Hannah moved on to the condiment cart as Amy poured Vickie's coffee and Christy sidled in next to me. 'I can only imagine how tough it is on Hannah. Her mom is failing a bit and Nancy had a stroke last year that limited her mobility. Neither has anybody else to take care of them.'

'Wah, wah, wah. People have strokes or heart attacks every day,' a voice declared from behind Christy. 'Or so it seems at the manor. Last night it was Matilda. Or was it Berte? They all look alike.' Sophie Daystrom blew a curl of gray off her forehead and held out her cup for a refill.

Sophie had moved into Brookhills Manor to be with her paramour, Henry Wested, who already lived there.

'I guess you have to expect that,' Christy said. 'It *is* a senior home.'

'Do you know there's a panic button in each room for emergencies? Even the residential apartments like ours have them, even though we're far from the "Help! I've fallen and I can't get up!" stage of life.'

'Until you do take a fall or something,' Christy reasoned. 'It's not like you have to use the button. It's just there if you need it.'

'They do force some people,' Sophie said. 'They have to flip a switch every morning so the desk knows they aren't dead. Can you believe it?'

'Again, it is a senior—' Christy started.

But Sophie wasn't through grousing. 'God's waiting room is what I call the place.'

Christy tilted her head to one side. 'I thought that was Florida.'

'Old is a state of mind, not a state of the union, is what I tell Henry,' Sophie said, nodding across the room. 'Especially these days when he's going on about his heart.'

I turned to see Henry Wested moving his signature fedora from the next chair to make room

41

for Vickie with her cup of coffee and cell phone. 'I didn't know Henry was having heart problems.'

'Oh, don't you start fussing now,' Sophie said. 'He's doing enough of that for all of us.'

'That's men,' Christy said. 'Ronny had a cold last month and you should have heard him complaining about the quality of the tissues in prison.'

My heart went out to the lunatic. But I was still thinking about Henry. 'What exactly is Henry's heart problem?'

'Oh, just a little angina.'

At least Henry still had a heart. I wasn't so sure about Sophie, given how she was talking. 'Are you and Henry doing OK?'

'*We're* fine. I'm just sick to death of living at the manor. Though I don't say that out loud there in case somebody hears me out of context and delivers it from my lips to God's ears.'

As she said it, the sleigh bells on the door rang and in came Brookhills' pipeline to God, Langdon Shepherd, pastor of Christ Christian Church.

'Over here, Pastor Shepherd,' Vickie trilled, setting down her phone. Langdon was tall, thin and a little stooped – think Ichabod Crane in a church collar. He lifted his hand in greeting to us as he passed on his way to the table.

Sophie signaled with a chin-cock that we should come closer. 'I'm starting to think that there's a wormhole between Brookhills Manor and Langdon's stomping grounds.'

'Christ Christian?' Christy asked.

'Not the church. Heaven and hell, depending

42

on which direction one is heading.' Sophie shrugged. 'I like to think I'd be going up, of course, but let's face it: nobody really knows until it's too late.'

'As in dead.' At least that part I was fairly sure I understood. 'By a wormhole, do you mean like in sci-fi movies? Shortcuts between space and time?'

'Or in this case, between Brookhills Manor and the after-life.'

'You yourself called the manor "God's waiting room,"' I told her.

'True, but it's getting creepy. Somebody falls and breaks a hip or gets a cough and, whoosh, off they go.' She scuttled her fingers across the countertop. 'Hurried off into the light like in that movie.'

'*Ghost Story*?' I guessed.

'That's the one, I—'

'Martha,' Christy interrupted.

We both looked at her.

The former piano teacher's bottom lip was trembling. 'The woman who had the heart attack last night and died – her name was Martha. Not Matilda. And not Berte.'

'And she was a friend of yours?' I asked, concerned.

'No, but people treat the elderly like they're invisible. We're handling the arrangements for Martha Anne Severson. She was ninety-three years old, had three children, ten grandchildren and two great-grandchildren. She deserves to have her name remembered.'

'I didn't mean any disrespect,' Sophie said in

43

her own defense, 'but I can't tell one of the old biddies from another. They all have gray hair, wrinkled skin and flirt with Henry.'

What was this all of a sudden? 'Flirting with Henry? Is that what this is about?'

'You mean am I jealous?'

'Well, yeah.'

Sophie didn't answer the question, at least not directly. 'If we'd moved into my house, instead of Henry convincing me to move in with him, it wouldn't be an issue. Thank God we're in the residential section facing the Poplar Creek woods, which is nice and private.'

'Is that a separate entrance from the nursing home and assisted living?' Christy asked.

Sophie ducked her head. 'Yes, though the new rehab wing shares our entrance. At least people like Gloria are mostly too impaired to go after my Henry.'

Sheesh.

'Are the residential units subsidized by the county?' Christy asked.

'Some of them,' Sophie confirmed. 'Which is one of the reasons why Henry was so adamant about staying there. It's cheap, though there's also the downside.'

'The women?' I asked.

'No. Well, yes,' Sophie said, 'that does bug me. There must be a dozen females for every male there. Feels more like a harem than a home, with Henry one of the only sheiks still standing. And technically he's single, so they figure he's fair game.'

'Have you ever discussed getting married?' Why

44

was I, of all people, asking? I was having enough trouble sorting out my own affairs.

'I have.' A flush crept up her cheeks.

'But Henry . . .?'

'Thinks things are just fine the way they are, thank you very much,' Sophie finished for me.

I felt my own face get warm. 'Just because he doesn't want to get married doesn't mean he doesn't love you.'

'You wouldn't know it by the way he preens under a little female attention.' She was trying to get Amy's attention.

An ill-timed laugh from Henry in response to something Vickie had said punctuated the point.

'But you were saying the downside of the residential facility isn't the male-to-female ratio?' I asked.

'Probably more the junkie-to-senior ratio,' Christy said.

While I appreciated the former piano teacher abetting my attempted change of subject to get poor Henry off the hook, once again I wasn't sure what she was talking about. 'Junkie?'

'"Recovering."' Sophie made air quotes. 'They have to let them in because, like I said, the county provides subsidies for the manor's residential units and finding housing for the addicts in the rehabilitation program is part of their mission. But before long, recovering turns into relapsed and they have to be evicted. And don't get me started on the outright criminals like the guy next door to us.'

'How do you know he's a criminal?' I asked.

45

'Because he freely admits serving time like it's some kind of badge of honor that he's come out the other side.'

'It is, in a way,' Christy said. 'Assuming he's now leading a productive life.'

'More reproductive, if you ask me.' Sophie was building a low burn. 'The man is nothing special but can certainly turn on the charm when he wants to. Has women over there practically every night. And don't think we can't hear every moan, groan and butt slap through the cardboard they call walls there.'

Lovely.

'No doubt those prison groupies,' Sophie continued. 'Never understood why women fixate on those lowlifes. Write them letters in prison, visit—' She broke off as she seemed to realize there was a groupie in our very midst.

But Christy was rocking forward on the balls of her feet. 'Oh, Sophie, you're so right. Like when I visit Ronny.'

Sophie and I glanced at each other. 'Oh?'

It seemed a safe response given that we didn't know where Christy was going to take this.

'Oh, yes. Ronny's cellmate is a serial killer and you wouldn't believe how much mail he gets. And the visits.'

Ronny was no angel, but, 'A serial killer? Last time I heard, his roomie was a drug dealer or something.'

'That one got shivved,' Christy said, waving it off. 'This one's a much better fit.'

'Like, how?' I couldn't help myself.

'Well, you know how creative Ronny is. Remember how when we met him he was dressing to celebrate a different era each day of the week? Greaser Tuesdays, Disco Wednesdays?'

How could I forget? Earlier this year, Ronny's Elvis Sunday had nearly put a permanent end to my week.

'He does that in prison, too?' Sophie seemed fascinated now, too.

'Not quite to that extent. Prisoners have to wear their jumpsuits, you know, so creativity is limited. But Ronny likes to do small things that signal the era. Like wearing his jumpsuit collar up for the nineties or wearing a work glove on one hand for the Michael Jackson look. Other inmates get a kick out of it and have started helping. Especially Lionel, the serial killer. He loves to sew, believe it or not.'

'All that practice making lampshades,' I said without thinking.

'Lampshades?' Christy asked. 'Isn't that what Jeffrey Dahmer did?'

'No, he ate people,' Sophie said. 'Maggy is talking about Ed Gein, a Wisconsin serial killer back in the fifties. He—'

'But please,' I interrupted politely. 'Tell us more about your serial killer, Christy.'

Pink rose in Christy's cheeks. 'He's not mine. Or Ronny's. And I probably shouldn't call him a serial killer. They've only found two bodies so far.'

I cleared my throat. 'How does a guy like this get hold of needles?'

Christy looked blank.

'For sewing,' I explained, since needles might have other connotations, especially in prison. 'Needles and thread for alterations?'

'Honestly, I don't know,' Christy said, eyes wide. 'But the prison population is amazingly creative. Ronny says—'

Time to turn the conversation away from Ronny & Company and back to semi-sanity.

'Interesting,' I said in response to whatever Christy had just finished saying. 'Speaking of prisoners, Sophie, your neighbor – the one with the noisy sex. Is he older?'

'Older than who exactly?' Sophie seemed offended. Or prepared to be offended. 'Are you insinuating people our age don't have noisy sex?'

'I was just asking if the guy next door is a senior.' I could dodge a question, too. 'He's living in a senior facility, after all.'

'So what? You think crooks just stop being crooks when they get old?'

I guess I kind of did. Or maybe that they were in jail or dead by the time they reached their golden years. Hard to live to a ripe old age when you're addicted to cocaine or robbing banks, I would think. But then, what did I know?

'. . . In his seventies, though I'm betting he's had work,' Sophie was saying.

'Ooooh,' Christy squealed. 'Maybe to hide his identity, like in *Face/Off*.'

'Wasn't that a whole face transplant?' Sophie said.

'To change John Travolta into Nicholas Cage and vice versa?' I said. 'It would have to be.'

48

'I assume this was a little tucking and lifting,' Sophie said. 'But who knows what the guy is into?'

'So exciting.' Christy was fanning herself with her hand, like she was going to pass out.

'Hopefully not for long,' Sophie said dryly. 'There have been strange men hanging around. Henry thinks they're cops but I'm betting it's mobsters out to whack him. If they do it next Tuesday, I'll win the pool.'

Wait. 'You have a betting pool on the date your neighbor dies? Like people do on the score of a football game?'

'Of course not.'

A relief.

Until Sophie opened her mouth again. 'We're not singling him out. We have pools for everybody. It's the only group activity I participate in at the manor. Sure beats trips to the Mitchell Park Domes like today's big adventure.'

For my part, I thought the horticultural center was charming. And 'sure beat' placing bets on when people are going to die.

'Don't be looking at me like that,' Sophie said. 'Everybody who bets knows that they're also being bet *upon*.'

I was having a 'soylent green is people' moment.

'It's the only fun we have in that place,' Sophie grumbled. 'And now you're making it sound dirty.'

Excuse me for not being a ghoul.

49

Four

Speaking of ghouls, Brookhills' aspiring ash-sweeper seemed to be on a conversational trajectory of her own.

'. . . Right to prohibit discrimination against somebody like your neighbor, Sophie,' Christy was saying. 'There are very strict guidelines so long as he meets the age requirement.'

Understandable, given the public funding. Still, it was worrisome to think of grandma and grandpa living out their golden years next to Larry the Torch or Danny the Corner Drug Dealer.

'I had no idea such a thing was possible when I moved in,' Sophie said. 'And Henry didn't think it was a big enough deal to tell me. Everybody deserves a second chance, according to him.'

'Amen to that,' Christy said fervently. 'Wouldn't it be awful if, when Ronny gets out, there was no place for him to go?'

Sophie raised her eyebrows. 'I assumed he'll be living at your house. I mean, you did sell his, after all.'

Christy flushed. 'Well, of course. I was speaking hypothetically, of course.'

From the look on Christy's face, I had a feeling that, as romantic as she imagined her relationship with Ronny was while he was in the slammer, she hadn't given much thought to his appearing at her tidy little doorstep in ten to twenty.

But Sophie was still grousing about *her* love. 'Go-along to get-along – that's what Henry does. We had a meeting the other day about the rates on the assisted living and nursing home wings of Brookhills Manor, and you think he'd speak up about the increases? By the time we need care we won't be able to afford it, and it'll serve him right.'

'What *does it* cost?' Christy asked. 'If you don't mind my asking.'

I wasn't sure it was a deliberate change of subject, but I was grateful. It's hard when mom and dad fight. Even if they're not *your* mom and dad.

'Nearly five grand a month,' Sophie said. 'And that's assisted living, not full nursing care. The new memory unit for Alzheimer's and dementia is going to be seven thousand a month, I hear.'

Christy glanced toward the table where Hannah had joined Langdon, Henry and Vickie. 'I suggested that Hannah consider the manor should the time come when she can't take care of the ladies anymore.'

'A retirement fund or savings would go fast at that rate,' I said. 'Are the fees covered by insurance?'

'Or the government?' Christy added.

'Government?' Sophie snorted. 'Not for what they call long-term care. That kicks in right around the time you're knock, knock, knocking on heaven's door.'

Christy cocked her head like a puppy. 'Isn't that a song?'

'Bob Dylan,' I said.

'You *are* an old soul, Maggy.' Sophie was nodding her approval. 'The man is in his seventies now – more my generation than yours.'

She had a point, though I couldn't think of Dylan that way. 'He's an icon, and icons are ageless.'

'Unlike the people at the manor.' Sophie wasn't going to let it go.

'Baggy?'

The word – though semi-recognizable as my name – was slurred. Gloria was holding up her cup shakily, Oliver grinning proudly next to her.

I went over and took the cup. 'The same, Mrs G?'

A head waggle, with an emphatic, 'Unleaded.'

I laughed. This wasn't a slip of the stroke-impaired tongue – unleaded had been Mrs G's term for decaf at the lunch counter. 'One unleaded coming right up.'

One half of her mouth curved into a smile as she turned back to Oliver and Mort.

'So, tell me who this woman is,' Sophie said as I handed the cup to Amy to fill.

'You don't know Gloria Goddard?'

'No, I've been living in a hole the last fifty-some years,' the octogenarian said testily. 'Of course I know Gloria. I mean the woman you two were talking to when I came in. She's sitting at the table with Henry and Vickie now.'

'That's the Hannah I was talking about,' Christy answered. 'Hannah Bouchard. She bought Ronny's house.'

'I saw you had it listed on Craigslist,' Sophie

said. 'Too big and too expensive for the likes of us.'

'You're really serious about moving?' I asked.

'Hell, yes. If Vickie's smart she'll start looking for a place, too, before the manor finishes sucking her dry. The woman has an efficiency apartment the size of a postage stamp two doors down from us and even that is costing her a fortune. If I'd thought more, maybe we could have bought the Eisvogel place together.'

I hadn't realized that Vickie lived at Brookhills Manor. Somehow she seemed too young, in spite of her seventy-seven years, but maybe that was the Botox and collagen doing their jobs. Or their purported jobs. 'You trust Vickie around Henry?' I asked.

'Hell, yeah. They've known each other for years and Henry's not remotely interested. Says Vickie's way too high maintenance.' She nodded toward the table where Langdon Shepherd was now laughing at something Vickie had said. 'Besides, she's had something going on with somebody for the last few months. I'm just not sure who.'

Which was likely killing her, if I knew Sophie. 'Are you thinking she and Langdon might be involved?'

'It has crossed my mind,' Sophie admitted. 'For some reason, she's being very closemouthed about it.'

'Vickie is working at Angel of Mercy now, you know.' I took Gloria's now-full cup carefully from Amy.

'This I do know,' Sophie said. 'I assume you have a point?'

53

I wondered if Sophie was getting sarcasm lessons from Sarah. Or vice versa. 'Just that if Vickie is dating Langdon while she's working at Angel of Mercy it could be awkward. Maybe that's why she's keeping it quiet.'

'I doubt that Father Jim would care,' Christy said. 'It's not like she's dating a priest or a married man or something.'

Like a convicted killer, for example. But I kept my mouth shut and went to deliver Gloria's refill.

'. . . By a difference in religion in this day and age,' Sophie was saying when I came back.

'It could be Langdon who doesn't want it made public,' Christy said. 'The ladies in the altar guild are wild about him. I wouldn't put it past half of them to quit if he started seeing somebody romantically. And then who would do the work?'

'The men, maybe?' Sophie suggested. 'But getting back to Vickie, she went off on a cruise two weeks ago and I'm certain it was with him, whoever it is.'

'I wouldn't be caught dead on a cruise. All those people and germs in a combined space.' Christy brightened. 'Though they do have those hand-sanitizer dispensers everywhere.'

Always an antibacterial lining somewhere for our little germaphobe.

'Cruises aren't my cup of tea either,' Sophie admitted. 'But Vickie came back glowing. Spouting all this nonsense about retiring on a cruise ship and seeing the world.'

'You mean living on a ship year-round?' I asked. 'Wouldn't that be awfully expensive? I thought you said the manor was already bleeding her dry.'

'You know, I've heard of this,' Christy said. 'Supposedly it's not that much more than the cost of assisted living. There are things to do, a doctor onboard if you get sick and your food is free – all you can eat, twenty-four hours a day.'

'Yeah, and who pays for the crane that has to lift you out of the room once you hit 400 pounds?' Sophie asked.

'But think of it,' Christy persisted. 'It would be like a floating senior home.'

Sophie snorted. 'Bad enough living in one on dry land. At least I can jump ship when I need a break away from all the old coots. And what happens when somebody dies? They throw them overboard?' Her eyes brightened at the thought.

'You're living among a different demographic than you were before – an older demographic,' I pointed out. 'And let's face it. Eventually we all die.'

'Spoken like somebody who *thinks* she's decades away from death,' Sophie said. 'And can I please get a refill here?'

She shoved her still-empty cup across the counter and Amy just about caught it with a bemused grin.

'Temper, temper,' a voice behind me said. 'Anybody need absolution? We have a Sunday special.'

I turned and saw Father Jim, whose entrance must have been covered by Sophie's whining. 'Sunday services are over already?'

'Father George took the ten o'clock,' Jim said,

55

moving up the counter. 'Which any of you sinners would know if you came to church.'

'Ahem.' Mort was raising his hand. 'You'll recall I was at the eight.'

'Indeed you were, Morton, and a fine tenor you were in the choir as well.'

Christy giggled. 'I love it when you speak Irish priest.'

'Don't encourage the faker,' I said. Jim and I had dated in high school, way back when. We'd been better friends than sweethearts, and I'd never had the nerve to ask him if the lack of electricity in our relationship had anything to do with him going priest.

'Ah, but the parish expects a Father Jim to be Irish, don't you know.' He wasn't going to stop.

'Despite the fact your family came from Eastern Europe. Romania, right?'

'Hungary, and thank you for remembering.' Jim was about six inches shorter than Langdon but had twice the energy and probably ten times the sense of humor. I was surprised people weren't converting in droves. 'How's the family back in Switzerland?'

'Norway.' Which he knew, of course.

'Oh, Father Jim,' Christy was digging in her purse and came up with a stack of leaflets. 'Vickie said to ask you if it's OK to put these in the bulletin.'

Jim took one. 'Buy-one-get-one-free cremations?'

Christy giggled again. 'No, it's just a reprint of the story on Mort that the *Observer* wrote.'

'I do appreciate the soft sell,' Jim said. 'Tell you what, it wouldn't be appropriate to go in

56

the church bulletin but I'll put it on the bulletin board.'

'That would be wonderful,' Christy chirped breathlessly. Maybe the omnist would be one of the converted. If you were in the market for an untouchable man, a priest was even better than a prisoner.

'Done,' Jim said, slipping the paper into his inside jacket pocket. 'Now, I didn't mean to interrupt. Sophie, you were threatening Maggy with death, I believe?'

Having gotten her coffee, Sophie seemed to have settled down. 'No, just telling her she had no idea what it is like to be surrounded by people who have one foot in the grave.'

'Or the cremation urn, should you choose that option. Would you like some of the leaflets to take back to the manor?' Christy was a dog who wasn't going to drop this stick. 'Or some of my business cards?'

I held up my hand as she slipped her purse off her shoulder again.

She stopped, hand in the bag, and looked up at me. 'Bad form, you think?'

'I think.'

She straightened up. 'Thank you. Sometimes I get carried away with my own enthusiasm.'

'Entirely understandable,' Sophie said, throwing me an 'is she crazy or what' look as she went to join Henry and company. Christy followed.

'Hello, Father Jim.'

'Good morning, Hannah,' Jim said, turning to greet our new neighbor. 'And how are you this fine morning? And you brought the lovely Celeste and Nancy, I understand?'

He just wasn't going to give up the brogue.

'That was the plan, but I'm afraid I had to take them home,' she said. 'Nancy's not feeling well today – coming down with the flu, she thinks. But the truth is that both she and my mother would rather stay at home with a good book or TV show anyway.'

'It's good of you to try to get them out. But I'm sorry to hear Nancy is under the weather. Would you like me stop in?'

'I'm afraid a visit from the priest would mean one thing to them.'

'Last rites,' I said, a shiver going up my spine. 'My grandmother was the same way.'

'I know it's silly,' Hannah said, nodding. 'But Mother was never a churchgoer, which is perhaps why I am.'

'We do sometimes go the opposite way of our parents,' Jim said, 'but whether we see them in church or not, we'll say a prayer. Nancy has been a godsend, virtually taking over as finance chair when Fred was taken.' He crossed himself.

'Wait. Fred Lopez died?' I didn't think I'd heard right. The man couldn't be more than fifty and he was a pillar of our banking community.

'Deported.' Vickie had an empty cup in her hand. 'And an awful shame, if you ask—'

Father Jim held up his own hand. 'A battle we've already fought and lost, sadly. I'm just glad that Nancy was willing to fill his shoes.'

'Did Hannah tell you that Nancy asked that you

check your email?' Vickie said in an I-told-you-so tone.

'Shame on me,' Hannah said. 'I came up to give you that message and it just went out of my head.'

'She's likely sent the report for this afternoon's meeting,' Jim said, pulling out his phone. 'It amazes me how technologically savvy Nancy is. Although that's true of a lot of our older parishioners these days.'

'I think Nancy prefers computers to people. She says she's sat through enough meetings for one lifetime.'

Jim was scrolling through his mail. 'I don't see anything new here. 'Do you know when she sent it?'

'I don't, but I can call the house. I wanted to check on them anyway.'

As Hannah turned away, Vickie put her cup in the dirty dish bin. 'If you forward the report to me as soon as you have it, Father, I can print and copy it for the members.'

'Hopefully you'll have time,' Jim said, and then broke off. 'Hannah, are you leaving?'

Our new neighbor turned, one hand on the door and a puzzled look on her face. 'Yes. Nancy's not answering the phone.'

'Maybe they're both lying down,' Vickie said. 'Or in the bathroom.'

'I'm sure it's fine, but . . .'

The door closed behind her.

Five

Uncommon Grounds closed at three on Sundays, so I'd invited Pavlik over for a late afternoon barbecue. When I got home a little before four, he was sitting on my porch steps, throwing the tennis ball for Frank.

Or faux throwing it. One of the sheriff's greatest joys was duping my poor sheepdog by sending him out for a long one: 'Are you ready? Are you ready? Huh? Huh?' And then palming the ball even as he pretended to toss it.

Frank, impeded by both the hair in his face and the trust in his heart, bounded blithely away and turned for the pass. Another arm chug from Pavlik would send the sheepdog first this way and then that, before the human – if not the adult – finally let the ball fly for real.

'Torturing my dog again?' I asked as Frank dove under the bushes for the ball.

Pavlik laughed and stood up, wiping his hands on his jeans. 'Frank loves it. Besides, he's a big dog living in a small house. He can use the exercise.'

'And you can use the laughs.' As Frank came running back to his tormenter, I intercepted him and grabbed the ball, intending to toss it properly for him. Instead, I dropped it. Predictably already slimy with dog drool, the trip under the bushes had added mud to the mix. 'Ugh.'

'You're right that I can always use a laugh, and I want to thank you for that one.' The sheriff leaned down to kiss me.

Pavlik has dark hair he wears just a little long so it curls over his collar. Today he was wearing a blue dress shirt, sleeves rolled up, and jeans. A soft brown leather jacket was draped over a Schultz's Market bag on the top porch step.

Despite my non-answer to the sheriff's marriage proposal, things hadn't cooled down on either side. In fact, if anything they were hotter. As if we were clinging to each other on a cliff, not knowing quite where our next move might take us.

'Did you bring the steaks?' I asked a little breathlessly as I slid my hand down to his very nice butt.

'I did,' he said into my ear. 'And don't think I'm unaware of the fact you're surreptitiously rubbing Frank slime onto my jeans.'

Hearing his name, Frank looked up from where he'd been nuzzling the dirt ball on the sidewalk. Even he seemed loath to pick it up, though given his hand was his mouth, that was doubly understandable.

'Blame him,' I said, indicating Pavlik. 'He's the one who threw it under the bush.'

Frank's tail waved.

'He loves me,' Pavlik said. 'I can do no wrong in his eyes.'

I lifted the jacket and moved the bag aside before settling down next to him, jacket over my lap. 'Nor mine. What a beautiful day.' I ran my hand over the buttery leather of the jacket and sighed.

Pavlik took the thing away from me and hung it over the porch railing. 'If you're going to fondle anything, fondle me.'

'Gladly.' I slid closer to him, laying my head on his shoulder and my hand on his thigh. 'I do love your jacket, but I love you . . .' I stopped.

'More?' Pavlik cranked his head around and down so he could see may face. 'Why are you afraid to say it?'

'I'm not.' I sat up and met his eyes. 'But it's kind of a . . . door.' I'd almost said Pandora's box. 'Once it's opened it leads to a whole lot of other doors.'

'Like marriage?'

'For one.' I laid my hand on his cheek. 'I do love you. I think you know that.'

He put his hand over mine. 'But?'

'But I feel like I've just now gotten my feet under me after the divorce. You know, so I can stand up on my own.'

'And you don't want to give up your independence.' Pavlik's eyes were a cloudy gray as they bored into mine. If he was trying to figure me out, good luck. I was as confused as he was.

'I don't know if that's it. I don't think so. But I do know I don't want to lose you.' I kissed his lips lightly.

After a moment, they responded and then got more forceful.

I was pressed back onto the steps and Pavlik's hand was up under my shirt when the sound of toenails up the steps was followed by a *bounce/plotch, bounce/plotch.*

62

A muddy tennis ball landed on my bare belly where the shirt was hiked up.

I jumped up. 'Oh, God, Frank. You have the worst timing.'

Pavlik was laughing as he stood. 'They do have a way of worming their way in, don't they? Muffin's the same.'

The sheriff had adopted a toothless pit bull rescued from a dog-fighting ring they'd raided when he was on the job in Chicago. Not fit for fighting, the pit pup was kept for breeding purposes. It was probably the only reason she was alive. That and Pavlik.

'How's Muffin doing?' I was holding up my shirt so it wouldn't touch the muddy sludge on my stomach.

'Not good,' Pavlik said, his eyes darkening. 'She's fourteen and feeling her age. Sleeps a lot and when she's awake she's not herself. I've taken her to the vet but he says it's just age. And what she went through before I got her. He doesn't think it'll be long.'

I let my shirt fall. Much as I complained some-times about Frank, he had been a lifeline after the divorce and, from what little Pavlik had said about his own split, I knew it had been the same for him. 'You gave Muffin thirteen happy years – time she'd never have had if you hadn't taken her home that day.'

'I know.' There was a trace of moisture in his eyes, something I'd never seen before. 'It's just hard saying goodbye. Or maybe knowing when to say goodbye.'

'Is she in pain?'

'Not that I can tell, which is why I haven't wanted to . . .' He let it trail off.

I laid my hand on his arm. 'Is she all right by herself? We could go get her and she could have steak with us.'

'That's nice.' Pavlik kissed me on the forehead. 'But Tracey insisted on taking her home this past weekend. Susan's not working, so there'll be somebody at home if something happens.'

Tracey was Pavlik's twelve-year-old daughter with his ex-wife, Susan. After the divorce in Chicago, Susan had moved to Southeastern Wisconsin for a job opportunity and Pavlik had followed, wanting to stay close to his daughter. As luck would have it, Susan's job hadn't panned out and she'd moved them back to Chicago. Pavlik, already in his own newly elected role as Brookhills County Sheriff, had stayed.

I hoped I'd been at least partly responsible for that decision. 'Muffin was well enough for the drive down to Chicago?'

Pavlik looked surprised. 'They're back in Milwaukee – I didn't tell you that?'

Not likely I'd forget, especially since Pavlik and I had just gone through a traumatic – if short-lived – break-up. My suspicious nature would have glommed on to Susan's return as the possible cause. Not that I'd so much as met the woman to assess the threat level. I kept my voice casual. 'No, when did that happen?'

'I found out just before we left for Florida, though at the time I didn't know why. I was too ticked at Susan for bouncing Tracey back and forth like this to ask. The one saving grace is at least now they'll have to stay put.'

'Susan's taken a job here?' For the life of me, I couldn't remember what the woman did.

'More like taken a husband with a job here.' Pavlik snagged his jacket and flipped it up over his shoulder before picking up the grocery bag.

Now I was certain Pavlik hadn't told me any of this. 'Susan's getting re-married. Are you all right with that?'

'Sure, why wouldn't I be?' He'd pulled open the screen door to the house and now he turned back. 'I'm happy for her.'

That's what all we divorced folk say. Well, except for me, who'd been slightly less accepting when my dentist husband had announced he'd been drilling his hygienist and was leaving me to marry her. All pretty much in the same breath.

But it had been a lot to digest in a short amount of time.

Kind of like when Pavlik did a 180 – or a full 360, really – first dumping me and then asking me to marry him all within forty-eight hours, which made me wonder if there was a connection. 'So, Susan moved back and then broke the news?'

'What news?' He continued into the house.

'That she's getting' – I caught the screen door just before it could slap me in the face – 'married.'

'Oh, that. The wedding invitation with a plus-one was in the mail when I got back.' He slipped the jacket over the door knob of the front closet.

'Ouch, that's cold.'

He shrugged. 'Like I said, I didn't give her much of a chance when she called to say they were back. I was on the way to pick you up for the airport.'

'What about Tracey?' I asked, following him and the groceries into the kitchen.

'I think Susan wanted to tell me herself.'

By way of an impersonal wedding invitation. 'I mean, how does she feel about the guy her mother is marrying?'

I hadn't told Eric about Pavlik's proposal, not because he'd object but because he'd push me to accept. I mean, the kid loved his dad but Pavlik treated Eric like an equal and an adult. Plus, he had a gun and a badge. How do you say no to that? And yet . . .

'. . . Says he's nice enough,' Pavlik was saying.

'Sounds like what Eric said about Rachel.'

'He was wrong on that score.' Pavlik should know, since he'd put Rachel away.

'Yes, as it turns out.' I got a bottle of red wine out of the cupboard, along with two wine glasses.

Pavlik was unloading a butcher-wrapped packet of meat and a bakery box that had a smudge of chocolate on the side.

The perfect man. Why was I even hesitating?

A buzz, and the sheriff reached into his jeans pocket for his phone. He read the message and slipped it back. 'I'm sorry.'

'You have to go?' Log that under 'dumb question.'

'A guy we've been looking for just turned up at his brother's place. Time to go smoke him out, much as I'd rather spend the afternoon with you looking smoking hot.' He pulled me toward him and kissed the top of my head before letting go to retrieve his jacket.

'Be careful,' I said as he slipped it on.

He raised his eyebrows. 'Don't want me to rip the jacket?'

In truth, I wasn't sure why I said it. 'You got it.'

'I know that I have,' he said, taking me in my arms. 'But it's you that I want.'

With that, the sheriff let me go and bounded down the porch steps.

Six

'His ex-wife moves back to get married and his dog is dying,' I told Sarah as we cleaned up from the next morning's commuter rush. 'I think there's a connection.'

Sarah scooped beans from the container labeled Kenyan AA into the grinder, spun the dial to 'drip' and pushed the 'on' button. 'Please don't tell me you think the ex-wife is poisoning the dog.'

'Why would I think that?' I shoved a plastic bucket under the chute just as the freshly ground coffee started to spill out.

'You said they're connected,' she said, repositioning it.

With effort, I ignored the grounds now glancing off the edge of the container and onto the counter.

'I didn't mean that Muffin's failing health and Susan's marriage are connected. Though her moving back here and the wedding certainly are. I was talking about Pavlik's proposal.'

'You can grind coffee yet you can't form a coherent sentence.'

'You're grinding the coffee,' I pointed out. 'And making a mess of it, I might add.'

'Done,' she said, turning off the grinder. 'Now explain yourself.'

'It's not hard to understand,' I said. 'Pavlik's feeling alone. Besides needing a plus-one for the wedding.'

'He doesn't have to marry you to take you to a wedding unless it's his,' Sarah said. 'I assume you're going to watch the ex get safely hitched?'

'Wouldn't miss it. I've only met his daughter Tracey once and never even laid eyes on Susan.'

'Time to meet the family, huh? Wonder how he'll introduce you. I'm betting it won't be as his plus-one.'

I thought about that as I swept the remaining spilled coffee grounds from the counter and into my hand. 'Good point.'

'If you're nice, you'll let him say "fiancée,"' Sarah said, holding out the waste basket.

I deposited the grounds and clapped my hands above it. 'I'm not sure that's being nice. I don't want to mislead anybody, especially Pavlik.'

'What is *wrong* with you?' She returned the basket to its place under the sink.

'I ask myself pretty much every day. But in this case, I assume you mean why won't I marry Pavlik?'

'You care about him, right?'

'Of course I do. I even told him I loved him yesterday.'

Sarah turned, astonishment on her face. But not for the reason I'd expected. 'You've been together for what – two years? That's the first time you've used the "L" word?'

'In my defense, he only said it for the first time in November. And that was when he was breaking up with me. And then, again, when he asked me to marry him.'

Sarah didn't seem to think it was important. 'So you said you loved him and . . .?'

'No "and." More of a "but."'

'Figures. "But" what?'

'But I still wasn't sure about marriage. That I'd just gotten—'

The sound of sleigh bells interrupted both my lame explanation and whatever Sarah would have said to counter it. Christy burst in. 'Did you hear? Hannah's mother died.'

'Oh, no,' I said. 'I'm so sorry. When?'

'Yesterday morning, after Hannah brought them both home. I guess Celeste was watching television on the couch and fell asleep. Or at least that's what Nancy thought until she tried to rouse her and couldn't.'

'Is that why nobody picked up when Hannah called home?'

'I guess Nancy was so shook up that she couldn't find the phone to call for help. The poor woman was nearly hysterical by the time Hannah walked in the door.'

'Are – or were – Nancy and Celeste a couple?'

Sarah asked. 'I started to ask but Maggy thought it was rude.'

As if that ever stopped her. An elbow to the ribs had been effective, though, as I recalled. 'I just don't think it's anybody's business, one way or the other.'

'You *know* I'm not judging, Maggy,' Sarah said. 'I was just curious.'

It was true. Both that Sarah wouldn't judge and that she was curious – aka nosy.

'Hannah refers to them as "partners,"' Christy said, 'though whether she means partners in the boutiques or domestic partners, I don't know. I believe they kept separate finances, in any case.'

'However would you know that?' And I thought Sarah was up in everybody's business.

'The purchase of the house was in just Celeste's name, for one thing. And when Hannah and I were talking about what she'd do if she couldn't care for Celeste or Nancy anymore, she said her mother has plenty of money but that Nancy's social security wouldn't go very far.'

'You'd think if they were life partners it would have been share and share alike.' By which I meant Celeste wouldn't let Nancy die destitute while she had private care or checked into the country club of nursing homes. Or maybe a cruise ship, a la Vickie.

'Exactly. But whatever the relationship, it was deep. Hannah says Nancy is absolutely devastated. That's what happens to committed partners, you know – one dies and the other's life light is dimmed. I know that's the way it would be for Ronny and me.' She put her hand over where her life light presumably was.

'Sounds to me like Hannah is the one whose light should be dimmed,' Sarah said. 'She should have never come back here after the old lady got sick.'

'Nancy told Hannah she was fine, just coming down with the flu, and encouraged her to come back,' Christy said. 'And, besides, Nancy's not the one who died.'

'Give the woman a break, Sarah,' I said. 'She couldn't have known.'

'Hannah doesn't like to talk about it,' Christy said, 'but I understand it's been a long haul since her mother started failing.'

'She did tell Oliver that Celeste got confused sometimes,' I said, 'like Gloria.'

'She wasn't even at the closing – the attorney had to sign the documents for her.'

At the mention of the closing she hadn't taken part in, Sarah's expression darkened further. 'Even more reason her daughter should have stayed home with her.'

Empathy is not one of my partner's strong points.

'That's not fair,' Christy said indignantly. 'Hannah takes – took – care of her mother and Nancy all day, every day. One time she runs out to get a cup of coffee—'

'And an old lady dies,' Sarah said.

'Get up on the wrong side of the bed this morning?' I asked.

'At least I got up,' Sarah said, turning. 'Which is more than I can say for Hannah's mother.'

71

'My goodness,' Christy said as she watched Sarah disappear into the back room. 'What does Sarah have against Hannah?'

'She's nice and people like her?' Not to mention she didn't need a real-estate agent for a house sale and purchase. Which meant Christy should watch out, too.

'You mean Sarah's jealous? But she certainly shouldn't be. People like her, too.' She thought for a second before adding, 'Mostly.'

Not being able to add to that, I just shrugged.

'It's true, though, that the people who bluster the most are the ones who are insecure. I'll have to keep that in mind when I'm dealing with Sarah, poor thing.'

Christy would be the 'poor thing' if Sarah got a whiff of pity off her. Compassion and under-standing ticked my partner off, too.

'Can I get you something?' I asked Christy.

'The brew of the day would be lovely but I'll take it in a to-go cup,' Christy said. 'I want to be at the mortuary for Celeste.'

'That's kind of you,' I said, lifting a pot to pour her coffee.

'Well, to be fair, it's my job.' Christy was slip-ping bills out of her wallet. 'But if I can help, I'd like to do that. Now that Hannah and Mort are dating—'

'They are? I don't remember them so much as speaking to each other yesterday.' Not to mention that Mort had to be nearly twenty years older than Hannah.

'It's new, so I think they're keeping it on the cutie.'

Cutie. 'The QT, you mean?'

Christy frowned. 'It's not cutie? Like isn't that cute?'

'No, just the initials Q and T. Short for "quiet."'

'Really?' Christy's face was puzzled. 'Why not just Q? I mean, if you're going to use the first and the last letter, why skip the three in the middle? Besides, QT is two syllables, so it's just as easy to say "quiet." That's two syllables, too.'

'I . . . well, I don't know.'

'No matter.' Christy seemed satisfied she'd stymied me. 'I introduced Hannah to Mort the day she moved in and thank the Lord. Not only did she tell me the position was open at the mortuary, but he was the first person she called when she found Celeste dead.'

I had no idea what you do if somebody just ups and dies a natural death. Most of my bodies met an untimely – and *un*natural – end.

'Mort notified the doctor,' Christy continued, 'and then arranged to move Celeste to the mortuary, before Nancy could get even more upset.'

'I'm not sure how I'd feel about dating a mortician.' I hadn't really meant to say it aloud, but there it was.

Christy cocked her head, not so much in the 'I don't understand' way, as the 'I'm ready for a fight and waiting for you to make the first move' way. 'What do you mean?'

Trying to suppress the 'yuck' factor, I said, 'I know that Pavlik deals with death on a daily basis, too. And you can add violence and criminals to that as well. It's just that I hope Celeste's death won't . . . shadow their relationship.' Lame, but heartfelt. Kind of.

Christy was shaking her head. 'Oh, no, I think trying times make couples stronger. Look at Ronny and me.'

Brrr. Nope, not going there. 'Well, I'm glad Hannah has Mort to lean on and help her through.'

'Even if she didn't, we have trained counselors on our staff.' Christy had her business hat on again. It was black and somber. 'Both for the emotional and business sides of death.'

'Business?' I repeated, handing her the change from her coffee.

'Of course,' Christy said solemnly. 'It's bad enough to lose somebody, but then there are all the notifications that have to be made. Not just to friends and family but to government agencies, utilities, charge card companies, credit agencies and the like. And then there's the estate and trusts and taxes. We provide checklists for the bereaved, detailing each step from death notices to estate settlement, complete with a directory of professionals who can help.'

And likely are paid for the privilege of being listed in that directory. Funeral homes were businesses, too, despite what Christy might like to think. And I was willing to bet that a mortuary business had a whole lot healthier profit margin than a coffeehouse did.

Though we arguably had more repeat business.

'Oh, dear,' Christy said, glancing up at the clock. 'I've been jabbering here and now I'm going to be late for our ten o'clock.'

'Sorry,' I said. 'If I'd known that was when you were meeting Hannah, I'd have reminded you. Please tell her how sorry I am for her loss.'

Christy was dropping loose coins into her purse. 'Hannah won't be there until later this afternoon to meet with Mort.'

It's like the woman's driving force was to keep me in a constant state of confusion. 'But you said—'

'That I wanted to be there with Celeste when she's prepared and cremated.' She snapped her purse closed. 'I'm hoping that if I'm a quick study Mort will give me the honor.'

'Of *cremating* her? You want to cremate somebody you *know*?' I think I nearly shouted it.

'Not necessarily, at least not yet.' Christy looked hurt. 'But I never even really met Celeste – not that I wouldn't be honored to perform this last service for her. But more importantly, I'm not qualified to handle the cremator. It takes far more experience than I have to do it right.'

Before I could inquire about the wrong way of doing 'it,' Sophie Daystrom trudged in from the side door.

'You're getting here late today,' I said, taking a mug from the rack. 'Did you sleep in?'

'I wish, but I was up all night. A stand-off, of all things, at the manor.'

'The dead versus the undead?' Sarah emerged from the back, arms held straight out in front of her like a zombie. 'Or maybe nearly dead.' The arms rotated down now, like she was inching ahead with a walker.

75

'That,' Sophie flopped into a chair, 'would be funny if it wasn't so close to the truth.'

'Oh, dear, has there been a death?' Christy was sounding far too eager for my liking.

I slid her to-go cup toward her so she could be to-gone, but Christy was busy digging through her pockets.

'No bodies,' Sophie said, holding up her hand, 'at least not when I left. So you can keep your cards right where they are.'

Christy's own hands dropped to her side.

'What happened?' I poured the brew of the day for Sophie and signaled for Sarah to deliver it to her table.

My partner living-dead walked it over. 'Zee zombie apocalypse, perhaps?' she lisped. 'Or maybe somebody looking for their mummy?'

Argh. 'Boris Karloff would roll over in his grave.'

'He can't.' Christy took the lid off her cup and sniffed the brew. 'He was cremated.'

Enough funereal fun facts for one morning. 'Didn't you say you're running late?'

'Oh, yes. With luck, Mort will let me help with something.' Her nostrils flared. 'Sweeping, even.'

Best hurry, then. I took the lid away from her and settled it on the cup so as not to slow the crazy little demon down. 'Off you go.'

'What can she possibly be that anxious to sweep?' Sophie was looking out the window as our neighbor rushed down the front porch steps.

'You don't want to know,' I said. 'So, tell me, what was going on at the manor last night?'

'I did tell you. A stand-off.' Sophie swiped at

her forehead and the springy gray curls flew up and then settled right back down where they'd been. 'With the law, of course. If your boyfriend hadn't waved us through we'd still be hunkered down.'

'Pavlik?' I asked.

'You have more than one?'

She had a point. But speaking of 'boyfriends' . . . 'Where's Henry?'

'Barber shop. Nearly missed his appointment and, if he had, that guy next door would have been the reason.'

I frowned. 'The ex-convict?'

'Bingo. Couldn't wait until Tuesday.'

But I wasn't thinking of Sophie's death pool. Pavlik had said somebody they'd been looking for had showed at his brother's place. Could that be the senior home? The sheriff hadn't come back, so Sophie's stand-off might be the explanation. Or at least the explanation that was the most flattering to me.

But also the most risky for him.

'Is this stand-off still going on?' I asked. And then, without waiting for an answer, 'And is this guy – the brother – dangerous?'

'Brother?' Sophie asked.

I probably flushed. At least, it felt like I flushed. I try hard not to repeat what Pavlik tells me, even if he doesn't preface it with a 'Don't tell anybody this!'

And yet, I did. 'When Pavlik left, he said some guy that they were looking for had shown up at his brother's place. I had no idea – *have* no idea – whether he was talking about Brookhills Manor.'

'Well, now you do,' Sophie said dryly. 'And if Pavlik's "guy" came out of the same womb as our neighbor, I'd say he's a very bad man.'

Before I could ask for more details, the door flew open, sending the sleigh bells rappelling hard against the glass. I opened my mouth to scold some kid but then recognized one of Pavlik's deputies. Specifically, Detective Mike Hallonquist.

Hallonquist was Violent Crimes and, the last time I saw him, he was paired with Al Taylor of Homicide, not one of my favorite guys. In fact, it was Al's sarcastic ribbing that was partially responsible for Pavlik breaking up with me in the first place.

Now, though, Hallonquist was alone, his face pale as he swept the brimmed cap off his head. 'Maggy, the sheriff has been shot. You need to come with me.'

Seven

'Officially, we notify the next of kin and emergency contact,' Mike Hallonquist said as we sped to the hospital. 'When I saw that you were down as neither, I thought I should get hold of you.' Hallonquist glanced sideways at me. 'I'm sorry.'

Sorry that Pavlik had been shot? Sorry his partner had been a jerk to me? Or sorry that I wasn't Pavlik's next of kin or emergency contact?

Whatever. 'Thank you.'

I thought to wonder who *was* Pavlik's emergency

contact. I assumed his next of kin was his daughter, Tracey. She was just barely twelve, though, so it was unlikely she was his emergency contact. His ex-wife? Parents? It occurred to me that I didn't know a whole lot about Pavlik prior to his moving to Brookhills. For some reason that mattered a lot right now.

'How did this happen?' I mean, Pavlik was the sheriff, for God's sake. Shouldn't it be his deputies out there taking the bullets? I didn't have the grace to feel guilty about the thought. 'Pavlik said this guy you were hunting showed up at his brother's place?'

'Brookhills Manor. We've been sitting on the unit for a week.' Hallonquist signaled a lane change and checked his mirror before moving over. 'Not as easy as you'd think. Nothing gets by those old folks.'

I could imagine. 'Weren't you afraid somebody would tip off the brother?'

'At first, but it turned out to be just the opposite. Our guy posted at the front desk said folks kept wandering by, asking when we going to get rid of Andersen.'

If I was using our chat to do anything but distract myself, I'd have asked if Sophie had been one of them. 'Andersen is the brother?'

'Both brothers. Jack Andersen has lived at the manor for about a year – since he got out of prison.'

Just as Sophie had said. 'What was he sent away for?'

'Jack? Fraud. But it's his brother, Pauly, that we were waiting to nab.'

'And what did he do?' To my ears, my question sounded casual and almost disinterested. The kind of thing you'd ask about somebody at a cocktail party rather than the guy who just shot your . . . well, the man you loved.

'Convicted of bank robbery. He escaped while being transferred upstate to serve his sentence.'

Upstate to state prison. 'Transferred from Brookhills County Jail?' If so, the escape would have been on Pavlik's watch and the county sheriff would have taken it very personally. But Pavlik hadn't even mentioned it.

'Yeah.' Hallonquist was looking straight ahead, his expression tight. 'Got hold of Al Taylor's service revolver.'

Dear God. 'Is Taylor OK?'

'Physically, but . . . well, you've met him.'

Taylor played bad cop to Hallonquist's good one with gleeful swagger, but I thought I'd caught a brief glimmer of compassion in the man. Once. 'I imagine he's devastated.'

'Devastated, humiliated, angry, depressed – take your pick. I wasn't sure Al would come back from it at the time and now there's' – a swallow – 'this.'

Pavlik had been shot trying to recover the prisoner that Taylor had lost. The prisoner who'd taken the detective's sidearm. 'It wasn't Taylor's gun that—'

A single nod.

So Pavlik had been shot by his own detective's gun. I closed my eyes as the reality of the situation washed over me. Then I opened them. 'How did it go down?'

I imagined Pavlik rolling his own eyes at my 'TV cop-speak' and the fact that Hallonquist didn't do likewise gave me a twinge. 'Pauly must have managed entry by waiting in the woods by Poplar Creek and then leaving cover to blend in with a group that had just come back from a bus tour.'

The trip to the Mitchell Park Domes Sophie had mentioned. And the door Hallonquist was talking about would be the entrance Sophie had said was shared by the residential and rehab wings and faced the woods. It would have been a good plan. 'You didn't have anybody at the door?'

'We did, but by the time he picked Andersen out of the crowd he was already in and on the move to his brother's apartment.'

'And you couldn't stop him without endangering the other residents.'

A nod. 'Andersen barricaded himself in, using his brother as hostage.'

Now there's a sibling you'd want to share Thanksgiving dinner with. Yet, 'I thought Jack is a bad guy, too.'

A reluctant nod. 'But one who served his time and was now supposedly being held against his will.'

So they hadn't been sure of that and still apparently weren't. 'You had to treat it as a hostage situation, then, rather than two criminals in cahoots.'

This time 'cahoots' did earn me a trace of a smile. 'Exactly.'

'Sophie, the customer I was talking to when

81

you came in, lives in the apartment next to Andersen.'

'I thought I recognized her. We were moving in when the perp fired shots through the walls into the corridor.'

The walls being none too thick, from what Sophie had said. 'One of them hit Pavlik?'

'Not then. But Pete Hartsfield took one to the chest and we all scattered for cover. Pavlik – Sheriff Pavlik – went in to pull Hartsfield out of the line of fire.'

'Did he?' To my ears the question sounded like polite conversation. Like, 'Oh, did he really? How nice.' When what I really meant was, *Did Pavlik have to take a bullet?*

Hallonquist answered the question I didn't ask. 'The sheriff dragged Pete around the corner so the EMTs could attend to him.'

'You said he was shot in the chest, too?' Pavlik, I meant.

Again, Hallonquist got it. 'Yes.'

'Was he conscious when he was transported?'

'Yes.'

I didn't ask if Pavlik had asked for me. Knowing he had would make me sad that I hadn't been there for him. Knowing he hadn't would make me sadder. 'Do we know . . . I mean, is there any word . . .'

'They took him in for surgery to remove the bullet is all I know.' Hallonquist turned the car into the hospital parking lot. I noticed the squads – not just Brookhills County Sheriff's Department but city police. Not just our city, but surrounding cities. And not just our county, but seemingly all of southeastern Wisconsin.

Hallonquist pulled into the physician parking by the emergency entrance. Leaving the flashing lights on, he came around and opened the door for me. 'We'll find out more inside.'

I climbed out of the squad and made for the sliding glass doors as Hallonquist closed the car door. I practically ran into the first automatic door and once that opened had to wait for the next.

It was as if the doors couldn't detect my presence – like the restroom faucet that you wave your hand under and get no water, the soap that won't dispense until you've removed your hand – but I couldn't blame the doors. I couldn't quite believe I was there either.

As I hesitated at the sight of a waiting room and corridor of uniformed officers, I felt a hand on my shoulder.

I turned, expecting to see Hallonquist, but it was Sarah. 'What are you doing here?'

For once, she didn't snap back as my terse question probably deserved. Truth was I was practically faint with relief at seeing my partner.

'I was in the back seat the whole way here. The deputy had to let me out. Those doors don't open from the inside, you know.'

I had no memory of her following me out of Uncommon Grounds or getting into the back of the squad. 'Thank you.'

'You're welcome. Now let's see who we can talk to find out Pavlik's condition.'

Some of the officers in the waiting room I knew, though it'd be hard for me to dredge up their names at that moment. As Sarah pulled me across the room, the uniforms seemed to part on both sides of us and I saw a blonde man in scrubs and a cap. He was standing with a tall brunette and a girl of maybe twelve who seemed to be doing most of the talking.

I stopped dead. 'That's Tracey and that must be Susan.'

'Pavlik's kid and ex-wife?'

'Yes. I've met Tracey but only seen a picture of Susan.'

'Well, you're meeting her now,' Sarah said, pulling me forward.

I was holding back, feeling awkward. 'I don't have any standing here. I'm just the girlfriend.'

As Sarah turned, likely to scold me or give me a pep talk, the girl broke away and ran up to me. 'Maggy, I'm so glad you're here.'

She gave me a hug and turned to her mother. 'Mom, this is Maggy. She and Dad are getting married.'

I didn't say anything but Sarah elbowed me anyway. And if her elbow could have spoken, it would have said, 'Go with it.'

So, I did. 'I'm sorry to meet this way. How's Pavlik?'

The doctor took it from there. 'I was just saying that he came through well.'

'The surgery.' Duh.

'Yes.' The surgeon pushed his blue cap up off his forehead. 'You can see him in recovery. Family only, of course, and just two people at a time.'

Pavlik's ex and I looked at each other. Not exactly a mirror image. I was wearing jeans, sneakers and an Uncommon Grounds T-shirt with a latte smooge on it. I smelled like coffee. Susan's jeans were designer, her boots high-heeled and her shirt was silk. No smooge. Oh, and she smelled like Joy. And no, not the dish detergent.

Given Susan had come here on short notice, too, I had to assume she always looked like this. Shopped like this. Worked in the garden like this. Hell, maybe she even slept like this. And if not, she probably wore something lacy with a matching robe, not something a hundred per cent cotton with a matching nothing.

But much as I wanted to engage in hate-envy, Susan had been married to Pavlik for almost ten years and was the mother of his child. And that child shouldn't have to walk into her dad's hospital room without her mom. 'You should go in with Tracey.'

But Susan shook her head. 'Jake will want to see you.'

'I—'

But Tracey was already pulling me toward the doctor, who was waiting for us at the end of the corridor. 'C'mon, Maggy.'

She apparently didn't think she needed her mother's support, so who was I to judge? And if I was not going to dissuade anybody from the idea that Pavlik and I were engaged, I might as well take advantage of it so I could see him.

I let Tracey zoom ahead into Pavlik's room and hung back to talk to the surgeon. 'Could you update Detective Hallonquist and the other officers in the waiting room?'

'Of course.' As he started past me back to the lounge, I put a hand on his arm. 'Pavlik is going to be OK?'

He smiled. 'The bullet broke a rib and did some tissue damage but no organ damage. The sheriff is going to be fine.'

I was glad I asked, because the sight of Pavlik lying in a hospital bed almost made my heart stop.

Tracey was already perched on the side of the bed. '. . . Going to bring Muffin in to see you.'

'I'm not sure how the docs would feel about that.' Pavlik flashed me a smile.

'Then I guess Frank wouldn't make the grade either,' I said. 'Though I can bring in a slimy tennis ball if you'd like.'

Tracey lit up. 'I'm dying to meet Frank. Daddy has told me all about him.'

I glanced over at Pavlik, who lifted a hand. I took it. 'He did, did he?'

'I did. You and he are my second favorite girl and dog combination, after all.'

'I take that as a compliment, since I know who number one is.'

Tracey giggled.

It seemed off, chatting like this with Pavlik lying in bed in a hospital gown, IV in one arm. He was always in control. Always doing something. Riding his Harley in his— 'Uh-oh.'

Pavlik squeezed my hand. 'I was going to tell you.'

'Tell Maggy what?' Tracey's freckled nose was wrinkled.

I pointed. 'Your dad's jacket.'

Draped over a vinyl upholstered chair was Pavlik's buttery leather jacket. It had a hole in it. And that wasn't the worst part.

'Cool,' Tracey breathed. 'Is that your blood, Dad?'

'Hard to tell,' Pavlik said. 'But probably most of it is Deputy Hartsfield's. At least what you can see.'

Meaning Pavlik's own blood would be on the inside.

'Ugh.'

Apparently your own dad's blood was cool. Somebody else's blood not so much.

'Have you heard what Pete Hartsfield's condition is?' Pavlik asked me.

'No, only that he'd been hit in the chest, too. And that you pulled him to safety.'

Now Tracey's eyes were big. 'Did you, Dad? You're a hero, just like in the movies.'

'Except those heroes never get shot themselves,' Pavlik said.

'Oh, they take bullets,' Tracey said, waving her hand as if it were nothing. 'You'll be back in action in no time.'

'Have they told you how long you'll be here?' I asked.

'No, but—' Pavlik broke off as a different doctor came in with a chart. 'Phyllis, thanks for stopping by.'

'Just don't make a practice of getting shot on my days off.' The doctor put her hand out to me. 'Phyllis Goode.'

87

'Maggy Thorsen.'

'Oh, you own Uncommon Grounds, don't you? I stop in sometimes with the gang from Goddard's. When I have a Sunday off, that is.'

'Hi, Doctor Goode,' Tracey chirped up.

'Hey, Tracey.' The doctor shook the girl's hand. 'You sure made it up from Chicago fast. Or were you already here visiting your dad?'

'Tracey and Susan have moved back,' Pavlik explained.

'Well, that's good.' The doctor flicked a curious glance toward me before continuing. 'I've missed you.'

Tracey, on the other hand, didn't miss a thing. 'If you're wondering, Doctor Goode, Maggy is my dad's *fee-ahn-say*.' Confusion crossed her face. 'Or is it *fee-ahns*? I looked it up the other day but now I can't remember.'

'Women are the double e,' Dr Goode said. 'Men are single. But they're both pronounced the same. *Fee-ahn-say*.'

'So, I was right,' Tracey said. 'Maggy is dad's fiancée. And he's hers.'

Pavlik threw a sheepish smile in my direction but didn't comment. 'Any word on Pete Hartsfield?'

Dr Goode shook her head. 'Still in surgery, I'm told. The bullet apparently nicked a lung, among other things.'

Pavlik grimaced, seeming to feel his deputy's pain. Or maybe some of his own.

The doctor noticed it, too. 'I can get you something. Now that the anesthesia is wearing off we want to keep ahead of the pain.'

Pavlik waved it off. 'I'm fine for now. When can I go home?'

'Not for a couple of days, at least,' the doc said, setting down the chart. 'After that, we like to get people out of the hospital as soon as possible, assuming there's somebody at home to care for them.'

'I can do that,' Tracey said. 'I'm a good nurse. And I can cook, too, right, Dad?'

'Best toaster pizzas in the land,' Pavlik said.

'I'm sure that's true, Trace,' Dr Goode said. 'But your dad is going to need somebody a little bigger to help him for a week or so. Otherwise we'll need to send him to Brookhills Manor.'

'Brookhills Manor?' Pavlik and I asked in unison.

'But that's for old people,' Tracey said. 'My great grandpa was there before . . .' She glanced over at her father.

'Before he died,' Pavlik continued. 'And that's not going to happen to me, sweetie. But you are right that Brookhills Manor is a senior facility.'

'With a new rehab wing,' the doctor corrected. 'It's not age-restricted and I know they have room.'

I could read the horror in Pavlik's face. It was bad enough to be shot and in the hospital with your fellow law enforcement officers waiting in the lobby. But having them visit you at the old folks' home?

And that's how Pavlik came to live with Frank and me.

Eight

'If the thought of Pavlik staying at your place weirds you out,' Sarah said back at Uncommon Grounds that afternoon, 'why'd you invite him?'

'I didn't say it weirded me out. It's just . . . well, it's a big step. And besides, I have one bed. Where should he sleep? With me? What if I roll over on him or something?'

'From what you told me, Pavlik's condition isn't that fragile. And it's not like you're some big lug like . . . Wait a second, are you worried about Frank?'

'Frank? I don't know what you mean.' I was running the cash register tape to get the day's totals so far.

'I mean that sheepdog that sleeps in your bed. Please don't tell me you're worried about kicking him out for Pavlik.'

'Don't be silly. Pavlik has slept over before.' I tore off the printed tape a little too aggressively, sending the remainder of the roll out of the register and across the room, unraveling as it went. 'Shit.'

'Easy, girl,' Sarah said, retrieving it.

'And, for the record, Frank sleeps on my bed, not in it.' I took the roll from her and rewound the paper on to it before slipping the roll back into the machine.

'Meaning he doesn't sleep under the sheet and

90

blanket?' Sarah asked, watching me. 'Thank God. Though that's probably more a function of his needs than yours.'

I folded the printed tape in sections and paper-clipped it to our journal before turning. 'I heard the words but I have no idea what you just said.'

'I'm saying that Frank wears a fur coat so he's always warm. He's certainly not going to crawl under the covers with you. But I'm betting if he was hairless and came snuggling, you'd let him crawl between your sheets.'

I tried to imagine Frank as a hundred pounds of hairless. 'I'm pretty sure not.'

Sarah squinted, thinking about it. 'He would kind of look like a giant rat, wouldn't he?'

'Don't let him hear you say that.' But yeah. With longer legs. 'Back to Pavlik, though – I just can't imagine him rehabbing at Brookhills Manor next to Gloria Goddard.'

'And don't let Gloria hear you say *that*.' Sarah picked up a pot and poured the cold coffee in it down the drain.

'You know I love Gloria. But Pavlik would hate it. Besides, Tracey was looking at me like he was going to die if he went there.'

'Not your kid.' Sarah set the pot she'd just rinsed on the warmer before swiveling to face me with a wry grin on her face. 'At least, not yet.'

'If you want to know something that *does* weird me out, it's that Tracey thinks Pavlik and I are getting married. Why is that?'

'Because he told her, I assume.'

'Maybe he told her he was going to ask me.'

I took the pot and gave it a thorough washing before placing it back on the warmer and pressing the brew button. 'I guess that makes sense. I mean, I'd probably run it by Eric before I asked somebody to marry me.'

'Yet you haven't told your son that Pavlik proposed.'

'Because I haven't answered.' I was already getting pressure enough from Sarah, thank you very much.

'And what about Pavlik moving in? Going to keep that a secret, too?'

'No.' At least, I thought I'd tell Eric. Assuming the subject came up before the week was over and the sheriff was back home. 'I wonder if Pavlik told Tracey he was going to ask me but didn't tell her I said no.'

'You haven't said no.' Sarah held up her index finger. 'You've said . . . maybe.' She let the finger go limp.

Enough.

Sarah must have read it on my face because she shifted gears. 'What happened to this Pauly guy? I wouldn't blame Pavlik's guys if they'd gunned him down on the spot.'

'Me neither. But Pauly Andersen escaped out of the window during the confusion that followed the shooting.'

'Are you telling me they weren't covering the back?'

'They were, but in the uproar . . .' I shrugged. 'We didn't get a chance to talk about it with Tracey there but I know Pavlik's not happy about it.' That was putting it mildly. And I wasn't happy about the guy that shot *my* guy still being out there somewhere.

'Oh!' I was waving my hand at Sarah like a kid waiting to be called on. 'Remember that gray-haired man who came out with the to-go cup when we were talking Sunday morning?'

'You mean the one you accused me of scaring away?' Sarah asked.

'That's the one. And now I wish you had. Pavlik says that's Pauly Andersen's brother, Jack – the one who lives at the manor. A detective followed him to our place and then back to his apartment, which they were already sitting on, of course.'

Sarah gave me the cop-speak eye-roll I deserved. 'The guy only bought one coffee, so his brother couldn't have been there yet.'

It seemed like a leap. After all, maybe Pauly Andersen didn't drink coffee. Or host Jack wasn't considerate enough to ask whether his brother wanted a cup when he picked one up for himself.

But as it turned out, Sarah was right. 'According to Hallonquist, Pauly didn't sneak in until the tour group came back from their trip to the Domes late afternoon. Though they think he was lurking in the woods before that.'

'What else do we know about the brothers grim?'

I tilted my head in appreciation. 'Brothers Grimm – good one.'

Sarah grinned. 'Thanks. I think it was the name Andersen that inspired it.'

Hans Christian Andersen. 'Did you know he

93

wrote his own fairy tales while the Brothers Grimm were lawyers and academics who compiled folk tales and other people's writing? There's some thought that the Brothers' collection inspired Andersen. He never—'

The eye-roll was nothing compared to the disgusted look I was getting from Sarah. 'Are you done?'

Obviously not, since she'd cut me off midsentence. But I digressed. Mightily. 'Anyway, Pavlik said the two Andersen brothers couldn't be more different. Pauly, the younger, has a long rap sheet of mostly violent crimes. Jack is the smart one – a charming con man who has bilked people out of millions over the years, yet managed to stay out of jail until eight years ago.'

'Millions of dollars and he was in jail for less than eight years?'

'Good behavior, supposedly. Told you he was charming.'

Sarah shrugged. 'Could have fooled me. All I saw was an old guy with a pink face.'

'I'm trying to think if I've ever seen him in here before, maybe with the Goddard Gang?' Though why would I remember Jack Andersen any better than the rest of our customers?

'Not as far as I know.'

'So maybe it was just chance that he came here. Or maybe Jack left his apartment thinking the detectives would follow him and Pauly could sneak in unseen, but it didn't work.'

'And why not get a good cuppa joe while eluding the cops.'

'So the man is both charming *and* smart.'

94

'Talking about me again?'

Father Jim was on the other side of the service counter.

'No, but you are both of those things,' I told him.

'And sneaky,' Sarah added. 'It unnerves me when people just materialize in front of us like that.'

'It's my ninja stealth,' Jim said, striking a pose with hands held out flat. 'And the fact your chimes on the side door are gone.'

'What?' I circled out from behind the service counter and into the side hallway that led to the train platform and parking lot. 'Somebody stole our sleigh bells.'

'Maybe they thought they were helping us. You know, taking down the Christmas decorations.' Sarah had followed me. 'It is March, after all.'

'They're not Christmas decorations,' I told her for maybe the umpteenth time since I'd put them up on both doors. 'They're just bells.' That happened to be round. And tied with a red ribbon.

'And yet you insist on calling them sleigh bells,' Sarah said dryly.

'All I care about is that the sleigh bells ring—'

'"Are you listening?"' Jim's tenor rang out. '"In the—"'

I gave him a stern look. 'You're not helping, you know. You're supposed to be on my side.'

'Well, if you've got God on your side I'm out of here before I can be struck down.' Sarah was undoing her apron strings.

'You were leaving anyway. Your shift was over at three-thirty.'

'And I'm only a priest, not God,' Jim said. 'Though we *are* confused a lot.'

'It's the eyes.' She patted his check and handed him her apron.

'She's a trip,' Jim said to me as the now bell-less door closed behind Sarah.

'Yes, she is.' I took the apron from him. 'Can I get you a drink?'

'Not really. I've probably had enough caffeine today. Besides, I really stopped by to see if you are OK.'

'You heard about the shooting.' It wasn't a question, since everybody in Brookhills would know by now what had happened. 'And Pavlik.'

I heard my voice shake at the end and Jim must have, too, because he wrapped his arms around me. 'I'm sorry, sweetheart. Is there anything I can do?'

'No,' I said into his chest. Tears were suddenly streaming down my cheeks and I couldn't quite figure out why. 'I know Pavlik is going to be fine. I'm just being silly.'

'You're being human. It's only now hitting you that you might have lost him. Just thank God,' he let go of me to make the sign of the cross, 'you didn't.'

'Yes.' I dug into my apron pocket and came up with an Uncommon Grounds napkin to mop my face. 'Well, anyway, like I said,' a sniffle escaped, 'I saw Pavlik at the hospital and we should be able to bring him home in a couple of days.'

Jim didn't raise an eyebrow at the 'we,' meaning

Frank and me. The priest knew the sheepdog and I were a couple and didn't judge. 'I'm glad to hear it. I stopped by his room at the hospital but the bed was empty.'

My heart gave a twist and I tamped it back down. What was with me all of a sudden?

Jim was watching me. 'I *meant* he was out of the room having tests. You sure you're OK?'

'Other than having watched too many bad movies with the "empty hospital bed means dead" cliché? Sure, I'm fine.' I made myself grin. 'Thanks for stopping by to see Pavlik. He's not even Catholic.'

'But he is a friend,' Jim said. 'Or at the very least, the friend of a friend. Besides, I was already there for Pete Hartsfield.'

Like Celeste and Nancy, I thought of last rites when a visit from a priest was mentioned. Talk about clichés. 'How is Pete doing?'

'Out of surgery but in the intensive care unit. Prayers are needed.'

'Done,' I said. 'You sure I can't get you a cup of coffee?'

'Thanks, but I need to go.' He checked his watch. 'I was due at the mortuary five minutes ago to discuss Celeste Bouchard's arrangements.'

'Has the day and time been set?' I asked.

'Not yet, but the cremation won't take place until tomorrow, so the funeral will probably be Thursday.' Jim was halfway out the door.

'But she was being cremated this morning. Or at least I thought that's what Christy said.'

'She must have confused the intake of the body with the actual cremation. That can't be done for forty-eight hours. Add that time to the actual procedure, cooling and packaging and—'

'Please.' I held up my hands palms out. 'I've heard enough from Christy on the subject to last me a lifetime.'

Or an afterlife-time.

Nine

It had been a busy day, both death and injury-wise, and it wasn't over yet. The day itself, I mean. Hopefully the deaths and injuries were done, but one can never tell in Brookhills.

It was after nine when I got home, after stopping by the hospital to see Pavlik, who'd been downright ornery in comparison with earlier. I figured that was at least partially because whatever meds he'd been on after the surgery had worn off, only to be replaced by the regular painkillers. Which, of course, he'd delayed taking as long as possible, despite the doctor's advice to 'stay ahead of the pain.'

I also knew that he'd wanted to reassure Tracey after the shooting. With me, he could be himself. And growl. 'A prisoner escapes thanks to Taylor losing his gun? Another deputy is so rattled by the sound of gunfire and the call, "Officer down," that he deserts his post and lets Andersen get away for a second time? Talk about amateur time.'

'It's not like the Brookhills County Sheriff's

Department has a lot of experience with shootings,' I said. 'Law enforcement here is different than in Chic—'

But Pavlik wasn't listening. He was too busy punching an email into his phone. 'This is my own damn fault, you know. I've been too easy on these guys.'

'What's going to happen to the brother – Jack Andersen?' I was trying to get him to focus on a subject that would require less self-flagellation than the second escape of Pauly.

'What's going to happen? Nothing. He claims he was a hostage and we can't prove otherwise. Another failure.'

Blessedly, visiting hours ended before he could take the blame for global warming and cancer.

'What do you think?' I asked Frank as he watched me pull the meat off a rotisserie chicken carcass I'd picked up at the grocery store. 'You OK with Pavlik coming to stay for a while?'

He growled and it took me a second to realize it was because I'd paused in dismantling the poor chicken and was waving a drumstick at him.

I dumped the chicken I'd pulled off into Frank's dish and added water and a scoop of dehydrated raw vegetable dog food that promised a well-balanced, holistic doggy diet. The stuff rehydrated into green goo and cost a fortune, but after both Frank and I had weighed in at a little over fighting weight at our respective doctors, I'd made a pact with myself that we'd eat better in the future.

I'd kept half the pact, at least.

Setting the dog's bowl on the floor, I poured

myself a glass of red wine and pulled a sleeve of butter crackers and can of spray cheese out of the cupboard. The meal hit the major food groups, or would have if I'd added the vegetable sludge. Not an option, given the cost of the sludge.

Frank glanced up from his dish, wearing a green vegetable beard and a disgusted look.

'You win,' I said, setting down my meal. 'Pizza it is.'

'Since when do you go to funerals?' I asked Sarah the next morning.

We were sitting at a table in our own coffee-house, enjoying lattes and sticky buns after the morning commuter rush.

'When it comes to the "Holy Hannah's Ladies of Ronny House," I'll make an exception.'

'Just what is your deal?' I took a sip of my latte.

'What deal?'

'I mean, why don't you like Hannah? She's a perfectly nice person.'

'Something's just . . . off.' Sarah pointed. 'You've got foam on your lip.'

I licked it off, lest it be wasted. 'Somehow I have a feeling the "something off" you're refer-ring to is not my foam mustache.'

'Good call. I'm talking about little miss perfect.' She stuck a leftover pecan from the long-ago devoured sticky bun into her mouth.

'Hannah, because she took in her mother and her mother's friend?'

'"As anybody of good conscience would do."'

It took me a second to realize she was mimicking Hannah. 'Are you going to say nasty things about me, too, when Pavlik comes to stay?'

'I already say nasty things about you.'

It was true. Not that she meant them. Or so I thought.

'Besides,' Sarah continued, 'I know you're going to be busting your butt, working and playing nurse to Pavlik.' A sly grin. 'Though that doesn't sound half bad, come to think of it.'

I ignored her fantasy. 'I was thinking I might take a few days off.'

'Yeah, well, think again. But you're making my point. Exactly how has the lovely Hannah made a living while she was caring for the oldsters in the house Celeste bought?'

I shrugged. 'How do I know? Maybe Hannah works from home. Or has family money or something.'

'I think that's probably just it. She's living off her mother. But here's another thing. Why didn't Hannah have the power of attorney?'

Now she'd completely lost me. 'What do you mean?'

'This is what got me thinking,' Sarah said. 'Remember Christy telling us about the closing on the house?'

'What about it?'

'The way it works is if you can't be present at a closing, the papers can be overnighted to you to sign. Or you can give your power of attorney to somebody else and have them sign in your stead.'

'Which is exactly what Celeste did, according to Christy.'

'But to a lawyer, not her daughter. Don't you think that's strange?'

'What I think is that you're ornery that Christy sold your cousin's house on her own rather than have you broker the deal.'

'Ronny is *not* my cousin.' Sarah jabbed her finger a tad too vigorously at an errant flake of bun on the table, sending it off onto the floor.

'OK, your criminal cousin by marriage.' I retrieved the crumb with a napkin as the bells on the front door jangled.

I jumped up. Nobody likes to see their servers having more fun than they are.

'Sit, sit,' Langdon Shepherd admonished, his hand gesture identical to the one that signaled people to take their seats in the pews. It was customary in most churches for the congregation to sit for the sermon. But at Christ Christian it was also self-preservation. Langdon's record was an hour and four minutes.

'How is your sheriff doing?' he asked, leaning down to give me a one-armed hug.

'I saw Pavlik last night and he's good, thank you,' I said, wincing as he squeezed. The man was all bones. 'Fixated on work, of course.'

Which was true, as far as it went. It also reminded me that I'd better check my Internet provider to make sure I had enough bandwidth to handle Pavlik's phone, tablet and computer. All up and running simultaneously, even when Pavlik couldn't be up *or* running.

'And the other officer? Deputy Hartsfield?'

'No update last night. But Pete was in intensive care yesterday, according to Father Jim.'

'Oh, is the father here?' Langdon asked, glancing around like he expected Jim to pop out from under one of the empty tables. 'I wanted to share some ideas for a joint Easter celebration we've been discussing.'

'Just missed him by eighteen hours,' Sarah said, getting up to gather our plates and cups.

'Jim was in yesterday afternoon,' I explained, standing myself. 'You'll probably find him at the church, though.'

'I'll have to stop by. Easter will be here before we know it and we'll need to get the word out if we're going to do something. You know, social media, advertising, press releases.'

I did know, given I'd done corporate public relations prior to opening Uncommon Grounds. I was just surprised that Langdon was embracing marketing. Traditionally, his approach was more . . . traditional. Like church bulletins.

'I can't remember the two churches ever doing something together,' I said.

'An entirely new endeavor,' the pastor said as I ducked behind the counter to make his cappuccino. 'Despite our differences in doctrine we are united in the need to bring people into church.'

I reemerged at the ordering window. 'I thought Christmas and Easter were the two holidays people did come to church. Why do a joint service then? Won't you be taking away from your own attendances?'

'Oh, this wouldn't be on Easter Sunday itself.

More of a festival on that Saturday, with the children.'

'Like an Easter egg hunt?'

'Exactly.'

Didn't sound like all that novel an idea, but maybe the real collaboration was not so much between the two churches as it was the Easter bunny and Jesus.

'Christmas, Easter, marry and bury, my father used to say,' Langdon went on, smiling a little painfully.

'Oh, was your father a pastor, too?' I picked up the portafilter and slipped it under the espresso grinder/dispenser, only to realize the bean hopper above it was empty.

'More agnostic, I'm afraid, laying out his parameters. My mother had to twist his arm to get him to attend church even for those milestones.'

Looking at Langdon, you'd imagine he came from a family with its roots in the bedrock of the church. 'Was it your mother who inspired you to become a pastor?'

Langdon smiled. 'Honestly, I think it was more my father's resistance than anything else. I was quite the contrary young man.'

Sarah appeared with a bag of espresso beans from the storeroom. 'That's hard to imagine.'

'That I was a young man or that I was contrary?' Langdon knew Sarah too well.

'Both.' Sarah grinned and dropped the five-pound bag of roasted beans on the counter.

'Did your dad ever forgive you for being holier than he?'

'I'm afraid not, though he did come to hear my first homily.' Langdon barely averted a roll of his eyes – an implied judgment I was sure he'd normally be loath to make.

'That was good, at least,' I said, using scissors to slice the bag so I could pour the beans into the hopper.

'I'll let you be the judge. He dropped a dime in the collection plate as it went around.' He held up his hands. 'Not that I'm saying God requires payment.'

'But . . .' Sarah was leading the witness.

Langdon allowed himself to look perturbed. 'My father was well enough off. To my mind, it was an insult. Like dining at a restaurant and leaving a penny as the tip for the waiter. It's worse than no tip at all.'

'And you were the waiter,' I said.

A wave of Langdon's hand said it was no matter. His face said otherwise. 'That's all in the past. But the fact is churches are in difficult straits because of people like my father, who partake but don't pay.'

'To be fair, your father didn't want to partake either,' Sarah pointed out. 'Or order, if you want to keep the dinner analogy going.'

Like Langdon, I thought maybe it was time to let this go. 'Is Christ Christian struggling financially?' I asked as I switched on the grinder.

'Most churches are,' Langdon said, not quite answering the question. 'Even at Angel of Mercy, which traditionally has done quite well, Father Jim says they're struggling.'

Since Jim was new to the church, that worried

me. And mystified me as well. I'd go to Angel of Mercy to hear Jim if I didn't have to work Sundays, and I wasn't even Catholic. I couldn't say all that to Langdon, of course, so I said, 'Why do you think that is?'

'I honestly don't know,' Langdon said. 'Father Jim is a gifted speaker and has brought young people into the church. Actual attendance is on the upswing but collections remain stagnant. The key, we both feel, is to get people involved so they join the congregation and have a stake in its future.'

'So why Easter?' I asked, switching off the grinder and going to pull the shot. 'Like you said, that's one of the times the churches are full. Why not concentrate on increasing attendance during the downtimes?'

'Easter celebrations bring in young families, which is important for growing our membership basis. If we get them in for an Easter or Christmas event, maybe we can keep them coming.'

'And paying,' Sarah said, and then listened. 'Is that your phone I hear vibrating?'

The irony of 'hearing' vibration. But I heard it, too. I fished my phone out of my apron pocket, but the vibrating had stopped and it read 'missed call.'

'Good morning,' Clare Twohig called out.

The owner of Clare's Antiques was small – maybe five feet tall, with blonde hair cut short – but you couldn't miss her melodic voice or the vintage pieces she wove into her otherwise modern style.

She was also a 'double latte, skim milk, no

foam', which she picked up on the way to the antiques shop every morning at about a quarter to ten.

Exactly what it was now.

I slipped my phone back into my apron and started Langdon's milk frothing. 'Morning, Clare. Can I get you your usual?'

'Please.' Today Clare was wearing a pillbox hat with jeans and a military-style blouse.

'I don't know how you do it,' I said, finishing up Langdon's cappuccino.

'Do what?' Clare was glancing around like she didn't know what I was talking about.

Which she didn't, of course, because for her the look was effortless. Me, I was lucky if I was wearing two of the same shoes. 'How you put together outfits like that.'

Sarah was passing behind me and backtracked so she could get a better look at Clare. 'Nice outfit.'

Not snide. Not sarcastic. A genuine compliment.

'Oh, this? It's nothing.' Clare tried to pirouette but fell out of it, giggling.

'It is very fetching, my dear,' Langdon said, taking the cappuccino and passing a five to me.

'Why thank you, Langdon,' Clare said. 'I thought since the pillbox hat that was so popular for women in the forties is believed to be inspired by military headgear, it would be kind of fun.'

'Well, I'm sure you wear the *chapeau* more beautifully than any soldier could have.' With that, Langdon bowed out. Literally.

'Did you all see somebody is moving into the

building across the street from me?' Clare asked as she set her wallet on the counter.

'That's where Penn and Ink, the graphic design firm was,' I said, pulling a gallon of skim milk out of the refrigerator.

'Penn dumped Ink,' Sarah informed Clare. 'It got messy.'

Clare laughed. 'I bet. Any idea what kind of business is moving in?'

'No clue,' Sarah said, 'but customers have been complaining about the trucks blocking the street in that direction.'

Clare's nose crinkled. 'It's just the one lane, leaving plenty of room for cars to get around.'

'You're not from here, are you?' Sarah asked.

'No, Minneapolis. Why?'

'In most cities,' Sarah was saying, 'a double-parked truck is business as usual. In Brookhills, it's a reason to call the cops.'

Clare grinned. 'I do get a kick out of the police report in the *Observer*. Did you see the one last week where somebody reported they were sure they'd left their car windows down but, when they returned, they were up?'

'That was good,' I agreed, 'but my all-time favorite one was the guy who is allergic to poppy seeds calling the police because his wife bought three-seed bagels and he decided she was trying to kill him.'

'Ooh, that must have been before I moved here.' Clare's blue eyes sparkled. 'And I love the way they're reported. In a kind of "just the facts, ma'am" way.'

'That's the work of one of my original

partners in Uncommon Grounds.' I poured milk into the frothing pitcher. 'Caron Egan. You might have seen her byline.'

'Caron Egan, of course,' Clare repeated. 'She wrote the article on the mortician, too.'

'Christy mentioned the article but I didn't realize Caron wrote it.'

'Front page this past Thursday. Either your friend Caron is a gifted writer or Mort the Mortician is fascinating.' Clare's eyes were bright as she leaned in to ask, 'Have you met him?'

'Sure.' I stuck the frothing wand into the milk and turned on the steam, moving the pitcher up and down to introduce air and get the froth the way I wanted it. 'He's part of the Goddard Gang that's here every Sunday morning.'

'Really.' She was thinking. 'I should come by to meet him.'

'You could go by the funeral home if you're really dying . . .' I stopped frothing. 'Sorry. Is this professional or personal?'

'You mean am I looking to date a mortician or hire one?' she asked with a smile. 'Neither. But what Caron called Mort's "thinking outside the box – or urn" in the article intrigued me. He believes both a funeral and a final resting place should make a statement about what was important in the deceased's life. Ashes sent up in fireworks' shells or stored in the departed's favorite brand of bourbon bottle. Rock and roll celebrations of life.'

'How about *Weekend at Bernie's*?' Sarah suggested. 'Now there's one I'd go to.'

'That's what I thought, too,' Clare said. 'Reading how creative Mort is, I thought my shop might have some . . . containers that might be perfect.'

'Have to be one big-ass antique to fit a body,' Sarah said. 'Steamer trunk, maybe?'

Clare was peering into the bakery case. 'Is that a sticky bun behind the muffins?'

'The last one.' I set the milk aside to rest. 'We had a run on them this morning.' And Sarah and I had eaten two.

'I was half hoping you'd be out of them,' Clare said ruefully. 'Save me from myself.'

'Better that you take it now than I take it home.' I picked up a pair of tongs.

'Says you. Anyway,' she continued, 'I have several items that would work for ashes. For example, a guitar for the rock and roll funeral. Or that vintage coffee urn you've been eyeing, Maggy, for the coffee lover.'

I stopped, tonged bun in hand. 'I said I liked it, not that I wanted to spend eternity in it.'

Clare chin-gestured for me to continue the roll's journey. 'But it is an interesting alternative to spending eternity in a plastic bag fastened with a twist tie, isn't it?'

It was indeed.

Ten

'Plastic bag and a twist tie? Really?' Sarah said as I slipped Clare's roll into a white paper bag, trying not to dislodge the pecans on top of it.

'Damn it!' A nut went flying.

'That's the way it's done, according to the article,' Clare's voice said as I ducked behind the counter to retrieve the pecan before it cemented to the floor or the bottom of somebody's shoe. 'A sturdy plastic bag, no doubt, and an industrial-strength twist tie.'

'That way the dead guy can't make a run for it.' Still bent, I tossed the pecan into the trash basket and missed. 'And stays fresh, in the bargain.'

Resurfacing, I saw Mort Ashbury.

He was grinning. A curse on whoever stole my bells/early-warning system.

'Mort,' I said, 'we were just talking about you. Well, not you, but your—'

'Stay-fresh containers, I heard. And what could be better on a Tuesday morning than being the topic of discussion for three lovely women.' The smile stayed on his face as he turned to Clare. 'Morton Ashbury, at your service.'

Given the wink that accompanied his words – as well as what the mortician's 'service' was – I had to believe that Ashbury was in on the joke, even if his new loyal follower, Christy, wasn't.

Whether the name had spurred his decision to dedicate his life to burying and cremating people or the choice had been a pure coincidence, Morton Ashbury had decided to embrace it with a certain *joie de vivre*. Which Ashbury would no doubt term *joie de mort*.

The thought made me smile right back. 'Clare owns the antiques and flower shop next door.

We were talking about the article on you in the *Observer*, and I was just saying that her shop might be the perfect place for people to find just the right . . . vessel for their loved ones.'

Of course, it had been the other way around – Clare had made the suggestion, not me – but I'd always found it more effective to have somebody else blowing your horn than to do it yourself. And you can take that any way you wish.

As for Clare, she threw me a grateful look before offering her hand to Mort. 'Clare Twohig. I must say that I'm fascinated by your idea of celebrating life, not mourning death.'

'I don't claim that it's a new thought,' Mort said. 'So-called celebrations of life are a dime a dozen in the funeral industry. The video presentations of a life well-lived, etc., etc. We try to go beyond that and – for cremations, at least – have the departed in a lasting reminder of that life. Now this shop of yours—'

A cell phone interrupted. Since I recognized the opening strains of 'Always Look on the Bright Side of Life,' I assumed it was Mort's.

As he went to answer it, Sarah said, 'I find myself disappointed his ring isn't "Another one Bites the Dust." You?'

'A little,' I admitted. 'But the man can't afford to be too obvious. He has a business to run.'

'It might come off as heartless.'

'You think?'

On the other side of the counter, Clare was looking on as Mort spoke into the phone. 'I'm so sorry. What a terrible waste. Yes, I'm sure

112

there'll have to be autopsies, under the circumstances. I—' He listened some more. 'Yes, right now.'

My heart was thudding as he went to slip his phone in his pocket. Reaching across the counter, I stopped him. 'Autopsies, plural?'

Pete Hartsfield was in a critical condition. But a second? Could Pavlik's condition have deteriorated during night?

There was a missed call on the cell phone in my apron pocket. The hospital? Or Hallonquist with even worse news than he'd already given me? I knew I should pull out my own phone and see, but I was afraid.

Mort seemed agitated by his call, especially for somebody who dealt with death on an everyday basis. 'I'm sorry, but Peter Hartsfield has died. And this morning—'

My fingers tightened on his. Inside I was screaming, but I could barely whisper, 'Pavlik?'

I felt Sarah's hand on my shoulder as Mort's expression changed. 'Pavlik? Oh, no. I'm so sorry if I gave you that impression. The second deceased is not the sheriff.'

'Oh, thank God.' The relief that swept over me made me light-headed as I let Mort's hand go. Sarah's hand back-stopped me.

I took a deep breath. 'I'm sorry. That was unkind of me, given Pete's death. And another family lost someone, too.'

Mort shook his head. 'I think you can be excused, under the circumstances.'

'Can we get you something to take with you, Mort?' Sarah asked.

'Thank you,' he said. 'Maybe just a black coffee?'

Sarah poured our brew of the day into a cup and fit the top on it.

As Mort fumbled for his wallet, I said, 'On us, please. You go do what you have to do.' 'Cause you couldn't pay me enough to do it. Be with people at the worst times in their lives? Over and over again.

As Clare followed Mort out the door, I turned to Sarah. 'Thank you.'

'What for?' She was wiping the counter.

'You know what. Having my back again, literally. I thought I was going to pass out.'

She turned, dishrag in hand. 'Doesn't that tell you something?'

'That you're a good friend?'

'And you're an idiot. I mean doesn't that tell you something about how you feel about Pavlik? Your world ended when you thought he'd died. I saw it in your eyes.'

'You couldn't see my eyes.'

Sarah's own warning glance was enough.

'OK, you're right. I . . . Well, I couldn't breathe. Couldn't even bring myself to look at my phone because I was afraid that call I'd missed was . . .' I let it go at that.

'So, tell him.' Sarah tossed the rag into the sink. 'Or I will.'

'Duly noted.' I stepped out onto the porch and punched up the missed call. It was from Pavlik. In fact, there were three from him, all seemingly in quick succession.

'I heard about Pete,' I said when he answered. 'I'm so sorry.'

There were voices behind him in the room. 'Hang on a second.'

Then, 'I wanted to get into the corridor.'

'Are you OK?' I asked. 'When Mort said there had been two deaths, I was so afraid—'

'Mort?'

'Mort Ashbury, the mortician. He was here at the coffeehouse when he got the call about Pete and somebody else. I was afraid . . .' I was afraid to put what I'd thought into words.

'That it was me? No, I'm fine.' Pavlik's voice was flat. He'd lost a man, and there was no getting past that.

'Then who was the other—' I had a thought. 'Did you find Pauly Andersen?' Not that I necessarily wanted the escapee dead, especially if it had been in a shoot-out with law enforcement. But if somebody had to die, Pauly was definitely the lesser of two evils. Or maybe, in this case, the greater.

'No, but we found a stolen car abandoned at the bus station in Milwaukee.'

'You think it's Pauly's?'

'We're working with the Milwaukee County Sheriff's Department to see if we can track him from there, but the timing works. The car was reported stolen from Brookhills Manor on Monday—'

I interrupted. 'Nobody was hurt when it was taken?'

'No, it was stolen from the back parking lot and turned up at the bus station fifteen miles away.'

'Then that's how Pauly got away.'

'It seems likely that it was during the confusion of the shooting.' Shot or not, Pavlik still
wasn't happy about confusion on his watch.

'So if the second death wasn't Andersen,' I
said, 'then it must be unrelated.'

'No.'

'No?' I think I looked at the phone.

'They took Pete Hartsfield off life support at
eight forty-three this morning.'

'I know. And it's awful, but you did everything
you could for—'

'At nine-oh-three, Al Taylor shot himself in
the head.'

Eleven

'One way or another, I'm bringing him home
tonight,' I told Sarah, who'd come out to sit with
me on the porch as we waited for the last
commuter train to arrive from Milwaukee so we
could close.

I'd been to visit Pavlik and then come back to
help Sarah. 'He needs to be away from that
hospital and the media and even his own deputies. He's just so sad. It's all just so . . . sad.'

'Taylor blamed himself for Hartsfield's death?'

I nodded. 'I know Hallonquist was worried
about him. First, his gun is stolen by a convict.
A humiliation. Then not only does the guy escape
but he uses the gun to shoot two of your fellow
officers.'

'And one dies.' She sneezed. 'Sorry, I think I must be coming down with what that Nancy woman has.'

'Bless you.' I rubbed my face. 'Pete Hartsfield has a wife and brand-new baby girl. Apparently Taylor left a note and one of those Internet wills bequeathing everything to Hartsfield's family.'

'Hope it stands up in court.'

'I hope so, too, but I doubt that's anybody's priority right now. Pete Hartsfield is dead. Al Taylor is dead.'

'And Taylor wanted to make amends as best he could. You don't have to give me that "how can you be so insensitive" look.'

'And I'm not. OK, maybe I was, but this is such a tragedy all around.'

'And Pavlik feels responsible?'

'Of course.' I ran my finger along a line in the table. 'His department. His officers. His responsibility.'

Sarah pushed out her chair and stood up. 'I'll close for you. Go break your man out of the hospital.'

As it turned out, it was easier said than done.

By the time I got there, there was no doctor on duty to sign Pavlik out.

'I'm sorry,' the petite nurse on duty said, 'but Doctor Goode won't be in until rounds tomorrow morning. I'll be happy to ask her to stop by first thing, though.'

'Fine, but I won't be here,' Pavlik said flatly.

Once I'd floated the idea of bringing him home, he was totally on board. So much so that, under the circumstances, I wished I'd spoken to the doc first.

On the other hand, his eyes were verging toward blue again rather than the stormy gray they turned when he was upset. And I wanted to keep them that way.

'Couldn't you just call Doctor Goode?' I asked. 'Maybe she could just run by.'

'Out of town.'

'Well, what about the surgeon then? What was his name?'

'Doctor Warren's daughter is having a first birthday party tonight. You wouldn't want me to interrupt that, would you?'

The one-year-old probably wouldn't notice.

Pavlik was pulling on jeans. 'There must be an ER doc on. Maybe he or she would be willing to sign the release.'

'I don't know,' the nurse said. 'They've been awfully busy down there today.'

Pavlik was buttoning his shirt.

'Why don't we give it a try,' I suggested to the nurse.

In the end, we all came to an agreement. We got hold of Dr Goode, who agreed to call the ER doc, who agreed Pavlik probably wouldn't bleed out if he left. Pavlik agreed he'd sign a waiver just in case he did, and Frank and I agreed that peperoni pizza two nights in a row wouldn't kill us.

We were sitting in the bedroom, Pavlik propped up in my bed, a plate with a slice of pizza on his lap. Frank was on the floor, chewing. I was sitting next to Pavlik, cross-legged, doing likewise.

And sipping red wine. It had been quite a day.

'Thanks for getting me out of there,' he said.

'My pleasure. You're going to have to break it to Frank, though, that he needs to split his pizza with both of us for a while.'

'He'll be OK with that,' Pavlik said. 'We're buds, right, Frank?'

The sheepdog grunted and went back to chewing.

'See? You're not company anymore so you don't get the royal treatment.' I rubbed his right shoulder. The position of the bullet wound and resulting broken rib made doing anything with his left arm difficult and painful. The rib was wrapped and the wound was bandaged, but I was still worried that either Frank or I would jostle him during the night.

'You have to promise me you'll take it easy. I'm going to have to run into work tomorrow for a while and I don't want to find you on the floor "bleeding out" as that doctor so charmingly put it.'

'I'll make sure that if I do bleed out, I do it in the bed.' He put his good arm around me and kissed the top of my head. 'Easier to clean up.'

'But not so good for the bed. I'll go by your place and pack some things. Any special requests?'

His eyes danced. 'Yes, but I think that would make me bleed out.'

'I meant so you won't have to wear Eric's clothes.'

'What? You think they don't look good on me? He held out his arms so I could see the skin-tight Gap T-shirt in all its glory.

119

'It looks excellent on you,' I said. 'But he's going to kill both of us if you stretch out his clothes.'

'Fine. Just bring me some jeans and a couple of dress shirts and T-shirts. You know the drill. Oh, and a toothbrush and razor. Shorts.'

'I should probably stop at the grocery store, too. As you've no doubt noticed, I don't keep much food here.'

'Pretty much nothing that doesn't have caffeine, cheese or fermented grape juice in it. Unless it's for Frank.'

'I know I spoil him,' I said, snuggling back in. 'But he completes me.'

'And what about me?'

I froze, then felt myself relax. 'You complete me, too.'

Twelve

'I'm so sorry,' Amy said the next morning.

'I know,' I said, pouring cream from the quart carton into our server. 'I have to say, she seemed fine yesterday, except for her attitude, of course.'

'And now she's gone.'

I nodded. 'It's for the best. Put an end to the suffering.'

Amy cocked her head. 'Hers?'

'Hell, no, mine. And yours. And anybody else who's around Sarah when she's not feeling well.'

My partner's sneeze of yesterday had turned

120

into a scratchy throat and sniffles. In her mind, that meant she was getting sick. In my mind, it meant I was getting a week of grumpy partner, followed by a week of being sick myself. Not to mention all the customers we'd potentially infect, as well as my new housemate. Pavlik didn't need to add that particular insult on his immune system to his current injury.

'I couldn't take it any longer and told her she should go home,' I continued. 'Thanks for coming in on such short notice.'

'I got the impression that you'd have gone it alone if I hadn't.' Amy screwed the top onto the cream pitcher and walked it over to the condiment cart.

'The sniffling was getting on my last nerve. And, every once in a while, she'd make this little whimpering noise.' I shuddered.

'Maybe she wanted you to send her home,' Amy said, circling back behind the counter.

'Believe me, I tried. Over and over again. Begged her for the sake of me and everybody else she was going to infect.'

'She hates being around people who are sick herself.'

Sarah routinely disappeared into the back to leave one of us to serve anybody visibly ill – or what she referred to as 'Patient Zero.' 'Yet she's happy to expose us when she's sick. The paradox that is Sarah.'

'She knows you have Pavlik to think about.'

'I did run out and take him lunch before you came. He and Frank were happily ensconced watching TV.' In fact, I'd been amazed at how

121

relaxed Pavlik had been. And not a computer, notebook or phone in sight.

'Well, that's good. I'm sure Sarah didn't want to leave you in the lurch.'

Or herself without a sympathetic audience. On Amy's arrival, my partner had gone into the office, presumably to get her coat and go home. But now . . . 'Was that a whimper?'

Amy lowered her voice to match mine. 'A whimper?'

'From the office.' I stuck my head around the corner. 'Damn. The door is closed. She must still be in there.'

Amy's lips twisted in a smile. 'What are you going to do?'

'Nothing. Apparently containment is all we can hope for.'

'Well, you fought the good fight.' Her expression changed. 'I haven't seen you since Sunday, but I wanted to tell you how sorry I am about the sheriff and especially the two deputies who died. What an awful thing.'

'It's been a tough few days. Did you hear that Hannah's mother died, too? Last Sunday morning, when we were all here.'

'Christy told me when she was in. She says the mother's friend – Nancy, I think? – is not in good shape. Nearly beside herself with grief.'

'I guess they were very close,' I said. 'And had been for years.'

'"Two peas in a pod" – isn't that a great old-timey expression? Christy is just so cool and retro.'

In my mind, coolly retro and frozen in time

were two different things. But who was I to judge? I was usually so late hopping on the bandwagon that I most often ended up chasing it. You've heard about Christy's new job?'

'At the mortuary?' Amy's eyes were big. 'Yes. Who knew she was such a . . .'

'Freak?' I said. Then added hastily when Amy's eyes widened, 'I mean that only in the nicest way.'

'Oh, I know,' Amy said, waving it off. 'Christy has a different way of going about things but she's very kind – have you noticed? Look at everything she's done for Sarah's cousin, his being in jail and all.'

'I think she's in love with him.' I got that icky feeling in my stomach at the thought.

'True, though I think that kind of developed, don't you?' Amy leaned on the counter. 'She started to visit him out of kindness and a need to do good and then fell in love. In a way, working at the funeral home is also providing a service to people in need.'

'Since the next step in her career path is sweeping out the cremators,' I said, 'let's hope she doesn't fall in love with somebody there.'

Amy stood up straight. 'Maggy, that's awful.'

'I know, but with Sarah in the office it seems up to me to make the inappropriate jokes.'

Amy cocked her head. 'Maybe next time it'd be better to just skip it.'

I'd take that under consideration. 'Well, anyway, I like Christy and I hope her new job makes her happy.'

As I said it, I spied Mort Ashbury taking the

front porch steps to the door. He pulled open the door and let Hannah Bouchard enter ahead of him. It was obvious she'd been crying.

As Amy turned to greet them, I heard the office door creak open and saw Sarah tiptoe out. Snagging a coffee mug from the counter, she filled it with hot water from the spigot on the brewer and snagged a salt shaker, all without acknowledging me. Then she disappeared again.

With a mental shrug, I poured milk into a pitcher to froth for Hannah's latte. Since Amy was handling the front of the house, it was the least I could do. 'I'll get your latte started, Hannah. And what about you, Mort?'

'. . . So sorry for your loss,' our barista was saying to Hannah.

'Double espresso,' Mort said, approaching the window. 'It's going to be a long day.'

It sure was. 'Three deaths in as many days. Unusual for a place the size of Brookhills.'

'Unprecedented in my memory.' Mort was rubbing his forehead. 'I'm sorry to have given you such a shock yesterday.'

'Detective Taylor and Deputy Hartsfield's deaths were a shock for everybody,' I said.

'Both relatively young and with full lives in front of them,' the mortician said.

'How do you do it?' I asked curiously.

'Do what?'

'How do you deal with death and grieving all day, every day? Psychologically, I mean.'

'In a way, living your own life is easier when you accept that death is the default position.'

I stopped mid-pour. 'What do you mean?'

He lifted his shoulders and let them drop. 'Just that death – ashes to ashes, dust to dust – it's what we all revert to. Nobody is immune.'

A sneeze from in the back.

I continued pouring as I thought about it. 'You're saying that *living* is the anomaly?'

'Exactly,' Mort said, nodding. 'We need to hang onto life with all we can, while we can. Because when we let go – whether it's because we're sick or hurt, tired or it's just time, we . . .'

I set down the pitcher. 'Revert to the "default."'

'Exactly, I—'

'We should take our drinks to go,' Hannah cut in. 'We told – what's her name, Mort?'

He turned. 'Clare Twohig.'

'Yes, we told Clare we'd be at her shop at ten and we're already late.'

I stuck my head out of the service window and looked up at the three oversized clocks above what had been the depot's ticket windows. Eight-ten, ten-ten and six-thirty – the first clock being Pacific Time, the second our Central time zone and the third – which was supposed to be Eastern – stopped, both hour and minute hands dangling at six. 'Clare usually comes by to pick up a latte on her way in just before ten but she hasn't been here today. Maybe she's running late as well.'

'Or she passed up *her* coffee to be there on time and here we are—'

'You *need* your coffee,' Mort said testily. 'As do I.'

'I'm sure Clare won't mind,' I said, pouring Mort's shots into a to-go cup and starting two more. 'In fact, if you'll wait a few seconds, I'll give you her drink to take to her.'

'Of course, happy to,' Mort said. 'Hannah is having a little trouble deciding where Celeste's ashes should be kept, and I thought Clare's shop might give us some ideas.'

'Is someone staying with Nancy?' Amy asked, and then blushed. 'I'm sorry. That's none of my business.'

'No, it's fine,' Hannah said, taking a tissue out of her bag. 'Doctor Goode gave her something to sleep.' She blew her nose.

Amy put her hand on the other woman's shoulder. 'The reason I ask is because Christy told me that Nancy is taking your mother's death very hard. If there's anything I can do, sit with her or whatever, please let me know.'

Amy really was too good for us, in so many ways. Kind and giving, with a love for the environment and an eye for marketing, she inspired Sarah and me to be better people.

So far we were fighting it, but maybe there was still hope.

'. . . Kind of you,' Hannah was saying, pushing an errant lock of hair out of her face. 'But I think we're fine. I tried to get her to come with us today to pick out the urn but she doesn't want to leave the house or even see anyone other than me.'

'She barely tolerates me.' Mort's smile was back. 'But I did think it important that Hannah get out and I thought she'd enjoy meeting Clare.'

'Clare's great,' I said, pressing the covers onto three to-go cups. 'Do you two think you can handle these or do you want—'

The sound of something akin to a cat choking on a hair ball interrupted me. Sarah in the office . . . gargling with saltwater?

I continued, 'A drink tray to—'

She hawked up something.

'Tell you what,' I said, untying my apron. 'Why don't I walk over there with you?'

Thirteen

Clare was grateful for the latte, though I had to admit bringing it personally was a poor excuse for escaping Sarah. And leaving Amy alone with her and her phlegm. Fact was, though, that our barista was far better – and infinitely more patient – at soothing the savage beast that could be Sarah than I was. I was hoping she'd soothe her right out of the door and home by the time I got back.

Clare showed Hannah around, stopping at the coffee and tea servers on the stairs. The shop smelled of lavender sachets and early-blooming fresh lilacs from the floral corner. The antiques themselves added a bit of a must and mildew, partly diminished by the fresh air wafting in from the front door, which Nancy had propped open with an antique flat iron – the kind heated on the stove and used to press clothes. Or so I heard tell. Ironing clothes, even in the age of electric irons, was not my thing.

The display of urns was as lovely as I remembered it, but I noticed for the first time that there was a velvet rope across the top of the staircase. Storage for the store, most likely, or maybe Clare had a private office or living space on the second floor.

'This is beautiful,' Mort said, pointing at an ornate two-handled urn set on a pedestal with four tiny ball-and-claw feet.

Clare smiled. 'You have a good eye. That samovar dates back to the seventeen hundreds.'

The urn, embellished with carved silver garlands of leaves and flowers, was a little gaudy for my taste. 'Is that a coat of arms?'

'Yes,' Clare said, lifting the thing. 'And there's a viscount's coronet here, too. Isn't it gorgeous?'

'It's the perfect size,' Mort said, taking it from her. 'Was your mother a tea-drinker, Hannah?'

'No – coffee-drinkers, both she and Nancy. They could go through pots in a day.' She was misting up.

Mort was admiring his find. 'I may get it anyway. It truly is the perfect vessel.'

It did look like something you'd put ashes in. Or maybe a genie. There was even a spigot for him or her to materialize from.

Hannah had moved on to the other side of the stairs. 'My grandmother had one just like this.' She indicated an engraved silver pot with handles and a spout.

'Another beautiful piece,' the shop owner said, picking it up to show her. 'Victorian.'

'Do you think Celeste would like that?' Mort asked, setting down the samovar to join Hannah.

Tears in her eyes, Hannah glanced at him and then down. 'I think she would.'

'Good,' Mort said. 'Then we'll take both of these.'

He lifted the samovar again and waved Clare and the coffee urn over to the cash register. 'Let's tally this up, and then can I get your business card? I'd like to put you on our list of recommended merchants.'

'Of course,' Clare said, picking one up from a porcelain dish on the counter. 'In addition to our antiques, we provide flowers for all types of . . .'

As the two talked, I focused on Hannah, who was still standing by the urns. 'How are you doing?'

She looked up like she'd forgotten I was there. 'Me? Sad. I feel like I'm losing both of them.' She reddened. 'First Mother and now Nancy to this sudden ennui. She's moody and angry, forgets things and seems to go in and out of focus. It reminds me of my mother sometimes, but not quite.'

'Triggered by Celeste's death, do you think?'

'That's all I can figure. It's like a switch has turned off in her.'

'Has Nancy been seen by a doctor?'

Her eyes flicked in my direction and then back. 'Not besides Doctor Goode, who Mort asked to give her something so she could sleep.'

'Professional courtesy,' Mort said, joining us.

A wan smile from Hannah. 'Neither Mother nor Nancy liked doctors. And hospitals are where people go to die. I guess I got some of that attitude from them. If Nancy doesn't want to see a doctor, I won't force her.'

129

'Even if she's not herself?' Mort asked. 'From what I've seen, she really is incapable of making those decisions at this point.'

'The dislike of doctors predates all this.' Clare's fists clenched at her sides. 'She – my mother, I mean – died peacefully at home. I'm grateful for that.'

'As am I,' Mort said with a little bow and checked his watch. 'Nearly eleven, my dear. You need to be at the attorney's office in twenty minutes and I need to get back to the mortuary with the urn if we're going to be ready for your mother's service at three p.m.'

'Today?' I asked. 'I thought it was tomorrow.' Hadn't Jim told me that?

'No, it's today at the mortuary,' Hannah said, checking her own timepiece. 'Oh, dear. I wanted to stop at the house and check on Nancy before I saw the lawyer.'

'Would you like me to run over to your house?' I asked. 'Or send Amy?' Better idea.

'That's nice, but—'

'It's no problem for me to stop by on my way to the mortuary,' Mort said. 'It's right next door and, as I've said, the old girl does tolerate me.'

'Not for long if you call her "old girl,"' Hannah said with a wan smile. 'But thank you.'

She turned to me. 'And thank you and Amy, too. It'll be better, though, if it's somebody she knows. I wouldn't leave her this long, but it's important I see the new lawyer and get to the bank, too, before the memorial.'

'Christy was saying how difficult dealing with the business side of death can be.'

130

'More so than I ever imagined,' Hannah said. 'And I, at least, have Mort to guide me. And the attorney, too, but he's being part of the problem. We have bills that are due and the funeral costs,' she glanced at Mort's back, 'aren't insubstantial. It's complicated because my mother's money is in a trust. Nancy is the trustee but she's so confused and distraught she's having trouble so much as signing her name.'

'I thought trusts were supposed to make things easier. At least that's what my lawyer friend Bernie is always telling me.' In truth, that's what he was always badgering me about. Not that I had anything to actually *put* in a trust.

'Bernie Egan?' Hannah looked surprised.

'He's a good friend and I worked with his wife Caron for years – both at First Financial and then in Uncommon Grounds.'

'He's the lawyer I'm going to see,' Hannah said. 'Small world.'

'Small town,' I countered.

'From what I can tell, his specialty is copyright law?'

'In the corporate world,' I said, wanting to reassure her, 'but now that he has his own practice he does a little bit of everything. Like I said, small town.'

'And a very nice one.' Mort slipped his credit card back in his wallet as Clare wrapped the urns in tissue paper and found a box to fit them in. I guessed the coffee urn would appear on Hannah's bill from the mortuary along with a markup.

'Well, I'd best be on my way,' Hannah said,

131

stepping out of the door. She was already down the path and on the front sidewalk when she turned and called up to Mort: 'I leave the back door unlocked so just go around and let yourself in, OK?'

'Will do, my dear. And don't worry about a thing.'

Hannah turned back, nearly colliding with a man walking in the other direction. She zigged and he zagged.

Mort hefted the box. 'Thank you so much. Will I see either of you at the service?'

'I'll try, if I can find somebody to mind the shop,' Clare said.

'I'll be there,' I told him.

'That would be wonderful,' Mort said. 'Given the Bouchards are new in town, we don't expect a large turnout. Hannah's afraid that nobody will show up at all.'

'Poor woman,' Clare said, watching Mort load the urns into a black Mercedes. Apparently the BMW wasn't his work car.

'You mean Hannah's mother?'

'Sadly, she's beyond sympathy now. I was talking about Hannah having to deal with all this.'

'She does seem anxious, doesn't she?'

Clare seemed surprised. 'Of course. Wouldn't you expect her to be?'

'I guess,' I said, watching Hannah's back disappear into the distance.

Fourteen

I left the antiques shop and walked slowly down the sidewalk toward Uncommon Grounds.

Hannah *had* seemed worried. Maybe even more worried than sad, but who was I to say? Like Christy had said, the emotional piece is only part of the puzzle you need to deal with when somebody dies.

But . . . if she thought Bernie only did trademark and copyright law – which he had at one time – why had she chosen him as her lawyer in dealing with the estate and trust?

I could hear Sarah's voice – probably raspy from her cold – saying in my ear, 'And why isn't Celeste's own daughter her trustee? Why Nancy?'

'I'll tell you why,' I said out loud. 'Because Nancy was her business partner, best friend and maybe more.'

A man getting up from a bench with an Uncommon Grounds' cup glanced over.

I touched my ear, like I was adjusting my Bluetooth earpiece, albeit an invisible one. He smiled and kept going, and it was only then that I recognized him.

Not only was he the man Hannah Bouchard had nearly collided with going the other way, but I'd seen him before. 'Jack Andersen.'

The man turned. 'Yes?'

Now what did I say? The man was a released felon and may have sheltered his prison escapee brother. In my book, Pauly Andersen was not only responsible for Pavlik's injury but Pete Hartsfield's and Al Taylor's deaths as well.

'You live at Brookhills Manor, don't you?'

'Yes?' The blue eyes above his now peeling nose were twinkling. 'Do I know you?'

'No, but my friends Sophie and Henry are your next-door neighbors.'

He cocked his head and then his eyes narrowed just a bit. 'You're the coffeehouse owner.' He held up the cup.

'Maggy Thorsen. I think you stopped in on Sunday, too, didn't you?'

'You know I did.' The voice and the eyes had turned cold.

'Jack,' a familiar voice called and the eyes snapped back to friendly.

Vickie LaTour was hurrying up the sidewalk toward us. 'Maggy, I didn't know you knew Jack.'

'I didn't, really, until now,' I said truthfully, though I thought I already had the man's number. Jack Andersen may play at being charming but I'd wager that underneath he was as much of a snake as his brother was.

Vickie hooked arms with Andersen. 'Isn't he handsome? Do you know he does his own Botox? Aren't we just a match made in heaven?'

Sure. I supposed a smooth brow and lack of expression was handy for a con man.

'Glad two of my favorite people have met,' Vickie was saying. 'Maggy owns Uncommon Grounds, Jack.'

134

'So I just realized,' he said pleasantly.

'Jack and I were going to meet there on Sunday but we just missed each other.'

'I was early, I'm afraid,' Jack said.

'And I was late.' Vickie smiled up at him. 'It's so us. We went on a cruise to the Bahamas and Jack was always up with the birds.'

'Seagulls, in that case,' he offered with a wide smile.

I laughed, since that seemed to be what was expected of me by the happy couple. 'Sophie mentioned you'd gone on a cruise.'

She wagged a finger. 'And don't you tell her I went with Jack or I'll never hear the end of it.'

'She doesn't like me for some reason.' Jack said it with a can-you-believe-it smile.

'I can't imagine why.'

I'd intended to just play along, but the words came out flat and Vickie gave me an uncertain glance. 'Oh, Maggy. You can't blame Jack for something his brother did.'

Yes, I could. And I did.

'That's not fair, my dear,' Jack said. 'Pauly has done some awful things. I've had to come to terms with the fact that sometimes I'm painted with the same brush.'

Vickie's eyes were as big as the Botox would allow. 'But you were held hostage, Jack. For hours.' The eyes swiveled to me. 'My Jack was a victim as much as your sheriff was.'

Now that was too much. 'Really? Was *Jack* shot? And why would Pauly have even come to the manor if he didn't think his brother would hide him?'

135

A nerve in Jack's jaw was jumping but he said evenly, 'I don't blame you for how you feel. But I can't control my brother or what he thinks. Believe me, I've tried.'

'We need to be away from him, go someplace where he'll never find you.' Vickie turned to me. 'I'm afraid that man is going to come through the window every night when we go to bed.'

Which meant that it was Vickie and Jack that Sophie was hearing through the walls between the two apartments.

'Botox Vickie's doing the convict, huh?' Sarah was sniffling.

We were just inside the door of Brookhills Mortuary. Despite her cold, Sarah had insisted on coming to the funeral with me rather than going home.

'Will you lower your voice,' I pleaded, looking around.

'Why? The place is a tomb. Literally. Helloooo . . .'

I shushed her. 'You realize you're shouting, right?'

'No, my ears are stuffed up. Besides, who's going to hear me anyway?' Sarah waved her arm at the empty hallway. 'There's nobody in the place except you and me.'

'Well, it's just quarter to three.' I stopped. 'Isn't that a song?'

'Isn't what a song?' She dug a tissue from her pocket and blew her nose.

'"Quarter to three." Isn't that Sinatra?'

'I don't know. Google it.'

136

'You say that when you want to shut me up.'

'But, alas, it doesn't work.' A half sigh, half sniffle. 'Are you sure it's today? Maybe you got me out of my sick bed for nothing.'

'You never even went to your sick bed. And if you had, I would have told you to stay in it. But no – you insisted on infecting everybody at the funeral.'

'Which is you.'

'Exactly my point.'

'I'm on antibiotics so I'm not contagious anymore.'

'Your doctor prescribed antibiotics for a cold?' I demanded. 'When? Your first sneeze was yesterday.'

'Actually, I realized it was Sunday. Remember I sneezed when we were outside unchaining the furniture?'

Unlike my partner, I didn't catalog each sneeze. But I did remember this one, because I'd nearly choked myself. 'That was Celeste's perfume, don't you think? But regardless, antibiotics aren't effective against viruses. You're—'

'Geez, will you relax? I had a few pills left over from last time so I took one. And you say *I'm* a pain in the ass.'

'Because you are.' I tapped a discreet card next to a doorway that read: Celeste Bouchard. I stuck my head into the room and saw a photo display at the back, the urn from Clare's the focal point in front. And, permeating everything, Celeste's floral scent.

I put my hand over my mouth. 'This is the place, though I don't see—'

137

'Maggy.' Hannah was approaching, arms wide, and enveloped me. 'Thank you for coming.'

'You're welcome,' I said, my face crushed up against the shoulder of her tailored navy dress. 'You remember my partner, Sarah.'

Hannah turned on Sarah, who is not a hugger under the best of circumstances.

'You may not want to get too close,' I started to warn, but it was already too late.

'It's so kind of you to come,' Hannah said. 'You barely know us.'

'And yet you're hugging me,' came the strangled reply.

'I'm sorry,' Hannah said, stepping back. 'To be honest it's not my nature, but my first husband came from a big Italian family so I got into the habit of going into the clinch first to get it over with.'

'Preemptive hugging,' I said.

Sarah blew her nose.

'Are you sick?' Hannah seemed to notice my partner's red nose and watery eyes for the first time.

'No,' Sarah said, stashing the tissue. 'I always cry at funerals.'

'That's so sweet,' Hannah said, her own eyes filling.

Sheesh. 'We knew that you were new to town, so we didn't know how many—'

The door to the mortuary opened and two men came in, hefting large sprays of flowers. Vickie LaTour and Jack Andersen were behind them.

'Oh, how lovely,' Hannah said. 'Who are these from?'

Vickie linked her arm through the crook of Jack's arm. The happy couple had apparently decided to come out. At a funeral. 'The roses are from us.'

A speculative 'hmmmm' came from Sarah.

Vickie threw an uncertain glance my partner's way as she continued, 'And the lilies are from Brookhills Manor. We couldn't let your mother go out without a proper send-off.'

Hannah's eyes overflowed and she started to sob.

Jack Andersen took a neatly folded handkerchief out of his pocket and shook it out before handing it to Hannah. 'We're so sorry for your loss.'

'Hannah, I don't think you've met my beau, Jack Andersen?'

The bereaved woman tried to pull herself together. 'Thank you for coming.'

Jack gestured toward the photo display – an album flat on the table with framed photos surrounding it. 'Your mother was a beautiful woman. Was she a model?'

'At one time, yes.'

'That was before she opened the boutiques?' Vickie picked up a photograph of a well-endowed brunette in a bikini on the beach, arms flung wide.

'Yes, but that picture you're holding was taken less than twenty years ago. She was nearly sixty, if you can believe it.'

'Good genes,' Jack said appreciatively, taking the picture and studying it. 'An enduring beauty and successful businesswoman. Vickie has told me what a good mind for numbers she had. It was kind of her to help the church.'

'Oh, no, dear,' Vickie said, putting her hand on his arm. 'That's Nancy. Celeste's friend.'

'Oh, I'm sorry,' Jack said, looking around. 'Is she here?'

'Nancy is resting in one of the anterooms. I . . . umm,' the tip of Hannah's nose tinged pink, 'thought I'd bring her in when the service starts.'

'Worried about another "accident," no doubt,' Sarah whispered to me.

I was impressed that she had the restraint to whisper rather than shout it, until I realized she was losing her voice.

'. . . A terrible loss for her,' Jack was saying as he set down one photo and picked up another to study.

There was something about the way the guy was studying a dead woman's glamour shots from long ago that gave me the heebie-jeebies. Hannah must have felt the same way because she took the photo. 'Oh, let me take that. I didn't mean for it to be out here with the others.'

As she tucked the snapshot away, I got a glimpse of two young women smiling and carefree, their arms linked. Probably Celeste and Nancy.

'Oh, there are Sophie and Henry,' Vickie said, waving.

'I thought you didn't want Sophie to know about . . .' I hiked my head toward Jack.

'Now that Jack's planning to make an honest woman of me, she can say all she wants,' the redhead said. 'I sure don't see Henry proposing anytime soon.'

'Jack proposed?' Because, of course, what else does one do when your escapee brother is on the lam after shooting his way out of your house?

I mean, if *that* didn't scream romance, I didn't know what did.

'There are quite a few people from the manor on their way,' Henry said as the two joined us.

'It'll take 'em a while,' Sophie said grumpily. 'All those walkers and canes.'

'We certainly can wait for them. Thank you so much for this.' Hannah gave Henry a kiss on the cheek and the man turned crimson.

'Sophie, Henry,' Vickie said, pulling the former convict over. 'You know Jack Andersen?'

'Know him?' Sophie spouted. 'His brother put a bullet through our wall and shot the sheriff. And the deputy. What's he doing here?'

'Jack is here as my guest.' She took his hand.

Sophie's eyes went wide. '*You*,' her index finger was tick-tocking back and forth between the two of them, like it, too, was trying to figure this out, 'are a couple?'

'We wanted to keep it quiet. You know how people gossip at the manor. But now that we're getting married—' Vickie shrugged.

'But, but . . . what about all the women in—' Sophie put her hand up to her mouth. 'That was you?'

Vickie simpered. 'I've always been a bit . . . noisy.'

'I'd say responsive, like a race car.' Jack draped his arm over her shoulder and they both laughed.

141

'But, but . . .'

I thought Sophie was going to explode all over us. 'Maybe we should take our seats,' I suggested. 'Henry and Sophie, why don't you sit with us?'

Sophie hesitated but Henry said, 'Come along, Sophie.'

Sophie relented and followed Sarah and me into the pew. 'This is just sick. The man is a felon. What can Vickie be thinking?'

'About what?' Christy was in the pew behind us, leaning on the back of ours.

'Just . . . umm, that particular shade of hair dye,' I said quickly. 'Sophie isn't a fan.'

'What I'm not a fan of,' Sophie said, 'is lonely women dating criminals.'

'I'm not lonely,' Christy said defensively.

'Well then, I must not be talking about you,' Sophie snapped.

'Oh, I guess not.' Christy sat back. 'Sorry.'

'Achoo!' came from Sarah on the other side of me.

'Why did you lie to Hannah about having a cold?' I asked, handing her a tissue.

'You're sick?' Sophie nudged Henry to move so she could slide away from me.

'Sarah's the one who's Typhoid Mary,' I told her as Sarah sneezed again. 'Not me.'

'Give it a day. You're probably already a carrier.' Sophie pulled a little bottle of hand sanitizer from her purse, squirting the goo into her palm before offering it to me.

I shook my head. The stuff smelled like rubbing alcohol crossed with the pink sawdust the janitor sprinkled on vomit in my elementary school.

142

'And you ask why I didn't advertise the fact I'm sick.' Sarah was searching through her pocket. 'Do you have another Kleenex? I blew through that one.'

'No. And I just think that warning people is the least you can do.'

'Or better yet, stay home.' Sophie sent a purse-sized pack of tissues sailing over my head.

Sarah caught it. 'I told you, I'm on antibiotics. Besides, the woman hugged me without permission.'

'And she apologized.' For hugging, for God's sake. 'Besides, her mother just died. Can't you cut her some slack?'

'Mine died, too, and you don't see me whining.'

I slid my butt back an inch into the space Sophie had vacated so I could turn to make better eye contact with Sarah. 'I'm sorry, I had no idea. When?'

'Last month.' Sarah sniffled, but I couldn't tell if it was from the cold or grief.

'Why didn't you say something?'

'She lives – or lived – with my sister.'

'I didn't know you had a sister.' Hadn't Sarah given me no end of grief last year because I'd never mentioned my reclusive brother? And she'd never mentioned her sister or her mother. 'Does she live in Brookhills?'

Sarah shrugged me off. 'In Milwaukee. And I don't get on with my mother or my sister, so don't make a big deal of it. Haven't seen them for years.'

Milwaukee was fifteen miles away. This went far beyond forgetting to call mom on Sundays.

'Is that why you don't like Hannah?' I asked, lowering my voice. 'She reminds you of your sister?'

Sarah turned on me. 'You're a psychiatrist now? Or is our omniscient, Christy, having visions?'

'Omnist,' Christy corrected from behind us. 'And I didn't know you don't like Hannah.'

Apparently I hadn't kept my voice down low enough.

'So I don't like martyrs,' Sarah snapped. 'Slay me.'

Two seats away, Henry chuckled.

Fifteen

'Why isn't her own daughter her trustee?' Sarah hissed in my ear. And, yes, her voice was raspy, just as I'd imagined it earlier. 'Why this Nancy person?'

'Nancy was her partner,' I said. 'It's not so unusual. Would your mother have made you her trustee?'

'Low blow.' Sarah snorted. 'But a good one. And no, she wouldn't have. My sister – that's another thing. And Ruth is the very last person my mother should have trusted.'

Lots of bad blood there and I wasn't about to wade in.

Luckily I didn't have to, because Sarah was still talking. 'I'm just saying that Celeste had better instincts. Remember? She gave the lawyer her power of attorney for the sale—'

'Shh!' Christy said from behind us.

I glanced to the front of the room to see Hannah guiding Nancy, dressed in a somber black maxi-dress and oversized vest today, to a seat in the front row. The older woman's face was drawn and tear-streaked, her gray hair limp.

'I feel sorry for her,' I said as Vickie and Jack made their way forward to pay their respects.

'Because of Celeste's death? Or because she's going to have to talk to those two?' Sophie asked.

'Now Sophie,' Henry said. 'Vickie is your best friend.'

'That was before she lost her mind. And we had to listen to her doing it every night.' She turned to me. 'Did she tell you how long this has been going on?'

'Not really. But she went on that cruise you mentioned with him. When was that?'

'Maybe two weeks ago? He must have been the one who filled her with all these ideas about retiring on a ship. And now she's going to marry the man, just like that?'

'Maybe Vickie and Maggy can have a double wedding.'

I kicked Sarah but it was Sophie who gasped. 'You're marrying the sheriff?'

I glared at my partner before turning back to Sophie. 'No, I'm not. Or at least I haven't decided.'

'Oh, I love weddings,' Christy said from behind us. 'Why don't you and Henry tie the knot, Sophie? We can make it a triple.'

'Good idea,' Sarah said. 'Add you and Ronny, too, and we have a movie title.'

I looked at her.

'"Four Weddings and a Funeral"?' Sarah wiggled an eyebrow at me. 'I'm surprised you didn't get that. It's one of your favorite movies.'

I do love me some Hugh Grant. But that was beside the point.

'People ask why Henry and I don't get married,' Sophie was saying, 'and I ask them why we should.'

'Not like you're going to have kids, I suppose,' Sarah said.

'That's what I say,' Sophie said. 'Shuts 'em right up. Though that probably won't work for you, Maggy. You're in your forties, right? These days women your age are still popping them out.'

'Not this woman. Eric, my one and only child, is twenty.'

I felt someone's breath on the back of my neck. 'Did you see the urn, Maggy?' Christy said into my ear. 'It was my idea to soak the doily underneath it with Celeste's favorite perfume. Mort seemed truly impressed with my suggestion. And did I tell you they let me sweep Celeste's ashes? Mort doesn't know, so keep it a secret.'

With pleasure.

'What about the sheriff?' Sophie was saying loudly into my other ear. 'Does he want children?'

Glad to turn my attention back to the living, even if they were haranguing me, I said, 'Pavlik already has a daughter. She's twelve.'

146

'Has he said he doesn't want more?' Sarah was being a huge help.

'No,' I said, letting them take that answer any way they wished. The truth was that Pavlik and I had never talked about having kids. Then again, we hadn't talked about marriage either, until he proposed. But having a baby at my age was so outside my—

Happily, Sophie had lost interest in my relationship and was digging into her purse. Coming up with an airplane-sized bottle of vodka, she held it up to Sarah. 'Kill a cold?'

Sarah ruefully shook her head. 'I can't drink on my meds.'

Or at least she didn't when I was around. Outside my orbit, I wasn't so sure.

'There's Clare,' I said, watching the little shop owner make her way to a seat halfway down. 'And Mort.'

The mortician had stopped at Clare's pew. As the two spoke, Hannah pulled Vickie and Jack away from Nancy to join them.

Sophie shook her head. 'I'm not surprised those two found each other. They're perfectly suited. He's obviously a player and Vickie is on men like white on rye.'

'I think it's white on rice,' I said.

Sophie sat back. 'Now what sense does that make?'

'I think it just means that rice is white, so you can't separate the white from the rice. It refers to two things being as close as they can be.'

'What about brown rice?' Sarah asked. 'Or wild?

147

'And what does that have to do with bread?' Sophie asked.

'It's not white *bread*—' I stopped myself and said, 'Google it.'

Sarah took out her phone but Sophie was still pouting. 'Guess she's part of the family now.'

There was a hurt tone to her voice, and I turned to see Vickie and Jack joining Hannah in the front pew. Mort was nowhere to be seen.

'Are you still thinking of moving from the manor?' I asked to change the subject.

'Henry won't agree to go. Though I'm starting to think just getting away from a round-the-clock version of Night of the Living Dead,' she nodded toward the procession of walkers, wheelchairs and portable oxygen tanks now making their way down the aisle to seats, 'might make the sacrifice worth it.'

'The sacrifice of Henry? Come on. That's not going to happen.'

'I suppose not,' Sophie said grudgingly as Henry slipped his arm around her shoulder.

'I am here, you know,' he said, giving her a peck on the cheek. 'And I'm not deaf like your last suitor.'

'Well, not *as* deaf,' Sophie admitted.

'You know what?' Sarah interrupted, raising her head from her phone. 'This rice thing makes no sense at all.'

'I told you,' Sophie said, sliding closer to see the small screen across my body. 'Does it say what white they're talking about, though? Is it bread?'

'Uh-uh,' Sarah said, holding it up.

'White is the absence of color,' Henry contributed.

'I think that's black.' Christy was leaning forward again, elbows on the back of the pew. 'Or is black the absence of light?'

'It depends whether we're talking paint color or—' I stopped myself as all four sets of eyes focused on me. This had all the trappings of a lose/lose, lose/lose argument.

So I just shrugged. 'Got me.'

It was almost as effective as telling them to Google it. Sarah went back to her phone and Sophie went back to her discussion with Henry. Christy just went back.

The service itself was short, but coffee and cookies had appeared in the foyer while we were in the chapel.

'I really couldn't have people at the house,' Hannah said, one hand at Nancy's elbow to steady her as they stood accepting condolences. 'And besides,' she lowered her voice, 'I had no idea so many would show up. Luckily Mort had boxes of cookies from the last funeral stashed in his storeroom and brought them out.'

'How many of these folks do you actually know?'

'Honestly, just you and Sarah, and Christy and Vickie, of course.'

'Had you met Jack before today?' I was keeping my voice down, too, since he and Vickie were just one mourner behind me in line.

'No.'

I read something in her expression. 'What?'

She shrugged. 'I don't know. He's just kind of pushy. Vickie is my friend, yet . . .'

'He acts like he's running the show,' I completed for her. 'For what it's worth, I don't like him either.'

She put her hand on my arm. 'Vickie told me your fiancé was shot. I'm so sorry.'

Then it was official. When I got home I'd ask to see the ring.

The person behind me let hunger outweigh speaking with the bereaved and stepped out of line to get a cookie. Jack stepped in.

'Again, very sorry for your loss.' Jack pumped her hand and then turned to the older woman. 'Nancy, is it?'

She squinted. 'Are you a doctor?'

'No, dear,' Hannah said. 'This is Vickie's friend. The doctor is the lady. The one who prescribed the pill to relax you?' She turned to us. 'I'm afraid she's taken to them a bit too . . . readily.'

'Do be careful about that,' Vickie said from behind Jack. 'Prescription overuse in the elderly is—'

'I don't like doctors or shots,' Nancy snapped. 'And I don't have a headache.'

'I'm glad you're feeling a little better,' I said to her.

I couldn't blame the woman for being testy. Everybody was talking about her like she wasn't here. Maybe Christy was right about people treating the elderly like they're invisible.

'I think my partner Sarah is coming down with

something, too,' I told her on the theory that her misery would like a little company.

Hannah blinked. 'Is she really?'

'There must be something going around,' Jack said. 'Happily, it doesn't seem to last long.'

Nancy shifted her weight from one foot to another. 'Can we go?'

'Are you tired, dear?' Hannah turned to us. 'If you'll excuse me, I think we'll take a little break.'

'Would you like us to drop Nancy at your house, Hannah?' Vickie asked. 'Then she can lie down in her own bed.'

'Thank you, but she just needs to sit for a bit.' As she started away with her elderly charge, Hannah seemed to remember something. 'Oh, Maggy, when I saw Bernie Egan this morning he said to say hello. Maggy's friend is the attorney overseeing mother's trust,' she said by way of explanation to the other two.

'Bernie's a good guy,' I said.

'Yes, he is, and I'm sure a good lawyer, too. We're just running into a bit of trouble accessing the trust in order to pay,' she glanced self-consciously at Vickie and Jack, 'expenses.'

'Funerals can be terribly pricey,' Vickie said.

'We all need to pay the piper eventually,' her paramour contributed.

Cheery thought. But I was wondering why Mort couldn't give Hannah some sort of friends and family discount, given their relationship. Or maybe an EZ payment plan. I mean, even Pavlik cut me a little slack when I was a murder suspect. And I do mean 'a little.' Like enough to hang myself.

151

'I know,' Hannah said, reddening. 'And I'm sure we'll get it worked out. It's just that Nancy needs to come with me tomorrow and it's difficult for her. Just being here has taken its toll.'

Hannah's eyes were wide and moisture-filled. I thought any moment they'd burst like rain-heavy storm clouds. And so I made an Amy-like offer. 'I'd be happy to go with you and help, if you'd like.'

'Or we could, right, Vickie?' Jack offered.

'Well, I suppose—'

But Hannah wasn't having any. 'That's very kind, but Maggy is an old friend.'

'It's good that you have somebody here,' Jack said. 'Somebody who knows you well, I mean. I was but a stranger in town until Vickie came along.'

Sweet.

Of course, Hannah had meant that Bernie and I were old friends, not she and I. But neither of us enlightened Jack Andersen. It – along with most everything else in Brookhills – was none of his business.

Sixteen

Leaving the mortuary, I realized I hadn't stopped by Pavlik's place yet to pick up the things he needed.

Passing my house on Poplar Creek Drive, I continued south to Brookhill Road and then turned west out of town and toward the Brookhills County administration complex, which included the sheriff's office, as well as the county's court and jail facilities. Kind of one-stop shopping for criminals.

Just past the complex on Brookhill was Pavlik's two-bedroom Cape Cod-style house.

Crunching up the gravel driveway, I parked my Escape and climbed up the concrete steps. Fetching Pavlik's key from my purse, I turned it in the lock and stepped into the living room. The main floor consisted of this room and the kitchen behind it, and on the other side of the house were two small bedrooms with a bathroom between them.

Built in the early fifties, the place would be 'retro' in Amy's opinion. I kind of liked it because it reminded me of the house I'd been brought up in, but with none of the supposed 'updating' of subsequent decades. This house was fifties' kitsch with no apologies.

Looking around, I tried to remember what I was supposed to get.

Toothbrush, of course, since the only spare in my house was Frank's, something I hadn't had the nerve to tell Pavlik after he'd plucked it out of the glass next to my sink and used it.

The toothbrush in his bathroom was worn, the bristles bent. I'd stop at the drugstore and pick up a new one on the way home. I did grab his tube of toothpaste. It was a different brand than mine. I preferred gel but Pavlik was a paste man. Can this relationship last?

We would see.

153

Pavlik would need a jacket now that his leather one was sadly destroyed. I sorted through the front hall closet and settled on a North Face that I laid across the back of the couch. Maybe I'd buy a new leather jacket for him. For us.

Moving to the bedroom, I found underwear and socks in one drawer. T-shirts in another. Jeans in a third.

I lifted out a pair. They looked like they'd been ironed. I sniffed. No. Could that be spray starch?

I collapsed on the bed. The made-up bed, I might add.

Don't get me wrong, I love a neat man. Ted had been a bit of a slob and Pavlik was fastidious by comparison. But . . . could I possibly take on the care and feeding of a man who starched his jeans?

Would Pavlik think I was a slob because I didn't iron my own jeans? Or even wash them each time I wore them?

Or every other time. They just started feeling comfortable after—

OK, Maggy, settle down. You are an adult. Pavlik is an adult. Neither of you is going to change your habits at this stage of life. And you're not expected to. For better or worse, you are now temporarily co-habitating.

Think of it as a fact-finding mission. A trial run. A weather balloon.

Yeah, that's it.

So reassured, I stood up and tried to think what else he might need. Absently, I pulled open the drawer next to the bed.

And closed it.

Then I opened it again.

A framed photo of Pavlik and Susan was smiling up at me. And he was wearing our leather jacket.

I pushed the drawer firmly closed, rocking the lamp on top.

I steadied it. So Pavlik had a photo of his ex in the night stand. Big deal. Susan had been a big part of his life. They'd been married for over a decade and were a couple longer than that. They had a child together.

And, I reminded myself, it wasn't like the photo was on the dresser or hanging on a wall. It had been put away.

In the night stand.

Why in the world had I looked in there anyway? Nobody keeps anything much in a night stand. Except things they need at night. Books. Sex toys. Pictures of their ex.

Argh. What was wrong with me? One moment I'm questioning our compatibility, the next I'm jealous. How exactly does *that* work? But . . .

Pavlik had moved to Brookhills, to this house, after his divorce. Wouldn't you expect that picture to have been packed away in a box somewhere? Why take it out?

Then again, maybe the night stand had been moved intact, drawers full, contents forgotten. I knew people who did that. Sure, that was probably it.

Or at least it was the explanation that would keep me from feeling . . . What was this I was feeling? Jealousy? Sadness? Or just plain ridiculousness? I mean, I probably had pictures of me

155

and Ted laying around my place. Pavlik was likely stumbling over them willy-nilly right this very moment.

I moved to the closet to pick out a couple of dress shirts that Pavlik liked to wear with jeans, the sleeves rolled up. A pair of khakis. Sneakers.

Stuffing it all in a white plastic garbage bag, I let myself out of Pavlik's house, locking the door behind me.

'You didn't have to make a special stop to buy me one,' Pavlik said, holding up the new toothbrush. 'I know mine is trashed but I was fine using your spare. It's practically new.'

That was because Frank didn't brush regularly. 'It was no problem,' I said, pulling a bottle of wine out of the pharmacy bag.

Pavlik slipped an arm around my waist. 'You know, it's not like we haven't swapped spit before.'

Frank lifted his head from his water dish and we exchanged looks.

'I was getting ready to retire that toothbrush to clean grout,' I lied.

'A woman who cleans grout with a toothbrush,' Pavlik said, kissing me. 'Be still, my heart.'

I had cleaned grout with a toothbrush. Once.

I sniffed the air. 'Is that tomato sauce?'

'Yes, though pretty basic. All I could find was canned tomatoes, garlic powder and basil.'

I was surprised he'd found that. 'I had basil?'

'Behind the shriveled limes.'

'Oh, yeah. I bought that by accident when I

had Sarah over for mojitos. I thought it was mint.'

'You didn't smell it?'

'Well, no. I was in a hurry.' See? It was already happening. I was making excuses for my perceived inadequacies. 'We substituted the basil and the drinks were pretty damned good, in fact.'

'It does sound good, actually,' Pavlik said, taking the wine. 'Want me to open this?'

'Can you do it with one arm out of commission?'

'I can try,' he said. 'If you'll keep the bottle steady for me.'

Maybe this living with somebody wouldn't be so bad after all. 'How was your day?'

Pavlik was rummaging in the drawer for the corkscrew. 'Shouldn't that be my line? You were the one off at work while I kept the home fires burning.'

'Oh, God,' I said. 'Please don't tell me you tried to use the fireplace. The chimney hasn't been cleaned for years and the flue—'

Pavlik was grinning up at me. 'Only an expression. Frank and I spent most of the day warming the couch.'

'Did you have any trouble with the Wi-Fi?' I said, holding the bottle so he could pull off the foil.

'I didn't use it.'

'Really?' I held out my hand for the foil. 'What a good patient you are.'

'Not really. I didn't have much choice. The county exec called to tell me I've been placed on leave.' He wasn't looking at me.

157

'Medical leave?'

'That's what they're calling it.' Now he met my eyes.

They were so dark that I couldn't read beyond them. 'But that wouldn't be unusual, would it? At the bank, if you were going to be out more than two weeks, I think it was, they had to put you on short-term disability so you got paid.'

'I know. Hold that.' He gestured to the bottle.

I wrapped my hands around it as he tried to turn the screw into the cork. 'What are you thinking?'

'I'm thinking that you'd be better off doing this by yourself.' He handed me the corkscrew.

I twisted it into the cork and pulled. 'You know what I mean. You were shot and the department has put you on medical leave. Do you think there's more to it?'

He slid out a chair and turned it around with one hand so he could straddle it backwards. 'I think there was a prisoner escape, a stolen police weapon and a shooting that left me wounded and a deputy dead. And God knows it could have been worse, given where it happened. And then, to top it all off, the detective whose weapon was stolen killed himself after refusing the psych evaluation I'd ordered for him.'

'Taylor was afraid he'd lose his job?'

'Or that they'd think he was becoming unhinged, which would have resulted in the same thing. Or maybe he'd just made up his mind and didn't want anybody to stop him.'

'From killing himself.'

Pavlik was gripping the back of the chair so hard his knuckles were white.

'We'll never know. Hell, if it were up to me I'd put me on leave.'

All the chatting about toothbrushes and spaghetti sauce – just bluster to cover what he was really thinking. 'It wasn't your fault. None of it.'

'Yes, I'm afraid it was. All of it.'

We drank the wine and ate the tomato sauce over noodles salvaged from a forgotten box of macaroni and cheese in the cupboard.

It wasn't a good night, but it was one I was glad we'd weathered together.

Seventeen

'Frank jumped in bed with us at about three,' Pavlik said, pouring a mug of coffee the next morning.

Sarah and Amy were taking the opening shifts for the next week or so, since getting both me and Pavlik showered and dressed with only three good arms and one bathroom between us was time-consuming. I had, though, promised to meet Hannah Bouchard at Bernie's office at nine.

'Oh, really?' I was searching through my purse for the car keys.

'Really. And don't pretend you slept through a hundred-pound sheepdog leaping onto the foot of the bed and then shoving his way up between us like a battering ram.'

159

'I had no idea,' I said innocently. 'In fact, I was shocked to find that it was Frank's nose pressed against the small of my back this morning.'

'I hope you were both shocked *and* disappointed,' Pavlik said, coming up behind me. 'Frank doesn't have much of a nose.'

Frank raised said fuzzy muzzle from his breakfast.

'You'd be surprised,' I said, leaning down to give the sheepdog a rub. 'It's just hidden under all that fuzz.'

Vindicated, Frank went back to his food.

'Soooo . . .' Pavlik said, wrapping his arms around me. 'Does Frank sleep with you every night?'

'Not usually.'

Frank threw me a dirty look but didn't stop eating.

'Not *usually*, I mean,' I restated, 'when I have a sleepover.'

'Which is why I've never had a hairy butt in my face before.'

'You had the butt end?' I asked. 'He was the other way around this morning.'

'Only because I made him switch. Though his breath is no picnic either.'

'I know.' I turned in Pavlik's arms and gave him a kiss. 'And I'm sorry. But I let him up on the bed after the divorce, when . . .'

'You were lonely.'

'I was going to say when he was small. Or at least smaller. But yes, I was lonely, too. It's just kind of morphed since then.'

'Well, it's your house and your bed, so your rules,' Pavlik said, letting me go. 'But if there are going to be three of us we're going to need a bigger bed.'

A new bed? That was a big move. 'Frank will sleep on the floor tonight. Right, Frank?'

He pfffted, blowing the hair out of his eyes momentarily, and stalked out of the room.

'I'll buy you a doggy bed,' I called after him. 'You'll like that.'

'Sure he will,' Pavlik said. 'If it's a California king. Which would probably be a good size, come to think of it. Want me to look online?'

'Sure,' I said, despite being anything but that. 'I'd better go now or I'll be late meeting Hannah.'

I gave him a quick hug and then pushed back to study his face. 'How are you, really?'

'Are you asking if I'm going off the deep end?'

'I guess so.' I hesitated and then added, 'Do you think you should talk to somebody?'

'A shrink? Maybe.' He tipped my face up to study it. 'Are you worried that your suggesting it is going to send me to my gun, like Taylor?'

My stomach twisted. 'No. Well, maybe yes, I did hesitate because of that. But not seriously. I mean, you never would. Right?'

It was a mish-mosh of a statement/question but Pavlik got it. 'You don't have to worry. And as for the psychiatrist, the department will probably require it before they have me back, anyway. If they have me back.'

'Please,' I said. 'Don't worry about things that haven't happened yet.'

'Because there are enough to worry about that have?' Pavlik said. 'You're right. I just need to find something to occupy myself. Sitting around watching television with Frank will drive me batty.'

A harrumph from the next room. Somebody had gotten up on the wrong side of bed. Which was pretty much impossible, since he'd been smack in the middle and exited over the footboard.

'Maybe I'll call Hallonquist and find out what's happening in the hunt for Andersen.'

'Excellent idea.' I slipped my purse over my shoulder. 'By the way, his smooth-talking brother is dating Vickie LaTour.'

'Botox Vickie?'

'The very one,' I said, starting for the door. 'And I said dating, but Vickie is talking about an engagement. I'm worried.'

'You should be. The guy has bilked a lot of women out of a lot of cash.'

I stopped. 'So Jack Andersen was some sort of a gigolo? When I heard "fraud" I assumed he's a Bernie Madoff type. You know, getting wealthy people to invest in his schemes and then taking off with their money.'

'Pretty much, but change "people" to "women" exclusively.'

'Aw, geez,' I said, rolling my eyes skyward. 'I'm going to have to tell Vickie. She'll be crushed. And Sophie triumphant.'

'Sophie?'

'Daystrom. Her foul-weather friend.'

'Foul—'

'I'll explain tonight. I'm late already.' I opened the door.

Pavlik put his good hand on it. 'So how many sleepovers do you have? I mean, that Frank doesn't join.'

'Not nearly enough.' I removed his hand. 'And they're all with you.'

I was thinking this cohabitating thing wasn't so bad when I arrived at Bernie's home office door. Finding it locked, I knocked.

'What?' Caron Egan swung open the door.

'Good to see you, too,' I said, giving Bernie's wife a hug.

'Oh, Maggy, I'm so sorry but you couldn't have come at a worse time. I'm on deadline and if it's not Bernie's door, it's his phone. The man needs to get a separate office. And a receptionist.'

'Which you've been telling him for years.'

'And he's been ignoring.' She shoved a strand of light brown hair behind her ear. 'Because he's cheap. Are you here to see him? He's in with somebody right now.'

'If it's Hannah Bouchard, I'm supposed to be in there, too. I'm late.'

'Adding another partner?' Caron asked with a grin. She'd been my first partner in Uncommon Grounds, along with Patricia Harper, who hadn't survived our first day of business.

And no, I'm not talking figuratively.

As for Caron, she'd opted out when the first Uncommon Grounds had been destroyed. Sarah, luckily, had opted in. 'Heavens, no. Sarah is more than enough partner for anybody.'

163

Caron grinned. 'And you also have my fabulous barista find, Amy.'

It was true that it was Caron who insisted we hire our rainbow-haired, multi-pierced rock star of a barista. 'And she remains fabulous. I don't know what we would do without Amy.'

'I wish I had one of her here. Or two.' She pointed to the closed conference-room door. 'Do you mind letting yourself in? I have twenty-two minutes to send this story in and I'm only half done.'

'Still living on the edge, huh?' I called after her as she hurried down the hallway.

'Yeah, right,' floated back to me.

Caron wasn't a risk-taker by any stretch of the imagination, but she had strayed off the straight and narrow once that came to mind. And it had frightened her right back into line.

Rapping gently first, I stuck my head in the door and Bernie waved for me to enter.

He sat on one side of the rectangular-shaped conference table, with Hannah across from him and Nancy next to her.

Bernie stood and hugged me. 'Hello, stranger.'

'I know,' I said, taking the chair beside him. 'It's been too long.'

'Did you see Caron when you came in?'

'She let me in. Did you know your outer door is locked?'

'No, I didn't,' Bernie said, rising again. 'Let me go fix that right now.'

'Thank you so much for coming, Maggy.' Hannah looked like she hadn't slept. And was about to cry. 'I'm not sure how much help you can be, though. Nancy won't even write her name and Attorney Egan thinks we need to get a doctor to—'

'I don't need a doctor.' Nancy seemed shrunken in her flowy dress.

Hannah saw my look. 'She's not eating. I picked up some of those protein drinks but . . .' She shrugged helplessly.

Bernie rejoined us, running a hand over his bald head. 'Now, where were we?'

'You were saying we'd need a court order, and probably . . .' she glanced at Nancy, '. . . an evaluation in order for me to become trustee.'

'Right now, you're the successor trustee to the successor trustee, who is Ms Casperson here. You can only take over if she is unable or unwilling to act.'

I realized I hadn't known Nancy's last name. 'Can't Nancy just request that Hannah take over as trustee?'

'No,' Nancy said definitively. 'And I can't sign my name on that line.'

'And there you have the problem.' Hannah was leaning forward, fingers splayed on the table. 'Despite the fact that Nancy's not capable—'

'I am, though.' Nancy was looking out the window.

I addressed Hannah. 'From what both you and Vickie have said, Nancy was . . . is very competent. Maybe if she has some time to recover from the shock of—'

'We don't have time.' Hannah's hands were pressing so hard on the table that her fingertips were white. 'We have bills, payments due.'

165

It was sounding more and more like Sarah was right and Hannah's only means of support – visible or invisible – had been her mother.

'Perhaps Ms Casperson could sign checks,' Bernie said.

'No, she can't,' Nancy said stubbornly.

'Do you see the problem?' Hannah nearly shouted. The woman was obviously at the end of her tether.

'Who's the beneficiary of the trust?' I asked and then flushed. 'Not that it's any of my business.'

'The two of us.' Hannah hiked a finger at Nancy. 'Fifty-fifty. But it does me no good if I can't get access.'

Again, I wondered whether Nancy and Celeste had been a couple. And, if so, where and for long? Some states recognized common-law marriages but I didn't know if that also included same-sex couples. Or whether that would change anything.

Bernie was leaning forward to appeal to Nancy. 'As trustee, Ms Casperson, you have a fiduciary duty to the beneficiaries, which includes *both* you and Ms Bouchard here.'

Nancy just folded her arms.

'You see what I'm dealing with?' Hannah said.

'I do. But when your mother died, the trust became irrevocable and the terms can't be changed,' Bernie said. 'As I told you, you have a right to petition the court for removal of the current trustee. But that will take time.'

Hannah jumped up. 'Who are you – or the court – to make that decision? It's my mother's trust and I'm the one who hired you!'

166

Bernie stayed seated and calm. 'I represent the trust. And, in that capacity, I am responsible to your mother and her wishes.'

'You didn't know my mother. You have no idea what her wishes are. Were.'

'That's true. I only know what she put in the trust agreement. And Nancy Casperson is the successor trustee to your mother. If there's anybody I work for besides your mother, it's her.'

I couldn't be sure, but I thought Nancy Casperson smirked.

Eighteen

'I'm starting to think you're right about Hannah,' I told Sarah when I got to Uncommon Grounds.

My partner was still sick but, germs or not, I was glad she was there. Not just because I didn't want Amy to have to open every day but because I was petty and wanted somebody to talk to about Hannah. Someone who . . . well, wasn't nice.

'That she has a martyr complex?' Sarah was dusting the shelves where we display coffee-related items for sale. Coffee makers, filters, cups and assorted bric-a-brac.

'Maybe that, but more that her mother was supporting the whole household.'

'Told you so. And now Mom's gone and Hannah of Brookhills gets the whole shebang.'

'Is Hannah of Brookhills supposed to be a play on Joan of Arc or Rebecca of Sunnybrook Farm?'

'The former,' she said. 'Would Joan of Brookhills have made the point better?'

'Probably.' And while we're talking about improvements, your dusting would be more thorough if you actually lifted something off the shelf.'

She held out the lambswool duster. 'Have at it.'

'No, thank you.' I'd been tricked before. Most notably when my ex had washed my whites with his red T-shirt so I'd never ask him to do the wash again. 'You're doing just fine.'

'Tell me what happened at Bernie's. Or can't you say because of lawyer/client privileges?'

I leaned back against the service counter. 'I think having a third person in the room – or in my case, a fourth – negates privilege. So we're good.'

'Did you learn that from Pavlik or on TV?'

'I honestly don't know. But I think it's true.'

'Good enough for me.' She ran the duster between two bone china cups, sending them both skittering sideways.

I didn't comment. On her dusting, at least. 'Can you believe Hannah had the nerve to tell me she thought Bernie was incompetent? Out of his depth is the way she put it.'

'Well—'

You know what I think? I think she went *looking* for an incompetent lawyer and is angry because she misjudged the little bald guy who works out of his house.'

'What did she want him to do?'

'Get Nancy to either hand over her role as trustee or sign checks so they can pay bills.'

'That doesn't sound so unreasonable,' Sarah said. 'I mean, if you discount the fact it's not Hannah's money and her mother gave it to Nancy in the first place.'

'Her mom made Nancy her successor trustee, meaning she controls the purse strings. The beneficiaries though are Nancy and Hannah, fifty-fifty.'

'Interesting.' Sarah jabbed the duster between the two cups again.

I grabbed them. 'Will you be careful? These are fragile.'

'Which is why nobody buys them. Who wants a tiny fragile coffee cup?'

She had a point.

'Anyway, Nancy may be a little unhinged by her friend's death but Hannah will have to prove that.'

'The old lady seemed OK to you?'

'Maybe not OK. She's very thin and Hannah says she's not eating. But there were a couple of times during the conversation that I thought she might be playing Hannah. Actually smirked when Bernie said he worked for the trust, and therefore Nancy, as successor trustee, was his client.'

'What does Hannah want Bernie to do? Decide that Nancy's incompetent and make Hannah the trustee?'

'That may be what she wants but it's not going to happen. According to Bernie, you must have

169

a court order or appeal or something and prove the person can't fulfill their duties if they're not willing to step down.'

'Why did Hannah want you there in the first place? Did she think you could sweet-talk Bernie?'

'Maybe. She made a big deal about our being old friends. Or maybe she thought I could help sweet-talk Nancy.'

'How? You've met the woman twice.'

'I know. Better to take Vickie. At least she knows Nancy. Oh! Which reminds me – Pavlik says Vickie's new boyfriend is a gigolo. Romances women out of their money. I think we should tell her, don't you?'

'Of course,' Sarah said, setting down her duster. 'And I want to be there when you do. Just leave instructions for your funeral.'

'Vickie will be angry, no doubt. But—'

'I'll be angry about what?'

I swung around and there, sure enough, was Vickie.

'Bitten in the butt yet again by the sleigh-bell thief,' Sarah said with a grin.

'Yes, where are your bells?' Vickie asked. 'I noticed they weren't on the side door but now they're gone from the front, too.'

Damn it. I stalked to the door and swung it open. Nothing. Except the sound of it hitting the condiment cart behind it hard.

I steadied the creamer. 'Somebody took them. Who would do that?'

'I'm not sure, but they are pretty annoying,' Vickie said. 'I don't know how you stand them all day, every day.'

OK, if she was going to pick on my bells, I was going to pick on her beau. 'How much do you know about Jack Andersen?'

Sarah and the duster took their seats at the nearest table to watch the show.

Vickie lifted her chin. 'I know that Jack loves me. That's all I need to know.'

'Did you have a tuck, Vickie?' Sarah asked.

'What?' Vickie said, distracted.

'Your chin. I can see it really well from down here and it's not wattly.'

'Wattly?'

'Like a chicken,' Sarah said. 'The skin looks tight.'

'Oh, well, thank you.' Vickie patted the place where wattle had lived. 'Last week Jack had a peel and I did a laser treatment. Do you think it helped?'

'I do,' Sarah said. 'No more jiggling. And speaking of jiggle-ohs, Maggy?' She swept her hand toward me in a 'your turn' way.

I took a deep breath. 'Jack Andersen is a gigolo who romances rich women and takes off with their money.'

Vickie burst into laughter. 'That's ridiculous. I'm not rich.'

There was that. 'Are you sure? Maybe a pension or something?'

Vickie was shaking her head. 'Sorry. Jack loves me because he says I embrace life with both hands. At this point in my life, I'm game for anything.'

As witnessed, at least aurally, by Sophie and Henry.

'Vickie, this is a man you've known less than a year. He's served jail time for bilking women out of their money. Why do you think you're different?'

'I told you, I don't have any money. Jack says we're in the same boat, sink or swim.'

'Telling Maggy about our cruise, honey?'

Yup. Jack. With no warning. Maybe I would be better off belling the people rather than the doors.

But Vickie, for one, looked like she'd scratch my eyes out. 'Maggy isn't interested in our trip, though she'd probably be surprised that you paid for it.'

'Really?' Jack draped his arm around his 'honey's shoulders and smiled. 'Don't you think my Vickie is worth it?'

'I think *you* think she's worth it.' The man set my teeth on edge for no good reason. Except the 'his-brother-shot-my-guy' thing. 'I'm just not sure why you think it.'

'Really.' Same word, different intonation. 'That's a rather rude thing to say about somebody who considers you a friend.'

'I *am* Vickie's friend,' I said, balling up my hands and planting them on my hips, a la Wonder Woman. 'Which is why I'm concerned about her well-being.'

'You don't have to—'

Jack interrupted Vickie's protest, moving closer to me. 'Her well-being doesn't need to concern you. You have your injured sheriff, who has his own problems. I'd save my concern for him if I were you.'

172

I started toward the jerk, even as Vickie put her hand on his chest and Sarah jumped to her feet, duster at the ready.

Jack held up both hands. 'I don't mean to start an argument. I was just defending my woman, much like you'd defend your man against any and all charges.'

'What charges are you talking about?' Sarah was pointing her duster at him.

'Not legal charges, of course. At least, not for now. But there are some who think the sheriff's decision to raid my apartment put innocent people in danger, including myself.'

'From *your* brother.' My teeth were so tightly clenched the words barely came out.

'Again,' the hands were up once more, 'not trying to start a fight. I think it's kind of you to open your home to the sheriff, like Hannah did for her mother and the other woman. I'm afraid I've forgotten her name.'

'Nancy,' Vickie said.

'Of course,' he said, pulling her close with an embarrassed laugh. 'I saw them driving home and waved, but I'm afraid I've met so many women of a certain age since moving here that it's hard to keep them straight. Except for my gal Vickie here, who stands out in a crowd.'

He gave her an appreciative look that made me queasy.

Vickie, though, seemed delighted. 'Oh, you charmer. Bet you say that to all the ladies.'

'Lady killer and lady chiller,' Sarah said under her breath.

Jack would have had to be deaf not to hear,

but he chose to address Vickie. 'Not true, my love. And you are the only woman in my life right now who counts.'

The woman in question giggled.

Jack gave her a squeeze. 'I'm not in the mood for coffee after all. You?'

'Maybe just a cup to go?' She stood on tiptoes to add in a whisper, 'I don't want to offend my friends.'

'No offense taken, Vickie,' I said. 'You know you're always welcome to come and go as you please here.'

'Without question,' Jack said pleasantly. 'It *is* a public train station, after all.'

'True,' I said. 'And I'm hoping to see you in another public facility very soon.'

The mask slipped a bit. 'I'm sure you would like that. But you and your friend have a glass house for accommodations. Maybe I have the rocks to bring it down.'

'Jack!' Vickie said. 'I'm sure Maggy only meant—'

'I *meant* exactly what he and his "rocks" think.' Anger could make me ballsy, too. Or was it just plain stupid? 'And just what glass house problem do you think I have, Jack? I'm not the one who's an accessory to a crime.'

Jack set Vickie aside to lean in close. 'You're not, huh? Well, play nice and maybe no one else needs to know better. *Capisce?*'

Capisce.

Nineteen

'Lady killer and lady chiller? Truly?'

Sarah and I formed a united front, standing shoulder-to-shoulder at the front window as Vickie LaTour and Jack Andersen retreated down the front steps to the sidewalk.

'Lady killer is self-explanatory. And "chiller" like on ice. I thought it was kind of clever. And apropos, as it turns out, given the *capisce* thing. The guy's a mobster.'

The adrenaline had ebbed; now fear was seeping in. 'Let's sit down before my knees buckle.'

'You were great,' Sarah said, following me to the high counter that faced the window.

I pulled out a stool and climbed up, watching the two move out of sight. 'He did threaten Pavlik and me, right? I mean, I didn't just imagine that?'

'The "glass house" and "rocks" thing was pretty clear, I think.' Sarah hiked herself up on the chair next to me. 'And what exactly was it that he whispered to you before the *capisce*? I missed it.'

Sure. This had to be the only whisper that nobody else heard. 'Something about playing nice and maybe nobody would have to know better.'

'About what?'

'Accessory to some crime. I have no idea what he means. And why bring Pavlik into it?'

'Could it have something to do with the reason they put him on leave?'

'Medical leave,' I said. 'Pavlik is a hero. He only got shot because he tried to save Pete.'

'I know that,' Sarah said. 'But you know how it is. Everybody has their own version of the truth.'

'I don't buy that. A fact is a fact, by definition.'

'And it's a fact that Jack Andersen thinks he's got something on you and Pavlik. Maybe when you go home to your house hubby you should find out what that is.'

'I honestly have no idea.'

I'd found Pavlik sitting at the kitchen table, a computer in front of him.

He sat back now. 'The bus station is a dead end so far. The security camera in the parking lot hasn't been working for a month, so we don't even know when the Chrysler was dumped. We do have a camera at the ticket window inside.'

'But no Pauly?'

'Nope. And not on the cameras on the surrounding buildings either. It's possible he jumped a train without a ticket, of course.'

'You said the stolen car was a Chrysler?'

'Yes.' He hit a few keys. 'And you, my dear, know the owner. Dark green Chrysler belonging to Gloria Goddard. Report filed Monday afternoon by Oliver—'

'Benson.' Small world, indeed. 'Well, that sucks. Gloria had a stroke, which is why she's

176

at the manor in the first place, and now her car was stolen?'

'From the rehab wing,' Pavlik said, nodding. 'She and Benson used the car on Sunday—'

'To come to Uncommon Grounds.'

'I didn't know that.' Pavlik made a note. 'You do have a finger on the pulse of this town.'

'Only the arteries that run by my coffeehouse.' I settled on the chair across from him. 'Are you back on the case?'

'Not officially, no.' He punched some keys.

'But you talked to Hallonquist.' I gestured at the folder next to the computer.

'One of my friends on the Milwaukee PD, since the train station is there. I decided I'd be putting Hallonquist in a bad position by asking him to keep me updated. I'm his boss – or at least was – so he'd feel an obligation even if he was instructed not to.'

'You think he's been instructed not to?' I asked.

'It's an ongoing investigation. More than one ongoing investigation. Pauly Andersen is one case, then there's Taylor's suicide, and also the question of whether the shoot-out at the manor was reckless.'

'You didn't start that – Pauly did. And you had evacuated people from the surrounding apartments. What were you supposed to do? Let him go?'

'I know. But a complaint has been filed so they have to investigate it.'

I frowned. 'Who complained?'

'Well, that's another interesting thing,' he said, leaning back in his chair. 'Vickie LaTour.'

'Who happens to be Jack Andersen's girlfriend.'

'Which I only know because you told me. And I thank you for that.'

'It's what I do.' I was chewing on this new information. 'Do you think Jack put her up to it?'

'I wouldn't be a bit surprised.'

'But Vickie is my friend,' I said. 'Why would she do this?'

'I doubt that she's thinking of it as something she's doing to you. And even if she is, she wouldn't be the first woman Jack Andersen convinced to abandon her friends as well as her scruples.'

'Geez, what's this guy got?' I asked. 'I just don't see it. The only things in his face that move are his eyes. And you should have seen them change when I challenged him.'

'You obviously pushed the right buttons. If you were one of his "ladies," he'd make that seem to be your fault.'

Like an abuser, who only hit you because you asked for it. 'And revert to charming, I suppose. Until the next time.'

'Exactly.'

I'd seen the chameleon-like change in the man. 'Could he be abusing her? Physically, I mean?'

'It's not his M.O. but there are other methods of abuse. Isolating somebody from their friends, for one.'

Or turning her against them. 'Do you think that's the leverage he thinks he has on you? Vickie's complaint?'

'Petty stuff for a guy like Andersen. Besides, a complaint would be public record. What's there to expose?'

'I don't know, but he said I had a glass house problem and he had rocks.'

Pavlik's lips twitched. 'He really said that?'

'He did.' I got up and opened the kitchen cabinet. 'Glass of wine?'

He nodded. I poured two glasses and handed one to Pavlik. 'For what it's worth, Hannah Bouchard likes Jack Andersen about as much as I do. Says he insinuates himself in situations and she's absolutely right.'

'What do you mean?

'For example, he offered to come to the lawyer with her instead of me. Who does that?'

'A con man.'

I'd been about to take a sip of wine but stopped mid-air. 'You think he's decided Hannah is a better mark than Vickie?'

'From what you've said, she's got money – or will, once she gets hold of it. That's one of his pre-requisites.'

'But Hannah is probably in her early forties. If Mort is twenty years older, tack on another ten or fifteen for Jack.'

'Age-appropriateness is *not* one of his requirements. One of his victims was in her thirties.'

Yikes. 'I guess at least he'd leave Vickie alone.' And likely heartbroken.

'And destroy Hannah instead.'

'True. Though I think she's more able to take care of herself. Besides, Vickie is a friend.'

Pavlik's eyebrows went up. 'I thought Hannah was a friend, too.'

'A very new friend, so if I had to rank her on

179

my concern-o-meter she'd have to be below Vickie.'

The sheriff grinned. 'Good thing you didn't go into law enforcement. You'd have to serve and protect people you didn't even know.'

'Oh, I would if I swore to.' I looked over his shoulder. 'What are you doing now?'

'Checking the layouts of the bus station and adjoining buildings to see if we missed something.'

'Somewhere he could have disappeared to.' I sat down. 'Didn't you say the Milwaukee police are on this?'

'They are, but I can provide an extra brain and set of eyes. I've studied Pauly and—'

My phone rang but I sent it to voicemail. 'Sorry.'

'Anyway, the MPD is happy to have me helping and it gives me something to do, which makes me happy.'

'And me.' I reached across the table and put my hand on his mouse. Which was where *his* hand was. 'I—'

The phone rang again and this time I glanced at the readout. 'Christy – both times.' Then, 'Hi, Christy,' I said into it.

'Maggy, did you hear? It's just the saddest thing. Nancy Casperson has died.'

'Died of what? I just saw her this morning.'

Pavlik's chin gestured, *What's going on?*'

I lifted my shoulders.

'I know you did, which is why I was sure you'd want to know. Hannah brought Nancy home after your meeting and then ran over to see Mort about the funeral expenses and all. When she got home an hour later, Nancy was dead.'

'She died in her sleep?'

'Yes, isn't it awful? Just like Celeste. *Déjà vu*.'

Or a horror version of the movie *Groundhog Day*. Except at Hannah's house, fewer and fewer people were waking up each morning.

Twenty

'So, Hannah finds out she can't remove Nancy as trustee, at least easily. A few hours later, Nancy is dead.'

We'd moved on to the second course of our meal, from the wine to peanut butter sandwiches.

'Convenient, but maybe too much so.'

I stopped smoothing my chunky spread onto the bread. 'Too obvious, you mean?'

'I mean she'd have to be an idiot to kill Nancy and think she'll get away with it.' Pavlik appropriated the knife and jar of Skippy from me. 'Is she?'

'I don't think so. But she is desperate.' I gestured at his sandwich – more a mutilated piece of bread. 'Can I please help you with that? Spreading peanut butter one-handed is not working.'

'Fine.' He passed the peanut butter to me and I took his plate. 'You don't have any Jif, do you?'

Jif brand peanut butter, instead of Skippy? Sacrilege. What was next? Pepsi over Coke? Decaf over regular?

But I just said, 'Sorry, no.'

'Or cracked wheat bread?'

Them's fighting words. 'Peanut butter on cracked wheat? That's un-American.'

'Not for this American,' Pavlik said, getting up and swinging open the refrigerator door. 'You have any decaffeinated Diet Pepsi?'

'Nooooooo . . .'

Frank raised his head and then cocked it, the doggy version of, *What the hell are you doing?*

Pavlik just asked, 'Was it something I said?'

'No, I'm fine. And I don't have any Diet Pepsi that's de—' I choked on the word, 'decaffeinated. But I can get some, if you like.'

'Nah.' Pavlik sat back down with a Diet Coke and popped it open one-handed. 'I just wanted to see what you'd say.'

I passed his sandwich of Chunky Skippy on white bread, thank you very much, to him. 'That was mean.'

'But kind of fun.' He put his hand over mine. 'I know that two people of our ages thinking about blending households . . . it isn't an easy thing.'

'But,' I ran my index finger down his palm, 'it's kind of fun.'

'I did mention to Pavlik,' I said to Sarah the next morning, 'that—'

'Wait,' she said, waving a dishtowel in my face, 'was this before or after sex?'

182

'Who said we had sex?' I snatched the towel.

'Your face.' She snatched it back. 'And your laid-back vibe.'

'I'm always laid back.' I opened the dishwasher and started to load in the dirty cups from the morning rush hour.

'That's clean,' Sarah said.

'Oops, guess we'd better run it again.' I added soap, closed the door and pushed the power button.

'See?'

'See what?'

'See how chill you are. Non-sated Maggy would have been ticked off at whoever didn't empty it, then ticked off at herself, for not checking before she put in the dirty cups.'

'I—'

Sarah held up her hand. 'I'm not done. Then you would have debated leaving the cups and taking out the clean dishes around them. Taking out one, you'd have sighed, put it back, finally slammed the door and re-started the machine.'

'You make me sound demented.'

'You are.' My partner was feeling better, with just the occasional cough to show she'd been sick. She chalked it up to the antibiotics. I just figured germs didn't stand a chance against her.

'Anyway,' I said, 'I told Pavlik that you and I both questioned Hannah's . . .'

'Martyrdom?'

'Exactly.'

'What did he say?'

'He seemed more inclined to give her the benefit of the doubt.' I felt myself blush. 'But

183

then we kind of got off the subject and didn't quite get back to it.'

'I'm sorry I brought it up.' Sarah hiked herself up on the kitchen counter.

Not sanitary practice, but what the hell.

I did the same.

'Returning to our regular G-rated programming,' Sarah said, 'what does Nancy's death mean for Holy Hannah?'

'Poof goes the problem of accessing the trust, for one thing.'

'That's awfully convenient.'

'Plus, they both died in their sleep? How lame is that?'

Sarah bobbed her head. 'To be fair, probably a lot of old people die in their sleep. If they're lucky.'

Since when was my partner fair? 'You have a point, but I'm not going to give up on mine.'

'I didn't think you would.'

'So Celeste dies . . .'

'In her sleep . . .'

'Or at least while napping,' I continued, 'on Sunday while Hannah is away.'

'And the same thing happens to Nancy four days later,' Sarah continued. 'Also when Hannah is away again.'

'You know,' I said, 'someone like Christy or Amy—'

'Somebody with a heart?'

'Well, yes,' I admitted. 'They'd say Nancy died of a broken heart.'

'Sweet,' Sarah said. 'And I'm sure it happens, but it's just too convenient. Don't you think?'

184

'I do. I asked Pavlik to see if there was an autopsy on Celeste.'

'Will he?'

'He would and he did. Believe me, Pavlik's looking for anything and everything to keep him busy.'

'And?'

'As he suspected, there was no autopsy, given her age and all.'

'Old people die.'

'They do. And the body's been cremated, so there's no going back.'

'What about Nancy?'

'You mean will there be an autopsy? Yes.'

'Then Nancy's death is considered suspicious?'

'Pavlik might have suggested that it might be.' I shifted my bum on the hard counter.

'You said he wasn't in touch with his department. That it wasn't fair or something I didn't quite understand.'

'Not fair for him to press his detectives – Hallonquist, in particular – on the shooting, which involves Pavlik and is still under investigation. He had no problem letting them know about the trust and what Hannah has to gain.'

'Which you told him.'

'I did.' I couldn't resist a satisfied smile. 'All of a sudden, we're like Nick and Nora, trading theories. It's kind of nice.'

'Don't get used to it. He'll be back to being sheriff and shutting you out in no time.'

I hopped down. 'True. But right now I'm enjoying having him around.'

'Aww.' Sarah tipped her head. 'Are those wedding bells I hear?'

I heard them too, except, 'Those are my sleigh bells!'

Mort Ashbury came around the corner dangling two red ribbons with bells attached. 'Look what I found.'

I took them. 'Where were they?'

'In the dumpster in the parking lot.'

Sarah slid off the counter, too. 'What were you doing in our dumpster?'

Mort looked surprised at the abrupt question. 'Well, I . . .'

'Don't mind Sarah,' I said. 'We've had trouble with people dumping things and then we're charged for the removal.'

'Get your own damn dumpster, I say,' Sarah said.

'Not you, Mort,' I said. 'I'm sure the mortuary has its own trash removal service.'

'And who knows what you put in it,' Sarah added.

Thankfully, Mort didn't enlighten her. 'To answer your first question, Sarah, I had an old to-go cup in the cup-holder in my car and dumped it to make way for the new one.'

Getting the hint, I set down the bells and picked up a cup. 'Today's brew is Sumatran.'

'Sounds good,' Mort said. 'It's going to be another busy day. Both the Hartsfield and Taylor services are scheduled for tomorrow.'

I assumed Pavlik would want to go. 'They're not at the same time, are they?'

'No, no. The Taylor service is at one o'clock at Angel of Mercy and the Hartsfield funeral

186

will be at four in our chapel. We knew people – especially law enforcement – would want to attend both.'

'Christy called to tell me about Nancy,' I said, pouring his coffee.

He sighed. 'Another tough one. The elderly die, of course, but so soon after Celeste? It's very hard on Hannah.'

'I bet,' Sarah said, the inflection somewhere in the wasteland between sympathetic and sarcastic. 'We hear there's an autopsy.'

'This morning,' Mort confirmed. 'It's unnecessary in my opinion, given she'd been ill and under Doctor Goode's care. But for whatever reason, it's been ordered.'

Pavlik and I were the whatever. 'Is Hannah worried?'

'I think more relieved than anything.' He opened his wallet and took four dollars out.

Sarah's head went up. 'Relieved that Nancy is dead?'

'Oh, heavens, no. That an autopsy is being done. She feels responsible, I think, and an official cause of death will give her closure. Well, thank you for this,' he continued, picking up his cup, 'and just put the change in the tip jar.'

'Thank you,' I called after him as he hurried out of the door. Then I turned to Sarah. 'That's interesting.'

'What do you mean?' She'd picked up the dishtowel and was wiping the ring Mort's cup had left.

'If Hannah killed Nancy, why would she be grateful for an autopsy?'

187

'Maybe she just told him that to cover her tracks. Or maybe he's in on it and he's just saying that.'

'Both possible, I guess.' I chewed on my lip. 'It's curious that Mort said Doctor Goode was Nancy's doctor when she'd only seen her once. And that time, according to Hannah, only to prescribe a sedative after Celeste died.'

'Maybe that's all it takes.'

My phone jangled. 'Would you please get a clean towel? You're just smearing around coffee smooge with more coffee smooge.'

Sarah looked skyward, and then went to the backroom to do as she was told. For once.

I checked my phone and saw that it was Pavlik. 'Hi, there.'

'The autopsy results are back.'

'And?'

'And there are petechiae in the eyes.'

Small hemorrhages. 'Nancy was strangled?'

'Suffocated. There were no ligature marks or bruising.'

'She'd been sick – a cold or the flu. Could congestion have caused it?'

'Struggling to breathe causes the petechial hemorrhaging, so theoretically, yes. But there's something else.'

Sarah had returned with a fresh cloth and held it out to me.

I punched up the speaker on the phone so Sarah could hear and mouthed, 'Pavlik.'

'Yes?' I said to the sheriff. 'You said there was something else?'

'We – or Hallonquist and his new partner

– think a pillow might have been used to smother her and there's a pillowcase missing.'

'The killer took the pillowcase?'

'A yellow flowered pillowcase, according to Hannah Bouchard.'

'Maggy,' Sarah whispered.

I waved her off. 'Why take the pillowcase and not the pillow?'

'Something on it, I assume. Something that didn't penetrate to the pillow, which was hers in the first place.'

'So finding Nancy's DNA on the pillow would mean nothing.'

'Most likely.'

'So why—'

The towel came flying across the room and fell at my feet.

Except it wasn't a towel. It was a pillowcase covered in yellow daisies. And with a red lipstick stain on it.

'I'll call you back,' I said into the phone.

Twenty-One

'Nancy wasn't wearing lipstick when I saw her,' I said for the third time.

'Oh, good,' Sarah said. 'The pillowcase isn't the murder weapon and we're off the hook for touching it.'

'You touched it,' I said, holding the thing by the wooden tongs we used for getting stuck toast out of the toaster. The sticky bun tongs were in the dishwasher. 'And I kind of doubt that a pillowcase would hold fingerprints anyway.'

'Good,' she said. 'Let's throw it in a dumpster. Mort's got one and who'd want to dig through that?'

'The last thing we need is for somebody – or some camera – to catch us disposing of it,' I said. 'We're not guilty. Why act like it?'

'Then why not tell Nick, Nora?'

I didn't think that was such a good idea, either. 'Pavlik may be on leave but he's not going to withhold evidence.'

'Yet we are.'

'Because it's evidence against *us*.'

'You might want to lower your voice,' Sarah said. 'Unless you want people walking down the street to hear us discussing this.'

I rubbed my forehead. 'How did it get here?'

'Well, there were no bells on either door. If we were behind the service counter or in the front of the store, somebody could come in the platform door and go right into the storeroom without us ever seeing them.'

'OK, so there's the how,' I said. 'And I don't want you ever to complain about those bells again, once I put them back up. But what's the why?'

'Why would the killer plant evidence on us? Got me. You're the one arguing with the Scandinavian mob.'

Jack Andersen. 'You think this is a crime that I was supposed to be accessory to? Maybe it had nothing to do with Pavlik.'

'Then who's the friend?'

190

'What friend?' I was casting about for some-where to put the pillowcase.

Sarah shook out a plastic garbage bag and held it out. 'Here.'

I dropped the pillowcase in. 'Your fingerprints will be on that bag.'

'Then we'll dump out the pillowcase and take the bag with us. At least we're protecting the evidence.'

'I think the police use paper bags. Or is that just for wet things?'

'Wouldn't you put wet in plastic?'

'It can degrade the evidence, I think. But this isn't wet.' I looked inside the bag. 'At least, I don't think it is.'

'Is the lipstick considered wet?'

'I'm not sure.' I had a different question on my mind. 'Why would somebody put lipstick on Nancy and then suffocate her?'

'It's evidence. They wanted to pin it on us and it's the only thing they could think of.'

'It's so cruel, though. Poor Nancy having this crazy person applying lipstick on her?' I had a thought. 'Speaking of crazy, maybe Pauly Andersen had a hand in this.'

'If he's still in the area after being responsible for two cops dead and one being wounded, he *is* crazy.'

'And it runs in the family, from what I've seen of Jack. He just has a shiny candy-coating over the rot.'

'I think you're making a mistake.'

'Not calling Pavlik, you mean?' I'd been hunkered over the bag and now I stood up.

'No, I'm fine with that. I think it's a mistake letting Hannah off the hook. She's the one who benefitted from both Celeste and Nancy's deaths.'

'True.' A lightbulb went off. 'Maybe she's the friend.'

'What?'

'You asked who the friend Jack referred to was, if not Pavlik.'

'Yeah, when he said something like "you and your friend have a glass house."'

'I assumed he was talking about Pavlik, since he had just come to stay at my place. But maybe Jack was talking about Hannah.'

'He thinks you and Hannah killed the old ladies?'

'That's the only thing that makes sense.'

'Hannah, I get. We suspect her, too. But why you? You barely know the woman and have no motive.'

'Maybe because Hannah wanted me to go to the lawyer with her and not him?' I had a thought. 'He threatened me. Maybe he's blackmailing her.'

'Hannah?'

'Yes, maybe that's why she's so hot to get her hands on the trust. She said she needed to pay Celeste's final expenses. Including blackmail?'

'If he's blackmailing her, that means she killed Celeste. And then, following that logic, she also had to have killed Nancy to get access to the money.'

'That means she's the one who put the pillow-case here. But why frame me?'

192

'She could be framing me,' Sarah said. 'Or isn't that in the realm of your possibilities?'

'Oh, for God's sake,' I said, picking up the bag with my toast tongs and holding it out to her. 'Are you jealous? Because if you want to be framed, it's fine with me.'

'I just don't like to be dismissed.'

'You have as much of a motive as I do, which is none. Yet somebody stashed Nancy's lipstick-stained pillowcase with our towels.'

'They folded it first.'

'So? Being neat doesn't preclude you from being a murderer.' I didn't understand any of it. 'I'm going to ask Pavlik to find out if Nancy's body had lipstick on it.'

'I thought you didn't want him to know about . . .' she gestured at the bag I was still holding, '. . . that.'

'I'm hoping I can finesse it.' I pulled out my phone with my free hand. 'Can you hold down the fort for a while?'

'If you do something with the evidence,' she said. 'Has it occurred to you that whoever framed us wants it found? The police or sheriff's department could be on their way as we speak.'

'Shit, no answer,' I said. 'OK, I'm going, but I'll hide this on my way out.'

'Are you going to see Pavlik?'

'No. I need to think about how I'm going to approach him on the lipstick thing. I don't want to invite questions.' I dropped my phone into my purse. 'I'm going to see Bernie.'

'Ah, the lawyer. Maybe you'll see Hannah there.'

'That's just what I'm thinking.' Taking my tonged garbage bag with me, I left through the side door.

Twenty-Two

But nobody was in Bernie's office, except for Bernie.

'Hannah called me this morning.' He waved me into a guest chair. 'But I can't tell you anything beyond that. And you know it.'

'I do.' I sat. 'But I was hoping you might bend the rules, since I was here with Hannah and Nancy just . . . Geez, was it just yesterday?'

'It was.'

'And now she's dead.'

'So I understand.'

'C'mon, Bernie,' I said, leaning forward to put my elbows on his desk. 'This has to smell as fishy to you as it does to me. Yesterday, Nancy was blocking Hannah's access to the trust. A few hours later, she's dead. And Hannah's already called here, presumably to get access to the trust to pay "expenses," right?'

'It would be within her rights.' He was my friend, but he was also her lawyer now, which meant he was measuring his words.

'Nancy was murdered.'

'What?' That had gotten his attention. 'By whom?'

'The autopsy says she suffocated.'

194

He was literally on the edge of his chair. It squeaked. 'Suffocated, or *was* suffocated.'

Potatoes, potahtoes. Lawyers and their words. 'Technically, she suffocated.'

'Geez, there you go again, Maggy. It's always got to be murder. An elderly woman died of suffocation. Maybe she choked on something.'

'Yes, a pillow. Then after she was dead she took off the pillowcase and stuck it in my storeroom.'

'Holy shit.'

'Yeah.'

'Are you hiring me?'

Since I'd just blabbed, I was torn between 'I don't need a lawyer' and 'yes, please,' which would get me confidentiality for a mere $400 per hour.

Then came a pounding at the door, which I'd locked behind me. 'Hello? Is anybody in there?'

Hannah. Bernie and I exchanged looks, and I had to assume my eyes were as big as his.

'If she hires you to represent her and I'm here, does that give me confidentiality about what I just told you?'

'What?'

'The pil—'

'Shhh.' He held up a hand. 'I don't know what you're talking about.'

Good enough for me. 'Should I let her in?'

Bernie threw out his arms. 'Why not?'

I opened the door.

'Oh, Maggy, did you hear? Poor Nancy was murdered and they think I did it.' She threw her arms around me and burst into tears.

195

I just stood there stiffly and let her cry it out on my shoulder, before leading her into Bernie's office.

After all, the woman might have killed two women and tried to frame me for one of the murders. No hugs for her.

Bernie poured a glass of water for her and then sat back down. 'What can I help you with, Hannah?'

'Didn't you hear me? Nancy was suffocated and I'm a suspect. The investigators are crawling all over everywhere looking for a pillowcase.'

Bernie's eyes flicked to me and then back. 'A pillowcase.'

'It's missing off one of the bed pillows. The pillow itself was next to Nancy on the bed. I noticed it when I got home and wondered where the cover was, but . . .

'You have to believe me,' she continued to Bernie. 'I didn't do this. I would never do this. She was . . .' She started to sob again.

The woman was in worse shape than when her mother died. I guess a murder rap hanging over your head could do that.

I was feeling none too chipper myself. 'Are you being blackmailed, Hannah?'

'What?' from both she and Bernie.

'How can you ask me that?'

There had been the slightest hesitation after the word 'how.' Had she started to ask how I knew?

'Just a feeling,' I said, watching her. 'Jack Andersen is a sleazeball and he gives me the creeps. I think you feel the same.'

'And so he must be blackmailing us? For what?' Her words were defensive but there was fear in her eyes.

'I'm not sure. Something about your mother's death, I think.'

That seemed to score, but maybe only half a point. 'I . . . I came here for help. Not to be accused.'

'If you're being blackmailed, you're the victim,' I said. 'Maybe Bernie and I can help.'

Bernie's face said he didn't want any part of this, but he kept quiet.

'I don't need your help. I came here to see my lawyer. In private.' She stood up.

I gestured for her to sit down and got up myself. 'I'm sorry. You're absolutely right. I'll go.'

When I got to the door, I turned. 'But when you said, "he must be blackmailing us," who is the "us"?'

'She didn't answer me, of course,' I told Pavlik over Chinese that night. 'And if looks could kill, Bernie's would have dissolved me right there and then.'

'Essentially, you just stirred her up and then left him to deal with her.' He was trying to get fried noodles out with chopsticks and the box kept moving away from him.

I took it and pushed a tangle of noodles onto his plate. 'I did. I called later and apologized.'

'Thanks,' he said. 'And I assume you also tried to worm more information out of him.'

'Would you expect any less?' I helped myself to orange chicken. 'But, alas, all he told me

197

was that he'd recommended a criminal attorney and that was pretty much that.'

'Bernie's a good lawyer. I'm sure after he'd gotten over his initial astonishment at the idea that his client might be a murderer—'

'Who might also be being blackmailed,' I interjected.

'He went back into professional mode. Did you get any sense of whether she was able to access the funds in the trust? If so, Andersen could get his money and be in the wind along with his brother.'

I was enjoying having Pavlik egging me on, rather than lifting his leg on my ideas. 'You think I could be right about the blackmail then?'

'A man like Andersen is always on the lookout for a new opportunity to make money. If he stumbled on information that made him think Hannah had something to hide, sure I believe it. I just don't know why he seemed to be threatening you as well.'

'For some reason, he believes that I'm in this with her. Whatever this is.'

'The "us."' Pavlik scored a piece of chicken off my plate. 'Could it be Hannah and Nancy?'

'They killed Celeste for her money? But if they're in collusion, why did Nancy refuse to let Hannah have access to the trust?'

'She wanted it all for herself maybe.'

'The woman fell apart after Celeste died – mentally and physically.'

'Guilt can do that.'

'True.' Greed and guilt wouldn't make good

bed partners. 'I wish we knew how much is in the trust.'

'Bernie would be disbarred if he told you that. And rightfully so.'

'Could a trust be subpoenaed?'

'Not a trust, because it's an entity. But a trustee probably could. There would have to be cause, though.'

'The trustee is Hannah now. I assume they're looking at her seriously for Nancy's murder.'

'More seriously, if they could find the pillowcase.'

I put down my chopsticks. 'What would that prove that the pillow can't? From what Hannah said, it was Nancy's pillow – and pillowcase – so her DNA will be all over them.'

'There could be a stain or something that didn't soak through to the pillow. But more than that, it's the absence of the pillowcase that's important. Somebody was there and took it for some reason.'

'Maybe to frame somebody else?' I leaned down to put my plate on the floor so Frank could slobber up the rest of my rice.

When I sat back up, Pavlik had an odd look on his face. 'Why would you say that?'

I tried for casual, but not push all the way to nonchalance. 'Like you said, taking the case only raised suspicion in the first place. Why not leave it and hope Nancy's death passed for natural causes?'

'I didn't say that, but it's a point. The case could also have traces of the assailant on it, meaning he or she would have been forced to take it.'

'What kind of traces? A pillowcase wouldn't show fingerprints, would it?' I wanted to confirm what I'd told Sarah.

'Not likely, but there could be blood, sweat, hair, that sort of thing. Thing is, if Hannah is the killer, those traces – except for the blood, probably – are easily explained by the fact she lived in the house.'

'And probably made the beds,' I added. 'Which is why, I guess, I was thinking there was another reason for removing the pillowcase.'

'We'll know when and if it's found.' He was studying me. 'You wouldn't know where it might be, would you?'

'Me? How could I know that? Oh, by the way, I saw Mort this morning. Did you know Al and Pete's funerals are both tomorrow?'

Pavlik's face dropped and I felt ashamed for changing the subject to the loss of his officers. Not that he could ever forget, but when we'd been discussing the case he'd been distracted and, seemingly, happy.

'Hallonquist told me when we talked,' he said. 'He'd be willing to come pick me up if you have to work.'

'That's nice of him. But I'd like to go with you. If it's OK with you?'

'Better than OK,' Pavlik said. 'Thank you.'

He took my hand and I felt ashamed all over again. This time for lying to him about the pillowcase.

Twenty-Three

I took the opening shift the next day so I could leave at noon to pick up Pavlik for the funerals. He was waiting at the door in full dress uniform when I pulled in.

'How did you get into that all by yourself?' I asked as he climbed into the Escape. 'I should have come home early so I could help you.'

'I can move my left arm, you know. It just,' he rolled it and winced, 'smarts a bit when I do this.'

'Then don't do this.'

Pavlik threw me the look the old gag deserved. I knew that it smarted more than a bit. I also knew he'd deny it.

'You know,' I said, backing out of the driveway, 'I was thinking last night—'

'When was that?' Pavlik asked. 'Before Frank jumped up and sat on my head or after?'

'After. Anyway, if Hannah is being blackmailed by Jack, like we talked about, that would have to be for Celeste's murder.'

'We don't know that Celeste was murdered.'

'And never will.' I pointed the car south on Poplar Creek Road toward Angel of Mercy, where Al Taylor's service was being held. 'But if Jack has something on Hannah—'

'Which he also thinks he has on you—'

This was the downside of being with – and

201

trying to keep things from – somebody as smart as the sheriff. Pavlik knew stuff. And figured out other stuff to go with it. I could almost see the sheriff slotting 'missing pillowcase' right up there next to 'Jack's leverage on Maggy.'

'It has to be something that pre-dates Nancy's death,' I continued.

'I'll give you that. Turn here.'

'But the church is on the next street down.'

'I know, but we'll park behind the church with the squads.'

I followed directions. 'But if our theory is that Hannah was already being blackmailed for Celeste's murder, she certainly wouldn't kill Nancy and give him even more of a hold on her.'

I expected him to correct 'our theory,' but he surprised me. 'When I hit a roadblock in a case, I step back to the various forks in the road and rethink my assumptions. Maybe we're wrong about the blackmail in the first place. Or it has nothing to do with the deaths of Celeste and Nancy.'

Like I said, he knows stuff. 'Other than that Hannah moved here with them in December, I don't know enough about her to guess what else Jack might have on her.'

'Who would?' Pavlik asked, unclicking his seatbelt as we pulled up next to a Brookhills' County squad car.

'Christy, maybe.' I shut off the engine. 'She sold Hannah the house here. Or, better yet, Mort. They're dating.'

'Mort and Hannah?'

'Yup.'

'That's interesting.' Pavlik had gone to open the door and now he sat back. 'Mort will be here today.'

'Want me to talk to him?'

'Let me,' Pavlik said, swinging open the door. 'You take Christy.'

'I'm not sure she'll be here,' I said, getting out and coming around the car.

'I am.' Pavlik pointed to the back door of the church, where Christy was talking to her boss. 'We'll divide and conquer, but not necessarily now. We have all day and two funerals. You catch Christy alone and I'll do the same with Mort.'

'Sheriff.' It was Mike Hallonquist. He was in full dress uniform, too.

'Mike.' They shook hands. 'You know Maggy Thorsen.'

'Of course. Good to see you, Maggy.'

'Same,' I said. 'I'm so sorry about Al.'

'He could act like a jerk but he was a good cop.'

I smiled. 'And here I always thought you were the one playing the good cop, to his bad.'

'It was our shtick,' Hallonquist said with a matching grin. 'We tried it the other way around, but I couldn't cut it.'

'I bet.' I shook my head. 'Despite Al's hard-ass act, I never questioned his heart, at least once I got to know him.' Which admittedly had been a rocky time.

As we approached the back door, Mort and Christy finished their conversation and Mort went inside. Christy started down the sidewalk toward us.

I thought I had my opportunity to talk to her, but Pavlik took my arm and said, 'Wait.'

Whether it was because Christy seemed in a hurry or Hallonquist was with us, I didn't know, but I followed his lead. 'Hi, Christy.'

'Oh, hi, Maggy. I'm running back to the mortuary to help prepare for the Hartsfield service. Will I see you there?'

'You will. You remember Jake Pavlik, and this is Mike Hallonquist.'

'I'm so sorry for your losses,' Christy said. 'We will do right by your officers. Mr and Mrs Taylor are inside if you'd like to greet them before the service.'

She hurried away with a sympathetic smile.

'She really has taken to this,' I said.

'To what?' Hallonquist asked.

To dealing with death was what I was thinking, but I said, 'Christy just started with the mortuary after years of teaching piano. It seemed quite a leap at the time.'

'They're both service industries, I guess,' Hallonquist said. And then, 'What the hell?'

We had rounded the corner to the front of the church.

'Now that's interesting,' Pavlik said.

I followed their gazes and saw Jack Andersen in a dark suit amidst a sea of blue uniforms. As we were watching, Vickie LaTour came out to meet him. 'Oh, that's not good.'

'Actually,' Pavlik said, 'it could be. Let's go say hello to your friend.'

I assumed he meant Vickie. Facetiousness wasn't Pavlik's thing.

'Oh, Maggy,' Vickie said, looking relieved to see a familiar civilian face. 'I'm so glad to see you.'

She seemed so adrift and panicked that I gave her a hug. And I'm not much more of a hugger than Sarah is. 'What are you doing here?' I whispered into her ear.

'Jack insisted,' she whispered back. 'To pay our respects. I'm . . . I'm appalled.' The woman was visibly trembling.

'Andersen.' Pavlik didn't take the man's proffered hand.

'Sheriff Pavlik.' He turned to Hallonquist. 'And Detective . . .?'

'Hallonquist,' Pavlik supplied. 'Al Taylor's partner.'

'Of course,' Andersen said. 'I'm so sorry.'

'If you're so sorry, tell us where your brother is so we can put him away for life,' Hallonquist said.

As he spoke, I saw officers stepping back. It took me a second to realize that if trouble started, they wanted time to react.

And get a good shot off. Out of the corner of my eye, I saw Father Jim move out of the narthex and, if not into the fray, near it.

Pavlik had seen him, too. 'Now, Mike, that's not fair. I'm sure Father Jim here would say that Andersen's not his brother's keeper.'

But Father Jim shook his head. 'I'm afraid that was what Cain said when God asked him where his brother Abel was.'

'That's right.' Pavlik cocked his head. 'And hadn't Cain killed his brother?'

'He had,' Jim said. 'Beyond that, though, we should all be our brother's keepers. In that light, Cain's denial was both against doctrine and an outright lie.'

'Because he knew very well where his brother was,' I said.

Pavlik nodded. 'Or at least where he'd left his body.'

Silence. One, two, three beats. Then, 'I killed my brother? That's the analogy you're going for?' Jack Andersen was smooth.

'Parallel, analogy.' Pavlik shrugged. 'Take your pick.'

'And why, in this work of fiction you're weaving, would I do that?'

'Money?' Pavlik ducked his head. 'I'm sorry to say that your brother Pauly is violent and uncontrollable. None too smart, either. You, on the other hand, are very smart. You plan, you pick your mark, you execute. But with him on the loose, you never know when he's going to show up and ruin one of your schemes. Like with Vickie here.'

Jack put out his hand and pulled Vickie toward him. 'There is no scheme this time. Vickie and I are in love.'

I wasn't sure that was true on either side, at least anymore. But she said, 'Let's get out of here, Jack. Please.'

Andersen held up his hands. 'What about it, Sheriff? Are you going to arrest me? Oh,' the hands went down again, 'I forgot. You're not sheriff anymore, are you?'

'He is as far as we're concerned,' a voice from somewhere in the blue-uniformed crowd said. 'All he has to do is say the word.'

'No, Andersen's right,' Pavlik said. 'I'm not in a position to take him down. Yet.'

'C'mon, Jack,' Vickie said, tugging at him.

Finally he relented and let her pull him away. As they did, the blue sea parted to let them through.

'What was that?' I whispered in Pavlik's ear as we sat waiting for the service to start. 'Are you telling me you knew Jack killed his brother all this time?'

'Of course not,' Pavlik said. 'It came to me when I thought of the Cain and Abel story.'

'Really?' I sat back. 'That's pretty cool.'

Pavlik tipped his chin. 'It is, assuming it's true and he takes the bait.'

Twenty-Four

Detective Al Taylor's service was short and sad. Taylor was divorced with no kids and his mom and dad, both in their seventies, seemed to be surprised and overwhelmed by the support from his fellow officers.

'But he took his own life,' his mother whispered to Pavlik in the receiving line afterwards.

'Al was one of my best detectives,' Pavlik said. 'He could be a pain in the butt, if you'll excuse me for saying—'

207

Next to his wife, Mr Taylor cracked a small smile. 'Nothing we don't always know, right, Helen? Remember all the trouble he gave us growing up? Always had to have the last word.'

She nodded once and a tear rolled slowly down her cheek.

'But we always knew he had our backs,' Pavlik said. 'He felt he let us down and didn't seem to want to hear otherwise.'

'And so he had the last word.' Mrs Taylor held up a shaky finger. 'One more time.'

Pavlik smiled. 'Your son was a good man.'

His father was folding and refolding the order of service. 'He left what he had to that poor widow and her daughter. I think . . . I think that was a very honorable thing to do.'

'Yes,' Mrs Taylor said, her voice breaking. 'Al did his best.'

'Now we'll do the same, Helen,' her husband said. 'And get through this. He never wanted us to hurt like this.'

We walked to the car in silence.

'Is it wrong for me to hope that Pauly Andersen is dead?' I said, getting in. 'And that he suffered as much as Al Taylor and his parents? And Mrs Hartsfield and,' I looked across the center console, 'you.'

'That's probably a question best asked of Father Jim. I'm more of an eye-for-an-eye man.'

'Don't give me that,' I said. 'You believe in justice, not vigilantism.'

'You don't know that. Maybe I'll go rogue if I'm not reinstated.'

I had no fears of Pavlik going rogue, but the

fact he was thinking of life after sheriffing broke my heart. 'Fighting for justice. Does this mean we're going shopping for a bat spotlight and a cape?'

'Please. I'm not a follower. I'll develop my own alter-ego.'

I grinned. 'Speaking of altars, I saw you talking to Father Jim.'

'Your old boyfriend? Yes, I was asking him for your hand.'

I swatted him.

'Ouch,' he said, wincing. 'Wounded, remember?'

'I'm so sorry.' I was mortified. 'Is it OK? Did I rip any stitches?'

'No, but my ego has sustained a terrible wound.'

'Your ego is just fine.' I put out my hand palm up.

He took it. 'Only if you marry me.'

'Maybe I will,' I said. 'Now tell me what you really were talking to Jim about.'

'First, I wanted to explain why I brought him into the discussion with Jack.'

'Which was?'

'I wanted Jack – and maybe Vickie, even more so – to know Father Jim was there listening.'

'It probably would give Vickie pause,' I said, taking my hand back and using it to turn the ignition key. 'Not only is she Catholic but she works for Father Jim. Jack, though, is another thing. He's perfectly brazen in front of fifty-plus law enforcement officers. Why would a priest make a difference?'

Pavlik pulled the seatbelt across and clicked it in. 'You never know. Maybe Jack was an altar boy. Or just has good old Catholic guilt, which is the other thing Jim and I talked about.'

'You have Catholic guilt?' I was waiting for traffic to clear behind me, so I could back out. 'But you were brought up Jewish.'

'We have the corner on guilt,' he said. 'But Jim was showing me a note that somebody put in the collection plate.'

I shifted my eyes from the rear-view mirror to Pavlik's face. 'Some kind of threat?'

'Just the opposite. An apology. For stealing.'

I sat back. 'Somebody receiveth rather than giveth when the plate passed by? That's pretty low.'

'And pretty hard to do without somebody seeing. Father Jim does say it explains why collections have been down.'

Which Langdon Shepherd had mentioned.

'Does Jim think it's an inside job?' I asked. 'I mean, one of the elders or the people passing the plate? It's obviously somebody inside the church.'

'He doesn't know but he gave me the note.' He reached into his suit pocket and held out a folded sheet of paper.

'Fingerprints?' I asked, hesitating.

'All over it, from what Jim told me. The elder who found it passed it around before giving it to him.'

'This person used cutout words,' I said, examining it. 'They probably wouldn't go to all that trouble and be stupid enough to leave prints.'

210

'My thought, too.'

I felt a twinge of gratification and looked down at the note. *We took money from collections. Will replace. Please forgive me.*

I handed it back. 'First "we," then "me" – did you notice?'

'I did. Interesting, though crooks don't necessarily have good grammar, especially when piecing together a note like this quickly.'

'Was this found in the collection plate on Sunday?' I asked.

'Today, but—'

'Well, that narrows things down. It has to be somebody here for the funeral.'

'Not necessarily.' Pavlik twisted his head around. 'I think you can back out now.'

I shifted into reverse. 'Why not necessarily?'

'Watch out.'

I was backing out of a parking spot amidst dozens of squad cars. Believe me, I was watching out, but apparently not enough.

'Maybe give it a minute,' Pavlik suggested. 'Anyway, the elder found it in an empty plate before today's service.'

Hmm. 'The pilfering might have been going on for a while. Vickie said she and Nancy were trying to track down some sort of discrepancy in the books. Maybe this was it.'

'When was this?'

'It would have been Saturday night, because Vickie mentioned it on Sunday morning. Nancy had just taken over the books from Fred Lopez. Maybe she was on to something.'

'And what? Fred killed her?'

'I think he's been deported, so probably no. Besides, Fred's a great guy with a family.'

'Great guys with families sometimes get in financial trouble and become desperate. But Fred or not, if Nancy and Vickie found this discrepancy on Saturday night why wait until Thursday to kill her? And what about Vickie?'

I shook my head. 'I don't know.'

'Do you know if we're ever going to back out? Because we're going to miss Pete's service if we don't.'

'Oh, right.' I put the car in reverse and this time pulled out successfully. 'I need to talk to Vickie. Without Jack around.' I shifted verbal gears this time. 'Do you really think Jack pulled a Cain on his Abel?'

'It's entirely possible.'

'The bait you mentioned. It's Jack knowing that you're on to him?'

'And doing something in reaction, like making sure the body is hidden or the weapon is properly disposed of.'

'How will you know? You're still on leave.'

'The department still has officers sitting on Jack Andersen's place in case his brother shows up. If Jack heads off into the woods around Poplar Creek to move his brother's body, for example, we'll know it. Or Hallonquist will and he'll tell me.'

The woods stretched the length of Poplar Creek from behind Brookhills Manor past the mortuary, Hannah's house and beyond. 'Has the area behind the manor been searched?'

'Not for a body.'

'Your theory is that Jack killed Pauly in the woods and then stole Gloria's car and abandoned it at the station to make us think he'd left the area.'

'Pretty much.'

'Your guys checked the trunk, right?'

Pavlik gave me stink eye. 'A little credit, please? And it was the Milwaukee PD, since the train station is in Milwaukee.'

I grinned and turned north on Poplar Creek Road to the mortuary, where Pete Hartsfield's service would start in twenty-five minutes. 'And the trunk of Jack's car?'

'Doesn't have a car, according to him. There's nothing registered in his name.'

This was the suburbs and public transportation except for the occasional bus from the city was nearly non-existent. How did the man get around? 'You said the MPD scanned the security footage around the bus station for Pauly. What about Jack?'

'Their focus was Pauly, though they should have had Jack's picture, too.'

'Maybe somebody picked him up. If a car pulled up at the front and Jack ducked out the door and into it quickly, they might have missed it.'

'You're thinking the somebody might be Vickie?'

'You mean is she Bonnie to Jack Andersen's Clyde? Got me. But she has a car and you say he doesn't.'

'Any idea what kind of car?'

'White Kia Soul.' I glanced sideways at

him. 'I think she's scared. Didn't you get that impression?'

'Honestly, yes. And eyes on the road. Please.'

I complied and Pavlik continued, 'Question is whether she's afraid for herself or for him.'

'Or both.' We passed my house. 'I wish we had time to stop and let Frank out.'

'I could cut you a doggy door. That's what I did for Muffin.'

'You know Frank. You've slept with Frank. If you cut an opening big enough for him to get through, there'll be no door left.'

'Yet he manages to squeeze himself into the two inches between us in the middle of the night.'

'I know. He's like a memory foam mattress. Arrives small and then splat, he's all over the place. Here we are.'

The mortuary driveway had a rope across it and Christy was directing traffic. 'Sorry, Maggy, but the lot is full. You can park at Hannah's if you like.'

'She's not home?' I asked.

'She's staying with Mort,' Christy said, waving to another car. 'The house is so empty now.'

'Happens when you kill off all your house-mates,' I said as I pulled up the driveway.

'You're ruthless, you know that?' Pavlik said.

'More cynical, I think. I just think bad things. Mostly, I don't even say them except to you and Sarah.'

Pavlik braced himself on the dashboard as we hit a pothole. 'Why us?'

'Sarah's even more ornery than I am. And you,

I love.' I stopped in front of a white frame house with green trim.

'See, did that hurt?' he asked, getting out. 'And you said it twice now in less than a week.'

'Trying to get used to it.' I went around the car and snuggled into his arms. 'You do know I care about you, right?'

'I do. And I think you're even getting used to living together.'

'Scary as that is, yes.' We started down the driveway hand in hand. 'Though technically you're living with me.'

'You're right. Living together demands more than one dresser drawer and just space enough on the bathroom counter for my toothbrush.'

'It is a little tight. Ouch!' I held onto his good shoulder to rub my ankle.

'Turn it?' Pavlik asked.

'Just a little – it'll be fine. This driveway needs to be paved,' I said as we started down it again. 'The house itself looks nice enough but it's set so far back into the tree line. We could have parked at my place and walked back from there easier.'

'Not to mention let Frank out.'

'Yup, thereby averting a possible doggy emergency.'

As we approached Christy again, I said, 'I'm going to stop and talk to her. Save me a seat?'

'Sure.'

Pavlik continued on up the hill to the mortuary while I waited for Christy to finish giving instructions to a driver in a blue car.

'There seems to be more of an equal number

215

of civilian and law enforcement cars at this service,' I said.

'I know,' Christy said. 'I don't think Detective Taylor had as many non-police friends or much family. I didn't stay but I imagine it was terribly sad.'

'It was. As Pete's will be.'

'Such a young family.' She sighed deeply.

'Is this getting to you?' I asked. 'All the deaths, I mean. Celeste, Pete, Al and now Nancy, all in less than a week.'

'Five days, actually.' Christy blew a lock of hair out of her face. 'Celeste died Sunday and Nancy on Thursday. Today is Saturday.'

I saw my opening. 'That's right. It was Monday when I almost made you late getting to the mortuary for Celeste. Were you able to help with the cremation?'

Her face lit up, God help us. 'I was, in fact. I just observed the body preparation and loading. But the technicians actually let me help sweep.' She frowned. 'I told you that, didn't I?'

She had, but I wanted to clarify what day the cremation was. 'Sophie was jabbering in my other ear.'

'Oh, yes, at Celeste's funeral. It was lovely, wasn't it?'

'It was. I haven't heard what arrangements have been made for Nancy.'

'The cremation is scheduled for tomorrow so the service will likely be Monday afternoon. I can let you know, if you like. Though I'm sure Hannah will tell you, since you're friends.'

Why did everybody think Hannah and I were friends? Even Jack Andersen had—

Andersen's name in connection with Celeste's funeral rang a bell. Hannah had said, 'Maggy is an old friend,' meaning I was an old friend of Bernie's. Jack Andersen, though, had misunderstood and assumed Hannah and I were old friends.

Neither of us had corrected him at the time, me figuring it was none of his business. But if Jack did think we were longtime friends, he might assume that I knew something about her that I clearly didn't. Maybe something that dated back to before she came to Brookhills.

'. . . Like to do them around one o'clock, but—'

'Why so long?' I interrupted.

'What's so long?' Christy asked, not understanding.

Not that I necessarily did. Which is why I was asking. 'Celeste was cremated the day after she died, but Nancy died on Thursday and isn't being cremated until Sunday afternoon. Why so long?'

I purposely didn't mention the forty-eight-hour waiting period Jim had told me about, wanting to see what Christy would say.

'Excellent question, Maggy. It is an interesting business, isn't it?'

Fascinating. Answer the question.

'There was an autopsy on Nancy, but that fell within the forty-eight hours we have to wait before cremating a body anyway. The extra day delay was because the Hartsfield service was being held here.'

217

Good of them not to smoke out the funeral guests. 'But what about the forty-eight hours for Celeste? She was cremated the next day.'

Christy's nose wrinkled. 'I know there are exceptions for special circumstances, so she must have fallen into that category.' Her handbag was hung over the fencepost and now she pulled out a paper and pen. 'You know what? I'm going to ask Mort about what exactly the special circumstances were.'

'No need to do it on my account,' I said hastily. If there was something hinky, I didn't want to tip him off.

'Oh, no bother,' Christy said. 'I need to know these things if I'm going to be in the business.'

She lowered her voice and beckoned me close. 'Don't tell anybody, but I think I'm going to go all the way.'

OK, it was an old-fashioned way of putting it. But then, like Amy said, Christy was retro. 'All the way with Ronny?'

'What?' She giggled as she got what I meant. 'Oh, Maggy, don't be silly. Ronny's in prison. No, I meant I'm really going to commit to this new career.'

'And that means?'

'I'm going to become – wait for it – a mortician!'

A booming organ signaled the start of the second funeral of the day.

Twenty-Five

'No Jack Andersen at this service,' I said to Pavlik as I drove us home.

'Hopefully he's busy burying the body.' He checked his cell phone. 'No messages to that effect, though.'

'I assumed he'd be a little stealthier. Like do it in the dead of night, perhaps?'

Pavlik was texting.

'I'm glad Jack wasn't at Pete's service,' I continued, 'but I was hoping maybe Vickie would be there alone.'

'She sounded like she wanted nothing to do with either funeral.'

'I'm sure she'll be at Nancy's. But that won't be until Monday from what Christy said. Oh!'

Pavlik looked up from his text. 'What?'

'Both she and Father Jim told me that there's a forty-eight-hour waiting period before a body can be cremated. Nancy's cremation is tomorrow.'

'OK.' He was back to texting.

'But Christy also said that Celeste's body was cremated on Monday morning – less than twenty-four hours after she died. That apparently there are exceptions to the rule. Is that true?'

'I can check.'

Switching from texting to Googling, he punched it up. 'Here it is. The Wisconsin statute on cremation. No person may cremate the corpse of a

219

deceased person within forty-eight hours after the death, or the discovery of the death, of the deceased person unless the death was caused by a contagious or infectious disease.'

I frowned. 'I don't think Celeste had an infectious disease. Or at least I hope not, or we were all exposed to it on Sunday.'

A chill went up my spine as I thought about Sarah getting sick, too. 'Could that be what also killed Nancy? A disease from Celeste?'

'Only if that disease causes pillowcases to disappear.' Pavlik was still studying his phone. 'It says that cremation requires a permit signed by the coroner or medical examiner, so the mortuary would have had to obtain that before proceeding.'

'No autopsy was done on Celeste,' I said.

'Not unusual if the death isn't suspicious. A doctor could pronounce death, too, and provide that information for the permit and the death certificate.'

'I don't know who might have done that in Celeste's case. Hannah said that both she and Nancy hated doctors and refused to see them. Though she did,' I drummed my fingers on the steering wheel, 'have your doctor—'

'Doctor Goode?'

'That's the one. Mort said Nancy was under her care, which seemed a stretch since Hannah said all she'd done was prescribe a sedative.'

Turning the car into my driveway, I turned off the engine. 'Doctor Goode is a friend of Mort's and part of the Goddard Gang.'

'My family practice doc is in a gang?'

220

'You know what I mean. It's what the group of people who used to meet at Goddard's for coffee – and now Uncommon Grounds – call themselves. They're pretty tight.'

'You're insinuating that Phyllis Goode did what?'

'Not insinuating. Just suggesting that Mort might have asked her to sign off on Celeste's death to save Hannah the heartache of having to have an autopsy. Celeste was old and apparently ill. It's not all that different than her calling the ER doc for us and having him sign you out of the hospital.'

'For one thing, I wasn't dead. For another, I was in my rights to sign myself out.'

'I know,' I said, patting his hand. 'But I didn't really want the liability of bringing you home like that. What if you'd bit the big one overnight?'

'What?' Pavlik put down his phone. 'You were afraid—'

'Water over the bridge,' I said, waving him off with a grin. 'But my point is that people bend the rules for friends. And maybe Doctor Goode bent the rules for Mort and Mort bent them for Hannah.'

'What about the permit required for the cremation? Mort certainly would have to have that.'

'True, but what's to stop him getting the permit for the cremation and then not waiting the forty-eight hours?'

'But what's to be gained by cremating a body a day early? Destroying evidence? Of what?'

I knew Pavlik had to be exhausted after the

funerals of two of his men, so I just shrugged. 'I don't know. What's say we go in, build a fire and have a glass of wine?'

'Sounds good,' Pavlik said, swinging open the car door. 'But first we'd better let Frank out before he goes firehose on us.'

Excellent idea.

Storms woke us up that night. Or first woke Frank, who then stepped on me to launch himself over Pavlik and off the bed.

'Ouch!'

I used to be a side sleeper, but since I'd let Frank on the bed I'd become a pretty-much-any-position-that-gives-me-a-few-inches-of-mattress-and-a-shred-of-blanket sleeper. My legs got more sleep than I did, since they were usually trapped under one of Frank's furry body parts and needed resuscitation in the morning. Add Pavlik to the equation – and the bed – and . . .

'Oooh, cramp, cramp.' I was frantically grabbing at my leg.

'What, what?' Pavlik was blinking.

'Charley-horse in my calf. Frank was laying on it. And it went to sleep.'

Pavlik sat up and gave it a rub. 'Was that thunder I heard?'

'Yes. That's what woke Frank up and set off this chain of events.'

'I didn't hear him.' He was working his thumb into my calf muscle.

'Mmmmm. That's because he sailed over you when he used me as a springboard to jump off the bed.' A flash of lightning followed by . . .

one one-thousand, two one-thousand, three one-thousand, four one-thousand, five one . . . a crash of thunder. 'Five seconds, so the storm is five miles away. I love a good thunderstorm.'

'Actually, that's not true.'

'I don't love thunderstorms?'

'No, I'm sure that you do. But it's not true that each second between the lightning and thunder means the storm is one mile away. Since it takes roughly five seconds for the sound to travel one mile, you need to divide the seconds you count by five.'

The theory behind it was beyond me at that time of night, but I could do the math. 'Five divided by five – so just one mile away, not five.'

'You got it.'

'A lifetime of storm-counting, shattered in an instant.' Stretching, I pointed my toe and the cramp seized again. 'Oww, oww, oww.'

'Who knew you were such a baby,' Pavlik threw a sideways glance my way, 'about leg cramps. You're so . . . stoic about other things.'

'Good attempt at bailing yourself out,' I said, giving him a pat on the cheek. 'But I'm not stoic about anything.'

He grinned. 'As I recall, you don't scream too much when facing down a python. Or an alligator.'

'Paralyzed with fear is a real concept. That's good,' I said as the cramp let up. 'Thank you.'

'You're welcome.' He lay back down. 'Can we go back to sleep now?'

'Not quite yet,' I said.

'Ohhh?' His eyes darkened playfully. 'What do you have in mind?'

Not that. At least, not right that second. But I needed Pavlik to find out something for me without tipping him off that I had the pillowcase. 'I was wondering do they remove makeup during an autopsy? It seems like they would in case it was concealing bruises or something, right?'

Pavlik groaned. 'I probably deserve this.'

'Deserve what?' I asked apprehensively.

'Your being fixated on something like that in the middle of the night. I probably did it often enough to Susan.'

Way to bring up the ex-wife.

He sighed and sat up. 'But in answer to your question, in my experience they would take photos and then make a careful examination, which I believe would include removing makeup. Why? Do you think Nancy was being abused?'

Since that was exactly what I hoped he'd think I was getting at, I said, 'Maybe. Do you think you could ask tomorrow?'

'About signs of abuse on the body? It would have been in the autopsy report.'

'Also the makeup itself. You know, whether she still had on foundation or eyeliner or lipstick.' Nancy had been wearing none of those things in Bernie's office, something that Pavlik couldn't know since he wasn't there. 'It might give us an idea how long she was home after she died. You know, did she have time to take off her makeup?'

I thought it was a masterful sleight of hand on my part, especially at 1:10 in the morning. But Pavlik's eyes narrowed. 'If I know you, you're after something else.'

He did know me. But I also knew him. 'Me?'

I said innocently, slipping back down onto my pillow. 'Well, maybe a little something else.'

As I pulled Pavlik down to me, Frank resignedly settled on the rug next to the bed.

Twenty-Six

Sunday was my day off, so Pavlik and I had breakfast together.

Which meant I made coffee and he made toast from the last of the white bread. 'Do you have butter?'

'Of course. Who doesn't have butter?' I swung open the refrigerator door. 'Well, maybe not.'

I was saved from his expression, since he was working on getting the heel of the bread out of the toaster.

'I have some wooden tongs,' I started to say and then realized they were at the shop. Or, more specifically, under the shop, along with the garbage bag containing the pillowcase. 'Or I had. Whatever did I do with those?'

'Probably hiding with the butter,' Pavlik said, unplugging the toaster and turning it upside down to shake. 'We need to do some grocery shopping. Or easier, just raid the fridge and cabinets at my place.'

Why did I get the feeling he had no plan to return to 'his place' any time soon? At least to live.

'You're getting crumbs all over,' I pointed out.

'But the crust came out.' He held it up. 'Which is good, because it and this,' he indicated a full piece of toast on a plate, 'are the only things we have to eat.'

Sure, if you discounted green sludge dog food and spray cheese.

'Tell you what,' I said, slipping my arms around him, 'I want to go by Brookhills Manor and talk to Vickie, so I'll run out to your place first for food and then stop at the manor on my way home.'

'Is it going to take long with Vickie?' he asked. ''Cause there's some really good ice cream in my freezer you could snag, assuming you don't plan on grilling the witness so long it melts.'

'I'll make it quick.' I let go of him and swung open the cabinet door. '*Voila!* Grape jelly.'

'It'll do,' he said, taking it. 'But why don't you grab my lingonberry while you're at my place.'

Lingonberry. Really? Next he'd be wanting cheese that didn't come in an aerosol can.

Pavlik's cabinets and refrigerator were admittedly a treasure trove of treats. And cheaper than a grocery store. First, I snagged the lingonberry jam and a loaf of bread – cracked wheat, naturally. Or unnaturally, as far as I was concerned. Also, a pound of butter, a jar of Jif and, much as it pained me, a twelve-pack of caffeine-free Diet Pepsi. Sensing that somebody who craved cracked wheat bread might also eat vegetables, I checked out the crisper. The bag of lettuce I found there was wilted so I tossed it. But the broccoli and carrots looked fine and Frank would eat the carrots if nobody else did. I also grabbed some Fuji apples, a Frank favorite.

Standing in the middle of the kitchen, I felt like I was missing something. The ice cream.

Sliding out the freezer drawer, I found two. Madagascar Vanilla and Bittersweet Chocolate. Yum.

And no need to decide. I'd take both. And hope I could catch Vickie at her home and be back at mine before the ice cream melted.

I found a brown bag from Schultz's market under the sink and loaded everything into it, ice cream on top.

Driving to the manor, I thought about how I should approach Vickie. And where.

'Call Sophie,' I told my cell phone, which was lying on the center console.

It beeped and that's it. Stopping at the signal on the corner of Brookhills Road and the manor, I scrolled to Sophie's number.

'Do you know if Vickie is home?' I asked when she answered.

'How would I know that?' she demanded. 'I'm at your shop.'

Well, that was good, if not helpful. The light turned green.

'Why don't you call her?' Sophie continued.

'I wanted to drop in unannounced. And when Jack Andersen is not around.'

'That'll be tough. From what I've been hearing next door, she's living with him.'

Damn. 'You don't think I can catch her at her own apartment?'

'You can try. Do you know the number? Eleven, which is the other side of Andersen's from us. Henry, I told you—'

The line went dead. Turning left into the Brookhills Manor parking lot, I pulled around back to the section closest to Poplar Creek. Getting out, I scanned the tree line. No sign of Andersen dragging a body, of course. Nor sheriff's deputies combing the area for that body, either. I was happy, though, to see Vickie's white Kia parked in the last line of cars, closest to the woods.

The rehab wing was to the left when you entered the building and the residential one was to the right. I knew Sophie and Henry's apartment was on the ground floor of the residential wing and had a door leading to a small patio facing the Poplar Creek woods. I had to assume Jack Andersen's set-up was the same, meaning he could have taken Pauly's body out that way and avoided the communal hallway and lobby.

As I went to lock the car, I hesitated, eyeing the ice cream on the passenger seat. It was already softening up. I probably should have dropped it off at my place but I'd been too busy talking to Sophie as I'd passed. Maybe I would take it in with me. If Vickie was home, I could stash it in her freezer as we talked.

I was in luck. As I stepped into the lobby, Vickie was coming out of the small store which also served as the post office.

'Maggy,' she said, seeing me. 'Why are you carrying two cartons of ice cream?'

'I didn't want to leave it in the car but I needed

to ask you a few things.' I glanced out of the lobby window and saw Jack Andersen walking through the parking lot toward the entrance. 'Could I stick these in your freezer so they don't melt?'

'I guess so.' She looked none too sure that she wanted to talk to me, much less store my frozen treats. 'But I don't know that I can help you.'

I was pretty sure she could. What I wasn't sure about was whether she would. I did know, though, that if I had any chance of prying any information out of her, I had to keep her away from Andersen.

'Can we get it in right now?' I asked, making a show of juggling the cartons. 'It's going to drip all over.'

'I guess so,' she said again, leading me down the hallway. We passed Sophie and Henry's number nine. There were bullet holes in the walls across from ten, so no question who lived there. Each hole was circled and numbered.

I noticed Vickie didn't look at them as we passed, instead searching through her purse. 'I know the key is in here somewhere.'

Finding it, she turned the key in the lock and I made it in just as Jack rounded the corner. Hopefully he was just heading to his apartment next door and hadn't seen us. If he had and had something to hide – something he didn't want Vickie to share – we wouldn't have much time.

'Sorry the place is such a mess.' She pushed some foil and a plastic bag aside to get at the microwave, which was flashing 12:00. 'The electricity must have gone off last night.'

'I'm not surprised – it really stormed. You weren't here?'

She finished resetting the clock. 'I've slept here all of two nights in the last month. Jack and I are talking about my giving it up and moving in with him.'

'This is it?' I put the two cartons down on the kitchen table. 'You're in love?'

If doubt does have a shadow, I saw it cross her face.

'Now why didn't I put these dishes away?' she scolded herself, plucking silverware from the dish drainer next to the sink and opening the drawer to put it away.

She was nervous, but with Jack in the hallway I didn't have the time to schmooze her. 'So do you think you're in love? Is that why you're sticking with him against your better instincts?'

'Maggy, it's sweet of you to be worried about me but you need to just . . . stop.' She pulled a large serrated knife out of the drawer and brandished it. 'For your own good.'

I backed up. 'What are you going to do with that?'

'This?' She looked at the knife like she hadn't realized she'd been holding it.

Yes, that. The big-ass frozen food knife in your hand. 'Please put it back in the drawer before you cut yourself.' And, more importantly, me.

'Uh-uh.' She gestured with the knife for me to move away from the table.

I stayed where I was. 'Pavlik knows I'm here.'

'So?' The gesture again, the tip of the knife drawing a circle in the air.

I say tip, but the one on this knife was a two-pronged stabby doo-hickey. I had a feeling it would hurt. More. 'I told him your Soul was in the parking lot. He wondered whether Jack has been using it?'

Vickie seemed surprised and the knife dipped a bit. 'Occasionally.'

'Any odd . . . smells?'

'Smells?' Her nose wrinkled. 'You and your imagination. It's amusing when you're talking about somebody else, but I must say you're getting downright annoying. Now will you move?'

This time I did, sliding right toward the patio door. 'Where are we going?'

'I don't know about you, but *I'm* not going anywhere,' she said. 'Jack will be here any minute.'

'Vickie, please—'

'I can't believe you think he killed his brother. Not that life wouldn't be simpler without Pauly around.' She shook her head.

Yeah, murderous future in-laws are a bitch. 'You heard what Pavlik said at the funeral. He believes Pauly is dead. And Pavlik is no fool.'

'No, unfortunately he's not.' Vickie was thinking.

It was better than stabbing me. 'He knows that you picked Jack up at the bus station in Milwaukee.'

That startled her. 'How does he know that?'

'He's the sheriff.' I said it simply, the implication being that Pavlik was all-seeing and all-knowing. Like, for example, he saw that Vickie had a knife and knew to send in the troops.

Though, at the moment, the sheriff had no

troops. I decided to ignore the knife and play it the way I would with my friend Vickie, who I believed was being duped. 'What was Jack doing at the bus station anyway?'

'Well, that's where they dropped him off, of course, after they questioned him.'

'Who?' I'd noticed a panic button – the kind Sophie had been grousing about – on the other side of the refrigerator/freezer. I'd have to reverse course to reach it.

'Your sheriff's detectives, of course. Jack texted me after all the ruckus that they had a few questions and he was going to the station with them.'

I ignored the reference to the double shooting as a ruckus. 'The bus station?'

'No, of course not. The sheriff's station.'

'But Pavlik's detectives are with the Brookhills County Sheriff's Department west of here. Why would they drop him fifteen miles east at the Milwaukee bus station?'

'Why . . . I don't know.' Vickie's eyes were uncertain and even her Botox couldn't keep her brow from furrowing this time.

I shook my head. 'That's not what happened, Vickie. Jack stole Gloria Goddard's car and drove it to the station to make it look like Pauly had abandoned it there.'

'Stop, Maggy. I don't want to hurt you.'

I froze as, with one swift movement, she lifted the knife . . .

And plunged it into the knife block on the counter to my left.

I put my hand up over my heart, which was

thumping wildly. 'You . . . umm, you just wanted to put the knife away.'

'Of course,' she said. 'It doesn't belong in the silverware drawer. What did you think I was doing?'

She didn't want to know. But maybe I should tell her anyway. 'I thought you were going to stab me.'

Her eyes went wide and filled with tears. 'I would never hurt you. I never meant to hurt anybody.'

Odd way of putting it. 'What do you mean, Vickie? Who got hurt?'

'It was only meant to be temporary, you understand? I—' She was nervously moving between the kitchen table and the refrigerator and back again. 'Oh, dear. Your ice cream is melting all over the table. Let me just put them—'

'Leave them,' I said. 'And tell me what was meant to be temporar—' A knock at the door interrupted me.

'Vickie?' Jack's voice called. 'Are you home?'

'We need to leave,' I whispered to Vickie. 'Now.'

'But what about the ice cream?' she asked, lowering her voice to match mine. 'Do you still want me to put it in the freezer?'

'Vickie.' I put out my hand as she picked up the Madagascar vanilla. 'We're going out the patio door. You won't have to explain. He'll never know we were in here.'

'Fine,' she said, not looking toward the door where Jack stood on the other side. 'But first let me—'

She swung open the freezer door and dropped the vanilla.

Pauly Andersen's head was staring back at us, wrapped in aluminum foil.

Twenty-Seven

My first thought was that Pauly must not have fit into the zip-lock.

My second was *get the hell out of there.*

Vickie was still staring open mouthed at Pauly and he at her. She moved first, backing away as Jack knocked on the door again. 'Vickie, sweetheart? Can I come in, baby?'

I grabbed her arm. 'Does he have a key?'

She nodded but I could have answered the question myself. The key was already turning in the lock.

'Come on.' I pulled her toward the patio door.

She resisted. 'We have to call for help.'

You think? 'No time. We can't get caught in here with him.'

'But—'

Enough. I yanked her toward the door as the hall door swung open. Jack Andersen may have been all sweetheart and baby for the benefit of people in the hallway, but as he moved into the room and took in the still-open freezer door, he slipped a gun from his waistband.

Parole violation, of course. But nothing compared to stashing a foil-wrapped bro-head in the freezer. 'Don't move.'

I'd learned many things from Pavlik. One of them was never obey a bad guy. The second was never let them get you alone. Third was that it's tougher to hit a moving target than a stationary one.

So I moved. One hand still on Vickie, I flipped the lock on the slider and tugged.

I'd assumed Vickie would keep it locked, so I was unlocking it.

I was wrong. Or maybe Jack, being a killer, had left it open in case he needed a little fresh air as he was sawing apart his brother with the frozen food knife.

'Jack,' Vickie said, like the man didn't have a gun in his hand. 'I was just showing Maggy the patio.'

I flipped the lock the other way.

'Nice try, but you forgot to close the freezer.' He gestured at Pauly with his gun.

With one movement, I slung open the door and used that momentum to sling Vickie out like a game of crack the whip.

She went flying across the patio and onto the grass. I was halfway out the door when a hand gripped my arm.

'Maggy!' I heard Vickie scream.

'Run!' I told her as he dragged me back in.

'Couldn't mind your own business, could you?'

Cliché. And though it probably wasn't the right time, I said, 'Cliché, much?'

235

'What?'

He shoved me against the kitchen counter and I flinched as the edge bit into my hip. 'Couldn't I mind my own business? C'mon, Jack. You're a con man, Jack. Can't you do better? Even your glass house and rocks was more original than that.'

'And yet you ignored it.'

'I did.' I was inching away from him in the direction of the refrigerator.

'Stop moving.' He was following me, gun pointed at my chest. The pistol was a semi-automatic like the one Pavlik carried and I saw no silencer. Which meant Jack would rather not shoot me right here. I kept going.

When my foot touched the ice-cream carton on the floor, I kicked it toward him and made my move for the panic button, slapping it hard.

Nothing happened.

Andersen's hand grabbed my shoulder.

Truly panicked now, thanks to the non-functioning panic button, I gave Andersen a hard shove, hoping the ice cream on the floor had melted sufficiently.

It had.

Jack Andersen took one backward step and then skidded. He was hitting the floor as I high-tailed it through the door into the hall and pulled the fire alarm.

Twenty-Eight

'Those panic buttons don't work,' I told Sophie, who'd come out of her apartment when the fire alarm went off. We were sitting on a picnic bench, watching the county's big crime-scene van pull up.

There was a freezer full of evidence for them to collect.

'Those things buzz in the office,' Sophie said. 'What did you think? They go off like the fire alarm just did? You'd give people heart attacks.'

'Even more heart attacks,' Vickie said, joining us.

I was hoping I hadn't done that. Though I thought maybe I could be excused. 'Detective Hallonquist finished with you?'

'For now,' she said. 'He doesn't seem to think I had anything to do with Pauly and the . . .'

'Dismembering,' Sophie supplied. 'How in the world did that man kill, butcher and package his brother in your apartment without you knowing?'

'He said he had to use the bathroom,' Vickie said. 'And don't you look at me like that, Sophie Daystrom. You said yourself how hard it is to get by with the one bathroom in these units. And you know how men are.'

'I'll give you that,' Sophie said. 'Can't jackhammer Henry off that toilet sometimes.'

Interesting, but I was thinking about Jack Andersen being led off in handcuffs, one pants leg creamed with Madagascar vanilla . . .

237

'What are you smiling about?' This voice was Pavlik's.

I stood up and hugged him as Vickie and Sophie thoughtfully moved to the next table. 'How did you get here? You're not supposed to drive.'

'Hallonquist picked me up. Are you all right?'

'I'm fine. But Jack Andersen is one bad dude. I never should have come here alone.'

Now Pavlik laughed. 'You're saying that so I can't say it first?'

'Yup.'

'Well, I wasn't going to. You had no reason to think you'd be in danger talking to Vickie here at the manor. And who knew he'd stashed his brother's body in the fridge?'

'Oh,' I said, my nose wrinkling. 'Not just the freezer?'

''Fraid not,' Pavlik said. 'Pauly was a big boy. He's even in the crisper.'

'Meat-keeper?'

'A little.' Pavlik held up his thumb and index finger, about two inches apart.

I laughed. 'Pauly dead and Jack, I assume, going away for a very long time. I'm good with that.' I chin-gestured to where Vickie and Sophie had been joined by Henry. 'What about Vickie? Will she face accessory charges?'

'It'll depend on where the investigation takes us. And what Jack tells us.'

'Do you think he'll try to pin it on her?' I hadn't thought of that.

'Andersen is slick,' Pavlik said. 'But don't worry; he's not going to get a deal on this.'

'I still don't understand what he thought I had to hide,' I said. 'I suppose I should have asked him that.'

'While he was holding a gun on you?' Pavlik said. 'That kind of thing only happens in movies. Or books.'

Right. Along with being framed by a pillowcase. 'Did you ever find out from the coroner if Nancy was wearing lipstick?'

Pavlik's head jerked quizzically. 'What made you think of that?'

'I don't know – loose ends? Remaining murderers on the loose?'

I wasn't sure Pavlik was buying it but he answered anyway. 'Nancy Casperson was wearing lipstick, though no other makeup.'

'Was the lipstick smeared?'

'Wildly. But she was smothered, so that's not surprising. Aren't you going to ask me if we found the pillowcase?'

I made my eyes widen. 'Did you?'

'No.'

'You keep saying "we." Did something happen on the inquiry?'

Pavlik's face darkened a tinge. 'Just old habit. I'm still on leave.'

'With Jack in jail and Vickie out from under his thumb, I'm sure she'll drop whatever complaint she filed.'

'We'll see,' Pavlik said, rolling his shoulder back and forth. 'Are you ready to leave?'

'Sure,' I said, standing up. 'Let's stop and get ice cream on the way home.'

Twenty-Nine

I opened the next day. Despite it being Monday, I knew the core of the Goddard Gang planned to show up, likely thinking they'd get the lowdown on what happened yesterday from the horse's mouth. Me being the horse.

Meanwhile, I'd been doing some thinking of my own and had decided the gang's attendance would save me the trouble of rounding up the suspects.

And, yes, I know that only happens in books.

Christy was the first to arrive. 'Are you coming to Nancy's service?'

'Wouldn't miss it,' I said truthfully. 'What time is it scheduled?'

'One-thirty. Mort let me help with the cremation yesterday. The sweeping and packaging.'

'Congratulations,' I said. 'How did it go?'

She looked around the empty store before answering in a low voice. 'Challenging. At the last moment we were told implant removal was needed.'

'What?'

She leaned over the counter and whispered. 'Silicone. Thank God it was caught in time.'

I'd bent over to hear her and now straightened up in surprise. 'Nancy had breast implants?'

'Yes,' Christy said. 'Nobody told us or we would have removed them earlier.'

'Then you must have removed Celeste's, too.'

'Celeste? No, she didn't have breast implants.'

Nor a communicable disease that would have required disposing of the body before the forty-eight-hour waiting period. Interesting.

Christy left for work before the rest of the gang showed up. First, Mort and Hannah, then Vickie – blissfully single – and Henry and Sophie. I was about to convene my planned meeting of the murder club when Father Jim arrived.

Vickie jumped up. 'I want to confess.'

I thought a priest would take confession in stride, but Jim backed up a pace. 'Excuse me?'

I had an inkling of what was coming, since Vickie had started to confess to me before all hell broke out with Jack.

'I'm the one who took the collection money. It was only a loan, and we were already paying it back with Jack's inheritance.'

'Inheritance?' I couldn't help myself. 'The man's in his seventies. Who was he inheriting from?'

'I don't know,' Vickie said, turning to me. 'Jack said it was an estranged relative.'

'Like Pauly?' Had Pauly given Jack the money from the bank robbery for safekeeping while he was in jail? If so, it explained why Pauly had shown up at the manor – and why he'd never truly left.

Vickie's eyes widened. 'I don't know. After you told me he was a gigolo, I started to think Jack had made it all up. That's why I left that note in the collection plate. I knew I'd been duped like all those other women. But instead of giving Jack my money, I gave him the church's.'

The woman fell to her knees and grabbed Father Jim's hand. 'Can you ever forgive me?'

For the embarrassment, probably not. 'Ah, well, we'll talk in private,' Jim said, pulling back his hand and awkwardly patting her on the head before moving away. 'There will have to be restitution, of course.'

'Of course,' she said, following him on her knees. 'I can't tell you how—'

'Oh, for God's sake,' Sophie said. 'Will you get up? You're making an idiot of yourself.'

As Vickie got to her feet, I decided to make a fresh pot of coffee and give Sarah a call.

She wouldn't want to miss the fun.

'What's the plan? Sarah asked.

'Refills,' I said, gesturing with the pot in my hand.

'And then what?' she hissed. 'Here's your coffee and would you like a jail term with that?'

'I like that,' I said. 'But given I don't know who did what, I probably shouldn't threaten them. Yet.'

'You know Hannah did something.'

'Something, yes,' I admitted. 'I'm just not sure it's everything.' I took a deep breath. 'Here I go. Wish me luck.'

'Luck,' Sarah said, and then took up the prime viewing spot behind the service window.

Hannah was at a table with Mort, Sophie and Henry. Father Jim and Vickie, who was trailing him like a remorseful puppy, were at the next

242

with Phyllis Goode, who'd just arrived with a woman I didn't know.

'Refill?' I asked, my pot hovering over Hannah's latte mug. While many of the gangers initially ordered espresso drinks, when time for refills came around they were happy to switch to free coffee.

'Oh, thank you, Maggy,' she said. 'Maybe just half a cup. We have to be on our way soon.'

'That's right,' I said. 'Nancy's service is this afternoon.'

'It is,' Mort said. 'But we don't really need to rush off, dear. Christy has everything under control.'

I saw my opening. 'She's been quite the hire, hasn't she? I understand Christy is already assisting with cremations. She was telling me the most interesting thing—'

'Christy's quite the worker,' Mort said, throwing an uneasy look at Hannah. 'Though given the recent losses, I'm not sure the rest of our assembly here wants to hear about the particulars of her progress.'

'I do,' Sarah volunteered from the window.

'Oh, dear,' Vickie said uncomfortably. 'I don't think that—'

But Sophie had her head cocked, eyes narrowed. She knew I was up to something. 'It's always interesting to hear what Maggy has to say. Isn't it, Henry?'

She elbowed him and he jumped as the bells on the platform door jingled. 'Yes, yes, of course.'

Father Jim didn't offer an opinion, nor Hannah,

243

who'd you expect to be the most squeamish given her recent loss.

I set my pot down on the next table. 'It's just the most interesting field. For one thing, I had no idea there was a forty-eight-hour waiting period before a cremation can be done. Though I guess that can be waived if there's a reason, like a communicable disease, as was done in Celeste's case.'

'The old lady had a communicable disease?' This was from Sarah at the window. 'She peed all over that chair.' She pointed to the one Dr Goode's friend was seated on.

I held up my hands as the woman started to get up uncertainly. 'No, no – Sarah has it wrong. It was Celeste's friend, Nancy . . . What was Nancy's last name, Hannah?'

'Casperson,' Hannah supplied. She was staring into her cup.

'Yes, Nancy Casperson who had the accident. But it's so easy to confuse people, isn't it?'

'I beg to differ,' Mort said, a little indignantly. 'Hannah's mother Celeste and Nancy couldn't have been more different.'

'You're right in a way,' I conceded. 'Celeste was the one with money who took great care with her appearance – fashionable clothes and full makeup every time she went out. Hannah even joked her mother had newer breasts than she did.'

Celeste's daughter tried to raise a smile and failed. She knew where I was heading.

'Now Celeste's friend, Nancy,' I continued, 'was more no-nonsense. A numbers person who

244

dressed in comfortable, flowing clothes and didn't bother with makeup.'

I pulled a chair over and turned it around to straddle it like Pavlik had done in the kitchen of my house. 'Which is why I was surprised when Christy told me that it was Nancy whose silicone implants had to be removed before cremation yesterday.'

Mort gave it another go. 'I don't think this is proper conversation, especially given Hannah's recent losses.'

'I'm so sorry,' I said to Hannah. 'You've been through so much in . . . was it just five days between Nancy and Celeste's deaths?'

'That's right,' Mort said crisply. 'Celeste on Sunday and Nancy this past Thursday.'

'You see, I keep going over that, but that's where I'm having the problem.' I was rubbing my chin. 'We know Celeste had breast implants, but Nancy—'

'Don't be ridiculous,' Hannah burst out. 'So both of them had breast implants. So what?'

'But that's the thing,' I said. 'Christy says Celeste didn't.'

Mort sat back. 'Christy wouldn't know that. She's—'

'Very eager to learn,' I said. 'She talked the technicians into letting her—'

'No, no.' Mort looked apoplectic. 'The breasts . . . I mean, the implants would have been removed before cremation, of course. Christy couldn't have known that.'

'In fact, she could. She watched the body preparation and was pretty emphatic that there

245

were no implants. She was also surprised that nobody told them about Nancy's breast implants until the last minute.' I turned to the rest of the gang. 'Apparently, silicone makes a terrible mess in the cremator if they're not removed.'

'Not something the little clean freak would likely forget,' Sarah said.

'You're right,' I said. 'What we're left with is two women – one is rich and has breast implants. The other is of more modest means and has none.'

'But,' Sarah piped up from the window, causing everybody to turn her way, 'the bodies were just the other way around, right?'

'Right.' They twisted back my way. 'It made me wonder if it really was Celeste who died on Sunday. We'll never know, of course, because Mort cremated the body before the forty-eight-hour period.'

'Mort?' This was from Dr Goode. 'Is this true?'

'Well, I . . .'

'He put you in a tough position, didn't he?' I asked. 'Apparent natural death of an old woman, family just moved to town. Why wouldn't you agree to sign off on the death certificate when an old friend asks you to?'

'Because I wasn't an idiot.' The doctor's eyes were shooting daggers at her old friend. 'But apparently I am. How could you put me in this position, Mort?'

'There was nothing suspicious about my mother's death.' Hannah had finally decided to enter the fray.

'But there was.' Quietly, from Vickie at the next table.

246

All heads swiveled.

'No!' Hannah said. 'She's just saying that because her "friend" was trying to blackmail me. But all I did—'

'No.' Mort put a hand on hers. 'All *we* did was . . .' He seemed not to be able to articulate it.

I could. 'You switched them. It was Nancy who died on Sunday and Celeste on Thursday.'

'But why?' This was from Dr Goode's friend, who seemed to be getting into it.

'Money, what else?' I nodded toward Hannah. 'Your mother was wealthy but had everything tied up in a trust with Nancy as the successor trustee. You needed money.'

'We all needed money,' Hannah burst out. 'My mother was fine with spending it on herself – on her clothes and wigs and cosmetic surgery – but she had no idea how much it cost to run a house. And then, to make matters worse, she started to lose it mentally.'

'Alzheimer's?'

She flung out her hands. 'Dementia of some kind, I assume. Not that she would see a doctor.'

'Did you really want her to?' I asked. 'Or were you fine with your mother just fading away mentally? Except there was the money.'

'I loved my mother.'

'Wait.' Sophie was waving her hand. 'We saw Nancy at Celeste's funeral.'

I smiled. 'You should be able to answer that one, Sophie. You're the one who told me all old ladies look alike.'

The hand went down. 'I did.'

'Think about it,' I said. 'Dress Celeste in a shapeless dress, no wig, no makeup.'

'She'd be Nancy,' Sophie said. 'You're right.'

Damn right, I was right. 'With the dementia progressing, Celeste couldn't even tell us who she was. And if she had, we wouldn't have believed her. At the funeral she confused Jack Andersen with Dr Goode, who'd prescribed her a sedative.'

'I didn't prescribe anything,' Dr Goode said.

'I just said that,' Hannah said, 'to explain mother's confusion.'

'Nancy had been a sharp woman. You used the drugs and grief to explain why she wasn't herself. And succeeded, largely. But then you were blackmailed.'

'By Jack,' Vickie said. 'Though I'm to blame.' She looked like she'd throw herself at Jim's feet again if she weren't sitting across the table from him.

'How did Jack know the identities had been switched?' I asked, and then it dawned on me. 'You'd been to the house and seen the real Nancy and Celeste the night before. In fact, you were the only person who'd seen the two women, right?'

'They were pretty much housebound,' Father Jim said. 'Or so we were told.'

Hannah shrunk under his glare. 'It's true that my mother wasn't well and Nancy didn't like going out. You have to believe that none of this was planned.'

Sarah was not going to let me forget this. She'd had Hannah pegged from the very beginning.

248

'When I found Nancy dead and called Mort to come over,' she was saying, 'he wasn't certain at first whose body it was.'

'And that gave you the idea.'

She hung her head. 'With Mother dead, we'd have access to the trust.'

'And with Nancy alive,' Sophie said, 'you'd also get her social security. A two-fer.'

'Well, yes.' The head didn't go up.

'You went along with this, Mort?' Dr Goode couldn't believe it.

'I . . . well, Hannah asked me to.'

'Doesn't hurt that she's twenty years younger than you, I'll wager,' Sophie said.

Henry sighed. 'Many a man has been led astray by a younger woman.'

Sophie slapped him.

But back to our dramatic reveal. 'After Celeste's death, things started to go awry. First, Jack and Vickie tried to blackmail you.'

Vickie looked about to object and then thought better of it. The woman had stolen from a church and been a co-conspirator in a blackmail scheme. Not a good day.

Hannah nodded. 'Jack called Sunday night and said he knew it was Nancy who was dead. He also knew that she was wealthy.' Hannah threw a dark look at Vickie. 'He demanded fifty thousand dollars to keep his mouth shut.'

'Which is why it was so important that I go to the lawyer with you and convince Bernie to let you get into the trust fund. Only problem was Bernie is ethical and Celeste was stubborn. She refused to sign Nancy's name.'

'So, after all this, Hannah couldn't get access to the money?' Father Jim had finally been sucked in.

'Nope,' I said. 'Not as long as "Nancy" lived.'

'She had to die.' This from Vickie.

All eyes – including Mort's – turned on Hannah. She held up her hands. 'I didn't kill my mother. I would never do that.'

'Yet she was murdered,' I said. 'Smothered with a pillow and the pillowcase was removed from the crime scene. It had lipstick on it.'

A single tear ran down Hannah's cheek. 'Mother loved her lipstick. First thing she did when I brought her home after our meeting at Bernie's was sit down at the vanity and try to put it on.'

So the lipstick hadn't just been part of the attempt to keep me quiet. But something else Hannah had said bothered me. 'Jack called you on Sunday night?'

'Yes.' She took a handkerchief from Mort.

'But there had been no funeral – not even the cremation.' I swiveled to Mort. 'Who would have seen the body?'

He sat back. 'Only me and one of my people who's been with me for years.'

'Then how could Jack know it wasn't Celeste who had died?'

Vickie wouldn't look at me.

The redhead said she'd seen Celeste in the living room the night she'd met with Nancy. Even that Celeste was all decked out – a fashionista, I thought she'd called her.

When Celeste/Nancy saw Vickie and Jack at

the funeral, she mistook him for a doctor. Why?

'So Jack was with you that night?' I asked Vickie. 'The night you met with Nancy about the Angel of Mercy's books?'

This seemed to be news to Father Jim. 'You met with Nancy to go through the books the night before she died?'

'She . . . umm, she left you a message about some discrepancies and I . . . um, happened to see it. I went there to try to set her mind at ease.'

'By killing her?' Sarah asked.

'No, of course not.' Vickie's face was as red as her hair.

'Wait,' Jim said, holding up his hands. 'The money you've confessed to stealing was cash from the collection plates. There would be no discrepancies – the money just wouldn't be there. Are you telling me you pilfered more?'

She nodded, and tears slipped over and ran down both cheeks.

'How much?'

'Umm, maybe twenty?'

'Twenty . . . ?'

'Thousand.'

'You stole twenty thousand dollars from my church?' The fire and brimstone in Jim's voice would have made God (the Old Testament, testy version) proud.

I held up my hand. 'I'm not sure that's the worst of it, Jim.'

'You think they killed Nancy?' Hannah asked, looking relieved at being off the hook for this

251

part, at least. 'But how? She was alive after they left.'

There was Celeste/Nancy's comment about a doctor at the funeral. Something about shots and headaches? 'Did you give her something?' I asked Vickie. 'A shot?'

'No, not me.' She was sniffling. 'But Nancy had a headache and Jack said he had something that could help.'

I felt my eyes go wide and my brow, thankfully, furrow. 'He injected Botox? I turned to Dr Goode. 'Could that have killed her?'

The good doctor seemed to be wondering what she'd stepped into. Her friend, on the other hand, was having a grand time. It was she who answered. 'In high enough doses, yes.'

'Who are you?' Sophie demanded.

'Pharmaceutical rep,' the woman said. 'Botox – in addition to its cosmetic use in low doses – is very effective in treating headaches. Like any other drug, though, it can be deadly if misused.

'What would the symptoms of overdose be?' the doctor asked.

Botulinum toxin is systemic, so it enters the bloodstream and spreads to all the muscles. It takes a tiny needle, so it can be injected anywhere.'

'Making it hard to find the site?' Mort asked.

'Yes. And the other thing is that it could take hours or even days for the victim to die. Symptoms would include things like weakness, blurred vision, trouble swallowing and breathing, maybe hoarseness, loss of bladder control—'

'Bingo,' Sarah said.

252

'Then it might present as natural death?' Dr Goode looked both relieved and horrified.

'And one following a flu-like illness.'

'But you must have known,' Hannah said to Vickie. 'You might not have realized what he was doing. But after the fact, and when he started to blackmail me, why didn't you speak up?'

Vickie's own Botox couldn't fight the lines in her face. 'I was so scared.' The words barely came out. 'And the blackmail – well, you were a criminal, too, switching those two old women.'

'And that made it OK?' Father Jim demanded.

'No, of course not.'

'What about Celeste?' I asked. 'I mean the real Celeste. Did he kill her, too?'

'I think so.' Vickie's voice was raspy and low. 'He said he'd seen Hannah drop Celeste off at home and go on to the mortuary. He knew somehow that the back door would be open. I think . . . I think maybe he snuck over.'

That day at Clare's, Hannah had called back to Mort that she'd left the back door unlocked, before nearly colliding with Jack. He would have heard.

'But why?' Hannah asked. 'Why kill my mother?'

Vickie swallowed hard, blinking back tears. 'When she mistook him for a doctor at the funeral, he decided that she had seen him inject Nancy. I tried to tell him that she was just a confused old lady and nobody would pay any attention to what she said, but he . . . he called her a loose end.'

253

A strangled sob from Hannah.

'So he killed her,' I said.

'And tried to frame us,' Sarah added, 'by stashing the case from the pillow that was used to smother her in our storeroom.'

'Oh, dear,' Vickie said, hand to her throat. 'I didn't know about that, either. He asked me a lot of things about you, Maggy. You have to get leverage on people, he said, because you never know when you'll need it.'

'Did he ask about me?' Sarah asked, looking a little miffed.

'No. And I didn't tell him any—' Vickie was trying to stand. The chair beneath her was wet.

'Call nine-one-one!' I yelled.

Pavlik joined Father Jim in catching her as Vickie toppled to the floor.

Thirty

'Botox.' Pavlik was shaking his head. 'Who knew?'

We were sitting on the couch in front of the fireplace, Frank at our feet and wine, yet again, in our hands.

'Vickie's drug of choice,' I said, 'and it almost killed her.'

'Good thing the good doctor, Doctor Goode, was there.'

'You didn't really say that.'

'I did.' He pulled me toward him. 'And I'm deeply ashamed.'

254

'If you're next line is "don't you want to punish me?" it's over between us.'

'Then I won't.' He rested his chin on my head. 'Now tell me about this pillowcase.'

When I'd called Pavlik from the shop, inviting him and the driver of his choice to my impromptu 'round up the suspects' party, I knew I'd have to own up to having the pillowcase. And, more importantly, to not telling him I had the pillowcase.

'I'm sorry I didn't tell you. But I knew that if I did, you'd have to relay it your guys.'

'You're right.'

I hesitated. 'That you'd be honor-bound to let them know?'

'Yes, and you were also probably right not to tell me. It would have made me crazy, but the only thing I could do, in good conscience, I wouldn't have wanted to do.'

'Rat on your sweetie?'

'Rat on my sweetie.' He kissed the top of my head.

'I'm still not sure why Jack went to the trouble of trying to frame me.'

Pavlik shrugged. 'The man's a con. He plays all angles and he prepares to play all angles.'

'I was just another angle?'

'And maybe somebody new to blackmail.'

'Me?'

'Or me. If I knew about the pillowcase, for example, and *didn't* pass it on.'

'Sheesh, I'm glad I didn't tell you then.' I snuggled down under his arm and then sat right back up. 'You know, I bet he was the one who snagged my bells. That first day we laid eyes on the man at Uncommon Grounds I remember something was jingling in his pocket as he went down the porch steps. I assumed they were keys. I can't believe I didn't recognize the sound of my own bells.'

Pavlik wasn't following. 'Your bells?'

'On UG's doors. First the ones from the track-side door were missing, then the front.'

'Maybe somebody got sick of hearing them all day, every day. Have you canvassed your neighbors?'

'I'm serious,' I said, turning to face him. 'If Jack played all the angles and prepared for all eventualities, like you say, he might have figured he'd have a reason to sneak into the shop. Which he ultimately did, to plant the pillowcase. Has the lab finished with it?'

'They have, but there was nothing on it beyond what you'd expect on a pillow.'

'Celeste's hair, lipstick. Any DNA?'

'We think so, though that will take more time. We have samples from the autopsy, which we can match with samples from her room and inside the wigs to make an identification.'

'Something you can't do for poor Nancy. What in the world was Hannah thinking?'

'It's fraud but thankfully it's not murder. I prefer to save that charge for Jack Andersen.'

'Along with money laundering through a church. He's worse than his brother, in my book.'

'I don't disagree.'

'Even though his brother shot you?'

'At least I knew what I was up against. Jack Andersen preys on people. He's a snake.'

'You should have seen him at the funeral, pretending he was confused about who was Nancy and who was Celeste. To Hannah, of course.'

'The woman he was blackmailing about the identity switch.'

'Which he only knew about because he'd killed Nancy that night, not Celeste. The man had the nerve to go to his victim's funeral and taunt Hannah. No wonder she was desperate.'

'I'm not sure Hannah deserves your pity,' Pavlik said.

'Oh, she's not getting that,' I said. 'I'm just trying to understand.'

'Don't,' he said. 'When you understand evil it's too easy to become it.'

'Ooh, nice. Original?'

Pavlik squinted, trying to remember. 'Probably an old movie?'

'Old movies and books were the inspiration for my rounding up the suspects, you know.'

'To be fair, you didn't really need to round them up,' Pavlik pointed out. 'They show up at your place every Sunday morning.'

'True, but this was Monday. And speaking of showing up at my place, I'm glad you're here.'

'Me, too, although the circumstances could have been better.'

'Like not getting shot?'

'For one.'

I knew he was also thinking about Al Taylor and Pete Hartsfield.

'I'm so sorry,' I said. 'About the deaths of Al and Pete, of course. But also about your being placed on leave. It's been a tough week for you and it's not fair.'

He pulled me down to him and kissed me. 'Thank you. In one bit of good news, pending medical clearance from the good doctor—'

'Don't say it!' I held up a warning finger.

'Anyway, I have an appointment tomorrow. If all goes well I should be able to go back to work. And my house.'

I felt an unexpected twinge. 'But I'd grown accustomed to your face on the pillow next to me each morning.'

'If it was this morning, that was Frank. I was in the bathroom. Right, Frank?'

Frank grunted agreement.

'OK,' I said, trying to scoot up again. 'But what I'm trying to say is . . . that I like living with you. And maybe your idea of our getting married isn't too crazy.'

'That may be the worst acceptance of a proposal I've ever heard.'

'I know. Sorry. Not that we have to do it right now, you understand.'

'You just said yes. Are you getting cold feet already?'

'You press your jeans,' I blurted out. 'And starch them.'

'I do,' Pavlik said. 'Old habit from the military and pressing my dress uniforms. I kind of enjoy it.'

'But they're *jeans*.'

'The bottom hem gets all bent. Doesn't that bother you?'

I thought about it. 'No.'

'Well, it does me. And as long as I have the iron out I figure I might as well do the rest.' He wrapped his arm around me and pulled me against his chest. 'Is this a deal breaker?'

I laughed. 'Honestly, I find it kind of endearing. It's just . . . I guess I'm afraid I won't measure up. I mean, if your jeans have to be perfect—'

'Will I iron you when you get wrinkled?' He settled his chin on the top of my head. 'No. Nor will I suggest Botox. Personally, I'm looking forward to getting old and wrinkly together.'

What does a girl say to that?

'We did pretty well living together,' Pavlik continued. 'So, let's continue taking baby steps. For example, I'd like you to meet my parents.'

'What?' My head snapped up, smacking him in the chin. The word 'baby' had nearly freaked me out but meeting the parents was scary, too.

'Damn,' he said, rubbing it. 'You could just say no.'

'No?' I tried.

Pavlik's face fell.

'It's not that I don't want to meet them,' I pleaded. 'It's just kind of . . . abrupt.'

'Abrupt? We've been dating for two years, I've lived here for a week, I've proposed and you've accepted. We've survived the pressed jeans crisis. How much longer do you think we should wait?'

He had a point. 'But don't they live in Chicago?'

'Yes. An insurmountable ninety-minute drive.'

259

I sighed. 'OK, I know I'm being silly but it sounds so . . . formal. Meeting the parents.'

Pavlik gathered me back against him. 'Maggy, I know you've been skittish about getting married and I respect that. But we're both adults – it's not like we need their permission to get married or not to get married. I just . . . well, I just want you to meet my parents.'

'You haven't met mine,' I pointed out.

'Your parents are dead.'

There was that.

Even so, it didn't seem fair for him to get off so easily. I opened my mouth to a put up more of a fight but realized I was being silly. From all accounts – which meant, essentially, Pavlik – his parents were nice people.

'Fine. Why don't you find a date that works for them and we'll go down and have dinner.' Ninety-minute drive there, two-hour dinner, ninety-minute drive back and we'd be done.

'I have a better idea,' he said, kissing the top of my head. 'How about I book a room in the Lakeshore East area for next weekend. Maybe the Blu or the Sofitel. We can have dinner with my folks on Saturday night, and then we'll have the rest of the weekend to ourselves.'

I perked up. I did love Chicago. Museums, parks, Michigan Avenue, me and Pavlik alone in a hotel room. What's not to like?

'Your parents wouldn't expect us to stay with them?' It had been a requirement with Ted's parents, which meant sleeping in twin beds in his childhood room when we were married and on opposite ends of the house before that.

Apparently it never occurred to them that if we were looking to fornicate we'd more easily be able to do it at home.

'My parents?' Pavlik said, eyebrows raised. 'No way. They've lived in a two-bedroom apartment on the fortieth floor of the Randolph since the building was built in the sixties. Once I was gone they turned my room into an office just so they can't have guests.'

My kind of people. I cranked my head around and up so I could see his face. 'And that includes you?'

'*Especially* me.' Pavlik grinned. 'I love my folks and they love me, but as adults we do not cohabitate. Besides.' He nuzzled me in the neck. 'There's just something about hotel rooms.'

'Room service?' I murmured.

He lifted his head. 'Yeah, that's it.'